THE PSYCHOLOGY OF CLASSROOM LEARNING

▶ THE PSYCHOLOGY OF CLASSROOM LEARNING

John M. Stephens

THE JOHNS HOPKINS UNIVERSITY

HOLT, RINEHART AND WINSTON, INC.

NEW YORK · CHICAGO · SAN FRANCISCO · TORONTO · LONDON

PREFACE

THIS TEXT DEALS with the psychology of the processes at work within the classroom. It applies psychological principles and data to the means that a teacher might employ to direct academic achievement, to promote the development of character, and to aid in the attainment of personal adjustment. In discussing these matters, of course, there must be some mention of child development. In general, however, this topic is left to the excellent systematic treatments of human growth to be found in other texts. These texts show the important development that takes place largely apart from the teacher's efforts. This book starts where they leave off.

In seeking to apply psychology to the processes at work within the classroom, we are free to tap the astounding array of data that have come to light within the past few years. During those years, verbal learning has become a whole discipline, and its classroom implications are exciting indeed. Reinforcement psychology has recruited its own camp of enthusiastic workers, and these researchers have turned out a flood of materials on programming, on the acquisition of skill and morality, and on the promotion of personal adjustment. The claims of structure confront us at every turn and, within a few years, the name of Piaget has rocketed from neglect to enshrinement. Creativity has become a way of life. The work on socialization and character formation has reached new levels of sophistication and rigor.

In applying this new work to the areas of academic attainment and the acquisition of skill (Part Two), I have pointed out some important modifications of traditional notions, especially in the fields of motivation and practice. In general, however, there has been even more emphasis on the impressive continuities uniting the bright new ventures with the older activities which, at times, have seemed to be trembling on the brink of obsolescence. These continuities are held to link the textbook with the teaching machine; the insightful grasp of structure with the rote memorization of arbitrary units; and the mundane acquisition of conventional material with the enthusiastic pursuit of creativity.

v

In looking at character development and at the converse problems of delinquency and prejudice (Part Three), we face abundance and confusion. The profusion of fascinating new evidence has itself arisen within a framework of contention between widely separated theoretical positions. Here I have spent most effort in trying to achieve a working synthesis, and in deriving defensible practical applications. In this area, more than in most, the transition from organized data to realistic and reasonable applications is troublesome and hazardous.

Throughout most of the book two powerful orientations have been at work. With one hand I have tried to do justice to the content and to the challenge of the new data. With the other I have tried to work out realistic classroom applications, never for a moment disregarding the well-remembered problems that press upon the classroom teacher. To provide an effective link between these two bracketing compulsions, it has been necessary to try to integrate the new data with the older, more general material, and to adopt, or to work out, some useful structure that will embrace both old and new.

The concern for the new evidence is, of course, inevitable. Once noted it could never be ignored. There is a danger, it is true, of suggesting that unless the data represent the very last word there is no need of bothering with them. When the new data are carefully integrated with the old, however, this risk of a misleading modernity should be reduced.

There is also a risk in the urge to provide realistic classroom applications for each of the main concepts. Unless the reader is clearly aware of the role of the data, the whole treatment may suggest a series of fatherly talks. This danger can be avoided, however, and in any case I am convinced that the risk is worth taking. Such down-to-earth applications, over and above their practical value, are tremendously useful in the clarification of theory. When confronted with an unusually stubborn piece of chaos, for instance, I find it most helpful to carry on an imaginary conversation with my more practical friends. It is only when I can explain the ins and outs to them that I feel I, myself, really understand it. Any fireside overtones detected in this book may well be an unintentional residue from this favorite stratagem.

This concern for the teacher and his problems appears in many places. The book begins with the teacher's job and functions. It ends with the teacher's emotional reaction to his work. Emotional reactions, be it noted, include not only worries that call for adjustment, but the positive feelings of zest, excitement, and satisfactions that are to be enjoyed and exploited.

The teacher-centered approach is also seen in the suggestions for dealing with individual differences (Chapter 15), and in the reminders of the spontaneous, primitive forces (Chapter 16) that the teacher unthinkingly brings to his difficult task. Here he is invited to release the educated man that he finds within himself in a veritable orgy of self-expression.

To call attention to the data from which the generalizations and the implications are derived, I have relied partially on parenthetical references and partially on the actual summaries of studies that appear in the occasional boxes. Both of these devices serve additional functions, as it happens, and each deserves a word of comment.

The detailed parenthetical references are directed primarily, of course, to the instructor and to any critical student who wishes to know more about the evidence underlying a given comment. This use of the references calls for a great deal of application, however, and many students may get more benefit from the general readings listed at the end of each chapter. A number of these are drawn from books of readings. A list of the books appears on page ix.

The boxed reports of research have a more varied function. In addition to serving as reminders that relevant evidence exists, they present actual samples of the crude, undigested data from which the discussion is derived. Like the chewy, unhomogenized chips that one occasionally encounters in an otherwise untextured medium, these intruders will, at itmes, be disregarded, or treated as minor inconveniences. At times, however, they may be relished or sought out, and may even serve as the focal points around which the encompassing medium is organized.

Clearly these boxes will be treated in different ways. Some instructors may merely treat them as the odds and ends that one puts on the bulletin board or leaves lying around the room—to elaborate a point, or to drive it home; to elicit a moderate, relevant puzzlement; or to introduce a salutary note of dissent when the tone of the discourse may sound too dogmatic.

There is much to be said for this easygoing approach. Students often get more out of such incidental items if we don't make too much of them, and if we are not too heavy-handed in pointing the moral. True enough, a really important item might be missed in this approach. Whenever a box deals with a crucial concept, however, that concept is also treated explicitly in the adjoining text.

But other approaches are also in order. Some instructors, for instance, may make systematic use of the boxes to remind the student that the interpretation of research is difficult and precarious, and that definite advice does not emerge automatically and unambiguously from the data themselves. To fit in with this important use, the box itself is typically limited to data and includes little or nothing in the way of interpretation. The student can thus be encouraged to draw his own conclusions and to see if these agree with the general treatment in the text. At times he will find that they do not.

Part of this discrepancy, of course, will come from the inevitable leeway in deriving conclusions. Some of it is contrived. A few boxes are deliberately selected to qualify or to modify the general trend of the exposition. In such instances, of course, the qualification is not considered essential. If it were missed the distortion would not be serious.

The instructor who stresses this function of the boxes may wish to supply more sophisticated statistics. Statistical significance is a case in point. Statements of significance are regularly reported, but there is no effort to develop the concept of significance. If skill in interpreting evidence is to be carried even farther, students should be asked to read such a treatment as Tyler (1956, Chapter 2), or the discussion in my own earlier text (Stephens, 1956, Chapter 2), or even the advanced treatments in Gage (1963).

Like the boxes, the occasional pictorial ventures can safely be ignored by the reader going single-mindedly down the course. The sketches carry out the idea, so frequently stressed, that genuine study calls for definite, overt reactions on the part of the reader. But not all reactions need be verbal, and the artist, Susan Blair, has been persuaded to react visually to some of the notions. The delightful sketches from her talented pencil are chiefly to be appreciated as illustrations of such visual reactions. It seems almost unthinkable, as a matter of fact, that such dainty creations should be put to work in the grim business of exposition. If the reader does linger to enjoy them, however, he will find that they often point up the moral in a graceful manner not to be accomplished by mere words.

The photographs, along with their ordinary function, are intended to call attention to some of the psychologists whose work is basic to the subject, but whose influence is inadequately documented.

My gratitude goes to Philip W. Jackson and to Dale B. Harris for reading and rereading, for helpful advice, and for a number of important but gentle vetoes. The editors must be thanked for their consistent encouragement, for the complete freedom granted, and for remarkable patience. To my wife goes the credit for getting the book done. Considering the complex process of getting ideas into print, one can properly say that she wrote the book. I merely supplied the copy.

J. M. Stephens

Baltimore, Maryland
January 1965

Books of Readings

As far as feasible books of readings have been used for general references or supplementary readings. The list that follows gives the title of each of these, preceded (in parentheses) by the code name used in the "Suggestions for Further Reading":

(Baller) W. W. Baller, *Readings in the Psychology of Human Growth and Development.* New York: Holt, Rinehart and Winston, Inc., 1962.

(Charters) W. W. Charters, Jr., and N. L. Gage, *Readings in the Social Psychology of Education.* Boston: Allyn and Bacon, Inc., 1963.

(Crow) L. D. Crow and Alice Crow, *Readings in Child and Adolescent Psychology.* New York: Longmans, Green & Co., Inc. Succeeded by David McKay Company, Inc., New York.

(De Cecco) J. P. De Cecco, *Human Learning in the School.* New York: Holt, Rinehart and Winston, Inc., 1963.

(Fullagar) W. A. Fullagar, H. G. Lewis, and C. F. Cumbee, *Readings for Educational Psychology* 2d ed. New York: Thomas Y. Crowell Company, 1964.

(Grinder) R. E. Grinder, *Studies in Adolescence.* New York: The Macmillan Company, 1963.

(Haimowitz) M. L. Haimowitz and Natalie R. Haimowitz, *Human Development: Selected Readings.* New York: Thomas Y. Crowell Company, 1960.

(Harris-Schwahn) T. L. Harris and W. F. Schwahn, *Selected Readings on the Learning Process.* New York: Oxford University Press, 1961.

(Kuhlen) R. G. Kuhlen and G. G. Thompson, *Psychological Studies of Human Development.* New York: Appleton-Century-Crofts, 1963.

(Morse) W. C. Morse and M. Wingo, *Readings in Educational Psychology.* Chicago: Scott, Foresman and Company, 1962.

(Noll) V. H. Noll and Rachel P. Noll, *Readings in Educational Psychology.* New York: The Macmillan Company, 1962.

(Page) E. B. Page, *Readings for Educational Psychology.* New York: Harcourt, Brace & World, Inc., 1964.

(Remmers) H. H. Remmers, H. N. Rivlin, D. G. Ryans, and E. R. Ryden,

Growth, Teaching, and Learning. New York: Harper & Row, Publishers, Inc., 1957.

(Rosenblith) Judy F. Rosenblith and W. Allinsmith, *The Causes of Behavior: Readings in Child Development and Educational Psychology.* Boston: Allyn and Bacon, Inc., 1962.

(Seidman) J. M. Seidman, *The Adolescent: A Book of Readings.* New York: Holt, Rinehart and Winston, Inc., 1960.

(Stendler) Celia B. Stendler, *Readings in Child Behavior and Development.* New York: Harcourt, Brace & World, Inc., 1964.

CONTENTS

PART ONE

▶ *The Child, the Teacher,
and the Scholastic Demands*

CHAPTER 1

▶ *What Teaching Is Like*

Being a Teacher

Many teachers have written of their experiences and other writers have prepared biographies of teachers. These accounts range from plodding recitals of events to sensitive narrations such as Jesse Stuart's *The Thread That Runs So True*.

Trying to Decide. The teachers who have written of their experiences have moved into the profession by many different routes. For some, teaching has seemed the only possible vocation from an early age. Others just happened to make a casual visit in the profession but found themselves remaining indefinitely. Some of these remained from inertia. Time went by and the teacher suddenly realized that this seemingly temporary job had become a permanent way of life. Others of these original birds of passage were surprised to discover great attractions or delights in the job of teaching and deliberately decided to remain.

We must not imply that "the call," once it occurs, always persists. Most of the published accounts are written by people who did remain in the profession. A substantial number of teachers, however, do resign each year, some for homemaking, some for careers in business or other occupations. Many of these, it is true, may never have really felt the appeal of teaching, remaining in the profession only for want of something better to do.

High school students planning to teach (Richey and Fox, 1951) give different reasons for their decisions. Sometimes there is a family tradition of teaching. Sometimes both the youth and his family had just taken it for granted that he would go into teaching. Others were influenced by the example of some admired teacher, or through some literary or dramatic work in which teaching was portrayed in an appealing way. Still others got their ideas from counselors or from discussions with teachers or principals (Stern, 1963).

Not all promptings toward teaching are of a pleasant or noble nature. Along with those young people who were in-

► *Some Books about Teachers and Teaching*

Adams, Henry, *The Education of Henry Adams*. Boston: Houghton Mifflin Company, 1918.

Aldrich, Bess S., *Miss Bishop*. New York: Grosset & Dunlap, Inc., 1940.

Barzun, Jacques, *The Teacher in America*. Boston: Little, Brown & Company, 1945.

Bowen, R. O., *The New Professors*. New York: Holt, Rinehart and Winston, Inc., 1960.

Braithewaite, R. R., *To Sir, with Love*. Englewood Cliffs, N. J.: Prentice-Hall, Inc., 1959.

Cattell, Ann, *Sixty Miles North*. New York: Comet Press Books, 1953.

Cotton, Ella E., *Spark for My People*. New York: Exposition Press, 1954.

Eggleston, Edmund, *The Hoosier Schoolmaster*. New York: Grosset & Dunlap, Inc., 1892.

Enslow, Ella, and Alvin F. Harlow, *Schoolhouse in the Foothills*. New York: Simon and Schuster, Inc., 1935.

Highet, Gilbert, *The Art of Teaching*. New York: Alfred A. Knopf, Inc., 1950.

Hilton, James, *Goodbye, Mr. Chips*. Boston: Little, Brown & Company, 1934.

Howard, S. C., *Alien Corn*. New York: Charles Scribner's Sons, 1933.

Hughes, Thomas, *Tom Brown's Schooldays*. New York: Harper & Row, Publishers, Inc., 1937.

Keller, Helen, *Teacher: Anne Sullivan Macy*. New York: Doubleday & Company, Inc., 1955.

McLelland, Isabel C., *Hi! Teacher*. New York: Holt, Rinehart and Winston, Inc., 1952.

Perkins, Virginia C., *The End of the Week*. New York: The Macmillan Company, 1953.

Rasey, Marie I., *It Takes Time: An Autobiography of the Teaching Profession*. New York: Harper & Row, Publishers, Inc., 1953.

Stuart, Jesse, *The Thread That Runs So True*. New York: Charles Scribner's Sons, 1949.

Weber, Julia, *My Country School Diary*. New York: Harper & Row, Publishers, Inc., 1946.

Kearney, N. C., *A Teacher's Professional Guide*. Englewood Cliffs, N. J.: Prentice-Hall, 1958.
See Chapter 17 for a biography entitled, "The Experience of Lucille Maxwell, Teacher."

Sharp, D. Louise, *Why Teach?* New York: Holt, Rinehart and Winston, Inc., 1957.
In this book a few teachers give short firsthand reports. Most of the book, however, is taken up with brief statements of well-known people commenting on the importance of teaching, and describing their own teachers.

Van Til, W., *The Making of a Modern Educator*. Indianapolis, Ind.: Bobbs-Merrill Company, Inc., 1961.
This is a collection of essays on the author's experiences, including his experience as a teacher.

spired by the example of an admired teacher, we must list others who entered the profession as a rebellion against some detested teacher (Rasey, 1953; Wright and Sherman, 1963), saying in effect, "You don't have to be like that to be a teacher. I'll show you!" Family influence, similarly, acted at times in a negative direction. In contrast to those who went into teaching because it was always expected of them, there are others who embraced the profession precisely because their elders so often decried it or belittled it. Among the less noble motives we find many that are pragmatic indeed. Often teacher-training programs are inexpensive and represent a cheap way of getting a degree. To some people, teaching seemed to be an easy way of getting started in a profession and of attaining independence. Other students found that by working toward teaching they could take longer to make up their minds, and many of these, in failing to decide on something else, just happened to end up as teachers (Haubrick, 1960; Lloyd-Jones and Holman, 1957).

There are more intrinsic motives. One young man, for instance, likes to work in the world of books or ideas, or has a strong interest in nature study and he thinks teaching may be an outlet for this interest. Another thinks he would like to work with children. A third finds himself getting some pleasure out of explaining things to others, and he, too, sees teaching as a natural outlet for this drive.

Taking the Plunge. The transition from college student to classroom teacher, like many other transitions, has its painful moments (Charters, 1963). Gone is the pleasant semi-anonymity that the student used to enjoy. No longer, when he feels like it, can he slump down in the back row of the class and be merely one of a large group. Now the spotlight picks him up, separates him from other people, and follows him remorselessly. He finds his rights and duties as a teacher vastly different from those he experienced as a student. Often he must leave a fairly liberal college campus, where, outside the classroom, if not within it, he was free to explore and sample an expanding world of ideas. Now he must concern himself with the more conservative job of inculcating a mastery of traditional ideas.

Some aspects of this painful transition are seen dramatically in the experience of student teaching (Iannaccone, 1963). The student is asked to give up his reliance on the abstractions he has mastered in class and to come to deal with the complex practicalities of teaching. In a sense he is even asked to abandon his loyalties and to go over to the enemy. Certainly the neatly drawn lines between "us" and "them" become blurred. Part of the time, at least, he must be one of "them." At the outset he finds himself extremely critical of the regular teacher to whom he is assigned. ("She actually gave one of the children a shaking!") Later, however, the psychological distance lessens. Instead of two people suspicious of each other, if not actually hostile, there appears to be a cooperating pair, and finally a clearly felt "we." "*We* had trouble with Jimmie and decided to do this." He finds himself adopting practices that he had earlier regarded as barbarous. He places less value on the things the textbooks emphasize and finds himself stressing those things that will get the job done and get the lesson completed. Now a procedure is good if it works, whether or not it accords with theory.

The first stretch of actual teaching will do much to complete this transition. After a few months of teaching a definite change in attitude can be detected. Again this is a change toward the practical. He is less likely to blame the school for all the inadequacies he finds in the child. He is more tolerant of the teacher who demands order and accomplishment. He is less insistent on honoring the rights and needs of children (Charters, 1963; Masling and Stern, 1963). Occasionally he may actually be disturbed by his own inability to sympathize with the interests and values of his adolescent charges (Smith, 1950).

The Steady Pull. The transition is over. Student days are left behind, to be regarded with an indulgent smile, or perhaps, with a sigh for an earlier, less responsible life. Most of the surprises are over. Many adjustments are made. What is teaching like now?

It's a busy and complex life, as we can see from the figures in Table 1.1. Notice that the average elementary school teacher puts in about a fifty-hour week, the secondary school teacher somewhat less. These, of course, are averages. Half the teachers put in longer hours, some much longer, and some work for shorter periods than those shown.

About half the time (a little more than half for the elementary school teachers) is taken up with actual classroom instruction. The remaining time is spent mostly in getting ready for the class-room or in doing things closely related to instruction. This work consists of correcting papers, or marking tests, making out report cards, preparing materials of instruction such as charts or displays, preparing work sheets and things needed for demonstrations. All told, this amounts to about an hour and a half each day or seven and a half hours per week. The average teacher spends another two and a half hours per week in reviewing the subjects he teaches or looking up details that he should know before going into class. About an hour each week is spent in giving help to individual students after class, and about the same amount of time in consulting with parents about the pupil's school work.

Not all the time outside the classroom is taken up with instructional matters. The typical teacher will spend from an hour and a half to two hours per day in incidental or miscellaneous duties that have little to do with his regular classroom responsibilities. The biggest item in this category is the chore of supervising playground, study hall, cafeteria, corridors, and bus loading or unloading. About two hours a week go into record keeping and reports; one class period per week is devoted to official meetings. Especially at the secondary school level,

TABLE 1.1. Hours Each Week Spent in Different Activities

	Elementary School Teachers	Secondary School Teachers
Classroom instruction	30	24
Other work directly related to instruction	12	13
Work not directly related to instruction	7	9
Total	49	46

SOURCE: *Teaching Career Fact Book* (Washington, D.C.: National Education Association, 1963).

some time each week will be spent with various clubs, or helping in athletics or extracurricular activities or projects.

In a number of schools, many of the noninstructional duties are taken over by teacher's aides (Thomson, 1963). These aides take attendance, keep other records, and take care of mimeographing. They also correct objective tests, look after films that must be located and returned, and run movie projectors. In some cases they help in preparing materials for display, and even coach children who have been absent for a few days.

Within the classroom much of the time is spent in presenting materials to students either merely by talking to them, by directing their attention to books on their desks, or by showing charts, demonstrations, or movies. Even more time is spent in listening to the students as the latter answer questions, recite, report on their assignments, or comment on the activities of other students.

In all this the teacher is chiefly trying to increase the academic attainment of his students, but other purposes or objectives also appear. Much of what he does is concerned just with keeping things going. He makes sure that students have their pencils and the appropriate books. He keeps some kind of order and deals with the minor emergencies of the moment (Stinnet and Haskew, 1962).

Still other goals or objectives are apparent as the teacher tries to get pupils to react more adequately to each other and takes steps to improve the group relations. At times he encourages a diffident child to speak out or persuades a more vigorous participant to wait his turn. Along with his ordinary instruction he helps the group to grasp the full force of some member's contribution.

Again, intermingled with his academic activities and his duties as discussion leader, he introduces a modicum of warm emotional regard (Hughes and others, 1959). This may range from a friendly arm across the shoulder to a fleeting smile of appreciation, a brief word of praise, or a chuckle at a well-turned jest. At a more formal level it may consist of a few statements indicating an appreciative feeling for some or all of the students. The activities of most teachers will also include some sharp disapproval or an emotionally toned reprimand.

Our list would be incomplete if we did not make room for sheer self-expression on the part of the teacher. On many occasions the teacher indicates his opinions, or asserts his views, or recounts his experiences even when these may have no clear-cut bearing on the academic objectives of the lesson. Typically, of course, many of the opinions or incidents mentioned by the teacher will have a bearing on the lesson. But often they seem to be purely spontaneous utterances.

In view of the multiplicity of things done by the teacher, it is not surprising that some specialization has taken place. In many schools you may see a team of teachers. One member of the team may deliver a lecture while other members pass among the desks to help pupils follow what is being said. Another member may conduct a brief demonstration for small groups of students or provide remedial instruction. At times each member of the team may work with small discussion groups (Lambert, 1963; Shaplin and others, 1964).

Most teachers find that before they have spent many years on the job there is some opportunity for change. In such a rapidly expanding enterprise as education, there is a great need for teachers who can take more and more responsibility. The teacher who is well regarded soon finds himself invited to become the group leader of a team of teachers, or to become department head. Some will be selected to become supervisor, vice-principal, principal, or director of some special division of the school system. A number of teachers become counselors, school librarians, or take other specialized jobs.

For those teachers who elect to stay in the classroom, and many do, there are frequent moves to different communities, the teachers with better reputations being offered jobs in the better-paying suburban communities. At one time this was a definite form of promotion or advancement—from slum to better and better communities with better salaries, better teaching conditions, and better living conditions. Since the early 1960s there has been a slight reversal of this process, however, as more and more of the high-spirited young teachers respond to the challenge of teaching in the slums, and actually seek jobs in such areas. All in all, young people entering the profession in the post-Sputnik days report a sense of adventure and challenge. Many of them sense the growing acknowledgment of the urgent importance of education and feel something like pioneers helping to develop a heretofore neglected area of life. Here there are new worlds to conquer and more challenge than is to be found in the grey-flannel, anthills of business.

THE TEACHER AND HIS ROLES

We have considered some of the things that teachers do and the way they feel about it. But in the larger context, what does this all amount to? What part does the teacher play in the general scheme of things? Psychologists, and especially sociologists, have given much thought to this problem (Charters, 1963; Grambs, 1957; Havighurst and Neugarten, 1962; Stiles, 1957) and have tried to discover the teacher's basic sociological function. What roles does he play at one time or another, and what other roles could he assume if he wished?

General Representative of the Adult World. In one sense the teacher may be considered as the adult who substitutes for parents when the latter are not available to act for themselves. There are, of course, many occasions when parents cannot do all that must be done. They cannot always get away from home when the child must venture forth. There are also specialized areas of conduct, such as in music, or the management of mathematics, or the intricacies of theology, which are beyond the parent from sheer lack of competence. Other limitations come from lack of time, lack of energy, or lack of sustained interest in such recondite or tiresome areas as ancient history or the multiplication tables.

For pupils in the lower grades, the teacher is chiefly the adult with whom they must spend much time and who has the power of making life cheerful or miserable, according to the mysterious and arbitrary currents by which adults are moved. He can offer emotional support or can act as a threat. The summaries of investigations (Allen, 1960; Witty, 1955) over a period of thirty years (Foster, 1933; Taylor, 1962) tell a fairly consistent story. Children in the early grades describe the teachers they like as kind, patient, cheerful, friendly, humorous. The teachers they dislike are simply cross, cranky, crabby, and bossy. Young pupils say little about the teacher as an instructor or a clarifier of intellectual mysteries. Specific pedagogical practices are seldom listed, though there is some mention of favoritism or fairness in discipline. Skill in teaching is more likely to be stressed in the upper grades, although even here the menace of the cross, crabby teacher never quite recedes.

Specialized Director of Learning. The teacher is not always seen as a sort of all-purpose parent substitute or authority figure. In the eyes of many people he is also a specialist in the art of directing learning (Fleming, 1958; Smith, 1960a; Woodruff, 1962). This role, important in itself, is also an important ally to other roles the teacher may be asked to take on. Later, for instance, we discuss the teacher's role as a symbol of culture. Now that role, in and of itself, does not necessarily demand the active direction of instruction. Anyone serving merely as a symbol of culture could, conceivably, adopt a purely passive role. He could conduct a culture column, so to speak, to whom anyone might write when in need of advice. Or he could manifest culture by other remote activities. And it is true in some cultures, the teacher—the rabbi, the guru, perhaps, fills precisely this role (Mead, 1943). When approached, he issues pronouncements or emits wisdom appropriate to the occasion. But he does not seek out converts.

In most conceptions, however, the teacher is seen as taking much more initiative. He does not merely dispense information or culture to those already moved to seek him out. On the contrary, he endeavors to inspire or persuade people, especially youth, to see the light and to become proficient in cultural matters. Often he sternly demands such proficiency. He presents cultural matters to those around him and asks for an appropriate reaction.

In the minds of some people, this ability to direct the learning process is some kind of free-floating skill. In this role the teacher is not exclusively oriented to youth. He may also apply his skill to the teaching of adults. At times, moreover, this skill is considered to be divorced from subject matter. According to this view, a teacher skilled in the art of instruction should be able to teach anything. "You can teach, can't you?" his superiors demand. "Then go ahead and teach this."

Success in this role has been a source of joy to many teachers. In warm and moving accounts we learn of the teacher's rich satisfaction in bringing to light, and to a functioning level, some talent that the student himself had neither much noticed nor greatly valued. The teacher also finds great satisfaction in seeing comprehension and appreciation develop in those who have listened to his explanations and have wrestled with his demands.

In their thoughts about teachers they knew, older students pay some attention to the teacher as a manager of instruction. It is true that the teacher as a parent or authority figure, so all-pervasive with young children, persists even into college days (Ofchus and Gnagey, 1963). Certainly older students agree with younger students in describing the detested teacher as cross and cranky, adding such items as sarcastic and bossy (Tiedeman, 1942). When describing the teacher they like, however, older students frequently stress the didactic arts (Isaacson and others, 1963). They speak of skill and patience in explaining, of the amount of work assigned, and of the intensity and consistency of the academic demands. There is some possibility, by the way, that this view of the teacher as director of learning may be more prominent among English students than among students in the United States (Taylor, 1962).

Symbol of Cultural Values. Along with other roles, the teacher has undoubtedly served as a representative of cultural things. Like the pastor, he served to remind people of things that they ac-

► *Teacher Qualities that Impress Students*

For the year 1959–1960, at a large state university, sixteen graduate students were assigned to teach introductory psychology. In 1960–1961 a new group was similarly assigned. In each year these beginning instructors spent the first semester leading discussion sections that were part of a large lecture class. During the second semester each of these instructors took complete charge of a class.

These graduate students had spent some time together and for any one year it was possible to get each of the sixteen to rate the other fifteen on a number of traits. From a factor analysis it appeared that these traits could be grouped under such categories as appearing to be a cultured person, agreeableness, surgency or enthusiasm, and dependability. Other data were also available from personality inventories taken by the instructors.

At the end of each semester each instructor was rated by his students. There are thus four "runs," two ratings each for two groups of instructors.

THE CHARACTERISTICS OF THE INSTRUCTOR AS THEY CORRELATE
WITH STUDENTS' OPINION OF HIS EFFECTIVENESS

Characteristics of Instructor	Average Correlation[a] for Four "Runs"	Number of the Four Correlations Significant at 5-percent Level
General Culture (Peer Rating)	.60	3
Student Rating of Instructor Culture	.48	—
Agreeableness (Peer Rating)	.44	3
Surgency (Peer Rating)	.51	2
Dependability (Peer Rating)	.14	0
Conscientiousness (Personality Inventory)	−.39	0

[a] See the Appendix for an explanation of correlation.

Most of the ratings are based on the general impression of the instructor's peers. A student rating for culture is also included, and one measure of dependability or conscientiousness from a personality inventory. Dependability, no matter how measured, seemed to have little relation—perhaps an inverse relation—to the students' estimates of effectiveness.

SOURCE: R. L. Isaacson, W. J. McKeachie, and J. E. Milholland, Correlation of teacher personality variables and student ratings, *Journal of Educational Psychology*, 1963, **54**, 110–117.

knowledged to be important but which, all too often, they tended to neglect. Merely seeing him around, or seeing the late lamp burning in his study, people would remember that there is a world of books and ideas, and of other values so easily ignored. In some cultures the teacher was venerated as the revered scholar or learned man. In other circumstances he might be regarded as a pioneer in the world of ideas, or certainly as having a command of ideas and cultural things that far exceeded that of the average man. Often he might act as arbitrator in arguments about intellectual matters.

To some extent, thoughtful adults may still think of the teacher largely as a symbol of culture. In judging the teacher, the adult may ask, "How does this person fit my concept of the educated man? Do I feel happy about him as a representative of the intellectual things I know about, or would like to know about? Or do I feel a little sad when I think of this person as a symbol of the world of ideas?"

As more and more people are receiving more and more education, the teacher may be losing his significance as an outstanding example of the world of culture. A great many people nowadays may equal or surpass the teacher in these matters. At this point, the teacher becomes, not an exceptional scholar, but merely one member of the group who happened to go into teaching instead of life insurance or embalming. He remains as a formal custodian of ideas, but his chief function is that of transmitting things already well understood by the general public. He is different from other people, not in knowing more, but in the sense of taking over matters that they are too busy to bother about, or at least, too busy to give the prolonged attention that is demanded. This is the traditional role that Mead (1951) attributes to grandparents in many primitive cultures. In such cultures, the immediate parent is perfectly able to transmit the tribal legends and ceremonial duties. But since the grandparent can also do this, and can do little else, and has little else to do, he may as well relieve the parents of this responsibility. Clearly in this role, the teacher ceases to be the revered scholar or honored arbiter of intellectual matters and becomes, instead, a parent substitute to whom is delegated certain minor but time-consuming chores.

But we must not overemphasize this possible change in the teacher's role as a symbol of culture. It is a role that he still fills to some extent, and a role that permeates other functions that he may be asked to perform. And it is a role that continues to give much satisfaction to many teachers. Over and over again we read of a teacher's surprise to realize that he is actually paid to read Melville and Conrad, or to keep up in his scientific interests. College teachers, indeed, often take a belligerent attitude in their guardianship of cultural matters (Bowen, 1960). They feel that they have to stand firm against the administration or others who might ride rough-shod over the precious realm of culture and the intellect. They boldly remind the administration that the professor, as the representative of culture, is really the central figure around whom other aspects of the university should revolve.

Symbol of Morality and Character. Along with his role as a representative of the intellect, the teacher has often acted as a symbol for some aspects of character. Like his cousin, the pastor, he has, at times, exemplified the unworldly, self-sacrificing, idealist. Here again he has been expected to symbolize traits that many people value to some extent but which they fail to stress as much as they ought. Although perhaps truer in the past, some of this image may still remain. The typical parent or citizen would probably be somewhat taken aback if he saw in the teacher the same sordid behavior, or the same evidence of grim self-seeking, that he may take for granted in other people or in himself.

However bright or tarnished the teacher may be as a symbol of a gentle

► *Impressive Teaching Takes Many Forms*

Love, Support and the Door to Insight. Helen Keller describes her teacher, Anne Mansfield Sullivan:

I felt approaching footsteps. I stretched out my hand as I supposed to my mother. Some one took it, and I was caught up and held close in the arms of her who had come to reveal all things to me, and more than all things else, to love me.

We walked down the path to the well house, attracted by the fragrance of the honeysuckle with which it was covered. Some one was drawing water and my teacher placed my hand under the spout. As the cool stream gushed over one hand she spelled into the other the word *water*, first slowly, then rapidly. I stood still, my whole attention fixed upon the motions of her fingers. Suddenly I felt a misty consciousness as of something forgotten—a thrill of returning thought; and somehow the mystery of language was revealed to me.

Teaching Intermingled with Family Living. John Stuart Mill is describing his education at the hands of his brilliant father, James Mill.

I went through the whole process of preparing my Greek lessons in the same room and at the same table at which he was writing; and as in those days Greek and English lexicons were not, and I could make no more use of a Greek and Latin lexicon than could be made without having yet begun to learn Latin, I was forced to have recourse to him for the meaning of every word which I did not know. This incessant interruption, he, one of the most impatient of men, submitted to, and wrote under that interruption several volumes of his *History* and all else that he had to write during those years.

But the lessons were only a part of the daily instruction I received. Much of it consisted in the books I read by myself, and my father's discourses to me, chiefly during our walks. From 1810 to the end of 1813 we were living in Newington Green, then an almost rustic neighborhood. My father's health required considerable and constant exercise, and he walked habitually before breakfast, generally in the green lanes toward Hornsey. In these walks I always accompanied him, and with my earliest recollections of green fields and wild flowers is mingled that of the account I gave him daily of what I had read

morality, he is typically expected to instill a measure of morality in his charges. A host of current writings (Charters, 1963; Havighurst and Neugarten, 1962; Warner and others, 1960) take it for granted that he is called upon to transmit the moral values that the middle-class citizens of any given era happen to hold. Whenever the middle class has held to the so-called Protestant or Puritan ethic, for instance, the schools have stressed work, ambition, success, independence, dependability, and prudent preparation for the future. Now that middle-class society may be worshiping the new god of sociability, togetherness, conformity, and group-thinking, the school's recent emphasis on sharing and group relations would seem a natural consequence.

In stressing the type of character necessary for success, whether that be sturdy independence or convivial conthe day before. To the best of my remembrance, this was a voluntary rather than a prescribed exercise. I made notes on slips of paper while reading, and from these in the morning walks, I told the story to him.

In my eighth year I commenced learning Latin, in conjunction with a younger sister, to whom I taught it as I went on, and who afterward repeated the lessons to my father: and from this time, other sisters and brothers being successively added as pupils, a considerable part of my day's work consisted of this preparatory teaching. It was a part which I greatly disliked; the more so, as I was held responsible for the lessons of my pupils, in almost as full a sense as for my own: I, however, derived from this discipline the great advantage of learning more thoroughly and retaining more lastingly the things which I was set to teach: perhaps too, the practice it afforded in explaining difficulties to others, may even at that age have been useful.

The Stern Teacher with a Powerful Sense of Duty. Louis Henri Sullivan, the revered mentor of Frank Lloyd Wright, reports on the welcome to new students accorded by Moses Woolson (1821–1896).

He was tense, and did not swagger—a man of passion. He said, in substance: "Boys, you don't know me, but you soon will. The discipline here will be rigid. You have come here to learn and I'll see that you do. I will not only do my share but I will make you do yours. You are here under my care; no other man shall interfere with you. I rule here—I am master here—as you will soon discover. You are here as wards in my charge; I accept that charge as sacred; I accept the responsibility involved as a high, exacting duty I owe to myself and equally to you. I will give to you all that I have; you shall give to me all that you have. But mark you: The first rule of discipline shall be SILENCE."

There may have been teachers and teachers, but for Louis Sullivan there was and could be only one.

SOURCES: Helen Keller, *The Story of My Life* (New York: Doubleday & Company, Inc., 1902); *Great Teachers*, Houston Peterson, ed. (New York: Vintage Books, Random House, n.d.); Louis Henri Sullivan, *The Autobiography of an Idea* (New York: Dover Publications, Inc., 1924).

formity, the teacher takes over a role often retained by parents themselves in primitive societies (Mead, 1951).

There has been some question, by the way (Charters, 1963), that the school's emphasis on middle-class morality necessarily represents docile compliance. It may be that the values of dependability, respect for order, and similar values attributed to the middle class are necessary for the smooth functioning of any organization such as the school. Even if school people happened to feel primary loyalty to lower-class values—to spontaneity, and gratification of impulse —they might well stress order and respect for authority in the school merely to make it possible to operate in moderate efficiency and comfort. In contrast to the cliché that teachers reward middle-class students and punish lower-class students, there is now some evidence that teachers reward any behavior that fits in with school values, whether the child comes from one side of the tracks or the other (Hoehn, 1954).

Gilbert Highet (1950) has made much of the dramatic success and dramatic failures of the great historic teachers in developing the moral character of their students. He is impressed by the remarkable success of Alexander, the pupil of Aristotle, and with the sorry performance of Judas, the pupil of Jesus, and of Nero, the pupil of Seneca. Even with such great teachers, the teaching of morality has proved to be a precarious enterprise. Indeed, Highet has implied that the enterprise is even more hazardous for the truly great man. He casts a tremendous shadow. To emerge from this shadow the pupil may be driven to desperate, and perhaps vicious, expedients.

Friend and Confidant of Youth. At times the teacher is perceived as one who is keenly alert to the needs of youth and who has a sympathetic interest in the problems of the young. This image fits in with the role of the child nurse as seen in primitive societies (Mead, 1951). Such a child nurse is sensitive to the wishes of her charge and tries to gratify them. She is not so much concerned with developing the child's ability as she is with indulging his present demands and in providing immediate happiness.

The exercise of this role has brought satisfaction to many teachers. They feel their own youth renewed as they share the comradeship of an adolescent group. Another teacher is rewarded when adoring eyes or a proffered sticky palm inform him that he has become a person of great consequence in the life of some child. There are frequent accounts of the thrill of encountering the occasional responsive mind, and the pleasure of genuine intellectual exchange when working with the more able students (Bowen, 1960).

Member of a Profession. There has been some doubt as to whether or not teaching really is a profession (Anderson, 1962; Havighurst and Neugarten, 1962; Lieberman, 1956). The problem of dealing with this question is discussed in Chapter 16. There is no doubt, however, that the teacher is a member of a definite vocational group. In his role as a member of a group of school people or of a school organization, the teacher has definite duties, rights, and sources of contact. He talks regularly with principal, department head, or supervisor. From each of these he can expect certain things. To each of these he has some obligations. He also has many contacts, both formal and informal, with colleagues of the same rank. In these contacts there may be much satisfaction and also many occasions for distress. To some teachers they mean a great deal. Often we get the picture of a coherent band of warriors in common cause against the perils to their craft, whether these be merely the inevitable difficulties of teaching, the shortages of equipment, or even the perversity of administrators.

The Teacher as a Person. The teacher, like nonteachers, is an individual with his own needs and foibles. Many teachers report much satisfaction in being able to follow, once in awhile at least, their own interests and to indulge their own needs (Bowen, 1960). The teacher, of course, cannot expect complete autonomy. But at times he is free to work things out his own way, and this privilege has been greatly prized. A few teachers gain some satisfaction from the very obscurity of their rewards. Just as in childhood we may have had a haunt made especially precious because it is known to us alone, so these teachers find additional satisfaction in the fact that the real joys in their work are those that no one else can realize.

The recollections of adults, in contrast to the statements of young children, often reveal the impact of the teacher as a person. The adult, now that he is no longer exposed to harassment, may even mention faults and foibles with appreciation. The personal qualities most frequently stressed are those closely associated with the teacher as a scholar, and with the teacher as a director of instruction. Students remember the histrionic teacher who infuses some dry subject with the surgency of his own personality. Harper of Chicago taught Greek grammar as if it were a series of narrow escapes. Leo Spitzer of Johns Hopkins could leave casual undergraduates tense and exhilarated by a dramatic analysis of some obscure nuance in Italian poetry. Adults remember other personal qualities ranging from astounding humility to violent moral indignation that sometimes brought life and color to the less formal relations between teacher and student.

Member of the Community. The teacher must play some role in his community. One of his many functions, indeed, may be to act as a link or interpreter between the school world and the general community. In many respects the teacher occupies the role of the stranger or the resident alien within the community. He is in the community but not quite of it. Literally, it is true, he is something of a transient. He is a transient in the profession. Fully 25 percent of teachers have had less than four years experience (Charters, 1963). He is a transient even within his profession in that he is likely to turn up after hours,

or on Saturday, in some second job. He is a transient in the community. Very frequently he moves to similar jobs in other areas. Whatever the important aspect of his transiency, he is often treated as some rootless person, a person on the move psychologically if not geographically.

DIVERSITY OF ROLES AND STYLES

Clearly, each teacher in his work plays many parts, and different observers see him from different viewpoints. Clearly, too, the teacher may be called upon to make some choice among the various roles he has a chance to fill.

In being so many different things to so many different people, the teacher faces many problems. Even the same person may expect different things from him at different times. A parent, acting as a member of the community, may think of the teacher as one who holds up academic standards and turns out an employable product. In thinking of the problem of his own child, however, the same parent may view the teacher as a solicitous friend of youth whose chief function is to smooth the troubled path of his pupils.

The teacher himself must vacillate in his view of his basic function. Many of the roles he may find himself playing are in conflict with each other. No one person can consistently fill them all. It is not unusual to hear the anguished wail, "Just what kind of a person am I supposed to be? What is expected of me?" Certainly to many teachers this has been a depressing problem.

But this diversity is not a complete evil. Since you must make some selection, since you cannot fill all these roles, you may well consider your own preferences. You may be especially competent in several roles and one or two of these you may enjoy. Why not play to strength, or inclination, and concentrate on the roles that best fit you?

Some Special Clusters of Roles and Attitudes

There has been a tremendous amount of research on the teacher's attitude toward children, and toward the profession. One instrument alone, the Minnesota Teacher Attitude Inventory (MTAI) has been used in scores of studies (Stern, 1963). Many other traits of teachers have also been studied (Ryans, 1960), and from the whole mass of data a few suggested patterns or clusters are beginning to emerge. The patterns, clusters, or dimensions include attitudes, personality traits, predominant role, and teaching style. These clusters or dimensions have emerged both from sober statistical analyses and from the lively recollections of articulate adults.

The Kindly, Interested Adult. In the first cluster we see the teacher both as a representative of the adult world and as a kindly companion to youth, keenly interested in the doings of young people. This general dimension or characteristic has appeared in Ryans's (1960) classical analysis where it is called the *friendly versus aloof* dimension. It also appears in the study of Solomon and Miller (1961) concerned with differences in teaching styles.

At one extreme in this cluster we have the adult who takes a warm and friendly interest in pupils. He tends to be more interested in students than in the subject that he teaches, regarding the latter chiefly as a means of helping the student to develop. He may get his chief pleasure from his interaction with the individual student. Or, like the fond parent warming to the spectacle of two children at play, he may get most of his satisfaction from the relations that develop between students.

The Businesslike Director of Instruction. The second cluster emphasizes the teacher in his role of director of instruction, but also includes a systematic attitude toward the management of learning. The teacher at one extreme of this dimension is orderly and efficient. Every problem has been foreseen and provided for, and the lesson proceeds with clockwork precision. We do not know what this teacher thinks about his students as people, but we do know that he takes a serious attitude toward the process of instruction. This appears as one definite dimension—*orderly versus disorganized*—in Ryans's analysis.

The Lively, Forceful Teacher. The vivacious, dramatic teacher turns up in students' recollections and in the statistical analyses. Here we see the teacher who comes alive in the classroom, who is expansive, stimulating, perhaps somewhat exhibitionistic. We know that this teacher enjoys his own performance, but we can be sure of little else. Underneath his lively presentation there may be a clear plan and a compact system, or there may be chaos and confusion. We know nothing of his attitude toward the students. He may be deeply concerned about each and every one as an individual, or he may regard each as an anonymous member of a mass audience that merely facilitates his act. We cannot tell whether the subject of instruction is important to him or whether it is merely something he can make use of in his performance. This trait has appeared as the *surgent versus dull* dimension in Ryans's analysis.

The Master of Subject Matter. This characteristic, although not conspicuous in Ryans's study, is clearly related to the teacher's role as a symbol of culture, and especially to his role as a respected scholar. However lively or dull, however systematic or confused, however friendly or aloof, this is the man who knows about his subject and cares intensely about it. His great satisfaction comes from the subject he teaches and from other things that serve or highlight his interest in the subject. Some of these devotees may also regard students as individuals important in their own right. Others may think of the students chiefly as instruments for developing and establishing the beloved subject matter. This dedicated specialist appears over and over again in the appreciative recollections of former students.

The Relative Importance of the Clusters

At the college level the successful teacher has usually been considered a master of his subject. Assuming a reasonable competence in subject matter, however, we find any one of the other clusters may be the basis for memorable teaching. In the more articulate descriptions of notable teachers (Highet, 1950), we hear of the eloquent, personable teacher, reaching into all fields of knowledge for the illustrations that enliven and clarify his discussions. Sometimes he is disorganized, sometimes on the trail of some intriguing digression he forgets what he was trying to illustrate, sometimes he is inaccurate. But always he is vivid, human, and interesting, and his students remember him as a great teacher. An equally able colleague may never utter a single wasted word, and may speak in icy, businesslike fashion, directing his remarks to the ceiling, and yet may hold his students by the logic with which he marshals and presents his ideas. Here we have the personification of the organized, businesslike cluster. There is no inaccuracy, no digression, and little eloquence or surgent vitality. Such a teacher may score low on the *friendly versus aloof* dimension. In testimonials to such teachers students often speak of this aloofness with admiration. Kitteridge collected his notes, books, and miscellaneous gear to the rhythm of his closing paragraph and was out of the door before even the most enterprising student could buttonhole him. Many students admired his skill in this art of avoiding small talk. Other students show admiration for the outstanding scientist who refused to permit casual chat to interfere with important research projects (Bowen, 1960).

Even the caustic critic may be admired, especially by adults no longer subjected to his ministrations. True enough, the more highly regarded of these critics used their biting remarks to provoke the student to a more careful analysis and to a more complete mastery of the subject. Perhaps they used their jibes skillfully. But however laudatory the goal, they exhibited little humanity or ordinary friendliness in the process. Other intensive questioners, however, stand high on the scale of kindliness. Socrates was noted for his patience and good nature. Indeed, in the written record, he seems to do his most effective work when, with equable temper and unfailing courtesy, he rides the storm of the student's antagonism and leads him to a rational decision.

Differences at Different Levels. The process of teaching as seen in the lives of Socrates and Seneca is probably a far cry from that process as it operates in English 8A in P.S. 16. Perhaps, indeed, these characteristics, drawn so largely from the teachers of adults, may be somewhat misleading when seen from the viewpoint of the teacher in the lower grades. For one thing, at the college and secondary school level, the clusters are largely independent or uncorrelated. Knowing where a teacher stands in one, we could not tell where he stands in any other. At these levels, moreover, a teacher can often succeed almost entirely through his strength in one of these clusters, even though he has only moderate standing in the others. The college teacher, for instance, can be unglamorous, aloof, even caustic, and still be successful, provided he is outstanding in one of the other clusters (master of subject or businesslike instructor). In the elementary school, on the contrary, the clusters cannot be so easily separated from each other. Here there is considerable correlation, and the teacher who excels in one cluster is likely to stand fairly high in the others as well. At this level, moreover, the teacher is less likely to succeed by concentrating on one of these clusters to the neglect of the others. In particular, no matter how outstanding he may be in the other traits, he cannot afford to be deficient in the friendly-supportive cluster.

College teaching may be distinctive in another respect. At this level, the concern for subject matter must often dominate. In many subjects the instructor's time is largely taken up with the sheer process of knowing what is true in his field. As a researcher he spends much time in original investigation. As a scholar he must cope with a continuous flood of books, journal articles, and oral reports bringing new information about his field. The psychologist, for instance, faces from 7000 to 8000 items *each year*; the biologist almost ten times as many. The college teacher must decide which of these to analyze carefully, which to read, which to glance at, and which to ignore. He must make sure that this information is organized into some struc-

ture. Either he does this himself or he must critically examine, and judge, what someone else has done.

Difficulties in Using College Teaching as a Model. In many instances, then, the college teacher is dominated by the thought of what he should tell the students and how it should be presented. At some levels, indeed, the college teacher's objectives begin and end here. In dealing with mature students in an honors program, the college teacher, having presented the material, need worry little about the task of directing the process of learning or inspiring or persuading his students. Clearly the teacher at lower levels cannot take this attitude.

In view of the great differences in the tasks confronting teachers of different age groups, you might be wise, in forming many of your views of the problems and tasks of teaching, to turn your back on the teaching that you now observe at the college level, and depend, rather, on your recollections of the teaching you experienced in high school and in the elementary grades. You should not necessarily regard these remembered incidents as models or as ideal procedures, but they should tell you about problems you will face. The tasks that present themselves to your college instructor, on the other hand, differ widely from those that you will face as a teacher in elementary or secondary school.

Various Routes to Success

In spite of the differences to be seen at different levels, we can find at each level many ways of being a good teacher, and we can take courage in remembering that good teachers vary tremendously among themselves (Jackson, 1962). The elementary teacher, although unable to ignore his role as a supportive adult, can find many different ways of being friendly and many different ways of offering adult support.

In the upper grades there are even more ways to be a successful and valuable teacher. Good administrators everywhere tend to welcome the wholesome diversity that can come when different teachers emphasize different facets of the profession (Stinnett and Haskew, 1962). Realizing that each student will come in contact with several different teachers, the principal of today is proud of the fact that most pupils will encounter the teacher in many roles, the kindly companion, the stern, uncompromising proponent of some subject, the skilled director of learning, and the excited, surgent purveyor of one subject or another.

Cultivate your own strength. Don't be too envious of the colleague who excels in a role that is not for you. But never minimize his contribution either.

SUMMARY

People go into teaching for many reasons—tradition, ideals, an intrinsic fondness for the work. A few just drift in. For the student, the entrance into the profession often brings problems. There are irksome responsibilities and a change of loyalties. The hours seem long, and the tasks go far beyond mere classroom obligations. In the classroom itself the teacher lives a varied and exacting life in which he provides stimulation, support, and an insistence on academic attainment. So many jobs are his, in fact, that

teams are often organized to provide specialists for the various chores.

In his broader work, the teacher stands as a representative of the adult world and of the general world of culture. Young pupils see him chiefly as the former. Older students also see him as a symbol of the intellect and as a director of instruction. To the teacher himself this is often a cherished role. To a certain extent the teacher may serve as a babysitter who takes the children off the mother's hands. In all this he must act as a reasonable representative of morality, must find his place in the community and in his profession, and must try to retain his individuality.

In playing any one of his many roles, the teacher can bring to his task a diversity of styles. Each teacher can be rated on a dimension ranging from *friendly* to *aloof*; on a second dimension ranging from *businesslike* to *disorderly*; and on a third dimension ranging from *lively* to *dull*. For the teacher of young children there must be something in the way of friendliness. At more advanced levels, notable teaching may be achieved by exceptional standing in any one of the dimensions. Among college teachers, of course, mastery of subject matter cannot be neglected. College teaching, by the way, may prove a misleading reference point for the student preparing to teach at a lower level. The teacher at any level should take advantage of the fact that the schools will welcome a great diversity in teachers.

SUGGESTIONS FOR FURTHER READING

American Association of Colleges for Teacher Education, *Roles and Relationships in Teacher Education*. 11th Biennial School for Executives, Washington, D. C.: The Association, 1963.

Bereday, G. Z. F., and J. A. Lawreys, eds., *The Education and Training of Teachers: The Yearbook of Education*. New York: Harcourt, Brace & World, Inc., 1963.

Englander, M. E., A psychological analysis of vocational choice: teaching, *Journal* of Counseling Psychology, 1960, 7, 257–264. Reprinted in Morse, pp. 7–12.

Fleming, Charlotte M., Teaching: A Psychological Analysis. New York: John Wiley & Sons, Inc., 1958.

Gage, N. L., ed., Handbook of Research on Teaching. Skokie, Ill.: Rand McNally & Company, 1963. See especially:

Wallen, N. E., and R. M. W. Travers, "Analysis and Investigation of Teaching Methods," Chapter 10.

Getzels, J. W., and P. W. Jackson, "The Teacher's Personality and Characteristics," Chapter 11.

Withall, J., and W. W. Lewis, "Social Interaction in the Classroom," Chapter 13.

Charters, W. W., "The Social Background of Teaching," Chapter 14.

Guba, E. G., P. W. Jackson, and C. E. Bidwell, Occupational choice and the teaching career, Educational Research Bulletin, 1959, 38, 1–12, 57. Reprinted in Charters, pp. 271–278.

Havighurst, R. J., and Bernice L. Neugarten, Society and Education. Boston: Allyn and Bacon, Inc., 1962.

Highet, G., The Art of Teaching. New York: Alfred A. Knopf, Inc., 1950.

Jackson, P. W., The teacher and individual differences, Yearbook National Society for the Study of Education, 1962, 61, Part I, 75–90.

Leeds, Carroll H., Teacher behavior liked and disliked, Education, 1955, 75, 29–37. Reprinted in Morse, pp. 12–18.

Lieberman, M., Education as a Profession. Englewood Cliffs, N. J.: Prentice-Hall, Inc., 1956.

Mason, W. S., R. J. Dressel, and R. K. Bain, Sex role and the career orientations of beginning teachers, Harvard Educational Review, 1959, 29, 370–383. Reprinted in Charters, pp. 278–286.

Ryans, D. G., Characteristics of Teachers. Washington, D. C.: American Council on Education, 1960.

Spaulding, R. L., Achievement, creativity and self-concept correlates of teacher-pupil transactions in elementary schools. (Unpublished) Printed in Stendler, pp. 313–318.

Stiles, L., ed., The teacher's role in American society, Yearbook John Dewey Society, 1957, 14. New York: Harper & Row, Publishers, Inc. See especially:

McGuire, C., and G. D. White, "Social Origins of Teachers—in Texas," Chapter 3.

Wattenberg, W., and others, "Social Origins and Teaching Role—Some Typical Patterns," Chapter 4.

Grambs, Jean D., "The Roles of the Teacher," Chapter 6.

Lloyd-Jones, Esther, and Mary V. Holman, "Why People Become Teachers," Chapter 17.

Stinnett, T. M., and L. D. Haskew, Teaching in American Schools. New York: Harcourt, Brace & World, Inc., 1962.

EXERCISES AND QUESTIONS FOR DISCUSSION

1. For each of the levels of education that you can remember (elementary, secondary, college) try to recall one teacher that you regard as outstanding and one that you regard as very inadequate. Try to determine the characteristics that distinguish between them. Are these distinguishing characteristics the same at all levels?

2. Consider some of the jobs in teaching that you have thought of for yourself. Which of the many possible roles of the teacher would you relish? What about those that you do not relish? Could you ignore these and still succeed in this situation?

3. Suppose that there is a great scarcity of teachers who are skillful in the process of directing learning. Which level (elementary–college) should have first choice of these scarce teachers? How do things work out in the practical situation?

4. What features of teaching, as you now see it, do you find attractive? What features do you find disturbing?

CHAPTER 2

▸ Development Apart from the School

In this book we are concerned chiefly with the things that the teacher can do in the classroom. In managing the classroom activities, however, we must realize that we do not work alone. By the time the six-year-old first reaches school he has taken tremendous strides in his progress toward maturity. From forces entirely outside the school, he has acquired an astounding working mastery of a whole language and much motor skill. Many of his basic attitudes have begun to take shape, and he is well on his way toward some degree of socialization.

The forces that have shaped the child before he reaches school by no means retire from the scene when we begin to exert our influence. The never-to-be-forgotten forces of physiology and body chemistry keep up their work. Interaction with parents continues with an intensity that we seldom approach in the classroom. The gang, the group, and the clique increase in their impact, interacting with our efforts in all areas, completely dwarfing them in some.

Aspects of Development Stressed in Classroom Contexts

Although general child development, as such, is not our basic theme, there are many issues in this field that are bound to receive extended treatment. The problem of motivation, for instance, takes on meaning only in the light of the child's needs, interests, and concerns. In discussing the whole area of learning, moreover, we must not only show how the process of learning depends on various aspects of child nature, but we must also show how learning acts to affect the general development of the child. The vital areas of personal and social adjustment can be understood only in the light of the basic process of child development acting from infancy on. Here we must consider the early forces that shape the child's adjustment and mental health. In this area, and in the area of character development, we have much to say about the detailed relations of parent and child, of the developing mechanisms on which

21

these relations rest, and of the shaping which these mechanisms receive in their own turn.

But these occasional treatments are bound to be spotty and incomplete. To place them in perspective, and to fill in the gaps, you should spend some time in reviewing your earlier study of human development (see "Suggestions for Further Reading"). The very general overview that follows may serve as a guide in such a review.

Methods of Studying Child Development

Our information about children comes from many different sources (Mussen, 1960). There are a number of reports in which a very few children, perhaps only one, have been studied very intensively (*intensive case study*). Typically such a study will cover many facets of the child—his physique, health, energy, ability, personality, and so forth. Other studies concentrate on only a few facets (independence or popularity or intelligence) but secure that information from a large number of children (*limited variables*). Similarly, in studying the changes in the child as he grows older, we can follow a given group of children through a period of years, observing the same children year after year (*longitudinal method*). We can, on the other hand, study a large number of different children at each age (*cross-sectional method*). Here we assume that this particular group of four-year-olds will reflect the behavior we can expect from our crop of three-year-olds when they become a year older.

Each of these approaches has its values and its limitations. There are obvious advantages, for instance, in the intensive study of a few people. This permits us to see many facets in relation to each other and to see changes in one facet in relation to changes in the other. But the results may not hold for the general run of children. There are obvious risks in the cross-sectional method. Our particular group of (say) twelve-year-olds may be drawn from a completely different population than (say) our group of four-year-olds. The introduction of an electronics plant in the locality, for instance, may have led to the influx of many young engineers, scientists, and technical workers having families, for the most part, in the preschool or kindergarten ages. The twelve-year-olds, on the other hand, may be largely the children of older residents with an agricultural background. The longitudinal approach avoids these dangers but even this approach is not without its difficulties. In addition to being expensive and burdensome, this method does not protect us from the danger that the particular children studied will not be representative. Typically we use only a small number of cases. Those used in longitudinal studies, moreover, must come from homes willing and able to have their children return for testing, year after year. Perhaps they are a special group.

THE CHILD AS HE COMES TO SCHOOL

As pointed out earlier, the child has attained a great deal of development by the time he enters school. In almost any area of educational growth he has progressed to some extent and is on the verge of still greater attainment. Let us look more closely at the growth he has reached in certain of these areas.

Health and Physique

The six-year-old has almost 90 percent of all the brain and neural tissue that he will ever have. Girls have attained over two-thirds of their ultimate height and boys almost that much. Both sexes have about one-third of their young-adult weight. Motor dexterity is well developed. At six the child can master the arts of bicycle riding, complex climbing, jumping, and hopping. His fingers can deal with knots, buttons, typewriter keys, and television control knobs. He can throw or toss a ball with some precision. And certainly he can tussle, although here energy is more pronounced than finesse or precision. His physiology has worked out some way of dealing with the substances that surround and infiltrate him. He now has an excellent chance of survival. In this he is a better risk than his two-year-old sibling. Deaths in the next decade or more are gratifyingly rare and come largely from accidents. His body is also changing in composition. By the time we meet him he has begun to get his permanent teeth, and, in scores of bony structures, centers of ossification have been established. From these, forces are set in motion to change the pliable and loosely articulated structures of childhood into the more rigid and tightly fused bones of adulthood (Tanner, 1961).

But there are some exceptions to this picture of advanced physical development. At the age of six, as we have said, the child lacks bulk, having only one-third or one-quarter of his total weight. More significant, perhaps, he lacks strength, having only one-sixth of his ultimate physical power. And apart from

---

▶ *Development of a Sense of Balance in School Children*

About 320 boys and 180 girls of varying ages were tested on their ability to walk along the edge of a twelve-foot 2 by 4 beam raised about 2 inches above the ground. There was some wobble in the middle part of the beam. Each child made three round trips. He was given a score of 1 for every time he walked the whole length without falling off. The total possible score was thus 6.

| | | Score | |
Age Range	Boys		Girls
4–6	0.1		0.5
6–7	0.9		1.6
7–8	1.6		2.1
8–9	2.5		2.0
9–10	2.8		2.1
10–11	3.0		2.4
11–12	3.8		2.5

Prior to the age of six very few children can make one successful trip. After six most children make at least one trip out of six without falling off.

SOURCE: G. W. Cron and N. H. Pronko, Development of a sense of balance in school children, *Journal of Educational Research*, 1957, **51**, 33–37.

a few chemical stirrings, there are few hints of the changes that will mark him as sexually mature. As you contemplate this individual, then, see him as still waiting for a moderate increase in height, the tripling of his weight, a sixfold increase in strength, and a complete transformation with respect to reproductive functioning. Add some inches to the length of a few bones, triple his bulk, multiply his physical power, endow him with reproductive possibilities, and physically he will be an adult.

Linguistic, Intellectual, and Cognitive Powers

Along with the attainment of almost his full quota of neural tissue, the six-year-old has made amazing intellectual strides. He has gone a great way toward mastering the language. In the course of a few months, during the second year, his vocabulary has exploded from some twenty words to one hundred or more. By the age of two this number has doubled, and it doubles again in another six months. At three he has almost 1000 words and by the age of six he is master of some 2500. This, by the way, is a most conservative estimate. Some studies, counting each variant as a separate word, have given the six-year-old credit for over 23,000 words. The true value is probably less than this but may well exceed 2500 (Carrol, 1960).

This substantial vocabulary represents words that he understands and that he uses with considerable precision. Most of them he pronounces in quite recognizable fashion although with a few childish or idiosyncratic inadequacies. He uses his words in regular sentences, averaging about six or seven words in length. He also uses complex sentences, having mastered the relation between main and subordinate ideas.

Distinguishing and Ordering. With his more precise mastery of the linguistic tools, the six-year-old can demonstrate his grasp of many important distinctions. He makes distinctions between little and big, the edible and inedible, yours and mine, rest and play, good and bad, male and female, past and present, near and far, many and few, left and right (in his own person). His comments deal fairly accurately with notions of space and time. He arranges things in order and can list the days of the week in their correct sequence. He counts, and has some rudimentary notions of addition. Often he can tell the time, basing his judgments on the over-all general position of the hands. Often, however, he must wait for another year before he is very accurate in reading the clock.

Mastery of Concepts. Not only can the six-year-old make distinctions between big and little, male and female, good and bad but he can treat these qualities as *concepts* and can talk about bigness as an attribute. He can discuss the advantages and disadvantages of bigness or maleness. He knows some of the things that go with goodness and badness. He can give you the *opposite* of "heavy" or "quick," without having to mention a heavy toy or a quick movement.

To say that a six-year-old can deal with many concepts is not to say that his mastery is precise or accurate. He can still bring smiles or embarrassment by speaking of Mrs. Jones as Mr. Jones's "mother." Here he is probably not so unchivalrous as to suggest that Mrs. Jones is much older than her husband. More plausible, he merely shows an inexact notion of the relationship of "mother." He may mean, "Are you the adult woman in the home to which Mr. Jones belongs?" (Stone and Church, 1957).

According to Piaget (Flavell, 1963), the six-year-old has mastered the *preconceptual* stage and has entered the *intuitive* stage of intellect. Even in the preconceptual stage the infant has been using genuine symbols. At this age, however, the symbols for an object consist of the actual movements that one makes in reaching for an object, grasping it, sucking it, dropping it, and so forth. These actual movements, or abbreviated versions of them, can be carried out even when the object is not present. Thus the child acquires genuine symbols which can be manipulated somewhat independently of the particular environment. These function before there is any mastery of words, and enable the child to have much more commerce with the objects. It is by virtue of this extended commerce that he experiences the object as existing even when hidden from his sight (*object conservation*). These same crude, fleshy symbols lead him to deal with objects purposefully and to treat the same object sometimes as a means and sometimes as an end.

We cannot afford to ignore the crude, muscular symbolisms that evolve from the child's physical groping. With the mastery of language, however, the child acquires symbols that are more precise and facile than the unwieldy physical gestures on which he has heretofore relied. There is then a vast increase in the range of experience to which he can be exposed. With his firm mastery of these linguistic symbols, the six-year-old is now in a position to grapple with the elusive problem of the basic external constancies. He can treat an object as if it really exists when his senses seem to say otherwise. Now he must learn to see that the number of marbles is not altered even when spread over a larger area (*conservation of number*), that the parts of a dis-

membered orange weigh as much as the intact object from which they were derived (*conservation of mass*), and that volume remains constant in spite of the difference in the forms that the substance may assume. But these notions are yet to come. Conservation of number may come shortly after the sixth year. *Conservation of volume*, however, may have to wait until near adolescence (Wallach, 1963).

In his general thinking about the world around him, the six-year-old often shows himself to have made a sudden improvement. In one investigation (Laurendeau and Pinard, 1962), children were asked what made dreams, why does it get dark at night, what is the difference between living and nonliving things, why do clouds move, and why is it that some things float in water whereas other objects sink. In only one of these did the authors fail to find a spurt at the age of six. In answering the questions about night, as it happened, there was only a gradual change from the age of four on. The youngest children gave no answers, or merely stated that it had to get dark (finalism). The explanations of older children stressed the usefulness of dark (because it is time to go to bed). By the age of six more and more children invoked some physical cause—clouds, fog, smoke, or the absence of the sun, but there was no spectacular improvement at this age.

Although the explanation of night improved in fairly gradual fashion, the other phenomena showed an abrupt improvement in understanding about the age of six. Naturally the explanations of the six-year-old left something to be desired. But in contrast to the previous year, we find a sudden increase in the number of children leaving one childish stage and moving up at least one notch in sophistication. It is at the six-year level that we first find reasonable accuracy in distinguishing between the living and the nonliving. Even here, of course, the distinctions are not one hundred percent accurate, nor will they be for many years (Simmons and Goss, 1957). In giving the reasons for his distinctions, moreover, the six-year-old is often in error. Very frequently he attributes life to a thing because it seems to move on its own initiative. But for all the imperfections, it is at this age that we first see some accurate groping toward a reasonable distinction between the living and the inanimate.

In explaining more specific physical phenomena, the six-year-old also shows a sudden and qualitative improvement over his younger sibling. In explaining why some objects sink and others float, the five-year-old resorts to notions such as, "It has to" (finalism); "It wants to (doesn't want to)" (animism); or "It gives itself a push—something holds it (pushes it)" (dynamism). The six-year-old, in contrast, uses more general explanations. These, although typically erroneous, are related to the properties of the object—its size, weight, or thickness —and can be used to predict (usually incorrectly) what an untested object will do. And these general explanations, however incomplete, represent a tremendous advance over the earlier statements which say in effect, "It did what it did for reasons operating at that particular time."

Emotional and Social Development

With his more vivid, but often fallacious, view of the world, the six-year-old has a volatile and rather tempestuous emotional life. He has a high level of activation and is extremely sensitive to the world, and especially to people and their attitudes. He detects subtle changes of expression in the faces of those around

him, and he reacts vigorously to what he senses. His intense and distorted perceptions may give rise to many fears. He is afraid of animals, of people under the bed or around the corner, of accidents, or of direct attack. Dreams and nightmares become prominent about this time. So do allergies and such compulsive tics as grimacing, nose-picking, and perhaps a recurrence of the two-year-old stuttering, and the chewing of clothing. He complains of aches and ailments. He has difficulty in making up his mind as to what he wants.

Along with his heightened emotional life there is much disorganized activity. He wriggles, drums on his chair with his feet, and throws his clothes around. To adults he is often a trial. In explosions of temper he tries to strike or kick the offending parent or teacher. He is quite free with epithets, vicious threats, and occasionally with curses. Often he fails to acknowledge a request or to respond to a greeting. A request, when heard, may be resisted and a defiant argument may follow. At times, when the adult can summon enough patience to wait a few moments, the young hopeful may carry out the suggestion, at the same time seeming to pretend that it was his own idea all along.

The temper explosions are likely to be set off by corrections, especially if the reprimand comes right on the heels of the misdemeanor. But a lesser occurrence, such as a seeming slight, or getting behind in a game, may also trigger the outburst (Gesell and Ilg, 1949).

Clearly the six-year-old is by no means a restful companion. But he is not a complete monster. He can be quite affectionate and can express his fondness most demonstratively. Although resisting overt instruction, he can be inveigled into a delightful cooperative arrangement in

Yale University News Bureau

Arnold Gesell

helping out with some adult activity. He loves to laugh, largely at slapstick, but now, more and more, at subtle verbal and intellectual incongruities. Zest for such incongruities now begins to show up in his creative exploits. And in other activities also he shows an appreciation of the grotesque or ludicrous. Some six-year-olds can embrace humor, even more intimately. By use of gentle teasing, the skillful adult can transform the somber or petulant mood into a laugh.

With his fellows the six-year-old is also turbulent, active, and changeable. Games show vigorous interaction, ranging from rough-and-tumble and amorphous competition and quarrelling to activities calling for cooperation (rope games, ball play), turn-about games, imaginative digging and deliberately assumed roles

(cop and robber). At this age there is some tendency to play in groups of two or three, but larger groups are becoming more frequent, and the threesome often elicits the traditional jealousy. Periods of peaceful play are still short. Indoors, a group of two or three do well to last half an hour before undirected pestering sets in. Outdoors, the group may remain on reasonable terms for a much longer period. But even under ideal conditions, quarrels, competitions, boasting, wanting to win, are quite conspicuous.

SOME OF THE FORCES AT WORK

Many forces have been at work to produce the child who comes to us at the age of five or six. We should get to know these forces. With no assistance from us they have induced a considerable development. Perhaps we can use them as models in our attempts to further the child's development. At the very least, these forces, already at work, will continue to operate even after we enter the picture and we should come to know them as members of a pattern into which we must fit.

Physique

Clearly the chemical and hormonal make-up of the body is an important force. These things affect the energy level, the fatigue states, the appetites, and other physical needs. Size and body build, themselves products of many forces, also have a powerful influence on other aspects of development. These things affect the experience that the child will have. They influence the age of sitting up and the amazing shift in perspective that then comes under the infant's control. Physique also has something to say about crawling and walking and the important experiences that come from these activities. In the years that follow, much of what the child does or does not do will be partly due to the body he happens to have at that time.

Physique also has much influence on the attitude that other people take toward the child. Children with different physical make-up will receive different kinds of attention from the people around them. The delicate three-year-old may be cuddled and protected, whereas his more robust, hulking age-mate may be expected to stand on his own sturdy feet. Because he is big, one child may find that independence and self-reliance, however unwelcome, are thrust upon him, willynilly. The boy who has attained puberty will be taken seriously by his classmates of both sexes. The less mature boy of the same age may be disregarded and can expect less success in his bids for leadership (Mussen and Jones, 1957). Early puberty for girls has less clear-cut advantage and may impose a slight handicap (Jones and Mussen, 1958).

Development is also shaped by the mechanisms responsible for supplying the body with its essential needs. Granted a normal environment, some of these mechanisms function quite well with no outside help. By virtue of these mechanisms, the child will secure oxygen and will get rid of carbon dioxide. Under normal conditions muscles will quiet down when fatigue products become too concentrated and will go into action when these are replaced by other chemicals. Most temperature needs are taken care of automatically. In the early months, elimination also takes care of itself.

These mechanisms that operate with little conscious attention from the adult world play some part in development. The child automatically securing his oxy-gen in the high Andes will develop differently from the child at sea level. The child exposed to one range of temperatures will develop one set of tolerances and controls, whereas his cousin in another climate will acquire a different way of responding.

Needs Requiring Adult Intervention

Not all the mechanisms used to fulfill crucial needs can operate on their own. Even the physiological needs for food or liquid call for the intervention of adults. So, often, do the needs for relief from the pains of sharp objects, biting insects, excessive pressure, cramped postures, itches, dampness, or excessive temperatures. Adult intervention is also needed when danger threatens. And at times, of course, adult attention and affection is the very thing that is needed.

To a tremendous extent the child's development is influenced by his experience in getting adults to help him with these needs. How much general success has he had? More important, what devices has he stumbled upon, or worked out, for securing the requisite adult attention? In attaining this all-important adult attention, the behavior of some children will be shaped into patterns of screaming insistence. Other children will develop an apathetic patience, and still others will go in for engaging strategems of cuteness and appeal.

Adult response to infantile demand is, of course, not entirely whimsical or random. Neither is later adult demand. Adult response and expectation varies systematically from culture to culture and from one social class to another. In one culture the baby will be in close physical contact with the mother throughout the whole twenty-four hours—while she works in the field, performs her house-

► *Social Class and Maternal Behavior*

Thirty-one mothers were observed with respect to the way they treated their children in the presence of an interviewer. The mother's behavior was later rated for several traits and was correlated with the social or economic status of the family.

A positive correlation (see the Appendix) means that mothers from the higher socioeconomic group were more likely to use the practice.

| | Correlation of Behavior with | |
Behavior of Mother	Mother's Education	General Socio-economic Status
Grants autonomy to child	.44	.28
Cooperates with child	.01	.19
Excessive physical restraint of child	−.35	−.28
Intrudes into child's activities	−.20	−.26
Use of punishment	.09	−.19

SOURCE: Nancy Bayley and S. Schaefer, Relationships between socioeconomic variables and the behavior of mothers toward young children, *Journal of Genetic Psychology*, 1960, 96, 61–77.

hold chores, while she eats, and while she rests. In another culture the baby may be bound to a board and given the minimum of nursing care. He may be cuddled and fondled by all and sundry or only by the mother or nurse. His demands may be met in easygoing but unpredictable fashion or according to a rigid, studied schedule. He may be weaned early and abruptly or after a prolonged period of nonchalant nursing. He may grow up with adults who give free and vigorous expression to every passing mood or he may have to seek out emotional significance by detecting subtle shades of expression that escape the restraint of those around him. In one culture, adulthood may creep up on him in almost imperceptible stages; in another culture some spectacular ceremony may suddenly transport him from the status of a child to the responsibilities of manhood. In one culture the adults may stress aggressive self-seeking, immediate gratification of impulse, and the virtues of direct action. In another culture the emphasis may be upon restraint of impulse, overt consideration for others, and the claims of the future needs.

The Child's Concept of Himself

Forces acting in these various ways must have a direct effect on the child's development. Along with this direct effect, they set up other internal conditions which also play a crucial part in development. Because of his experience and of the forces acting on him, the child acquires a clearer and clearer self-concept. He sees himself in relation to others and in relation to the prevailing social demands and values. He must make his peace with the values that he takes seriously. He may try to meet them. He may falsely picture himself as meeting them well, even when he does so most imperfectly. He may stress the values that he is able to meet and disown or disparage those that he cannot see himself attaining. Through these processes he develops a self-concept (Wylie, 1961) that, by one means or another, is clearly linked to his value system. This self-concept he will try to preserve, and much of his future development will come from the efforts he makes to preserve a favorable self-concept. By the time we meet him he will have a self-concept that is largely the product of his history. And this self-concept, as it develops, will act to en-

hance the continuity of that history. The course he has followed up to this point will help determine his compass setting. And this compass setting will have something to say about any course that he can be induced to follow in the future.

PATTERNS OF DEVELOPMENT

Growth does not take place in perfectly uniform fashion. Some aspects of development come earlier and some later. Students of early development, for instance, have made much of the *cephalo-caudal gradient* and the *proximo-distal gradient*. The first refers to the fact that, typically, development in the region of the head is more advanced than development in the region of the tail end of the

▶ *Mental Deficiency and Climate during the Fetal Period*

This study is based on all the children admitted to a state home for the mentally deficient during a period of thirty-six years (1913–1949). The investigators studied the records of all those who would have been in the third fetal month during the summer months. They also determined whether that month for that particular year was warmer than average or cooler than average. Finally, they found out what proportion of all children for each fetal condition were later admitted to the state institution. From among the children of the "cool June" condition, for instance, there were 1.4 admissions for every 10,000 births. The table gives comparable figures for the other conditions that obtained during the third fetal month.

PROPORTION OF CHILDREN ADMITTED TO THE STATE INSTITUTION

	Number per 10,000 births		
Temperatures at the time that the child was in the third fetal month	Children whose third fetal month occurred in		
	June	*July*	*August*
Warmer than average	1.40	1.62	1.50
Cooler than average	1.41	1.29	1.20

SOURCE: B. Passamanick, "Determinants of Intelligence," in S. M. Farber and R. H. L. Wilson, eds., *Conflict and Creativity* (New York: McGraw-Hill Book Company, Inc., 1963).

organism. By the second gradient, we mean that development in the region of the trunk is often farther along than is development in the hands, fingers, or toes.

Growth by Fits and Starts

In early development there is some suggestion of turn-about growth. One part of the organism spurts ahead while the rest of it remains relatively quiescent for a time. This is conspicuous during the prenatal period. Such specialized development has received great stress in recent years. Any disease or unfavorable metabolic condition (lack of oxygen, high temperatures) present while one structure is developing may impair that structure in irreversible fashion (Passamanick, 1963). Maternal measles at one stage may bring permanent deafness to the child. Unfavorable conditions at another period may impair sex differentiation. Harmful drugs working at one period may prevent the development of arms and legs.

After the child is born, the fits and starts continue. Tooth development may remain quiescent for a time, waiting to push ahead rapidly later on. The three- or four-year-old in the process of slimming out may gain considerably in height with very little change in weight. The rapid increase in weight and muscle will come some years later.

Development by Differentiation

Much development is characterized by differentiation. The broad, general structure or skill appears first and fine detail develops later. So long as the cells are relatively unspecialized, for instance, tissues from one area may be transplanted into other areas and will blend into this new environment. Later on, after some specialization has taken place, transplanted tissue will retain some of its individuality even when placed in a new setting. The change from the broad, general to fine detail is also observed, much later, in verbal behavior. The two-year-old uses the general form of a sentence (beginning, middle, end) even though many of the individual words are gibberish. Having started out with this broad, general patter he later supplies the details and fits the individual items or words into the already accomplished global pattern.

Regularities in the Sequences of Development

In the early years, certainly, and perhaps in the later years as well, there is a surprising uniformity in the sequence of development. We have already stressed the sequence in physical development. There is a similar sequence in the development of behavior (Hooker, 1952; Mussen, 1963). In any fetus, for instance, the head can be turned before there is any ability to extend the hands.

After birth, the regular sequence of physical development continues, and with it a corresponding sequence in the type of acts that the child can perform. At an early age he can hang on to a ring pressed into his hand, and it is only later that he can reach out and grasp a ring that is some distance from him. He can hold his head steady in an erect position before he can maintain his body in a sitting position. He can roll from back to side before he can roll from back to stomach. He learns to stand before he learns to sit down.

In language and thought a similar pattern appears. There is a fairly regular progression from simple words, to phrases, simple sentences, compound sentences, and finally complex sentences. He can tell you what a simple object is used for before he can tell you what it is made of. He acquires skill in the overt use of language before he can do much thinking without muttering to himself, and this muttering period must come before he can make efficient use of truly silent speech in problem solving or in creative fantasy.

In many cultures there is a comparable progression of interests, fears, worries, and attitudes. We can expect, for instance, that some negativism will develop in the terrible two's. Parallel play precedes true rough-and-tumble interaction and this in turn precedes organized turn-about play and the later team activities. The childhood play group is transformed to the mischievous childhood gang, and still later to the adolescent crowd with its endless conversing and socializing. The six-year-old's interest in stories about cute animals changes to interest in sports, adventure, and romance. The preschooler's worry about sickness and violence is transferred to a more realistic worry about school failure, social inadequacy, or moral shortcomings.

Factors Underlying the Regular Sequence

To some extent this regular sequence may come from the sheer organization of the external world. It is only when you are in a standing position that you are able to go through the act of sitting down. You can't speak a complete sentence unless you can say some words. Part of the sequence, moreover, may come from regularities in the experience to which children are subjected. The child's attention may regularly be directed to animals and their doings before he is asked to contemplate the techniques of the ball player or the romantic activities of the latest movie star.

Interaction of Internal and External Forces. Along with the external regularities that may call for a predetermined path of development, we must consider the possibility of some internal states or conditions that lead to one line of development rather than another. To see this possibility we consider, first, an extreme analogy.

A frantic stranger deposits a ticking parcel on your lap, tells you that it is a bomb, and asks you to deal with it. At this point you are not dealing with some inert object, such as a stone or a book. What happens from now on does not depend entirely on what you do. The events to follow are determined partly by the organized activity already taking place within the parcel. Those self-contained activities, or your view of them, will affect what you do. They will also have some effect no matter what you do.

Obviously, the organized and directed activity now going on within the parcel must not be regarded as some mysterious force that appears full blown from out of the blue. At one time, no doubt, the materials now at work were much more passive. At that time they were not clearly directed toward some definite and worrisome end point. This directed activity is the result of some other forces that have already been working upon those materials.

Our relation to the frightening bomb is not unlike our relation to the less formidable packet of energy that constitutes the child. The more subdued explosions we will experience while in his company will come not only from forces that we apply but also from the forces already at work within him. Here again, as in the case of the bomb, it would be wrong to think that the forces working within the child were mysteriously and knowingly laid down at some remote beginning, and that they work in some immutable fashion to a predetermined end. If we go back far enough, the child may well be the completely passive product of some chemical or electrical activity (Beach, 1955). For practical purposes, however, we must realize that, at any given time, there will be forces already at work within the child, pushing toward one change rather than another. We must also realize that some of the interaction that takes place between him and his environment will come from these forces, whatever their origin, now at work within him. Some of the interaction, of course, will be due to the environment.

This interaction between the internal forces and the environment is seen in sheer physical development. What the child absorbs from the environment is determined both by what is there to be absorbed and by the chemical and structural organization of the beginning organism. What he does absorb changes that chemical and physical structure, and this in turn has its influence on what he will absorb from now on. In carrying on this interaction, moreover, the child produces changes in the environment, depleting this substance and increasing the concentration of some other material.

Clearly this interaction is observed in intellectual and emotional development. Whatever the underlying reasons, different children very early come to behave in somewhat different fashion. These different ways of behaving will elicit different reactions from the mother, with the result that different children will receive different treatment. This difference in the treatments, brought on in part by the child's own activity, will now

affect the subsequent behavior. Parents shape their children, we cannot deny, but children also shape their parents. Two identical mothers, arbitrarily assigned infants having, at the time of assignment, radically different dispositions, might readily develop different attitudes toward children and might adopt different child-rearing procedures.

It is all too easy to ignore this possible shaping of parents by the existing tendencies of children. We learn, for instance, that creative children are treated in more responsible fashion by their parents and are taken more seriously as individuals in their own right (MacKinnon, 1962). Immediately we conclude that this treatment by parents helps promote creativity. But what kind of children get to be treated as significant and responsible people in the first place? Some qualities already within the child may elicit this treatment from adults, and these self-same qualities, already incorporated into the child, may be responsible for the later creativity.

At any point of development, the inner forces, from whatever source, will be acting at that time. These in conjunction with fairly regular features of the environment can produce behavior with very little help from deliberate adult instruction. At an early age, for instance, the infant's eyes will follow a moving spot of light. By the time he can crawl, a child will stop short when he comes to a cliff (really, a pattern that is made to look like a cliff), even though he has had no direct experience with such declivities (Gibson, 1963).

Maturation and Instruction

It is important to realize that some kinds of behavior can appear with little, if any, deliberate instruction. It is even more important, however, to realize that a degree of internalized development is necessary before certain kinds of instruction can have much effect. Prior to a certain age, instruction in walking or in stair climbing is practically wasted. And even in less critical areas, instruction can often be considerably more effective if it is delayed until the internalized processes are well developed (Tyler, 1964).

In pointing out that instruction in, say, the art of typewriting is more effective at age seven than at age five (Wood and Freeman, 1932), we must not seem to urge that most subjects should be deferred until we are sure that the relevant internalized processes are ready (Tyler, 1964). Some experience may be vital for the very development of those internal processes. According to Piaget (See Hunt, 1961), even unsuccessful experience may be necessary for the development of some mental structures. At times it is from failures themselves that the all-important *accommodations* develop. In the classical theory of Hebb (See Vernon, 1958), there is also a suggestion that early challenging experience, forcing the child to strain for success, is crucial for the internalized processes. The work on imprinting in animals may also suggest the possibility of a golden critical period. During that period we should strike while the iron is hot, or we may be foredoomed to failure (Hess, 1959; Moltz, 1960). At times, moreover, we may choose to disregard considerations of efficiency. Even when we would obtain more efficient learning by waiting for a time, we may choose not to wait. A seven-year-old will learn to read more readily than a five-year-old. But the skill that the five-year-old does acquire, however inefficiently, may have great significance for him as a five-year-old and as a

six-year-old. And, of course, these essential satisfactions of the five-year-old are not to be taken lightly. His experiences as a five-year-old are important not only for what they will help him become at the age of seven, thirty-five, or seventy. As the followers of Dewey have so urgently stressed (Chapter 4), these childish experiences are important in themselves. Even at that tender age he is a person with legitimate privileges and rights. These must be considered along with his obligation to the world and to his older self. Significant experience at this or any age is important, right now, apart from its implications for the future.

SUMMARY

Some aspects of general development must inevitably be treated in a book on classroom learning, but these treatments are spotty and disjointed. A brief review of the whole topic would be useful. Do not overlook the difficulties of getting an accurate picture of child development.

To make your review more pointed, you might imagine a child as he first comes to school, thus demonstrating the forces that work apart from the school. In many physical aspects, especially those related to neural processes, he is well advanced toward maturity. In others (height) he has passed the halfway mark. In still others (sexual maturity) he has hardly begun. He has acquired an amazing mastery of language and shows the rudiments of a realistic grasp of the world around him. He is restless, turbulent, and lively.

The forces that have shaped the child so far have come from his physique and physiological make-up, his pattern of needs, and his relations with parents, siblings, and general community. These things have combined to produce, among other things, a working self-concept, and this self-concept now acquired will play a part in his future development.

Growth both before and after school entrance often follows a fairly definite sequence of rapid growth alternating with a quiet period. In much of development, the child first acquires the broad, over-all skill (walking) and later development is concerned with adding precision and refinement to this broad pattern. The regular, predictable sequence, when observed, could be due to several factors. Maturation may supply some of these. The growth of physical structures may lead to the appearance of certain behavior at fairly regular periods. These internal forces may affect the child's relative readiness for different kinds of learning. The teacher should know about such readiness but need not be its slave.

SUGGESTIONS FOR FURTHER READING

General Textbooks and Handbooks in Child Development

Baller, W. R., and D. C. Charles, *The Psychology of Human Growth and Development*. New York: Holt, Rinehart and Winston, Inc., 1961.

Breckenridge, Marian E., and Margaret N. Murphy, *Growth and Development of the Young Child*. Philadelphia: W. B. Saunders Company, 1963.

Breckenridge, Marian E., and E. L. Vincent, *Child Development*, 4th ed. Philadelphia: W. B. Saunders Company, 1960.

English, H. B., *Dynamics of Child Development*. New York: Holt, Rinehart and Winston, Inc., 1962.

Goodenough, Florence L., and Leona E. Tyler, *Developmental Psychology*. New York: Appleton-Century-Crofts, 1959.

Hadfield, J. A., *Childhood and Adolescence*. Baltimore: Penguin Books, Inc., 1962.

Kawin, Ethel, *Parenthood in a Free Nation* (3 vols). New York: The Macmillan Company, 1963.

Martin, W. E., and Celia B. Stendler, *Child Behavior and Development*. New York: Harcourt, Brace & World, Inc., 1959.

McCandless, B. R., *Children and Adolescents: Behavior and Development*. New York: Holt, Rinehart and Winston, Inc., 1962.

Mussen, P. H., ed., *Handbook of Research Methods in Child Development*. New York: John Wiley & Sons, Inc., 1960.

————, *The Psychological Development of the Child*. Englewood Cliffs, N. J.: Prentice-Hall, Inc., 1963.

————, J. J. Conger, and J. Kagan, *Child Development and Personality*, 2d ed. New York: Harper & Row, Publishers, Inc., 1963.

Pressey, S. L., and R. G. Kuhlen, *Psychological Development through the Life Span*. New York: Harper & Row, Publishers, Inc., 1957.

Solnit, A. J., and Sally A. Provence, *Modern Perspectives in Child Development*. New York: International Universities Press, Inc., 1963.

Stevenson, H. W., ed., Child psychology, *Yearbook National Society for the Study of Education*, 1963, **62,** Part I.

Stone, L. J., and J. Church, *Childhood and Adolescence*. New York: Random House, Inc., 1957.

Vincent, Elizabeth L., and Phyllis C. Martin, *Human Psychological Development*. New York: The Ronald Press Company, 1961.

Treatment of Special Phases

Ausubel, D. P., *Theory and Problems of Child Development*. New York: Grune & Stratton, Inc., 1958.

Barker, R. G., ed., *The Stream of Behavior: Explorations of Its Structure and Content*. New York: Appleton-Century-Crofts, 1963.

Erikson, E. H., *Childhood and Society.* New York: W. W. Norton & Company, Inc., 1963.

———, ed., *Youth: Change and Challenge.* New York: Basic Books, Inc., 1963.

Harris, D. B., ed., *The Concept of Development: An Issue in the Study of Human Behavior.* Minneapolis: University of Minnesota Press, 1957.

Hess, E. H., Imprinting: an effect of early experience, *Science*, 1959, **130**, 133–141. Reprinted in Kuhlen, pp. 60–81, and Stendler, pp. 47–60.

Murphy, Lois B., *The Widening World of Childhood.* New York: Basic Books, Inc., 1962.

Mussen, P. H., and Mary C. Jones, Self-conceptions, motivations, and interpersonal attitudes of late- and early-maturing boys, *Child Development*, 1957, **28**, 243–256. Reprinted in Stendler, pp. 419–428, and Baller, pp. 377–394.

Scott, J. P., Critical periods in the development of social behavior in puppies, *Psychosomatic Medicine*, 1958, **20**, 42–54. Reprinted in Rosenblith, pp. 222–224.

EXERCISES AND QUESTIONS FOR DISCUSSION

1. Observe two children, one about to enter school and the other three or four years of age. Notice the motor skill of each child. What can the six-year-old do that the younger child cannot? Notice also the length and accuracy of sentences, the words poorly articulated.

2. How do you think the school's influence would compare with that of other forces (maturation, home, street) in teaching a child (a) to carry himself in graceful fashion, (b) to be friendly in his behavior, (c) to spell, (d) to tell the truth?

3. Discuss the dangers and possible advantages in having a child start *at an early age* to learn to read; to learn to appreciate good music; to learn to speak a foreign language; to learn the meaning of "reciprocity."

CHAPTER 3

▶ Measuring Promise and Attainment

In almost any vocation, measurement plays an important part. The cook must cope with weights, volumes, and temperature. The carpenter deals endlessly with lengths, strengths, and angles. Much of the work of the manufacturer and engineer is concerned with standards and with tolerated departures from these standards. And it is only by extremely intricate measurements and calculations that the navigator can begin to carry out his task.

PLACE OF MEASUREMENT IN EDUCATION

In our profession we are constantly enmeshed in the matter of measurement. As with the navigator, it is often only through complex measurement that we can have any idea where we are. We can seldom merely take a brief look and see what we have accomplished and learn what is still to be done. At times, more-over, the things we hope to measure are elusive and tricky. Not surprisingly, the problem has received a tremendous amount of attention.

Conditions Demanding Testing

Tests are of especial importance at two stages of the teaching process. First, at the outset of any teaching activity, we will wish to know whether or not the pupil is ready for the teaching we have in mind. What does he know about the subject already? What aptitude does he have for school work in general? And for this project in particular? What interests or aversions does he bring to this task? And are there any special facets of his make-up that we can use to facilitate our work? Or does he have some characteristics that will make this topic difficult for him? At the conclusion of any segment of instruction we also test to see what, if anything, the pupils have learned. The tests we use for either purpose may be

37

quite simple or highly elaborate. But simple or complex, we must usually take some steps to see where we stand. The results of these tests may merely be used to tell us whether we can leave this topic for a time or whether the instruction should be continued. Such tests, on the other hand, may have more serious implications. Through them we may have to decide whether or not the student passes the course, whether he gets a certificate of proficiency, and whether he is to advance to a new grade or a new level.

Possible Overemphasis on Testing

In spite of the obvious necessity for some testing there has been considerable questioning lately as to whether the entire process has been carried too far. Many laymen are becoming somewhat restive about the emphasis given to testing and the frightening use that may be made of test results (Berdie and others, 1962; Black, 1963; Gross, 1962; Hoffmann, 1962; Langemann, 1961).

Problems of Intangibles. Most of the worry, undoubtedly, is concerned with the highly standardized objective tests and the problems that arise when these tests are used to measure elusive or intangible values (Powell, 1963). Some of the things we teach are so elusive, indeed, that many people think it futile and perhaps pretentious to worry about the problem of accurately testing the matter. We may hope, for instance, that we can help the student ultimately to achieve an adult serenity and a sense of oneness with the significant aspects of the universe. Here we should frankly admit that we are operating in the realm of faith. Any illusory conviction that we knew how far we had progressed toward this goal might be the cause of actual harm.

With respect to any goal, we should encourage honest efforts to see if there is any hope of assessing the accomplishment of our pupils. If, after an open-minded scrutiny, we do see hope, we should make cautious use of whatever measures may come into being. If, as yet, there seems no basis for such hope, we should avoid an unfortunate reliance on pseudomeasures.

The General Impact of the Testing Program. In setting up a testing program we may have no purpose other than that of obtaining useful information. We can be sure, however, that in spite of our limited purposes, the effect of the testing never quite stops there. The mere fact of taking a test or expecting a test is bound to have many different effects on students. For one thing, testing can act as a form of teaching. In taking the test the student may learn something about the course he is about to study. Certainly by taking the test he may be alerted or sensitized to the topics that are to be stressed, and he may thus be led to pay more attention to these matters when he encounters them (Entwisle, 1961). Ordinarily we would expect this to help in his subsequent learning. At times, however, the test has seemed to hurt. Perhaps the student, in setting down an erroneous answer, becomes more committed to that answer and may have more difficulty in overcoming it.

As every student knows only too well, testing can also set up extreme emotional tension. A whole literature (Chapter 14) has grown up around the idea of test anxiety and the emotional stress that may result from being tested. Certainly the teacher knows about the test. The imminence of a system-wide test, or a test given by some outside agency, may affect his efforts and his actual objectives as well as his morale. The administrator also knows about tests and is tremendously concerned over the standing of his system as compared to some group. Under certain circumstances the general community may also be concerned about the test standing of the local school as revealed by testing programs (Findley, 1963).

The Teacher's Responsibility for Testing

In many school systems there are special bureaus of testing, and in many schools someone, perhaps a counselor, will act as a testing specialist. In these situations, of course, the teacher's responsibility for testing is limited. In other schools, however, the classroom teacher may have to arrange for almost any testing that is to be carried out.

Let us assume the more optimistic conditions, namely that there is some specialized service available to the teacher. Just what would his responsibilities be in that case? Very often the teacher can expect the special testing office to take much of the initiative in the testing of various broad, general traits that may have a bearing on many aspects of school success. The special office, for instance, often initiates testing programs covering intelligence, some special aptitudes, and perhaps broad ranges of interests. This office may also initiate an occasional system-wide test of achievement in core subjects. Often, however, these are given only every three or four years and serve only as very general guides of academic progress.

Although the teacher does not typically take the initiative for these broad, general testing programs, he must frequently assist, perhaps by giving tests,

perhaps by providing other services. These services will be less onerous and more useful if he has a fairly clear idea of the nature of the tests to be used and some idea of the principles of testing.

Certainly it is to be hoped that the teacher will make considerable use of the actual test results. To be able to do this he must know something of the different tests used, of the kind of information they supply, and of the uses and limitations of this information. He should also know enough about these general tests to enable him to supplement them with other information if that should appear useful or necessary. Since much of the information often comes in a sort of technical shorthand, the teacher should be able to interpret the various scores and ratings that he comes across.

So important is the matter of measurement, and so involved are the procedures that, at some time or other, you should make a detailed study of the topic. Perhaps the best time to undertake this more systematic study would be after you have had a little experience in teaching and after you have a more intimate knowledge of the topics stressed in your teaching field. When seen as a source of help for some clear-cut, practical problems, the topic may seem less formidable and more meaningful. At this point we merely consider some of the concepts necessary to understand classroom learning and to provide some general orientation that may be helpful as you begin your teaching career.

MEASURING READINESS FOR LEARNING

To determine the extent to which a pupil is ready to begin the study of a given topic, you may wish to know something of his general ability, his special aptitude, and his interests. Much of this information may have been secured by the testing office and may be already in the files. Some of it you may have to secure by yourself.

Performance and Ability

It is somewhat more difficult to get a good measure of *ability* than to get a dependable measure of *performance*. Suppose, for instance, we wish to know how quickly a boy *does* get dressed for school (performance). Here we would merely have to observe him often enough to get a reasonable sample of his behavior. To find out how quickly he *can* get dressed for school (ability), however, we would have to make sure that he was really trying, or that he was highly motivated during those observations.

Most of our tests of ability actually are performance tests that are given when we feel reasonably sure that the pupil is really exerting himself. Under most circumstances, fortunately, this is not hard to arrange. Ordinarily, most students will exert themselves when they know that "this is a test." Sometimes, as we shall see, they may even try too hard. There may be times, however, when either from discouragement or from some emotional quirk, a few pupils do not really try, and if this should happen, we would have no real measure of their ability.

Intelligence as an Index of Ability

In discussions of general psychology, or of human development, there is considerable emphasis on the nature of intelligence. For a thorough study of intelligence, as an important thing in itself, we should know whether intelligence is a single unitary thing or a weird conglomeration of many different things. It is also important to know the extent to which this trait is determined by the genes and whether or not it fluctuates wildly as the pupil moves from one experience to another. Such important questions, however, are not our concern in this treatment of classroom learning. We merely consider intelligence tests as one possible index of ability to do school work, or, more accurately, as one possible means of predicting success in school work.

As it happens, intelligence tests turn out to be fairly useful in predicting who will get through school with reasonable success. If you want to know, in very general fashion, whether or not this child is ready to undertake school work at one level or another, then his performance on an intelligence test will prove a valuable, but by no means perfect, index.

Individual Tests of Intelligence

For the most accurate measurement of intelligence, your testing office or school counselor will want to use one or more individual tests. These tests are given to one child at a time and permit the examiner to adapt his procedures to the child and to make sure that the general directions are understood. As a teacher you may never give one of these tests unless you also specialize in psychological testing. But you should know something of how they work.

For the younger child, the individual tests most likely to be used are the *Stanford Revision of the Binet Test* (Stanford-Binet) or the *Wecshler Intelligence Scale for Children* (WISC). In each test the pupil is asked to do many different things: answering questions of fact, giving the meaning of words, detecting similarities and differences in words and figures, working with simple designs and figures. In the WISC these are classified into verbal tasks and performance tasks, and the pupil can be given a separate score in each field. In the Stanford-Binet all tasks are combined to give a single score.

Group Tests of Intelligence

Most teachers will probably have some experience in giving group tests of intelligence. At times you may be asked to administer such tests as part of a larger testing program. At times you may give one of them on your own to get some

---

► *Some Intelligence-Test Items*

Look at the following words given below:
    If the word contains A, E, and N, mark it with a 1.
    If the word contains A and E, but not N, mark it 2.
    If the word contains A and N, but not E, mark it 3.
    If the word contains E and N, but not A, mark it 4.

Eaten	Nation
Elated	Plenty

In the lists given below, the numbers count up or down in some way, but in each list there is one and only one wrong number. Find the wrong number.

X	4	6	8	9	10
Y	9	8	7	6	4

From each of the lists given below, find the three words that are alike in some way:

    walk, rest, hike, wart, tramp

    sob, smile, laugh, frown, grin

In the examples below, fill in the missing signs (plus, minus, times, or division).

$$4 \_\_\_\_ 2 \_\_\_\_ 3 = 11$$
$$7 \_\_\_\_ 5 = 2 \_\_\_\_ 10$$

The words in the lists given below could be changed around to make a good sentence. Pick out the word that would be the first word in the sentence.

    my   not   is   book   that

    ran   several   boys   the   street   down

SOURCE: *Kuhlmann-Anderson Test*, Seventh Edition, Booklet G, 1960. Reprinted by permission of Personnel Press, Inc., a subsidiary of Ginn and Company.

supplementary information that you wish.

Unlike individual tests, the group tests can be given by any sagacious person who can read directions and follow them. There are many such tests available for almost all grades. Anyone reading this text must have taken a number of group tests during his student days. A few items from the *Kuhlmann-Anderson Test* appear in the box as reminders of the kinds of tasks used.

A group test may have anywhere from four to ten subtests. Each subtest presents a different type of task. As the accompanying illustrations suggest, the questions are typically in multiple choice form. Answers are usually placed on a separate answer sheet, and these can be scored either mechanically or by hand.

The Problem of Academic or Cultural Bias

Many of the tests used in the schools have a strong academic flavor and include exercises that call for ability to read and to compute. They also call for a certain amount of scholastic information. For the specific purpose of predicting later scholastic success, this academic flavor may be all to the good, provided, of course, that the children have had some experience with the content. In using the tests for this narrow purpose, we are not passing judgment on the student's basic intellectual powers or on his moral worth, but are merely trying to make a better estimate of his probable success in some academic task.

For some purposes in testing this academic bias may be a nuisance, and several tests have been devised which do not lean heavily on school tasks. In the *Goodenough-Harris Drawing Test* (Harris, 1964), for instance, the child is merely asked to draw a man or a woman. The test is then scored according to the number of concepts and relationships that the child seems to have grasped. The *Raven Progressive Matrices Test* (Burke, 1958) makes use of a series of abstract designs unlike anything that is stressed in the typical school. Other tests, such as the *Davis-Eells Games Test*, have also tried to eliminate the highly academic flavor, but have been even more interested in avoiding the social class bias. These tests make much use of cartoonlike drawings. Although the Davis-Eells tests have been available for some time, it is still impossible to say whether they are really any better than the traditional tests in predicting subsequent academic performance for children who have lacked normal schooling (Macarthur and Elley, 1963; Wallen, 1962).

Interpreting Test Scores

After a child has taken a test we must find some way of giving meaning to his performance. It is not very helpful to know merely that Joe got a score of eighteen or Susie a score of twenty-two.

Age Scores. One of the major breakthroughs in the field of intelligence testing came early in the century when Alfred Binet suggested the use of age as an index of intelligence (see "Suggestions for Further Reading"). Thinking now of the preteen years, we can see that age provides a valuable, if crude, indication of ability. Most of us have a general idea of some four-year-old powers that are beyond the two-year-old. Similarly, there are performances that might seem natural for a six-year-old but that would be surprising in a three-year-old.

The Stanford-Binet test relies heavily on this concept of age. Each of the tasks is assigned an age score. Some tasks, for instance, can be performed by most four-

TABLE 3.1. Mental Age Equivalents for Raw Scores

Raw Score	MENTAL AGE	
	Years	Months
33	7	1
34	7	2
35	7	2
36	7	3
37	7	4
38	7	6
39	7	6
40	7	7

year-olds but by only a few three-year-olds. A child passing these tests, but going no farther, would be considered to have a *mental age* of four years. A child's total mental age is a sort of composite based on the mental-age level of all the tasks he has passed. If he gets a mental-age score of eleven years three months, we know that, in general, he can do the tasks that the typical child of eleven years and three months can do.

Especially in the intermediate grades, the teacher may well pay quite a bit of attention to the mental age obtained from an intelligence test. Within limits, it should give a fair idea of the level of work of which the child is capable.

Mental Age Norms. The Stanford-Binet test yields mental-age scores automatically. The crude raw score we get from group tests, however, and from some individual tests, merely indicate the number of correct items, perhaps with some correction for guessing. At this point we have a *raw score* of (say) thirty-six. To translate this into a mental age we consult a table of norms. A simple illustration appears in Table 3.1.

From Table 3.1 we see that thirty-six corresponds to a mental age (MA) of seven years three months (7–3). This

merely means that thirty-six is the score obtained by the *average* child seven years and three months of age. Some children of this age would get a higher score, others a lower score. This score is the *arithmetic mean* of children of this age. If you have any idea of the mental abilities of the *typical* child of seven years and three months, you now have a clearer notion of the mental ability of the child just tested.

Notice that in getting the pupil's mental age we did not need to pay attention to his actual chronological age. The pupil who got a mental age of seven years three months in our example could have been six years old or seven years old or ten years old. Whatever his chronological age, his mental age is that of the average child of seven years three months.

Suppose that tomorrow our pupil takes the same test over again and at this time gets a score of only thirty-three. Looking at our table of norms, we see that this gives him a mental age of 7–1. *His mental age is now two months less than it was the first time he took the test.* This shows that we must not be misled by the word "age" in the term "mental age." True age, alas, can never be less tomorrow than it is today. But if the

Lewis M. Terman

pupil's score fluctuates wildly from day to day, his mental age will fluctuate just as wildly. Mental age must not be considered as something as substantial and regular as chronological age but merely as a convenient device for giving meaning to a raw score. It has no more stability or dependability than the raw score from which it was derived.

Although age scales, when interpreted judiciously, can be useful in giving meaning to the scores of younger children, they become less useful as we approach adulthood. Most of us have no vivid picture of the differences in the intellectual powers of the twenty-eight-year-old as compared to the twenty-six-year-old. Perhaps there is no difference whatever. To make intelligence-test scores meaningful for adults or older students we have to abandon the idea of age and make use of the notion of rarity or relative standing. Rather than asking, "What

age group does our eighteen-year-old Arthur resemble?" we ask, "How does Arthur compare with other eighteen-year-olds? How far is he above or below the average for his age-group?" This notion of relative standing, by the way, can be used at any age level. We can ask, "How does this five-year-old stand in relation to other five-year-olds?" and we can ask, "How does this adult stand in relation to other adults?"

Intelligence Quotients. As now used, the intelligence quotient, or familiar IQ, is a measure of relative standing. More precisely, it is a form of *standard score* (see the Appendix). It tells you where a child stands with respect to his age group.

This current use of the IQ is a departure from its original meaning. When first introduced, the IQ was a genuine quotient obtained by dividing the child's mental age by his chronological age. A ten-year-old child with a mental age of 12 would have an IQ of 120, showing him to be in advance of his years. A second ten-year-old with a mental age of 7 would have an IQ of 70, indicating worrisome retardation.

The original form of the IQ was in use for half a century and during that time it acquired a number of definite meanings or connotations. To fit in with these connotations, the new IQ, commonly called a *deviation IQ*, has been calibrated so that the numbers mean about the same thing as the older form of the IQ. As presently calculated, an IQ of 115 or 116 means that the pupil is one *standard deviation* above the average for his age group. A score of 68 or 70 would mean that he is two standard deviations below the average for his age.

To determine the deviation IQ you consult a table of norms. To use this table you will need to know the pupil's score on a test and his age (see Table 3.2).

TABLE 3.2. Deviation IQ's

Total Score	CHRONOLOGICAL AGE										Total Score
	5-9	6-0	6-3	6-6	6-9	7-0	7-3	7-6	7-9	8-0	
41	112	104	97	92	88	85	82	79	77	76	41
42	114	105	98	93	89	86	83	80	78	77	42
43	115	106	99	94	90	87	84	81	79	78	43
44	116	107	100	95	91	88	85	82	80	79	44
45	117	108	101	96	92	89	86	83	81	80	45
46	118	109	102	97	93	90	87	84	82	81	46
47	119	110	103	98	94	91	88	85	83	82	47
48	121	112	105	100	96	93	90	87	85	84	48
49	122	113	106	101	97	94	91	88	86	85	49
50	123	115	108	103	99	96	93	90	87	86	50

SOURCE: Modified from Manual, *Kuhlmann-Anderson Test*, Seventh Edition, Booklet A. Reprinted by permission of the Personnel Press, a subsidiary of Ginn and Company.

TABLE 3.3. Some Representative Intelligence Quotients

IQ	SD's from the Mean	General Description
180	5	Perhaps reached by 50 people in a million.[a] May be typical of outstanding geniuses of the past.
150	3	Mean of honor graduates of topnotch graduate professional school. Perhaps reached or exceeded by one person in a thousand.[a]
140	2½	Mean of men listed in *American Men of Science*. Attained by five people in a thousand.
130	2	Mean of PhD's.
120	1¼	Mean of college graduates.
115	1	Mean of freshmen in typical four-year college.
110		Mean of high school graduates. 50–50 chance of graduating from college.
105		Has 50–50 chance of passing academic course in high school.
90		Adult can learn moderately complex machine.
75	−1½	50–50 chance of reaching high school. Adult can run small store.
50	−3	Adult can do simple carpentry, domestic work. Great difficulty in learning to read. About five people in 1000 fall below this IQ.

[a] These proportions are taken from Sir Cyril Burt, Is intelligence distributed normally? *British Journal of Statistical Psychology*, 1963, **16,** 175–190.

Suppose that a pupil of five years and nine months gets a total of 48 items right. Going down the column for 5–9 until we come to 48, we find that this would give him a deviation IQ of 121. If an eight-year-old had obtained this same score of 48, his IQ would be 84.

Representative IQ's. In Table 3.3 we see a list of certain IQ's together with the *general* level of achievement they represent. Remember that these are based on very general averages. They must not be regarded as hard and fast cutoff points.

village." In using the *percentile rank* (see the Appendix) you say instead, "My house is farther out of town than 80 percent of the houses. Only 20 percent of houses are farther away." Each of these approaches gives some idea of distance from the average, but gives it in slightly different ways.

In Table 3.4 we see a typical means of providing percentile ranks. A student with a raw score of 110 on the *Concept Mastery Test*, for instance, would exceed 79 percent of the education majors at X

TABLE 3.4. Percentile Ranks (Approximate) for Concept Mastery Test

	REFERENCE GROUPS		
Raw Score	450 Education Majors in X University	98 Engineers and Scientists Applying for Special Grants	1500 Adults from Terman's Study of the Gifted
130	92	74	35
120	88	68	25
115	85	63	20
110	79	60	17
105	77	57	14

Other Standard Scores. The IQ, or some approach to it, is still the most popular standard score for indicating relative standing on an intelligence test. Some tests, however, such as those administered by the College Entrance Examination Board, use a standard score with a mean of 500 and a standard deviation of 100. A student with a score of 400 would be one standard deviation below the mean. For an intelligence test this would correspond to an IQ of 84. (For a more detailed comparison see the Appendix.)

Percentile Ranks. The standard score is intended to be a measure of distance. By using it you say, in effect, "I live a mile and a half from the center of the

University. A student with a score of 115 would exceed 85 percent. Percentiles for intermediate scores are usually given. In using this brief table, however, they would have to be estimated.

Notice how the percentile rank of a score differs from group to group. A student with a raw score of 110 would exceed 79 percent of the education majors but only 60 percent of a particular group of practicing engineers and scientists, and only 17 percent of a special group of gifted students selected for an elaborate follow-up study. When you set out to use percentile ranks to give meaning to raw scores, be sure to use a reference group that makes sense for your purposes.

TABLE 3.5. Percentile Ranks for Scores in Specified Subtests

Percentile Rank	History	Arithmetic Computation	Speed of Reading
75	48	62	28
70	45	58	25
65	43	55	23
60	41	53	22

Not all tables of percentile norms follow this form precisely. In Table 3.5, for instance, things are turned around, but the same information is presented. Here you would locate a student's raw score in the appropriate column and then read across to the left to get his approximate percentile rank.

Tests of Study Skills

In deciding whether or not a pupil is ready for a certain task, you may wish to know how well he goes about the business of studying. How well can he use the library, for instance. Can he read a map accurately? a statistical table? or a simple graph? How systematic is he in managing his homework or in carrying out his independent assignments?

The California Study Skills Test, to take one example, includes 150 questions covering not only specific habits or study skills but also morale and general attitude toward school. Not surprisingly, such tests show that, at the secondary school or college level, the good students are those who do considerable planning. When preparing for a class they also try to anticipate the kinds of questions they may have to answer. They deliberately drill themselves on difficult material and test themselves out. As might be expected, they are more likely to use some kind of outline in preparing reports.

From evidence of this sort, we must not jump to the conclusion that it is the good study habits that lead to success. For all we know, the kind of person who goes about things in a systematic way may be the kind of person who would do well anyway. There is a chance, however, that good study habits may play a part, and it is comforting to realize that many of these could be taught. Naturally we would not want to overdo this matter and transform all our students into robots who lived their entire lives according to plan and schedule (Maddox, 1963). For most of our students, however, this is not a serious danger, and almost all could become somewhat more systematic with profit. Obviously tests of skill in studying are not merely useful tests of readiness. They are also important tests of achievement and tell us how much a student has accomplished in this important area.

Diagnostic Tests

In addition to knowing a student's general scholastic ability, you may want to detect any specific weaknesses that he may have. By the use of *diagnostic tests* you may be able to identify specific words that give difficulty in spelling, or, at a more ambitious level, detect detailed difficulties in reading. Diagnostic reading tests attempt to determine whether a pupil's difficulty is in ability to distinguish between sounds, in lack of skill in phonic analysis, in failure to look for larger and larger units, and so on.

The more elaborate tests, of course, are typically given and interpreted by the school psychologist or the reading specialist. The results, however, should be extremely useful to the teacher who needs more detailed information regarding one or more of his pupils.

Tests of Special Abilities

Some programs of study may call for special aptitudes over and above the general ability to get along in school. Tests of such special aptitudes are available. *The Differential Aptitude Tests,* for instance, gives separate scores for clerical speed and accuracy, spelling, language usage, verbal reasoning, abstract reasoning (seeing patterns and systems in nonverbal material), mechanical reasoning (Figs. 3.1 and 3.2), numerical ability, and ability to reason about spatial relations. Other tests, such as the *Flanagan Aptitude Classification Tests* and the *General Aptitude Test Battery,* are constructed along the same lines.

Creativity. Whenever we have fairly able students to begin with, the typical intelligence test does not help greatly in distinguishing between those who are creative and those who are merely successful in absorbing traditional material. Many people are working on tests that will detect the creative students (Taylor and Holland, 1962; Thorndike, 1963b), and in the near future useful devices may be available. Even now we have some instruments which, although not strictly tests of creativity, do seem to select children in grades one and two who can do well in the more ambitious science programs offered for the elementary school (Lesser and Davis, 1960).

Interests and Morale

In determining whether or not a student is ready for a given task, it may be important to know his interests in that sort of thing. We may also wish to

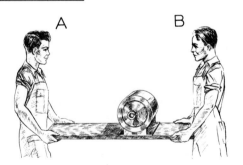

Do not make any marks in this booklet	MECHANICAL REASONING	Mark your answers on the separate Answer Sheet

X

Which man has the heavier load?

(If equal, mark C.)

Fig. 3.1. Example of test of mechanical reasoning. From Differential Aptitude Tests, Form L, Booklet 2. Reproduced by permission. Copyright 1947, © 1961, 1962, The Psychological Corporation, New York, N. Y. All rights reserved.

SPACE RELATIONS

DIRECTIONS

Find the place for Space Relations on the Answer Sheet.

This test consists of 60 patterns which can be folded into figures. For each pattern, four figures are shown. You are to decide which **one** of these figures can be made from the pattern shown. The pattern always shows the **outside** of the figure. Here is an example:

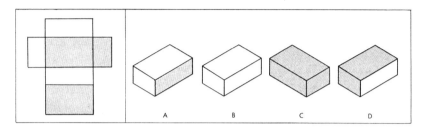

Fig. 3.2.   Example of test of space relations. From Differential Aptitude Tests, Form L, Booklet 2. Reproduced by permission. Copyright 1947, © 1961, 1962, The Psychological Corporation, New York, N. Y. All rights reserved.

know his general need to achieve, his willingness to persist in the face of difficulties, his level of independence and maturity, and perhaps his freedom from excessive worry. Some of these things come under the heading of tests of personality and are discussed in Chapter 13.

To determine a widespread pattern of interests for the purpose of advising students about future studies or suitable vocations, the counselor is likely to use a formal inventory of interests. One of the oldest and most elaborate of these is the *Strong Vocational Interest Blank for Men* (there is a separate blank for women). In this inventory the student expresses interest, indifference, dislike, preferences, and so on, in connection with some 400 specific activities. These activities range from "going for rides in an amusement park" to "making a speech about a new machine." Successful people

in various occupations have already taken this inventory and, by an elaborate scoring method, we can find how well the pattern of interests of our particular student matches the pattern of those who succeed as public accountants, YMCA secretaries, physicists, salesmen, and forty-seven other occupations. The inventory also permits us to get a measure of the maturity of the student's interests and the degree to which they match a typical feminine pattern or typical masculine pattern.

The Kuder Preference Record is somewhat simpler than the Strong Vocational Interest Blank both in administration and in scoring. A student is asked to imagine that he has an opportunity to:

Collect Autographs   1   3
Collect Coins   1   3
Collect Butterflies   1   3

He is asked to indicate his preferences

by marking out the 1 for the activity he most prefers, and he marks out the 3 for the least preferred activity. He repeats this for a number of clusters. From the total pattern of choices we can determine his general interest in each of the following clusters of interests: outdoor, mechanical, computational, scientific, persuasive, artistic, literary, musical, social service, clerical.

Choosing Tests of Scholastic Aptitude

Typically the tests used to determine readiness for learning will be selected by a central office. Teachers, however, should know some of the problems encountered in deciding about the usefulness of different tests.

Naturally enough, the first thing to ask about a test is whether or not it measures what you want to measure. Common sense will help a great deal, but some technical data will also prove useful. Use as much of this as you can get and understand. Don't place too much reliance on the mere labels or titles of the tests. Some of the labels turn out to be a trifle ambitious. You might think, for instance, that a test of mental ability or of intelligence would include such a thing as creativity. As we have seen, however, the typical intelligence test is not very useful for selecting highly creative people.

Predictive Validity. In looking for a test to assess a child's readiness to begin a program of study, the most important thing is the test's *predictive validity.* From the scores on this test, can you estimate how well the pupil will perform in the task you wish him to undertake? (Cattell, 1964.)

The degree of this predictive validity is usually given by the correlation between test scores and some measure of later success (see the Appendix). The test

manual will often tell you, for instance, that score on this test correlates .70 with later success in grade-four reading, or .60 with success in arithmetic, or .65 with average academic achievement. Coefficients of predictive ability may well reach these levels, particularly at the elementary school level. They are likely to be lower at the secondary or college level. Remember, however, that predictive validity can be quite specific. A test may do well for reading but not so well for spelling.

Most teachers will not wish to make unduly fine distinctions between validity coefficients. Suppose, for instance, one test correlates .45 with world history in grade eleven when the latter is measured by teachers' grades. Another test correlates .55 with standard test scores in the same subject. Actually the first test may really have higher general predictive power for world history. The lower correlation comes from the greater unreliability of the teachers' grades. Even a perfect test could not get consistent agreement with a standard if that standard itself wobbled around in helter-skelter fashion. Other technical considerations also play a part, and unless you are prepared to go into these in some detail, do not base your decision on slight differences in validity coefficients.

You will be more reassured by a high coefficient of predictive validity if the group on which it was based should resemble your students. There is a slight risk that results from a radically different group would not hold for your group.

Face Validity and Content Validity. It is true that when you are interested in determining readiness for learning you should try to find out about predictive validity whenever you can. At times, however, you may not be able to get a precise measurement of this predictive validity and you must use other measures.

Sometimes you can use *face validity*. Suppose, for instance, you want to find out how well a pupil can weld two pieces of pipe together. You give him two pieces of pipe to weld and test the result for strength, smoothness, and so forth. Such a test would have face validity. It is the very thing you want to know about. It might be a very inadequate sample, might be hard to measure objectively, and might have poor reliability. But in its essential nature, it would represent what you are trying to get at. *Content validity* is a form of face validity. It is more likely to be used with achievement tests than with tests of aptitude or of general scholastic promise. To determine content validity you check items in the test to see that they agree with the topics to be covered in your course of study.

Accuracy and Reliability. If you can find several tests that cover the material you want to measure, try to pick one that is reasonably accurate. One test may give a fairly precise score that would be duplicated with little discrepancy whenever the same student repeated a similar test. Another test, given on two occasions, might come up with scores that have little relation to each other.

As one means of determining reliability, we might give two forms of the same test to the same group of students. If the test is *reliable* the student who does well on one form should also do well on the other. This would be indicated by a high coefficient of correlation. For well-designed intelligence tests it is not unusual to find reliability coefficients as high as .92 or .93. From these top values the coefficients may drop to the mid .80's for a homemade test. The dependability falls off rapidly as the coefficient falls below .90 or so. When a test has only one form, reliability could be measured by repeating the test with the same students.

Other more technical methods can also be used.

Reliability or accuracy is affected by several things (Cronbach and others, 1963). Obviously it would be reduced by simple mechanical errors in scoring. It is greatly affected by the number of items. We can increase the reliability of a test merely by adding more items even though the new items are no better than the ones already there. We can also increase the reliability by correcting ambiguous items or by improving the individual items in other ways.

One of the woes of life is reconciling ourselves to the fact of inaccuracy. All statements or measures are inaccurate to some extent, although sometimes, of course, to a negligible extent. The realist, and especially the scientist, knows about this inevitable inaccuracy and regularly takes steps to deal with it. But he is not thrown into a panic by the realization of error that pervades all his activities. He is content with the prospect of gradually reducing the error and obtaining better and better approximations.

In general, try not to be disturbed by honest statements of inaccuracy. When you see such a statement you can deal with the error that is estimated and announced. Without such a statement you can be sure you have inaccuracy but you have no idea how much.

Realizing the fact of inaccuracy, you will not attach unrealistic precision to test scores. A score of 51 is not *the* score, but is an *estimate* of the score that would be given by an ideal, or theoretically perfect, test. This ideal score can never be known for sure. Any score that you actually get probably departs from the ideal by some amount. To remind you of this harsh feature of the real world, many test constructors provide a *standard error of estimate*. Suppose, for instance, that

▶ *The Inevitability of Error*

There might be some temptation to dream of the scientist's world as being beautifully precise and conveniently purged of all error. Actually, even in the most precise fields, the work of the scientist is dominated by the fact of error. In presenting a general view of physics, Dr. Oppenheimer, wartime director of the famous Los Alamos laboratory, stressed, among other things, the physicist's preoccupation with error. In a sense the physicist's work is organized around the search for error and around the attempt "to see how error can give way to less error, confusion to less confusion, and bewilderment to insight." Note that Dr. Oppenheimer talks about error giving way to *less* error, and not to complete absence of error.

In physics the worker learns the possibility of error very early. He learns that there are ways to correct his mistakes; he learns the futility of trying to conceal them. . . . The refinement of techniques for the prompt discovery of error serves as well as any other as a hallmark of what we mean by science.

The work of science is disciplined, in that its essential inventiveness is most of all dedicated to means for promptly revealing error.

Dr. Oppenheimer regrets that some of the followers of Freud, and perhaps of Marx, have worked out techniques to protect those theories from the revelation of error. He states, "The whole point of science is to do just the opposite; to invite the detection of error and to welcome it."

SOURCE: J. R. Oppenheimer, Physics in the contemporary world, *Bulletin of the Atomic Scientists*, 1948, **4**, 65–68; 85–86. Courtesy of the Educational Foundation for Nuclear Science, Inc.

the test we used has a standard error of estimate of 2.3. This means that, in this test, two-thirds of the obtained scores (or estimates) would depart from the theoretical *true* score by 2.3 units or less. To get a picture of this situation, imagine that, by some impossible magic, we had thirty people each of whom was known (again by some impossible magic) to have a true, or ideal, score of 70. We also know (never mind how) that the standard error of estimate is 2.3. We now test these thirty people on a *real*, that is to say, a fallible, test and see what sort of an index or estimate of the true score we would get. If the test were perfect, each of the scores would be 70. But with any existing test, we will get a *range* of scores. This range will cluster around 70. Two-thirds of them should fall between 67.7 and 72.3. The rest would fall beyond these limits, one-sixth being above 72.3 and one-sixth below 67.7.

From this imaginary situation we can say that there are two chances out of three that any obtained score we actually get will be within 2.3 units of the "true" score—the one that in actual practice we can never know. We can turn this around and say that there are two chances out of three that the *true*, unknowable score will be within 2.3 units of the score we get. We can thus use an obtained score as an estimate of the theoretical true score. We know that there are two chances out of three that this elusive true score will be within 2.3 units of the score we actually get. Obviously there is one chance out of three that the true score may be above or below these limits. Just how far above or below it really *could* be, we can never say.

In reporting their results many test publishers now give you a *percentile band* or a *stanine band* (see Fig. 3.6). This means that there are two chances out of three that the true percentile, or stanine, of this person would be within the band reported.

The Emphasis to be Placed on Accuracy. Although we must accept the fact that we can never get complete accuracy, we will obviously try to get as much as we can, or as much as we need. Accuracy is more vital in some circumstances than in others. In one situation, for instance, we might be trying to decide whether the class as a whole is ready to start a certain unit of work. Here a test with only moderate reliability will give us fairly dependable information about the group. The errors for one student will cancel out the errors for another. In another situation, we might merely be making a tentative decision, about either one child or several, and might feel quite free to change our plans if our decision turns out to be wrong. Here again we would not be greatly worried about moderate inaccuracy in our test. In some other situation, however, we might be trying to decide whether some drastic change should be made in the program of a single student. Should he leave college or should he transfer to a different school? Here a mistake can be quite serious, and a satisfactory correction unlikely. In this case we should try to get an accurate test even if it is expensive or more unwieldy. If we cannot find a single test that is sufficiently accurate, we may be able to give the student several comparable forms of the inaccurate tests. Here the random errors in one test tend to cancel out those in another.

Accuracy should never be stressed at the cost of validity. The most important thing is to try to decide whether the test measures what we want to measure. After that we try to get a measurement that is as reliable or as accurate as possible. Unfortunately, however, there is a real risk that this emphasis may be reversed. In their search for reliability, test makers may occasionally be led to concentrate on some easily observed facets of the person's behavior, and this easily observed behavior is not always the most relevant for our purposes. In rating a teacher's performance, for instance, we would get considerable reliability by concentrating on the number of times he used the chalkboard. But this may have little to do with his actual competence.

General Suitability of the Test. Besides providing an accurate measure of your objectives, a test should be convenient. It should have tables of norms that can give you information applicable to your students. It should be suitable to the age of your students. Many modern tests provide a variety of forms, each geared to a certain age range (Findley, 1961). Perhaps you would also like a test that gave separate norms for rural and for urban children, or for children from different regions. You might also have to worry about physical handicaps in your class and wish special norms for the children so afflicted.

The manual should be clear and helpful, providing instructions for giving the test, for scoring the papers, for interpreting the results, and for using the norms. Consider also the time limits in relation to the time available to you. Don't forget about relative costs but don't let this problem dominate.

Sir Cyril Burt

MEASURING ACHIEVEMENT: SOME GENERAL PROBLEMS

We must not overemphasize the difference between testing for promise and testing for achievement. Basically the two processes overlap to a considerable extent. Most tests of readiness do, in effect, measure previous achievement. Many regular tests of achievement, moreover, will prove most useful in estimating promise for the future.

There are important differences, however. The teacher faces different questions. In testing for readiness he asks, "Can we safely start this topic or this line of work?" In testing for achievement, he asks, "Can we safely leave it?" And in spite of the basic overlapping, the particular instruments used differ in practical detail.

The Crucial Role of Objectives

There are times, as we point out, when the achievement test may be used chiefly as an indication of readiness for new learning. Here, then, our concern is with predictive validity. More frequently, however, we really wish to know how much our student has learned, and here our chief concern is not with predictive validity but with some more essential aspect of validity. Presumably, at this point, the teacher, or someone else, has a fairly clear idea of what the pupil should know. Now we must ask if his score on this test really tells us what he is supposed to know. Does it cover our objectives?

To get at this all-important issue, we must first specify, as clearly as possible, just what *objectives* have been set up for this unit or this course. Notice that we say, "as clearly as possible." If the objective or goal of your teaching is basically general and vague, do not distort it by making it spuriously precise (Powell, 1963). But, obviously, the more vague and general the goal, the more trouble you will have in constructing a valid test for it, and the more difficulty you may encounter in directing your teaching toward it (Englehart, 1961). Considerable work has already been done in translating general statements of objectives into narrower units of behavior that might lend themselves to testing (Bloom, 1956; French and others, 1957).

Essay vs. Objective Tests

To bring up the topic of testing is to let loose a great deal of argument about the merits of essay tests as opposed to the objective variety. Teachers hold strong views on this subject (Torbet, 1957). These arguments, it is true, may enliven a dull session in the teachers' lounge, but on the whole they tend to be a bit unfortunate. As we shall see, each of the testing devices is well adapted for some things, but clumsy and awkward when used for other purposes. To ask which is better *in general* is like asking a plumber to decide whether he prefers a wrench or a hammer. Surely he would ask what the tool is to be used for.

Essay Examinations

The familiar essay examination has many advantages. It is relatively easy to construct. True, it takes time to phrase a really good question, but the teacher who knows his subject can turn out some kind of an essay examination in a short space of time. Some instructors, indeed, have been suspected of making out their questions on the way from the parking lot to the examination room. With the essay examination, moreover, elaborate mimeographing or printing, although to be recommended, is not an absolute must. Our casual instructor could, if nothing better offered, merely write his questions on the chalkboard.

Going beyond mere convenience, we find that, for some purposes, the essay test has a high degree of validity. There is no other way, for instance, to find out how well a student can express himself in writing. It also serves as a more natural test of the student's ability to structure and organize his ideas, and to produce something on his own. It may permit or require him to make subtle distinctions. There is no need to be satisfied with a flat-footed "Yes" or "No." The essay test, moreover, offers less temptation to guess. The different possibilities are not neatly lined up, asking for an eeny-meeny-miney-moh approach. Many students report that they study for essay examinations in a way that stresses

organization. They look for broad, general concepts and for relations between concepts. They are less tempted to memorize isolated elements.

But the essay test also has disadvantages. On the practical side, it is exceedingly laborious to grade or score. The grades, once attained, tend to be very subjective. For years the educational literature has reported instances of tremendous disagreement when several qualified examiners all mark the same papers. Such disagreement, although frequent, is by no means universal. On short essays, dealing with factual material, there can be marked agreement, reaching coefficients of 0.98 between raters (Grant and Caplan, 1957; Pidgeon and Yates, 1957). When the essays are longer and are scored for comprehension and general mastery, the agreement drops sharply to a correlation of .80. Ironically, it appears that the essay test may be least dependable when doing the very thing for which it is chiefly valued.

Ordinarily the essay examination permits only a very limited sampling. Of all the topics covered in the course, we can ask questions about only a few. In discussing those questions, moreover, the student, although discouraged from guessing, may be tempted to bluff. For some people it is easy to write persuasive nonsense about almost any subject. Even when no deliberate bluffing is intended, the general style and expression, including neatness and punctuation, may have an undue effect on the grade.

Setting the Examination. Some of the worrisome undependability of the essay examination may come not from weakness in the scoring as such but from the students' uncertainty about what is required. If you wish the student to deal with a fairly specific task, spell it out in some detail. "Discuss the use of rating scales in the classroom," for instance, is rather general. To be more specific one might say, "Point out several (at least two) classroom situations in which rating scales might be especially useful. Mention two difficulties in the teacher's use of rating scales and show in each case how one might deal with these difficulties."

As far as sheer reliability is concerned, it would be better to have quite a few questions, using a variety of forms. By chopping the examination up into too many questions, however, you may give up some of the advantages to be expected of the essay test.

From the point of view of dependability or reliability, there is little to be gained by the use of optional questions or by the use of open-book examinations.

Such things, it is true, may make for better morale or a better feeling between teacher and student. They do little to reduce inequities, however. For one thing, the better student has more ability to find his way around in the text. Often, therefore, the open-book procedure merely permits the better student to increase his lead (Green, 1963).

For ambitious essays, especially where the quality of writing is a crucial issue, some writers (Diederich, 1960) would recommend distributing the assignment over two days. On the first day the pupil chooses a topic, prepares an outline, and writes a rough draft. To reduce the temptation to get unauthorized help, the teacher keeps these outlines and drafts and returns them the following day. The pupil then completes a finished

► *Judging the Quality of Essays*

One hundred and fifty freshmen at three eastern colleges wrote essays on "Who Should Go to College?" and another 150 wrote on "When Should Teen-Agers Be Treated Like Adults?"

The 300 essays were submitted to 53 judges selected as being outstanding representatives of the following fields: college English teachers, social and natural scientists, writers and editors, lawyers and law professors, and business executives. Each of the 53 judges read all 300 papers, assigning each a grade, and commenting on what he liked or disliked about each paper. None of the judges saw the comments or grades of the others. The judges were not given a key or a set of objectives to go by. The grades assigned could range from 1 through 9.

Maximum disagreement would be shown if the 53 grades for an individual paper ranged all the way from the very lowest to the very highest. This actually happened for 100 papers or one third of the total. For another 100 papers the marks assigned by the 53 judges ranged over 8 of the 9 grades. For the single paper showing the *greatest* agreement, the marks ranged over 5 grades.

The ratings given by college teachers showed no more agreement among themselves than those given by people in the other professions. Among the judges, editors and writers showed somewhat more agreement than did other groups.

SOURCE: Judges disagree on qualities that characterize good writing, *Educational Testing Service Developments*, 1961, **9**, 2.

paper during the school period. This provides an opportunity for moderate reflection without which it would be unreasonable to expect anything in the way of acceptable writing (Cousins, 1963).

Scoring the Papers. Several procedures have been developed for increasing the consistency of scoring essay tests. Almost all of these are time consuming and somewhat complex. In actual practice you will have to decide, on a realistic basis, whether the greater reliability is worth the considerable trouble involved.

Reliability will be increased if two people read each paper. Three people will be slightly better but not a great deal better than two. If the stakes are such as to justify two or more graders, there is something to be gained from a preliminary analysis of the points to be looked for and the weight to be given each. The examiners should be sure they agree on these weightings, and there should be a few trial scorings followed by discussion. This procedure of clear-cut weightings is more appropriate for some essay questions than for others.

A second procedure emphasizes a more global approach and urges you, in effect, not to strive for undue precision. Under this procedure the examiner, working with one question at a time, makes a very rough preliminary sort for that question. In one variation (Diederich, 1960), you first sort the papers into three rough piles—those that attract favorable attention, those that are not distinctively bad or good, and those that strike you as poor. You may gain some precision if you go over the piles and reshuffle them so as to get half of the papers in the middle pile, one-quarter in each of the other two piles.

When this is done each of the three piles is again sorted into three more groups, making for nine groups in all.

Since this grouping fits the stanine values (see the Appendix) you may gain further precision by again shuffling papers until they approach the proportions in each of the regular stanines, namely:

Stanine   1 2 3 4 5 6 7 8 9
Proportion   1 2 3 4 5 4 3 2 1

The use of stanines, of course, is not an integral part of the procedure. Both in your crude preliminary sort and in your more detailed sort, you could use any number of categories that seemed convenient.

To avoid being biased by your previous impression of the student you may wish not to know the name of the students while you are grading. Have them write their names on the back of the booklet. To secure the same result, some teachers use fairly elaborate code systems. You could have each student, for instance, choose a six-digit number, write it on the upper right corner of page one, tear it off, and write his name on the slip torn off. He then also writes the number on the left side of page one, leaving this number on the paper. After marking you can match numbers to get the names. If two numbers should be the same, the fit of the slip should settle the matter.

Objective Examinations

To a great extent the objective tests are strong where the essay examination is weak, and weak where it is strong. Unlike the essay examination, the objective test is difficult to construct. This problem is treated in detail later on. We have to go to a great deal of trouble to construct even an ordinary objective examination. A good one is a real undertaking. For objective tests some form of reproduction is almost essential. Even with liberal office facilities, this often means preparation

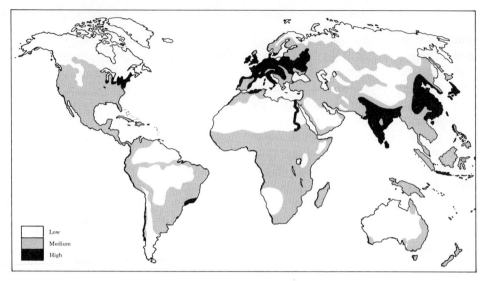

The shading on the above map is used to indicate

(A) population density
(B) percentage of total labor force in agriculture
(C) per capita income
(D) death rate per thousand of population

Fig. 3.3. An illustration of a multiple-choice question calling for interpretation. Reprinted with permission from "Multiple Choice Questions: A Close Look," copyright 1963, Educational Testing Service, Princeton, N. J. (A is the correct answer.)

well in advance. Without such facilities the preparation means great trouble or expense. The scoring of most objective tests, on the other hand, is beautifully simple. At times it can be done by machine. With reasonable supervision it can be done by an assistant or by any adult relatives who may be coaxed or coerced into assisting. Many teachers find it feasible and profitable to have the students themselves do the correction, using the time-honored procedure of exchanging papers.

It was the issue of dependability or reliability that first led to the development of objective tests, and it is not surprising to learn that they are excellent in this respect. With few exceptions, there is little likelihood of disagreement when several scorers mark the same paper. Although reliability is not automatically guaranteed, by taking a little trouble we can usually come out with objective tests that are fairly reliable. Objective tests permit wide sampling. They discourage the bluffer. But they do encourage guessing.

There is one argument frequently leveled against objective tests that we must take seriously. Many critics hold that such tests can reveal only the mechanical recollection of isolated facts. Clearly there is an element of truth in this accusation. It is easier to frame objective questions that deal with isolated facts. And it is true that many students in preparing for such tests do look for isolated factual nuggets and ignore broad, general principles. The proponents of objective tests, on the other hand, insist that the tests are not limited to this mechanical procedure. They hold that by using your ingenuity, or by taking advantage of the ingenuity and efforts of other people, you can get objective test items that are thought-provoking to a high degree. Notice the questions in Figures 3.3 and 3.4, for instance. Neither of these merely asks the student to repeat something that he has studied. Each, on the contrary, demands that he should make use of his information by applying it in logical fashion to some new problem.

Preparing True-False Questions. To obtain the potential benefits of the objective test and to counteract some of its defects, we must give considerable thought to the selection of the topics and the preparation of the items (Green, 1963). To take advantage of the opportunities provided for good sampling, for instance, we must be sure that the bulk of the items are not drawn from one or two units of the course.

Avoid the tendency to lift individual sentences directly from the text. This favors the student who has slavishly memorized the actual words of the assignment. It is better to construct an item that calls for the sense of a paragraph or larger unit. Even if one sentence in the text does summarize this general meaning in neat fashion, the actual wording should be changed.

Be sure that the truth or falsity of the item hinges on an important idea, not on some incidental or parenthetical phrase. Be careful about "give-aways" or specific determiners. Even a fairly naïve pupil can sense that, on the average, it takes more words to phrase a true statement. He is also alert to the fact that such terms as *all, always, never, none, no,*

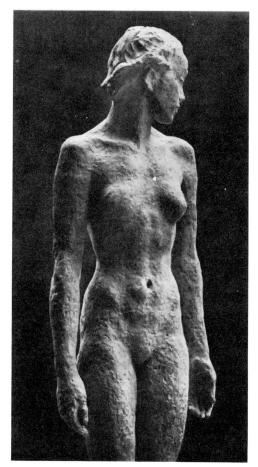

In which of the following centuries was the piece of sculpture shown above most probably produced?

(A) The fifth century B.C.
(B) The fourteenth century A.D.
(C) The sixteenth century A.D.
(D) The eighteenth century A.D.
(E) The twentieth century A.D.

Fig. 3.4. An illustration of a multiple-choice question calling for interpretation. Reprinted with permission from "Multiple Choice Questions: A Close Look," copyright 1963, Educational Testing Service, Princeton, N. J. (E is the correct answer.)

only, alone are typical of false statements. As in all testing, go over the items to eliminate ambiguity. If the answer hinges on the meaning of such a word as *large* or *many*, see if you can change it to something more definite (*over .80; at least 75 percent*). Try to avoid negative statements. Suppose, for instance, we say, "Objective tests are not limited to the testing of factual material." Since objective tests do not have this limitation, the general idea is false. The precise wording, however, makes the statement true. Unless you want to test the student's ability to deal with such technical niceties, it would be better to say, "Objective items are limited to the testing of factual material." Here the statement is false both generally and in its technical phrasing.

If a statement is open to dispute, include some authority or reference. "Writers on test construction (Chauncey, for instance) hold that multiple-choice questions can be used effectively to test ability to interpret and to apply general principles." Try to use a general authority, such as the author of the textbook. Otherwise a student may know that the statement was made but may not be sure that it was made by this particular man.

Preparing Multiple-Choice Questions. As compared to true-false items, the multiple-choice questions take longer to prepare and take up more room. They also take slightly longer to answer. Typically this will mean fewer items and consequently less adequate sampling. With multiple-choice questions, however, the temptation to guess, although still present, may be less pronounced. Having more alternatives, the multiple-choice question can also call for finer shades of discrimination. From the point of view of scoring, there is nothing to choose between the true-false and multiple-choice test. Both are completely objective.

The problems of constructing true-false items also apply to multiple-choice items. Here, as with true-false items, we have to worry about "give-aways" or specific indicators. Here again, such flat-footed terms as *never, always,* and so forth, betoken the false answer. The correct choice is often stated more cautiously and at greater length.

In constructing multiple-choice items, we typically work out a correct choice and then arrange for a number of plausible alternatives or decoys. Be careful not to give things away by sheer grammar as in the following example: "The word *readily* is most frequently used as an (1) adverb; (2) participle; (3) verb; (4) pronoun." Here "adverb" is the only word that would follow "an." Obviously the decoys must be plausible. A response that no one would ever accept is completely useless. In constructing the test we should try to avoid this possibility. In revising a test that has already been taken, we should find a substitute for alternatives never chosen.

Try to make sure that the plausibility does not hinge on a general familiarity with the course. Suppose, for instance, that an item would appear plausible only to someone generally familiar with the course. In that situation, the poor student would never see it as plausible and would never be tempted. A somewhat better student, however, may know enough to see its plausibility, and will thus run the risk of entrapment. We should avoid decoys which will attract only the better students.

All the alternatives should be mutually exclusive. Otherwise more than one answer could be correct. Avoid items like the following: "Group tests: (1) are almost always objective; (2) can be given

► *Examples of Short-Answer Questions*

Completion: The forced-choice rating technique is designed to counteract the tendency to _____.

True-False or Alternate Response: (Circle the T if the statement is true, the F if false.)

T F Whenever the rater is likely to be very uncertain of his judgment, it is important to provide a large number of categories or divisions to permit him to express his uncertainty.

Multiple-Choice: (Circle the letter of the correct choice.)

In determining the number of categories in a rating scale, we should:

   a. Stay within the number of discriminations that the rater can be expected to make.

   b. Be sure that there are enough categories to take care of the unusual student.

   c. Use any convenient odd number of categories.

   d. Adjust the number of categories to the age level of the student.

Matching Questions: (Each of the devices to the right is intended to deal with one of the common defects of rating scales listed on the left. Write the letter of the device on the line before the appropriate defect.)

Frequent Defects	*Techniques*
_____ Rater may hesitate to give anyone a low score.	A. Combining the independent ratings made by several people.
_____ Considerable unreliability in many rating scales.	B. Describing traits in terms of concrete behavior. ("Usually makes own bed.")
_____ Rater not sure of difference between "outstanding" and "superior."	C. Forced-choice technique.
_____ Rater not sure of your meaning of such a word as "initiative."	D. Giving percentages of specified groups to determine cut-off points. ("In the top 3 percent of college graduates.")
_____ Halo effect.	E. Scaling the ratings on the normal curve.
	F. Warning rater about the halo effect.

by the typical teacher; (3) are more reliable than individual tests." In any one question, moreover, it is better to use a homogeneous group of alternatives. In the example just given, for instance, all choices should deal with reliability, or with ease of administration, or with some other single feature.

Arranging Items in Order. Most students get along more easily if all the true-false questions are in one section, all the multiple-choice in another section, and so forth. Under such arrangements there is no need for a frequent change of set or general attitude. This is by no means an inviolable rule, however, and if you have some reasons for placing two or three kinds of items close together, do not hesitate to do so.

The ordering of items within a section is of some importance. In arranging the true-false items, avoid any clear-cut or detectable alternation between the true and the false. Ideally it would be best to follow the toss of a coin. But in any case, try to arrange for a random or unpredictable pattern. In your general sequence of testing, try to avoid any marked preponderance of either true or false. In any one test, however, it is not necessary, or even wise, to arrange for precisely equal numbers of true or false items.

In arranging multiple-choice questions, you also want to avoid any clearly detectable pattern for the correct choice. With these questions, moreover, it is also important to make sure that one position is not unduly favored for the true answer. Go to some trouble to make sure that the correct choice is not usually item "b" or item "c." In some questions there will be a natural progression of alternatives. For instance: "A good intelligence test might attain a reliability of .45; .60; .75; .90." Start with questions that have a natural order such as this. Then juggle the order of the remaining items so that, on the average, the correct choice occurs just as frequently in one position as another.

Standard Tests

There is much to recommend the standard, ready-made tests whenever they apply to our course material and whenever the occasion justifies the expense. The makers of standard tests are very conscious of the matter of accuracy or reliability. Examinations are pretested and then improved until they attain a high degree of reliability. And in this age of gimmicks, the standard tests are often the last word in general convenience and in ease of scoring. In getting an adequate sample of the content to be tested, moreover, and in the careful phrasing of the actual items, the expert will do a better job than anything the typical teacher can hope to accomplish.

The problem of objectives becomes crucial in deciding about standard tests. There is always the possibility that the things stressed in the standard test do not fit the objectives of your school. Sometimes, and especially in some subjects, there may be an admirable match. Sometimes the two sets of objectives may have little in common.

There can be several undesirable results from the use of a standard test that does not fit the local objective. Results may be misleading. Both teacher and pupils may become resentful. Finally, if such tests are used over a period of years, teachers may gradually abandon the stated local objectives and direct their teaching to the things actually stressed in the tests (Mahler and Smallenberg, 1963; Tyler, 1963). If the tests are not made to follow the stated objectives, the *actual* objectives may come to follow the tests.

Making Use of Norms. Like the tests of intelligence, the standard achievement tests provide norms of attainment. By the use of these norms you can compare your class with some specified group. You can find out, for instance, how your grade-six class compares with the average for grade-six pupils throughout the country. By using such norms you can also tell how much your class has improved over a given time.

In applying the norms to your group you will need to know the group from which the norms were obtained. With achievement tests, it is also important to know the month in which the norms were obtained. Norms based on a test given in May would be different from those based on a test given to the same group in the previous October. Most manuals will give the information on both these points.

Norms for achievement tests may come in the form of the age scores, percentile ranks, or standard scores already discussed. They may also be reported as *grade scores*. By consulting the grade-score table, for instance, you may find that a raw score of 87 is equivalent to a grade score of 9.1. A pupil who gets this score is doing about as well as the average child who has spent one month in grade 9. A grade score of 9.9 would mean the typical score of a pupil in the ninth month of grade 9. Since schools are seldom open for more than nine or ten months, grade scores are limited to a range of ten months in each year (say, 7.0 to 7.9). Age scales, on the contrary, range up to eleven months and may be expressed in a form such as 7-11. Apart from this difference, you will find a neat correspondence between age scores and grade scores. With each year the *average* child increases both his age and his grade by one year.

Norms, however expressed, can be very useful provided their limitations can be kept in mind. They tell you how a student or a class stands in relation to some definite comparison group, and this is often useful and important to know. Naturally, however, norms cannot always tell you what your particular group should be expected to accomplish. For some groups the norms would be quite unrealistic, for others, much too easy.

Selecting Suitable Standard Tests. The selection of a suitable standard test is probably a job for the specialist. The problems are much the same as those faced in choosing an intelligence test except that, in choosing an achievement test, the suitability of objectives is even more crucial. If you must take some responsibility for this task, try to consult one of the standard texts on psychological and educational tests (see "Suggestions for Further Reading"). These texts give a brief analysis and critique of many of the better-known tests. For a more complete list consult *Tests in Print* (Buros, 1961). This is a most comprehensive list. It will give you the names of the tests and, when possible, will refer you to reviews of the tests that have been published in a series of *Mental Measurements Yearbooks,* also edited by Buros. A list of some of the test publishers, and of the tests they publish, appears at the end of this chapter. If you already have some idea of the tests you are interested in, order specimen tests.

General Impression and Anecdotal Records

To some extent, your opinion of the pupil's progress will be based on a very general impression. You may be unable to give precise reasons, but you will have a definite conviction that this student is doing well, whereas another is having a great deal of difficulty. For some purposes this device may be eminently suitable. It may serve quite well, for instance, when judging energy, politeness, or good humor. On other occasions this approach may be less efficient but may be chosen because it is the convenient method at hand.

Whenever you do rely seriously on general impression, there are a few general precautions that should help.

1. Purely random errors can be reduced by repeated observations. The effect of the *individual bias* of one observer will be reduced by getting the

independent observations of several people. When one person is making all the observations by himself he can get better results if he repeats his own observations. The accidental circumstances which may be present during one observation are not likely to reappear in other observations.

2. Do as much as you conveniently can to maintain some sort of record.

3. In making the record, distinguish between (1) the pupil's actions, (2) your reaction to them, and (3) your interpretation of the cause of the action.

We see a record such as the following: "Jimmie felt left out of things and because of this tried to make trouble during the seat-work period." Here we get an interpretation, and the teacher's reaction, but very little information about Jimmie's behavior. It would be better to say, "Jimmie raised his hand three or four times but I called on someone else. A few minutes later, during seat-work, he broke his pencil and went to the sharpener three times within a few minutes, looking at me out of the corner of his eye. (I was annoyed but tried to remain casual.)"

Here the teacher's reaction, if given at all, is indicated in parentheses. An *interpretation* or a suspected cause of the behavior might also be given this way if it seemed necessary or useful. In general, however, try to concentrate on the actual events. If you have a reasonable record of the events, you, or anyone else, can interpret them at any time. If you have largely a record of interpretations, it will be difficult either for you or for anyone else to recapture the actual events.

Be realistic in this matter of collecting such anecdotal records. It can be quite an exacting and tedious matter during the hectic business of teaching. Decide how much of it is necessary and how much you can really carry out, and do this systematically. Some teachers concentrate on a few pupils at a time. If you are going to do much of it, you may find some prepared forms or record blanks useful.

Rating Scales

Most of us have had experience with rating scales. They come in many forms (Remmers, 1963b). To describe a student's promise as a graduate student we might be asked to use a scale such as any of those shown in Figure 3.5.

The scales in Figure 3.5 happen to have five steps. The number of steps, of course, is rather arbitrary. A scale could range from two steps, as in a checklist, (yes-no; better-worse) to any number. The number of steps should be related to the rater's probable confidence. If he can only make a crude estimate anyway, it is better not to have too many subdivisions.

Although rating scales may often be the best measure we can get, they do leave much to be desired. Frequently the typical rater does not know what standard is to be applied. He may also have only a slight knowledge of the person being rated. To the extent that he does know him, we face the problem of the *halo effect*. This refers to the tendency to rate a person favorably in each and every trait whenever you think highly of him in general. Even if he does not have a definite favorable opinion of the person being rated, a generous person may be reluctant to rate anyone on the low end of the scale.

To get around this understandable generosity, some test constructors have developed forced-choice rating scales. To get estimates of a person's promise for leadership, for instance, we might present

A. Much Below   Average   Above   Much
   Below Average   Average   Above
   Average   Average

B. Poor   Might succeed Good chance Should pass Outstanding.
   Risk   but odds are of getting with superior One of the
      against him degree   record   best people
                         likely to be
                         seen

C. Reference Group_____

(Which group do you have in mind when you are rating this student?
Undergraduate majors in_____? First-year graduate students?
Successful graduate students?)

Compared to the group indicated above, this student is:

Trait	In the top 5% of the group	In the next 20%	In the middle 50%	In the lowest 25%	(No basis for rating)
Knowledge of Subject					
Originality					
Ability to do Independent Work					
Ability to Persevere					
General Intelligence					

Fig. 3.5. Sample scales such as this could be used in rating prospective graduate students.

the rater with four brief descriptions such as the following:

 reasonably free from annoying mannerisms

  confident of his evaluation of others
  friendly with subordinates
  punctual in keeping appointments

The rater selects the statement that best describes the person. (Sometimes he also selects the statement that least describes the person.) Notice that all the statements are favorable. One of them, however (say number two) has been found to be a characteristic of the good leader. The others, let us assume, have less to do with identifying the good leader. If the rater selects statement two as the best description, he is, in effect, but unknowingly, giving the person a high rating for leadership.

Vague terms and exceedingly general statements make for unreliability in rating scales. To get around this we can use concrete examples of what we mean by average talent, or as in the last example of Figure 3.5, we can define outstanding talent in terms of percent of people who attain that status.

Checklists. In some respects, a checklist is a rating scale reduced to a "Yes" or "No" response. It is often used in evaluating shop work or the performance of technicians. In shop work, for instance, we could check off the questions such as the following:

He had the necessary tools within reach before starting.   Yes   No

Used the vise rather than fingers for holding the work.   Yes   No

Checked the measurement before beginning to saw.   Yes   No

Ratings by Pupils. The ratings of classmates can be a useful indication of some kinds of achievement. Indeed, for the determination of popularity, sociometric ratings by fellow-pupils serve as the most natural device. These are discussed in Chapter 12. Even for some phases of academic development, the estimates of fellow-students may be quite useful. Ullman (1957), for instance, found that, in junior high school, classmates were just as accurate as teachers in predicting who will attain the honor roll, and in Keislar's study (1957), high school students were remarkably successful in predicting the academic achievement of their fellows.

We must not be too surprised to learn that pupils do well in this matter. Over and over again we find that the amateur often equals the expert in the use of rating scales (Stephens, 1959). Perhaps the expert, feeling excessively confident, spreads his ratings over too wide a range. The more timid amateur stays close to the average thereby incurring fewer risks of exceptional error.

TREATMENT OF TEST RESULTS

Test results may be used to see how an individual child stands now in relation to his earlier performance, and to see how his accomplishment in one field compares to his performance in other areas. Such results are also used to get a picture of the class as a whole and of the performance of the individual pupils in relation to the group performance.

Seeing the Class as a Group

To get a picture of the class as a group you will find the frequency distribution (see the Appendix) one of the most useful devices. If you take kindly to diagrams, you may also profit from constructing a *frequency polygon* or *histogram* for such a distribution. The distribution, with or without its graphical counterpart, gives you in one "eyeful" a picture of the range of the scores. It also shows where the students tend to pile up, and what proportion fall above or below any selected cutoff points. Two such distributions provide an excellent means of comparing your group with a different group, perhaps a normative group, or with its own status at some previous time. A comparison of the two distributions tell you, for instance, whether the difference, if any, is found all along the line or whether it is due to a few exceptional students in one group, or in one testing.

Test Results for the Individual

Test results for a single pupil mean more if they can be linked up in some way with other tests he has taken. Many

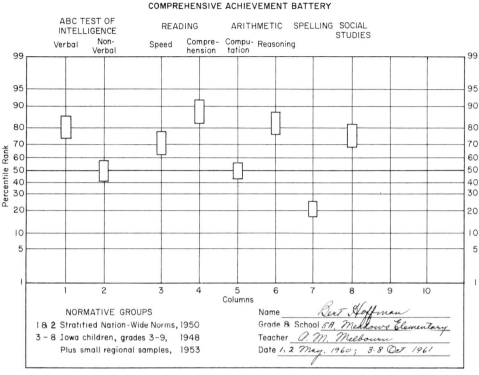

Fig. 3.6. Illustrating a profile of test performance.

teachers find that the *profile* is a convenient device for this purpose. Figure 3.6 shows a hypothetical profile for a child in grade five. This happens to be given in terms of percentiles. Notice that the scale for the percentile values expands as it moves away from the middle. The reason for this modification is discussed in connection with standard scores in the Appendix. Not all profiles employ percentiles. Some use standard scores, or stanines (see the Appendix).

In this profile the student's status is indicated by a *band* or range rather than a single score. In making use of the band, the publisher reminds us of the inevitable uncertainty in any obtained score. The band makes use of the standard error of estimate discussed earlier. We can be reasonably sure that the true

score on this test has a two to one chance of falling within the limits of the band, but we must be less certain about the student's position within the band. In the face of such uncertainty, we would be reluctant to say that this student is definitely better in reading comprehension than in arithmetic reasoning. Similarly, we hesitate to decide that he is better in arithmetic reasoning than in social studies. We would feel little doubt, however, that his performance on the verbal part of the intelligence test exceeds that of the nonverbal part.

The profile shows at a glance that the general level of performance is well above average. It also shows at a glance the difference between subjects. This student, for instance, is close to the 90th percentile in reading comprehension, but falls behind in spelling and numerical computation.

Underachievement and Overachievement: Some Cautions. A profile such as this permits us, indeed tempts us, to compare a student's academic performance with his intelligence. This may be useful provided we keep a few cautions in mind, and provided we do not make too much of the comparison. In our illustration it would appear, for instance, that in general the student does about as well on the achievement tests as he does on the intelligence tests.

In making such comparisons we should have an eye to the norms. There is nothing to prevent different test constructors from using different groups in setting up their norms. When this happens the percentile ranks or standard scores for intelligence may be derived from one normative or standardization group, and the percentile ranks for achievement from quite a different group. Clearly, it is possible that any differences we find may merely reflect differences between these two normative groups. Conversely, of course, actual differences could be hidden by differences between the standardization groups.

There are other dangers in reading too much into the relation between intelligence and achievement. The typical intelligence test shows how well the student has mastered the tasks encountered in everyday life. Not surprisingly, his success with everyday things often indicates, to some extent, how well he will do in school. The correlation may be as high as .70. This is a useful level of prediction, but far from perfect. With a correlation of .70 many people are bound to differ sharply from the achievement test score predicted for them.

Most people are aware of this useful but moderate predictive relation between intelligence and achievement. Other people, relying on the general terms used to describe these things, assume that a thing like "intelligence" should surely be the chief factor in determining a thing like "achievement" (Coleman and Cureton, 1954). At any rate, there is much to suggest that many people have made too much of the relation between intelligence and achievement. They have assumed that intelligence tests, in addition to providing a rough empirical indication of expected achievement, actually give us a fairly precise measure of the student's capacity to achieve. They feel that intelligence tests tell what a pupil "ought" to achieve. We know, for instance, that a student just exceeds 80 percent of his age mates in his ability (a) to define common words, (b) to detect logical absurdities, and (c) to separate animals that run from animals that fly (typical items on an intelligence test). It is assumed that this is a precise measure of his general intellectual power and that he should therefore also exceed 80 percent of his age mates in arithmetic, reading, history, or any academic task he may undertake. If he exceeds only 60 percent in arithmetic he is not working up to his capacity in arithmetic. If he exceeds 90 percent in literature, he is, in some mysterious fashion, doing better in literature than he is really able to do. Actually, both of these departures from the 80-percentile level merely underline the well-known fact that the prediction is imperfect and that, as pointed out earlier, some students are bound to do better than predicted and others worse. When the student's achievement is better than that predicted from his intelligence, nobody worries, although sometimes he is called an "overachiever." When, equally inevitably, some students fall below their predicted attainment, they are labeled "underachievers," and

TABLE 3.6. The Use of Standard Scores in Averaging Several Scores
for the Same Student

	Quiz Oct. 1	Quiz Dec. 1	Total	Course Average
Class Mean	80	90		
Class Standard Deviation	7	2		
Jones, Raw Score	66	94	160	80
Smith, Raw Score	94	86	180	90
Jones, Standard Score	30	70	100	50
Smith, Standard Score	70	30	100	50

people suspect that some real force must be at work to prevent this student from achieving up to his capacity (Dulles, 1961; Levy, 1962; Stephens, 1956; Thorndike, 1963a; Various, 1963).

Using Standard Scores. The profile gives us a graphic picture of the student's performance in a number of areas. But it does not give us one single number to show his over-all average. And often we will need such an average. This happens, for instance, when a student has taken several quizzes in a single course and we want to work out a single average for the course. We also need such a single average when we want to combine the grades in several courses to find who is eligible for Phi Beta Kappa, the dean's list, or draft deferment.

To get such a combined average, many people merely average the raw scores. Others may weight the raw scores according to their importance, and then average these weighted scores. Either of these simple procedures, however, could cause serious injustice. In Table 3.6 we have an illustration of what can happen. Notice that the two means of the two quizzes differ somewhat and the standard deviations even more so. Notice, too, that Jones did well in the first but poorly in the second, whereas for Smith the picture is the other way around. Averaging the raw scores will give Jones a grade of 80 and Smith a grade of 90. Should this be? Is Smith really the better student? If we look at the scores in relation to the standard deviations we see that each student was two standard deviations below the mean in one quiz and two standard deviations above in the other. Taking into account the distributions for the two quizzes, the two students should have the same average. But Jones's fall from grace happened to bring him down to a very small number (in raw score), whereas Smith's misfortune brought only a slight numerical penalty. These differences, however, came from accidents in the particular distribution. As is seen in the last two lines, the use of standard scores would prevent this injustice. Such scores would express each performance in terms of the mean and the standard deviation of that performance. No student would have an advantage from doing well where it accidentally helped to an unusual extent, nor would he be penalized unduly for doing poorly at the wrong time.

Some form of standard score should be used in combining the various scores of one student whenever we want to find his over-all average. This is especially important whenever one teacher may be a stiff marker and another extremely lenient, or whenever one teacher gives grades all across the board whereas another restricts himself to a narrow range of grades.

The use of standard scores does not prevent the deliberate, intelligent use of weighting. On the contrary, it makes possible a more equitable form of weighting. Suppose, for instance, that, in our example, we wish to give the December quiz twice as much weight as the October quiz. A quick glance tells us that Jones did better on this more important quiz. Clearly he ought to get the higher score. If we merely weight the raw scores, however, Jones comes out behind, getting only an average of 85 as compared to Smith's average of 89. By weighting the *standard* scores, on the contrary, Jones gets 57 and Smith only 43. This is the way things should be if we really think the December quiz is twice as important. Don't worry about the fact that these are both low numbers. With arbitrary standard scores you can raise or lower the general average any amount you please.

Reporting to Parents. The problem of maintaining communications with parents is, of course, a problem in administration or in general public relations. The psychologist has been concerned, however, about the wisdom of divulging individual scores to parents (and to others) and in the last few years a whole literature has grown up around this contentious subject. *Must* the school divulge results to parents? What if it appears unlikely that the parents can interpret the results? When should the results be given to the pupil himself? When withheld? Many people would take the position that certainly parents have a right to know anything that the school knows about a child, but that any information given should be in clearly understandable form. Very often bald numerical scores will convey little to parents and what is conveyed may be misleading (Fischer, 1961; Ricks, 1959).

SUMMARY

Measurement, so crucial to our craft, has recently come under a cloud. Many people suggest that it has been overdone. Other students of the problem seek to preserve its essential function and to reduce such harmful side effects as undue test orientation and the restriction of initiative.

The typical teacher must do much informal testing on his own and may be asked to assist in more ambitious programs. In any case he should know about tests and should be able to use test results. Intelligence tests are the devices most frequently used to indicate readiness to undertake a program, and the teacher may have some occasion to use the more familiar group tests. Intelligence test scores, group or individual, are often translated into age scores (MA). Although giving a dangerous suggestion of stability, such age scores are useful. The familiar intelligence quotient, formerly derived from the MA, is a useful index of relative standing. Percentile ranks also indicate relative standing.

To obtain additional measures of readiness (or of actual attainment) we might use tests of study skills, or tests of special aptitudes in engineering, business, music, art, or, more recently, creativity. There are also tests of interests and morale.

Any test used should clearly match our purposes (validity) and should give us the relevant information as accurately and dependably as possible (reliability). Don't select a test that measures the wrong thing, just because it measures that wrong thing very accurately. Spend some time in trying to decide what you really want to find out. Be conscious of the inevitable error in all tests, and deal with it as one of the facts of life.

In achievement testing, even more than in intelligence testing, a clear idea of purposes is essential. Naturally it is easier to construct the test when these objectives are stated in testable form. For some objectives, the familiar essay test may be the natural or inevitable device. For other purposes, some of the technical advantages of the short-answer tests (reliability, sampling, objectivity) may have great appeal. Don't be too hasty in dismissing any form of testing as utterly useless. At times, even the teacher's general impression may be a useful measure. Sample anecdotes, if carefully kept, may also help, but extensive reliance on these devices calls for many precautions and a great deal of effort. Most teachers will also make use of rating scales and checklists.

Setting suitable examination questions is quite an art. Essay questions become more *reliable* as they become more specific and detailed, but this feature may defeat your purpose. Often we can grade essay examinations more satisfactorily if we content ourselves with broad groupings of acceptability. When accuracy is very important there should be more than one reader. In preparing objective items it is important to avoid mechanical or incidental giveaways. Obviously we should take advantage of the opportunity for good sampling.

When standard tests match your objectives they will be found to be technically excellent, convenient, but fairly expensive. They also provide norms that you can use to judge the progress of your students.

To get a picture of the performance of the class on any test you can use a frequency distribution, average, or other statistical device. A profile often helps in the study of a child, since it permits you to compare his performance in different subjects and to compare achievement with presumed aptitude. In the latter comparison, however, there is a danger of reading too much into the two separate measures. To get a combined score showing a student's general performance it is often better to use some form of standard score.

SUGGESTIONS FOR FURTHER READING

General Discussion of the Problems of Testing

Adams, Georgia S., and T. L. Torgerson, *Measurement and Evaluation in Education, Psychology, and Guidance.* New York: Holt, Rinehart and Winston, Inc., 1964.

Ahmann, J. S., M. D. Glock, and Helen L. Wardeberg, *Evaluating Elementary School Pupils.* Boston: Allyn and Bacon, Inc., 1960.

Freeman, F. S., *Theory and Practice of Psychological Testing,* 3d ed. New York: Holt, Rinehart and Winston, Inc., 1962.

Gerberich, J. R., H. A. Greene, and A. N. Jorgensen, *Measurement and Evaluation in the Modern School.* New York: David McKay Company, Inc., 1692.

Nunnally, J. C., *Educational Measurement and Evaluation.* New York: McGraw-Hill Book Company, Inc., 1963.

Remmers, H. H., N. L. Gage, and J. F. Rummel, *A Practical Introduction to Measurement and Evaluation.* New York: Harper & Row, Publishers, Inc., 1960.

Schonell, F. J., E. Roe, and E. G. Middletone, *Promise and Performance.* London: University of London Press, Ltd., 1963.

Thomas, R. M., *Judging Student Progress.* New York: David McKay Company, Inc., 1960.

Thorndike, R. L., and Elizabeth Hagen, *Measurement and Evaluation in Psychology and Education.* New York: John Wiley & Sons, Inc., 1961a.

Tyler, Leona E., *Tests and Measurements.* Englewood Cliffs, N. J.: Prentice-Hall, Inc., 1963.

Vernon, P. E., *Intelligence and Attainment Tests.* New York: Philosophical Library, Inc., 1961.

Special Aspects of Testing

Binet, A., and T. Simon, The development of the Binet-Simon Scale, *L'Année Psychologique,* 1905, **11,** 191–244. Reprinted in Rosenblith, pp. 286–290. Describing the early development of this classic scale.

Coleman, W., and E. E. Cureton, Intelligence and achievement: the "jangle fallacy" again, *Educational and Psychological Measurement,* 1954, **14,** 347–351. Reprinted in Remmers, pp. 475–477. Lamenting the confusion arising from attaching too much significance to the words "intelligence," and "achievement."

Dyer, H. S., On the assessment of academic achievement, *Teachers College Record,* 1960, **62,** 164–172. Reprinted in Morse, pp. 353–359.

Findley, W. G., ed., The impact and improvement of school testing programs, *Yearbook National Society for the Study of Education,* 1963, **62,** Part II.

Goslin, D. A., *The Search for Ability: Standardized Testing in Social Perspective.* New York: Russell Sage Foundation, 1963.

Dyer, Findley, and Goslin deal with the fears that education has suffered from an overemphasis on testing.

Harris, C. W., ed., *Problems in Measuring Change.* Madison, Wis.: University of Wisconsin Press, 1963.

Harris, D. B., *Children's Drawings as Measures of Intellectual Maturity.* New York: Harcourt, Brace & World, Inc., 1963.

Remmers, H. H., Rating methods in research on teaching, in N. L. Gage, ed., *Handbook of Research on Teaching.* Skokie, Ill.: Rand McNally & Company, 1963b, pp. 329–378.

For Help in Selecting Published Tests

Anastasi, Anne, *Psychological Testing.* New York: The Macmillan Company, 1961.

Buros, O. K., ed., *Tests in Print: A Comprehensive Bibliography of Tests for Use in Education, Psychology, and Industry.* Highland Park, N. J.: Gryphon Press, 1961.

Cronbach, L. J., *Essentials of Psychological Testing.* New York: Harper & Row, Publishers, Inc., 1960.

Educational Testing Service, *Selecting an Achievement Test: Principles and Procedures.* Princeton, N. J.: Evaluation and Advisory Service Series, No. 3, 1961.

Joint Committee on Testing, Some features to consider in choosing a published test, *Psychological Bulletin,* Supplement, 1954, **51,** 1–38. Reprinted in Remmers, pp. 458–464.

This report was prepared by a committee drawn from the American Psychological Association, the American Educational Research Association, and the National Council on Measurements Used in Education.

Many of the general textbooks on measurement also treat this topic. See Remmers, Gage, and Rummel; and Thorndike and Hagen.

For Help in Constructing Tests

Educational Testing Service, *Making the Classroom Test: A Guide for Teachers.* Princeton, N. J.: Evaluation and Advisory Service Series, No. 4, 1961.

Green, J. A., *Teacher-Made Tests*. New York: Harper & Row, Publishers, Inc., 1963.

Wood, Dorothy A., *Test Construction: Development and Interpretation of Achievement Tests*. Columbus, Ohio: Charles E. Merrill Books, Inc., 1961.

See also the general textbooks on measurement. A section of essay testing drawn from Remmers, Gage, and Rummel is reprinted in the readings by Remmers, pp. 490–494.

Interpretation of Test Scores

Diederich, P. B., *Short-Cut Statistics for Teacher-Made Tests*. Princeton, N. J.: Educational Testing Service, Evaluation and Advisory Service Series, No. 5, 1960.

Lyman, H. B., *Test Scores and What They Mean*. Englewood Cliffs, N. J.: Prentice-Hall, Inc., 1963, Chapter 4, also Glossary, p. 193.

Townsend, E. A., and P. J. Burke, *Statistics for the Classroom Teacher*. New York: The Macmillan Company, 1963.

See additional textbooks on statistics in the "Suggestions for Further Reading," in the Appendix.

Publishers of Representative Tests of Intelligence, Aptitude, and Achievement

California Test Bureau, Del Monte Research Park, Monterey, California.

(CTMM) *California Short Form Test of Mental Maturity*, Grades[a] Kg–Adult.

California Achievement Tests, battery for basic subjects, Grades[a] 1–14.

Cooperative Test Division, Educational Testing Service, Princeton, New Jersey, or 1947 Center Street, Berkeley 4, California.

(SCAT) *School and College Ability Tests*, Intelligence, Grades[a] 4–14.

(STEP) *Sequential Tests of Educational Progress*, Achievement battery, Grades[a] 4–14.

Harcourt, Brace & World, Inc., Test Department, 757 Third Avenue, New York 17, New York.

Davis-Eells Tests of General Intelligence. (Intended to reduce culture bias.) Grades 1–6.

Otis Quick Scoring Mental Ability Test, Grades[a] 1–College.

Terman-McNemar Test of Mental Ability, Grades 7–12.

Goodenough-Harris Drawing Test, Grades Kg–9.

Metropolitan Achievement Tests. Battery, Grades[a] 1–9.

Stanford Achievement Tests. Battery, Grades[a] 2–9.

Essential High School Content Battery, Grades 9–13.

Houghton Mifflin Company, 432 Park Avenue South, New York 16, New York.

Iowa Test of Basic Skills, Achievement battery, Grades[a] 3–9.

Personnel Press, Inc., 20 Nassau Street, Princeton, New Jersey.

Kuhlmann-Anderson Intelligence Tests. Grades[a] Kg–12.

The Psychological Corporation, 304 East 45th Street, New York 17, New York.

(DAT) *Differential Aptitude Test Battery*. Grades 8–12.

Science Research Associates, Inc., 259 East Erie Street, Chicago 11, Illinois.

SRA Tests of Educational Ability, Grades[a] Kg–12.

(FACT) *Flannigan Aptitude Classification Tests*. Grade 12 and beyond.

SRA Achievement Series. Battery, Grades[a] 2–9.

(ITED) *Iowa Tests of Educational Development*. Achievement battery, Grades 8–13.

[a] Total range of grades. Different forms provided for different grade levels.

Publishers of Additional Tests

Acorn Publishing Company, Inc., Rockville Centre, Long Island, New York.

The Bobbs-Merrill Company, Inc., 1720 East 38th Street, Indianapolis, Indiana.

Bruce, Martin M., 340 Oxford Road, New Rochelle, New York.

Bureau of Educational Measurements, Kansas State Teachers College, Emporia, Kansas.

Bureau of Educational Research and Service, State University of Iowa, Iowa City, Iowa.

Bureau of Publications, Teachers College, Columbia University, New York 27, New York.

Center for Psychological Service, 1835 Eye Street, N. W., Washington 6, D. C.

Committee on Diagnostic Reading Tests, Inc., Mountain Home, North Carolina.

Consulting Psychologist Press, Inc., 577 College Avenue, Palo Alto, California.

Educational Test Bureau, 720 Washington Avenue, S. E., Minneapolis 14, Minnesota.

Institute for Personality and Ability Testing, 1602 Coronado Drive, Champaign, Illinois.

Ohio Scholarship Tests, State Department of Education, Columbus 15, Ohio.

Personnel Research Institute, Western Reserve University, Cleveland 6, Ohio.

Psychometric Affiliates, Box 1625, Chicago 90, Illinois.

Scholastic Testing Service, Inc., 3774 West Devon Avenue, Chicago 45, Illinois.

Sheridan Supply Company, P. O. Box 837, Beverly Hills, California.

C. H. Stoelting Company, 424 North Homan Avenue, Chicago 24, Illinois.

Western Psychological Services, 12035 Wilshire Boulevard, Los Angeles 25, California.

The following films are available from the Cooperative Test Division of Educational Testing Service, Princeton, New Jersey or 1947 Center Street, Berkeley 4, California. (16 mm., black and white, sound, $50.00.)

Selecting an Achievement Test
Interpreting Test Scores Realistically
Using Test Results

EXERCISES AND QUESTIONS FOR DISCUSSION

1. In comments made by laymen, have you heard much concern about what testing is doing to the schools? Analyze and evaluate the arguments you have come across.

2. What is your own attitude to the part that testing plays in a teacher's work? a necessary evil? no more worrisome than the rest of the teaching job? a challenge?

3. Suppose that someone has convinced you that the XYZ test is not a good test of intelligence. What significance would you attach to your new conviction? That the test would not be a very good predictor of academic achievement? or that the test may have seriously injured someone by giving a distorted picture of his worth? or both?

4. Compare the usefulness (values and limitations) of percentile rank, mental age, and intelligence quotients as norms.

5. Outline your attitude to the argument about essay and objective tests, and your conclusions, if any, about the questions being argued.

PART TWO

▶ *Promoting Learning*
in the Classroom

CHAPTER 4

▶ *Motivation and Practice*

Motivation is a topic that we encounter over and over again. Motivation, need, and drive are the chief topics that concern us when we treat the problems of promoting personal adjustment. And motivation is an important consideration when we deal with social adjustment.

In this section, motivation is treated largely as a *process* or device. Here we speak of using motivation (a) to get the student into a situation in which learning can occur, (b) to energize him, activate him, or keep him reasonably alert, (c) to keep his attention directed to one part of the situation rather than another. In addition to these basic functions of motivation, we might hope that what we do will lead him to perform an act (take his seat quietly) that is part of the learning task, and that it might also make him more readily influenced by whatever rewards are in store.

In considering motivation chiefly as the process whereby the teacher influences pupils, we clearly betray a classroom orientation. Most psychologists, in using

the term motivation, would refer, not so much to the things we do to motivate a pupil, but to the nature of the motivated state. They would be concerned with telling us what it is like to be motivated. In describing the nature of the motivated state, some theorists (Brown, 1961) would pay most attention to the physiological conditions responsible for such things as hunger, thirst, pain, and sex drive. Other theorists (Hilgard, 1963; Leeper, 1963) insist that this would give a very inadequate view of the motivated state. The latter psychologists hold that interests, emotions (pleasure, enjoyment), perceptual sets (looking at this rather than that), and actual resolves or decisions also play a part in motivation, and that these other things are not always clearly traceable to physiological conditions.

Fortunately we are not required to take a definite stand in this controversy regarding the precise nature of the motivated state. For us, the motivated pupil is the one who *behaves* in alert fashion and who keeps his attention fairly closely directed to one feature of the environment. To manipulate this behavior, we will sometimes appeal to things that would be classed as interests. At times we will rely on social needs, and at other times we make invoke drives that have a clear physiological basis.

Much of our motivating is done to get pupils into the situation in which learning can occur. We use various devices to get pupils to enroll in the appropriate course, to get them to come to class, to sit down at the typewriter, or to enter the swimming pool. Along with these efforts, we go to some trouble to keep activation at a reasonable level. Typically, of course, we try to make sure that activation does not get too low. During examinations, however, or on similar occasions, we may try to keep it from getting too high. With activation at a reasonable level we must often go to some trouble to be sure that attention is directed to the chalkboard, the textbook, and the work at hand.

These are the facets of motivation that you will find stressed in the more specialized psychological treatments of motivation (Bindra, 1959; Brown, 1961; Hall, 1961; Young, 1961). In general, we can expect little or no learning unless pupils are in the right general situation, are reasonably alert, or at least awake, and are attending to the approprite materials.

MOTIVES FOR CLASSROOM USE

For classroom use, the most dependable, most natural, and most efficient motives are the basic urges, needs, or interests of the children. Powerful needs, when they are at work, automatically take care of the conditions necessary for learning. A hungry child is likely to be active and restless. He is also likely to keep his attention directed to things having to do with food. Similarly, a boy with an intense urge to become an astronaut or jet pilot will stay around places where aeronautical matters are discussed, will come to life when these topics are mentioned, will direct his attention to matters dealing with aeronautics, and will ignore many distracting stimuli such as a summons to come to dinner.

Unfortunately there is no precise agreement among psychologists regarding the basic needs acting on children. Different psychologists prepare different lists. In the discussion that follows we will make much use of the list prepared by H. A. Murray (1938) and his associates.

Some Ego and Activity Needs

The ego needs seem directly related to classroom work. They refer to the student's needs to preserve an acceptable concept of himself, to see himself as worthwhile in some important way. They also refer to his need for *activity*, for *experience*, and the contrary needs for *rest* and for the *reduction of sensory experience*.

These activity needs should not be neglected. At one time many psychologists spoke as if activity and complex experience were always forced upon us. They suggested that our goal was always to reduce the complexity of the stimulus barrage and to attain quiescence. Obviously, however, these goals or needs work only part of the time. At other times we crave activity and an increase in the flow of stimuli. For some people, prolonged sensory deprivation may become intolerable and may induce hallucinations and other distortions (Brownfield, 1964). This need for stimulation is shown in children's *curiosity*. Children will go to some trouble to watch novel or off-beat

Henry A. Murray

events (Berlyne, 1960) or to keep interesting sights in view (see Piaget, 1952, in "Suggestions for Further Reading"). According to White (1960), the urge toward activity and the urge to see interesting sights become combined in the need for *effectance*, which is the need to manipulate or to produce interesting changes in the environment.

A number of the needs listed by Murray clearly seem to belong with these ego and activity needs:

Need	*Description*
Achievement	To accomplish something difficult
Counteraction	To make up for failure, to overcome weakness
Order	To put things into precise or tidy order
Understanding	To ask or answer general questions
Play	To take part in sports, games, relaxation
Sensuous Experience	To observe, watch, listen, or to experience events

Some Social Needs

There is no sharp distinction, of course, between ego and social needs. Many of the needs discussed above, however, could function on the proverbial desert island. Those needs about to be considered, on the contrary, refer primarily to relations with other people.

In so far as these needs are in operation, they will have much to say about the pupil's willingness to be influenced by the teacher, to accept help or criticism from him, or from classmates, and about his tendency to contribute to the class or to help classmates.

Need	Description
Deference	To admire, support, or yield to a superior
Affiliation	To be close to some other congenial person. To work with him
Succorance	To receive help, sympathy, consolation from an ally or protector
Abasement	To accept blame, misfortune, or injury
Exhibition	To impress, shock, or amuse others
Autonomy	To be independent, to avoid domination or coercion, to be free to follow impulses
Dominance	To control, persuade, or direct others
Nurturance	To help, support, or console the young, the unhappy, or the unfortunate
Aggression	To oppose in a forceful manner, to attack, injure, or seek revenge
Rejection	To avoid or to dismiss a disliked or inferior person

Physiological Needs

Along with the needs listed, Murray considers the need to avoid pain or injury, and the need for release of sexual tension. He also takes into account the needs for air, water, food, urination, and defecation. These more physiological needs often play a great part in determining the student's behavior, but they are seldom actually utilized to motivate him toward the school tasks. Many of them, as a matter of fact, far from being useful, merely present problems to us. The pupil's need to go to the toilet, for instance, may be something we have to take into account, but it is seldom actually utilized to motivate him toward school tasks. Similarly, we are unlikely to make deliberate use of the hunger needs, or the need to avoid the pain of a headache, or the physiological needs of sex. At the best, we settle for an intellectualized form of these primitive needs. To develop interest in safety education, it is true, we may appeal to the pupil's general desire to avoid death. Some other activity may be linked to his long-term urge to marry. But the first is not the same thing as the vivid fear of death in its urgent, primitive form, and the second is very different from the imperious demand for immediate sexual release.

It is not the physical and physiological motives but the social, intellectual, and ego motives to which the teacher appeals in most direct fashion, and which he uses most freely. The teacher is free to utilize the child's need to be with people, his need to secure the attention of other people, his need to influence people and to help them, his need to have people think well of him, his need to move things around, to manipulate, his need to rearrange ideas, his need to express himself, and his overpowering need to think well of himself.

Using Ego and Achievement Needs

The achievement need is seen most clearly in the student who must continually test himself and who is always ready to take on a difficult task merely because it is difficult. For such students, as McClelland (1953) and his associates have shown, it is often enough to know that is is hard to make a good grade on

► Curiosity Is Aroused by the Unusual

Each pair of pictures in the table is intended to bring out a difference of some kind. In the first pair, for instance, the lower picture has more material in it. In the second pair there is no difference in the number of items but the first picture shows those items arranged in more regular fashion. The remaining pairs bring out differences in homogeneity and in regularity of shape.

Many pairs such as these were shown to college students, ten men and ten women. Each person was tested individually. During the test, a pair of pictures would be shown on a screen. Behind the screen, hidden from the student, there was an observer who watched the student's eyes and kept a record of the time spent in watching each picture in the pair. The experimenter made sure that each picture in the pair would be on the left for some students and on the right for others. He also made sure that the observer behind the screen did not know which picture was to the left or to the right.

Type of Picture		Average Number of Seconds Spent in Watching Each Type of Picture	
		Simple or more regular picture	Complex or less regular picture
Less Material		3.4	
More Material			4.3
			0.9 (Difference)
Regular Arrangement		3.4	
Irregular Arrangement			4.6
			1.2 (Difference)
Similar Elements		3.2	
Diverse Elements			4.9
			1.7 (Difference)
Regular Shape		3.1	
Irregular Shape			4.7
			1.6 (Difference)

On the average the students spent a little over three seconds looking at the more conventional or more regular pictures and more time (4.5 seconds) on the less conventional designs. The difference in these averages was significant.

SOURCE: D. E. Berlyne, The influence of complexity and novelty in visual figures on orienting responses, Journal of Experimental Psychology, 1958, 55, 289–296.

this assignment, or that a certain problem is considered insoluble. This trait is probably an outcome of an early childhood training that emphasized achievement or independence. This need for achievement can be enhanced, especially in boys, by pep talks or by stories of men who have succeeded in spite of serious handicaps.

It is possible, by the way, that this achievement need is too often neglected. When children complain about school, they are much more likely to complain that things are boring than that the subjects are too difficult.

Closely associated with a continuing need to test oneself are the persisting ego needs, the need to think well of oneself, especially in the areas of life that really matter. When a student can be made to feel that his performance on a certain task is a measure of his real worth as a person, he will exert himself tremendously (Alper, 1946; Kausler, 1951). For many college students, such motivation can be brought about by the mere announcement that the assigned exercise is a dependable test of intelligence. Failure on a test which really measures intelligence is something which no student can contemplate with indifference.

There are numerous ways in which the teacher may enhance the amount of ego-involvement experienced by the students. One method is to encourage the feeling of initiative. If the student feels that he thought of a project or an idea, he will feel more responsibility for it, and will accept it as a part of himself (Fig. 4.1).

As you might expect, the use of ego-involvement can be overdone, especially in the case of people who are tense or anxious to begin with. Such people may do worse when "put on the spot." There is also the problem of understress and

the occasional risk of a crushing sense of failure or guilt. The judicious teacher must encourage the student to distinguish between those tasks which call for everything he has, and those needing only casual interest. In many problems, such as problem solving, the great task for the teacher is to reduce ego-involvement (see Chapter 7).

Long-Range Urge for Success. In every student, presumably, there is a need to make a success out of life, a need to amount to something. This may mean success in a specific vocation, or it may be a generalized urge to avoid being a nonentity. The student may see himself achieving recognition specifically as a scientist, actor, or basketball player, or he may merely have visions of himself as being famous for some undisclosed reason.

These long-term drives toward success are useful to motivate young people to attend school, or to take a certain course. They may be less useful, however, in providing day-by-day, or hour-by-hour incentives for the more detailed tasks that must be mastered. Most of us know only too well that we can have a powerful urge to get a good grade on a final examination and still defer essential tasks from day to day. Perhaps we should save these long-term interests as motives for long-term decisions and not bring them up day after day to motivate the pupil for each and every lesson. Even if they did work well for these day-by-day tasks, the pupils may get tired of hearing about them. We might then find them less useful as motives for long-range planning.

Manipulation, Exploration, and Knowledge of Results. In listing ego and activity needs we placed much stress on curiosity and manipulation. The teacher can make good use of the urges to move things around and to see things happen,

Fig. 4.1.   Fantasies of achievement.

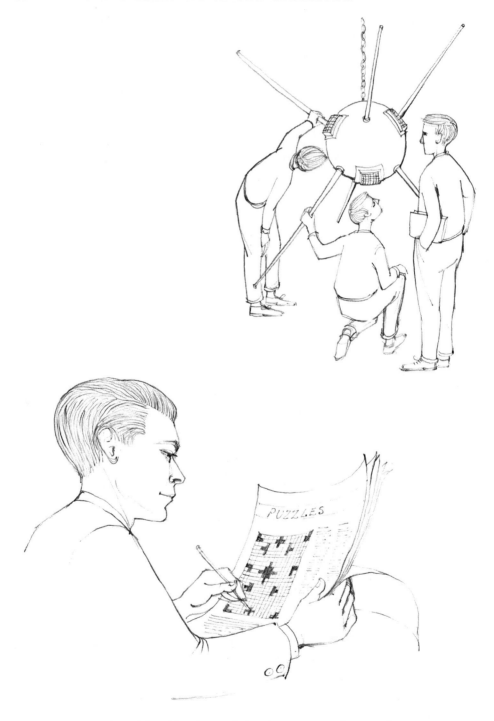

Fig. 4.2.   Novelty, and the chance to produce results.

and the related urge to get a closer and more detailed view of complex and novel situations. These are powerful urges in animals, children, and adults (Fig. 4.2). Rats are rewarded by entering a runway that is merely complex and interesting. In Harlow's (1953) classic experiments, monkeys regularly work hard to solve puzzles for no other reward than the pleasure of moving bolts and levers, or of seeing a toy train going around on a track. Infants manipulate spoons, blocks, or paper with endless zest, and few of their elders can resist the temptation to "monkey" with gadgets, pinball machines, or other devices that produce interesting results. Nor are these attractions limited to interesting physical manipulation. It is also fun to do crossword puzzles, to simplify an algebraic expression, to analyze a sentence, or to guess at the outcome of a story.

In general, these manipulative activities become more intriguing when the results produced are immediate and fairly clear-cut. The student is especially likely to try harder when there is definite and objective evidence of how well he is doing (Wolfle, 1951). A student squeezing on a bulb will squeeze harder when a pointer is used to show the score that is reached. Students keeping a graphical record of the scores in arithmetic or typing will usually perform better on the next test.

Providing knowledge of results is an excellent way of motivating students to apply themselves to the task at hand. It is an honest, intrinsic form of motivation, calling for no elaborate pep talks or farfetched rationalizations. It is a fairly safe method. Knowledge of our previous performance tends to make us compete against ourselves. And for most of us, this is a contest in which we can hope for considerable success. We are not asked to match the record of the best student in the class or some unattainable ideal. We are merely asked to beat our own previous score.

In addition to being safe, this motive is often readily available. Indeed, it may be hard to avoid. When a student answers a question in class, the teacher's facial expression or the reactions of the other students may clearly tell him whether he is right or wrong. In mechanical work, in penmanship, or art, he can often tell whether his performance is satisfactory or not.

These simple, manipulative urges constitute almost the sole source of motivation used in teaching machines (see Chapter 5). In these devices the pupil is quite active. He moves things around, pulls levers, and manipulates. Almost immediately after each response he finds out how well he has done. Under these circumstances children appear to work eagerly, and the teacher does not find it necessary to give a pep talk or to invoke the more deep-seated, long-term interests.

When the results of each act are not automatically revealed, deliberate steps should be taken to make the knowledge of results as definite and immediate as possible. By the use of tape recorders, students can often hear their pronunciation of foreign words played back to them. Sometimes students can mark their own papers from a model as soon as they finish their exercises. Papers marked by the teacher can be returned as promptly as possible.

Frequent Tests. One way to make a student's performance apparent to himself, and to the teacher, is to give a test. Will a student perform better under a program of frequent tests? At the college level, there is little advantage either way (Stephens, 1956). In high school, however, there is a slight advantage for fairly

► Do Frequent Quizzes Help?

The groups in this experiment consisted of four sections in a course in educational psychology. Students had been allowed to choose their own sections whenever schedules permitted. The students in the different sections did not differ significantly in age, sex, intelligence, or general class standing. All were taught by the same instructor. All four sections were given a pretest, a midterm test, and a final. One section, the control, had no further tests, but the other three sections were given a total of thirteen weekly quizzes, or activities of a quiz nature.

Procedure in Weekly Quiz Period	Possible Contributions from Each Procedure	Mean Score on Examination		
		Pre-test	Mid-term	Final
Group A, 30 students Traditional: Instructor grades and returns papers, keeping a record No weekly quizzes	1. Increased familiarity with subject 2. Knowledge of results 3. Desire to get good grades on quiz	33.9	66.2	101.7
Group B, 28 students Papers graded and kept by students. Not seen by instructor	1. Increased familiarity with subject 2. Knowledge of results	34.9	63.9	94.4
Group C, 14 students No real quiz. Instructor merely reads out the question and gives the answers	1. Increased familiarity with subject	36.5	59.7	97.5
Group D, 32 students No weekly quizzes		33.9	59.4	92.4

The midterm results were corrected (analysis of covariance) to allow for the observed differences in the original test. On these corrected scores, Group A was significantly ahead of Group D. No other midterm differences were significant, and none of the differences in the final examinations were significant.

It would seem that the quizzes had no lasting effects. Some conditions may have had a transient effect.

SOURCE: L. W. Standlee and W. J. Popham, Quizzes' contribution to learning, *Journal of Educational Psychology*, 1960, **51**, 322–325.

---

frequent tests, but even here there are some important cautions. First, don't overdo this matter of frequent tests. Tests given every day are not so effective as tests given every two weeks. Indeed, it may be that daily tests are worse than no tests at all.

As a second caution, we should not

put our faith in surprise tests as opposed to tests that are announced ahead of time. The results so far suggest that at the end of the term, the students working under a system of surprise tests learn less than those who know in advance when the test is to occur.

Using the Social Motives

Whether he wishes to or not, the teacher is bound to invoke many of the social needs. The child has a powerful need to be noticed by adults, and preferably to be noticed favorably, and to be liked. To a certain extent the teacher may try to reduce this pronounced dependency, but he cannot overlook it, and up to a point, he is likely to use it (Sears and Hilgard, 1964).

The teacher, of course, is not the only one whose opinion matters. In many school situations, indeed, the approval of classmates or of members of the gang, may outweigh that of the teacher. Rather than try to make any precise distinction in this matter, we may merely assume that the typical student is concerned about appearing well in the eyes of others and will exert himself to this end.

Announcing a Standard to be Met. By letting a student know that a certain amount or quality of work is expected, we invoke his need for approval. Whether we stress the point or not, we intimate that this is what he must do to get our approval and that of the world we represent. Typically we do this ourselves, telling a student that he is expected to type 25 words a minute, or to know 850 Spanish words. Such standards, of course, should be set individually and should be based on the student's previous performance. Often students can be encouraged to set reasonable standards for themselves, setting a new goal as soon as each

standard has been reached (Leuba, 1930). At times teachers have offered a material reward to each pupil who meets the standard assigned to him. This definitely boosts performance but does not seem feasible as a regular procedure and may have undesirable effects on character.

Observing the Work of Others, but Working Privately. This is the situation which prevails when one or two good students are working at the board and the other children are at their desks. When this pace-setter arrangement is in effect there is some increase in speed of output but no increase in the quality of the output. The presence of the pace-setter induces the children at their desks to do more exercises but does not prevent them from making errors.

Being Observed by Others. If the child is working at the board where all the class may see (and perhaps comment) will he perform better than he would if working at his desk? The answer is twofold. Under such obtrusive observation the quantity of routine work will increase markedly. The number of decisions regarding difficult issues will be reduced. So will the quality of the routine work.

Competition. Competition can be depended on to increase output. Working in New York schools, for instance, in one experiment, Maller (1929) urged grade-six children to see who could make the greatest gain in adding number couplets. The class gained some thirty-two examples. This is more than the total gain that ordinarily takes place between grades five and eight. Of course, their skill did not increase that much. They merely made better use of skill they already had.

In the experiment just mentioned, it was found that individual competition was much better than group competition.

► *Making Decisions While the World Looks On*

In this experiment, a college student, working alone with the experimenter in a small laboratory, was shown a phrase such as, "a musical composition." As soon as he had read the phrase, the experimenter showed him a pair of words such as, "concerto-symphony." The student had to decide which of these two words best fitted the phrase he had just read. Unknown to the student, a record was kept of the time he took to make the decision. Each student was given some choices that were easy and others that were hard. Some choices were relatively neutral or objective; others made room for preferences, fears, or prejudices.

The laboratory had a large sheet of glass in one wall, and this made possible different audience conditions for different students. Under one condition the student could easily see some four or five people watching him from behind the glass, and he knew that they were also listening. Under a second condition, the lights on the glass were arranged so that the audience could not be seen, but the student was told about this unseen audience behind the glass and he knew he was being observed. Under the third condition, the glass was covered by a curtain and there was neither an audience nor the suggestion of one. In all 120 students took part, 20 men and 20 women working under each condition.

The results shown in the table were obtained for the *first half* of the experiment.

	Time Taken To Make a Choice		
	No Audience	Seen Audience	Unseen Audience
Difficult Choices, Personal Tone	179	204	248
Difficult Choices, Neutral Tone	178	207	254
Easy Choices, Personal Tone	137	168	171
Easy Choices, Neutral Tone	117	119	150

In general, the differences between "no audience" and the "unseen audience" were significant at the 5-percent level. The other differences were of questionable significance. These differences did not hold up for the last half of the experiment. Apparently the students adjusted to the audience condition.

SOURCE: S. Wapner and Thelma G. Alper, The effect of an audience on behavior in a choice situation, *Journal of Abnormal and Social Psychology*, 1952, **47**, 222–229.

The children performed at a higher level when each child was trying to excel all other children. When, on the other hand, one class was trying to excel another class, the influence of competition was less marked. Group competition was fairly effective when a group of boys tried to excel a group of girls. The whole problem of competition is highly controversial, of course, and has proved difficult to investigate in an objective fashion (Myers, 1962; Phillips and De Vault, 1957; Smith and others, 1957).

Competition is a device which may be used to give life to such tasks as a spelling drill, especially if the class is a trifle apathetic. Here the students are working with words that are fairly familiar. For most of the words there is relatively little chance of error. We should also bear in mind that in this type of competition, most students will ultimately miss *one* word. There are likely to be many losers. No one loser is likely to feel markedly conspicuous or inferior.

Praise and Blame. In the extreme case of social approval or disapproval, the teacher overtly praises the student for his good work or administers a reprimand for poor performance. In general, we should present school tasks to students in such a way, or in such sequence, that he will succeed in the great majority of those tasks. (This problem is discussed in detail in Chapter 5.) If we manage things this way, there will be little occasion for overt blame. In spite of our best efforts, however, we are bound to encounter work that is a mixture of good and bad. At this point, we cannot be sure whether praise or blame will have the greatest effect in bringing about an improvement in the future. The reports (Murphy and others, 1937; Schmidt, 1941) of the earlier material reveal a great deal of inconsistency from one study to another. Later studies (Grace, 1948; Thompson and Hunnicutt, 1944) have not completely eliminated the confusion, but they suggest the possibility, if not the certainty, that blame might be quite bad for people who are very tense to begin with. Blame may have a valuable effect, however, for people who are too easygoing or lethargic. There is some evidence to support the common-sense notion that what will work for one teacher might not work for another. In general it would seem wise to let nature take its course, avoiding undue reliance on either praise or blame. In the long run we might aim at a balanced diet with success and praise predominating. On the occasion of a lapse, however, we might very well act in a way that seems natural, perhaps ignoring the lapse, perhaps administering a good-natured, but definite, rebuke.

Using the Expressed Interests of Pupils

Presumably the motives already discussed are basic and widely distributed. They are the inner forces that can be depended upon to move people. But these are not the surface interests that children ordinarily talk about. However fiercely he may feel the urge, the child does not go around freely discussing his need to be loved or to gain the approval of others. He does talk freely about baseball, science fiction, or TV programs. These arc examples of the child's expressed immediate interests, derived no doubt from his basic needs, but not directly expressing themselves as such.

There are scores of such specific interests. In any one culture, some interests (in animals, aeroplanes, or stories) may be found in almost all children. Other interests may be limited to a few cultural groups, but can readily be detected by the teacher. These interests, when detected, can be enlisted to provide motives for school work. A lesson in chemistry, for instance, can be linked to a known interest in photography; the physics of combustion with a known interest in "hot rods;" refraction of light with a known interest in skin diving; political history with a recently aroused interest in current politics. Such interests should be used whenever convenient and feasible. Provided that you link them up in a convincing manner, there is everything to be gained from this approach. By linking up your subject with lively existing interests you automatically lead the child to come into the presence of the materials for instruction, to become activated, and to attend to the lesson.

Strategies for Using Interests. If we can convincingly link our subject with powerful existing interests of the children, our problems in motivation are largely solved. But how to do this?

One solution, of course, is to reverse the traditional approach. Rather than trying to find interests or needs to motivate our preselected topics, we could start with the interests and needs to be found in the children and let these determine the subjects to be taught at any given time. This position is adopted, in one degree or another, in each of three general programs. In the *complete child-centered* curriculum, the immediate interests of the children determine what is to be taught and when it is to be taught. In the less extreme program of *flexible timing*, the school decides what should be taught, but the teacher is governed by the immediate interests of the pupils in deciding when each topic is to be taught. Elections, for instance, must be understood sometime, but they will be introduced when pupils show an interest in the topic. In a much more conservative policy of *using expected interests*, the school decides what shall be taught, and to a great extent, when it should be taught. In deciding on the sequence of topics, however, the curriculum makers take into account the typical interests of each age group. If it is known, for instance, that twelve-year-olds frequently show an interest in politics, we could schedule some election topics for grades six or seven.

Controversies Regarding the Strategies. You will notice that, in listing these different approaches, we are in the middle of a tremendous controversy that has rocked the educational world and the general public as well (Cremin, 1961). The proponents of the complete child-centered approach believe that this approach not only solves the problems of motivation but that it is also an approach demanded by ethical considerations. They believe that the needs and interests of children are not merely laughable foibles. Such interests and needs are very real and important in their own right and the school has a moral obligation to meet the needs felt by the pupils at the moment.

Obviously many people take violent exception to this approach. They claim that there are certain subjects that should be taught and that the school has the responsibility for deciding this matter. It cannot delegate this responsibility to anything as undependable as the spontaneous interests of children.

Flexible timing runs the risk of violating the inherent unity in some subjects. It may also disregard the definite sequence (algebra before analytic geometry) found in other areas. There is also the very down-to-earth possibility that some teachers, excellent in most respects, may just lack the agility that is needed to keep jumping from one facet of the subject to another.

Confusion Regarding the Word "Needs". If you do become involved in a discussion of the general merits of the three general approaches, you will probably encounter much talk about meeting the needs of youth. To avoid unnecessary confusion, the psychologist would urge you to remember that the word "need" is often used in two quite different senses (Komizar, 1961). From his bedroom, Jimmie calls, "I need a drink of water." He expresses a simple *organismic* need. The drink is something he really wants. Perhaps it is something his body requires. His mother says, "That child *needs* to learn what bedtime means." Here the word "need" is used in quite a different sense. It refers to something that Jimmie ought to do, or that his mother would like him to do. This is often called a *normative* need.

In many educational discussions the organismic and the normative needs are lumped together as if they were the same things (Low, 1953). At times, when people are talking about meeting the needs of youth, they mean meeting organismic needs, helping children get the things they actually want. At other times such people mean meeting normative needs, or teaching the child what we think he ought to know, or what will be good for him later on. This latter interpretation, of course, represents the age-old purpose of the schools and is a far cry from the policy of meeting immediate, organismic needs.

For the curriculum maker, there may be some justification in lumping together the normative and organismic needs. The school may feel equally obligated to take care of both kinds of needs. When we set out to deal with these needs, however, we must realize that psychologically speaking, they are oceans apart. The organismic needs are self-motivated. The normative needs, on the other hand, may be completely lacking in motivation. Much of our work consists of taking the things that the pupil *should* learn, and linking them up in some way with what he *wants* to do.

Intrinsic vs. Extrinsic Motives

To supply a motive for any given task we might be able to call upon a need intrinsic to the task, or we might have to use some extrinsic need (Hilgard and Russell, 1950). For the washing of hands, for instance, a child's need to get

News and Publications Service, Stanford University

Ernest R. Hilgard

rid of that grimy feeling would be an intrinsic motive. His need to avoid a scolding from his mother would be an extrinsic motive. Or, to take an academic example, his wish to be able to read would be an intrinsic motive, whereas his hope to gain the teacher's approval would be extrinsic.

There is an important practical difference between intrinsic and extrinsic needs. An intrinsic need can be met only by the behavior in question—only by washing the hands or by learning to read. The extrinsic needs can be met by various roundabout devices. Or, more accurately, a person may *try* to meet these needs by roundabout devices. Without washing his hands, the small boy may *try* to avoid trouble with his mother by staying out of her way, by pretending illness, or by keeping his hands well up into his sleeves. Without learning to read, the child may *try* to curry favor with the teacher by lavish use of apples, babyish behavior, or by acting as teacher's little helper.

Obviously, the intrinsic need leads more directly to the behavior that we desire. When we use this motive, moreover, there is less need for supplementary restraints to prevent roundabout behavior. Try not to be too rigid about using intrinsic motives, however. In the hurly-burly of teaching you may not always be able to lay your hands on an appropriate intrinsic motive. Here it would be better to use some safe and suitable extrinsic motive than to do nothing. It is always possible, moreover, that an activity, like reading, originally brought about by some extrinsic motive, may later become an intrinsic interest in its own right. More will be said about this when we discuss *functional autonomy*.

THE MECHANICS OF MOTIVATION

Motivation is needed to get students into the general situation in which learning can occur, to keep them awake and reasonably active, and to keep their attention directed to the task at hand. To accomplish these things we should use basic needs and interests when possible. For controlling activation and directing attention, however, there are also some rather simple, mechanical things that we can do.

Controlling Activation

Performance is at its best when activation or arousal is at a moderate level (Malmo, 1959). We should avoid drowsiness at one extreme and panic at the other. If we feel that our pupils are too indolent, we may have to arouse them a bit. If we feel that they are already too jittery or alert, we may need to induce a more relaxed condition.

As we all know, sheer physiology has a great deal to do with the general level of wakefulness, activation, or level of arousal (Duffy, 1962). Much recent interest in this problem, as a matter of fact, has been set off by the intensive study of one portion of the brain stem, the reticular division, that controls the level of arousal or degree of activation (Magoun, 1958). The activity of this part of the brain stem is closely related to the general blood chemistry which is, in turn, affected by fatigue, poisons, hormones, or drugs.

The physical environment also plays a big part. We are all familiar with the lulling effect of subdued and distant sounds. Monotony and regularity are the especial enemies of wakefulness. We are most likely to doze when the stimuli follow a rhythmic or predictable pattern, when there are no unexpected events to disrupt the pattern, when the broad and level turnpike brings no surprises. Drowsiness is especially likely to set in when we are listening to someone read, or listening to a mechanical recording. In this situation, the sounds often have less range or variety than when people talk spontaneously, and we can depend upon it that the reader or recording will present few abrupt changes in tempo or inflection. Wakefulness or arousal is brought about, on the other hand, by intensity, variety, or the threat of the unexpected. Even when the blood chemistry would bring about sleep, we can push people into wakefulness, if not into panic, by intense stimuli such as bright lights, loud noises, cold water, pain, or rough handling. To maintain wakefulness in the classroom, variety or the unexpected may be more feasible than sheer violence or intensity. A switch from one group of stimuli to another can work wonders. Pupils drowsing through a lecture may come awake with the mere introduction of another voice, as when a student asks a question.

Controlling Attention or Directness

Clearly the student must look at some features of the situation and must ignore others. He must look at the Latin text and ignore the charms of the girl in the seat just ahead. He must attend to the music on the piano and ignore the conversation in the next room. Directedness means something more than merely passive watching. It means that the pupil's activities will change as the nature of the task changes. The pupil who is really directing his attention to the lesson in the teaching machine, or to the management of the car, will show appropriate changes in his behavior as he encounters changes in the task.

Anything new or different is likely to attract attention. When the familiar and the novel are side by side, the novel will win out. Attention is even greater when the new thing goes against our expectations, the automobile with three wheels, or is incongruous—a large, burly man with an exceptionally quiet voice.

The louder sound or brighter light has a stronger pull on our attention. This is especially true if the intense stimulus stands out from its background. The elaborate, complex gadget is more likely to attract attention than is its simpler counterpart.

Coordinating Activation and Attention

Ordinarily activation and attention go hand in hand. Whatever we do to boost one will also boost the other. An unexpected bang in the chemistry lesson, for instance, will attract the attention of the students and get them somewhat excited. And again, ordinarily, an excited person has his mind fixed on one thing. Conversely, anyone intently watching a single event will find himself tense and activated. There are exceptions, of course. A man half asleep may keep his indolent efforts consistently directed to the annoying fly or to the blanket that is slipping off. Conversely, we may observe someone all keyed up and nervous, but dominated by no definite purpose and with his attention at the mercy of any chance stimulus.

For efficiency in most tasks, the two facets of attention and activation must be more or less in step. An increase in one may cause trouble unless it is matched by an appropriate change in the other. In some rather monotonous tasks, for instance, attention may be at a reasonable level, but the student may be getting exceedingly drowsy. At this point we should do something to bring him to life or to activate him, even if what we do might distract his attention from the task in which he is engaged. The attention is of little use unless it is matched by an appropriate activation level. For this reason, it is not surprising to learn that, for monotonous work, a slight distraction may actually lead to an increase in efficiency (McBain, 1961). We see this when the high school student is doing his homework with jazz blaring from the radio. There is some interference with his attention, but this is more than overcome by the fact that he has a higher degree of activation.

We face a more serious problem of keeping the two facets in step with each other when we reach the higher levels of activation. As we have seen, efficiency is likely to fall off when the degree of

► *When Distraction May Help*

Some of the members of the Canadian Air Force were assigned to the monotonous task of printing a sequence of 7 pairs of letters, KT, LH, IM, XF, KV, TZ, IW, over and over again for a period of 42 minutes. The letters had to be printed on a tape that was advanced one line at a time at a fixed rate. Memory was not stressed, since the sequence was printed on a card and the subject could glance briefly at the card at anytime. The task proved difficult, however, as the letters could easily be confused. Whenever a man thought he had made an error he was supposed to press a button with his foot.

To reduce the variation in stimulation as much as possible, the room in which each man worked was covered with a black drape. Outside noises were masked by the hum of a large exhaust fan.

After some preliminary experience, half the men continued to work under these quiet conditions. The remaining men, however, worked while a record of a speech was played backward. At times, short snatches of music, or intelligible speech were added to this meaningless noise.

The men working with only the steady hum of the fan made 16.4 errors per thousand responses, whereas those working with meaningless noise made only 12.2 errors. The difference of 4.2 is significant at the 5-percent level. The latter group, however, were no more accurate in reporting their errors, reporting 55 percent of such errors as compared to a 56-percent report on the part of those working under quieter conditions. This difference of 1 percent is not significant.

SOURCE: W. N. McBain, Noise, the "arousal hypothesis," and monotonous work, *Journal of Applied Psychology*, 1961, **45**, 309–317.

arousal passes a certain point. This decrease in efficiency will become much more pronounced if the increase in activation is not matched by a clear-cut focusing of the attention on the task at hand (Eason and Branks, 1963). Indeed, some psychologists (Duffy, 1962) hold that increase in activation would bring no decrease whatever if attention were appropriately focused. However that may be, we should try to be sure that marked arousal is accompanied by appropriate concentration of attention. At this point, ironically enough, we face the problem that in trying to sharpen the focus of attention so as to match the activation

level, we may further increase the degree of activation itself.

We run the risk of marked inefficiency when activation greatly outruns the degree of attention. Assuming a reasonable degree of activation to begin with, however, we face little risk from the converse problem. *Provided we can keep activation within reasonable bounds*, that is to say, there is little danger of getting too much attention; typically, the more the better.

In general, whenever either member of our team is markedly ahead of the other, we should do something to bring the laggard into line, even at the cost of

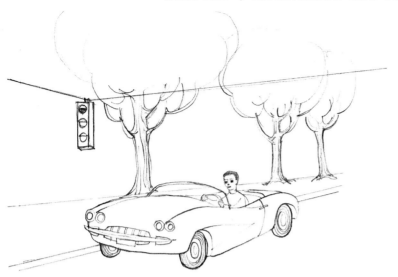

Few competing responses

Many competing responses

Fig. 4.3.   Tasks differing in the likelihood of error.

curtailing the leader. Beyond the middle ranges of arousal, it is especially important to see that activation does not outrun attention.

ADJUSTING MOTIVATION TO THE TASK AT HAND

It is obviously true that we must have a certain amount of motivation if learning is to take place. It is also true that motivation can be overdone and that we can push the level of activation to the point where learning becomes inefficient. Are there some rules to help us to keep motivation at the proper balance?

Probability of Error

In some tasks there is little likelihood of serious error. In other tasks, however, some error is extremely likely or almost inevitable (Fig. 4.3). In learning to press the brake of a car when we see a red light, for instance, we are not likely to do many wrong things. We can be too slow, or we can "beat the gun," but we do not have to choose between many rival responses. When first learning to hit the letter "e" on the typewriter, however, there are a great many wrong responses we can make—and will!

Spence and his students (Farber, 1955) have made much of this difference. Their experiments suggest that whenever mistakes are extremely likely motivation should be kept at a low level (Castaneda and others, 1956b). With great probability of error, high motivation can hurt in several ways. When tense or worked up, we are more likely to blurt out any answer that is on the tip of the tongue, to let go with any response that presents itself. And in this situation, the answer on the tip of the tongue could easily be the wrong answer. Furthermore, when we

are extremely anxious or worked up, there is often some relief or reward even after making a mistake. When we are terribly worried about a situation it is a relief even to know the worst, and a mistake brings this kind of relief. Finally, of course, the person who is intensely worked up and anxious to succeed may quit completely when he encounters frequent failures.

The Specter of the Unmotivated Class

In general we should go to some trouble to keep motivation at a low level whenever we suspect that the pupils are inclined to be a bit anxious about school in general, that they are more excited than usual, and that the subject is one in which errors are likely.

Can we go too far in cutting down on the motivation? Under the circumstances just mentioned, this is not a serious danger. To be sure, there must be enough motivation to get the student to go through the motions which make learning possible. But once he is going through the motions in adequate fashion, there is not too much danger of undermotivation. Even listless or lackadaisical practice will produce considerable learning at this stage of development.

Not only is it possible that some learning takes place when the student addresses himself to his task in somewhat listless fashion, but the experiments on incidental learning suggest that some learning can take place even when people have no intention to learn and have no idea that learning is expected of them (Adams, 1957). Without trying to, you come to remember frequently encountered telephone numbers or addresses, or snatches of television commercials. By using the well-known Greenspoon effect (Krasner, 1958), you can induce uncon-

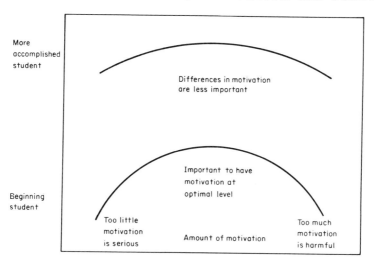

Fig. 4.4. Influence of motivation at different levels of competence.

scious learning in other people. By smiling or "coming to life" when your fellow-diner scratches his ear, or arranges his tie, you can make him "learn" to carry out these actions to an absurd extent, even though he has no idea of why you are "coming to life" or why he himself has acquired this compulsion. When taking part in a formal experiment, of course, he may suspect something (Farber, 1963). The evidence suggests that some learning can take place when people are in bed and practically asleep—have no recollection of having been awake—although there is no learning when they are in a really sound sleep (Emmons and Simon, 1956). People trying to break a code, or to work out the key of a complex puzzle, often lose nothing whatever when encouraged to adopt a relaxed attitude at the outset (Deese, 1958).

Notice that there is some disagreement on this matter. It is still quite possible that vigorous, zestful practice will be more effective than the indifferent, heel-dragging performance we so often

deplore. Certainly the highly motivated behavior is more pleasant to observe. It is possible, moreover, that grudging, indifferent practice may lead to a habit of lack of effort. In view of all this, there is much to suggest that we should encourage a reasonable degree of effort on the part of our students. The additional effort may do some good. Within limits, it should do no harm. But let us not be too disturbed when an exceedingly indolent performer proves to have learned as much as his more conscientious classmates.

Motivation at Different Levels of Competence

It is clear that it is when the student is a beginner in any subject that we should be careful to keep motivation at a fairly low level. At this stage, mistakes are more likely to occur. As the student acquires skill, however, the likelihood of error is less and at this stage it might be wise and would certainly be permissible to bring motivation to a higher level.

Actually the whole problem of motivation takes on a different significance as we move from the early to the later stages of learning (Fig. 4.4). At the outset of any learning, motivation is likely to be a serious problem. When considerable skill has been acquired, however, there is less need to be concerned about the matter of motivation one way or another. Consider a student just beginning piano lessons. To combat drowsiness we may go to some trouble to arrange for practice at a favorable time of day. If he has little genuine interest, we may wish to add some extrinsic motive such as the need for approval or even a material reward. But we will keep the eagerness at a moderate level and will try to make sure that he is not too nervous or anxious. At this stage we will be especially careful to eliminate possible distractions such as interesting conversation or a television program. We may have to make repeated attempts to get the pupil to attend to the music and to strike the keys.

After our student has learned to play well, many of these matters can be ignored. The distractions against which we had to protect him in earlier times now present no problem. When he is really engrossed in his playing we may actually find it hard to interrupt him. There is little need to worry about keeping alertness within the narrow optimum range. He plays reasonably well within wide ranges of activation, when half asleep at one extreme, or in the panic of recital nerves, at the other.

Very often the skilled activity, originally induced by bribes or other extrinsic motives, later becomes a motive in itself. It becomes something which the student does for its own sake and which is now so attractive that it acts as an incentive for intermediate steps. Now the student may do many other things just for the pleasure of playing the piano.

It is not at all unusual to find that an activity which originally had to be developed by all sorts of extrinsic motivation later becomes attractive in its own right. When this happens, we say that the activity has acquired *functional autonomy* (Seward, 1963), a notion that has been greatly stressed in the writings of Professor Gordon Allport.

When the various school subjects do acquire some functional autonomy, do no hesitate to use them as real motives. After acquiring some competence, many students actually enjoy reading, problem solving, or even just thinking. If these become needs in their own right, there is often no necessity of bolstering them up with more remote or farfetched needs.

Harvard University News Office

Gordon W. Allport

TYPES OF PRACTICE OR ACTIVITY

Learning comes from the acts that the pupil performs, from the circumstances to which he is attending, and from the events that follow his actions. The chief purpose of motivation is to guarantee that he will be acting in a given way at the time he is attending to a given situation or symbol. This process is seen in the recitation, when the student becomes aware of the teacher's question, or flash card, or the work on the chalkboard; when he comes up with some kind of answer or response; and when he encounters the teacher's comment or some new situation or result. The process is also seen when the student is practicing on the typewriter, or on a musical instrument, or working on one of the teaching machines. In each case he becomes aware of some symbol, makes some sort of movement, and encounters some new situation or result.

Reading or Listening

There are some situations in which the activity considered necessary for learning is not apparent at first glance. A closer look, however, shows such activity to be present in a very lively fashion. A student quietly reading a book, for instance, really is carrying on a lively program of activity. Having read (attended to) the first part of the sentence, he is almost bound to run ahead a bit and guess at _____. When his eyes catch up, he finds out whether or not his guess (the rest of the sentence) was correct. This is typical in all reading. In fact, one very good way to judge the "readability" of a given selection is to find out how well the typical student can guess or anticipate the next word or so when you stop him in the middle of a sentence (Rubenstein and Aborn, 1958). If he can anticipate too many words at any point, the reading becomes boring and too easy. But if he can't anticipate any words, he will find the reading quite difficult.

The reacting that goes on in reading is not only this business of guessing what is coming next. As a matter of fact, this is probably the simplest and most mechanical form of reaction. We do other and more interesting things as well. Reading about present-day speeds across the Atlantic, for instance, the student may think of many other things—the time taken in the past, probable speeds of the future, or a host of other items. An author may take pleasure in trying to make us think of something that he doesn't quite say, as when he *speaks* of the Bard of Avon but forces us to *think* of Shakespeare.

Listening is very much like reading except, here, the timing is under the control of the speaker. As in the case of the reader, the listener is making many silent responses to the statements he hears. The lecturer should allow for the many silent responses which are being made to his remarks. When he introduces a novel idea (and surely many of the ideas he introduces will be somewhat novel) he should not pass over this idea too quickly. He should linger over it, repeat it in slightly different words, state it this way and state it that way, and dwell on it for some time. By thus holding the idea before the students for a considerable length of time, and holding it before them in a stimulating way, he permits them, and, indeed, actually impels them, to make several reactions to the idea. One of these responses has a chance of being the right one.

► *Lecture vs. Discussion*

For one division of a class in college mathematics, the instructor taught two small sections of twenty to thirty students each, using the lecture-discussion approach. Each section met for three such sessions each week. The instructor also met the students in smaller groups for a one-hour laboratory session each week. Later in the year, the same instructor taught seventy students in one large class. He used the straight-lecture approach. There were three lectures per week supplemented by *two* one-hour laboratory sessions meeting in small groups. Unlike the previous class, these latter laboratories were led by student assistants.

Achievement was measured by an objective test covering manipulation and understanding of mathematical concepts, and by an essay test on the nature of mathematics. The mean scores at the beginning and the end of the course are shown in the table.

	Objective Test			Essay Test		
	Initial	*Final*	*Gain*	*Initial*	*Final*	*Gain*
47 students taught in small lecture-discussion group	115.6	192.8	77.1	17.0	22.7	5.7
59 students from the large lecture class	113.9	187.8	73.9	18.6	24.9	6.3
Advantage for small classes			+3.2			−0.6

Neither of these differences is significant

In a poll of student opinion, the instructor received a higher rating from the students who were taught in small sections. The laboratory sections accompanying the large sections were rated more favorably than those accompanying the small classes. Both procedures were rated as better than the college average.

SOURCE: Ruth Churchill and Paula John, Conservation of teaching time through the use of lecture classes and student assistants, *Journal of Educational Psychology*, 1958, **49**, 324–327.

Class Discussions

When a discussion is going on, some of the students will make their reactions out loud, and in those cases the teacher can quickly tell whether or not those students are on the right track. But he can only tell about the student who has just spoken. Each of the other students also makes silent reactions to what the instructor has said. Each is also making some reaction to the student's contribution. It may happen that the student who first makes a comment may be completely off the track. His comments, in turn, may elicit reactions from other students, some out loud, others silent, that are even farther astray. This complex interaction is very hard to control. Many an instructor finds it easier to control the host of silent reactions of the students when the instructor himself is doing most of the talking.

The management of a discussion is a tricky business. In spite of the expected advantages of the discussion method, indeed, the typical college instructor gets no better results from the discussion than he does from the lecture method (Mc-Keachie, 1963; Stovall, 1958). We have little evidence as to how the two approaches compare at the high school level. It would be natural to suppose, by the way, that it is chiefly the "communicating" student who profits from discussion. For the silent student, who merely listens anyhow, it may be better to *listen* to the typical instructor than to *listen* to the typical fellow-student. Whenever we do use the discussion method we should keep this in mind and try to be sure that as many students as possible take part (Walther, 1941). (See Chapter 12 for a discussion of the related problem of the group-centered approach.)

GRAPHICAL RECORDS OF LEARNING

Many teachers encourage pupils to keep a graphical record of their performance from day-to-day or week-to-week. Pupils, for instance, can keep a plot of the books they have read by using devices such as that in Figure 4.5.

Whenever the performance can be given as a numerical score, as in speed of reading, number of words spelled correctly, or number of arithmetic problems completed, the record can take the form of a graph of learning. The bars shown in Figure 4.6 may be more convenient for younger children. The curve, Figure 4.7, may give a better picture of continuity.

Such graphical records serve several purposes. They provide knowledge of results in moderately dramatic form. Most children keeping such records definitely try to beat their own previous performances. Such records can also be useful to the teacher. They show at a glance whether or not performance is improving, and whether or not the rate of improvement is changing. The section of the curve from *a* to *b*, for instance, shows increased performance throughout, but varying rates of growth.

The General Pattern of Learning Curves

In looking at a curve of learning for any one student we are bound to wonder how this compares with the "typical" or average curve. This should not concern us too much since each child may improve in a somewhat different way. Such curves have a few features that occur fairly regularly, however, and these features should cause us no surprise when we see them.

In many curves you will see a very rapid increase at first, followed by a more gradual increase thereafter. This is especially likely to happen, as in reading, when much practice has occurred before, and when the first stages of the graph merely bring out what the pupil already knows. Such a rapid initial increase is also seen when, as in memorizing a foreign vocabulary, the student masters the easy items in the first few trials and must deal with the more difficult items later.

This rapid initial increase, although frequent, is by no means universal. In some kinds of practice, as a matter of fact, there is little or no growth at first, followed by a snowballing effect when

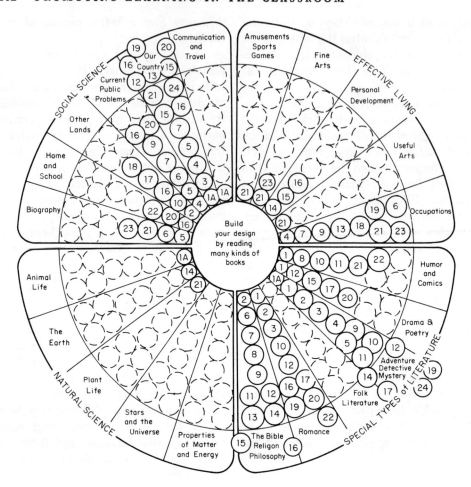

Fig. 4.5. My reading design: A device to provide a graphic record of books read. From "My Reading Design," Form D, by G. O. Simpson. Copyright 1962 by G. O. Simpson. Published and distributed by the Ward Division of The Hubbard Company, Defiance, Ohio.

some improvement does occur. A curve like this is likely to occur when starting a task that is quite new, swimming, for instance, and when there is no store of related skill on which we can draw. It may also occur when success depends largely on catching on to one or two key items or acts. If the task to be mastered has an arbitrary limit, as in learning the names of the students in a class, this increased rate of learning may continue to the end. If there is no arbitrary limit, however, as in speed of swimming, we can be sure that ultimately daily improvement will come at a slower and slower rate.

When a curve begins to level off, say, after several years of typing, we must remember that further improvement is becoming increasingly costly and we should ask if the additional skill is worth the increased cost. It might well be. But

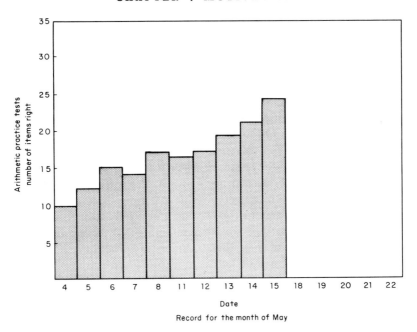

Fig. 4.6. Bar graph showing improvement in arithmetic.

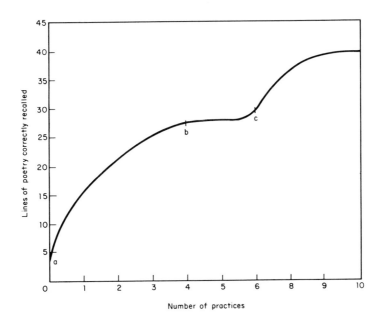

Fig. 4.7. Learning curve showing progress in memorizing a poem.

in that case we should be prepared to pay the heavy cost of exceptional attainment.

In Figure 4.7 the portion of the curve from *b* to *c* shows a leveling off period, or a *plateau*. Again, such temporary halts in improvement are frequent but by no means universal. Often they will cure themselves. If such a plateau should persist it may be that the student has been using an inefficient method all along (adding by counting on his fingers) and has now gone as far as this method will take him. It may mean that some new concept (the meaning of a mathematical limit) is still to be mastered. It may be boredom or loss of interest.

In the matter of discouragement or lack of interest, we face a vicious circle. Whenever a prolonged plateau does occur, discouragement and lack of interest are likely to follow. To combat this difficulty, try to get the pupil to look at the whole graph from the beginning. In this way he can see his long-term progress. You may be able to convince him that this recent lack of improvement, which now looms so large in his thoughts, is a minor matter in the light of his long-term improvement.

A Final Caution

Practice, or experience with the material to be learned is, of course, essential. But we can place too much reliance on it. In the first place, we might be tempted to assume that since some practice is essential, more would be better. Very often this is not the case. Beyond a certain minimum, we often gain little from greater amounts of practice. In an interesting experiment, Rock (1957) had students attempt to memorize pairs of words such as one finds in a vocabulary list. Each student read over the list of pairs once and then tried to give the second (response) word of the pair as soon as he saw the first (stimulus) term. Each student would get some pairs right on this first test, but would miss a good many others. Rock kept the pairs that were right, but took out all that were wrong and substituted completely new but comparable pairs. The student would then read this new list made up of pairs already learned and other pairs seen for the first time. A test followed this reading, and again Rock made up a new list containing only successes and new pairs. Under this procedure, if the student was to learn a given pair at all he had to learn it the first time he saw it. If he missed it he would never see it again, but would encounter a new pair on the next trial. Here, then, there was no chance for practice or repeated experience to operate in the learning of the pairs. Yet students working in this way did just as well as comparable students who saw the same pairs over and over again. As you might imagine, there has been a great deal of controversy (Lockhead, 1961) over the full implications of Rock's work. It suggests, however, that practice may not function by successive additions of strength to a response or association. Practice, on the contrary, may merely provide an additional chance for the learning to occur. Practice may be like the process of extracting money from a piggy bank. After fifty shakes, true enough, you have got more out than you had after three shakes. But each shake, or practice, does not bring any single coin farther through the slot. It merely gives each of the coins that re left an additional chance to appear.

Perhaps repeated practice is not always an absolute necessity for learning. Long before Rock's provocative experiment, Rice had shown that, when extended beyond a certain minimum, we often gain little from longer periods of practice in spelling, writing, or English composition. In any case, practice can do nothing in and of itself. At the very best it can merely provide the occasion in which other forces such as reinforcement or insight can come into the picture. These other forces frequently do come into the picture when practice is provided, but unless they do, additional practice will accomplish very little.

SUMMARY

As it is in so many topics in psychology, motivation turns out to be an important problem in managing classroom learning. Our problem here is to make effective use of motivation to get the child to engage in learning, to keep him alert, and to keep his attention appropriately directed. To do this we try to engage his urge to achieve, to be active, and, conversely, to rest; his need to think well of himself, and a host of related ego and activity needs. To a moderate extent we appeal to his urge to make a success out of life. Curiosity and the needs to explore and manipulate have proved to be effective motives. These are even more effective when the student is frequently or continuously aware of how well he is doing. Routine records of performance may be better than frequent formal examinations.

To some extent the school must make use of the pupil's need to secure the approval of teacher, classmates, and the world in general. In stressing this need, we can usually boost total output but sometimes at the cost of quality. Such increases have come from the announcement of standards to be attained, from pacing, working under observation,

competition, and from outright praise or blame. It is hard to point to any clear advantage of any one of these devices over the other.

The deep underlying urges typically express themselves in the form of interests in hobbies, games, and other activities. The teacher can make use of these as motives. In one controversial approach, indeed, all teaching is organized around the pupil's expressed needs and interests.

Motivation involves both activation and attention. In managing activation we should avoid both the extreme of drowsiness and the other extreme of panic or frenzy. Activation is somewhat under the control of chemicals and hormones, but can be increased by the variety and intensity of the stimuli and by the urgency of the needs at work. These same factors work for sustained attention. Indeed, in straining for the desired attention we may push activation to an undesired level. Conversely, things that interfere with attention may make up for their distracting effects by enhancing activation.

When beginning a new task, and whenever he is quite likely to make an error, the pupil should be kept at a low level of motivation. As competence increases, however, and as the likelihood of error becomes less, motivation can be sharply increased. As competence becomes greater, as a matter of fact, motivation becomes a less crucial problem.

To learn, a pupil must go in for some activity and must make a number of responses to the material being studied. Much of this activity will take place, however, when the pupil is merely reading or listening. A flood of overt discussion is no guarantee of superior learning.

The effects of practice can be portrayed graphically as learning curves. These provide a convenient record and can be used as motives. Some recent work has led to the re-examination of the function of practice. Unless some favorable forces are working at the time, practice in and of itself can do little to bring about improvement.

SUGGESTIONS FOR FURTHER READING

Bindra, D., *Motivation: A Systematic Re-interpretation.* New York: The Ronald Press Company, 1959.

Brown, J. S., *Motivation of Behavior.* New York: McGraw-Hill Book Company, Inc., 1961.

Castaneda, A., D. S. Palmero, and B. R. McCandless, Complex learning and performance as a function of anxiety in children and task difficulty, *Child Development*, 1956, **27**, 328–332. Reprinted in Haimowitz, pp. 471–474.

Duffy, Elizabeth, *Activation and Behavior.* New York: John Wiley & Sons, Inc., 1962.

Hall, J. F., *Psychology of Motivation.* Philadelphia: J. B. Lippincott Company, 1961.

Hilgard, E. R., Motivation in learning theory, in S. Koch, ed. *Psychology: A Study of a Science*, Volume V. New York: McGraw-Hill Book Company, Inc., 1963, pp. 253–283.

Mednick, S. A., *Learning.* Englewood Cliffs, N. J.: Prentice-Hall, Inc., 1964. See Chapter 5, "Motivation and Learning."

Page, E. B., Teacher comments and student performance: a seventy-four classroom experiment in school motivation, *Journal of Educational Psychology*, 1958, **49**, 173–181. Reprinted in Charters, pp. 219–225, and Noll, pp. 264–276.

Piaget, J., *The Origins of Intelligence in Children.* New York: International Universities Press, Inc., 1952. Chapter 3 reprinted in Stendler, pp. 146–154, "Making Interesting Sights Last."

Rethlingshafer, Dorothy, *Motivation as Related to Personality.* New York: McGraw-Hill Book Company, Inc., 1963.

Rock, I., Repetition and learning, *Scientific American*, 1958 (Aug.), **199**, 68–72. Reprinted in Morse, pp. 210–215.

Sears, Pauline S., and E. R. Hilgard, The teacher's role in the motivation of the learner, *Yearbook National Society for the Study of Education*, 1964, **63**, Part I, 182–209.

Smock, C. D., and Bess G. Holt, Children's reactions to novelty, *Child Development*, 1962, **33**, 631–642. Reprinted in Stendler, pp. 155–163.

Terrell, G., Manipulative motivation in children, *Journal of Comparative and Physiological Psychology*, 1959, **52**, 705–709. Reprinted in DeCecco, pp. 98–107.

Thompson, G. G., and C. W. Hunnicutt, The effect of repeated praise or blame on the work achievement of "introverts" and "extroverts," *Journal of Educational Psychology*, 1944, **35**, 257–266. Reprinted in Noll, pp. 245–254, and Remmers, pp. 357–363.

White, R. W., Motivation reconsidered: the concept of competence, *Psychological Review*, 1959, **66**, 297–333.

Young, P. T., *Motivation and Emotion.* New York: John Wiley & Sons, Inc., 1961.

EXERCISES AND QUESTIONS FOR DISCUSSION

1. In the old one-room school and in the modern ungraded school, one group may be working at their seats while another group is engaged in discussion. What about distraction under these circumstances? Can you think of any circumstances under which casual eavesdropping would be an advantage?

2. Try to recall some course that fitted

in with lively interests that you already had. Recall a class that had no relation to your pre-existing interests. Comment on the problems and opportunities facing your teachers.

3. What is your reaction to the results of the experiments on the lecture versus the discussion method? Suggest some hypotheses to account for these results. How could you test the truth of some of these hypotheses? Do you think that the type of examination has anything to do with the results? Describe a type of examination on which you would expect superior results from the students taught by the discussion method.

4. Discuss the advantages and disadvantages of competition as a motive in producing immediate performance; in the development of long-term attitudes; in preparing for life as the student will face it.

CHAPTER 5

▶ *Maintaining a Schedule of Success*

Suppose that we have undertaken to help Jimmie learn the following things: to say or think "7" when he sees $4 + 3$; to spend some of his time reading for pleasure; to be reasonably cheerful around the home; and to take an interest in nature.

The basic rules for teaching these things are rather simple. In the first place, whenever the conditions are appropriate, we must get him to perform the acts in a successful or acceptable way. By one means or another we must get him to say "7," or to sit down with a book, or to smile, or to look at what the robins are doing. Secondly, whenever he does one of these things more or less adequately, whenever he comes up with a success, we must be sure that he is rewarded or *reinforced*. When he says "7," the teacher should accept this answer in an enthusiastic manner. When he spends some time in reading we should be sure that he encounters satisfaction. When he acts in a cheerful manner we should commend him or be sure that things are pleasant for him (Fig. 5.1).

The Basic Steps

Somehow or other we must arrange things so that, when the conditions are appropriate, the child is led to act in the desired way and that, thereupon, he receives some reinforcement or encounters a pleasant state of affairs. Just how do we do this?

The Conditions Appropriate for the Behavior. At times we do not need to worry a great deal about the conditions appropriate for the act we have in mind. Under just what conditions, for instance, do we want Jimmie to be cheerful around the house, to read for pleasure, or to take an interest in birds? It is hard to say. Here this matter of conditions is not especially critical. Within a wide range of conditions, we would like to get him to do these things fairly often.

Actions of this kind, which are not presumed to be set off by one specific stimulus, are often described as *operant responses*, or *operant behavior* (Skinner, 1953). It would be wrong, of course, to suggest that operant behavior is not in-

Whenever the conditions are
appropriate . . .

. . . do something . . .

. . . to bring out an acceptable
response . . .

. . . and accept or reinforce that
response

Fig. 5.1. The basic steps in reinforcement.

fluenced by stimuli. Skinner and his associates spend much of their time in studying how operant behavior varies with different stimulating conditions. The young couple, for instance, may go in for one kind of operant behavior when other people are present, and may exhibit a different kind when alone. Clearly the stimuli provided by other people play a part. But the behavior is not the direct result of these specific stimuli (Hill, 1963). That behavior is affected by so many things that, in the view of Skinner, it is pointless to link it up with a single instigating stimulus.

At other times the appropriate conditions are very specific indeed and are easily identified. One of the conditions for saying "7" is when Jimmie sees $4 + 3$. It is when he sees h-o-u-s-e that we want him to say, "house." It is when the student is asked the boiling point of water that we want him to say, "212° F." It is when he is concerned about the capital of Brazil that we want him to think of Brasilia. In many kinds of school work we can be fairly specific about conditions or situations that call for equally specific responses.

The term *respondent behavior* is often used to describe behavior in which a given response is regularly set off by a specific stimulus. "Given the stimulus, the response occurs automatically. Respondent behavior is made up of such specific stimulus-response connections called reflexes. We are born with a number of reflexes, and we acquire others through the process of conditioning." (Hill, 1963.)

ARRANGING FOR REINFORCEMENT

Obviously we cannot reinforce a pupil's response until he makes that response. Theoretically, therefore, we should first consider the problem of getting the pupil to make an acceptable or reinforceable response. The two problems are closely interrelated, however, and it will be simpler to consider reinforcement first.

Kinds of Reinforcement

It has been very difficult to define reinforcement in any rigorous fashion (Deese, 1958). But from the practical point of view, that is not especially serious. Most of us, when we see an act performed, can usually tell which things are likely to lead to a repetition of the act and which things are not. In general, the things that will lead to a repetition are things that will relieve distress (pain, hunger, thirst), or things that are pleasurable, or biologically valuable. We will not be very far off if we think of reinforcement as a reward.

Reinforcement from Within the Body. The nerve endings in the muscles, tendons, and other tissues provide a good deal of reinforcement. To make some movement and to feel the normal "feedback" from such a movement is moderately pleasant. Babies get fun merely from waving arms and legs and feeling them move. Even adults get a moderate thrill from swimming or walking in which arms and legs move and are felt to move.

Automatic Reinforcement from Outside the Body. Along with the reinforcement arising from the body itself, there are other forms of reinforcement that are automatic or almost inevitable. Such automatic or inevitable reinforcement is often found in the schoolroom. A student, in learning to type, usually knows when he strikes the wrong key or when he strikes a second key before the first has returned. A student of music, who has any ear at all, can tell when he has played the wrong note. Similarly, in an endless number of activities the correct and incorrect reactions will bring about striking differences in reinforcement.

We must not forget this mechanical feedback that comes from the musculature itself or from the world in which we operate. These sensations play an important part in acquiring skill. To see how dependent we are on the automatic feedback, it is only necessary to interfere with the normal flow of stimuli that ordinarily follow our behavior (K. U. Smith, 1962). Any such disruption is most disturbing and markedly reduces our skill. By ingenious electronic devices, for instance, we can arrange things so that the student hears his own voice only after a brief interval. As a result he stammers, grows tense, and shows much disturbed behavior (Yates, 1963). In other experiments a student is required to write out words while his hand is hidden behind a barrier. He sees his hand move through a television screen. When a delay is introduced between a movement and the sight of the movement, there is a marked reduction in performance (Smith and others, 1960).

It is not only in acts of bodily skill that effects may be automatic and striking. In solving a mathematical problem, for instance, it is often obvious that we are on the wrong track. In translating from a foreign language, a mistake may reveal itself by the failure of the subsequent context to make sense. We can tell that we must have made a mistake somewhere. This is also true in ordinary reading. An erroneous interpretation of a word or phrase will produce the effect of confusion or nonsense or the feeling that something is amiss.

Casual Reinforcement. Very often the teacher will apply the appropriate re-inforcement with no effort whatever. If the pupil makes an incorrect response, the teacher's eyebrows may rise, or an expression of surprise or annoyance may cross his face. If the pupil is right, the teacher's facial expression often shows pleasure or relief.

The teacher, of course, is not the only one who reacts unconsciously or spontaneously to the responses which occur in the classroom. The other students inevitably indicate their attitude by a variety of expressions. These may include the guffaws or snickers which greet a real boner, or the violent shaking of hands offering to supply the right answer, or a quiet acceptance of a proper response.

Along with these clear-cut, though often unintentional reactions to the pupil's behavior, there is a built-in system of reinforcement which is at work whenever the teacher gives an extended explanation. As we point out in Chapter 4, a pupil in listening to an explanation is seldom completely passive. He reacts to what the teacher is saying, often running ahead of what is said and guessing what is coming next. The succeeding statements of the teacher let him know whether or not his guesses are on the right track. If he is on the right track, he experiences considerable reinforcement.

Deliberate Reinforcement. We can be very grateful for the useful reinforcement that is bound to occur whether we do anything about it or not. But we should not rely exclusively on this free reinforcement. An essential part of teaching is to provide an efficient schedule of reinforcement and one that goes far beyond the haphazard reinforcement which occurs apart from our efforts.

Traditionally, the teacher has provided deliberate reinforcement by overtly accepting or rejecting the statements made by the students. He constantly emits such comments as, "That's right," "Good," "Right so far. Anything to add?" "True, but what about . . .? Much of this, of course, is quite spontaneous. The teacher makes these comments with little effort. Often, indeed, he would have to use considerable will power to avoid making them. Some of the comments, however, are quite deliberate, and the teacher may give some thought as to just what he should say in this or that circumstance.

In one sense, we could include, as reinforcements, the marks, grades, or comments that the teacher places on the student's written work. These certainly follow the response of the pupil, and they often function as a reward or lack of reward (Page, 1958).

▶ The Effect of a Delay in the Reinforcement

In this experiment the subject sat facing a screen. His arm projected through a curtain in the screen and he held a small pencil-like stylus in his hand. His task was to learn to hit a small one-inch target in a rectangular plate lying flat on the table. He had to work by pure trial and error. If he hit the target a light would flash. If he missed there would be no light. For fifty trials the light flashed as soon as he made contact. For another fifty trials either a hit or a miss would cause a ball to roll down an incline. If the target had been hit, the light would flash when the ball reached the bottom. If the target was missed no light would flash. The ball rolled anyway. The rolling ball made for a delay of about two seconds in the flashing of the light. For twenty-eight students the delay condition came first. Another twenty-eight worked first with the immediate light and then with the delayed light.

When the subject saw the light flash, he should, of course, return to the same square on the next hit.

	Number of Times Next Hit Was Made to			
	Same Square	Different Square	Total	Percent to Same Square
No delay in light	684	688	1372	49.8
Light delayed 2 seconds	552	842	1394	39.6
Diff.				10.2

(The hits for all 56 subjects are lumped together.)
The difference is significant.

Even this brief period of delay seems to reduce the effect of the reinforcement.

SOURCE: J. M. Stephens, The influence of different stimuli upon preceding bonds, *Teachers College Contribution to Education*, No. 493, 1931.

Problems of Delayed Reinforcement. Such comments may well provide motivation for further work, or may provide guidance which can be used in new work. There is some question, however, as to whether or not such comments function as true reinforcement. The chief problem is the long delay between the student's behavior and his receipt of the teacher's comments. In laboratory studies we learn that a delay of even a few seconds will interfere with the rapid acquisition of skill or knowledge (Bourne, 1957). For the long-run retention of this skill or knowledge, it is true, immediate reinforcement may not be so important. Indeed, one study (Brackbill and Kappy, 1962) suggests that people will *remember* slightly better if they learn with delayed reinforcement. But instructors' comments on student papers represent an entirely different order of delay. This may extend to days or weeks. Probably we should not class these with the automatic or casual reinforcements that typically follow right on the heels of the act.

To supplement the teacher's own efforts, many people, throughout the years, have worked out devices by which the student can easily secure his own reinforcement. For years people have provided answer sheets or "cribs" so that the student can quickly look at the back of the book or at the approved translation and find out whether he is right or wrong. More recently, interest in such devices has been linked up with the general problem of *automated instruction* and *programmed learning*. We consider these devices in detail in a later section.

Possible Functions of Reinforcement

A person cultivating his garden may be firmly convinced that the tillage will help the plants. He may be quite uncertain, however, about just exactly what the tillage may be doing. Does it provide its benefits by killing weeds, by aerating the soil, by reducing evaporation, or by all of these? In the same way, we as teachers may be clearly aware that reinforcement is a good thing, but may be uncertain about the crucial feature that actually benefits the learning process. Just what is accomplished when the teacher says, "Seven. That's right," after Jimmie has given "7" as the answer to $4 + 3$?

Promoting Insight The teacher's comment may well help Jimmie acquire some sort of *insight* or *expectation* or *cognition* as to what leads to what. As a result of this experience he might come to realize that "saying '7' in this situation leads to the teacher's approval." Consequently, if the situation occurs again, and if he wants the teacher's approval, he knows what to do. To make the most of this aspect of reinforcement it is important to be sure that the pupil understands just what it is that leads to what. Insofar as we rely on such realizations and cognitions, we should go to some trouble to sharpen his insight into the relation between what he does and what happens. We point out, "It isn't the total energy that sends the badminton bird across the net. It's the final flick of the wrist."

Automatic, Physiological Strengthening of Connections. Along with the insight that it may develop, the teacher's comment could also act in a purely mechanical or automatic way. When the infant is learning to walk, for instance, or when the older person learns to skate, hundreds of little responses are continually being made. Some of these lead to good results, such as regaining one's balance. Some lead to a tumble. Gradually the learner becomes more likely to make the responses that lead to good results, and less likely to make those that

▶ *Possible Roles of Reinforcement*
(For a more detailed statement see Hilgard, 1964; Hill, 1963.)

Situation Acting on the Pupil	Response or Answer Elicited from Pupil, by one Means or Another	REINFORCEMENT (Teacher's Comment)
4 + 3	7	"Seven! That's right."

Different Things That the Reinforcement Might Accomplish:

1. The teacher's comment could develop an *insight* or *cognition* as to what leads to what.

The comment occuring at this time produces the idea of *cognition* or *insight* that "in this situation saying, '7' leads to the teacher's approval." If the student is in this situation again, and if he wants the teacher's approval, he knows what to do.

This interpretation has been stressed by the late E. C. Tolman (1951). For a more sophisticated treatment see Miller and others (1960). Cronbach (1962) shows how this view may be applied to education.

2. The teacher's comment could also act in an automatic, physical, or neurological manner to strengthen the connection between seeing 4 + 3 and saying, "7." Whether the pupil has any clear thoughts on the subject or not, such a comment is just the sort of thing that makes people more likely to repeat responses. This is in line with the views of B. F. Skinner (1953).

B. F. SKINNER

Fabian Bachrach

Wide World Photos   Yale University News Bureau

EDWARD L. THORNDIKE   CLARK L. HULL

Or perhaps the sheer *satisfaction* of hearing the teacher say, "That's right," may be sufficient to go back in a purely physical or neurological way and increase the strength of the connection between 4 + 3 and 7. This would happen whether or not the pupil had any clear memory of the teacher's comment. This was suggested by E. L. Thorndike at the beginning of the century (see Hilgard, 1956).

Some people think that satisfaction is a rather vague term and one that is hard to define. Clark Hull suggested that the thing that produces the reinforcement is the reduction of some need, or perhaps a stimulus of some kind that has been regularly associated with need reduction. Adult approval often goes along with getting food when hungry and with the consequent reduction of hunger. Because of this, the teacher's approval, when it occurs, has the power to strengthen the connection (4 + 3 = 7) that has just been in operation. It could do this in a purely mechanical way, whether or not the pupil has a clear idea of the relation between his answer and the teacher's comment. Spence (1956) has extended and systematized many of Hull's views.

3. There are still other ways in which the teacher's comment might work. It could serve to prevent the undoing of an association that has already been formed. According to the late E. R. Guthrie (1952), the real learning takes place when the pupil comes to say, "7" while the situation 4 + 3 is acting on him. As a general rule, any response that the pupil makes gets tied up with any situation acting on him at that time. This happens in an automatic way, with-

out any effort or conscious thought on his part. But what does the teacher's comment do? It more or less wipes 4 + 3 off the slate and thus prevents this situation from getting linked up with some rival response. Suppose nothing remarkable happened after the pupil said, "7." In this case, the situation 4 + 3 would still be acting on him, although with diminished force. If the pupil now made some new response, such as saying, "12," this *new* response would get linked up with 4 + 3, just as 7 earlier got linked up with 4 + 3. The teacher's comment, however, or any other important event, will push 4 + 3 out of the pupil's experience, or at least isolate it, and thus prevent it from getting linked up with responses occuring after that event. The teacher's comment thus serves to preserve or protect the already-made association between 4 + 3 and 7.

The views of Guthrie, first advanced in the 1930s, have been developed into a highly sophisticated statistical theory of learning by W. K. Estes (1959) and others. In this theory, as in Guthrie's, the chief function of the teacher's comment is to terminate the experience, or to take the experience that included 4 + 3 and 7 and wrap it up in a little parcel somewhat separated from the experience that is to follow.

University of Washington News Services

EDWIN R. GUTHRIE   W. K. ESTES

lead to discomfort. But he probably has no clear realization of just which movements lead to which results. This means that to some extent the reinforcement is working in an unconscious, mechanical fashion.

To make the most of this feature of reinforcement, we need worry little about sharpening insight, but would concentrate on a consistent pattern of forceful and immediate reinforcement.

Separating One Episode from the Next. Along with its other functions, the teacher's unmistakable comment may say in effect, "That's that. Now let's go on to something else." It may wrap up the experience that included 4 + 3 and 7, and separate this episode from the new experience that is bound to come. In this way the teacher's comment may serve chiefly to protect or preserve the learning that always takes place whenever Jimmie says, "7" during the time that 4 + 3 is acting on him. To promote this function of reinforcement we might make the separation even more pronounced. After making the reinforcing comment, for instance, we might pause for a second before introducing any new experience. (Of course there will be *some* new experience whether we introduce it or not.) Or we might erase the couplet 4 + 3 from the board, or we might move to a different section of the board for the next activity. Anything to encapsulate the association between 4 + 3 and 7, to set it off from other experience, and thus to protect the learning that has already taken place.

Disagreements about the Role of Reinforcement

Since reinforcement could work in so many different ways, it is natural that there should be some disagreement as to which of its functions is most important.

Indeed, especially in the past, there has been a tremendous argument on this matter, one theorist seizing on one way in which reinforcement could work, and holding this to be the only thing that matters, and another theorist making similar exclusive claims for another feature.

Although these controversies by no means dominate the field of learning as much as they used to, we still face the problem of what to do about them and of how much attention to give them.

First of all, these rival theories still have considerable scientific and even philosophical interest. For practical purposes, it is true, we can merely go ahead and cultivate our gardens and let the cultivation produce its benefits in any way it wants to. As thinking people, however, we must be curious about just what is going on. The controversies regarding reinforcement have an even stronger claim on our attention, and thoughtful teachers and educators frequently turn to these broader theoretical issues. The 63d Yearbook of the National Society for the Study of Education (Hilgard, 1964), for instance, is largely given over to these general theoretical problems.

You will notice that some of the functions of reinforcement place an emphasis on understanding or thoughtful deliberation. Other features stress a mechanical, automatic process. To some extent, therefore, the controversies are linked up with the questions as to whether man should be regarded chiefly as a rational human being or chiefly as an exceedingly complex machine or as a highly developed animal. If you are interested in these semi-philosophical questions you may be concerned about the arguments over the role of reinforcement. A chart is provided to give additional information on this topic.

Secondly, it would be useful, in a practical way, if we ever could find out just which of the functions of reinforcement are really important, and which, if any, could be ignored.

Finally, however, we should realize that from the practical point of view, the agreement greatly overshadows the controversy. In our day-by-day teaching we should make much use of reinforcement, expediting any and all of its functions as circumstances permit.

The Amount of Reinforcement Required

According to those who stress reinforcement in learning, the child's success in any task depends largely on the number of reinforcements he has received in performing that task. For this reason we should be prepared to supply reinforcement in lavish doses. But it is not as simple as that. The pattern of reinforcement is important as well as the quantity. And there are limits in the quantity that we should feel obliged to supply. There is no need, for instance, to be sure that each and every response is reinforced.

Partial Reinforcement. It is fortunate that we are not required to reinforce each and every response that the student makes. It would be utterly impossible for the teacher in the typical classroom to make a suitable comment after each and every response of each and every pupil (100-percent reinforcement).

Apart from practicality, however, what should be our aim in this matter? As far as the immediate acquisition of skill is concerned, a rich diet of reinforcement, even up to 100 percent, would be preferable, and certainly at the outset of learning we should attempt such a rich diet whenever possible (Lewis, 1960; Salzinger, 1959).

When we turn from the immediate acquisition of skill, however, and consider the problem of retention, we encounter a different story. Students learning under 100-percent reinforcement may be easily discouraged when they later encounter a series of trials that give no reinforcement whatever. Under this condition the learned response may be quickly extinguished. Suppose, up to now, your car had *always* started (100-percent reinforcement) when you turned the key. After that experience, a series of failures might quickly lead you to give up completely. If you had *always* been used to partial reinforcement (sometimes yes, sometimes no,) however, you may keep on trying in spite of a long series of failures. The schedule of partial reinforcement helps prevent extinction or discouragement when reinforcement is withdrawn. Retention of what is learned may thus be favored by a program of partial rather than 100-percent reinforcement.

In general, we should aim at a generous schedule of reinforcement, especially at the outset of learning. We should avoid being too rigid, however. A slip into partial reinforcement, although reducing the rate of original learning, would help prevent the temporary discouragement and forgetting that might later follow if the student encountered a long series of unreinforced trials. As competence develops there will be a greater total output of reinforceable responses. Even if we reinforce only a fraction of this large output of responses, the total amount of reinforcement will be substantial. At this stage, therefore, we may well consider tapering off the amount of reinforcement, and asking the student to get along on a more lean and Spartan diet.

► *The Effects of Different Schedules of Reinforcement*

In the Vineland Social Maturity Scale there are a number of tasks and each is assigned to a given age level. In this experiment, thirty-four college students learned to give the appropriate age for the separate tasks. Each student mastered four lists of eight tasks each. Each of the four lists was studied under a different condition.

Under the condition of *Reinforcement plus Guidance*, the student was given (guided into) the correct answer as soon as he made his response. In one of the lists he studied, this happened after *every response*. In another list this happened only after *every other response*. Under the condition of *Reinforcement Only* (*Over-all Grade*), the student was not given the correct answer but was merely told "Right" or "Wrong" after he gave his answer. In one list this happened after every response, in the other after every other response. At the completion of the list, the student was given an *over-all* grade, or indication of success, for the whole list.

All thirty-two students worked under each of the four conditions, the sequence of conditions being counterbalanced so that each came first for some students, second for others, and so forth.

The table gives the number of trials required to master each list of eight items.

| | Treatment Applied After | |
Treatment (or Condition)	Every Response	Every Other Response
Reinforcement *Plus* Guidance	5.6	6.8
Reinforcement Only	13.3	31.5

The differences were significant.

A recall test two days later failed to reveal any significant differences.

source: N. M. Chansky, Learning: a function of schedule and type of feedback. *Psychological Reports*, 1960, 7, 362.

GETTING THE PUPIL TO MAKE AN ACCEPTABLE RESPONSE

As competence develops, acceptable responses may pour out so profusely that we can well decide to reinforce only a fraction of these. At the outset of learning, however, we usually face a very different problem. Here we are often hard put to elicit a single response that we feel prepared to reinforce. And unless a pupil comes up with a number of reinforceable responses, how can we provide a liberal amount of reinforcement?

To provide a reasonable amount of reinforcement at the outset, we must get the student to make acceptable responses at the outset. And how do we do this? How do you get him to say, "7," for instance, the very first time that he encounters $4 + 3 = ?$ Being now firmly resolved to reinforce the child whenever he acts in cheerful fashion, how do you get him to act cheerfully and thus to permit you to apply the reinforcement? There are several answers. First, we could merely change our minds about what constitutes an acceptable response. At the outset we could be prepared to reinforce almost any response the child makes. Later, of course, we could become more demanding. This widely used procedure is called *shaping up*. Second, we could find some means of *guiding*, or leading, or maneuvering the student into giving more adequate answers—answers that can be legitimately commended or reinforced. Finally, we could use meticulous *programming*. This means that the tasks presented to the student are arranged in a careful order, beginning with very easy exercises and moving by one small step at a time to more complex problems. Programming and programmed learning are discussed in a later section on automated instruction. The other two procedures are treated below.

Shaping Up as a Classroom Procedure

The process of shaping up has been stressed in the work of B. F. Skinner (1953) and of Staats and Staats (1963). It is a process that you adopt without thinking when a child first begins to pronounce words, or when a first-grader turns in his first crude art work. In either case the production will fall far short of perfection. Using an absolute standard, you could find little to commend. But you do commend, often with enthusiasm, and thereby provide the necessary reinforcement (Fig. 5.2).

The shaping up that is often used spontaneously in dealing with young children has also been employed in highly deliberate fashion for the training of animals. Suppose you want to teach a young chimpanzee or other ape to do interesting finger painting. You select some reinforcement that is effective for chimpanzees. Perhaps approving attention will do, or perhaps a grape or raisin.

At first you will applaud or supply a raisin as soon as the ape even looks toward the paint pot. You can depend upon it that the paint pot will soon become a frequent object of regard. Now you raise your standards. You give the reinforcement only when the ape makes some motion toward the paint—leaning, reaching out, or taking a step in the right direction. At each stage of progress you become more and more exacting. In successive stages you commend or reward only when the paint is actually approached, touched, applied to *some* surface, applied to an appropriate surface, applied in some reasonable manner, or applied in the manner of Van Gogh rather than in the manner of Cézanne—if you think the latter stage of development feasible and desirable.

There are times, of course, when you may be reluctant to use the technique of shaping up. It is easy to be somewhat flexible in your judgments of art work, compositions, or social elegance. But what can you do when the pupil takes liberties with such factual material as the sum of 8 and 9, or the date of Columbus's first voyage? You may not find it feasible or morally justifiable to accept or reinforce such incorrect answers. If you wished, you could, of course, commend the general approach. You could say, "That's close, but . . .," or, "You're on the right track," but flatfooted commendation might seem out of the question.

Guidance as a Classroom Procedure

Theoretically, we could use the shaping up technique to teach Jimmie to say, "house" whenever he saw the letters h-o-u-s-e. At first we could reinforce him for saying almost any word, then for say-

Fig. 5.2. Techniques of shaping up are not always difficult to use.

ing any word that began with an "h" sound, and so forth. But this would be an awkward and roundabout procedure. In this situation we would be more likely to use some form of guidance. To guide a pupil who sees the letters h-o-u-s-e, we need merely *find, and use, some situation or experience that is already capable of making him say, "house."* We might use a picture of a house. We might ask him what Mr. Brown is building down the street, or we might merely ask him to repeat the word "house." When, *by one means or another,* we succeed in getting the correct answer, we promptly reinforce this correct response by commendation or in some other way. In the same manner we can use this simple type of guidance to get a child to spend time in reading, or get him to be cheerful. Again, a simple request might get him to sit down with a book. A lively, jolly approach might lead him to smile. When these desired acts occur be sure to reinforce them.

The Conditioned Response as a Model. Guidance of the type described represents one form of the *conditioned response*. In his original work on this process, Pavlov presented the dog with some new stimulus, a ringing bell, and then applied an old stimulus (dry food powder in the mouth) that was already capable of making the dog salivate. When he had done this several times, the bell itself came to make the dog salivate quite regularly.

It was not until the twentieth century that the conditioned response was studied in a scientific way, or that the technical terms came into use. The principle itself, however, is an age-old device and one that teachers and others have used almost automatically ever since teaching began. Suppose we observe a child reading out loud. He encounters the letters d-o-g and comes to an awkward halt. Few of us can resist the temptation to supply some extraneous stimulus that will guide the child toward the word for which he is groping. We say, "What barks and has four legs?" hoping that this extraneous condition will lead him, or force him, to say, "dog." This is also a device that teachers turn to quite naturally when they must teach a new word. You want the child to say, "cat" when he sees the symbols c-a-t. First, find something which is already adequate to make him say, "cat." Perhaps the sight of a real cat will do. Perhaps a picture of a cat. Perhaps, if you are tired or if your ingenuity is at a low ebb, a simple request, "Say 'cat,'" will do. Now you must first present the symbols c-a-t and then present the stimulus which you have chosen to force him or lead him to say, "cat." Present the symbols c-a-t, then a picture of a cat. This common-sense procedure is a direct use of the conditioned response.

Other illustrations abound. You want the student to think *now* when he sees the French word *maintenant*. Formula:

find some situation which is already capable of making him think *now*. Perhaps, if you do not mind being obvious or hackneyed, the English word *now* will do. Present the word *maintenant* and an instant later present the word *now*. Do this several times and he will think *now* whenever he sees *maintenant*.

You want the student to smile rather than sulk when he has been defeated in a game. Find something which you know will lead him to smile (perhaps a jolly approach on your part) and apply this as soon as he has experienced defeat.

The political candidate wants the voter to feel well disposed whenever he hears the name *Senator Fearing*. He must find something that is already capable of making the voter feel good and arrange that this magic something will act on the voter after he hears the name *Fearing*.

The form of guidance just discussed is very mechanical and arbitrary. The guidance is very positive. We almost force the student to make the correct response. We try to find some situation which will leave him no alternative. For all its mechanical rigidity, however, this type of guidance may prove useful on occasion, especially in such straightforward activities as learning a new vocabulary, or in a numbers drill, or in learning to spell.

Manual Guidance or Tuition. The teacher is by no means restricted to the arbitrary form of guidance provided by the simple conditioned reflex formula. There are many additional procedures which are much more elaborate and which are less rigid. They point the way to the correct behavior, or they lead the student toward a better way of doing things. By means of these devices we take some steps to prevent the student from merely floundering along on his own.

When a student is learning to write

or to draw or to use an instrument of any kind, the teacher may provide ordinary physical guidance. The teacher may place the pencil in the student's hand so that he holds it properly. Or he may move the student's hand so as to form the letter correctly. He may help guide the saw. In teaching physical education, he may move the student's body to a position which gives a more adequate posture. When students in a laboratory are learning a pencil maze, the experimenter may take the learner's hand and guide it around the correct path. These are merely illustrations of what is meant by manual guidance. These procedures do not always bring about good results. Sometimes this mechanical guidance is extremely irksome to the learner. There are other times, as we shall see, when guidance of any sort is of little use.

Rereading of Material To Be Memorized. When material has finally been memorized a whole host of tendencies or habit units have been formed. When, for instance, we hear, "Mary had a little lamb," we are led to think, "Its fleece was white as snow." One idea suggests the other. The question is, how to use guidance in forming these associations or tendencies. It happens that the simple process of rereading the material provides perfect guidance (Forlano, 1936). If, after reading the first line, we immediately proceed to read the second line, we are getting a maximum of guidance. We are being led to make the correct response to the first line. On the other hand, if we covered up the second line, we would be deprived of that guidance. Theoretically, our next response could be anything in the way of a guess. With the line uncovered there is no guess, but almost perfect guidance.

Learning Vocabulary by Looking rather than Guessing. In learning a vocabulary list, a student will get the maximum

amount of guidance if, after looking at the foreign word, he looks immediately at the English word. In this way he will be prevented from making the wrong response. He will be guided into correct association for that particular foreign word (Forlano and Hoffman, 1937).

Use of Rhetorical Questions. Teachers very frequently answer their own question. This practice, of course, can be overdone and may even reach the stage of becoming an annoying mannerism. Nevertheless, it is a form of guidance. The teacher asks the question. Before the student has a chance to give a wrong answer, the teacher provides the right answer thus guiding the student inescapably toward the correct behavior. An instructor of aerial navigation, for instance, may ask, "What is that town off toward four o'clock?" Then, when the students are still frantically trying to identify the town from their maps, he may add, "It is obvious that this town must be Centerville. See how the railway comes in from the northwest, crossing a loop of the river on the two bridges."

Recitation in Unison. The ancient practice of having the whole class recite in unison—now upgraded to "choral reading"—provides a type of guidance. When any member of the class begins to falter he is bound to be guided back to the right path by the statements of the rest of the class. Each student is thus guided or forced to respond in conformity with the majority. Of course, if the majority should be wrong, this would provide guidance in the wrong direction.

Hinting or Prompting. As we have seen, hints can be used to get the child to think of a word that he cannot recognize. Hints and prompting are also used at a more advanced level. If a student cannot give the formula for heavy water we may ask him the formula for ordinary water, hoping, by the use of this supple-

▶ Guidance vs. Trial and Error

Strings of diamond-shaped patterns such as those shown in the table were printed on strips of paper. As the paper moved past a slot, students were required to follow the correct path. The wrong path was shown by two little cross lines. The sixty students had been randomly assigned to three different groups. For the *first four* trials, the different groups received different treatment. For one group the cross lines were toward the end of the wrong path. The student could not see them until after he had made his choice and had begun to follow one path or the other. For the other group the cross lines could be seen before the choice was made. These students were thus guided into the correct path before they had had a chance to make a mistake. During these first four trials, the third group saw *only* the correct choice.

Following the first four trials, all students worked on mazes like that to the left. During those trials they had to make their choice before knowing which choice was correct.

Procedure During First Four Trials

	Right & wrong choices shown after choice is made	Right & wrong choices shown before choice is made	Only right choice shown
Trials needed to learn	24.2	10.4	18.8
Errors after 4th trial	76.3	15.8	52.1

All differences are significant.

SOURCE: J. M. Von Wright, A note on the role of "guidance" in learning, *British Journal of Psychology*, 1957, 48, 133–137.

mentary question, to give him some hint. At times, instead of asking a supplementary question, we merely suggest, "Remember, this man lived in the seventeenth century," or, "Don't forget that it is the altitude of the parallelogram that determines its area."

Preventing Competing or Erroneous Responses. One way to get a child to respond in the way we have in mind is to make it difficult for him to do anything else. If there is very little else that he can do on this rainy afternoon, Jimmie may read. You might get him to say "house" or "36" by warning him away from any other answers you think he is likely to make. When first asking about the capital of Maryland, for instance, you could remind him that it is not Baltimore.

We often face this problem of preventing competing responses when we are constructing examination questions of the completion type. We want our students to think of Marlowe as one of the outstanding dramatists of the Elizabethan period. If our question merely reads: "One of the outstanding dramatists of the Elizabethan period was _____?" we are likely to get Shakespeare or Ben Jonson. To take care of this problem we may write, "Along with Shakespeare and Ben Jonson, one of the outstanding dramatists of the Elizabethan period was _____?" This procedure is called *pre-empting* the responses we wish them to avoid.

The Overlapping of Guidance and Reinforcement

It is difficult to apply reinforcement without also providing some guidance. True enough, it can be done, but one must go to some trouble to arrange it. By the same token, it is difficult to provide guidance without at the same time providing reinforcement. Let us think of the dog learning to salivate when he hears the sound of a bell. At the outset the meat powder acts as guidance. It forces the dog to salivate which is, of course, what we want him to do when he hears the bell. But, later on, this same meat powder will act as reinforcement. With practice the dog will come to salivate as soon as he hears the bell, and the meat powder will not appear until the act of salivation has begun. Under these conditions, the meat powder functions as a type of reinforcement. If the dog has already salivated and the meat powder is then put into his mouth, we have a good result and the tendency to salivate will be strengthened. If, on the other hand, the salivation occurs but no meat powder follows, we would have a bad or useless condition, and the tendency to salivate would be weakened.

Even in the basic formula for the conditioned response, then, the meat powder can act either as guidance or as reinforcement. It can either point the way to a new kind of response, or it can confirm a response that has just been made. Which of these roles the meat powder assumes depends on the timing. If it is presented *before* the dog makes any response, it will act as guidance. If it is presented *after* the dog has made a definite response, it will act as reinforcement.

Just as the meat powder may act either as a guide or as reinforcement, so may the teacher's comment act in either way. When the students are learning a list of French words, for instance, the teacher can supply the correct translation immediately or he can wait for a short interval (Fig. 5.3). Suppose that the teacher says, *la maison,* and *immediately* thereafter says "house." During that brief

The Overlapping of Guidance and Reinforcement

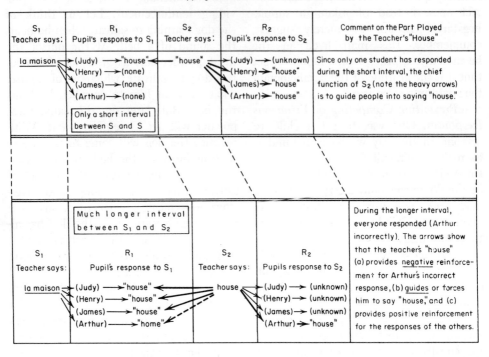

Fig. 5.3. Chart showing the overlapping of guidance and reinforcement.

interval few, if any, students will have had a chance to make any response at all. Consequently, the English translation "house" can only serve to tell them what the answer is, or, more technically, to guide them into the correct response. Again the teacher says *la maison*. This time, however, he hesitates an appreciable time before he says "house." During this longer interval many, perhaps most, students will have made some silent response. For these students, the teacher's announcement of "house" coming on the heels of some response, will act as reinforcement of some kind. If, during that interval, a student has silently responded "house," the teacher's announcement of "house" will act as confirmation or positive reinforcement. It is possible, of course, that some student may have responded in some other way during the period of the teacher's silence. In that case, the teacher's announcement of "house" will point out the error (negative reinforcement) and will also *guide* him into the correct answer. But this feature of guidance will be present only for those students who have failed to make the correct response during the interval between the teacher's two statements. For the other students, the teacher's second remark will serve as reinforcement.

As in the vocabulary lesson, so also in many other activities, the teacher can switch from guided learning to reinforced learning merely by altering the timing of his comments. After posing a question, for instance, the teacher may rush in to give the answer, or he may hesitate and give the students a chance to answer silently before he himself gives the correct answer. In a straight lecture, after beginning a statement, the teacher may complete the statement immediately, or he may hesitate a few seconds, in which time the students may silently complete the sentence, and then go on to finish the statement. If the students have finished the statement for themselves, the latter part of his comment would constitute a form of reinforcement.

Values and Limitations of Guidance. Clearly guidance is a most important technique and one that the teacher ought to strive to use effectively. At times guidance is almost essential. At other times it is a valuable supplement. It is, moreover, a rational, humane and intelligent device. Learning which is deprived of guidance, and which is reduced to sheer trial and error, appears to be a stupid, cruel, and perverse form of learning.

In considering these things, however, we must not be misled by the claims of gentility or niceness. The fact that guidance seems less brutal and more intelligent should not blind us to the harsh fact that guidance has limitations. It is very seldom that the student can reach perfection or even acceptable proficiency through guidance alone. In almost all learning there comes a stage when the student can improve only by a certain amount of trial and error on his own (Kittell, 1957; McGeoch, 1942). We can guide his hand while he forms the letters, but we can help in this way only up to a point. After awhile he must try out different movements on his own, and, after a certain amount of blundering, he will come to produce letters which have a more acceptable appearance. Similarly, we can do much to guide the movements of the student swimmer. We can tap him when it is time to breathe. We can place his arms in this position or that. But be-

fore he becomes a skilled swimmer he must flounder around a bit, trying this device and that, until he finally hits on a cue for breathing at the right time. For the student learing to speak in public, we can provide much guidance. We can signal him to use more gestures or to cut down on his gestures, or to tell a joke, or to launch into his final statement. But ultimately he must experiment on his own and try this method and that, getting different kinds of reinforcement from different approaches.

Guidance is a most valuable tool. But, like other valuable tools, there are times when it should be used and times when it should be laid aside.

AUTOMATED INSTRUCTION, PROGRAMMED LEARNING, AND TEACHING MACHINES

To illustrate some of the procedures used in programmed textbooks, a sample program is provided beginning on page 128. Consult this to see how various procedures are arranged. Before leaving this section, moreover, actually work your way through it. The programmed material deals with punishment and reward, a topic treated at the last of this chapter.

Linear Programs

Much of this chapter has been concerned about the problem of securing a generous supply of reinforcement, which means, of course, securing a reasonable number of reinforceable responses. This also happens to be the great objective of B. F. Skinner (1958) and others who advocate linear programming. People using this kind of program try to make sure that almost every response will be reinforced. Not all psychologists, of course, agree that it is wise, or possible, to make

A PROGRAMMED TEXTBOOK

You will notice that the questions in this exercise are not arranged in the usual order. On page 129, for instance, Question 5 follows Question 1. Whenever you go from one step to the next, you must turn a page. After filling in the blank for Question 1 you turn to page 130 and look at the right answer. Then you go on to Question 2 on page 131. There are detailed directions for each step. Starting with Question 18, the jumping around will be even more erratic. Here, again, you will get detailed directions for each step.

With this procedure you could peek, of course, if you wanted to. And this might be all right once or twice if you are really stuck. Ordinarily, however, you should write down, or check off, some answer before going on to the next step.

sure that the student is guided into each response with no room for uncertainty or error (Wohlwill, 1962). As we point out in the discussion of problem solving (Chapter 6), a period of uncertainty may be necessary for some kinds of learning. But the advocates of linear programmes hold to their position and try to make sure that almost every response will be reinforced. They try to do this by arranging for a graded series of tasks in which the student moves ahead only one very small step at a time. The first task is so easy that practically no one could fail to get the right answer or fail to make a reinforceable response. In the first exercise at the top of page 129, for instance, it is assumed that from the title and from common sense, everyone would be able to write in "reward" or some such word. Another introductory task might be one such as the following: "In training a dog to sit up and beg we should make use of some reward or reinforcement. If the dog is hungry, the simplest reinforcement is _____?" It is assumed that no one could fail to write "food." If a fair number of people did write some other word, the item would be revised so that "food" would be even more obvious as an answer. After the student has written in a word ("food," we hope) he finds out right away whether or not he is right. With the text, he gets this information by turning the page. With the machines, this is done mechanically. The correct answer ap-

SYMBOLIC PUNISHMENT AND REWARD:
A PROBLEM IN REINFORCEMENT

We begin the discussion of symbolic punishment and reward with this example. *Question 1.* A pupil is asked the sum of 6 + 9, replies, "15" and hears the teacher say, "Yes, that's right." The teacher's comment is an illustration of symbolic _____. Look at Answer 1, Page 130.

IGNORE QUESTION 5 AT THIS TIME

Question 5. When (a) _____ are very weak to begin with, symbolic (b) _____ can be expected to strengthen them. Look at Answer 5, page 130.

Question 9. By administering this symbolic punishment the teacher hopes to_____ the pupil's tendency to say, "Reno" when asked the capital of Nevada. Look at Answer 9, page 130.

Question 13. The most logical use of symbolic punishment is for the purpose of (a) _____ tendencies that are (b) _____ but which lead to undesirable behavior. Look at Answer 13, page 130.

Question 17. Just as symbolic reward is superfluous or useless when a tendency is already very (a) _____, so symbolic punishment is superfluous or useless when a tendency is already very (b) _____. Look at Answer 17, page 130.

Answer 20c. Your answer was, "to weaken some tendencies but to strengthen others." You must have misread the question. There is no theoretical reason to suspect that punishment would ever strengthen a tendency. Go back to Question 20, page 134.

---

pears as the student advances his own answer under a transparent shield.

Provided the programmer has anticipated matters correctly, the student will find that his first response has been right. This positive reinforcement should develop or strengthen some new association, such as that which links the idea of "reinforcement" to the idea of "food for a hungry animal." Because of this experience, the learner could now readily attempt a new task such as, "If a hungry animal encounters food after making a response, we could say that the response has been _____?" By virtue of his experience with the first question he should now be able to give "reinforced" as the proper answer.

Branching Programs

As we have said, the linear program is aimed at getting a great many reinforceable responses and avoiding responses that cannot be reinforced. In other programs, such as the branching programs, however, there is less insistence that every response be reinforced. A number of errors are to be expected, and special arrangements are provided to take care of these. In our illustration, a branching program is introduced with question 18 page 130. If you make no errors from this point on you will find this program to be very much like the linear program you encountered at first. You just go from one question to the next. If you do choose a wrong answer, however, you will find that

Answer 1. reward or *reinforcement*. Go on to Question 2, page 131.

Answer 5. (a) *tendencies* (b) *reward* or *reinforcement*. Go on to Question 6, page 131.

Answer 9. weaken or *reduce* or *discourage*. Go on to Question 10, page 131.

Answer 13. (a) *weakening* or *reducing*. (b) *strong*. Go on to Question 14, page 131.

Answer 17. (a) *strong* (b) *weak*. Go on to Question 18 immediately below.

NOTICE THE NEW SYSTEM, STARTING WITH QUESTION 18

Draw a circle around a, b, or c to indicate the best answer.

Question 18. Going entirely by the theoretical possibilities, we would expect symbolic reward to:

    a. strengthen all tendencies. Look at Answer 18a, page 135.

    b. strengthen weak tendencies but to have little effect on very strong tendencies. Look at Answer 18b, page 136.

    c. strengthen some tendencies but weaken others. Look at Answer 18c, page 133.

Answer 20a. Your answer was, "weaken all tendencies." It is true that the only useful thing punishment can do is to weaken tendencies, but we wouldn't expect it to weaken *all* tendencies. If a tendency is already as weak as it can get, we would not expect punishment to weaken it any further. Go back to Question 20, page 134.

---

you are given special instructions as to what to do from then on. These special instructions send you off on a branch program, or detour. In our illustration this detour merely returns you to the question you had just missed. (If you really make no natural errors, by the way, make a point of getting one wrong just to see what happens.) It is hoped that you get the question right on the second try. If you don't, the *third* try is bound to give you the right answer, since only one answer would be left. Not all branching programs treat errors by merely sending you back to the question you just missed. Some of them send you on a "remedial loop" in which you get some supplementary instruction, or practice, before rejoining the main program.

Constructed vs. Ready-made Answers

In our linear program, we ask you to make up your own answer and then to compare your constructed answer with the answer given on the next page. It would have been possible, even in this linear program, to use a different procedure and to provide several alternate, multiple-choice answers, and then merely ask you to select the correct answer. Some programmers, however, believe that such a selected answer is not a good indication of genuine mastery. They hold that the constructed answer means much more.

When, starting with question 18 we begin the branching program, we change from constructed answers to

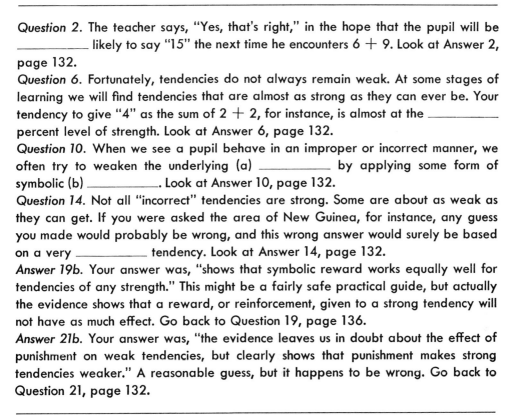

Question 2. The teacher says, "Yes, that's right," in the hope that the pupil will be _____ likely to say "15" the next time he encounters 6 + 9. Look at Answer 2, page 132.

Question 6. Fortunately, tendencies do not always remain weak. At some stages of learning we will find tendencies that are almost as strong as they can ever be. Your tendency to give "4" as the sum of 2 + 2, for instance, is almost at the _____ percent level of strength. Look at Answer 6, page 132.

Question 10. When we see a pupil behave in an improper or incorrect manner, we often try to weaken the underlying (a) _____ by applying some form of symbolic (b) _____. Look at Answer 10, page 132.

Question 14. Not all "incorrect" tendencies are strong. Some are about as weak as they can get. If you were asked the area of New Guinea, for instance, any guess you made would probably be wrong, and this wrong answer would surely be based on a very _____ tendency. Look at Answer 14, page 132.

Answer 19b. Your answer was, "shows that symbolic reward works equally well for tendencies of any strength." This might be a fairly safe practical guide, but actually the evidence shows that a reward, or reinforcement, given to a strong tendency will not have as much effect. Go back to Question 19, page 136.

Answer 21b. Your answer was, "the evidence leaves us in doubt about the effect of punishment on weak tendencies, but clearly shows that punishment makes strong tendencies weaker." A reasonable guess, but it happens to be wrong. Go back to Question 21, page 132.

ready-made, multiple-choice answers. Constructed answers would be very hard to use in the branching program. They call for very elaborate devices such as providing lists of all *possible* wrong answers. If your answer was among these you would know it was wrong, and you could also be directed to a special branch program that would help you with that particular error.

In actual use, the branching program makes use of a few plausible, preselected alternatives from which the correct answer should be chosen. These are stated as in a multiple-choice question. One choice requires you to turn to one page, a different choice asks you to turn elsewhere. After turning to the designated page you find out whether or not your choice is correct, and you are then instructed to proceed along one branch if you are right, and along a different branch if you are in error.

Size of Step

Programs vary in the size of each step. In one program you may proceed by very easy stages. In others, you may be asked to make a bit of a jump in going from one question to the next. For obvious reasons, the users of linear programs stress small steps between questions. A small step maximizes the chance of getting the next question right. It thus increases your chance of securing the all-important reinforcement. Conversely, if, by some mischance, a student misses a

Answer 2. more. Go on to Question 3, page 133.

Answer 6. 100. Go on to Question 7, page 133.

Answer 10. (a) *tendency.* (b) *punishment.* Go on to Question 11, page 133.

Answer 14. weak. Go on to Question 15, page 133.

Answer 20b. Your answer was, "weaken strong tendencies but to have no effect on weak tendencies." This is correct. This is what we would expect from theoretical considerations. Go on to Question 21, below.

Question 21. You will remember that our expectations regarding the influence of reward were largely confirmed by the evidence. When we look at the evidence regarding punishment, however, we will not find quite so much support for our expectations. Actually we find that: (make your best guess)

    a. the evidence clearly shows that punishment has little influence on weak tendencies, but leaves us in doubt about the influence of punishment on strong tendencies. Look at Answer 21a, page 134.

    b. the evidence leaves us in doubt about the effect of punishment on weak tendencies, but clearly shows that punishment makes strong tendencies weaker. Look at Answer 21b, page 131.

    c. the evidence clearly shows that punishment can make strong tendencies weaker and can also drive a weak tendency to below zero strength. Look at Answer 21c, page 136.

---

question, there is nothing specific the linear program can do about it. He is merely sent on to the next question. Obviously this will give him less trouble when he misses a little step than when he misses a big step. With the branching program, on the other hand, the student can be advanced by fairly large steps, and special treatment is provided if he does make a mistake.

There has been much argument and research (Feldhusen, 1963; Lumsdaine, 1963) regarding the merits of these different procedures. From the little we know at present it would appear that either approach will work quite well, and that there is little likelihood that one has marked advantages over the other.

Autoinstructional Machines

Programmed textbooks, of course, are not the only means of presenting programmed learning. Indeed, when programmed learning first caught the public eye, it was typically assumed that the programming would be done by a machine of some kind. To some people, programmed learning and teaching machines have meant almost the same thing.

Long before programmed learning was discussed, many people were intrigued by the possibilities of using machines in teaching. It was obvious that mechanical devices could be used to make reinforcement more immediate, more vivid, and to make sure that it followed a regular and predictable schedule (Lumsdaine and Glaser, 1960). It was also obvious that machines could free the teacher from many routine tasks. You are probably familiar with the Auto Bridge device for practicing the game of bridge without the help of a teacher. Here the player makes a choice, moves a slide and finds whether

Question 3. Speaking technically, symbolic reward is used to _____ the pupil's tendency to say "15" when he hears 6 + 9. Look at answer 3, page 134.

Question 7. When a tendency is already about as strong as it can possibly get, any additional symbolic reward can have _____, if any effect. Look at Answer 7, page 134.

Question 11. Sometimes the tendencies responsible for incorrect answers are quite strong. When asked to name the first man to fly across the Atlantic, for instance, many people will answer, "Lindbergh." This answer is wrong. But for those people this wrong answer is probably based on a fairly _____ tendency. Look at Answer 11, page 134.

Question 15. The only useful thing that punishment could possibly do to such a tendency is to _____ it. Look at Answer 15, page 134.

Answer 18c. Your answer was, "strengthen some tendencies and weaken others. It is true that we would expect symbolic reward to have different effects, but there is no reason to expect that reward would ever *weaken* a tendency. Go back to Question 18, page 130.

Answer 19c. Your answer was, "fails to show any dependable effect." You probably misread the question. Things are not quite that vague. The strengthening effect of rewards on weak tendencies is one of the most dependable facts we have. Go back to Question 19, page 136.

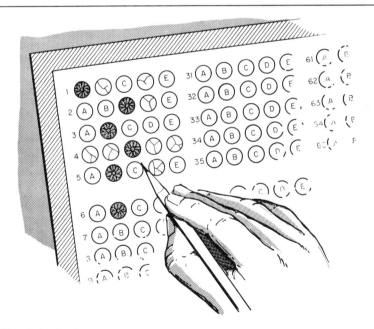

Fig. 5.4. The SRA Self-Scorer. (A red dot appears whenever the correct answer is punched.) Drawing based on copy provided by Science Research Associates, Inc., Chicago, Ill.

Answer 3. strengthen or *increase* or *reinforce.* Go on to Question 4, page 135.

Answer 7. little. Go on to Question 8, page 135.

Answer 11. strong. Go on to Question 12, page 135.

Answer 15. weaken. Go on to Question 16, page 135.

Answer 19a. Your answer was, "clearly shows that symbolic reward strengthens weak tendencies and also suggests that the effects of symbolic reward become less as the tendencies become stronger." This is correct. This time, the evidence is in line with our expectations. Go on to Question 20, below.

Question 20. From strictly theoretical considerations, we would expect symbolic punishment to:

    a. weaken all tendencies. Look at Answer 20a, page 130.

    b. weaken strong tendencies, but to have little or no effect on weak tendencies. Look at Answer 20b, page 132.

    c. weaken some tendencies, but to strengthen others. Look at Answer 20c, page 129.

Answer 21a. Your answer was, "the evidence clearly shows that punishment has little influence on weak tendencies but leaves us in doubt about the influence of punishment on strong tendencies." This is correct. Punishment is useless when we are dealing with a tendency that is already weak, and there is some doubt about its value for a tendency that is fairly well established.

---

or not his choice is correct. Punch boards have also been used for the same purpose. There is a group of possible answers. The student selects one of these and indicates his choice by punching the proper hole in the answer sheet. A color or symbol is found at the bottom of the hole, and this indicates whether or not the choice is correct (Fig. 5.4). Invisible inks have been used in the same fashion. A student marks his choice with a special moistener and immediately a symbol emerges, or the paper changes color, and in this way the correctness of the choice can be indicated. In other devices a student pushes a button to indicate his answer and one light flashes if he is right, another if he is wrong. In some machines, pushing the right button will cause the next question to move into place. If the wrong button is pushed, the questions stays put. Such "self-teachers" have been on the market for a good many years and have been used both for experimental and instructional purposes.

Many of the early machines presented the questions in rather haphazard fashion. Almost all of these early machines, moreover, used only predetermined or ready-made, multiple-choice answers. Following Skinner's (1954) proposals, however, there was a tremendous increase in the interest in teaching machines, and, in this new interest, the machines were thought of in connection with programming. In this new development, moreover, the chief emphasis was on machines that permitted the use of constructed answers.

There are now available several kinds of such machines (Fig. 5.5). They vary tremendously in cost, complexity, and versatility. For the use of the constructed answer, the machine typically provides a slot through which the question appears. There is a second opening through which

Question 4. The strength of a tendency changes with experience. At the outset, a child's tendency to give "15" as the answer to "6 + 9" is probably very _____. Look at Answer 4, page 136.

Question 8. A pupil is asked the capital of Nevada, replies, "Reno." and is told, "No. It isn't Reno." This comment, far from acting as a reward, is really a form of symbolic _____. Look at Answer 8, page 136.

Question 12. Whenever an undesirable tendency has considerable strength to begin with, we might expect symbolic punishment to _____ that strength. Look at Answer 12, page 136.

Question 16. If a tendency is already about as weak as it can possibly get, an additional symbolic punishment would have practically _____ effect. Look at Answer 16, page 136.

Answer 18a. Your answer was, "strengthen all tendencies." This may be a fairly safe practical guide, but it is not a strict interpretation of the theoretical possibilities. If a tendency is already as strong as it can be, additional reward could have little, if any, effect. Go back to Question 18, page 130.

the student writes in his answer, either on the same sheet as the question or on a separate tape. There is also some arrangement whereby the learner can move a slide to uncover the correct answer. In the simpler machines this is done when the student advances the paper to the next question. The same movement covers his own answer with a glass slide. In this way he can compare his own response with the correct answer, but he cannot alter what he has written. He can then move the next question into view. The machine is so arranged that one question must be completed before the next question can be seen.

Claims for the Different Devices

Obviously, there are advantages and disadvantages in each device. The machines can use constructed or predetermined answers, and they prevent the stu-

Fig. 5.5. A learning device in use. From B. F. Skinner, Teaching machines, *Science,* 1958, **128,** p. 971.

Answer 4. weak or *slight.* Go back to Question 5, page 129.

Answer 8. punishment. Go back to Question 9, page 129.

Answer 12. reduce or *weaken.* Go back to Question 13, page 129.

Answer 16. no or *zero.* Go back to Question 17, page 129.

Answer 18b. Your answer was, "strengthen weak tendencies but to have very little effect on very strong tendencies." This is correct. This is certainly what we would expect from theoretical considerations. Go on to Question 19, below.

Question 19. Having studied the theoretical expectations, let us now see if the experimental evidence confirms these expectations. The evidence from these experiments:

    a. clearly shows that symbolic reward strengthens weak tendencies, and also suggests that symbolic reward becomes less and less effective as tendencies become stronger. Look at Answer 19a, page 134.

    b. shows that symbolic reward works equally well for tendencies of any strength. Look at Answer 19b, page 131.

    c. fails to show that symbolic reward has any dependable effect. Look at Answer 19c, page 133.

Answer 21c. Your answer was, "the evidence clearly shows that punishment can make strong tendencies weaker and can also drive a weak tendency to below zero strength." This is an interesting idea, and there may be some indirect evidence for it from experiments on extinction. But studies of symbolic punishment show no such trend. Go back to Question 21, page 132.

---

dent from jumping around from one question to another. In the same way, they prevent him from peeking at the answer before he completes a question. At the very practical level, many of the machines are fairly economical in the use of paper, the students' responses being written on a small separate tape, and the questions being used over and over. On the other hand, the machines themselves are somewhat expensive and fairly elaborate, although there is a tremendous range in both respects. Unless a machine is very complicated it does not permit the use of a branching program.

With the scrambled textbook, the student could cheat but obviously he would have to go to a good deal of trouble to do so. In original cost such books are less expensive than machines. They may also seem less artificial than a machine. As we have seen, with the branching program that is used in this type of book larger steps can be used than with either the typical machine or the programmed textbook. On the other hand, since a book can only be used once, these books use up paper at a rapid rate. They call for a great deal of page turning and are restricted to predetermined answers.

Although the textbook with linear programming could use predetermined answers, it seldom does so. The constructed answer is much more frequent with this device. Like the scrambled text, this device calls for a great deal of page turning, but the student proceeds in more straightforward fashion with a minimum of searching and turning back. The chief objection raised against this linear textbook has been the ease of cheating. If

▶ *Conventional Teaching versus Programmed Instruction*

Computer service men took a 16-hour course on an IBM 7070 computer. Of these men, 42 began the course in September and studied by conventional classroom methods. Six classes (70 men) enrolling after October were taught one section of the course (a total of 15 hours instruction) solely by programmed text books. The instructors merely explained the procedure and passed out one or more of the five "chapters" in the various sessions. In the conventional classes, this material was covered in 15 hours of regular instruction. The men using the programmed texts worked one three-hour period and two four-hour periods but were free to take the books home. The instructors were told to avoid any suggestion that this programmed learning was an experiment or that it was unusual in any way.

All students were given an aptitude test at the outset. Later the final examination scores were adjusted to take care of any differences between the groups in aptitude score. For the programmed instruction group, the mean of these adjusted scores was 94.7 and for the conventional group 86.9. The difference was significant at the 1-percent level.

DIFFERENCES IN DISPERSION

	Scores ranging from			
	60–79	80–89	90–94	95–99
Percent of conventional group in each range	16	39	33	12
Percent of "programmed" group in each range		11	22	67

Notice that two-thirds of the "programmed" men scored 95 or better, and that only 11 percent fell below 90. The conventional people are spread out over a much wider range.

Eighty-three percent of the men in the programmed learning stated in an anonymous questionnaire that they would prefer to use this method in future courses.

SOURCE: J. L. Hughes and W. J. McNamara, A comparative study of programmed and conventional instruction in industry. *Journal of Applied Psychology*, 1961, **45**, 225–231.

the student is so inclined he can easily turn the page, look at the answer, and then turn back and write it in. Whether much cheating will occur, it is hard to say. Theoretically, there should be little temptation to cheat if each step is very easy. There should also be little cheating if the student is really trying to make the best use of his time. Notice, moreover, that such cheating automatically provides guidance. In "peeking" the student gets the same kind of guidance as when, in learning the foreign vocabulary, he looks at the English word before trying to answer. Early in the game, a certain amount of looking at the answer might be all to the good. For this reason, many psychologists are not greatly disturbed by the danger of cheating. Other psychologists point out, however, that this freedom to look ahead is available to the student at all times and is not something which is permitted him only when it would be useful, and which is withdrawn when it interferes with learning.

Experiments on Programmed Learning

Such are the issues regarding the use of the devices for programmed learning. The evidence bearing on these issues is exceedingly difficult to assess. Beginning in the early 1960s there has been a veritable flood of research, analysis, and discussion. Any statement made at one moment runs the risk of being outmoded a few weeks later. ("See Suggestions for Further Reading" for general summaries.)

At the outset, certainly, most students rather enjoy programmed instruction (Eigen, 1963). As we might expect, opinions differ widely, but the consensus is somewhat favorable. College students and graduate students tend to get tired of the approach after a time (Roth, 1963). Elementary school children, however, may retain their eagerness. Even after thirty-four weeks of studying spelling by use of machines, sixth-grade pupils in one experiment showed no loss of zest (Porter, 1959).

There is much controversy about the effectiveness of autoinstruction (Feldhusen, 1963). Adults using programmed instruction often equal or surpass those exposed to the traditional classroom situation (Hughes and McNamara, 1961). As in any arrangements for individualized teaching, some of those using programmed instruction saved a great deal of time, and a general saving was observed for the group as a whole.

Since autoinstruction is essentially individualized instruction, we should compare it with other forms of independent study. How does it compare, for instance, with independent study involving reading and note taking? For college students and graduate students, there is little difference either way (Whitelock and others, 1963). In one study (Poppleton and Austwick, 1964), however, the machines were better at the high school level.

Whatever the over-all effect of programmed instruction, it is certainly too soon to decide which feature of the process is essential (Silberman, 1962). So far the highly elaborate details have not seemed important. Students merely reading the statements in the program do about as well as those conscientiously writing in responses or checking off answers (Feldhusen, 1963). It even seems doubtful that we need the meticulous arrangement of programmed steps. When such a careful sequence is sliced into separate questions and the questions presented in scrambled order, students seem to do just as well (Levin and Baker, 1963; Roe and others, 1962).

In our final consideration of these devices, we should try to see their inherent psychological properties and should pay less attention to the novel physical features. Compared with other forms of individualized instruction the new devices seem to be neither an inhuman plunge into technology, nor a miraculous dispensation for revolutionizing the basic processes of learning. Consider two students, one reading a textbook all alone in the quiet of his room, the other cranking away on a teaching machine. For the time being, both are (cruelly?) deprived of physical human interaction. On the positive side, each one is being stimulated by some words in

► *The Teaching Machine as an Aid*

When an evening-school class had completed three of the nine assignments, the sixty-six students were divided into pairs that were matched on their performance up to that point. One member of each matched pair was then randomly assigned to an experimental group and the other to the control group. Members of the experimental group met separately for about twenty minutes. They were told about teaching machines and were allowed to sign up for as much time as they wished for practice on the machines outside the class. Members of the control group were told nothing of teaching machines and were not permitted to use them. There was nothing to stop them, however, from learning about such machines from their classmates.

	Average Scores		
	First Three Assignments (Before Machines Introduced)	Final Exam.	Final Exam. Plus Last Six Assignments
Teaching Machine Group	54	81.6	181.1
Control Group	54	78.4	176.1

The differences were not significant.

All those in the teaching machine group had the opportunity to use the machines, but some students made more use of them than others. A second comparison was made of those who used the machine at least ten times and their mates in the control group. The differences favored the teaching machine group but, again, were not significant.

According to their comments, most students believed that their experience with the machines had helped.

SOURCE: W. F. Oakes, Use of teaching machines as a study aid in an introductory psychology course, *Psychological Reports*, 1960, 7, 297–303.

the text. Each one is responding, one by a silent thought, or by writing notes, the other by writing a response. Both find the adequate responses reinforced. For the student with the textbook, this comes about when he anticipates the ideas to be presented and later finds that he is right. For the student at the machine, the reinforcement comes in a more mechanical way. But from a psychological point of view the two processes are highly similar.

All in all it would be amazing if the programmed devices did not turn out to be useful in teaching spelling, the mastery of factual material, and the grasp of concepts that can be clearly formulated. Whether or not they can also be used to teach less tangible things is still a matter of debate. If the evidence for them continues to be favorable, it might turn out that such devices could free the teacher from much routine drill on cut-and-dried factual material and leave him free to concentrate on those areas that demand enthusiasm, inspiration, and flexible guidance. The machine can regularly, accurately, and tirelessly reinforce the overt responses of the student. As yet, however, only a teacher can take into account the hesitancies, doubts, or assurances that accompany those overt responses. And it would take an exceedingly complicated machine to provide useful guidance based on the subtle cues coming from the student's behavior.

EXTINCTION AND PUNISHMENT

In the material used to demonstrate programmed learning we have already considered some general ideas about punishment and reward. At this point we give more detailed attention to the critical problem of punishment.

Unfortunately it is not always sufficient to build up the strength of tendencies—to make Jimmie *more* likely to say "7," or to be cheerful, or to read for pleasure. At times we must also try to weaken a pupil's tendency. We try to make him less likely to say "x^8" when he sees (x^2) (x^4), to write "neccesary" instead of "necessary," or to think of Spanish as the language of Brazil. How do we do this?

The simplest device is *extinction* or withdrawal of reinforcement. Such extinction might occur, for instance, if Jimmie should say, "12" instead of, "7," and thereupon other people should fail to react in any way whatever. In animal training it is often easy to use extinction. We can arrange things so that the hungry rat fails to get a food pellet when he presses the lever, or that the thirsty animal fails to get a sip of water. Under these circumstances, the act deprived of reinforcement is typically weakened or extinguished and comes to occur less frequently.

The Problem of Using Extinction in the Classroom

In the classroom it is often difficult to rely exclusively on extinction. A pupil, for instance, trips another pupil as he goes by the desk. We wish to discourage such behavior. We can easily refuse to commend or reinforce. But does this mean the complete absence of reinforcement? By no means. There is the automatic reinforcement as the victim stumbles forward. There may be considerable immediate casual reinforcement as other pupils snicker or gasp. Under these circumstances the teacher cannot be sure of extinguishing or weakening the tendency merely by refusing to supply reinforcement.

The social situation in the classroom, moreover, makes it difficult merely to withhold reinforcement. What do you do when the pupil makes a response you wish to extinguish? Just say nothing? This is awkward, if not actually churlish. Make some ambiguous comment? This is very likely to be interpreted as a commendation. Pretend not to hear? This would be all right if it worked, but most people can see through such a stratagem.

Reproof or Verbal Punishment

When confronted with behavior that should be discouraged, most teachers are inclined to add a note of reproof or verbal punishment. This inclination may come partly from the awkwardness of saying nothing, or from a conviction that we cannot depend on sheer absence of reinforcement, or from a more primitive, widespread, spontaneous tendency to speak out when we see behavior we do not like. Whatever the reason, teachers often administer a reprimand, or arrange for other unpleasant consequences when they observe an act that should be discouraged. Does such punishment, verbal or physical, mild or severe, have the effect of reducing the strength of the tendencies? Regarding this question there is still considerable uncertainty (Jones, 1961). Some psychologists hold that a boy punished for throwing stones through a window, for instance, may refrain for a time, but after this delay the tendency will function just as often as if he had never been punished (Estes, 1944). Other writers claim that verbal punishment applied to a strong tendency will definitely reduce its strength (Stephens, 1941).

Practically, it would seem wise to assume that punishment merely keeps the punished act in abeyance for a time. In that case, if we wish to effect a lasting improvement, we should try to use that period of abeyance to teach the student some other way of behaving—a way of behaving that would replace the act we do not desire. While he is staying away from "x^8" teach him to see that $(x^2) (x^4) = x^6$. During the period

---

► *Reward vs. Punishment*

The children in each of three grades (two, four, and eight) were divided into three groups for different kinds of treatment. Every child was presented over and over again with two rectangular blocks, each one divided by a diagonal into a white and black triangle. The children had to select the "correct" block which, in this expriment, was always the one with the white triangle long side down. This was just as likely to be on the child's right as on his left.

One group of fifteen children found a candy under the block when they made a correct choice. Nothing happened for a wrong choice. A second group was subjected to a loud noise (ninety-eight decibels, considered by the children as really "awful") after a wrong choice. Nothing happened after a correct choice. The third group got the candy for the correct choice and were subjected to the loud noise for the wrong choice. Each child had a total of sixty choices.

PERCENT OF CORRECT CHOICES IN SUCCESSIVE BLOCKS OF TRIALS

	Trials				
	1–12	13–24	25–36	37–48	49–60
Percent Correct for:					
Group receiving loud noise only	58	64	78	80	81
Group receiving noise and candy	57	51	51	60	74
Group receiving candy only	54	57	50	56	54

In the trials twenty-five to thirty-six, the loud-noise group is significantly ahead of the other two. At the end, the noise group and the noise-and-candy group are both significantly ahead of the candy group, but there is no significant difference between the first two.

SOURCE: R. K. Penney and A. A. Lupton, Children's discrimination learning as a function of reward and punishment, *Journal of Comparative and Physiological Psychology*, 1961, **54**, 449–451.

that his fingers hesitate to write "neccesary," teach him to write "necessary."

So far we have spoken of what happens with the onset of punishment. We must also consider what happens when the punishment ceases. Typically this is tremendously reinforcing as is suggested by the anecdote of the man who kept hitting himself on the head because it felt so good when he stopped. When the punishment ceases, the effect should be to reinforce whatever the pupil is doing at that time. This problem has received considerable stress in theories of character development and is developed within Chapter 9. Meanwhile, we should realize that in imposing punishment we inevitably set the wheels in motion for the cessation of punishment. And this cessation is almost bound to reinforce any act occurring at the time.

In these, as in so many other problems, we must not be completely swayed by feelings and by sentiments. Punishment has a harsh and medieval sound. It would be nice if we could get along without it. Perhaps we can. Perhaps we should. But the decision should not be based entirely on our feelings of what would be pretty or nice. To some extent we should be guided by the evidence. If the implications of that evidence call upon us to do things which violate our integrity or our basic principles, we can, of course, deliberately turn our backs on it. But we should do so knowingly and deliberately.

SUMMARY

To get a student to become more likely to behave in a certain way, we must have an eye to three conditions. (a) Whenever the circumstances are appropriate, (b) we must elicit the behavior from him and (c) make sure that the behavior is reinforced. At times the appropriate conditions consist of a specific stimulus $(3 + 2)$ which should be followed by a given response (5) (respondent behavior). At times the appropriate circumstances consist of very general conditions (Monday through Friday) when the behavior (going to school) is appropriate, but these conditions are not considered to elicit the behavior or response (operant behavior).

A great many events may serve to reinforce any behavior that does occur. An act may be reinforced by the normal feedback from sensations arising within the body; by automatic feedback from the external world; by casual social reactions (attention, smiles, admiring glances), and by the deliberate approval of the teacher or of some other person. Automatic reinforcement tends to be more immediate, and for this reason, it may be more effective.

There is much contention about the actual process by which reinforcement helps learning. It may merely help the student remember which result follows from which act (Expectancy theory of Tolman). The reinforcement, on the other hand, may act quite apart from consciousness and may merely automatically strengthen some connection (Hull) or some response (Skinner). It may function chiefly to initiate a new response (Guthrie) or to separate one learning episode from another (Guthrie, Estes). It may do all of these things.

In general it will be wise to arrange for generous amounts of reinforcement throughout learning. When only a few reinforceable responses occur, this may be difficult. As the number of correct responses increases, however, we can afford to reinforce only a fraction of these and still be sure of a generous amount of total reinforcement (partial reinforcement).

At the outset of learning the great problem is to get the pupil to make any acceptable or reinforceable responses whatever. Here we may employ shaping up. At first we reinforce anything remotely resembling the desired behavior and gradually tighten our standards. We may also use guidance, prompting, or the conditioned-response technique. The teacher can provide this help by giving manual guidance, by having students look at the answer before responding, by giving the answer to his own questions, by recitation in unison, or by pointing out the likely errors that are to be avoided.

The process of getting the correct response from a pupil often merges with the process of reinforcing the response. When a teacher announces that the correct answer to the question is "Jefferson," he provides a prompt for the child who has not come up with any answer. At the same time he provides reinforcement for the child who has already thought of "Jefferson." By waiting longer and longer before he supplies the correct answer, the teacher can gradually shift from an emphasis on guidance or prompting to an emphasis on reinforcement.

Devices for programmed instruction came about to provide more systematic reinforcement. Such devices come in many forms and vary both in methods of dealing with the problem of error and in the types of responses elicited. Such differences seem to have minor influence on achievement. Programmed instruction in general is essentially a form of individualized instruction. It involves largely the same psychological principles and has about the same success as other forms of individualization. For younger students, the programmed devices may even slightly surpass traditional methods. Students vary in their attitude, but are generally favorable at first. Older students may later lose their relish.

An undesired way of behaving can sometimes be eliminated by withholding all forms of positive reinforcement. But at times this is not feasible and some form of correction or reprimand is often used. Such corrections or reprimands may inhibit the act for a time.

SUGGESTIONS FOR FURTHER READING

General Principles of Reinforcement and Guidance

Birney, R. C., and R. C. Teevan, eds., *Reinforcement, an Enduring Problem in Psychology; Selected Readings*. Princeton, N. J.: D. Van Nostrand Company, Inc., 1961.

Estes, W. K., Learning, *Encyclopaedia of Educational Research*, 3d ed. New York: The Macmillan Company, 1960, pp. 752–770.

Hilgard, E. R., Theories of learning and instruction, *Yearbook National Society for the Study of Education*, 1964, 63, Part I. See especially

Hill, W. F., "Contemporary Developments within Stimulus-Response Learning Theory," Ch. 2.

Underwood, B. J., "Laboratory Studies of Verbal Learning," Ch. 6.

Pressey, S. L., "Autoinstruction: Perspectives, Problems and Potentials," Ch. 15.

Lumsdaine, A. A., "Educational Technology, Programmed Learning and Instructional Science," Ch. 16.

Hill, W. F., *Learning: A Survey of Psychological Interpretations*. San Francisco: Chandler Publishing Company, 1963.

Lawrence, D. H., and L. Festinger, *Deterrents and Reinforcement: The Psychology of Insufficient Reward*. Stanford: Stanford University Press, 1962.

Salzinger, K., Experimental manipulation of verbal behavior: a review, *Journal of General Psychology*, 1959, **61**, 65–94.

Skinner, B. F., Reinforcement today, *American Psychologist*, 1958, **13**, 94–99. Reprinted in Rosenblith, pp. 65–70.

Staats, A. W., and Carolyn K. Staats, *Complex Human Behavior*. New York: Holt, Rinehart and Winston, Inc., 1963.

Programmed Instruction

Frý, E. B., *Teaching Machines and Programmed Instruction, an Introduction*. New York: McGraw-Hill Book Company, Inc., 1963.

Keislar, E. R., and J. D. McNeil, Teaching scientific theory to first grade pupils by autoinstructional device, *Harvard Educational Review*, 1961, **31**, 73–83. Reprinted in Morse, pp. 226–231.

Lumsdaine, A. A., Instruments and Media of Instruction, in N. L. Gage, ed. *Handbook of Research on Teaching*. Skokie, Ill.: Rand McNally & Company, 1963, 583–682.

Lysaught, J. P., and C. M. Williams, A *Guide to Programmed Instruction*. New York: John Wiley & Sons, Inc., 1963.

Silberman, H. F., Self-teaching devices and programmed materials, *Review of Educational Research*, 1962, **32**, 179–193.

Smith, W. I., and J. W. Moore, *Programmed Learning: Theory and Research, an Enduring Problem in Psychology*. Princeton, N. J.: D. Van Nostrand Company, Inc., 1962.

There is a group of articles on programmed instruction in *Educational Research*, 1963, **5**, 163–200.

A similar series appears in the March 1963 issue of *Phi Delta Kappan*, Volume 44, No. 6.

Delay of Reinforcement

Renner, K. E., Delay of reinforcement: a historical review, *Psychological Bulletin*, 1964, **61**, 341–361.

EXERCISES AND QUESTIONS FOR DISCUSSION

1. Show how and at what stages you would use the two mechanisms of guidance and reinforcement in memorizing a poem; in teaching a student to appreciate a concerto; to pronounce *pleurer*; to saw a board in a straight line.

2. In general, do you expect that your students will be more likely to want to remain too long in the guided, conditioned-response stage of learning or to be too eager to plunge into the trial-and-error, reinforcement stage?

3. Can you think of any recent experiences in which you had to learn by trial and error, even though you felt the need of guidance? Can you think of any experiences in which someone insisted on "showing you how" when you would have preferred to puzzle it out on your own?

4. List five teaching tasks in which conditioned-response techniques could be used with very little modification.

5. Get someone to read a book in a room that is dark enough to need a light. Have him follow the words with his finger as he reads. At intervals turn out the light and ask him what he thinks is coming next. Then turn on the light and have him go on. Compare this procedure with a textbook using a linear program. With ordinary reading.

6. Using materials from the subject you expect to teach, construct a brief programmed text similar to that found in the insert.

CHAPTER 6

▶ *Structure and Meaning in Learning*

Most people need little urging to believe that meaningful learning is better than arbitrary or rote learning. We are all convinced that it is more interesting and more worthwhile to learn and to teach in a meaningful way than it is to rely on sheer memory. Some people, indeed, feel that there should be little place in the school for material that cannot be presented and grasped in a meaningful way. In his very influential book on this topic, Professor Bruner (1960), has called attention to important structures that can be appreciated at quite early ages and has urged us not to neglect the opportunity to develop these useful concepts.

Granted that everyone admits the importance of making teaching more meaningful, we still face the task of finding out just how this can be done. We also ask why it is that the meaningful approach is more effective. At times, moreover, we might adopt a cautious attitude and ask if there is any danger of going too far in our reverence for meaningful material and in our scorn for rote learning.

Characteristics of Meaningful Material

When we speak of making material more meaningful we probably have several different things in mind (Underwood and Shulz, 1960). We may mean that the individual items to be learned are more *familiar*, less bizarre. Looking at the items listed on page 146 you will agree that list two is more meaningful than list one. Each of the words in list two is familiar to you, whereas the items in list one are strange, perhaps strange to the point of being offensive.

Along with their greater familiarity, the words in the second list are richer in their *association value*. Each of them evokes a number of images and calls forth a number of associated ideas. The syllables in the first list, on the contrary,

145

1	2	3	4
XAH	RIVER	FOOT	HELP
YIX	DOOR	MILK	BRING
ZEQ	PEOPLE	HAND	THOSE
PYB	GENERAL	WATER	WEARY
QAJ	BLOW	EAT	SAILOR
COJ	HOUR	ARM	MEN
YOF	GIRL	EYE	SAFE
GYK	EARTH	DRINK	AGAIN
VEF	CALL	FOOD	TO
XUW	BOOK	EAR	SHORE

are unlikely to call up many associations. It is this idea of association value that many people have in mind when they speak of material having meaning. According to some psychologists, a meaningful word is merely one that calls up many associations.

Meaning can also come from the relations between items. The items in the third list, for instance, are probably no more familiar than those in the second list. But some of these items are more closely related to each other. To see this more clearly, read over the third list two or three times and then try to write down all the words you can remember. Don't worry about the order. Just try to repeat as many words as you can. Do this now before you read any farther. When you have finished compare the words you recalled with the list as given.

Do you find that you have tended to put parts of the body in one group and the food items in another? Many people do. This is an example of *clustering* (Bousefield and Cohen, 1955). It shows that these categories really lead you to organize the items into groups, even when you don't intend to.

At times, when people speak of material as being meaningful, they may refer to the fact that it is *easy to organize* or becomes organized almost automatically or is even already organized. The items belong together in some sort of unified pattern or structure.

The words in the third list have some implicit structure or pattern. In the fourth list, however, the pattern or structure is more prominent. In fact, you may find it difficult to think of this as a "list" of separate words. It may strike you as a single idea or sentence.

The Prevalence of Basic Pattern or Structure

Most of the time when we experience anything, we become aware of that thing as part of a pattern or structure. The pattern may be simple and primitive, as when we see a splotch of mud on a white wall, or it may be extremely complicated, as we become aware of pattern imposed on pattern in a musical composition or other work of art. But, however simple or complex, the pattern or structure is typically an important part of our experience. The splotch of mud would be experienced quite differently if it were not on the white wall.

According to the adherents of *gestalt psychology*, or *field psychology* (Köhler, 1947; Prentice, 1959), structure or pattern is the basic feature of all experience. The structure is experienced first, the details later. In the musical selection we first become aware of the general melody, and only later, if ever, do we notice the individual notes. In reading the words on this page, you first become aware of a word or phrase, and you may never notice individual letters that make up the word. In our experience, moreover, the general pattern remains fairly constant even when many or all of the details are changed. The melody is the same even if it is transposed to a different key and an entirely different set of notes are employed. The word is much the same whether printed in roman type or italics, in this type face or that, whether printed or written. As any proofreader will attest, it is even the same, all too often, when one of the letters is inadvertently left out, or two letters are transposed.

When a pattern is compellingly grasped, essential details may be experienced whether they are there or not (Fig. 6.1). The last few notes of the melody may be "heard" even if the sound is turned off. The punch phrase of a well-structured Limerick may be grasped even when the reciter hesitates to pronounce it. Just as essential details supply themselves with little or no effort, so less essential but helpful details are grasped with great ease. When we are aware of the *general* pattern of large lakes between the St. Lawrence and the MacKenzie rivers, we can easily learn the location of the individual lakes that make up the pattern. When clearly aware of the general pattern of the poem, we can easily memorize the individual words that fit in with the pattern.

USE OF STRUCTURE AND MEANING IN PRESENTING NEW MATERIAL

When presenting new material that has a clear and obvious structure, it is wise to present the general pattern first. If the student is to learn a new musical

psychology   *psychology*

PSYCHOLOGY

PSYCHOLOGY

Psyhcology

Fig. 6.1. A constant pattern in the face of varying details.

selection, let him grasp the entire melody before he works on the detailed passages. If he is to learn a play, let him understand the plot before he begins to memorize separate lines. If he is to learn to swim or to play badminton, be sure that he knows the *main* points to be kept in mind before he concentrates on the details. If he is to study the history of a certain culture, let him see something of the broad, general outline. If he is to learn to read, let him master the sentence or some other structural unit before he has to master the individual letters.

The Problem of Elusive Structure

Some pattern is bound to be noticed at the outset of any experience. But the most obvious pattern is not bound to be the one that is most interesting or the most useful. In Figure 6.2, for instance, you will undoubtedly see some structure or arrangement. You may merely see a general L-shaped arrangement, or perhaps a dog with his head cocked to one side. After someone gives you a hint, however, you may clearly see a boy on a tricycle. As soon as you do see a boy on a tricycle, this pattern should be very compelling and should dominate any future experience with the picture. Clearly, it also provides a more interesting and a better structure.

In most of the material we teach, we can see simple, naïve, banal structures, and on top of these, structures that are more inclusive, elegant, and useful. In presenting new material, should we try to develop these more complete structures, or, at the outset, should we be content with the more simple structure that is already perceived? Here we must use our judgment. At times, as with the boy on the tricycle, we can bring out the better and more elaborate pattern by a simple hint or by directing the attention to a key point or by a wave of the pointer. At times, moreover, the new or more inclusive structure will be convincing and compelling from the moment it is discerned. Under these circumstances, of course, it would be wise to go to some trouble to bring out this more inclusive structure at the outset of our lesson.

But there are times when the essential structure of the new material may be very difficult for the students to grasp. If the new material is a symphony, for instance, it may be possible that the over-all "architecture" is beyond the younger students. Yet there may be individual passages which such students can readily master and appreciate. Similarly, a pupil in grade six would probably find it hard to understand the reasons for each step he takes in extracting the square root of a number. Yet there are many recurring minor patterns in that process that are easily within his grasp.

When the complex structure, so intriguing to the teacher, is beyond the immediate powers of the students, it is foolish, of course, to try to use it as an aid in presenting new material. Often, new material presented so as to emphasize an elaborate and important structure proves no easier to learn (Munro, 1959) or has only a slight advantage (Binter, 1963) than the same material presented in an arbitrary or rote fashion. In one experiment, for instance (Newman, 1957), had students learn the meaning of the symbols used in electrical wiring. For some students, these symbols were grouped in a very logical pattern. Other students were given the same symbols grouped in helter-skelter fashion. The latter students actually came out ahead.

An insistence on a structure which fascinates the teacher but which eludes the child, far from aiding the student, may merely place an additional burden on his shoulders. One teacher, for instance, in using the *development lesson* as a device for bringing more meaning

Fig. 6.2. Illustration of an incomplete structure. Redrawn by permission of the publisher from *A Gestalt Completion Test*, by R. F. Street, Teachers College Contribution No. 481 (New York: Bureau of Publications, Teachers College, Columbia University, 1931), Item 11, p. 61.

► *The Structure Developed by the Teacher Does Not Always Help*

A total of thirty airmen who had just completed basic training were randomly assigned to one of two groups. Both groups were given a pretest on identifying twenty electrical symbols (a capacitor, a transformer, and so forth). The fifteen airmen in a "free-style" study group were then merely given the twenty symbols, not in the same order as in the test, with the name appearing after each symbol, and told to study the list.

The other group was given an organized presentation. Here the symbols were sorted according to some predominate feature. Five symbols all featuring a wavy line, for instance, were placed in one group. Five others, all having a prominent circle, were placed in another group, and so forth. The instructor presented these by groups, being sure that the symbols in one group were mastered before the next group was presented. The common feature in each group was stressed. Seven of the airmen went over the lists once (about eight minutes), and eight went over the lists twice (about twelve minutes).

In both cases the initial test was given again immediately after the learning exercise.

Airmen Studying for		Average Number of Symbols Recognized
8 minutes	Free-Style Study	13.1
	Organized Presentation	9.6
12 minutes	Free-Style Study	17.0
	Organized Presentation	13.5

For both time periods, the superiority of the free-style study was significant. The greater attainment for the longer period of study was also significant.

SOURCE: S. E. Newman, Student vs. instructor design of study method, *Journal of Educational Psychology*, 1957, **48**, 328–333.

into teaching, attempted to derive the whole history of Minnesota from an intriguing structure composed of three things: (a) the western grain fields, (b) the northern lumber industry, and (c) the falls on the Mississippi River at the site of Minneapolis. As the lesson went on it was apparent that the children were learning the facts of the history, but they were making scant use of the elaborate structure. At intervals they would "drag in" the deductions just to make the teacher happy, but these deductions, instead of being an aid, were merely additional things to be learned. In many other subjects, children also solve the problem as best they can and then obligingly give the approved reasons for doing it as they did.

Difficult Structures as Objectives. Obviously we should not ignore or discard these elaborate and complete structures just because they lie beyond the immediate grasp of the student. Although useless or harmful for introductory purposes, such structures make up the important final goals of teaching. Treat them as such. Regard the more elaborate structures as ultimate goals and not as mere introductory aids. Use minor patterns and structures to develop some understanding of the symphony or play, and then, when a moderate understanding is attained, try to bring out the larger structure or architecture. Use minor recurring patterns to help the student acquire some proficiency in extracting a square root. After that, try to develop an understanding of the underlying reasons, if this understanding is important in its own right.

But it is only in exceptional cases that we have to worry a great deal about this problem of elusive structure. By and large, the basic meaning in the new material will be within the grasp of the students and can be stressed from the outset. Even when its advantage is not clear in mastering the material at hand, the meaningful approach often shows a later superiority when the student turns to more difficult problems of the same general type. Provided the structure or meaning can be readily grasped by the student, seize upon it at the outset, and build the rest of your teaching around it.

New Material Related to an Established Pattern

It is seldom that the material to be presented is completely new. More often it is a continuation of something already considered. In this situation some sort of structure already exists. The material already dealt with is organized in some manner. Here, of course, the additional material should be presented as a part of the existing structure. It is presented as one of the details which help to round

Asuc Photography, Berkeley, Calif.

W. A. BROWNELL

out, or complete, or enrich, the patterns which the students already have in mind. After having learned how to solve the quadratic equation by factoring, for instance, the student can be encouraged to see the method of completing the square as an alternative method of achieving the same result. Or, having discussed the Industrial Revolution and its general effects, the teacher can present any given event as one special example of those general effects.

Additional material will be much more readily digested if there is a structure already waiting for it. Often, as it happens, such additional material will come not as an extra task to be mastered but as a welcome completion or refinement of a structure that is incomplete. It may come as the final note to an incomplete chord or as the denouement of an exciting story.

► *Providing Structure before Learning Begins*

College seniors majoring in education were assigned a brief article on the physiology of adolescence. After twenty minutes of study they were examined for mastery of the material. The students were then matched or paired on the basis of this examination. One member of the pair was assigned to an "advance organizer" group. The other was assigned to an "historical introduction" section. Later both groups were to study an article dealing with the metallurgical properties of carbon steel. Prior to studying this major article, however, the advance-organizer groups spent two five-minute periods, (fourty-eight hours apart), in reading a passage which set forth the main categories of the major paper (differences between metals and alloys, advantages and limitations of each, and so forth). During the same two five-minute periods the historical group read a selection on the historical evolution of methods of making iron and steel.

After these different orientations, both groups spent thirty-five minutes in studying the basic paper on steel. Three days later all students were given a test on the basic paper.

The two groups had already been matched for performance on the earlier paper. After further matching on sex and field of specialization there were forty students in each group.

	Final Score
Advance Organizer Group	16.7
Historical Introduction Group	14.1

The difference was significant between the .05 and .01 levels.

SOURCE: D. P. Ausubel, The use of advance organizers in the learning and retention of meaningful verbal material, *Journal of Educational Psychology*, 1960, 51, 267–272. Reprinted in Rosenblith, pp. 463–466.

Using Meaningful Relations within the Material

There is usually some external pattern into which our new topic can be shown to fit. Clearly we should make use of this. Often, there is also a definite internal pattern or structure within the new topic itself. When this is brought out, students may master the material more readily (Ausubel, 1960). To use this we should bring out and emphasize any latent, meaningful relation that can easily be grasped by the students. Cause and effect relations are extremely useful.

Analogies may help. When there is no convincing or intrinsic structure waiting for us to bring out, we can always analyze our material into main topics and subtopics.

VALUABLE FEATURES IN MEANINGFUL MATERIAL

When meaningful material does prove more easy to master than arbitrary material, what aspect of meaning plays the crucial part? Offhand, this may sound like a foolish question. The sheer fact that the material is meaningful would seem to be sufficient explanation. There is some point, however, in trying to explore the features responsible for the superiority of meaningful material. In so far as we can detect these valuable features, we may be able to emphasize them whenever they are found within material that is already meaningful. More important, perhaps, if we can find useful factors, apart from the meaningfulness itself, we may be able to apply some of these factors to material that is devoid of meaning.

Chunking or Recoding

The process of *chunking* and recoding has been emphasized in the work of G. A. Miller (1956b). Something like it is often used in a parlor game or trick by which you and a confederate might astound your friends. Suppose that there are several (six or seven) people that you and your confederate both know, and that you are both quite familiar with the telephone numbers of each of these people. You both know that Sam's number is 413 2964, Mary's number is 825 6351, and so forth. Your confederate starts the game by innocently speculating on how many separate numbers people can recall after one hearing. The other people, of course, have no notion that these numbers will have anything to do with telephone numbers. He reads out 413296, which is the beginning of Sam's number. Most people will get that one without any help. Next he gives Mary's number, 8256351. This will be possible for some people, difficult for many. For you it is simple, "Mary's telephone number." At 8 or 9 digits many people will drop out. With your secret knowledge, however, you may be able to go on 25 or 30 digits. You will hear:

72841568256351413296448373291

but you will group them 728 4156 825 6351 413 2964 483 7291 and will name each group Bob Mary Sam Ellen

As you listen to the digits being read, you must first of all be able to group them or hear them in a *chunk*. You must then quickly think of the *name* of that chunk. Next you must remember each name in order. You could probably remember as many as 5 or 6 names in order, giving you perhaps 35 to 42 digits. But much of your attention will be taken up with identifying the familiar chunks, and the effort necessary for this may limit you to 4 or 5 names.

In giving the numbers back, you think of the names in order, and as soon as you think of the name or code, you translate it into the numbers.

Our parlor game is a bit of a cheat in that your confederate has to give you numbers that are "prechunked." If any other member of the party started giving you numbers at random, you would be in trouble. The same principle, however, can be used in real life situations provided you can find some rapid way of chunking the material or provided you can deal with material that is on the verge of being chunked.

Our familiar decimal system of numbers is not suited to modern computers and they must employ the *binary* system instead. The binary system uses only 0's and 1's. We use 0 in binary for our ordinary 0, and 1 for our 1. When we come to our 2, however, we have used both 1 and 0 and since we cannot use any other numbers, we must use these again in a new combination, namely 10. Going on, 11 in binary is our 3. 1000 in binary is our 8.

You can see that you will soon run into a long string of digits. Our ordinary 35, for instance, appears as 100011, the number 1069 as 10000100011. To remember the binary equivalent of even a modest ordinary number becomes a very difficult task. To solve this problem, some workers have learned to break binary numbers up into chunks of (say) 3 digits each, and to give names to the 8 different chunks that are thus produced. Instead of remembering a long string of digits, they merely have to remember a few code digits or a few syllables. If they could learn to recall a series of 7 or 8 such digits or syllables, for instance, they could thus remember 20 to 24 binary digits.

To use chunking in an efficient way, we must be quick in giving names to the chunks. The names we do give, moreover, should be those that are easily recalled. If the naming is partly done for us, and if the names used are meaningful for us, much of the problem is solved. The letters TLY or BTL all by themselves, for instance, would be difficult to remember. If they are presented as hoTLY, or as douBTLess, however, they come already chunked (last part of "hotly") and more or less named. Under these circumstances they will be more readily remembered (Lindley, 1963). When the letters are meaningful as they stand (WAS, for instance), the addition of other letters adds nothing and tends to produce confusion. Since the letters were already chunked and named, the added letters merely introduce a second rival name.

We can see how much easier it is to master arbitrary things when we can recode them or chunk them into larger units. This principle of recoding, which can be deliberately or laboriously applied to arbitrary things, is almost automatically and effortlessly applied to any material that has meaning in it. Meaningful prose either comes already chunked or is very easy to break up into chunks. "Bobby hit Jimmie and then Jimmie hit him back and soon there was a real fight that Mother had to try to stop." In hearing this, the chunks used and the names given to each would vary from person to person, but some chunking would occur and each would be given something like a name. In this material, moreover, unlike our task in remembering numbers, we do not have to work hard to get the chunks in the right sequence. They fall into a natural order—an order that we have already "learned" to expect.

Familiarity

As we have pointed out, one of the things to be found in meaningful material is familiarity. Most of the words or items that we find are old friends. They do not seem strange. And this is one feature of meaningful material that may make it easier to master. Familiarity, or more extensive acquaintance with material, will help even if the items continue to be arbitrary or nonsensical (Riley and Phillips, 1959). After several repetitions of a list of nonsense syllables, for instance, you would be less appalled at the prospect of using them as names. It is true that some help may come from the fact that you began to see some meaning in the labels (Underwood, 1959). But even apart from this, sheer familiarity or further exposure would help.

Respecting Traditional Sequences

Just as there are customary sequences of thoughts or phrases, so there are traditional sequences of words that we have come to expect. Any departure from these will give us a jolt and distract our attention. You read the words, "There is no doubt that many people kettle chain and hock." The word "kettle" gives us a jolt, not because it is a strange word, but because it does not seem to belong here.

► *Making the Individual Items More Familiar*

Each of the twenty college students in this experiment was required to learn four lists of twelve nonsense syllables each. Prior to this experience each student had spent some time each day for four days in becoming familiar with the twenty-four individual syllables that were to be used in two of the lists. They had no such experience with the syllables on the other two lists. In this familiarization process the student looked at a card on which was printed the first two or the last two letters of a nonsense syllable. He then attempted to supply the missing letter. Whatever the result, the card was turned over and the correct spelling shown. This was repeated until all twenty-four syllables could be completed without error.

The cards were shuffled after each run so that the syllables would not appear in the same order from one trial to another.

After being familiarized with the individual syllables on two of the lists, the students learned these two lists in a precise serial order. They also learned two similar twelve-syllable lists containing syllables not seen before.

The average student required 7.2 trials to achieve a reasonable mastery of the lists with unfamiliar syllables, but only 5.8 trials to learn the comparable lists made up of familiar syllables to the same level of mastery. This difference was significant between the 5-percent and 1-percent levels. To attain a more exacting level of success, the students required 19.4 trials for the lists of unfamiliar syllables but only 15.2 trials for the lists of familiarized items. This latter difference, however, was not significant.

SOURCE: D. A. Riley and Laura Phillips, The effects of syllable familiarization on rote learning, association value, and reminiscence, *Journal of Experimental Psychology*, 1959, 57, 372–379.

Now it is possible to honor these expectancies, to avoid any major jolts, and still to write nonsense. Consider the following: "Won't do for the members what they most wanted in the course an interesting professor gave I went to at one o'clock stopped at his front door and rang." (Miller and Selfridge, 1950). This says nothing meaningful and yet no single word is especially out of place. No single word violates our customary expectancies.

When the material to be learned approximates ordinary English sequences, it is, of course, less annoying. More important, however, it is also more redundant. In reading ordinary English, as has been pointed out so often, we regularly anticipate what is coming. In so far as we can correctly anticipate the next few words, these words, strictly speaking, are unnecessary. Even without seeing them we already had the information they provided. In other words, they are redundant. But such redundancy provides exceedingly valuable and relevant reinforcement whenever we anticipate correctly. And this ability to anticipate correctly becomes more pronounced as the nonsense material comes more and more to approximate the structure of English prose (Salzinger and others, 1962).

What happens when we are asked to memorize familiar words that fail to make sense but which still honor the ordinary dependencies of speech? Most students get along just about as well with such nonsense material as with material that actually conveys a meaningful message. Provided we can move smoothly from one word to the next, or from one small group of words to the next few words, we find the passage relatively easy to repeat and to recall.

To summarize, it seems that some of the advantages of meaningful material may come from the fact that we do not have to deal with each item separately. We can deal with them as ready-made "chunks" or units, such as words, ideas, or master principles. Further advantage comes from the fact that the items are more familiar and each item is richer in the associations it can call forth. Finally, meaningful material is less disturbing, and the sequence of items presents no rude jolt.

TEACHING ARBITRARY MATERIAL

It is not always possible to meet our obligations merely by bringing out the inherent meaning in the material we teach. Some of the things we must teach actually have little inherent meaning or structure to bring out. There is little inherent meaning in the alphabet. Counting has little structure for young children. Spelling must often be mastered on a rote basis. The names of countries, capitals, and oceans are quite arbitrary.

Fortunately, as we have seen, many of the useful features in meaningful material can be applied to arbitrary items. Arbitrary material can be grouped, coded, and named, thus giving it some structure. It can be encountered more and more often and thus acquire some fa-

miliarity. At times such material can be arranged so as to avoid unwelcome jolts or unaccustomed sequences.

Supplying Artificial Structure

When the material to be learned has no usable, inherent structure, good teachers often provide an artificial structure into which the arbitrary material may be organized. This artificial structure, of course, should never be used instead of the genuine or essential structure if that is available to the student. On the other hand, it should not be spurned. Do not hesitate to use jingles or diagrams or other *mnemonic aids* to help the student with rote material. Do not be afraid to let the student learn, "Thirty days hath September," "In 1492 Columbus crossed the ocean blue," "*i* before *e* except after *c*," and countless other jingles which have helped students to master material which is purely arbitrary. The alphabet has often served as the system or organization into which isolated material has been fitted. A student who could not remember whether or not Madison preceded Monroe as President was reminded that *Ma* precedes *Mo*. Another student knew that the rods and cones of the eye had specialized functions, one serving in daylight and the other in twilight. He could not, however, remember which was which until it was pointed out that the *c* of cones and the *d* of daylight belonged together in the alphabet while the *r* of rods and the *t* of twilight had a somewhat similar proximity.

In these latter illustrations, it will be observed, there are also meaningful and inherent cues which could have been used. After all, an adequate view of the whole structure of early nineteenth-century American history would have provided a framework into which Madi-

► A Classical Account of Insight at Work

Sultan, a male chimp, has been trying to reach a piece of fruit outside his cage. He has two sticks but one is so made that it could be joined with the other to make a longer pole. Neither single stick is long enough. He has been trying to push one stick toward the fruit and, for a time, seems to feel some accomplishment if he can make this one loose stick touch the fruit. The experimenter tries to show him how to join the sticks, but nothing comes of it. The experimenter tosses the sticks back into the cage and leaves, asking the animal keeper to watch Sultan. The keeper reports:

Sultan first of all squats indifferently on the box, which has been left standing a little back from the railings; then he gets up, picks up the two sticks, sits down again on the box and plays carelessly with them. While doing this, it happens that he finds himself holding one rod in either hand in such a way that they lie in a straight line; he pushes the thinner one a little way into the opening of the thicker, jumps up and is already on the run towards the railings, to which he has up to now half turned his back, and begins to draw a banana towards him with the double stick. I call the master: meanwhile, one of the animal's rods has fallen out of the other, as he has pushed one of them only a little way into the other: whereupon he connects them again.

The experimenter now takes up the story:

The keeper's report covers a period of scarcely five minutes, which had elapsed since stopping the experiment. Called by the man, I continued observation myself: Sultan is squatting at the bars, holding out one stick, and, at its end, a second bigger one, which is on the point of falling off. It does fall. Sultan pulls it to him and forthwith, with the greatest assurance, pushes the thinner one in again, so that it is firmly wedged, and fetches a fruit with the lengthened implement. But the bigger tube selected is a little too big, and so it slips from the end of the thinner one several times; each time Sultan rejoins the tubes immediately by holding the bigger one towards himself in the left and the thinner one in his right hand and a little backwards, and then sliding one into the other. The proceeding seems to please him immensely; he is very lively, pulls all the fruit, one after the other, towards the railings, without taking time to eat it, and when I disconnect the double-stick he puts it together again at once, and draws any distant objects whatever to the bars.

SOURCE: W. Köhler, *The Mentality of Apes* (New York: Humanities Press, 1926), pp., 131–133.

son and Monroe would have fitted with no room for doubt. Similarly, there are reasons why the cones are especially responsive to certain ranges of light intensity. For the final outcome this more meaningful grasp is infinitely to be preferred. But for a quick mastery of an individual fact, the complete structure is sometimes an expensive aid.

Although the standard devices listed above are not to be scorned, they are perhaps less useful than devices which the student works out for himself. In the first place, the devices which help one person may actually get in the way of another person. The stunts used by our friends to remember telephone or license numbers are weird and mystifying to us, but they do help our friends. In the second place, there is always the possibility that the very act of working the material into a device will help the student learn the material itself.

MEANING AND INSIGHT IN THE APPLICATION OF REINFORCEMENT

So far we have discussed the role of meaning in presenting material to the student. It is easier to motivate students to study meaningful material. After they are motivated and have begun to practice or study, the meaningful material is much easier to learn and to remember. But meaning and structure not only facilitate motivation and practice; meaning also enhances reinforcement.

The word "insight" as used here will refer to meaningful reinforcement. It refers to the fact that after some kinds of reinforcement the student gets a clear picture or idea of "what leads to what." After some kinds of reinforcement the student is able to say, "Immersing your head well into the water (behavior), gives you increased buoyancy" (reinforcement), or, "Keeping the violin bow parallel to the bridge reduces the danger of a horrible screetch," or, "Starting the detective story before doing homework leads to disaster." Each of these represents an *insight*. Each of these illustrations suggests a compact idea in which a certain kind of behavior is tightly linked with a certain result or reinforcement. These two form an integral pattern. When we think of one, we think of the other. When we think of the behavior, we think of the corresponding result. When we think of the result, we think

of the behavior which will produce it. Under these conditions the reinforcement has become meaningful.

Not all reinforcement is meaningful. The toddler, feeling himself about to fall (situation), takes some corrective action (response or behavior), and finds himself still on his feet (reinforcement). He does not clearly realize which particular movement or response produced this desirable reinforcement, and yet this blind reinforcement does work. To take a different example, the adult finds that the key sticks in the lock. He twists and pulls and rattles things around (behavior), and the key turns (reinforcement). Here again, he cannot always tell you just what response leads to this reinforcement. Nevertheless, with continued experience he will find himself doing the right thing more and more regularly (Prentice, 1949). In these illustrations we have learning but very little insight.

WOLFGANG KÖHLER

The Importance of Insight

Whenever it does occur, insight should prove most helpful. According to the cognitive psychologist, indeed, the whole problem of learning hinges on some crucial insight. In some forms of parlor games, for instance, the whole trick is to select the code or to "catch on" to some double meaning in the directions that we get. As soon as this relation is understood, the problem is solved and often solved at the 100-percent level. In such an instance, the successful insight is the determining thing. Lacking it, our score is zero. Attaining it, our score is 100. In a great many athletic or gymnastic activities, a certain kind of insight may be noticed. We suddenly "get the hang of it" or "catch on," and from that point on our improvement is very rapid.

Enhancing Insight

A certain amount of insight will come about from the student's unaided efforts. It is natural, however, that the teacher can help out in this phase of learning. For one thing, the teacher can often call attention to potential reinforcement which may escape the child's attention. The mother may say, "See, the dog doesn't growl when you pat him on the head." The teacher of English may be able to show that by using an outline the student has produced a much clearer theme. Any one of these results may have escaped the student's attention. The teacher brings these results into the foreground and at the same time links them up with the act or behavior which brought them about.

Ready-made Insights vs. Student Discovery

In addition to helping the student verbalize and sharpen his own vague insights, the teacher often supplies insights that have been handed down from generation to generation. These ready-made insights range from profound and inclusive principles to the common maxims or catchy slogans. Such rules as *more haste, less speed; out of sight, out of mind; God helps those who help themselves*, for instance, are intended to serve as insights. They point to a way of acting. They suggest that if we want to achieve a certain goal, we should act in this particular way. They serve to remind us that this way of behaving will lead to a given reinforcement.

In the history of psychology there have been many arguments about the value of such highly verbalized cultural insights. In a renewed discussion of this ancient issue a number of writers (Bruner, 1961; Hendrix, 1961) have claimed that principles or rules have genuine meaning only when they are independently discovered by the student himself. To expect a student to comprehend important principles from straightforward explanation is regarded as a hopeless venture, if not as an improper, arbitrary, authoritative exercise of adult power.

One might urge a more moderate position. The data (Ausubel, 1961a) suggest that completely independent discovery, even if feasible, is seldom as effective as learning with reasonable amounts of direction or help. As pointed out in Chapter 5, too much guidance or direction can interfere with mastery of a principle. But the lack of any guidance whatsoever is seldom advantageous either.

Although the evidence does not give clear-cut support to the more extreme demand for learning by discovery, there is something to be said for the general atmosphere of discovery. We often do find superior learning when there is an emphasis on student activity and initiative, when the search for a principle is clearly kept in mind, and when many examples are provided. This general approach, however, includes many features over and above sheer independent discovery on the part of the students. Any one of these features, moreover, may account for the frequent superiority of the general approach (Ausubel, 1961a). Among other things, the greater ego involvement may lead students to spend more time in practicing the tasks, or thinking about them, outside the formal practice periods (Kersh, 1962).

Clearly it seems unwise to make a fetish of unaided student discovery. It is to be hoped that many important principles can be grasped without asking the students to go through all the efforts that led to the original discovery of those principles. On the other hand, some emphasis on discovery, coupled with features often associated with discovery,

---

► *Helping the Student vs. Letting Him Discover the Principle for Himself*

A group of seventy-six college students worked on some twenty problems of coding. Ten of the twenty problems were like this: "For each letter of the sentence write the letter that follows it in the alphabet."

EXAMPLE: They need more time

UIFZ OFFE NPSF UJNF

Now write the following sentence in the same code:

Give them five more

In the other ten problems the rule was not stated and the student was given only the sample sentence and the coded sentence.

Each of the twenty problems used the same illustrative sentence (They need more time), and the same test sentence (Give them five more), but employed a different code so that students practiced on twenty different codes.

A week later there was a second test on the same twenty codes. This time, however, the code was given, followed by a short English sentence, followed in turn by one correct coding of the sentence and three incorrect versions. The students had to select the correct coding.

	Score on Original Problems	Score on Similar Problems One Week Later	Difference between First and Second Tests
Problems for which the code had been given	8.6	7.7	−0.9
Problems which student had to work out for himself	5.4	8.1	+2.7

SOURCE: G. M. Haslerud and Shirley Meyers, The transfer value of given and individually derived principles, *Journal of Educational Psychology*, 1958, 49, 293–298. Reprinted in Harris, pp. 335–341.

should be valuable. With respect to a grasp of ready-made maxims or rules, for instance, we might expect more success when such rules are used to organize and enhance the vague insights which the student has already come to feel in a nebulous sort of way as a result of his own experience. When a student has already behaved in a certain way and has encountered a given kind of reinforcement, he is likely to experience some vague feeling of "what leads to what." As this feeling struggles, so to speak, for a more compact structure, the neat, catchy phrasing of a standard maxim or rule may prove exceedingly valuable. It may crystallize and clarify the general insight which the student has already begun to experience. It is possible that many of the delights of great literature spring from this process. The great writers put into precise and glorious language the vague and confused thoughts toward which the rest of us have groped. As a result of our own experience, each of us has formed vague and fuzzy insights regarding the pangs of remorse or the tragedy of indecision. It remains for Shakespeare, however, to thrill us by picking up these vaguely felt presentiments and returning them to us as insights that are neat, compact, and magnificently ordered. But even here there is some disagreement. Hendrix (1947) holds that the neat, verbalization of such insights may actually interfere with later transfer to other tasks.

In the face of this controversy we suggest the same general rule that is used frequently throughout this text: Provide a reasonable schedule of reinforcement throughout. Even at the outset, try to get the student to make a reinforceable response, or to achieve an acceptable understanding. If, within a reasonable time, he can do this through independent discovery—wonderful! Under these circumstances you can reinforce both the understanding attained and the tendency to try to discover principles. Perhaps, however, his independent efforts are not likely to produce much in the way of a reinforceable achievement within a reasonable time. Here it would be better to provide some guidance or direction. Don't let him go on indefinitely with no reinforcement.

MEANING AS A PRIME GOAL OF TEACHING

Meaning, insight, and organization are important devices to be exploited in teaching factual material, and most of us use meaning and structure as means to help to achieve whatever goals we have in mind at the moment. Obviously, however, meaning is not simply a device for the attainment of minor goals. Neither is it merely a means for achieving more important aims. The attainment of rich meaning and comprehension and understanding, on the contrary, is itself one of the major goals of education.

A rich store of meanings, of comprehensive understandings, and of functioning insights is one of the greatest gifts that the school can bestow on the student. True enough, the facts which he learns in the school are important too. But if those facts can be contained within a few highly structured, general principles, the latter are infinitely more valuable. A relatively few scientific principles, for instance, clearly comprehended, can give meaning and direction to a whole host of practical problems in engineering, in homemaking, in agriculture, and in healthful living. Other principles actually understood enable the banker or businessman to think about his problems in more intelligent fashion. Similarly, a somewhat larger number of less-structured principles from psychology may help in teaching and in the more complicated business of getting along with people.

A rich store of meaningful principles, in addition to pointing the way to the solution of practical problems, also contributes directly to sheer intellectual satisfaction. The need for understanding is a real need. It functions at different levels in different people and is much stronger in some people than in others. But it is present at some level, and in some degree, in all of us. We are bound to work out some principle to help us organize the haphazard world around us. That "principle" may be crude and childish ("People never understand me") or elaborate and sound ("Don't expect that people will always act in strictly logical fashion"). But some principle will prevail. Since that need is present, and since it must be partially filled in one way or another, the teacher should make sure that the principles attained are as comprehensive and as valid as possible. Some students may be able to comprehend and absorb principles that are exceedingly complex and inclusive. Others may have to be content with rather simple principles. But for each student, the teacher can do much to help him attain a more adequate set of principles, insights, and understandings.

Dangers of Premature Closure

Some difficulties confront us when we cease to use meaningful relations as devices and begin to consider them as ends in themselves. When we use these meanings and structures primarily as helpful aids, we have no worry about premature closure. A definite and convincing structure, even if not quite valid, may serve quite well as a working structure in helping the child in comprehending the subject. When teaching the meaning as an end in itself, however, it is important that the structure be valid. At times, moreover, things are better when the structure does not come too soon. The ultimate grasp of the meaning may be better if the student endures a period of uncertainty (Smedslund, 1961). A neatly closed structure, early accomplished, may strenuously resist disruption or modification.

The Role of Maturation

In teaching some broad, general concepts we may have to gear our efforts to the broad stream of development (See Chapter 2). Many ideas such as causality, or the extent of past history, are exceedingly difficult to develop in younger children, but seem to come automatically for older children. If Piaget is right in his notion of stages, we would be foolish to try to force matters (Flavell, 1963).

Using the Standard Mechanisms of Learning

To bring about growth in the student's understanding and in his comprehension of meanings, the teacher can use the rules already stressed for teaching in general. Motivation, practice, reinforcement, guidance, and insight will serve just as well in teaching students to grasp a general principle as in teaching them to spell "anxious," to draw a book, or to sing a song.

To motivate the tendency to seek out meanings and general principles, the teacher should exploit the student's existing need to see relations. With very little encouragement, students will seek out similarities, analogies and general relations. In studying the history of Brazil, they may comment spontaneously on parallels to the history of the United States. In studying the rhythm in poetry, they may be reminded of some of the properties of rhythm in music. It will be the unusual class in which some child is not reminded of some other matter which can be related to the structure of his present experience.

Encourage this general tendency. Even when the actual principle announced by the student is farfetched and questionable, the *tendency* itself can be encouraged. Be enthusiastic about the fact that the principle was stated, but ask the pupil to regard it as tentative until more cases have been examined.

It is not enough merely to take advantage of the spontaneous expression of the student's need for broader principles. Stimulate that need. By your actions show that you too are interested in these generalities. Let the search for generalities pervade even the most ordinary teaching. The teacher of French can ask, "Does that remind you of anything in Latin (or English)?" The teacher of geography can ask for analogies or contrasts between the pampas in South America and the plains of the United States. The teacher of music can stimulate the amateur tune detective who can spot passages from Handel or Scarlatti in the current popular hit.

These illustrations, of course, represent the incidental uses of motivation that accompany the daily teaching. At the more overt and intellectual level, students can also be motivated to master general principles. The teacher can show how a mastery of these principles aids in earning a living, in contributing to human welfare, in attaining the esteem of one's fellows, and in experiencing a very real intellectual satisfaction.

In using the mechanism of practice to help develop meaningful relations, we should rely more on emphasis and less on formal practice sessions. In teaching most material, there are numerous occasions when general principles can be stressed and when meaningful relations can be brought out. It is much more important to seize upon these natural opportunities and to develop them than it is to arrange for more formal practice sessions devoted exclusively to the study of general principles. Otherwise we may disrupt the natural intricate relation between fact and principle.

The mechanism of reinforcement is easy to use in the development of meaningful relations. Commend with enthusiasm the student who sees the material being discussed as part of a larger structure or who can see the analogy between this usage in French and a related usage in Latin. Be especially zealous to commend the student who can summarize the main point of a lesson in a pithy and precise insight.

The mechanism of guidance can be used with great effect, especially in pointing out the many minor principles of generalizations that we hope our students may attain. Much can be done by the mere arrangement of the material. Simply by placing rainfall maps of North America and South America side by side, for instance, we may have automatically arranged things so that the general principle is almost staring the student in the face. Similarly, in biology, there are many parallel sketches of the skeleton of man and horse (Fig. 6.3), or parallel diagrams of frog and man, and these can be depended upon to point the way to the mastery of some of the general principles of anatomy or physiology. Naturally, we will not expect 100-percent success from these devices. Even the most ingenious sometimes fail to work (Koller, 1957).

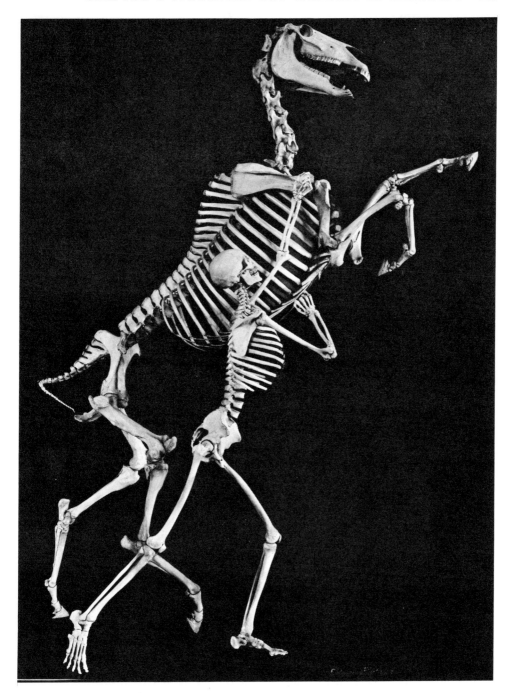

Fig. 6.3. A skillful arrangement of materials can bring out important relations. Photograph of skeleton of man with skeleton of horse, courtesy of The American Museum of Natural History.

SPECIAL PROBLEMS IN THE DEVELOPMENT OF MEANINGS AND UNDERSTANDING

Although the teaching of meanings is essentially the same as any other kind of teaching, there are a few details which become especially important when we turn to the more complex area of meanings and abstractions and general principles.

Meanings Arise from Experience

Meanings can never far outrun direct concrete experience. At least, they can never do so safely. A meaning that is not closely anchored to some clear experience is likely to be wide of the mark. In one of her novels, for instance, Gene Stratton Porter made interesting use of the kind of misconception that is likely to arise when a word or meaning or concept is not tied up with actual experience. In this story a neglected waif was rescued from her squalid surroundings and moved to a better home. Here she became inordinately fond of milk and extended her affection to cows. She had never seen a cow but learned of them as the givers of the delectable food. She heard a great deal about the function, the utility, and the disposition of the cow, but nothing of its size. Her first encounter with an actual cow was traumatic. She expected something small and round and cuddly, perhaps like a rabbit. She was in no way prepared for the behemoth which welcomed her with an uncouth and monstrous noise.

Similar misconceptions are encountered by every teacher. The pedagogical literature is filled with amusing examples of such incidents. A grade-four youngster, for instance, reads about the army officer who provided his men with "quarters for the night." We can easily understand his visual picture of the officer handing each soldier a twenty-five-cent piece to pay for his lodging. A second student is said to have stated the "furlough" meant "mule." To support his unorthodox definition he produced a picture of a soldier riding a mule, underneath which was the unmistakable caption *Civil War soldier going home on a furlough.* The writer once asked his grade-six class to write out the story of Lochinvar. In one place Lochinvar declaims,

> I long woo'd your daughter, my suit you denied.
> Love swells like the Solway but ebbs like it's tide.

One student paraphrased the first line thus: "I long woo'd your daughter but you wouldn't give me back my clothes." One wonders at the background structure of the student's impression within which this misconception was formulated. But it is a reasonable interpretation of the denial of a suit.

In each of these illustrations, the student was called upon to deal with a word or a concept before he possessed the general background or structure into which the word would fit. In each case, we asked the student to attain a meaning which at that time was too far in advance of his concrete experience.

It would be ridiculous, of course, to imply that meaningful ideas must always be anchored *directly* to concrete experience. One can often proceed a few steps from concrete experience and still avoid serious misconceptions. The tutors of the little girl could have given her an adequate idea of the cow's size if they had made use of her concrete experience with horses or ponies or other large objects. The teacher of history could have found a chain of concepts from "quarters" to tourist camps or to some idea of lodgment which came within the child's actual experience. By the use of analogy or of similarities within our own experience, clever writers are often able to give us a very accurate concept of things we have never experienced. Intensive reading, for instance, is alleged to have given Rex Stout such a vivid picture of Manhattan that the city held no surprises for him when he visited it. Similarly, on the basis of sheer verbal description, he was prepared for everything he actually encountered when he heard his first symphony. Few psychologists will be completely convinced that unaided verbal description can do so much. It is possible, however, that a large number of parallel descriptions, each giving somewhat different illustrations, can give a fairly accurate picture of an unfamiliar scene.

Rather than depend too much on intermediate links to anchor the new meaning to concrete experience, the teacher should use photographs, moving pictures, and other visual aids when the actual concrete experience is lacking. Records and sound films can also bring the song of the skylark (a bit insipid after reading Shelley), or the roar of Niagara. As yet there are no artificial or substitute devices which will stimulate the taste of champagne or the odor of Naples. It is quite possible, moreover, that the student who has encountered these things only in literary descriptions may be in for a bit of a shock when he experiences the real thing.

Although our discussion has centered around the meanings of individual words, we must remember that we are seldom called upon to deal with words in isolation. Words are usually encountered in a sentence or in a phrase or in another context. And, typically, the broader structure determines the meaning which we attach to the word. The "tear" in her eye is a very different thing than the "tear" in her dress, but ordinarily the difference would cause us no trouble. It is the entire phrase that determines the meaning, and the same words really mean different things in different contexts.

These contextual clues are to be utilized. It is a great help when the new word is encountered in its proper context. The context provides important guidance and almost forces the student to interpret it more or less adequately. He is able to react to the passage as a whole and is not held up while he stumbles around trying to deal with an individual word. When he reads that "The cruel bombing left Warsaw a reeking shambles," he can readily surmise the "reeking" and "shambles" describe the destruction wrought by the bombing. These new words will not prevent him from grasping the main idea. So long as these words remain in their present context, they will cause no difficulty. It is only when the student wishes to use either one in a new context that he may encounter trouble. At that time he will need to know whether "shambles" means "litter" or "blood," and whether "reeking" means "smoking" or "odoriferous."

Attaching Meaning to Abstract Concepts

Mastering the meaning of such concepts as "justice" or "squareness" or "democracy" is much more difficult than mastering the meanings of such terms as "money," "cow," or "trireme." In teaching the abstract concept we cannot find a single object in the child's experience—we cannot show him a picture of "justice" or present a sound recording of "democracy."

And yet, if students are to acquire any understanding at all of abstract concepts, they must acquire that understanding largely from experience with concrete objects. To a limited extent, of course, we can use a group of abstract concepts, such as the three normal dimensions, as a basis for speculating about a fourth dimension which we have never experienced. But our grasp of those concepts which go beyond our experience is very uncertain and vague. Typically we cannot go many steps beyond our concrete experience if we are to understand an idea in a dependable manner.

A grasp of abstract concepts, of course, must come from experience with many objects (Dienes, 1959). To understand *squareness* the student must see square papers and square boards and a square drawn on the chalkboard. He must see red squares and white squares. In other words, he must see a variety of concrete objects, all having the common property of squareness. He must also see a large number of concrete objects somewhat similar to the above but which lack

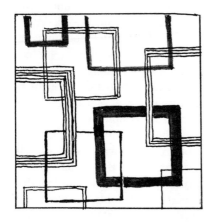

Fig. 6.4. The concept (squareness) should be conspicuous when first presented.

the property of squareness (Fig. 6.4). To understand the concept of *rhythm* as an abstract idea, the student must encounter rhythm in one selection after another. He must also encounter somewhat similar selections in which the element of rhythm is lacking. To understand the term *justice* in any precise fashion, the student must encounter a large number of situations, real or hypothetical, each of which exemplifies justice. He must also encounter similar situations in which justice does not appear, but in which are to be found such things as kindness, sympathy, or unselfishness with which justice may be confused.

In teaching abstract concepts, choose those concrete materials in which the abstract idea is fairly prominent. The squareness of a piece of paper may be more prominent, for instance, than the squareness of a room. The paper would therefore be preferable for beginning the teaching of squareness. Similarly, the rhythm in a waltz may be more prominent than the rhythm in a tone poem. Choose the waltz at the beginning of the instruction. The concept of justice versus mercy may stand out more clearly in *The Merchant of Venice* than in *The Brothers Karamazov*. Choose the former to begin with.

When first presenting an abstract concept try to be sure that there is as little as possible to interfere with that concept. When first teaching squareness, try to be sure that the feature of squareness stands out, and also try to arrange things so that no other feature is especially prominent. We would avoid striking colors, or extremely unusual material. Such competing features would reduce the prominence of the concept to be developed.

Especially when teaching young children, we should be sure that there is nothing in the *atmosphere* of the material that interferes with the concept. It may be hard for young children to realize that the girl in Figure 6.5 is *lonesome* if she is wearing a pretty dress (Honkavaara, 1958). If you are teaching young children the difference between living and not living, avoid using attractive non-living objects at the outset. Children may readily consider a car to be alive if it is attractive. They would be less likely to think this if the car were drab or decrepit.

Although we wish that the quality to be taught shall stand out, we should never try to isolate that quality, even if we could. Never try to present pure rhythm. Let it always appear in a fairly natural context. Do not seek for a literary situation from which all extraneous details have been removed and in which the concept of justice is presented with almost no irrelevant background. The natural context should be there, but at the outset it should be in the background, and the abstract quality should be quite prominent.

Use many concrete examples chosen from a wide variety of settings. Justice as portrayed in one play could easily be confused with incidental qualities which appear in the same play. Use many literary selections or other examples. If you have to teach the concept of individual differences, for instance, use examples of individual differences in height, weight, hair density, and wealth. Never let the student feel or infer that individual differences refer only to differences in intelligence or any other single trait.

Use a multitude of practical examples in testing as well as in teaching. And provide much opportunity for testing. The mastery of abstract concepts depends, after all, on the student's own activity. You cannot do everything for him. After an initial guided approach,

TRACK 15

ARRIVAL

2:47 P.M

7:22 P.M

DEPARTURE

3:02 P.M

7:51 P.M

Fig. 6.5. For young children an attractive detail may outweigh a somber mood.

let him try himself out frequently with many different kinds of examples. Let him pick out the square face of the pyramid, the square pane of glass, the square in the pattern of some cloth. Let him beat out the rhythm in a song, in a poem, in rhythmic prose, or perhaps in a graphic pattern. Let him point out the rival claims of justice, mercy, and expediency in newspaper reports of trials, in fables, and in the problems before the United Nations. His *final* mastery of these concepts will come largely from his own trial-and-error efforts and from the reinforcement and insight which follow these efforts.

DEVELOPING SKILL IN THE USE OF ABSTRACT CONCEPTS

We have laid down certain rules for teaching new words and for teaching the *meaning* of abstract concepts. These rules also hold when we are helping the students to develop skill in the manipulation of abstract concepts. They hold, for instance, when we are teaching students how to manipulate the abstract x's and y's of algebra. At first, make sure that the problems deal with concrete materials well within the student's experience. The student is less likely to make a mistake in manipulating these familiar materials. The materials themselves provide the guidance so necessary in the early stages of the acquisition of skill. If, by some chance, he should begin to go astray in using familiar concepts, his error is likely to become immediately and glaringly apparent, thus providing the automatic reinforcement which is so helpful to learning at all stages.

To illustrate the difference between reasoning in the abstract and in the concrete, consider two syllogisms. Here is one that is highly abstract:

All S's are M
All P's are M
$\therefore$ all S's are P's

True or false? How sure do you feel? Now try it in concrete form:

All (S)cotchmen are (M)en
All (P)ortuguese are (M)en
$\therefore$ all (S)cotchmen are (P)ortuguese

What is your reaction? And how sure do you feel? Actually, there is probably no comparison in your reaction to the two problems. Any child who knows the meaning of the three terms can see that

the last conclusion is fallacious. Many a college student, on the other hand, may fail to see that the first conclusion is invalid. To render a fallacy glaring and apparent, merely translate it into familiar and common sense content. When this is done, a child of seven can detect the most complex logical fallacies.

So much for the beginning stages of teaching the manipulation of abstract concepts. But we cannot keep on using familiar material forever. To do so would negate our goal. Gradually we must withdraw the guidance supplied by the familiar material. As some skill develops, we try to get the students to feel more at home with the abstract symbols, so that now they need only refer occasionally to familiar material to see if their conclusions check with common sense. Ultimately, a very few students may acquire such competence in dealing with abstract symbols that they can proceed accurately even when the material has no relation to common sense or when the assumptions are in direct contradiction to common sense.

Ability to think in this way represents the stage of *propositional thinking*, or *formal operations*, in the Piaget system (Flavell, 1963). This is the realm in which the physicist must operate when he reasons about the characteristics of a fifth dimension. He can receive little guidance from common sense or from concrete operations. Nor can he spend much time in worrying about whether or not there *really* is a fifth dimension. But genuine facility in this realm comes only with much experience. If Piaget is right, moreover, it cannot be expected of young children no matter how much experience they have. For the young child, and for the beginner at any age, we should be generous in providing the guidance that comes from concrete illustrations.

► The Effect of Context on Reasoning

Eighty-one college students were given a test of syllogistic reasoning. The test contained a total of 240 items. There were four different kinds of materials, 60 items for each kind. The syllogism consisted of two statements (or premises) and three proposed conclusions. A conclusion was to be marked valid if it followed necessarily from the premises, even if it were false in actual fact. Conversely, a conclusion was to be marked as invalid if it did not follow necessarily from the premises, whatever its truth in actual fact. To get credit, all three conclusions had to be marked correctly.

Type (and Sample) of Items	Mean Number of Items Completed Correctly Out of a Possible 60
A. Familiar Material All the rugs sold in that shop are expensive. Some of my rugs are sold in that shop. (a) Some of my rugs are expensive (b) All expensive rugs are mine (c) Some of my rugs are not expensive	50

B. Symbolic Material
All x's are y's. Some z's are x's.
    (a) Some z's are y's (b) All y's are z's
    (c) Some z's are not y's
	43

C. Unfamiliar Material All tigerlini are coniferra. Some zoolidi are tigerlini. (a) Some zoolidi are coniferra (b) All coniferra are zoolidi (c) Some zoolidi are not coniterra	40
D. Material Familiar but Misleading All members of this club are undertakers. Some florists are members of this club. (a) Some florists are undertakers (b) All undertakers are florists (c) Some florists are not undertakers	46

SOURCE: Minna C. Wilkins, The effect of changed material on ability to do formal syllogistic reasoning, *Archives of Psychology* (New York, 1928), No. 102.

The Dangers of Unanchored Abstractions

Abstractions have proved of stupendous value in our lives. We are greatly attached to them, and properly so. Sometimes, too, we regard them as pretty things in their own right, and this attitude has much to commend it. Sometimes we regard them as *actual* things in their own right. Plato, of course, held that we should. In actual practice, however, an unclothed abstraction may be dangerous. When using such an abstraction we should frequently come back to earth and make sure that our abstraction is firmly anchored to something concrete and objective.

To see the dangers inherent in unanchored abstractions we have only to look at the concept of intelligence. This is an abstraction. It is a quality which pervades a great many acts. It also, unfortunately, is a concept that has value connotations. It is a "good" word or a nice-sounding word. No one likes the sound of being called "unintelligent," no matter what the user *meant* by the term. Very frequently students will use the term "intelligence" over a period of time without ever asking themselves for a concrete example of what is meant by intelligence. When they do realize that the concrete process most often implied is merely getting a score on an intelligence test, they feel a bit of a jolt.

There are many abstractions which cause us endless trouble if we fail to bring them back to earth at frequent intervals. We hear that a man is dishonest. Honesty or dishonesty in an abstraction. They are words describing aspects of many ways of behaving. To get any *clear* idea of what is meant, we should ask our informant for a concrete illustration. In commenting on his wife's new hat, for instance, the man may merely have expressed an enthusiasm which he did not genuinely feel. He may have used some of the office stationery for his own personal correspondence. He may have defrauded a trusting widow. Each of these concrete acts could be classified as dishonest. Until the abstract word is clearly anchored to some such concrete act, it has little meaning. Unanchored, it is also a dangerous word. It could lead to serious misconception.

Try to get students to probe behind the sound of ever-present abstractions. Get them to give concrete illustrations of what they mean by *undemocratic, liberal, progressive,* or *sophisticated.* Get them to demand such concrete illustrations from those who would seek to sway them by words that have a pretty sound but which may fail to convey any precise meaning.

SUMMARY

When we say that material is meaningful we could mean that the items are familiar and rich in association value, that the items readily cluster into different categories, or that the items are incorporated into a few large structures. These large structures, characteristic of all experience, are clearly to be utilized. Whenever the student acquires a convincing grasp of an important structure, the teaching process may become virtually transformed. A useful but elusive structure can often be brought out by a simple device. At times we can present new material as part of an existing structure. At other times we can bring out the structure within the material itself. In helping the student to grasp material, we can make use only of a structure that he can readily grasp. Stress on difficult structures will not help *for this purpose,* and may get in the way. Such difficult structures should be considered as goals and not as helpful introductions.

When meaningful material does prove easier to grasp, the advantage may come from the greater familiarity, from the fact that it can be more easily structured into manageable "chunks," or from the fact that in dealing with familiar sequences of words we are more likely to benefit from the reinforcement that comes when we correctly anticipate oncoming phrases. The more closely nonsense material approximates English prose, the more likely we are to make such anticipations.

In teaching material that lacks structure or that lacks a structure the child can grasp, we should make use of artificial structure or mnemonic aids.

Just as we can use meaning and structure in presenting new material, so we may also use them in applying reinforcement. When reinforcement is thus insightful, the student has a clear idea of just which kind of behavior leads to which kind of result. Some psychologists maintain that all such insights should come from the child's own discovery. Others hold that some guidance is essential, or certainly useful. As a compromise we might rely on student discovery when it can be expected to bring reasonably prompt success.

Meaningful relations are not only tools to help in presentation and reinforcement but are often the prime goals of teaching. To develop them we try to interest children in them. By displays, hints, and other devices we guide pupils toward the necessary comprehension, and we hasten to reinforce even the first hints of such a comprehension. A grasp of abstract principles always arises from concrete experience and usually needs frequent correction by our appeal to such concrete experience. The concrete experience provides the early guidance and the later reinforcement so necessary in learning. In furthering the acquisition of dependable abstractions, we should use a diversity of concrete examples, emphasizing, at the outset, those in which the abstract idea is prominent. Gradually, provided he has the necessary maturity, we may partially wean the pupil from his concrete illustrations and help him acquire skill in the manipulation of the abstractions themselves.

SUGGESTIONS FOR FURTHER READING

Ausubel, D. P., *The Psychology of Meaningful Verbal Learning; An Introduction to School Learning.* New York: Grune & Stratton, Inc., 1963.

Brownell, W. A., and H. E. Moser, *Meaningful vs. Mechanical Learning; A Study in Grade III Subtraction.* Durham, N. C.: Duke University Press, 1949.

Bruner, J. S., *The Process of Education.* Cambridge, Mass.: Harvard University Press, 1960.

———, The act of discovery, *Harvard Educational Review,* 1961, **31,** 21–32.

Henle, Mary, ed., *Documents of Gestalt Psychology.* Berkeley, Calif.: University of California Press, 1961.

Hilgard, E. R., The place of gestalt psychology and field theories in contemporary learning theory, *Yearbook National Society for the Study of Education,* 1964, 63, Part I, 54–77.

Katona, G., *Organizing and Memorizing.* New York: Columbia University Press, 1940.

Miller, G. A., Information theory and memory, *Scientific American,* 1956, (Aug.), 195, 42–46.

Osgood, C. E., G. J. Suci, and P. H. Tannenbaum, *The Measurement of Meaning.* Urbana, Ill.: University of Illinois Press, 1957.

Peel, E. A., Learning and meaning, *Bulletin of the British Psychological Society,* 1962, **48,** 1–9.

Underwood, B. J., Verbal learning in the educative process, *Harvard Educational Review,* 1959, **29,** 107–117.

———, and R. W. Schulz, *Meaningfulness and Verbal Learning.* Philadelphia: J. B. Lippincott Company, 1960.

Brief Classical Articles

Miller, G. A., and Jennifer A. Selfridge, Verbal context and the recall of meaningful material, *American Journal of Psychology,* 1950, **63,** 176–185. Reprinted in DeCecco, pp. 367–380.

Piaget, J., How children form mathematical concepts, *Scientific American,* 1953 (Nov.), **189,** 74–79. Reprinted in Morse, pp. 193–198, and Stendler, pp. 333–337.

EXERCISES AND QUESTIONS FOR DISCUSSION

1. Suggest some devices by which you could quickly bring out the basic structure of a sonnet, of a musical theme, of an electronic computer.

2. (a) List two or three topics which you feel sure should be taught in a meaningful way from the outset. (b) List two or three topics or activities (extraction of square root?) which have a meaningful basis, but which you might first teach on a rote basis.

3. Thinking of the subject you expect to teach, list a few structures which would be so apparent that they might be used in the first presentations. List some structures that might better be considered as ultimate objectives.

4. A student has stolen some money from a classmate and later voluntarily confesses to you. You want to reinforce one act but not the other. How could you structure the application of the reinforcement so that the student would know what is being reinforced and what is not?

5. When teaching students to use a new and complex process, be sure that they use it at first in connection with familiar material. This familiar material acts as a form of guidance which keeps the student on the right path.

Illustrate this point as applied to the teaching of algebra; as applied to the teaching of syllogistic reasoning.

6. Two wordings are suggested for the title of a debate:

(a) Resolved that the nation's interest would be best served by encouraging at least 50 percent of the general population to continue formal education until the age of twenty-two. (b) Resolved that higher education should be democratic rather than aristocratic.

Discuss the advantages and disadvantages of the two wordings. Prepare a third statement which is an improvement on either.

CHAPTER 7

▶ The Higher Uses of Intellect

It is important to help the student grasp the meaningful relations and established principles that have already been worked out and which lie ready and waiting for him to make his own. But this is not the whole of thinking. After he has come to understand the geometrical theorem that is presented to him in detail, the student must also be able to work out an "original" for which no solution is offered. In a sense, of course, this is a spurious original, since the student knows that a solution has been worked out and is merely being kept from him in almost teasing fashion. To progress farther in the use of his thinking power, therefore, he should attempt genuine original problems for which there is no existing solution so far as he knows, or perhaps, so far as anyone knows.

PROBLEM SOLVING

In undertaking to solve an original problem we do not abruptly enter a new world. Many of the things we are required to do now are things that we have

already been doing when we undertook to comprehend a theorem or principle that had already been worked out. Even when the theorem or principle is clearly in front of the student, and when he has merely to comprehend, he often goes about this task by the use of a trial-and-error, or problem-solving approach. Suppose you, yourself, encounter Sir Frederick Bartlett's (1958) definition of thinking: *Thinking is the extension of evidence in accord with that evidence so as to fill up the gaps in the evidence: and this is done by moving through a succession of interconnected steps which may be stated at the time, or left till later to be stated.* Do you merely say, "Ah! Yes," and immediately feel that you have a grasp of the process of thinking? Probably not. Spend some time trying to get the significance of Professor Bartlett's statement and you will probably find yourself guessing, trying out one idea after another, and applying the definition to a variety of concrete examples (Duncan, 1959).

174

The squirming around that you go through in trying to grasp or understand a new definition is found in much school work. Observe a young pupil wrestling with the problem of $1 + 3$. He repeats the problem to himself, hoping, with some justification, that the answer may just come to him. He guesses, and finds that this does not give the approved answer. He changes the question around, wisely as it happens, to the more familiar form of $3 + 1$. If this fails he may resort to counting—a laborious and discredited device, but one that has brought success in the past.

Differences between Comprehending and Problem Solving

Along with the things that are common to the two processes, there are some features that are much more prominent in problem solving than in the mastery of a principle that is already worked out. Take the matter of orientation. In trying to understand the definition of thinking, you had little doubt about where to direct your attention. You also had a fairly good idea about the first few steps to take. In solving a genuine problem, however, the whole crux of the matter may lie in this problem of orientation. If you are lost in the woods, for instance, the key decisions might be, "What do I look for? What do I do first? Of all the possibilities in this situation, on what do I concentrate my attention?"

The problem of orientation is not our only worry. In solving a complex problem we can expect very little reinforcement or guidance from our early efforts. When trying to get out of the woods, you may pick one "trial" path and go for a long time before you have the slightest hint as to whether you are finding your way out or whether you are

actually getting deeper into the woods. In trying to understand things that have already been worked out, on the contrary, the reinforcement or guidance is more immediate and more definite. If your first guess is on the right track, you can usually see it, and can profit from this reinforcement. If the guess is getting you nowhere, you usually see that dismal fact fairly soon and are thus guided away from the unprofitable attack.

Finally, the teacher's part in the two processes is quite different. When you are trying to grasp the meaning of a definition, the teacher can readily take a very active part. He need feel no hesitation in offering all the help and guidance within his power. When you are trying to solve an original problem, on the other hand, the teacher must restrain himself. Even when he knows the correct approach, as in a textbook original, he must often stand by and let you

SIR FREDERICK BARTLETT

Fig. 7.1. When the search model is clearly in mind, the needed solution may seem to call attention to itself.

fumble around on your own. The essence of the task lies in your independent discovery.

As we have suggested, the matter of orientation is often crucial in problem solving. We must often make some effort to keep our attention on the problem. More important, we must try to select the key feature of the problem, and having done so, must again keep our attention directed to that key feature.

Strategies in Problem Solving

When confronted with a problem, we seldom make conscious decisions about which of several strategies or approaches to use. But the steps we find ourselves carrying out really do belong to one or another strategy, and the merits of these various approaches should be considered.

Relying on "Resonance". In solving a jigsaw puzzle you may form a general picture or *search model* of the particular piece you need, and then merely let your gaze wander over the various pieces until suddenly, for no clearly specified reason, one of the pieces becomes more vivid, or seems to stand out (Fig. 7.1). In real life many problems have been solved by this seemingly mysterious, unconscious "resonance" (Ghiselin, 1952). A more complete analysis, of course, may show that this resonance comes from more prosaic features, but meanwhile we must acknowledge that, to the people involved, the solutions to many problems emerge in this way.

Systematic Elimination. Theoretically, in solving a jigsaw puzzle, you could systematically try out each remaining piece for the particular spot you need to fill. Or, in playing a game such as

"What's My Line?" you could rapidly try out every conceivable occupation. This is a logical and sure-fire method. Fantastic as it sounds, moreover, it is a fairly good method provided each test or trial can be made very rapidly and provided that there is some way to keep track of the results of each trial. An electronic computer, of course, can often make hundreds of trials per second and can keep a perfect record of the results. Human beings, however, cannot make such rapid tests, and few human beings can hope to remember all the results. Consequently, whenever the number of possibilities is large, this method, however logical, proves to be far too cumbersome.

Guessing with Much or Little Risk. Since the sure-fire, but laborious, method of logical elimination is seldom feasible, we must ordinarily use some more risky strategy. We guess, perhaps conservatively, perhaps taking a great risk. In playing "Twenty Questions," for instance, you might proceed cautiously— "Is it in the northern hemisphere?" Here you get little information, but you are bound to get some. A wrong guess gives as much information as a right guess. On the other hand, you might take a greater risk, asking, "Is it in New York City?" If you are right, you get a tremendous amount of information, and at one swoop you eliminate a host of possibilities. If you are wrong you have gained practically nothing.

Of the three methods considered, fairly conservative guessing works best for most people (Bruner and others, 1956). Most people do better by using a series of guesses and by following one line of thought systematically until it pays off or plays out. People are especially likely to use this conservative approach when the going is tough, or when they have had hard luck in their more venturesome attempts. After a series of successes with this more conservative approach, however, many people become emboldened and try a more risky play.

We should be careful, by the way, not to judge these approaches by the labels given to them. "Logical" and "systematic" sound good. "Gambling" sounds bad. Unconscious resonance has a mystical connotation. But in problem solving, the strictly logical approach is often out of the question for anyone but a superman or computer. Gambling is often efficacious. And we owe many of the glories of civilization to something like unconscious resonance.

Making More Systematic Use of Strategies. It is true that few people ever ask which is the best strategy to use, or indeed, give any conscious attention to strategy. You may wish your students to become more sophisticated in these matters, however, and may wish to have them consider which is the wisest approach to use in the particular situation. To get a student to make a deliberate choice between strategies, you need merely ask him to tell you in advance just what his next move or next line of questioning is going to be (Ray, 1957). Few people, apparently, can announce a decision without giving some rationale along with it. Upon being asked what they propose to do, they seem impelled to consider reasons that are in line with the decision.

Using Trials To Secure Information

Often, when experienced people are trying to solve problems, they use up a few trials, not in the hope of succeeding in those particular trials but merely to obtain useful information. The gunner fires a few shots just to get the range (Fig. 7.2). The expert bridge player leads a card,

► *Getting the Student to Announce His Strategy*

Air force trainees were given the job of finding out how to extinguish a light bulb by manipulating a panel of seven switches. The successful solution called for the simultaneous manipulation of two switches. Each man worked at the problem individually.

There were two sets of conditions, each involving sixty-four men. Under one condition (verbalizing group), each man was told that before he touched a switch he should tell the experimenter just what he was going to do. If the experimenter was not sure about the man's intentions, he asked, "Exactly which one?" or "And what would you do next?" The subject did not touch the switches until he finished his comments. These men took, on the average, 7.3 trials to solve the problem.

The men in the second (nonverbalizing) group were not required to talk about their plans before working the switches. They took 8.7 trials on the average. The difference is significant.

Speed of reaching the correct solution is not the whole story. We might also ask whether the men made use of a wise strategy in their efforts to discover the solution. At the outset no one would have any reason to suspect that two switches must be used. The most efficient strategy would be to explore the hypothesis that one particular switch would do the job. At the outset this simple hypothesis would be just as probable as any other. It would also be a useful solution, if it turned out to be correct. It would be easy to modify or build upon if it turned out to be wrong. Finally, it is the easiest hypothesis to test. One need merely try one switch after another.

In their talk, 63 percent of the verbalizing group showed that they were using this most efficient initial hypothesis. By the time they got around to working the switches, however, only 36 percent of this group actually used the most efficient strategy. Even so, they were ahead of the nonverbalizing group. Only 20 percent of these used the most efficient strategy. These differences are significant.

SOURCE: W. S. Ray, Verbal compared with manipulative solution of an apparatus-problem, *American Journal of Psychology*, 1957, 70, 289–290.

not primarily in the hope of winning that particular trick but expecting to find out which of his opponents holds a crucial card. The army commander initiates a probe, not caring especially whether he captures this area or not but chiefly concerned with learning about the strength of the enemy in that sector. Each one of our problem solvers, of course, would be grateful for a success if that should occur, but such a success would be a secondary bonus and not the prime reason for the move.

Unlike the expert, you may find it difficult to adopt this cold-blooded, businesslike attitude toward your guesses. In extreme cases, you may stake your entire ego on each and every play. Each minor win is a triumph and a vindication of your judgment. Each loss is a crushing

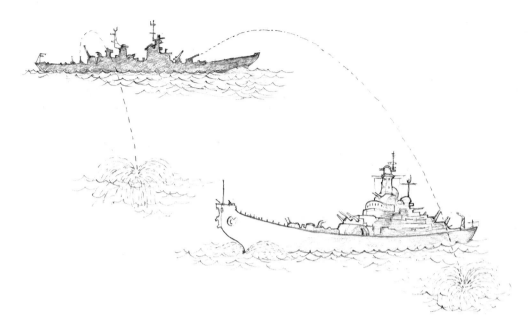

Fig. 7.2. Early trials are used to get information, not to achieve a hit.

defeat and a humiliation that you may be unwilling to accept.

You will do much better in problem solving if you can regard each guess or move as a potential source of information and not as a test of your ultimate worth as a person. If your mind is dominated by the thought that you are right or that you are wrong, you may fail to notice all the information that your move has brought you. Extreme ego involvement is especially likely to prevent you from making efficient use of your wrong guesses. As the game of "What's My Line?" progresses, for instance, you get a powerful hunch that this person is a member of a husband-and-wife theatrical team. You ask, "Are you related to someone who is prominent in the entertainment world?" The answer is "No." If you take this at its face value, you would abandon your hunch and move to a more profitable line of inquiry.

Being so wrapped up in your theory, however, you refuse to give it up. Instead, you try to convince yourself that you are still right, but that your respondent misunderstood what you meant by "related to."

Reducing Ego Involvement in Problem Solving. To get students to feel less ego involvement in each and every move, you should try to avoid any show of impatience in yourself as you watch them floundering around. This may be easier to do if you have a record of the time taken by previous students to solve similar problems. You could then base your expectations on these records and not on your subjective feelings of how easy the task is. To help the student even more, you can remind him in advance that the process will take some time and will involve many guesses that will turn out to be wrong but which can be used to provide valuable information. In extreme

► *Reducing the Worry About the Success of Each Trial*

From earlier experiments of problem solving, the authors were convinced that in solving problems, people give most of their attention to the success or failure of each trial. So much attention is given to this feature, as a matter of fact, that important cues, hints, or regularities in the problem are never noticed. The authors reasoned that their subjects would do much better if they could be led to follow a systematic pattern of responses and thus be freed from having to make a new decision for each trial and from having to worry about the success or failure of that decision.

The task consisted of playing a "two-armed bandit." At a signal the student could press one of two keys, left or right. One of these keys would release a token, the other would not. On some trials the key on the right would be correct. On other trials it would be the key on the left.

The students were not told that any definite pattern of payoff would be used. To bring about a regular system of responses, however, the experimenters had one group working under a condition of simple alternation. If "left" was correct this time, "right" would be correct next time. After some 49 trials, on the average, the 20 members of this group came to follow this regular pattern. For a second group the left key was always the correct one, and this response was regularly used after an average of only 6 trials.[a] These two groups with

cases, you may even encourage the student to pretend for a time that he is merely a spectator (Heidbreder, 1924). If he really could be a spectator, he would feel less emotion over the success or failure of each move and would be more aware of the information provided.

The General Problem of Wrong Guesses

In any difficult problem we can expect a large number of wrong guesses. At times, but not always, these erroneous guesses contain information that the astute worker may notice and use to some extent at least. In some problems, such as getting at the meaning of a new concept, a few wrong guesses, or negative instances, are absolutely essential. It is difficult to learn what *democracy* really is unless we learn some of the things that it is not.

But for all their potential usefulness or importance, we should not go to any trouble to arrange for wrong guesses or erroneous trials. In the first place, there are bound to be plenty of them anyway. In the second place, although they are useful or essential at times, there are other occasions when they contribute very little. They are likely to be useful when there are only a few possibilities to deal with. Your opponent has a five-letter word in mind, for instance, and you are trying to guess the word. You know it must contain one of the letters a, e, i, o, u, or y. Since there are only six possibilities, a few wrong guesses, five at the most, can solve this part of the problem for you. Wrong guesses are less useful when there are a great many possibilities of error. Imagine trying to give a person an idea of democracy merely by having him learn *all* the things that it is not!

definite response patterns were now given a purely random series in which it would be impossible to predict the correct sequence. A control group also took this random series. After the random series, the two definite-response-pattern groups and the control group encountered a patterned series of left-right payoffs. This, of course, was precisely the pattern that one group had adopted prior to the random trials, and this group mastered this final pattern in 8.0 trials. For the second group, however, this final pattern differed from the one originally developed. Nevertheless, the members of this group mastered the different pattern in only 9.5 trials. The controls, who had never been induced to adopt a regular pattern, required 17 trials. This was significantly greater than either of the other scores.

The experimenters conclude that a systematic pattern of responses prevents people from getting all disturbed about each and every response and enables them to concentrate on other aspects of the problem (looking for regularities or cues). This is true even when the systematic pattern used happens to be at odds with the one that must be mastered.

[a] A third group was used but the results are not included in this brief abstract.

SOURCE: Jacqueline J. Goodnow and T. F. Pettigrew. Some sources of difficulty in solving simple problems, *Journal of Experimental Psychology*, 1956, **51**, 385–392.

Finally, it is the rare person who can make very efficient use of the valuable wrong guesses that do occur. Extreme ego involvement, as we have seen, may actually prevent us from realizing that our guess is in error. And even when we do admit that the guess is wrong, it is difficult to be strictly logical about the matter. Suppose you are looking for a misplaced key. You look in one drawer and convince yourself that it is not there. You make other guesses or trials and find that these are also wrong. Now, unless you are unusually methodical, you will find yourself going back to one of the places already eliminated. In this respect, our students are no better, and no worse, than their teachers. Over and over again we will find them making guesses or trying out solutions that, logically, they should have known were foredoomed to failure. Try to reduce this illogical behavior, but don't feel horrified when you see it. Regard it as further evidence that people seldom make the most efficient use of wrong guesses.

In general, since wrong guesses are sometimes useful, and occasionally essential, we should not be disturbed about those that are bound to occur. We cannot be sure, however, that any given group of errors will turn out to be useful, and for this reason we should not deliberately try to increase the number of wrong guesses or negative instances. We should, of course, give students more skill in extracting useful information from the guesses that do turn out to be wrong. This means more careful planning in formulating the guesses. It also means keeping ego involvement at a low level.

Sets and Their Management

Have a friend listen while you spell out m-a-c-m-a-h-o-n, then ask him how to pronounce the word. He should give

► *Sample Exercises in Problem Solving*

WATER JAR PROBLEMS: These are like the problem faced by the man who needed 3 ounces of water but had no 3-ounce measure. He did have a 7-ounce measure and a 4-ounce measure, however. All he had to do was to fill the 7-ounce measure, and from this fill the 4-ounce measure. He would now have precisely 3 ounces left in the 7-ounce measure. Look at the first illustration. You have 3 jars with capacities of 4, 10, and 3 ounces respectively. You need 7 ounces. There are two ways to get this. First, fill up the 10 and pour off 3 $(10 - 3 = 7)$ or, empty 4 ounces into the 10-ounce jar and then add the contents of the 3-ounce jar $(4 + 3 = 7)$. In the second illustration the solution is slightly more complicated.

Solve the remaining problems, indicating your solution at the right.

	Jars Available			To Obtain	Steps in Solution
	A	B	C		
Illustration (a)	4	10	3	7	$B - C$ $(10 - 3 = 7)$ or $A + B$ $(4 + 3 = 7)$
Illustration (b)	42	71	5	19	$B-A-C-C$ $(71-42-5-5=19)$
Problem 1	21	127	3	100	_____
2	14	163	25	99	_____
3	18	43	10	5	_____
4	20	59	4	31	_____
5	23	49	3	20	_____
6	15	39	3	18	_____
7	28	76	3	25	_____
8	17	43	3	20	_____
9	9	42	6	21	_____

TRIANGLES: You have 6 matches, each 3 inches in length. Arrange these to form 4 equilateral triangles each 3 inches to the side.

BUS STOPS: Try this on someone else. When the bus came to its first stop 8 people got on. At the next stop 6 people got on. Next, 4 people got on and 1 got off. At the next stop 5 got on and 3 got off. Then 6 got on and 4 got off. (Pause) How many stops did the bus make?

Turn to the end of the chapter for comments on these problems.

SOURCE: Adapted from Olga W. McNemar, An attempt to differentiate between individuals with high and low reasoning ability, *American Journal of Psychology*, 1955, 68, 20–36.

you MacMahon. Continue with MacGill, MacDonald, asking for pronunciations. Now try m-a-c-h-i-n-e-r-y. You may get MacHinery instead of machinery. Such a response will come from the *set* you have developed by spelling out the "Mac" names.

Notice that the set proved to be both a help and a hindrance. The second and third names were easier to deal with because some set had developed. But the last problem was made more difficult. This dual role of set is typical. So long as the problems remain fairly constant, a very specific set may be most helpful. When the problem changes, such a set often gets in our way. Often the whole problem consists in avoiding or surmounting a natural set. Take the riddle:

As I was going to St. Ives,
I met a man with seven wives,
And every wife had seven sacks
And every sack had seven cats
And every cat had seven kits,
How many were going to St. Ives?

Here there would be no problem if the wording and the suggestion of complex arithmetic had not induced a misleading set.

Ideally, to be good at problem solving, a student should be able to acquire a set fairly easily and also be able to get rid of it quickly when it becomes a nuisance. Unfortunately these two things do not always go together. People who are good at acquiring a set are not necessarily good at breaking away from it. To be safe we should be prepared to help our students both in the acquisition and in the elimination of sets.

Creating a Set. Perhaps the surest way to develop a set is to provide the student with a series of problems all of which are solved by the same approach. Pronouncing the "Mac" names is a simple illustration. Such direct experience is not the only means, however. In one classical problem a student is shown two strings hanging from the ceiling and is told to fasten them together (Fig. 7.3). They are so far apart, however, that he cannot reach both at the same time. An ordinary clamp happens to be lying nearby. The student has only to tie this to one of the strings and thus create a pendulum. By setting this pendulum in motion he can readily solve the problem. Many things could be done to give him a set toward this solution. If, before coming into the room, he had seen a string and clamp lying close together he would be more likely to use the clamp as a pendulum bob. Even if he had not seen the actual objects, but had merely learned to associate the words "clamp" and "string"

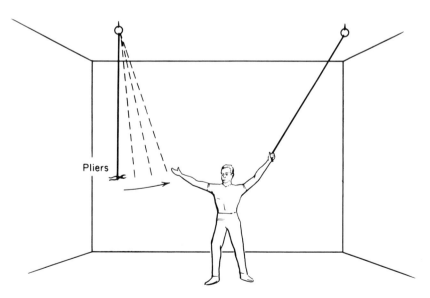

Fig. 7.3. The problem of trying to join the two strings. Adapted by permission from S. A. Mednick, *Learning.* © 1964, Prentice-Hall, Inc.

he would be more likely to use the two objects together in the solution of the problem (Judson and others, 1956). The order in which events are presented can establish the set. A student reads "prayer, temple, cathedral, skyscraper," and is asked to eliminate the word that does not belong. He is likely to cross out "skyscraper." If the order had been "skyscraper, temple, cathedral, prayer," however, he would be more likely to eliminate "prayer" (Judson and Cofer, 1956). Here, of course, he would also be influenced by his basic interests or drives. A religious student would be less likely to eliminate "prayer" no matter what the order. Set, in other words, is also affected by basic attitudes.

All in all, it is fairly easy to establish a set. Sets are likely to develop even when the teacher has no intention that they should. A set will develop more quickly if you give many experiences and give them close together. If you want the set to carry over to a new experience, you should make sure that the practice sessions resemble the new experience. As you might expect, students will be more likely to develop a set if you urge them to hurry or tell them that they have only a few minutes left or otherwise subject them to stress (Duncan, 1959).

Obviously, if you wanted to avoid the development of a strong set, you would spread the practice sessions farther apart and would cut down on the speed or general stress. You might also introduce some variety into the practice. In the earlier example, for instance, you could spell out words like "machinery" early in the game.

Eliminating a Harmful Set. When he has to use a clamp as a pendulum bob, the student is handicapped by a set arising from his general experience with clamps. This interfering set, technically called *functional fixedness* (Chown, 1959; Duncker, 1945), could be made worse, if, just before encountering the problem, the student has been required to use a clamp for its customary purpose. If you wanted to reduce this earlier set instead of strengthening it, you could ask the student to list all the uses to which a clamp might be put. In thus thinking of unorthodox uses, he might partially break away from a set toward a single use (Staats, 1957). On some occasions, a very general admonition such as, "Don't be blind!" has helped students avoid a harmful set which had just been built up.

To help the student get rid of a harmful set, we should, of course, avoid stress (Stevenson and Zigler, 1957) or any emphasis on speed. Such an emphasis is likely to reinstate an old set which is just about to be given up.

A Set to Break a Set. It is true that much of problem solving consists in breaking away from a harmful set. But we might give the student a governing set to help him in this (Bloom and Broder, 1950). With some guidance, for instance, he might develop "a set to break a set," or might learn to be on the watch for the possibility of a misleading set. After considerable experience he may regularly say to himself, "Is there some other way of looking at this? What things am I taking for granted? Should some of these be questioned?"

Some Useful General Sets. As part of the general set, we may try to get the student to adopt a general problem-solving attitude in which he tells himself that he can expect a period devoid of success, that the failures should not be regarded as evidence of stupidity, but should be used as possible sources of information, and that in spite of the initial failures, final success is to be expected.

It would be useful, by the way, if,

► *Correlates of Skill in Problem Solving*

A test of reasoning ability, judged to cover the abilities needed in problem solving, was given to 308 men and 180 women registered for college courses in psychology.

The average score for the men was 39.4, for the women 32.7. The difference is significant.

The upper 15 percent of the men and the upper 15 percent of the women were selected as a high-reasoning group, whereas the lowest 15 percent for each sex constituted the low-reasoning group. All students in both groups were given word-association tests. These tests were administered to groups of four or five. For all these tests, the students were told to write as many associations as possible, not worrying about handwriting or spelling.

Type of Task	Score of High-reasoning	Score of Low-reasoning	P-values of Difference
1. Write as many words as possible: just any words will do	67.6	66.6	.6
2. Write as many words as possible that begin with the letter "P"	36.2	33.4	.006
3. Write as many words as you can which *begin* with "S" and *end* with "L"	11.0	8.7	.0002
4. Write as many words as you can which have about the same meaning as this word ———: (Repeated for a total of eight stimulus words)	43.6	37.6	.00003
5. Write the word "pearls" as often as you can (three minutes)	82.3	86.1	.01

Any P-value of .01 or *less* is considered significant; the lower the value, the greater the significance.

SOURCE: Olga W. McNemar, An attempt to differentiate between individuals with high and low reasoning ability, *American Journal of Psychology*, 1955, 68, 20–36.

as part of this general set, students could be induced to include more and more experiences under the head of problem solving. Matters which they often regard as evils to be borne in silence, or as items to be complained about, might better be considered as problems to be solved.

Individual Differences in Problem Solving

Those who are good at problem solving differ from those who are less successful in several ways (Harootunian and Tate, 1960). As we might expect, the people good at problem solving are more intelligent. But this is not the only factor. A group of people all having an IQ of 140, for instance, would exhibit a wide range of ability to solve problems. The boys would be somewhat better than the girls (Duncan, 1959, pp. 412–413). The more masculine minded of the girls would be better than the more feminine girls (Milton, 1957). Those good at problem solving would be no more fluent in giving out strings of words in general, but would do better in rapidly listing a large number of words having some special feature, words all beginning with "w," for instance, or words relating to oceans. The good problem solver would not necessarily be blessed with more information about the problem, but would be better in sorting out the relevant from the useless information. The successful students would probably be no better in the rapid acquisition of a set, but would be better in breaking away from a set that proved to be a hindrance (Duncan, 1959; McNemar, 1955). In some cases those good at problem solving may be somewhat more negative, obstreperous, and less conforming or docile. This may be a factor in the superiority of boys over girls in problem solving.

The Teaching of Problem Solving: Resumé

In setting out to teach problem solving we must not expect miracles. Some systematic attempts in this work have drawn blanks, and some others have had to be content with moderate success. A few, fortunately, have shown favorable results (Duncan, 1959, p. 401), and this hope of probable success makes the effort worthwhile. A very slight gain in the arts of discovery, even if experienced by only a few, would be worth the time, the effort (Rosenbloom, 1959), and the ingenuity demanded.

From the evidence presented, it would seem that students should increase their skill in solving problems if they could be lead to make more conscious use of strategies; to plan their probes with a view to collecting information; to make use of the information that does become available from their efforts, especially from the efforts that fail; to try to keep ego involvement within reasonable bounds; to be on the lookout for misleading sets and for the chance to break a prevailing set.

Arranging for Early Success. We can often do something to speed up the appearance of the first successful response. True enough, this is something we should not overdo. As is pointed out in Chapter 6, perhaps some uncertainty is necessary or helpful for the successful solution of a problem. Too prompt a solution may close the mind to a host of useful alternatives. But for many students this is not a serious problem. Typically we face little worry that our students will be too precipitous in coming up with a reinforceable response. For the most part our problem will be to get the pupil started on that series of successful performances from which an increase in skill may follow.

To promote early success in problem solving we should, first of all, try to use familiar materials (Fig. 7.4). Success would be more likely with a jigsaw presenting a familiar scene than one portraying a bizarre or strange design. The familiar material provides useful guidance and makes it easy for the student to know immediately whether a given move is right or wrong.

Typically, students are more likely to succeed in problems dealing with concrete materials than with highly abstract concepts (Duncan, 1959, p. 408). It is easier to figure out if this man's occupation is steam fitting or accounting than

Fig. 7.4. Familiar material makes the problem easier to solve.

it is to discover if this particular x is in the class of x_1 that includes x_2. When dealing with concrete matters, we are often warned immediately when we begin to consider ridiculous possibilities.

Naturally it helps in problem solving if the central problem stands out clearly and does not have to be selected or separated from a mass of irrelevant or distracting items. At the start, too, a simple problem is to be preferred to one that is more complex or which asks the student to solve two or more problems at the same time (Anderson, 1957).

These aids, of course, are to be stressed when the student first encounters

problems or attacks some new area. To continue such aids indefinitely would be to defeat many of our objectives in teaching problem solving. We hope that ultimately our student will be able to deal effectively with unfamiliar material, to isolate the nub of the problem from a mass of irrelevant material, to tackle complex problems, and to be at home with problems that are presented largely in abstract or symbolic form.

CRITICAL THINKING

In different discussions, and even in formal tests, you will find that critical thinking means many different things (Ennis, 1962; Rust, 1960). At times it is used to include almost any thinking that the student does on his own or any careful use of logic (Dressel, 1955). In this section we will concentrate on one limited aspect of critical thinking, namely, the tendency, or *set*, to adopt a cautious, questioning attitude. We have in mind the tendency to ask, "How do we know?" "What are the facts in this case?" "What are the reasons for coming to this conclusion?" These are the questions that the student will ask himself when he has acquired some skill in critical thinking (Smith, B. O., 1960b). He is especially likely to ask such questions when he encounters important or significant claims (Henderson, 1958).

Keeping Critical Tendencies within Bounds

Obviously you could go too far in developing this set. You don't want to reduce yourself to a quivering mass of indecision. Nor do you want to let this doubting-Thomas attitude prevent you from becoming a congenial companion when circumstances call for sociability rather than serious decisions. In practical matters, moreover, you must usually take it for granted that the staircase will bear your weight, or that the food you are about to swallow will prove edible. In matters of great moment, too, you must often accept unquestioningly the sincerity of your lover's admiration, or the truth of some religious doctrine.

To protect us against the excesses of critical thinking there are built-in restraints. Many people find it most uncongenial to have to stop and ask for evidence, or for factual data, when they are all "set" to buy the new car or to make some other important decision. Here, of course, critical thinking is needed, but it is still uncongenial. Furthermore, critical thinking often makes us unpopular, temporarily at least. Many people become annoyed when asked, "How do you know?" or when told, "I'll have to wait until I examine the accuracy of your claims."

Removing Excessive Restraints

One of the first tasks in the development of critical thinking is to overcome the student's reluctance to use it. To overcome this reluctance we might do well to reassure him that critical thinking is called for only in a limited number of situations, but is most important in these cases. The fear of being surly or insolent can be reduced through the use of debates and mock trials in which the game calls for challenge and for an attack on the other fellow's logic. In real life, you can often find some simple method to reduce the emphasis on personal attack and to shift the attention to the objective problem to be solved. Instead of saying, in effect, "I want to see if *you* are a competent workman," you can properly say, and think, "I want

to see if this product will meet my particular (peculiar) needs."

An Illustration

The procedures for critical thinking vary from one area to another. The detailed procedures which serve well in buying a house might not apply in analyzing political arguments. To be sure of having an example that is common ground for teachers of varying specialties, we turn to a problem in child development.

A psychiatrist interviewed some 300 children all of whom were known to have some serious neurotic symptoms. He found that 35 percent of these neurotic children were addicted to horror stories in movies, television, or comics. Now we may be tempted to conclude from this evidence that excessive exposure to such horror stories induces neuroticism in a fair number of children. This is plausible and in line with our general notions. But we would show a serious lack of critical thinking if we immediately reached such a conclusion on the basis of this evidence. There are a number of important questions that we should raise.

First of all, the earnest critic will ask himself about some preliminary general matters. He would want to know the basis for selecting these 300 children, the definition of an addict, the chance that this was just a "freak" sample, and so forth. But these are general and preliminary matters. The heart of the problem calls for more detailed consideration. Our serious critic will want to know, for instance, what percentage of *normal* children are addicts of horror stories. For all we know, perhaps 35 percent of any normal group we came upon would be considered addicts if the same criterion was used. In that case there would be no

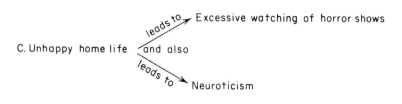

A. Excessive watching of horror shows ———→ neuroticism
leads to

B. Neuroticism ———→ excessive watching of horror shows
leads to

leads to → Excessive watching of horror shows

C. Unhappy home life < and also

leads to ↘ Neuroticism

Which is true ?

Only A ?   Only B ?   Only C ?   A and B ?   A and C ?   B and C ?   A, B and C ?

Fig. 7.5. Rival hypotheses regarding what is causing what.

connection between neuroticism and interest in horror stories.

What next? There are at least two possibilities. Many people would say, "If the investigator has not enough sense to take care of this important matter, why should we be expected to have anything more to do with it?" This attitude suggests that we are playing a game with the investigator and since we have caught him "out at first," we have won the game. But this is not a very businesslike attitude. Ordinarily we do not read the investigation because we want to be fair to the investigator. We read it because we really want to know the answer to his question. It is too bad that he did not provide all the information we need to help us get an answer. But he didn't, and we still want to know. So we try to see what we ourselves can do to take care of the matters the investigator neglected. According to this approach, critical thinking is not a matter of making a personal attack on the investigator. It is an honest, searching, critical attempt to find out just what we can safely conclude from his results.

In an attempt to get all the dependable information we can, we ourselves try to decide whether or not it is reasonable to expect that 35 percent of all normal children of a given age group and a given social group, and so forth, would be considered horror-story addicts. To answer this question we may even consult other sources of data. Suppose we do so and find that the figure for comparable non-neurotic children is about 20 percent. Suppose, further, that a statistical computation shows that this difference of 15 percent would be extremely unlikely (about one chance in 100) to come about by accident or some fluke of sampling (Fig. 7.5).

As a result of our own efforts, we have now taken care of our first important worry and we have found that our worry can be dismissed. But we do not stop here. We admit now that there is *some* connection between neuroticism and addiction to horror stories. But what brings about addiction in the first place? Could it be that it is neuroticism that leads children to be interested in the horror stories? This conclusion would seem just as valid as the conclusion that the horror stories lead to neurotic symptoms. Or, could it be that some other conditions—such as neglectful parents or too much emotional stress—lead *both* to neuroticism and to an excessive interest in horror stories? It may be that neither of these things is causing the other, but that something else is causing both.

So long as there are several rival and independent ways to interpret the same data, a cautious critic could not legitimately conclude that any one of these interpretations has been proved to be correct. At this point he could, as before, try to find ways to test these several interpretations or hypotheses. Until this is done, however, he would have to accept a degree of uncertainty about the results. Notice that his uncertainty is made up of a number of alternatives or hypotheses.

He now believes that the truth is either A, B, C, or some combination of these hypotheses.

In many ways, you are better off when you can express your uncertainty or doubt in the form of a cluster of rival hypotheses. In the first place, since there are several rival interpretations or hypotheses, it is clear that no single one of them has been proven to be true. Secondly, when you have a list of hypotheses, you know what to look for when you read or encounter further work on the question. Third, when you phrase your doubts in the form of definite, positive hypotheses, you will find it easier to decide just how plausible each is. Often, after expressing your worry in complete and unambiguous form you won't take so kindly to it, and you will then be able to reduce the number of hypotheses or

---

► How Much Do Teachers Stress Critical Thinking?

How much of the teacher's work is concerned with the problem of helping students think correctly? To get an answer to this question, Smith and his associates secured tape recordings of 85 high school classes. An observer was present during these classes to note relevant facial expressions or other visual cues that might help interpret the significance of the actual words. These records were analyzed into *episodes*, each episode consisting of a transaction between two or more members of the class. Typically the teacher was involved in these episodes.

Most episodes were concerned with describing material (25 percent); giving the correct names for objects or ideas (15 percent); announcing programs of activity (7 percent); presenting unexplained opinions (5 percent); or merely reporting what was in a book or other source (3 percent). Some 30 percent of the episodes, however, had a clear relation to the correct use of reasoning. Some 13 percent of the episodes were concerned with explanation or cause and effect relations. Another 7 percent had to do with the problem of making legitimate inferences from stated conditions. About 5 percent of the episodes dealt with evaluation and the factors underlying value judgments. A total of 6 percent involved classifying (including the justification for a given class) and locating similarities or differences between items.

SOURCE: B. O. Smith, Critical thinking, *13th Yearbook American Association of Colleges for Teacher Education*, 1960, pp. 84–96.

alternatives. Finally, a structured, organized uncertainty is just a more comfortable thing to live with than the vague infinite uncertainty of a simple, "I don't know." We are still in the dark, but it is a better dark.

Let us again urge upon you the value of this structured approach. First decide where you agree with the statement, and where, on the other hand, you feel some doubt or reservation. Express that doubt as a list of independent, positive, flat-footed hypotheses. Examine the plausibility of each.

Go over the points raised in this illustration and try to work out a similar set of questions that you can use whenever you read or hear about investigations or claims in your own field. After the analysis of a few investigations you will probably be impressed by the number of things that you formerly accepted on faith, but which you now consider to be open to serious question.

CREATIVE THINKING

Creative thinking stresses the kind of thing that is observed in invention or in the production of works of art. Like problem solving and critical thinking, these activities call for independent efforts, and for the discovery of something new. In creative thinking, however, there is usually the additional requirement that the thing discovered or produced should have some merit or should be prized in some way. In problem solving or in critical thinking, of course, this requirement does not hold. The problem could be a trivial brain teaser. Critical thinking could be applied to some formal textbook problem.

In creative thinking there is also more stress on genuine novelty. The student solving a problem may know that a solution has already been worked out by someone else. In criticizing a logical argument he may be aware of a completed criticism reposing in the teacher's notebook. In writing a poem, or in painting a picture, or proposing a new constitution for the United Nations, however, the student does not feel that he is merely redoing something already accomplished. True, he may later find that the melody he has composed or the device he has invented was achieved long ago. But he is not aware of this while he is working on his project.

Typical Stages in Creative Thinking

There are a few typical stages which are reported over and over again by those known for their creative achievements (Ghiselin, 1954; Patrick, 1935). One of these stages is a period of *incubation*. When he first begins to work on a problem, the creative worker does a great deal of analysis, makes sure that he has a clear grasp of what he wants to do, and makes sure that he understands the minor problems that need attention. Then he tries to put the whole matter into the back of his mind to allow it to incubate. At this stage he gives it occasional consideration but little systematic thought.

With luck, the period of incubation is often followed by a fairly sudden *illumination*. A solution appears, often out of the blue, often in the midst of some other activity (Archimedes in his bath). We say that *a* solution appears. Unfortunately this does not always turn out to be *the* solution. After some *evaluation* the author decides that this ending to the story will not work. The inventor finds that the gadget he visualized has some bugs in it. When this happens, he must revise the solution or perhaps reject it completely and start over again.

Perseverance

Although the experience of illumination is exciting and encouraging, the other two stages call for unusual determination and persistence. Prior to the illumination there is the familiar problem of lack of reinforcement. The creative worker can see no apparent progress that might reward and sustain him. Confronted by such an apparent standstill, most people will give up. It takes tremendous determination to continue. Even more determination is demanded when the creative worker must ultimately discard the "solution" which seemed so promising when first conceived and must face another stretch of unrewarding incubation with the risk of a second false illumination.

To persevere in the face of an obstacle does not mean to concentrate our attention unremittingly on that single obstacle. Many poets, baffled by an awkward phrasing, will go on to other lines, leaving the awkward problem until later. An artist may skip over the part of his picture that presents problems and go on to the rest of the composition, coming back later to the section that gives trouble.

General Set toward Originality

Many people already show a set toward originality or modification. Some people find it difficult to copy a sentence in its original form even when it is important that they do so and when they intend to do so. Many people cannot be content with a furniture arrangement they have inherited. Along with this spontaneous set to improvise and modify, there is a general climate in our society which puts a high value on self-expression, originality, or do-it-yourself. Not only do we value the creativity which leads to discoveries and inventions that are genuinely new and useful, but we also value self-expression for its own sake, even if the thing "created" has less merit than something already available or is merely an inferior copy of something readily available. These widespread pressures from within and without should help us develop in students a set toward originality or creativity. It should not be difficult to show how society benefits from performances that are genuinely creative. It should also be easy to show the personal satisfaction to be obtained from the self-expression involved.

In all this we might try to maintain the distinction between acts that are genuinely creative and those which merely involve the satisfaction of self-expression. In creative efforts the phase of evaluation must never be neglected. After our "brain-child" has arrived, bringing the delightful sense of achievement, we must, if we are to be creative, coldly ask if this really differs in any important and useful way from that which is already available. In mere self-expression, on the other hand, we face no such obligation. Along with Touchstone, we can properly say, "A poor thing, but mine own." We can realize that our production is really a somewhat inferior substitute for something already produced, but we can still enjoy the fun of producing it. The thing we must not do is to regard it as genuinely superior just because we produced it.

Although the general culture provides strong support for creative activities, we must not shut our eyes to the fact that some schools, and some teachers, are far from enthusiastic about the child who is strikingly creative (Torrance, 1961a). Such children, with their individualistic notions and their fondness for an unconventional slant (MacKinnon, 1962) may readily worry the teacher whose chief responsibility is the development of traditional, conventional subject matter. If you yourself became firmly convinced that, within reason, you must foster creativity, you may even find that the conventional teacher within you will occasionally take a dim view of the creative outbursts of your students. In your efforts to cultivate creativity you will find much support in the general atmosphere and in the child's inner nature. But do not expect to find similar support regularly in your colleagues or even, on all occasions, in your work-weary self.

Developing Specific Abilities

As a result of their own urges and of the pressures applied to them, many students will be eager to do something original. We can best help them in this ambition by working on a few specific abilities known to play a part in creative work (Parnes and Meadow, 1960; Torrance, 1961b; Wilson, 1958).

Practice in Detecting Problems. People vary in their sensitivity to problems. How many important problems in your own field—education—can you list? Some people could quickly fill several pages with such problems. Others could think of only one or two. Similarly, we vary, one from the other, in our awareness of esthetic problems, or problems in design (the fact that this piece of furniture does not fit in); or intellectual problems (why do people have an urge toward originality?); of practical problems (a possible widespread shortage of water). Since awareness of a problem, of a gap, or of an inconsistency is often the first step toward creativity, you will want to help students see or detect such problems. To provide this help, you could give the students practice in answering such questions as, "What problems would arise if the ocean rose two feet? if you had to build a theater to use odors as well as sound and sight? if all insects were suddenly exterminated?" For each example, the students should try to list as many problems as possible.

Encouraging Ideational Fluency. Your students are more likely to come up with one original idea if they can think of many different ideas. The more ideas they can get down on paper, the larger the pool of ideas from which they can later select one that may be original. You might give students practice in such things by asking them to list all the different uses they can think of for a brick; all the different uses for a pair of pliers; all the different natural foods they can think of that might be found in a meadow; all the different things that might be done to reduce traffic congestion in cities; all the different things they would like to create. Use your own ideational fluency to extend this list. Before reading any farther, jot down a few additional problems. In your actual teaching, of course, you will also consult lists that have been thought up by other people.

Practice in Thinking of Novel Items. Look over the ideas for problems that you have just written down. Unless you are unusually endowed with the spontaneous urge to be different, you will find that the ideas that you first produced bear a strong resemblance to the illustrations that were provided for you. Ordinarily you will not come up with highly original ideas until the trite and ordinary ideas have been eliminated (Maltzman, 1960). To many theorists, this is the crucial point in the production of novel ideas. Keep people giving out one idea after another until they have used up all the customary, frequent notions. Then, and only then, will they start to produce ideas that have some claim to novelty. To speed up this process, you could deliberately rule out, or *pre-empt*, the familiar or traditional ideas that people ordinarily think of first. Give the students a cartoon along with several ordinary, trite titles and ask them to supply additional titles.

Practice in Improvising. Improvising often involves the breaking of a set. You can give practice in this by presenting problems such as the following: how to open a can without a can opener; how to draw a right angle without a square or protractor; how to move in a zero-gravity situation, the atmosphere offering no resistance (answer: sneeze, or take a penny from your pocket and throw it).

Mastery of Traditional Material: Pros and Cons

A student embarking on creative work may readily rebel when required to master the classical work in the field. After all, the overpowering need is to be original, and now the teacher is chiefly concerned with having him digest and remember what has already been done! But genuine, objective originality is an informed originality. It consciously pushes beyond what is already known. The great innovators, by and large, have been masters of the traditional material from which they departed.

There are several ways in which a creative worker can profit from a knowledge of what is already known. Unless he knows what is already available he cannot know what is really new. Only by knowing older forms, moreover, can he hope to combine those older forms in a new pattern. A knowledge of the traditional material might also help in the important process of eliminating the trite

and ordinary responses. As we have seen, we are unlikely to think of something new until we have exhausted the usual and most familiar ideas. Perhaps those people who are steeped in existing concepts have already, in some vicarious way, eliminated most of the ordinary and familiar items from the pool of their associations. Even when there are some trite ideas left in the pool, it should be easier for the sophisticated person to get rid of these in one or two well-organized packages. He can then quickly get on with the uphill job of producing less familiar items.

Obviously, familiarity can be overdone. By spending too much time with the traditional forms and solutions, we could develop a series of sets from which it would be hard to break away.

Providing General Support for Originality

In most school activities, the student is asked for customary, orthodox reactions and for answers that can easily be obtained from textbook or lesson. In urging him toward creative work, however, we are asking him to think up and announce suggestions that are unorthodox, unusual, and elusive. It would be natural if he should need a great deal of support in this unfamiliar activity (Buzzeli and others, 1959). To provide this support, first of all, help the student to realize that he as a person is not on trial. His acceptance as a person is assured no matter what he says. Second, make sure he understands that, in this activity, individuality and individual differences are valued. The pressure toward conformity should be eliminated as far as possible. Third, in contrast to the usual situation, criticism should be ruled out during the actual production of ideas

Fig. 7.6. The innovator is often a master of the traditional. Left, *Portrait of Gertrude Stein*, Pablo Picasso, 1906. The Metropolitan Museum of Art, New York. Bequest of Gertrude Stein, 1946. Right, *Girl Before a Mirror*, Pablo Picasso, 1932. Collection of The Museum of Modern Art, New York. Gift of Mrs. Simon Guggenheim.

or suggestions. Many years ago Samuel Johnson advised authors to "Compose in fury, and correct in phlegm." Get the words down while almost anything you write seems good. For some writers the attraction of alcohol lies in its power to lull the critical tendencies. Under these conditions, many ideas otherwise destined to die at birth may at least be given a hearing.

After ideas have been safely committed to paper or otherwise recorded, it is necessary, of course, to turn on the critical facilities and correct in cold blood. Now, every idea must pass severe scrutiny before it can be preserved.

A group version of this procedure is seen in the process of brainstorming (Parnes and Meadow, 1959). A problem is presented. Suggestions are invited. The call is for as many suggestions as pos-sible, and for as many novel or original suggestions as possible. The more off-beat the better. During this phase, no one is permitted to offer an objection or even to make a questioning grimace. Everything is enthusiastically accepted. You are encouraged to elaborate on your neighbor's weird idea, to extend it, to build it up, but you must never restrict it or tone it down. Here the elimination of the trite and familiar is speeded up by group action. Novel ideas thus appear sooner, and these are written down or otherwise captured. When this is safely accomplished the grim business of evaluation begins. Even here, however, the process should be as impersonal as possible. The person whose idea is finally rejected should not feel inhibited on the next occasion. This danger is less serious, of course, if the brainstorming period

► *Using the Brainstorming Technique in Teaching Creativity*

College students were asked to think of all the possible uses for an ordinary wire coat hanger or for a broom. Half of the students (26) worked on the hanger problem first and the other 26 worked on the broom problem first. At each session, and for each problem, half the students were given "brainstorming" instructions. According to these instructions they were urged to list *all* ideas that occurred to them and to forget about the quality of the idea. When thinking of the ideas they were to make no attempt to evaluate. The other students were told to list all the *good* ideas they could think of. They were told that they would be scored by the total number of good ideas.

The arrangements were rotated so that the student who worked on the broom problem using brainstorming instructions during the first session would work on the hanger problem under "quality" instructions in the next session. Similarly, all students would shift to a different problem and to a different set of instructions from the first to the second session.

Each student worked individually and was allowed five minutes to write down all his ideas. Each idea written down was later rated for its uniqueness and for its usefulness, and the scores for each idea were combined into a total rating. In assigning a score, the rater had no knowledge as to which group the idea came from. Ideas getting a total rating of 5 out of a possible 6 were classified as "good."

During the first session the brainstorming people (involving people working on both problems) produced an average of 3.7 "good" ideas. Those working under quality instructions produced 3.0 "good" ideas. For the second session, those who changed to brainstorming instructions boosted their average to 4.8. Those who changed from brainstorming to quality instructions dropped to an average of 2.0. Lumping both sessions together, the brainstorming instructions brought out 4.3 good ideas, and the quality instructions 2.5. These latter differences are significant at the .001 level.

SOURCE: S. J. Parnes and A. Meadow, Effects of "brainstorming" instructions on creative problem solving by trained and untrained subjects, *Journal of Educational Psychology*, 1959, 50, 171–176.

has been successful in producing a number of fantastic ideas. In that case, everyone will see most of his ideas rejected in the evaluation session, and nobody should feel conspicuous just because some of his ideas failed to pass the test.

SUMMARY

Although similar to ordinary learning in some ways, problem solving presents more difficulties in the way of orientation, provides little reinforcement for early efforts, and requires the teacher to withhold guidance. In solving problems we may choose to rely largely on resonance or may resort to systematic elimination of each possibility. The most reasonable course, however, is a program of guessing so arranged that each guess, right or wrong, brings a moderate amount of information. Beginners are seldom aware of the strategy that they actually do use and are often unlikely to make effective use of the information that is produced by each probe. They are particularly likely to overlook the information produced by faulty guesses. This is especially true when people are highly ego involved and thus deflated by an error.

Sets play a great part in problem solving. At times success hinges on the rapid acquisition of a set. More often, however, the crucial point is the breaking of a prevailing set. A set can be engendered by sheer association of ideas or other suggestions. At times it can be broken by establishing a counter set toward variability or toward looking at many possibilities. In teaching the art of problem solving we face the problem of getting some reinforceable or successful responses *reasonably* early in the game. (They should not come *too* early.) We can provide some guidance at the outset by using familiar subject matter involving concrete materials in which the crux of the problem stands out fairly clearly.

Success in problem solving is related to intelligence, masculinity, ideational fluency that involves some restriction, and to the ability to break a set.

By critical thinking we refer to the tendency toward critical scrutiny of serious statements encountered. This has an important, but restricted, place in the life of the student. When possible, the student should be encouraged to structure his criticisms. He should show exactly where his hesitations or doubts begin, and he should structure these, in turn, as a series of alternate or rival interpretations that could adequately replace the interpretations that he challenges.

Creative thinking goes beyond ordinary problem solving in that it refers to a solution that has not yet been achieved. Creative work typically involves periods of incubation, illumination, evaluation, and, so very frequently, a repetition of the whole series when the evaluation reveals a flaw. This means tremendous but flexible perseverance.

In promoting creativity we can rely on a prevailing set toward originality in the world at large, but we cannot assume that all teachers will relish creativity in their students. We can give help in detecting new and elusive problems, in thinking up many diverse and novel modifications of traditional ideas, and in improvising resourceful solutions. To some extent novel creations may come from the exhaustion of the trite, and here a study of traditional material should help.

When first producing the awkward brain-child, the student should be encouraged to keep his critical tendencies in abeyance. Brainstorming has been used to accomplish this. Later, of course, the new creation must be exposed to the most ruthless evaluation.

SUGGESTIONS FOR FURTHER READING

Anderson, H. H., ed., *Creativity and Its Cultivation*. New York: Harper & Row, Publishers, Inc., 1959.

Bartlett, Sir Frederick C., *Thinking: An Experimental and Social Study*. London: George Allen & Unwin Ltd., 1958.

Duncan, C. P., Recent research on human problem solving, *Psychological Bulletin*, 1959, 56, 397–429.

Duncker, K., On problem-solving, *Psychological Monographs*, 1945, 58, No. 5.

Ennis, R. H., A concept of critical thinking, *Harvard Educational Review*, 1962, 32, 81–111.

Gardner, M., *Mathematical Puzzles*. New York: Thomas Y. Crowell Company, 1961.

Getzels, J. W., and P. W. Jackson, *Creativ-*

ity and Intelligence, Explorations with Gifted Students. New York: John Wiley & Sons, Inc., 1962.

Ghiselin, B., *The Creative Process.* Berkeley, Calif.: University of California Press, 1952.

Gruber, H. E., G. Terrell, and M. Wertheimer, *Contemporary Approaches to Creative Thinking; A Symposium.* New York: Atherton Press, 1963.

Humphrey, G., *Thinking: An Introduction to Its Experimental Psychology.* New York: John Wiley & Sons, Inc., 1951.

Johnson, D. Mc. E., *The Psychology of Thought and Judgment.* New York: Harper & Row, Publishers, Inc., 1955.

MacKinnon, D. W., The nature and nurture of creative talent, *American Psychologist*, 1962, **17**, 484–495.

Mearns, H., *Creative Power: The Education of Youth in the Creative Arts,* 2d rev. ed. New York: Dover Publications, Inc., 1958.

Mednick, S. A., The associative basis of the creative process, *Psychological Review*, 1962, **69**, 220–232.

Peel, E. A., *The Pupil's Thinking.* London: Oldbourne Press, 1961.

Rugg, H. O., *Imagination.* New York: Harper & Row, Publishers, Inc., 1963.

Smith, B. O., Critical thinking, *Yearbook American Association of Colleges for Teacher Education*, 1960, **13**, 84–96.

Stein, M. I., and Shirley J. Heinze, *Creativity and the Individual: Summaries of Selected Literature in Psychology and Psychiatry.* New York: The Free Press of Glencoe, 1960.

Torrance, E. P., *Guiding Creative Talent.* Englewood Cliffs, N. J.: Prentice-Hall, Inc., 1962.

Vinacke, W. E., *The Psychology of Thinking.* New York: McGraw-Hill Book Company, Inc., 1952.

Wertheimer, Max, *Productive Thinking,* 2d ed., Michael Wertheimer, ed. New York: Harper & Row, Publishers, Inc., 1959.

Williams, J. D., Teaching problem-solving, *Educational Research*, 1960, **3**, 12–36.

Wilson, R. C., Creativity, *Yearbook Na-*

tional Society for the Study of Education, 1958, **57**, Part II, 108–126.

Discussions of Creative Ability

Barron, F., Creative vision and expression, in Frazier, A., ed., *New Insights and the Curriculum, Yearbook Association for Supervision and Curriculum Development.* Washington, D. C.: National Education Association, 1963a, pp. 285–305.

——, *Psychological Vitality and Creative Freedom.* Princeton, N. J.: D. Van Nostrand Company, Inc., 1963b.

Coler, M. A., ed., *Essays on Creativity in the Sciences.* New York: New York University Press, 1963.

Golann, S. E., Psychological study of creativity, *Psychological Bulletin*, 1963, **60**, 548–565.

Guilford, J. P., and R. Hoepfner, Current summary of structure-of-intellect factors and suggested tests, *Reports from the Psychological Laboratory, University of Southern California.* Los Angeles: 1963, No. 30.

Hammer, E. F., *Creativity: An Exploratory Investigation of the Personalities of Gifted Adolescent Artists.* New York: Random House, Inc., 1961.

Brief Articles and Abstracts Available in Reprints

Barron, F., The psychology of imagination, *Scientific American*, 1958 (Sept.), **199**, 150–166. Reprinted in Morse, pp. 183–188.

Birch, H. G., and H. S. Rabinowitz, The negative effect of previous experience on productive thinking, *Journal of Experimental Psychology*, 1951, **41**, 121–125. Reprinted in Rosenblith, pp. 459–462.

Maier, N. R. F., Reasoning in humans, *Journal of Comparative Psychology*, 1930, **10**, 115–144. Reprinted in Harris, pp. 31–41.

Maltzman, I., and others, Experimental studies on the training for originality, *Psychological Monographs*, 1960, **74**, No. 6. Reprinted in DeCecco, pp. 287–310.

EXERCISES AND QUESTIONS FOR DISCUSSION

1. Start a collection of some of the puzzles that you come across in your casual reading. For each one, try to decide just what makes it a puzzle. Does it invoke a misleading set?

2. Arrange to play the "word" game with a patient fellow-student. Each of you selects a five-letter word having no repeated letters. You propose any five-letter word (black) to your opponent, and he replies "two," meaning that the word "black" contains two of the letters in the word you are trying to guess. He then proposes a word to you, and each of you takes a turn until one of you solves the problem.

After each attempt keep a record of (a) the information provided, (b) possibilities suggested but not established, (c) possible words to propose next time, and (d) the information that would be obtained from each possible reply to your probe.

3. Go over the things that a teacher might do to promote problem solving. Which of these would seem to be most useful in the type of teaching you expect to do? which would be hard to use?

4. Select some published study dealing with the influence of some factor (size of class) on pupil attainment and adjustment. Analyze it to show just how much of it you accept as established and how much you think is open to question. Express each doubt as a list of specific rival interpretations.

5. Prepare an outline for a talk on "Creativity in the Classroom." List both the opportunities and the difficulties that you see in this area.

COMMENTS ON PROBLEMS ON PAGE 182

WATER JAR TEST: Go over your solutions to problems 5–9. For problems 5 and 6 you could use either the solution you had been using $B - A - 2C$, or a simpler solution, $A - C$ for 5, or $A + C$ for 6. Did you notice the simpler solution when you first tried these two problems? if not, why not? After you tried Number 7, did you go back over previous solutions? How many solutions did you discover for 8? for 9?

TRIANGLES: The problem in this puzzle hinges on your set to use all the matches in the same plane. To solve the problem you must form the six matches into a pyramid, using one triangle as the base.

CHAPTER 8

▶ *Effectiveness in Learning*

In the previous chapters we have examined the basic processes by which knowledge and skill can be developed. But we must deal with a vast number of facets of knowledge and skill. Now we must ask how we can teach all these facets without wasting too much time, without placing unnecessary strain on ourselves or on our students, and without letting the many things we must teach interfere too much with each other. In these matters we are concerned with the problem of efficiency in learning. We also want to be sure that when the skill or knowledge is developed it will turn out to be useful in the future and in as many circumstances as possible. Obviously, a student's skill or knowledge can be used in future situations only to the extent that such skill or knowledge stays with him. We must, therefore, try to promote this necessary retention and to reduce the all too prevalent forgetting.

FACILITATION AND INTERFERENCE IN LEARNING

In some jobs we might undertake, the separate minor tasks have little effect on each other. We can drive one stake or picket of a picket fence, for instance, and then go on to the next with little fear that what we do to the one will have much effect on the other. Laying bricks is somewhat the same, but here there is a chance that the bricks just being laid might disturb the earlier work, or, in some cases, provide additional support for the work already done. In other jobs, on the contrary, it is almost impossible to perform one minor task without introducing side effects that may either help or hinder in other minor tasks. It is difficult to drive two or three steers out of a herd of cattle, for instance, without taking others along as well. We may not object to these others coming along, or we may want them to stay. If we want them to stay and try to drive them back, we may find that one or more of those we do want are also driven back.

In teaching, as in herding cattle, side effects are bound to occur. Some of these will be all to the good. They will be things we wanted to do anyway. This makes for facilitation or useful transfer. Other side effects may be neutral. Still others of these side effects may create conditions we do not want. In taking care of these harmful conditions, moreover, we may well undo some of the useful things we have just accomplished. Here the side effects make for interference.

The Interaction between Two Tasks

Look briefly at Figure 8.1. It suggests that in certain areas of teaching we need give little thought to the possibilities of interference or facilitation. In other areas, however, we find distinct opportunities to reap the rewards of facilitation. In still other areas there are serious risks of interference. When can we ignore the problem of facilitation or interference? And when must we give serious attention to these matters?

Material That is Highly Structured. Insofar as we have been successful in using structure or meaning in our teaching, we need give only moderate attention to the possibility of facilitation or interference (Hall, 1955). When we have succeeded in developing a clear-cut structure, each of the different things we have taught will occupy its own neat place in that structure. So long as this structure is the conspicuous feature in the student's mind there is little danger that the individual items within it will affect each

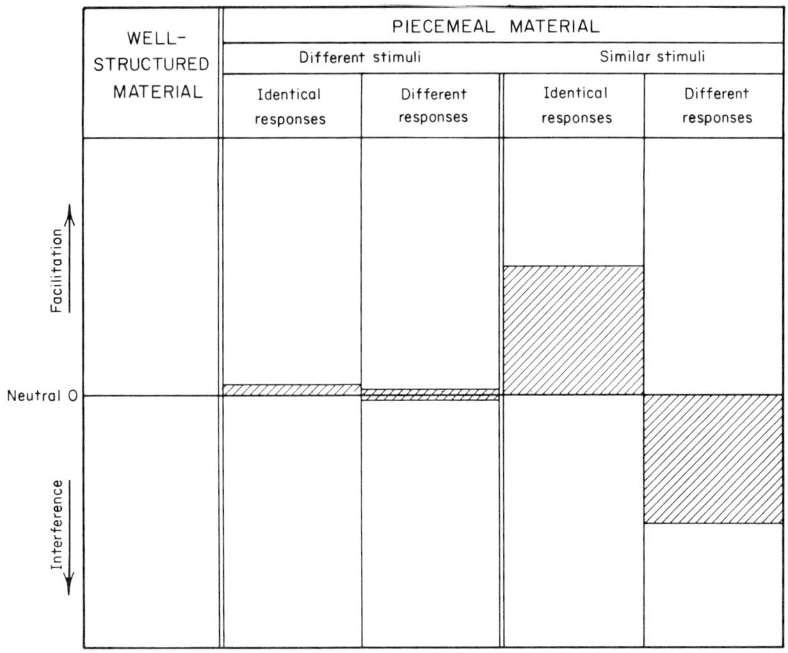

Fig. 8.1. Showing when experience with one task affects the mastery of another.

other in a worrisome way. If some new item disturbs the structure, however, as new items sometimes do, we may well find a reduced mastery of the things that make up the structure. If the new item fits neatly into the existing structure and helps complete it, the net effect will be an increased comprehension of the structure and of the items making it up. But these effects are incidental to the problem of creating and maintaining a useful structure. If we can really accomplish this latter task, the matter of facilitation or interference, although present (Entwisle and Huggins, 1964), is not especially important.

Piecemeal Tasks. As we have seen so often, it would be unrealistic to assume that we can teach everything in highly structured form. In the first place, many of the things we have to teach do not fit into any very impressive structure. In the second place, although we *present* some items in structured form, the student may actually perceive those items as an aggregate of separate piecemeal tasks. And in some, but not all, piecemeal tasks, there is the possibility that these separate tasks may have some effect on each other. Figure 8.1 shows when this is likely and when it is not.

The independent separate tasks which have possibilities for interference or facilitation can readily be expressed in stimulus-response form. Consider such tasks as $8 \times 7 = 56$; capital of Australia —Canberra; Water—H_2O; Canis—dog. Each of these tasks can be separated into something that we encounter (stimulus, question, problem) on the one hand, and some behavior that is required (response, answer, solution) on the other. To simplify the discussion we use the term *stimulus* to cover all the things we might encounter. The term *response* is used for any action that might be expected of us.

Tasks Having Different Stimuli. Suppose you had to learn the names of a number of people, as in a college class. When you see a certain young man, for instance (stimulus), you should respond by thinking, "Kenneth Brown" (response). Upon seeing a young lady (stimulus) you may want to be able to say, "Hilda Maxwell" (response). Here the stimuli of the two tasks are quite different and so are the responses. Neither of these tasks should get in the way of the other, nor will either be of any use to the other. In the same way, we need be little concerned about facilitation or interference when our students learn *canis* —dog and shortly afterward encounter $a^2 - b^2 = (a - b)(a + b)$. For tasks having such different stimuli and different responses there is little likelihood of an effect in either direction (Fig. 8.2).

It is possible that two quite different stimuli could call for the same response. Two young men (stimuli) having no resemblance to each other could both be "Mr. Brown" (response). *Canis* and *der Hund* could both call for the answer "dog." For both "$4 \times 25 = ?$" and "number of senators?" the proper reply could be one hundred. Even in such cases, however, there will be little interaction between the two tasks. If anything, each may help the other slightly. But the responses do not matter so much. So long as the stimuli are different, the two tasks have little chance to affect each other one way or the other.

Similar Stimuli and Identical Responses. In learning the names of a college class you encounter a young lady, and to this stimulus you should respond by saying, "Miss Perkins." This is only one of many such associations or tasks that you must master. Suppose your score on this particular task is just about 50 percent. Half the times you see her you

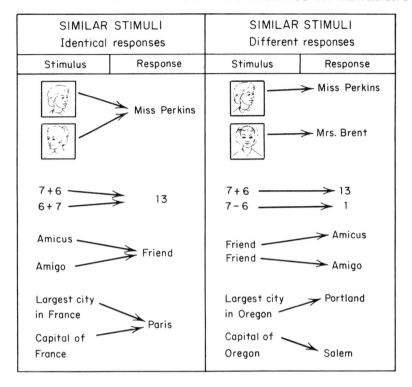

Fig. 8.2. Illustrations of mutual facilitation and interference arising from two separate tasks.

think of her name. Half the time the name eludes you.

Now you meet a sister showing considerable resemblance to the first Miss Perkins. In mastering this new task, or in making this new association, do you think the first association, with its moderate strength, would help or hinder? It would help. Your experience in trying to call the first lady "Miss Perkins" would help you to use the same name for the look-alike sister. This is an illustration of *proactive facilitation*. In such facilitation an early experience works forward to help you with a somewhat similar task in the future.

There is also a second kind of facilitation. What would be happening to the first association while you are learning the name of the second Miss Perkins? Before you met the sister your score in this first task was about 50 percent. What would it be after you had learned to call the sister by her proper name? It would be much higher. Your experience with the second task would work back to strengthen the rather tentative earlier association. This backward-working process is called *retroactive facilitation*.

Mutual facilitation, both forward or backward, is to be expected *whenever the two tasks have similar stimuli and call for identical responses*. In classroom work, for instance, the two tasks, $3 \times 4 = 12$ and $4 \times 3 = 12$, have somewhat similar stimuli, or questions, and call for identical responses. The two tasks *amigo* 'friend,' and *amicus* 'friend,' also have similar stimuli and call for identical responses. Each would facilitate or support the other.

Similar Stimuli and Different Responses. Life would be much more simple, and also duller, if similar stimuli always called for the same response. But as it is, our dog may be petted, but the similar strange dog must be given a wide berth. Mushrooms are to be eaten, but the similar toadstool is to be avoided.

Let us go back to the time when you knew only one "Miss Perkins" and did not know her very well. Now you meet a third sister, also resembling the first, but going by the name of "Mrs. Brent." As in the other illustration, she is one of many people you meet and you must make some effort to remember her name. Will it be easier or harder for you to call Mrs. Brent by name from having known the somewhat similar sister as "Miss Perkins?" It will almost certainly be harder. You would find it easier to call this third sister by her name if you had never known the first sister as "Miss Perkins."

This sort of interference in which early learning works ahead to hinder later learning is called *proactive inhibition.*

Interference can work backward as well as forward. After spending some time in learning to call this third sister "Mrs. Brent" you will find that you will be less successful than before in calling the first sister by her right name. This troublesome process goes by the name of *retroactive inhibition.*

This sort of interference is often encountered in the classroom. A pupil encounters the symbol d o g and must learn to say, "dog." Shortly afterward he meets d a y, which, to him, is exceedingly similar. Now, however, he must come to say, "day." Each of these tasks will get in the way of the other. The second task, d a y—day, will be more difficult to master because of the experience with the combination d o g—dog. The partial mastery of the first will be reduced by the experience with the second (Postman, 1961). The tasks $4 \times 3 = 12$ and $4 + 3 = 7$ also have stimuli that appear similar to the young child. They call for quite different responses. Here again we can expect each to interfere with the other.

Conditions That Augment Interference

Whenever two tasks have similar stimuli that call for different responses, we face the risk of some interference, both forwards and backwards. Such interference is especially likely when the different responses are *incompatible, easily confused,* and are *important in their own right.* Let us consider each of these conditions.

Incompatible Responses. At times, whenever one of two responses to a stimulus is correct, the other must be wrong. If "Mrs. Brent" is the correct response, "Miss Perkins," though forgivable, must be wrong. If "12" is the answer to 3×4, "7" must be wrong. At other times, two responses could be different but still quite compatible. We could think of the young lady as "Margaret" or "Maggie" or "Peg." These responses are different but one is not incompatible with the other. At one time the fire ranger may respond to the sight of the fire by calling "Fire!" At another time he may be required to press a button. Again these two responses are quite compatible. He could do both at the same time. Doing one would not prevent him from doing the other.

It is when the two responses are incompatible with each other that we can expect the greatest interference. When the two responses are compatible there may be no interference whatever. Indeed, in some cases we may find a slight facilitation (Deese, 1958, p. 223).

Responses Easily Confused. In some tasks, the different responses to similar stimuli are quite different. In other tasks, the two responses could easily be confused with each other. Your friend Jones, for instance, lives in Mifflinburg, and you

have formed the association *Jones-Mifflinburg.* He moves to Sacramento and you must form the new association *Jones-Sacramento.* Here the two responses are easily distinguished and you would probably experience only slight interference. Suppose, however, he had moved to Mifflintown and you had to change from *Jones-Mifflinburg* to *Jones-Mifflintown.* Here the responses are easily confused and the resulting interference could be very great (Bugelski and Cadwallader,

---

▶ *Response Generalization as a Form of Facilitation*

In all, 63 college students began this conditioning experiment, each student being tested individually. The student sat with his hand strapped palm down on a board, with the fingers resting on an electrode. The fingers could be raised easily. The experimenter sounded a tone to be sure that this did not cause the subject to raise his fingers. He then applied three shock stimuli. These separate presentations were followed by 130 paired presentations of tone-shock. By the time they finished these 130 paired presentations all but four of the 63 subjects were regularly raising (extending) the fingers as soon as the tone sounded. These four were not used in the rest of the experiment.

After conditioning had been established, the hand was turned over and strapped down so that the back of the fingers rested on the electrode. Now the only way to escape the shock was to flex the fingers. Then 27 of the subjects were given 10 trials with the same tone that had been used in the training series. The other 32 subjects received 10 trials with a tone one or two octaves removed from the training tone. At this stage neither group received any further shock.

	Subjects Tested with the Training Tone	Subjects Tested with a Tone Different from Training Tone
Percent of Subjects Giving No Response	7.4	31.2
Percent of Subjects Flexing Fingers	77.8	68.8
Percent of Subjects Extending Fingers (as in training trials)	14.8	0.0

SOURCE: D. D. Wickens, Stimulus identity as related to response specificity and response generalization, *Journal of Experimental Psychology,* 1948, 38, 389–394.

1956). To take another example, suppose you learn *fressen* 'to feed on' (horses feed on hay) and now encounter *essen* 'eat' (people eat bread) (Deese and Hardman, 1954). It would be easy to confuse these two different responses to the somewhat similar stimuli. Under these conditions we might get a great deal of interference. There should be less trouble from interference if *fressen*— 'feed on,' were followed by *fassen* 'grasp.' Here the stimuli are somewhat similar but they call for responses that can easily be distinguished from each other.

Responses Important in Their Own Right. Some responses are regarded as correct or incorrect regardless of the consequences. Calling a person by the wrong name, for instance, makes you feel foolish whether or not the person takes offense. Stopping at a stop light is correct, whether or not this enables you to avoid a collision or escape a fine. The answer to "3 × 4" is "12," no matter what might follow from this response.

Other responses are not important in their own right, but are merely incidental steps by which we accomplish results that really are important (Kendler and D'Amato, 1955). The specific response by which you sound the automobile horn, for instance, is not important. The important thing is, that by one means or another, you get the horn to sound. You may do this with your thumb, with the heel of either hand, or with a forearm. A few minutes later you may not remember which movement you used.

It is when the different, incompatible responses are important in their own right that interference is likely to occur. When each response is merely an incidental means of accomplishing the same major results, we may get little interference or even facilitation. When the rain starts coming in the car window, for instance, you rotate a handle clockwise and shut the rain out. You change to a different car and now you must use a counterclockwise motion to obtain the same important result. How much interference will you encounter from these two tasks, each calling for a different response? Probably very little. Sometimes one may help the other.

Reducing Interference

Figure 8.1, summarizing what we have just said, suggests that interference becomes a problem only under very special conditions. We face serious risks only when the material is made up of separate, unstructured tasks; and when these tasks present similar stimuli, which in turn call for responses that are different, confusable, incompatible, and important in their own right. Actually, however, we will find many school tasks that fit this seemingly narrow category. On second thought, this is not surprising. These tasks that are so subject to intereference are, for that very reason, difficult to master and they call for much application. The other tasks can be mastered with less effort or attention. Since the school is specifically charged with the direction of learning, it would seem reasonable that it should be made responsible for important tasks that call for sustained application.

However that may be, we do find within the curriculum many somewhat isolated tasks that have similar stimuli, "Sioux Falls; Sioux City" that call for responses, "South Dakota; Iowa" that are different but easily confused. Typically, only one of these could be correct for a given question, and its correctness is a final thing in its own right, not merely a means to some other end.

All in all, interference is a most serious problem in school work. Interference can be blamed for much of the difficulty we face in learning a new task. It is also chiefly responsible for the forgetting of material after it has once been mastered (Postman, 1961).

Develop Structure. It is when the tasks are separate and free-floating, so to speak, that interference is likely. If each task is conceived as an integral part of a larger structure, there is less to worry about. Even when we cannot incorporate the whole of each task into a structure, however, we can often work out some usable structure. We can sometimes connect each of the two different responses with its own proper structure. At one time the student must learn to think 'friend' *amicus*. At another time he may have to think 'friend' *amigo* (Fig. 8.3). There should be little interference, however, if the student has a clear feeling for Latin and Spanish as different structures, and if *amicus* is unmistakably a part of Latin and *amigo* as unmistakably belongs to the structure of Spanish. If a student can clearly see why the rule for multiplying powers differs from the rule for multiplying digits he will not let $3 \times 4 = 12$ get in the way of $a^3 \times a^4 = a^7$.

It may often happen, of course, that we cannot lay our hands on two different convincing systems to which we could assign each of the responses. Even here, however, we can sometimes achieve the result we wish by using the very inconsistency or paradox as the basis for our structure. "Since morphine quiets dogs, you would think it would have the same effect on other carnivores such as cats. Actually, however, morphine tends to excite members of the cat family." "You would think that 'ague' and 'plague' would rhyme, but . . . ." "From other constructions you might think that *ne que* means 'not only.' Really it means

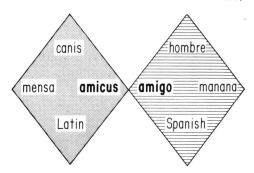

Fig. 8.3. Interference is less when the different responses are firmly embedded in separate structures.

'only'." In such instances the very discrepancy, which would ordinarily lead to confusion, can be made the basis for a structure into which the contrasting responses can be effectively fitted.

Spaced Practices. Although structure should be used for predictable and important sources of confusion, it is too much to expect the teacher to take care of the major share of interference in this way. In the rote learning that is going on, each student will experience thousands of stimulus-response associations, and the possibilities for interference will often differ from student to student. Clearly the teacher cannot work out an elaborate structure to take care of each possible case of interference.

To combat this random, unpredictable interference, it is often, though not always, useful to try to arrange for frequent breaks in the practice sessions (Underwood, 1961, 1964b). If a student is about to memorize his lines in a play, urge him to study in periods of not more than ten to fifteen minutes each. At the end of each period he could do one of two things. He could merely rest for a minute or so. Rest periods of this length accomplish about as much as longer rests. Or he could interrupt his practice for a longer period and use this longer time to study something else.

We might advise our student that almost any reasonable system of spacing his practices will work fairly well. If he wants to go farther in his search for efficiency, he should perhaps cut his practice periods down to the minimum consistent with the practical circumstances. A one-minute practice, for instance, might be quite efficient under some circumstances. It might be impractical, however, if it took him five or ten minutes to get his desk cleared of other material, to get the light and papers arranged, and to develop a set for memorizing. If he is to spend five or ten minutes in the incidentals, he might spend almost an equal amount of time in practice. When our student has worked out a practice period that is reasonable and short, he can adopt almost any convenient schedule of intervals between practices.

In general teaching, by the way, there are many times when we can use exceedingly short practice periods to great advantage. A lively one-minute drill could accomplish a good deal. By the same token, we can be grateful for the many brief rest periods that circumstances provide. In some kinds of learning, a rest period of a few seconds may prove very valuable. Students seem to have some built-in intuition of this fact and are very often able to work out brief rests, or brief periods of inattention, with little help from us.

In straining for further efficiency, we might ask about the best sort of activity for these rest periods. As far as the material being memorized is concerned, sleep would represent the ideal way of spending the rest periods (McGeoch and Irion, 1952). If this is impractical, some less extreme relaxation is helpful. If other responsibilities prevent complete relaxation, then the rest period should at least be free from activity that involves stimuli similar to the stimuli of the material being memorized.

TEACHING FOR RETENTION

The student's failure to remember one item is due largely to the interference from other learning. Some interference comes from the things he learned before he came across the item in question (Underwood, 1957). Additional interference comes from the things he learned after he experienced that item.

The student's failure to remember may also come from active repression of material that is unpleasant (McGeoch and Irion, 1952, pp. 384–389), uncongenial, or threatening to the ego. As we have long suspected (see Chapter 11), a person is more likely to remember things that are flattering or that boost his ego than things that are derogatory (Taft, 1954).

Extent of Forgetting

Whatever the cause, forgetting of classroom material is quite prevalent (Sterrett and Davis, 1954). As might be expected, there is marked forgetting of more technical and advanced scientific material that is little used in everyday life. In one study, for instance, almost 75 percent of college botany was forgotten in one or two years. There is somewhat less forgetting for material that we often come across in reading or in ordinary experience. Some studies report a drop of only 20 percent or 30 percent in grade-school history or introductory psychology (Benschoter and Charles, 1957; McKeachie and Solomon, 1957). This, of course, is still a substantial amount of forgetting.

► *Retention of General Psychology*

Some 35 students completed a course in general psychology in June and then enrolled in a course in educational psychology in September. A test given to these students early in September included 19 items that had been in the final examination taken the previous June. The average score on these 19 items in June was 14. In September, after a lapse of three to four months, the average score was 13.4. The score on these items before taking the course in general psychology was 10.3.

SOURCE: W. J. McKeachie and D. Solomon, Retention of general psychology, *Journal of Educational Psychology*, 1957, 48, 110–112.

There are a few bright spots, however. In the first place, general principles or other meaningful material may be retained with little loss (McDougall, 1958) or even a definite gain. These are the general principles which the student grasps thoroughly and which he may review over and over again in his reading and thinking.

In the second place, material that has been learned and seemingly forgotten is seldom completely forgotten. Even when it cannot be recalled outright, it can often be relearned much more quickly than when first studied. In one experiment (Burtt, 1937), passages from Greek drama were read, in the original Greek, to a boy of fifteen months. Seven or eight years later the boy memorized both these passages and comparable selections to which he had never been exposed. He took 30 percent less time to learn the selections read to him as an infant.

Material that cannot be clearly recalled or reproduced can often be recognized. When someone mentions the "Diet of Worms," for instance, we can at least remember that this is one of the things that we have studied. And even this modest sense of familiarity is worth something. In relearning this recognized subject we would feel more confidence than in learning some new subject that may hold unknown terrors.

Forgetting during the Summer Vacation. The facts revealed by the many investigations of summer forgetting fit in readily with our common sense expectations (Parsley and Powell, 1962; Stroud, 1940). When the skill acquired during the school year is consistently employed during the vacation, as in the case of reading, there is very little forgetting and there may even be marked gains. Naturally enough this is especially true for older children and for brighter children who do more reading anyhow. The summer vacation does less harm to meaningful material than to material that is learned by rote. Ability to solve arithmetical problems, for instance, suffers only a slight loss, although some loss does occur. Arithmetical computation, on the other hand, often undergoes a severe decrement. In one investigation, the summer loss was not made up until December of the following term. There is some evidence, by the way, that specific training at the close of the school year may reduce the summer loss in arithmetic. Spelling ability, like ability to compute, also decreases during the vacation. The loss is especially severe for the younger students who presumably make less use of spelling in their vacation activities.

Factors Affecting Retention

As we have seen, retention varies considerably from material to material and from one condition to another. Let us look at those conditions which affect retention and, in so doing, try to determine what the teacher can do to obtain a reasonable degree of retention on the part of his students.

Speed of Learning. In the world at large there is a belief that the rapid learner is sort of a "flash in the pan," that he learns quickly and forgets quickly. This same belief holds that the slow learner has superior retention. People often remark, "It takes me a long time to learn anything, but once I do get it, I never forget."

What is the truth about this hare-and-tortoise philosophy? If we take different people we find that the fast learner tends to retain things better. But the fast learner is also a better learner in the first place. He gets more out of a single practice than the slow learner. That is what makes him a fast learner. Consequently, the fast learner begins his forgetting with more to go on. He could forget more and still come out ahead. If we allow for this difference in original mastery, and arrange things so that the fast learner and slow learner start their forgetting at comparable levels, we find little difference in the rate of forgetting (Underwood, 1954). All in all there would seem to be no advantage in encouraging any given child to learn at a slower rate.

Meaning or Structure. Of all the factors which affect memory, meaningful structure is perhaps the most important

for the teacher to keep in mind. If the material is sufficiently meaningful, there may be no forgetting whatever. An important governing principle, like the old idea of the conservation of energy, may so help us organize the rest of our ideas that it stays with us for life. Content that is not so brilliantly structured, but which still has much meaning, will be remembered in proportion to its meaning (McGeoch and Irion, 1952, p. 383). Nonsense material is headed for extinction before the last syllable is uttered. Much of the advantage of meaningful material may come from the fact that it is better learned to begin with. There is some suggestion that when rote or nonsense material is as well learned as meaningful material it may be retained just as well (Postman, 1961; Underwood and Postman, 1960).

The more the student can be made to see the material as an organized group of large governing principles, the better he will remember. The moral is obvious; the practical application is difficult. Large (and true) governing relationships are sometimes hard for young students to see. And, remember, it is the student who must see or experience these relations and not merely the teacher. Sometimes the teacher may labor at relations or principles which are beyond the grasp of the students at their particular level of maturity. All in all, however, the gains from clear understanding and from a sure grasp of principles are so great that the teacher may well lean over backward to try to secure them. The steps that enhance meaning and insight (Chapter 6) are the surest guarantee of more permanent learning.

Motivation. The motivation that is present during learning has a marked effect on retention. Students who learn material under a high degree of ego-

► *What Happens When Motivation Is Applied after the Learning Is Completed*

The material for this investigation consisted of a 1400-word passage on opiate addiction. Two equivalent tests of 28 items each were constructed. During the fall semester a control group of 53 people studied the material at normal reading rate (about 8 minutes) and used the rest of a 25-minute period to memorize the facts and concepts. The subjects knew they would be given a test at the end of this period. They were also told that grades would not be influenced by performance on this test, although each student would receive his own marked test and would be able to compare his score with the class average. Two weeks after taking this test, they were given the other form of the test. They had no hint that such a follow-up test would be given.

Next term the same exercise was given to an experimental group of 44 students. These students, however, were told *immediately after taking the first test* that a follow-up test would be given in two weeks.

	Average Score on Immediate Test	*Average Score Two Weeks Later*	*Percent Retained*
Group Expecting a Follow-up Test	19.5	13.6	54
Group *Not* Expecting a Follow-up Test	20.1	13.2	48
None of the differences were significant.			

SOURCE: D. P. Ausubel, S. H. Schpoont, and Lillian Cukier, The influence of intention on the retention of school material, *Journal of Educational Psychology*, 1957, 48, 87–92.

involvement show a higher level of retention throughout than students who learn under more prosaic motivation (Alper, 1948). But it is the motivation that is present during learning that counts, and not the motivation that the student feels after the learning is over. After a student has finished his study it does little good to tell him that he should expect to be tested (Ausubel and others, 1957). Such a statement before he begins his study, however, may well increase his retention.

Overlearning. Retention is clearly affected by the amount of practice during learning. If we have spent much time practicing one set of material and little time on another comparable set, we shall find that our retention at a later date will be in almost direct proportion to the amount of practice.

For both teacher and student, it is important to realize that practice carried on *after* we have first reached mastery of the material is of great value to retention (Krueger, 1929). This additional practice is called *overlearning*. Overlearning, by the way, takes a bit of "selling." Students who have achieved mastery are reluctant to go on practicing. When a student has studied a number of foreign words until he has gone through the list once without a mistake, it is most natural for him to assume that the job is done.

He will not be happy about any suggestion of further practice. In spite of his feeling, however, he should not stop here. If he will go over the list many more times—even spending as much time after learning as he did before (100 percent overlearning) he will have a much better chance of remembering the list in the future.

Review. It is to be expected that review of material learned will aid in retention. Review may be of two general types. It may consist of a test in which the student is required to recall what he has studied. On the other hand, it may be a restudy of the material. We repeat here what we have previously said about the most efficient use of these two types of practice. Both types of review will help retention. Each method, however, has its own special value. Immediately after learning there should be a recall test in which the student is required to reproduce the material or to answer questions about it. At this stage, such a test will be more valuable than a mere rereading or restudy of the material, although the latter will be of some use. Later on, the test becomes less useful as an aid to retention. When as much as two weeks have gone by, it will be better to use the method of rereading or restudying in order to secure maximum retention (Sones and Stroud, 1940).

UTILIZING AND PROMOTING TRANSFER OF LEARNING

The interfering side effects of learning are important and must occupy a good deal of our attention. Fortunately, however, they are not the whole story. Some side effects are useful, and these we should utilize when possible and should do our best to foster. By taking advantage of the automatic transfer that is ours almost for the asking, we can help the pupil acquire information and skill at a more rapid rate and with less effort all around. By taking steps to produce additional transfer, we can make sure that the skill and information which he does acquire will be useful in a wide variety of situations in and out of the classroom.

General Views about Transfer

Transfer of training has been one of the more controversial topics in education and in psychology. At one time people expected fantastic things from transfer. Samuel Johnson is reported to have said, "If a man can walk, he can walk east as well as west." By the same token, if he can remember one set of things, he can remember another. If a man spent much time in memorizing Chinese words, for instance, this experience would be expected to develop some general memory "power" or faculty of memory. The memory faculty thus developed could then be used to help him remember any item whatever. By virtue of his experience with Chinese he should be more adept in remembering historical dates, telephone numbers, poetry, wedding anniversaries, or batting averages.

Such an extreme view was bound to produce a reaction. Some psychologists questioned the very existence of such a thing as general memory power, or a faculty of memory. They produced data to show that *not all* the gains achieved from the study of one thing (judging areas of circles) would transfer to a similar task (judging the areas of triangles).

Apparently it proved difficult merely to say, "There is not as much transfer as people commonly assumed." This rather moderate warning gradually became changed to read, "Transfer occurs only rarely." For many years teachers were warned not to depend on transfer but to take specific steps to teach every separate thing the students should know.

The excesses in the early controversy have largely disappeared. Only a few people still expect miracles from transfer (Trow, 1958). Almost everyone realizes, however, that some transfer occurs. Sometimes there is a great deal, sometimes very little. All learning and all teaching are based on the assumption that transfer works to some extent. As we move from one day to the next, or from one lesson to the next, there are always some differences in the situations facing the student. Yet we assume that in this new situation he will be able to make use of the material he studied yesterday or last month.

At present the serious question is, "Under what conditions does transfer occur and how can such transfer be augmented?"

Taking Advantage of Automatic Transfer

As we learned earlier, some transfer is almost bound to occur whenever two similar situations call for the same response. Having almost learned the name of one Miss Perkins, we were well on our way to learning the name of her sister. Having learned to say "dog" when he sees his own spaniel, the child, with no further teaching, will say "dog" when he sees the neighbor's terrier. Having learned to say "6" when he sees 2 × 3, he will require little, if any, additional instruction to say "6" when he sees 3 × 2. Having learned to say "house" when he sees the letters *house,* he will have learned, almost if not quite, to say "house" when he sees the letters h o u s e. When we have taught him that the *largest city in France is Paris,* we have

almost, if not quite, taught him that the *capital of France is Paris,* since for many people "largest city" and "capital" are all too readily confused. When we have taught him that this particular combination of winds, ocean, and mountains produces the grasslands of Nebraska, we have almost taught him that a similar combination produces the grasslands of Argentina.

Types of Transfer Frequently Observed

In view of the many forces at work to promote some transfer, it is not surprising that most investigations report fairly large amounts of useful transfer whenever people have looked for it. Naturally enough, the amount observed depends on the methods of measuring (Gagné and others, 1948). In some of these reports the teachers were making a deliberate attempt to induce transfer. At other times, transfer seemed to occur with little deliberate effort.

Arithmetic. In arithmetic it has been observed that children who practice only 110 of the 200 addition and subtraction couplets do about as well on the other 90 couplets as children who have practiced all 200 (Olander, 1931). Another similar experiment (Knight, 1924) dealt with the addition of fractions. Some 18 denominators between 2 and 30 were chosen for test purposes. One group of children practiced all 18 denominators. Another group practiced only 6 of these. Both groups did equally well on the final test using all 18 denominators.

Spelling. In spelling we find that children who learn to spell "reflect" have also learned, with no additional practice, to spell "reflects," "reflected," and "reflecting." There is also some transfer between words less clearly related. Learn-

► *Transfer from Language Study in High School*

Of 1647 entering students in one college some 953 had had no foreign language in high school, 148 had had less than two years, and 546 had had two years or more. All students had taken a scholastic aptitude test which provided a score on quantitative tasks and another score on verbal abilities. To reduce the part played by general intelligence, the records were sorted according to the score on the *quantitative* part of this scholastic aptitude test.

The information given in the table applied to the students in the top 10 percent of the quantitative test, to those in the middle 10 percent, and to those in the lowest 10 percent.

Amount of Foreign Language in High School	Average Grade-point Score for the First Quarter		
	Lowest 10%	Middle 10%	Top 10%
Two Years or More	.82	1.22	1.64
Some, But Less Than Two Years	.77	1.17	1.63
None	.60	.89	1.18
(A = 3; B = 2; C = 1; D or F = 0)			

SOURCE: R. B. Skelton, High-school foreign language study and freshman performance, *School and Society*, 1957, **85**, 203–205.

ing to spell "se*a*rch" may help a pupil to spell "le*a*rn." English spelling being what it is, however, we must expect some interference along with the very considerable transfer. Although "se*a*rch" may help with "le*a*rn," it makes for difficulties in spelling "j*ou*rney." And although "reflected" may help with "reflect," "excelling" may hurt with "excel."

Fortunately there is even some transfer from the study of spelling rules (*i* before *e* except after *c*). Rules are especially useful when only a few simple rules are taught and when these do not have too many exceptions (Breed, 1937).

Foreign Languages. At one time Latin was considered *the* foreign language. It was supposed to have tremendous transfer powers and was thought to in-duce almost all the intellectual virtues. Although these great hopes have not been borne out, it does appear that Latin can be used to increase a pupil's ability to spell and to read English words, and to help in the mastery of other languages. This transfer is more likely to occur if, during the study of Latin, pupils are deliberately encouraged to apply their new knowledge to aspects of other languages (Jordan, 1956, pp. 304–314).

Students who have taken several years of high school Latin or French get along better in college than students who have had no foreign language, or very little (Cook and Martinson, 1962; Skelton, 1957). The more recent investigators, of course, have been careful to secure groups of comparable intelligence, and with such controls we find that the students who take French or Latin are significantly ahead of their intellectual peers who take no language in high school. The superiority is most marked in college languages but is also found in nonlinguistic subjects. Although this superiority could not be due to "tested" intelligence, it is possible, of course, that it is due to some of the qualities that induced the students to take languages in high school. Such things as academic-mindedness or parental pressure may have led students to take languages and may have also led to superior college grades. These possibilities should be considered before finally accepting the very plausible hypothesis that foreign language contributes valuable knowledge, skill, or habits of study.

Science. Even when taught as straight subject matter, a study of science will bring about some increase in ability to use scientific concepts and facts in a functional way. Such transfer is increased when the possibility of practical application is stressed throughout the teaching (Babitz and Keys, 1939). As yet there is considerable doubt about the contribution of high school science to college performance in scientific subjects. The many investigations are about equally divided, half showing some advantage and half showing none.

Mathematics. There is some evidence that geometry, when specially taught, can bring about a definite improvement in ability to think logically about materials in other fields (Hartung, 1942; Ulmer, 1939). There is a suggestion that students who take a fair amount of mathematics in high school will perform better in college mathematics. This is true even when the influence of intelligence is controlled (West and Fruchter, 1960). So far, however, there has been no control of interest in mathematics, academic-mindedness, academic drive, or the like (Byrns and Henmon, 1935). We cannot tell whether high school mathematics actually helps or whether the high school course merely selects people who would do well anyway.

Learning How To Learn. Perhaps the most striking and important form of transfer is the development of a general *set* toward learning which results in learning how to learn. This has been shown dramatically when a monkey learns to solve a series of similar mechanical puzzles or problems in discriminating between similar objects. After much trouble with the first task, the monkey will stumble upon a general response, or approach, or *set* that gets results. With each succeeding similar task he will more and more rapidly invoke this general approach or response, solving the problem in much shorter time (Harlow and Warren, 1952). As with monkeys, so with pupils. After much wasteful movement in their early trials at problem solving, pupils will work out a more businesslike approach and will readily use this new approach or general response when they encounter somewhat similar problems.

Presenting Similar Tasks in Close Succession. Occasionally something studied now (*amicus* 'friend') may help in learning something else (*ami* 'friend') that is studied months or years from now. For the most part, however, such effects will be more powerful if the two tasks are experienced in close succession. Some of the factors involved are rather short-lived and if we want to use them we should make sure that the two experiences occur close together (Underwood, 1961). The couplet $3 \times 2 = 6$, for instance, is more likely to help $2 \times 3 = 6$ if the two occur close together. Whenever other conditions permit, we should try to promote transfer by making sure that the similar situations that call for similar treatment can be experienced close together.

"Whenever other conditions permit" —this qualification is important. Other conditions may readily upset our rule. You will notice that, naturally enough, the rule for using transfer is precisely the opposite from the rule for avoiding interference. To avoid interference between two tasks we should separate the tasks. To use the positive transfer between tasks we should present them close together. What should we do when the two tasks have clear possibilities for both transfer and interference? Here it is wiser to try to prevent interference than to try to take advantage of the opportunities for mutual support. When both mutual support and mutual interference are likely, it would be better to space the practices.

The possibility of interference is not the only thing that may make it unwise to present similar things together. You have taught the students how to spell "manufacture." To take advantage of positive transfer you could now show how the similar sounding word "fracture" is also spelled with this ending. But you may be more concerned at the moment with other features of the word "manufacture." You may wish to stress its relation to "factory" or to "manual" and you may well decide that this latter structure, or meaning, is more important than the gains to be had from the more mechanical transfer.

Emphasizing the Similar Features in the Two Tasks. Positive transfer is available when two similar situations call for the same response or approach. To take advantage of such transfer we must be sure that the pupil perceives the similarity in the situations (Fig. 8.4). Sometimes, of

Fig. 8.4. Bringing out similarities in the two tasks.

course, this is no problem whatever. To the infant, the terrier is clearly similar to the spaniel as, indeed, is the cat. To many pupils 2×3 is hard to distinguish from 3×2. By the same token "was" is hard to distinguish from "saw." For some other stimuli, however, the similarity may not be so obvious, and in that case something should be done to bring it out. Often the latent similarity can be brought out quite simply, perhaps by placing the

two stimuli close together *house* / house or

sometimes by a simple sweep of the pointer over two similar arrangements on a map. At other times the similar features can be stressed and the dissimilar elements played down, as in bringing out the common theme of two musical selections. By other arrangements of bold and subdued effects one could enhance the similarity between written and printed letters, or between comparable patterns of mountain, sea, and wind.

As the similarity between the stimuli becomes more and more obscure, more effort, of course, will be required to bring it out. We may have to go to a good deal of trouble to show that the altitude of a parallelogram is similar to the width of a rectangle, or to show that

$$r_{xy} = \frac{N\Sigma XY - (\Sigma X)(\Sigma Y)}{\sqrt{[N\Sigma X^2 - (\Sigma X)^2][N\Sigma Y^2 - (\Sigma Y)^2]}}$$

is just another form of

$$r_{xy} = \frac{\Sigma xy}{N\sigma_x\sigma_y}$$

At some point or other we will have to decide whether the gains to be had from natural transfer will justify the effort required to bring out the similarity in the two stimuli.

Transfer Values in Principles and Formulas

Often the feature that is similar in two tasks lies not in the similarity of the stimuli or in the similarity of the basic notions (capital of a country; largest city in a country), but in a common basic principle or rule (Hendrickson and Schroeder, 1941). Transfer is likely to be most effective when it is based on a grasp of common principles, or formulas, or rules. Naturally, we will get more transfer payoff from principles or rules that have many applications.

It is reassuring, but not surprising, to learn that it is in principles and meaningful generalizations that the great benefits from transfer are to be found. It is only common sense to suppose that the great universal truths, if thoroughly grasped, may enable a person to master many tasks for which he has had no formal courses nor any specific instruction whatever.

But there is a very worrisome catch in this reassuring truth. It is only those principles or formulas that are adequately grasped that are likely to prove useful in transfer. And the great universal principles are often quite difficult to master. For this reason we may get more transfer from a rather limited and inelegant rule which a pupil really grasps than from a much more complete principle that he can repeat but may not fully understand. In algebra we may get more transfer from the *mechanical rule* which says, "change the sign when you transpose," than from an ordinary understanding of the underlying theorem that when equals are subtracted from equals the remainders are equal. Over and over again, when working with average students, we get our most dependable transfer (Overman, 1930) from devices, rules of thumb, or from practical applications of principles. Figure 8.5, for instance, shows a graphic scale that you might use to help pupils grasp the time between events in American history. A pupil could readily transfer such a device to the study of ancient history or even to geology. Such transfer is also observed when a camper is learning to estimate distance across water. He learns that it is farther than it looks. He can now use this simple correction when he comes to estimate other distances over the water. The boy learning skeet shooting finds that he must "lead" the target. He can use this rule when he later shoots at ducks or enemy planes. In these illustrations, the principle involves a "constant error" (Gibson, 1953) that must be corrected, and this correction can be expressed in a fairly simple rule.

► *Transfer from the Study of General Principles*

This study attempted to redo a classical experiment on transfer (C. H. Judd, The relation of special training to general intelligence, *Educational Review*, 1908, **36**, 28–42). This older study has played a great part in discussions of transfer for over half a century.

Three groups of 30 junior high school boys practiced shooting at a submerged target using an air rifle. The three groups were about the same age on the average (14 years) and about the same intelligence.

One group, the control, received no instruction but merely shot at a target submerged to a depth of 6 inches. After three consecutive hits each student changed to a target 2 inches below the surface. Here again the criterion was three hits in succession.

A second group received a brief explanation of the general principles of refraction, accompanied by a simple diagram using a rock in a lake as an example. The boys in this group studied the explanation for as long as they wished prior to the practice.

A third group received the same explanation plus the following working rule: "It is easy to see from the diagram that the deeper the lake is the farther the real rock will be from the image rock."

In each case the score is the number of trials needed to reach the first of three consecutive hits.

Help Given the Groups	First Problem 6 Inches	Second Problem (Transfer Task) 2 Inches	Percent Gain
Control—No Explanation	9.1	6.0	34
General Principles Only	8.5	5.3	36
General Principles plus Working Rule	7.7	4.6	40

The only significant difference was that in the second problem between the score of 6.0 for the control group, and the score of 4.6 for the group receiving both the explanation and the working rule.

SOURCE: G. Hendrickson and W. H. Schroeder, Transfer of training in learning to hit a submerged target, *Journal of Educational Psychology*, 1941, **32**, 205–213.

Obtaining Transfer from Meaningful Generalizations

Following our own advice, we will present this topic in the form of a series of fairly definite rules.

1. Take into account the intellectual level of the students. A class of bright students in high school or college might obtain a thorough grasp of a broad and complex principle. Younger or duller students might do little with such a principle.

2. Be sure the principle or rule is thoroughly grasped (Duncan, 1953). There are several ways to bring this about. Some psychologists hold (Chapter 6) that you should have the children formu-

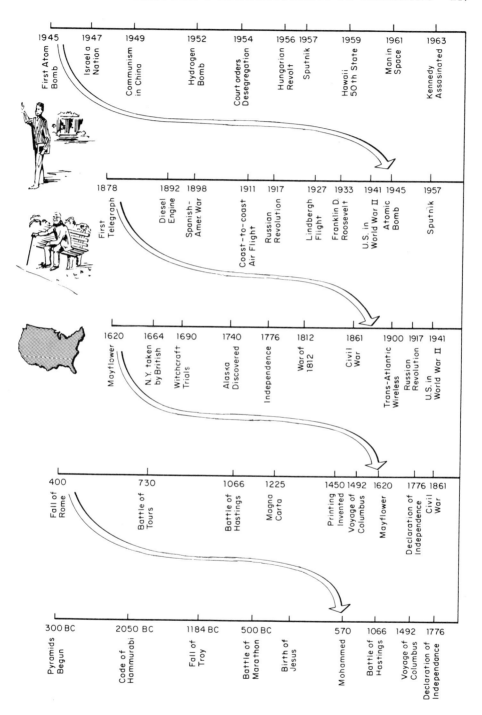

Fig. 8.5. There is transfer value in time scales.

late the principle or rule themselves. By providing appropriate examples, you may be able to get the pupils, for instance, to approximate the rule that winds blow clockwise around a meteorological high, or to work out rules about the polarity of an electrical helix, or about Congressional elections in midterm, or the sequence of *i* and *e* in English spelling. Don't expect these rules to be as complete or elegant as those found in the textbooks. Be sure they are not in error, but if you are chiefly concerned about transfer, tolerate a little awkwardness. An awkward rule that the pupil grasps will have more transfer effect than a more elegant rule not so well understood. Naturally, if your main concern is not transfer but a grasp of the more elegant principle itself, the procedure would be different.

To be sure of a thorough grasp of the rule or principle on the part of as many students as possible, you may have to settle for a more limited, concrete version of the principle, and give up your hopes for the more general and more abstract form of the principle. You may have to settle for "*i* before *e* except after *c*," and give up your hopes of deriving the rule from basic etymology.

3. After some work with the general principle, provide much practice in applying the principle to a wide variety of situations. After teaching about the refraction of light in water, help the student apply the principle to the problem of hitting underwater targets at *different* levels, to the placement of underwater lights in a swimming pool, and so forth. The guidance that you give in these varied applications should help the more able students get a more thorough grasp of the general principle. For the less able students, the entire transfer value of the lesson may reside in such guidance. From such guided application they may come up with specific rules ("It's deeper than it looks") that may transfer, whereas the general principle may not have registered. Having developed the idea, for instance, that, in adding, units must be added to units, tens to tens, and so forth, be sure to spend some time in guiding the pupils into the application of the principle—the importance of a straight right hand column, for instance. If you must neglect either the exposition of the principle or the guided practice in application, slight the former. To follow our own advice, we should give more space in this text to these practical rules than to the earlier discussion of the general principle of transfer.

For most effective transfer, this guided practice should be given in a wide variety of fields. If you want the logic of geometry to have wide transfer, give the students practice in using it in mystery stories, ethics, and puzzles. If you want him to make wide use of his ability in critical thinking, have him use it in the analysis of editorials, proposed reforms, or justifications for the status quo.

4. Develop a "set" for the use of the principle. Even when the student is capable of using the principle or rule in a new situation, is he likely to do so? To be sure of this, he will need to be looking for chances to use the principle. To develop a set of this sort, we should present him with problems in which the principle is useful, but in which its application is less and less apparent. Whenever he attempts to make sensible use of the principle, commend him. If he fails to use it, point the way to its use, and give him an opportunity to use it again on his own.

Relying on Transfer

It is assumed that we will make much use of transfer. We will use a certain amount whether we intend to or not. By taking a few pains we can use much more. But there are still some questions left. When we have a choice, for instance, should we always arrange for direct practice? Or are there times when transfer might be preferable?

Often, of course, we have no choice. Direct practice is not always available. We cannot provide direct practice in the use of an electronic computer as yet unbuilt to solve problems that have not yet been stated. And yet we may wish to have some competence developed by the time the machine is available or as soon as the problems are set. There are other times when the deliberate provision of direct practice is almost unthinkable. We are unlikely to bring ourselves to provide practice for children in dealing with intense grief or the full fury of an atomic attack. We would be reluctant to let the young surgeon do his first practicing on the live human being. For such early practice we might wish him to use cadavers or animals, hoping that a considerable amount of transfer will have occurred before he operates on his first patient.

To Avoid Costly Practice. Even when direct practice is possible and is morally justifiable, it may turn out to be enormously expensive. In estimating this cost we should consider the time during which the machines or facilities have been diverted from production and used for training. We must consider the time of instructors, the cost of materials used up, and the risk of damage to the machine, to the student, or to other people (Lawrence, 1954). At times it may pay us to have the student practice in a less costly situation and hope that there will be considerable transfer. Students needing skill in woodworking, for instance, can acquire some proficiency by working with less costly cardboard (Crofton, 1957). Through his practice in the less costly situation he may be able to start off on the more expensive materials or equipment with a higher level of skill. Or, even better, he may be able to master the more costly machine at a more rapid rate.

To Secure Valuable Concomitants. Even when the total cost of transfer is clearly greater than that of direct practice, and even when direct practice is feasible, we may prefer to rely on transfer for the sake of some concomitants not considered likely in the direct practice. Latin may be more costly than direct practice in inducing a mastery of English. In the minds of some people, however, this greater cost may be offset by the intrinsic familiarity with Latin to be had from the indirect practice, or by the feeling of kinship with other educated people. In the final assessment of the claims of transfer versus direct practice, we must also keep in mind the possibility that the attitudes or general approaches induced by the more expensive transfer may persist longer than those generated by direct practice (Woodworth and Schlosberg, 1954).

To Hasten Reinforcement. We may find it wise to rely on transfer rather than direct practice whenever the ultimate task is so very difficult that the student could expect no success whatever from direct practice (Baker and Osgood, 1954; Lawrence and Goodwin, 1954). A beginner plunged into the real business of wine testing, for instance, might never make a single correct judgment. Similarly, a rank beginner starting to operate a complicated power shovel on a fixed time schedule, might never load a single truck. In these cases there would be none of the intrinsic success or reinforcement so important in learning. For this reason direct practice might be almost useless.

Whenever direct practice is likely to lead to very little initial success, we might well use other tasks and base our hopes on transfer. This can be done in two different ways. First, we could simply use an easier version of the basic task. If a student is hoping to take shorthand at a rapid rate, we could have him practice for a time at a slower rate. During this easier practice a reasonable amount of success and reinforcement could be expected. The final gain from such a modified task would be much greater than the gain from practice on the more formidable genuine task (Lawrence and Goodwin, 1954). This is one instance in which we may gain more from transfer than from direct practice.

As a second substitute for practice on an extremely formidable task, we could have our student practice on separate features of the more complex task.

▶ *Does it Pay To Take Time Out To Differentiate between Similar Stimuli?*

A total of 107 pupils in four grade-six classes were given tests in spelling and in word discrimination. They were then drilled in discriminating between similar collections of letters, "up" versus "uy," "banana" versus "banona." In each case the pupil merely indicated whether the two items were the same or different. Neither during the test nor in the subsequent drills was he asked to concern himself about the correctness of the spelling. Following the first tests, the pupils practiced on similar word discrimination tasks for ten minutes a day. These periods were scheduled five days a week for two weeks, then three days a week for four weeks, and twice a week for five weeks.

A control group of 97 pupils from three grade-six classes took the initial tests in word discrimination and in spelling. While the pupils just described were practicing word discrimination, the control pupils received *regular instruction in spelling.*

At the end of the eleven-week drill or practice period, both groups took the two tests over again using comparable forms.

	Tests of Word Discrimination			Tests of Spelling		
	Initial	Final	Gain	Initial	Final	Gain
Discrimination Training						
Plus Spelling	24.5	28.4	3.9	26.2	30.1	3.9
Spelling Practice Only	26.8	28.6	1.8	27.4	29.7	2.3
Difference			2.1			1.6
Both differences are significant						

SOURCE: G. P. Mason, Word discrimination and spelling, *Journal of Educational Research*, 1957, **50**, 617–621.

If the complex task of driving a car is too much for him, we could get some value from the separate practice of such things as braking, steering, accelerating. Practice on even one of these components will frequently transfer to the complete task. Indeed, if we have little time for practice, it would be better to select one key component, say braking, and give much practice in that, than it would be to spread our time over a number of components (Eckstrand and Wickens, 1954).

To Utilize Predifferentiations. In many of the complete tasks encountered in the school, the pupil must distinguish between two similar stimuli. He must make one response to *bay* and a different response to *day*. When this task is difficult, the teacher can help by giving preliminary practice in merely attending to the two words or to the two crucial letters. Such *predifferentiation*, even when the pupil is not asked to give a response, often transfers to the complete task of correctly naming the words (Arnoult, 1957).

When To Choose Direct Practice

Ordinarily we would do better to use direct practice whenever it is available, safe, not too expensive, when it provides the desired concomitants, and when it permits a reasonable amount of success in the early stages. To illustrate the last of these conditions, let us suppose that a boy should be able to drive a gearshift car as well as a car with an automatic shift. Should we start him out directly with the gearshift? Or should we let him use the automatic shift at the outset? If the gearshift car permits a reasonable amount of early success, we would do better to have him work with this from the start. The skill he acquires in this more complex task should transfer almost completely to the simpler task (Day, 1956; Holding, 1962). After mastering the automatic shift, however, he would still have much to learn in handling the gearshift. If, however, we could expect little or no early success with the gearshift car, we would get more over-all transfer from initial practice with the automatic transmission.

RULES FOR EFFECTIVE STUDY

To be sure of a reasonable amount of transfer, we should not stop with general principles. We should translate these into specific rules or applications. To follow this rule, we try to work out a few highly concrete rules which embody the general principles discussed in the previous chapters. These take the form of rules for effective study—rules that you may find useful in your own study and that you can use to provide the help your students will so often need.

As pointed out in the discussion of tests of study skills (Chapter 3) we do not want to overdo this matter and thus transfer ourselves or our students into mechanical automatons (Maddox, 1963). But we might systematize the matter somewhat.

There is certainly a great need for help in this process of studying. When students have had no special instruction in the process, they seldom get more than half of what they read (Morgan and Deese, 1957). Even a second reading adds only slightly to the yield. Most students, on the other hand, improve somewhat after getting systematic help on methods of study (Entwisle, 1960). The more complete treatments of this topic, of course, cover many special features such as effective use of the dictionary and of the library, skill in reading graphs, in taking notes, and in the general arrangement of study conditions. You might do well to get one of the books that offer help in these matters and give it careful attention (Morgan and Deese, 1957; Robinson, 1962; Tussing, 1962). Meanwhile, here are a few rules that come from our study of the learning process.

1. *Adopt an active role.* Study is not the simple process of letting your eyes wander over the printed page—as you might do while perusing a magazine in a doctor's waiting room. It is more like the directed effort you feel when trying to get to your friend's house and fearing that you are lost, you reread the letter which sets forth the directions. In the latter case, the level of activation may be a bit too high, but for the most part, study should be more like this active search for information and less like casual browsing.

2. *Set specific immediate goals.* Your general motivation is probably fairly high. You want to succeed in college or to get a good grade on this course. But these goals are rather remote and general. They are not as immediate as the need of the motorist to get to his destination. Divide your long-term goals into small units—to master a certain number of pages each week, to finish Chapter 12 tonight.

3. *Get an early grasp of the general structure* (SURVEY). Try to understand the general pattern of what you are reading. When starting a book, look over the Table of Contents and see if you can get a picture of the over-all pattern of what is covered. When about to read a chapter or part of a chapter, study the headings of each section. Try to organize the different headings into a group. Try to guess the general pattern of what will be said.

Naturally enough, you should try to work out some structure that makes genuine sense. If the material is too strange or novel, however, you may not find a very meaningful structure from the headings alone. In that case, an arbitrary structure (for example, beginning, rise, and fall) should be better than nothing.

4. *Devise questions to be answered* (QUESTIONS). Our lost motorist had a very definite question to answer. He was actively reading with a purpose in mind. To develop such a set in yourself, try to phrase questions that you could answer from the material being studied. The easiest, routine way to do this is to turn the heading of each section into a question. If the heading says, "Origins of Children's Needs," you could turn this around and say, "What are the origins of children's needs?" Now READ the section, trying to get answers to your question.

After you have read the section you may find that the question you first formed out of the heading is not a very appropriate question. In that case you might well try to work out a new and better question. Write this down, either in the book itself or in a notebook you keep for this purpose. If you use a notebook, be sure to note the page in the text to which the question belongs. The very effort of trying to phrase a new question may help you turn the section into a new and better structure. The very act of phrasing the question should help even if you do nothing further with it— but, of course, you should do something further with it.

5. *Answer the questions* (RECITE). Here we urge you to give up the comfort of guidance and to plunge into the uncongenial trial-and-error stage of learning. With the text covered, try to an-

swer the questions you have phrased, and then jot down a few *cues* or *key phrases* to remind you of the answers. Write them clearly and arrange them systematically, but don't try to make them complete. Keep them brief and in the form of cues that will bring the complete answer to your mind when you look at them later. After you have written down the cues, check to be sure that they suggest the right answers. If they do, enjoy the reinforcement you get. If not, absorb the guidance you got by looking, then cover the book and try again. Check over your notes or cues to see if they need to be corrected.

6. *Review.* After you have gone over a few sections in the way suggested, go back over the whole group, recalling the questions, if convenient, or looking at the questions, if necessary, and for each question, try to recall all the answers you can. Whenever you seem to draw a blank, keep trying to recall for a few moments and then, if you are still stuck, look at the cues you have written in your notes.

Repeat this REVIEW for larger and larger units as often as you can find the will power to do so.

The words in solid capitals in the previous sections are the key words of Professor Robinson's (1962) well-known system of study. People often refer to the system as SQ3R. This may serve as a convenient cue or mnemonic device to help remember the rules.

7. *Practice even where understanding is incomplete.* By all means seek out the meaning in your new material. Try to see the general process and the rationale underlying the task you are about to attempt. Get a general picture of the dancing steps you are to learn, of the words you are about to pronounce, of the problems you are to solve. But do not insist on perfect understanding be-

fore you begin to practice. Get a reasonable amount of familiarization. Then plunge in. If you are learning to dance, get up on the floor and try to dance. If you are studying mathematics, start doing the exercises even though you do not understand everything the text says. Understanding often follows manipulation. In writing an English exercise, do not wait for the muse to visit you with a perfect theme. Start to write. At first you will probably write rubbish, but it may get you into the swing of writing, and anyway, you may be able to salvage something from it when you correct it later on, as, of course, you must. People who insist on a perfectly complete understanding of the underlying reason before they make a single move often fail to make that first move.

8. *Handle distractions systematically.* Do not use up too much time or energy in trying to overcome distractions by sheer will power. Physical distractions may often be avoided altogether. Try to find a place where you do not hear other conversations, speeches, or plays from the radio or television. Casual music probably will not bother you a great deal. Neither should meaningless noise unless it is too intense or unpleasant.

It is not only with physical distractions that you will have to contend. Most people probably lose more time through the intrusion of their own irrelevant ideas than from outside physical distractions. There is no single method for handling these internal distractions. One psychologist used this system: whenever he found an irrelevant idea cropping up with bothersome frequency, he used to jot it down in a "commonplace book" he left on his desk. If, while marking papers, for instance, he found his mind occupied with ideas for constructing a new piece of apparatus, he would make a brief sketch in the notebook. Even more frivolous, persistent ideas would be dealt with in this same way. He might write down, "Tell Bill story about . . .," or "Dean . . . had no business making me take over that extra section," or, "Try to make up to Mary for the dirty crack I made about her hair-do." His theory, of course, followed something of a Freudian trend. He believed that any idea which kept bobbing up must have had some powerful drive behind it. Suppressing a powerful drive will, of course, be difficult. By writing it down, he promises, in a sense, to give it due attention later on.

SUMMARY

In helping a student with one task, we are exceedingly likely to affect his mastery of some other task. The net result may be facilitation or interference. Facilitation is likely to appear when the two tasks have similar stimuli and identical responses. Interference may result when the stimuli are similar but the response different. Here, however, there are exceptions. Neither facilitation nor interference is likely in well-structured material or in tasks that have markedly different stimuli.

To combat interference we can try to embed the two tasks in some structure or structures, or we can space the practices in which the similar stimuli occur.

Forgetting is largely a result of interference between tasks. In some school subjects much of the material learned may be forgotten over the summer or in a year or so. In other subjects most of the material is retained. Much that is forgotten can be rapidly relearned. Structure aids retention. So does high moti-

vation during learning. Overlearning will help, and so will frequent review.

Positive transfer is one form of facilitation. Although transfer cannot produce miracles, it can greatly add to the total contribution of the school. Within many subjects automatic transfer makes it unnecessary to teach every single item. There appears to be substantial transfer from high school experience to college attainment. From many kinds of learning we may learn how to learn.

To take advantage of transfer, we should present similar tasks in close succession, bringing out the similarity. If several tasks can be seen as part of one principle, the knowledge of the principle should aid in those tasks. There may be more payoff from a well-understood working rule than from a more elusive principle. In any case, there should be much varied practice in applying the principle.

Transfer is often, but not always, a second best. At times, however, it may be better than direct practice when that practice is dangerous, costly, or offers little early reinforcement. The substitute for the direct practice (transfer task) may also have something of value in itself.

It is difficult to decide whether to plunge into a complicated task or to begin with an easier version. Probably the former is better whenever there is a reasonable certainty of early reinforcement.

From knowledge of efficiency we can work out rules for effective study. These rules call for *active* studying, the use of *specific* goals, the search for *structure*, the *devising* of questions on the material, the *answering* of these questions, and a program of *review*. They also urge the student not to be too desperately concerned about distractions, his own sensitive ego, or even these rules.

SUGGESTIONS FOR FURTHER READING

Bugelski, B. R., *The Psychology of Learning.* New York: Holt, Rinehart and Winston, Inc., 1958.

Cofer, C. N., ed., *Verbal Learning and Verbal Behavior.* New York: McGraw-Hill Book Company, Inc., 1961.

————, and Barbara S. Musgrave, eds., *Verbal Behavior and Learning: Problems and Processes; Proceedings.* New York: McGraw-Hill Book Company, Inc., 1963.

Deese, J. E., *The Psychology of Learning.* New York: McGraw-Hill Book Company, Inc., 1958.

Estes, W. K., Learning, *Encyclopaedia of Educational Research,* 3d ed. New York: The Macmillan Company, 1960, pp. 752–770.

Ferguson, G. A., On transfer and the abilities of man, *Canadian Journal of Psychology,* 1956, **10**, 121–131.

Grose, R. F., and R. C. Birney, eds., *Transfer of Learning, an Enduring Problem in Psychology.* Princeton, N. J.: D. Van Nostrand Company, Inc., 1963.

McGeoch, J. A., and A. L. Irion, *The Psychology of Human Learning,* Rev. ed. New York: David McKay Company, Inc., 1952.

Mednick, S. A., and J. L. Freedman, Stimulus generalization, *Psychological Bulletin,* 1960, **57**, 169–200.

Morgan, C. T., and J. E. Deese, *How To Study.* New York: McGraw-Hill Book Company, Inc., 1957.

Postman, L., and Lucy Rau, Retention as a function of the method of measurement, *University of California Publications in Psychology,* 1957, **8**, 217–270, No. 3.

Robinson, F. P., *Effective Study.* New York: Harper & Row, Publishers, Inc., 1946.

————, *Effective Reading.* New York: Harper & Row, Publishers, Inc., 1962.

Stephens, J. M., Transfer of learning, *Encyclopaedia of Educational Research,* 3d ed. New York: The Macmillan Company, 1960b, pp. 1535–1543.

Tussing, L., *Study and Succeed.* New York: John Wiley & Sons, Inc., 1962.

Underwood, B. J., Forgetting, *Scientific American,* 1964a (March), **210**, No. 3, 91–99.

————, Laboratory studies of verbal learning, *Yearbook National Society for the Study of Education,* 1964b, **63**, Part I, 133–152.

Woodworth, R. S., and H. Schlosberg, *Experimental Psychology.* New York: Holt, Rinehart and Winston, Inc., 1954.

For a brief review of the whole field see:

Gagné, R. M., and R. C. Bolles, A review of factors in learning efficiency, in E. H. Galanter, ed., *Automatic Teaching: The State of the Art.* New York: John Wiley & Sons, Inc., 1959. Reprinted in De Cecco, pp. 30–51.

EXERCISES AND QUESTIONS FOR DISCUSSION

1. Make a list of some of the specific things you may be teaching. From this list select (a) those things which are not likely to be affected by either facilitation or interference. Also list (b) some items for which interference may be a problem. Indicate the activities which might produce the interference. (c) Select these things from which you might expect transfer to some other activity.

2. Is there anyone whom you tend to call by the wrong name? Can you track down the reason for this?

3. Think of several subjects that you have not studied for two or three years. Jot down some things that you recall readily, and some things that you think you should be able to recall but which elude you. Can you suggest any reason for the differences?

4. Under what conditions could you urge your pupils to spend time in overlearning? How might you motivate them for this activity?

5. Think over several of the recent general articles or editorials on education that you have read. Did these articles make any assumptions regarding the amount of transfer that we can expect?

6. You are advising a student about the high school subjects that might help him most in college. List the points you would make from the evidence now available.

7. Go over the section in Chapter 7 that deals with critical thinking. In developing this skill in your students you wish it to transfer to many things that they will read. What should you do to increase the likelihood of such transfer?

8. A student who has been ill for some weeks finds that he must quickly learn the English meanings of some 120 French words if he is to go along with the class in regular fashion. He is anxious to make the best use of his study time and comes to you for advice.

First of all, for your own guidance, list the factors in the situation which are favorable to his objective. List the factors which will handicap him.

Work out with him a list of detailed, concrete rules that should help him in his task. Use everything that you have learned that will apply to his particular problem.

PART THREE

▶ *Promoting Character and Personal Well-Being*

CHAPTER 9

▶ *Character and the Major Theories of Socialization*

From one point of view, perhaps we should not make too much of the difference between teaching for character and teaching for other forms of attainment. To a great extent the two processes overlap. To some extent one form of attainment hinges upon the other or would be undesirable without the other. Many of the processes involved in promoting academic attainment, moreover, will be seen to be also at work when we turn to the area of character development.

But there are some differences. In setting out to teach character we may find marked disagreement about the goals. Should we aim, for instance, at conformity or at rugged individualism? If we should reach agreement about the general goals, we would still find it difficult to specify those goals in terms of measurable behavior. Character, even more than academic attainment, moreover, is an area in which other agencies have an exceedingly vital stake. In seek-

ing to promote this vital area, the teacher will find himself most intimately enmeshed with other powerful forces, any one of which may work to supplant, to bolster, or to nullify his efforts.

NATURE AND MEASUREMENT OF CHARACTER

Morality, character, or social worth are terms that mean different things to different people. Rather than attempt a rigorous definition to describe the process to be considered, we will attempt to list the various facets that seem to emerge whenever we set out to study character in a systematic way. These are the facets that turn up from the factor analysis of existing test instruments. Such an analysis, of course, can only bring out those things that the instruments can pick up. In using this procedure we would completely miss any aspects of character not tapped by existing tests or other devices.

231

Some Facets of Character

From one investigation (Peck and Havighurst, 1960), employing some thirty test instruments, we find six separate factors, each of which keeps turning up in one test or another. To get a picture of the student's performance on this whole cluster of tests, we would not have to look at every single score, but would merely need to know his standing on each of these six factors.

Outward Conformity to Rules and Laws. Ordinary conformity seems to be a factor by itself. At the one extreme of this factor, or dimension, we find the person who cheerfully goes along with most rules and regulations, and, at the other extreme, the sullen delinquent who seems to regard every social requirement as something to be violated or evaded, or at least as something that does not apply to him.

Friendliness in Outward Behavior. No matter whether he abides by rules or breaks them at every opportunity, the student could display an attitude of outward friendliness and helpfulness to those around him, or, at the other extreme, he could be indifferent, cold, or condemnatory. He could regard the individuals he knows as being important in their own right, or he could feel that these people were important only as they fitted in with his needs.

Freedom from Inner Hostility. It is unfortunately true that the person who acts in a friendly fashion does not always feel the friendliness that he portrays. The outward helpfulness may cover an intense inner dislike. Conversely, in literature at least, we frequently encounter the rough, scolding critic whose captious behavior really hides a heart of gold. This inner good will, as opposed to sullen hostility, or suspicious prejudice, is often considered as an important aspect of character, irrespective of the person's outward behavior.

Zestful, Spontaneous Commitment. Some people do good, or evil, from a nagging sense of guilt or inadequacy. Those who do good may do so in reluctant, fearful fashion, asking all the while, "Have I met my quota? Will this serve to keep me from feeling guilty?" Similarly, those who do evil may do so to quiet a nagging fear. They may violate the law, or attack an associate, chiefly to prove that they are not frightened, or to cover up some disturbing feeling of guilty inadequacy. Other people do what they do, for good or for evil, in spontaneous, positive fashion. The reasonable citizen helps this person or this cause because he feels a positive urge to help. The delinquent high in this spontaneity steals not to cover up his fear of being a sissy, but to get the car he really wants. He attacks his neighbor not to protect himself from the fear of cowardice, but in a simple, wholehearted effort to get revenge.

Naturally enough, current discussions of character place little stress on commitment to a course of evil. Commitment to some worthy cause, however, receives much attention, and the lack of such zestful commitment is frequently deplored (Sachar, 1961). This lack of commitment is considered to be a special hazard for the thoughtful, fair-minded student, who, through his very perceptiveness, may be led to believe that nothing really matters, or that there is so. much to be said on both sides that there is no point in trying to get at the truth. The same discernment that may tempt one to a stultifying neutrality may also induce a sense of helplessness in the face of the size and complexity of social problems. This, again, detracts from the feeling of social responsibility. Such a feeling of futility and impotence (McGinley, 1961) is at odds with the concept of vigorous, confident, and spontaneous commitment.

Susceptibility to Inner Controls. Most people can act in fairly decent and cooperative fashion when actually under the eye of some authority. Most people also respond fairly adequately to responsibilities unmistakably present on their doorsteps. They may act less acceptably, however, when no one is watching, or when the responsibility can easily be disregarded. Such people, of course, are lacking in the inner controls necessary for adequate character.

In most discussions of character we find much emphasis on the importance of inner controls. It is held that internal controls should gradually replace external controls. Some structures, or ideas, or ideals that the student carries around with him should come to replace the physical presence of the parent, the teacher, or the policeman. In gradually replacing the external forces, moreover, it is to be hoped that these inner controls will change in character. Primitive anxiety in the face of the imagined punishment, for instance, should give way to controls based on a rational decision, motivated perhaps by a genuine desire for the happiness and well-being of others.

Understanding the Implications of Behavior. To understand the implications of his behavior, the student must have some power of rational self-criticism. He must foresee, to a reasonable extent, the outcome of his acts. And he must see and judge all these things in the light of the moral person he thinks he is, or should be. As he falls below these requirements he would get a lower rating on this one facet of character.

Notice that none of the six dimensions explicitly mentions religion. Many people, of course, would hold that any genuine character the pupil attains must be organized around his religion. If not a formal religion, his character must include his considered view of the universe and his relation to the guiding principles he sees at work.

The Measurement of Character

The facets just discussed have emerged from the tests already used to measure character. We now turn to a closer look at these tests and to the general problem of obtaining measurements in the field of character.

Disagreement about Objectives. As suggested earlier, the problem of measurement is made difficult by the lack of agreement regarding the proper objectives of character education. Conformity provides one issue regarding which we can expect much dispute (Riley and others, 1961). A similar dispute is to be found regarding the stress to be placed on the sense of commitment. Surely we will work hard to develop an attitude of open-mindedness and the ability to withhold a decision for a time (Smith, 1960a). But, how much open-mindedness, and for how long? In this, as in so many problems, we are faced with some compromise between the Hotspur, roaring into action completely committed to a half-considered view, and, at the other extreme, a Hamlet endlessly mulling over ethical niceties.

As in many other areas, we can probably get more agreement when we talk of character traits that we should avoid than when we adopt a more positive approach and consider the ideal character that we should strive to attain. Almost everyone is against sin, against the most

MARK A. MAY

obvious kinds of delinquency, and against prejudice in its gross and vicious forms. Suppose we reduce these evils, however, and attain a state where we are free to follow positive goals. At this point we cannot expect the same consensus in deciding how we should utilize this freedom.

Some Representative Tests. As we are so frequently forced to realize, it is hard to draw a fine line between character and the other aspects of personality. Certainly the basic problems of measuring character resemble the problems of measuring personality. These underlying general problems are treated more systematically in Chapter 13.

One of the early investigations of character (Hartshorne and May, 1928–1930) made considerable use of *performance* tests. To test honesty, children were

asked to close their eyes and put dots in the middle of circles on a paper. Success was practically impossible unless the child peeked. In other tests of honesty, students took a test containing a mixture of items that are very easy, and others—number of diesel locomotives built in 1948—that are almost impossible to answer. The child is given a key, and scores his own paper. If he credits himself with more than one or two of the difficult items, he must have cheated. In one ingenious performance test, children made purchases at a drug store and were intentionally given too much change. What does the child do? To get at altruism, students were given attractive kits of tools. Later they were told that the kits for an adjoining room had not arrived and each student was asked to indicate how many things from his own kit he would donate. Persistence was measured by having a child read through material that calls for more and more effort as he goes along.

Performance tests are often unwieldy, and must be carefully disguised. If the child knows he is really being tested, his performance will indicate very little.

Prejudice or *ethnocentrism* has been measured by the famous F-scale described in *The Authoritarian Personality* (Adorno and others, 1950). Here the person taking the test indicates his agreement or disagreement with statements such as "Obedience and respect for authority are the most important virtues children should learn." "An insult to our honor should always be punished." Projective tests are also used to measure ethnic attitudes. These tests use pictures that are deliberately vague or general and the person being tested must project into it things that are part of himself. (See Chapter 13 for a further description.)

Earlier attempts to measure attitude

► *Tests of Character, Attitudes and Values*

As with tests of achievement and intelligence, certain tests of character come prepared for classroom use. These may be ordered from the publisher. (See Chapter 3 for address of major publishers.) Some examples:

Study of Values: A Scale for Measuring the Dominant Interests in Personality (Allport-Vernon-Lindzey). Boston: Houghton Mifflin Company.

Child Personality Scale, Grades K–9, (Sister Mary Amatora). C. A. Gregory Company, 345 Calhoun Street, Cincinnati 19, Ohio. Includes measures of punctuality, courtesy, cooperation, generosity, honesty, neatness, thoughtfulness, dependability. Some strictly religious items. Based on ratings of self, teacher, and peers.

Gordon Personal Profile, Grades 9–adult level, New York: Harcourt, Brace & World, Inc. Measures responsibility and sociability.

Personal and Social Development Program, Grades K–9, Chicago: Science Research Associates. Based on critical incidents technique.

There are other tests of character which are not neatly packaged for use, but which are published in reports of specific studies. The OSS Assessment Staff (1948), for instance, describes various tests of initiative, resourcefulness, and dependability. Watson (1925) describes one of the earliest instruments used in testing fair-mindedness. See also Adorno and others (1950) for a description of the tests used in *The Authoritarion Personality*; Harris (1957a) for a social attitudes scale dealing with responsibility; Hartshorne and May (1928–1930) for a variety of tests used in the *Character Education Inquiry*; and Peck and Havighurst (1960) for a description of a variety of formal tests and interview techniques.

toward other groups made use of the *social distance* scale. Would it bother you to think of a (Canadian) as a neighbor on your street, a member of your club, a visitor in your home, a roommate in college, a relative by marriage, a wife or husband? These steps are scaled, and the distance a student insists on maintaining is used to indicate his prejudice or lack of tolerance (Stern, 1963).

From their general experience in using some thirty different instruments over a period of years, Peck and Havighurst (1960) came to the conclusion that the interviews and the projective tests, as managed by trained people, gave the most useful information. The more objective and more easily used inventories were of less value in providing data for their research. For the average teacher, however, this information, important as it is, cannot serve as a very practical guide. Lacking the training to use these less structured tests, the typical teacher will have to restrict himself to simple inventories, checklists, ratings, and instruments of the "guess-who" variety (Harris and others, 1954).

The Constancy of Character

Character, as measured by the various tests, turns out to be fairly constant. Although all children change as they grow older, they tend to retain about the same relative standing. The excessive delinquent in his midteens turns out to have been an unusually unruly child in the earlier school grades. The child who has more than average self-control at age ten will turn out to be above average in the same trait at age seventeen (Peck and Havighurst, 1960).

THE PLACE OF THEORY IN THE STUDY OF CHARACTER

For several reasons, the wise teacher will wish to be informed about the major theories of socialization or character development. Many of our data have been gathered from investigations designed to test this or that aspect of one of the major theories. More than most psychological theories, moreover, these theories are in the air. Parents encounter them at every turn—in the newspaper column, at the sewing circle or cocktail party. In gearing his efforts to the other forces at work, the teacher will wish to know something of the basic views which play a part in directing those forces.

The Problem of Rival Theories

Unfortunately, at present, there can be no neat, clear-cut answer to the question about the mechanisms of socialization. There are several vigorous, rival theories in the field and, in spite of the many data pouring in, it is still too early to decide between the rival views.

In the face of this problem we present each theory in its own right, setting forth the assumptions and the claims of each as if they could be accepted. Later we try to see where the rival theories overlap, and the points at which they remain in conflict. We then develop the implications of the various theories, stressing those implications to which most of the theories seem to point.

To a great extent this position of suspended judgment or eclecticism comes from the lack of crucial data. Even if the data were much more unanimous and clear-cut, however, we would still face vigorous disagreement on the part of the proponents. For one thing, there could be some doubt about the adequacy of the tests from which the data are derived. For another thing, some of the theories are based on large, general convictions that, to some extent, defy the conventional notions of proof or of scientific test. People are not likely to abandon such broadly held principles because of a few negative experimental results.

The theories to be considered are (1) the Freudian or psychoanalytic theory with its emphasis on the psychic conflicts and the unconscious alignments of the id, ego, and super-ego; (2) the complex social-learning theory of the Hullians, laying great stress on complex drive-states such as anxiety, dependency needs, and frustration; (3) the direct-reinforcement theory of the Skinnerians with its attempt to avoid the use of elaborate hypothetical things like acquired drives, and with its reliance on the concept of direct reinforcement; and (4) the cognitive theories, such as those of Piaget (1932) and Kohlberg (1963a), which hold that character or socialization arises from the child's improved understanding of moral matters and of the results of his interactions with other people.

PSYCHOANALYTIC THEORIES OF SOCIALIZATION

According to Freud and his followers, there are three separate aspects of the mind which are at work in the process of socialization. At the base there is the powerful *id*, the source of psychic energy and of impulse and desire. At birth the child is all id, a creature with psychic energy directed to the pleasure

SIGMUND FREUD

principle and to the immediate gratification of impulse. With the increase of physical strength, however, complete control by the id would lead to injury or death. As every mother knows, the untrained infant seems determined to accomplish his own destruction—by swallowing or half-swallowing harmful objects, or by hurling himself at declivities, or by other lethal pastimes.

The Ego as the Servant of the Id

Not only is the id deficient in its inability to distinguish safe gratification from that which is dangerous. It is even unable to distinguish between gratification that is real (actually securing nourishment, for instance) and a pseudo-gratification which is completely illusory. For the purposes of the id, an image of

food will serve as well as the real thing. To keep the id from squandering its precious psychic energy in this illusory fashion, a second agency gradually develops. This is the *ego*, the rational guardian which tries to make sure that the energy of the immature id will be spent only upon real sources of satisfaction, and upon those that do not invite destruction. This servant of the id examines the images put forth by the id, and tries to match these with something real (and safe) in the objective world. If nothing in the outside world meets this condition, the ego vetoes the action. In searching for a match, and in deciding whether a safe and feasible match has been found, the ego must use judgment and the whole range of logical powers. These logical faculties belong to the ego and to the ego alone.

The Role of the Superego

But the ego is no real preceptor. It never decides about the propriety or morality of the id's desires. Like the worldly-wise and completely indulgent servant of a capricious princeling, the ego will only say, "This will not work," or, "It would be better to wait," or, "Wouldn't this safer alternative do just as well?" It never says, "This is wrong."

Something, however, does arise to assume the role of moral arbiter. The *superego* gradually develops from the id and the ego. Just as the ego is exclusively concerned with what is safe, effective, and feasible, so the superego becomes exclusively concerned with what is proper, moral, and in keeping with current social code. The superego includes the *conscience*, which keeps the child from doing what his parents would prohibit, and also the *ego-ideal*, which impels him toward conduct that parents and society would approve.

Stages in the Development of the Superego

The superego is the last and the least primitive of the structures of mind. It develops from the primitive id and from the ego. To get a clearer picture of this development we must take a brief look at the transitional stages leading up to the emergence of the superego. The Freudian theorists, by the way, are nothing if not specific. And they have specified these stages in great detail. We must remind ourselves that this is only one theory and that many people violently disagree. Recent authors have been especially critical of some of the far-reaching tendencies alleged to stem from experience in these early specific stages (H. E. Jones, 1960; Murphy, 1962).

For the first year of life the child is held to be in the oral stage. During that time the pleasure-seeking urges of the id are focused on the mouth and its activities. Dependency feelings are intense. There is pleasure from sucking, drinking, eating, and later from biting. From the primitive sources of pleasure, Freud holds that there may develop a later joy in general intake or in acquisition of things or of ideas or of beliefs. From the primitive pleasure of biting there may develop

► *Elaborations, Appraisals, and Critiques of Freud*

In an analysis of Freud's idea of psychosexual stages, R. W. White holds that this theory "will stand in the history of thought as an astonishing first approximation to a theory of growth in its dynamic aspects." He reminds us, however, that Freud's latest statements were completed almost forty years ago, and that failure to change or modify them will hold us back. More recent Freudians have attempted such a modification by adding interpersonal needs to the simpler instinctual needs stressed by Freud. With the possible exception of Harry Stack Sullivan, however, these neo-Freudians still treat the interpersonal needs as linked to the earlier Freudian needs and stages.

White thinks that no revision of the Freudian drives will enable them to explain the tremendous human concern with the problem of competence. Much of our behavior is motivated by *effectance*—the motive that leads us to produce changes in the environment. (This is related to Thorndike's motive of "being a cause," to Stephens' and Courts' idea of the reward-value in seeing "something happen" and to Sheffield's work on rewards that do not reduce drive.) As the child realizes his own part in producing deliberate effects, we have the motive of *efficacy*. These two motives are organized around the idea of competency. Competency motivation cannot be usefully derived from the drive-theories stressing visceral tensions and tissue deficits. It provides a more convincing explanation of the tremendous increase of skill in doing the world's work. In contrast to the Freudian view, this theory of competence would not regard great objective achievements as merely modified ways of expressing psychosexual drives.

SOURCE: Based on R. W. White, Competence and the psychosexual stages of development, *Nebraska Symposium on Motivation*, 1960, 8, 97–141. Reprinted in Rosenblith, pp. 213–221.

an adult delight in sarcasm or in argumentation.

During the second year of life, the *anal stage* supersedes the oral stage. The pleasure from defecation is important and may become the basis for similar urges later on as when the adult goes in for spluttering abusiveness or for a disorderly life. Toilet-training attempts to insist that this pleasure must be controlled and postponed, and this control, in turn, may lead to later obstinacy and stinginess. A tremendous concern about bowel movements may be the basis for adult productivity or creativity.

By the end of the second year the child enters into the *phallic stage*, enjoying genital stimulation and indulging in erotic fantasies. In these latter fantasies, by the way, aggression may play some part. Soon this interest is focused on the opposite-sex parent, and the *Oedipus complex* is in full swing. During this phase the boy's love for his mother becomes quite erotic in nature, and he jealously wishes to get rid of his father. The developing ego, committed to realism, anticipates the outraged father's violent retaliation. It even exaggerates this menace until the fancied punishment culminates in the threat of castration. It is to meet this menace, and others like it, that the superego develops. With its constituent parts of conscience and ego-ideal, this new structure evolves from the ego, and part of the id. It evolves for the sole purpose of dealing with urges that threaten to bring down the wrath of parents or of society in general.

Our account has dealt exclusively with the boy. In the *Electra complex* the girl acquires a corresponding love for the father and a jealousy of the mother. For girls, however, the whole problem is more subtle and indirect. And, as we shall see, it is resolved in less compelling fashion.

The Superego and the Other Basic Structures. We now have three basic structures. The primitive id has remained relatively unchanged while giving rise to the two other structures. Completely devoid of morality, rationality, or logical considerations, the id is still directing its energy to one attractive pleasure outlet after another. Equally illogical, and equally devoid of realism and rationality, the new superego is concerned only with what is moral or immoral. Its prohibitions and its proddings have nothing to do with reason or feasibility. They consist of the insistent pressure of the ego-ideal toward noble outlets, however, unrealistic, and of the negative, fearful veto of the conscience as it issues its arbitrary, "Thou shalt not."

The ego remains the sole executive officer. It has the final decision as to which outlets coming before it will actually be sought out, which suggested acts will finally be performed. It is much more than a neutral executive officer, however. Although indifferent to moral issues, it urges its own claims in the interests of what is feasible and prudent. With development of the superego, moreover, the ego assumes the role of an arbiter, balancing the surgent, primitive drives of the id against the fussy prohibitions and naggings of the superego. In carrying out these functions, the ego can make full use of the reason, logic, and consistency that are denied to the id and to the superego.

Processes Involved in Socialization

It is the irrational, arbitrary superego, with its conscience and its ego-ideal, that is most significant in socialization. The ego-ideal and, to some extent, the conscience, do some of their work in the conscious, open court of the ego. Here

► *Are Children Especially Likely To Imitate the Powerful Controller of Rewards?*

This is a report of the behavior of thirty-six boys and thirty-six girls from three to five years of age (most of them about four years old). Each child was brought into a playroom where he met the adult who was represented as owning the playroom (adult owner), and the attractive equipment (toys, juice dispenser, and cookies). He also met another adult (adult visitor) who expressed a desire to play with the equipment and to get some of the refreshments.

In one situation (adult rewarded-child spectator) the adult owner allowed the adult visitor to make use of the facilities while the child sat off to one side playing with rather dull toys. The two adults played with more adult toys (pinballs), the owner clearly in the dominant situation. The owner also provided refreshments and promised to procure some more attractive play equipment. The child was ignored.

In another situation (child rewarded-adult spectator), the adult visitor sat by ignored while the adult owner played with the child, fed him, and promised him even more attractive toys.

Each session was followed by a game in which each adult performed a number of distinctive acts. One, for instance, wore his hat with the feather up whereas the other wore the feather down. One marched clockwise, the other

---

they exert pressure on the realistic ego to seek a nobler outlet or to avoid one that is shameful. This is the obvious phenomenon, on open display, that we often observe in ourselves as we struggle with some moral problem.

Identification. In its basic work, the superego is complexly involved with the mechanism of identification. This important process is partly responsible for the very existence of the superego. In the shattering struggles of the Oedipus complex, the young boy, fearing the wrath of the outraged father, comes to identify with him, seeming to follow the maxim, "If you can't lick them, join them." Rather than sitting fearful and helpless before this powerful menace, the boy links himself with the father and, in his mind, takes on some of the father's power. He feels a sense of personal achievement in the accomplishments of

the father. Punishment, real or threatened, is administered jointly by himself *and* the father. Through this identification he shares in the father's intimacy with the mother. As he identifies more and more with the father, his attitude toward the mother is more and more colored by those aspects of tenderness which the father openly displays toward her. His feelings lose something of their crude, erotic cast, and he acquires the beginning of true socialization.

Modified Theories of Identification. Other theorists (McCandless, 1962) have pointed out that the boy's fear of the powerful father would lead to identification even without the underlying Oedipus complex. This theory merely assumes that orders and punishment are easier to take if they are partially self-imposed, if they come from "us" and not from "him." According to this view, to make sure counter clockwise. After these adult performances, the child had his turn and his behavior was observed to see which of the adults he imitated.

In the table, the adult *"owner"* always dispenses the rewards. The adult *"visitor"* may receive the rewards or may be ignored. When the "visitor" is ignored the child himself is rewarded by the "owner."

Condition Observed by Child	Number of Times the GIRLS Imitated the Adult When the Adult Was:		Number of Times the BOYS Imitated the Adult When the Adult Was:	
	Owner	Visitor	Owner	Visitor
Male owner rewards female visitor	29.0	9.7	30.1	18.7
Male owner ignores female visitor	22.0	16.2	29.2	16.7
Female owner rewards male visitor	26.0	10.0	22.3	16.2
Female owner ignores male visitor	31.8	22.2	26.8	34.5

SOURCE: A. Bandura, Dorothea Ross, and Sheila A. Ross, A comparative test of the status envy, social power, and secondary reinforcement theories of identificatory learning, *Journal of Abnormal and Social Psychology*, 1963a, 67, 527.

that the boy achieved a satisfactory identification with his father, and with the male role, it would be important to be sure that the father is the dominant member of the household. Otherwise, the boy might reject the male role, identify with the more powerful mother, and cling to a female role. As we shall see later, there has been some suspicion that many disorders in males (schizophrenia, delinquency) come from the combination of a dominant mother and a weak, ineffectual father.

Whatever its underlying basis, the mechanism of identification has helped to shape the superego into an inner embodiment of the things that parents punish or approve. As the superego matures it makes use of this mechanism, responsible for its very being, to direct the energy of the id toward outlets which the parents would approve or toward those which the child thinks the parents would approve.

Repression and Displacement. In carrying out its mission, the superego can argue in the open court of the ego, and it can also make us of indirect and unconscious devices. The conscience, especially, is likely to make use of repression and displacement. At times, of course, the conscience has no need to resort to indirection. When, for instance, it sees the id focusing on a moderately worrisome outlet (a boy about to make faces at his father's photograph), the superego may feel confident of taking care of the situation in direct fashion merely by urging the ego toward a more worthy outlet. If it should lose out in that rational, realistic court, no great harm would be done. But not all issues permit this indulgent attitude. And when the id's energy is streaming toward some really hideous outlet, the superego cannot afford to take its chance on the triumph of reason and prudence in the court of the ego. It takes steps to make sure that this outlet will never come to the attention of the ego. If the superego is successful, the reprehensible outlet will be *repressed* and will never rise to the level of consciousness. The claims of this outlet will never be scrutinized in the light of reason.

When this repression is successful, the ego will never have a chance to deal with an urge that is focused on an erotic relation with the mother or on the destruction of the father. Through the mechanism of repression, these outlets will be denied admission to the ken of the ego. But things are not as simple as they seem. We must still reckon with the resources of the remarkable id. This primitive, amoral, a-logical energy system is extremely fluid. Denied release through one outlet, it can get some measure of release if the energy is displaced to some other outlet. If the desire for the father's death cannot get a hearing, the energy might even be partially released if displaced to a desire for the father's well-being. Logical inconsistency gives no trouble in the realm of the unrealistic, a-logical id, and it is not unusual to find that an outlet which shocks the superego is displaced toward the very opposite of the prohibited outlet. This is called *reaction formation.*

Not all displacement follows the pattern of reaction formation. The inadmissible hate for the father could be displaced to some object that, through coincidence or otherwise, just happens to be associated with the father. It could, for instance, take the form of an inordinate dislike for the father's favorite food. Later on, with the acquisition of more subtle generalizations, the aggressive energy could be displaced toward some intangible thing, such as injustice or tyranny whenever encountered.

As with the aggressive urges, the energy from the erotic impulses within the id must also frequently be displaced toward morally acceptable outlets. The unacknowledged erotic interest in the mother could be displaced toward some other woman who resembled the mother, provided the resemblance is not too obvious to the superego. Later on, with increased capacity for generalization, erotic energy directed to the mother might be refocused on some abstract attribute which the mother exemplified; gentleness, humor, or a warm concern for others.

In all this we must not suggest that displacement always follows some describable pattern. Actually this process, conducted below the level of consciousness and rationality, can be quite capricious and fanciful. We cannot tell which weird outlet will come to serve as a substitute for the primitive object that is hated or loved. Some of these displacements lead to harmless and frivolous activities, such as toying with coins. Some lead to grotesque and incapacitating delusions. Others lead to astounding creative achievements or acts of moral grandeur.

The Latent and Genital Stages

In its culminating effort, the superego and its constituent parts succeed in repressing the Oedipus complex, and the child becomes unaware of these horrible urges. This victory over the Oedipus complex usually takes place around the age of five, and, with this victory, the phallic period comes to an end. Now begins a long *latent period.* The warring factions, having taken the measure of each other, are now in a state of almost peaceful co-existence. This quiet period is to persist until the juices of adolescence initiate new turmoil.

Some important activity, of course, is going on during the latent period. Certainly some displacements and new outlets are coming into effect. No new major realignment is to be expected during this time, however, and it is only in the fourth or *genital stage* that the full moral significance of the pattern of displacements (or of identifications) becomes apparent. At the beginning of adolescence, the id impulses become more turbulent and also become more capable of focusing in altruistic fashion on other people as persons in their own right. Heretofore these urges have focused merely on the narcissistic sensuous delight to be had from others and on the general "usefulness" of people (reality principle). With this stronger flow of energy, oriented to people as ends in themselves, we see more clearly the full significance of displacements earlier acquired. With this greater energy, additional patterns of displacement are needed. With the more vigorous social transactions, the character of the youth takes on more definite form, and his style of socialization, good, bad, or indifferent begins to assume its adult cast.

CHARACTER FORMATION AS LEARNING: DRIVE-STATE AND REINFORCEMENT

A number of psychologists, notably Dollard and Miller (1950), have been quite impressed with the various processes that Freud has described (displacement, identification, the operation of guilt or anxiety) but have been worried about the basic theory or the "model" from which these processes are derived.

These psychologists have hesitated to assume the existence of an id, an ego, and a superego, with their seeming rivalries and schemings. Instead they have placed their reliance on learning. They hold that the child learns to be decent or delinquent, to be anxious or dependent, in the same way that he learns to solve an equation or to translate a Latin phrase. The learning theory that they adopted was that of Clark Hull (See Chapter 5) with whom many of this group worked.

The Hullian Concept of Drive

Freudians talk of a single reservoir of psychic energy located in the id. This energy, like pressure in a steam boiler, can achieve release through a variety of outlets. When the pressure is discharged through one outlet we can expect a reduction in the pressure at other points of possible eruption.

In contrast to this view, the advocates of the learning approach assume that there are a number of separate drives or sources of energy. In Hull's view, moreover, these drives are closely related to such physical things as hunger (lowering of the blood sugar), or pain (the presence of some noxious substance). These things are drives in the sense that, when they are active, the organism will do one thing after another until the stimuli associated with the drive are reduced in intensity.

The Role of Stimulus Generalization

Stimulus generalization (See Chapter 8) is an important concept in the explanation of transfer and interference in learning. The child who learns to say "cat" when he sees his own pet will also be somewhat more likely to say "cat" when he sees a larger cat or even when

NEAL E. MILLER

he sees a dog. An infant who comes to feel joy when he sees his mother will feel something of the same joy when he sees his nurse, his aunt, or the casual guest. A boy who feels hostility toward his father may react to the gardener or male teacher in much the same way.

With this concept of stimulus generalization, the Hullian psychologists are in a position to explain the Freudian process of displacement. In coming to love his mother, the child comes to love those who resemble her. When she is not present or available, he expresses this already-existing love for the others. The boy who hates his father also hates the doorman and can express this derived object of hostility when it is impossible or unwise to attack his father (Miller, 1948).

Reinforcement

From the reduction of the stimuli associated with a strong drive comes the all-important reinforcement, discussed in Chapter 5. Whenever an act is followed by such reinforcement, that act will be more likely to be repeated in the future. In using this familiar theory to explain character development, Dollard and Miller (1950) go beyond simple drives and simple reinforcement and rely heavily on the ramifications of these processes as seen in stimulus generalization, secondary reinforcement, and acquired or secondary drives.

Secondary Reinforcement. To get a picture of secondary reinforcement we might imagine a young infant wet and cold. The cold, wet condition sets off a train of stimulation from his skin. At this time, for some reason or other, he calls, "Mamma." Thereupon (a) his mother appears and about the same time (b) there is a sudden reduction in flow of stimuli from his wet, cold skin. This latter constitutes primary reinforcement. The reduction in such stimuli will directly and mechanically strengthen his tendency to call "Mamma." He is now more likely to make the same call if he is ever in the same predicament again. Secondary reinforcement comes from the fact that the mother is prominently in the environment at the time that the unpleasant stimuli are reduced. Through a process very similar to conditioning, the mother's presence will now come to have somewhat the same effect as the actual reduction of unpleasant stimuli. Because of this process, reinforcement is exceedingly contagious. Not only will it spread to the mother but also to any seemingly neutral stimulus—the squeak of the door, an increase in illumination, an increase in the intensity of the sounds from the living room. By this process of secondary reinforcement, each child acquires countless sources of reward. Many of these, such as the presence of the mother, would be quite predictable and would hold for almost any child. Other sources of reward, however, would be unique to each child and would come barging out of the environment to reinforce him under circumstances that would mystify the onlooker.

Acquired or Secondary Drive-States

We have seen how primitive reinforcement, such as the rapid decrease in discomfort or pain, can be transferred to a neutral stimulus such as the squeak of a door or the odor of perfume. In the same way, a primitive drive-state can become attached to some new condition. The child's cold, wet skin brought about direct physiological distress. But this distress acts during the absence of the mother. By virtue of this association, the sheer absence of the mother may come to induce somewhat the same distress as that originally produced by the cold, wet clothes. This new distress caused by the absence of the mother becomes a real drive-state. The child has now acquired the secondary drive-state of dependency. This drive-state is held to be associated with some characteristic flow of stimuli, probably from the child's own internal organs. The mother's presence will reduce this flow of stimuli and will act as reinforcement.

There is no limit to the number of new drive-states that could be acquired in this way. From all the acquired drives that could occur, different theorists have laid great stress on one or more of the following: *dependency*, the need to be near the parent or other adult and to experience that adult's approval; *aggres-sion* and *anger* toward hitherto innocent objects; *frustration*, arising when some other drive is prevented from operating; *anxiety* and the flow of internal stimuli that go with it; bewilderment or *cognitive dissonance*, arising when we must reconcile two conflicting things (the good mother behaving in a bad way; all the care I lavished on this project and so little to show for it) (Chapanis and Chapanis, 1964; Festinger, 1964, 1957).

Clearly, many of these suggested new drive-states no longer seem to have a definite physiological anchor. Many theorists, however, assume that these conditions do arise from definite physiological conditions. Terms like cognitive dissonance are used as convenient labels for the complex cluster of stimuli that make up this drive-state.

Phenomena Explained by the Derived Processes

With this array of acquired drives standing ready to be reduced, and thus to generate reinforcement, and with this source of reinforcement augmented by limitless secondary reinforcement, the Hullian psychologist is now in a position to explain a great many things, including the phenomena of identification and imitation.

Identification and Imitation. Suppose that a boy comes into the presence of his father and thereby reduces a dependency need. At this moment, moreover, the father happens to be sawing wood and producing the distinctive odor of cut lumber. He may also be exhibiting a particular stance or uttering a characteristic phrase. Each of these circumstances, having been present when the dependency need was reduced, becomes a form of secondary reinforcement. Later, when the boy is alone, he may happen to saw a

▶ *Acquiring a Dislike for a Neutral Object*

This study involved 68 boys and 40 girls between the ages of 4½ and 6. Each child played a card game with the experimenter. The child's object was to win enough chips to buy a small toy. There were ten cards in the pack, five of them being blank and five being figure cards, each carrying an ink drawing of a boy (when a boy was playing) or of a girl (when a girl was playing).

The game was manipulated so that each child was bound to lose. Some children, however, started out with almost enough chips (seven) and ultimately lost all but two. This was supposed to induce *high frustration*. Others started out with only two chips and, after a series of losses and wins, also ended up with two—*mild frustration*. In each case the child lost chips when the figure card was present and won when the plain card was present. The high-frustration group lost two chips for each figure card, whereas the mild-frustration group lost one. In a control group, each child started out with two chips and lost equally to plain and to figure cards, ending up with two chips.

After he finished the card game, each child took part in a target shooting exercise in which he could shoot a pop gun at various cards. As *one part* of this exercise, the figure card was used as the target and the child was told he could take as many bonus shots at this target as he wanted. During the actual shooting he was reminded that he could quit any time he wished. The investigator com-

board. The sight of the cut board (or the smell of sawdust), having been established as secondary reinforcement, will now make him more likely to saw boards in the future. The same thing will happen if he utters a phrase that is characteristic of the father, and hears himself utter it. All in all, when he himself does the things the father did, he encounters the same stimuli that were present when his dependency need was reduced. He comes more and more to do the things the father did and to find satisfaction in the process. Insofar as these processes lead the boy merely to behave as his father does, we have the phenomenon of *imitation*. Insofar as he receives internal reinforcement from merely thinking as (he thinks) his father thinks, or feeling as he thinks his father feels, we have the additional phenomenon of *identification*.

Imitation, of course, can be encouraged by direct reinforcement as well as by the more subtle kind of internal reinforcement we have stressed. The boy, for instance, may be overtly praised for imitating his father. By deliberate imitation, moreover, he may achieve valuable, need-reducing results. By following his father's activities, the board is cut more neatly, the ball is thrown farther, the opponent is more readily cowed.

Bizarre and Devious Side Effects. With this vast store of acquired drives and subtle reinforcements, we can see how, under certain circumstances, almost anything a person does may be reinforced from one source or another. It would be hard to imagine a moment in the life of the individual when some itch is not being allayed, some anxiety is not being reduced or some frustration is not being alleviated. Any such event would produce puted the average number of bonus shots taken by boys and the average number taken by girls. As shown in the table, each child is reported as being above average (for his sex) or below average in the number of shots taken.

| | Percentage of Children Who Took More Than an Average Number of Shots at the Figure Card | |
	Boys	Girls
When the figure card had been associated with high-frustration	80.9*	50.0
When the figure card had been associated with low-frustration	28.0*	30.7
When the figure card had not been associated with frustration	45.0	69.3

* These values differ significantly from 50 percent. If nothing were at work, of course, we would expect, in each case, that half of each group would be above the average and half below.

SOURCE: Shirley G. Moore, Displaced aggression in young children, *Journal of Abnormal and Social Psychology*, 1964, 68, 200–204.

reinforcement, and this in turn would spread to any incidental stimuli present. Many of these casual reinforcements, of course, will be promptly offset by equally casual and equally pervasive extinction. It is not likely, however, that all effects will be neatly balanced out, and some weird and complex outcomes may be expected.

Other peculiar or paradoxical results may arise from two basic factors that affect the efficacy of reinforcement. First, immediate reinforcement is more effective than the reinforcement which comes after some delay. Second, a sudden or precipitous decrease in the intensity of stimulation makes for the greatest reinforcement. A more gradual decline has less influence. The superiority of immediate overdelayed reinforcement often brings unfortunate results. Our rash outburst of temper may bring ultimate cen-

sure or loss of friendship. Right now, however, it reduces the stimuli associated with our anger or frustration. It may thus become likely to be repeated in spite of its serious, but delayed, social consequences. The effect of a precipitous decline in stimulation is dramatically shown when the tortured prisoner is suddenly released from torment. This tremendous reduction in the flow of aversive stimuli constitutes pronounced reinforcement. By the mechanism of secondary reinforcement, moreover, we would expect that any person or object, present at that time, would take on some of those reinforcing properties. The tormentor himself, if he were conspicuously present during the rapid cessation of pain, could easily become a source of reinforcement and could evoke in his victim the same attitude that the mother evokes in the infant she succors. Allegiance, then, goes not necessarily to the considerate and faithful provider and protector but so frequently to the bully or tormentor who merely arranges for periodic remissions of distress while he himself is present.

SOCIALIZATION AS DIRECT REINFORCEMENT

The theories of both the Freudians and the Hullians have become quite complicated. Both theories rely on intricate devices such as ego, superego, and the id, in the case of the Freudians, or on a host of acquired drive-states such as dependency, anxiety, cognitive dissonance, and perhaps a drive toward imitation in the case of the Hullians. Both theories stress such processes as displacement and identification.

The Search for Simpler Mechanisms

Reliance on elaborate and intricate mechanisms does not necessarily condemn a theory. Inevitably, however, many people must wonder if all the complexities are necessary. This is especially likely to happen when the inferred mechanisms are quite removed from direct observation. At any rate, B. F. Skinner (Chapter 5) and his associates have held that whenever possible, we should describe character formation and other phenomena in terms of things we can actually observe. We observe the baby crying, for instance. We can see him being fed. We can see that he stops crying. Why not, ask the Skinnerians, try to describe the results in terms of the things we see? If we do find it convenient to invent new shorthand labels, they would urge us to remember that these are only convenient labels that we have made up. We should not regard these labels as something actually occurring in

nature, something that we have discovered. Under many conditions, for instance, we see a child acting in a manner that we might call dependent. To simplify things in talking to each other we might group these acts together under the heading of *dependent behavior*. But in applying this label we would be advised not to give the impression that there is some single, real force within the child that could be called a dependency urge. In the same way we could, for convenience, talk about "traffic-light" behavior, without in any way implying that there is a single, identifiable urge to deal with traffic lights.

Special Problems in Social Reinforcement

Psychologists influenced by Skinner's views (Bandura and Walters, 1963b; Buss, 1961), rely heavily on direct reinforcement to explain character formation or socialization. They lay great stress, however, on the fact that, in this process, the basic reinforcement is of a social nature. Much of the relevant reinforcement comes from being noticed rather than ignored, from receiving a smile rather than a frown or a blank look, from being praised rather than scolded. Such reinforcement is by no means the same as the reinforcement that follows the acts of eating food, escaping from pain, or achieving sexual release.

Unpredictable Sequences in Social Reinforcement. Social reinforcement is notoriously unpredictable. The ingestion of food produces a fairly dependable change in the flow of stimuli. So does the removal of cold, damp clothes. Blowing a bubble of saliva, on the contrary, or coming out with a cute statement can have no such predictable consequences. At times the adults in the vicinity may smile and gurgle in delighted fashion. At times they may take no notice and at other times they may turn away in disgust. Social reinforcement varies not only in this chance or random fashion. It also changes systematically as the child grows older. The seeking of the breast, which at first is followed by tender reception, is later met by a rebuff. The cute performance, smilingly admired in the two-year-old, is scolded in the four-year-old. Some of these changes may come from changes in the standards or expectations that we attach to children of different ages. Other changes come from the fact that social reinforcement is reciprocal. Not only does the parental reinforcement shape the later behavior of the child, but the behavior of the child partially determines the pattern of parental reinforcement. Consciously or unconsciously, parents and other adults change their ways of reacting to the behavior of children. The delighted surprise that greets the infant's first peek-a-boo loses some of its zest and spontaneity after fifteen performances in a row. The patient admonition that follows one upset glass of milk may yield to an irritated scolding after a dozen such episodes.

Selective Features in Social Reinforcement. Clearly the pattern of social reinforcement is intricate and complex. From such an intricate pattern, moreover, peculiar things may develop. A young child, for instance, begins to whimper. Hoping that this is merely transitory, we pay no attention. The crying grows more and more intense, however, and finally we show our concern. In this illustration, mild crying has received no social reinforcement. Intense crying has been rewarded. Are we thus training the child to abandon mild protests altogether and to replace them with screams of outrage at every inconvenience?

The Termination of Punishment. This bewildering intricacy confronts us in almost any interaction with the child. Detecting some misdemeanor, we begin to scold the child. Now, as we saw in Chapter 5, we are not sure just what happens when a scolding is begun. There is no question, however, about what will happen when a scolding ceases. The termination of a scolding is reinforcing. Whatever the child happens to be doing at that moment, he will be more likely to repeat in the future. Perhaps he was weeping as the scolding stopped. Weeping will become more strongly entrenched. Perhaps, instead, he was muttering murderous threats against the scolder. Such mutterings will be reinforced. Perhaps the overt scolding continued unabated but it lost its impact because the child "tuned it out." "Tuning out" will be reinforced.

It is not surprising that, in spite of our best efforts, children learn the most peculiar things. Neither is it surprising, fortunately, that by and large, in spite of bewildering detours, they do gradually become more and more socialized. The pattern of reinforcement, for all its intricacies, does tend in that direction.

The Role of Imitation

Along with the complex contingencies of reinforcement, some members of this group, Bandura and Walters (1963b), for instance, also place great stress on the gross, observed fact of imitation. However one may feel about the machinery responsible for imitation, these authors hold the phenomenon itself has been irrefutably established. Children consistently imitate behavior they observe in others. As we see later on, this is more likely to occur under some conditions than others. It is more likely to occur, for instance, if the hero has been rewarded for his attack on the villain, if the physical risk has lead to admirable results. But in any case, we must include it as a factor in character development.

By means of imitation the child is provided with types of responses he might never stumble upon otherwise. Left to his own devices he would probably never invent the hammer-lock of the professional wrestler. Having observed this, however, he may try it out when opportunity offers. If used successfully, it is followed by a host of consequences. Some of these are purely physical. To a certain extent, his opponent moves in response to his efforts, just as a stone would move when pushed. The most important effects, however, are social. He senses his ascendancy over his victim. On one countenance or another, there may be expressions of surprise, admiration, regret, or anger. He is likely to encounter overt comments of approval or disapproval or both. And it is this pattern of reinforcement, and the pattern that occurs on subsequent occasions, that will determine whether or not he will go around applying hammer-locks of one form or another to the people around him.

CHARACTER FORMATION AS THE DEVELOPMENT OF UNDERSTANDING

To explain the facts of character development, many psychologists place their chief reliance on the mechanisms of thought and cognition. Rokeach (1960), for instance, holds that most of the mechanisms advanced by Freud and the Hullians can be linked up with the *beliefs* that a person holds, with the things he expects to happen, and most importantly, with the extent to which his system of beliefs and expectancies is open

to new experience or new evidence. Kohlberg (1963a) also suggests that to a great extent character develops as the child comes to grasp more and more complex ideas of the relation between conduct and results; as he comes to understand the important aspects of social conduct and of the social results of that conduct; and as he makes finer and more accurate discriminations in these matters. Most important, perhaps, character develops as he reaches a clearer idea of the self that he is and would like to be.

The outstanding proponent of this emphasis on mental structures as the basis for socialization is Jean Piaget (1932), the famous Swiss investigator of child development. For Piaget, moral development comes from the child's increasing grasp of the actual principles that make for acceptable social relations and from his greater internalization of these rules. As the child gets older he acquires a better grasp of the rules that determine reasonable behavior with respect to others, and he also becomes increasingly able to use those rules by himself, without depending on external cues from parents, teachers, or other adults.

Piaget's Heteronomous Stage

Piaget claims that by the time the child comes to school he is still in the heteronomous stage. He has a high intellectual regard for rules. True enough, he does not by any means always follow these rules, but he talks a lot about them. Much of the playtime conversation is concerned with what is fair and what is not, with what you can do and what you can't do. But these rules are considered as sacred, inflexible things, laid down by adults and not to be questioned (though not always to be obeyed). An act is bad if it breaks one of these rules and leads to bad consequences, especially if it leads to the danger of punishment. This is true regardless of the intent or the line of thought lying behind the act. When an accident has occurred, the whole group of preschoolers may scurry from the scene, whether or not they have done anything that adults would judge to be wrong. In their minds, wrongdoing is that which gets, or invites, punishment. Virtue and duty lie in complying with these arbitrary rules. The breaking of a rule demands pain or suffering rather than making good the harm that has been done. This suffering, moreover, follows naturally from wrongdoing. There is something in the nature of things to make sure that sin will be punished, the punishment coming essentially from the same authority that laid down the unchallengeable rule.

These ways of regarding things, Piaget believes, come partly from the child's inherent egocentricism during this heteronomous stage. The young pupil is intensely aware of the rules that affect him. He may also be aware of the rules that he can invoke to deal with age mates. But he cannot grasp the fact that other people, or inanimate objects for that matter, have any significance apart from his own wishes and his own fears or concerns. Until he catches some glimmer of other people as ends in themselves, with their own desires and feelings apart from him, he cannot hope to attain a genuine altruistic attitude.

Autonomous Stage

As this egocentricism begins to decline, and as the child becomes more and more able to see others as individuals in their own right, he can now grasp some of the rules by which separate coequals deal with the relation between their wishes and concerns. He no longer sees morality as a one-way obedience to authority, but as a mutual problem between equals. Punishment is not imminent, but is arranged by the group. At this stage, the child can also grasp his own responsibilities in dealing with the legitimate concerns of others. As befits one associated with the Institute of Jean-Jacques Rousseau, Piaget has no doubt that the highest morality comes from a clear understanding of the "social contract" by which each person grasps his reciprocal rights and obligations with respect to others. For Piaget, "merit lies from man to man, and not from man, Oh Lord, to Thee." In true morality, the only authority that counts is that which is derived from the requirements of group living in its broadest sense.

The adolescent's actual grasp of these principles, according to Piaget, will come largely from vigorous interaction with others of his age. Piaget is pessimistic about the teacher's power to influence these things in any direct, significant way. As teachers, of course, we can try to be sure that each student does have the necessary association with his fellows. We can also try to arrange things so that these groups of students will encounter social problems, and that these problems will include many facets of the relations between individuals. But, in Piaget's view, we cannot hope to control this process in any precise fashion.

In describing this emphasis on the social group as the source of morality, as in describing so many things in this section, we are discussing a theory. As we shall see later, the evidence is not unambiguously in its favor.

THE GENERAL CONCEPT OF STAGES

In both the Freudian and the Piaget theories, stages play an important role. They also play a part in other theories.

▶ Stages of Character Suggested by Different Theorists

Age	FREUD	ERIKSON	HAVIGHURST	PIAGET	KOHLBERG
1	(1) *Oral:* Basis for acquisitiveness, oral aggression	(7) Should learn trust, but could become distrustful	(12) *Impulsive:* Nor moral or immoral	(16) Few clear moral concepts	
2	(2) *Anal:* Basis for avarice, tantrums, creativity	(8) Should learn autonomy and control (self-will and negativism); could learn shame	(13) *Ego-centric, Expedient:* Learns some necessary control; learns how to please		
3	(3) *Phallic:* Erotic pleasure from self and others				(20) "Being good" means conforming to superior power and avoiding punishment
4	(4) *Phallic* (continued) Development and resolution of Oedipus complex	(9) Should learn initiative and imagination; but could learn guilt, fear, dependence		(17) *Heteronomous:* Believes in blind obedience to inflexible rules, but breaks rules. Act is bad if it has bad results (is punished). Punishment is expiative and follows from sin. Unilateral obligation to adults	
5			(14) *Outward Conformity and Irrational Conscience:* Conforms to most rules without thought. Feels irrational guilt or pride		
6					
7					
8		(10) Should learn industry, but same pressures working badly could lead to a sense of inferiority. Needs discipline and games with definite rules			(21) "Being good" means conforming to power and doing what is necessary to get what you want
9	(5) *Latent Period*			(18) *Intermediate:* Believes rules are partly based on mutual agreement; does not follow rules	
10					
11					
12					
13			(15) *Rational Conscience:* Choosing in the light of probable moral consequences. Preference for the moral. Less likely to do bad things from good intentions	(19) *Autonomous:* Rules are internalized. Seen as based on mutual agreement. Rules obeyed. Wrongdoing depends on intention. Justice seen as retributive and permits some mercy. Obligations extend to peers as well as to adults	(22) "Being good" means liking and helping others and living up to what others have a right to expect
15		(11) *Overcoming Identity Diffusion:* Should acquire self-confidence and a clear picture of larger self (including a consistent set of ideals), but may fail to settle the question of "Who am I?" Success calls for much experimenting			
14	(6) *Genital:* Genuine love for others as persons in their own right. Can become reality-oriented, socialized adult				
16					
17					(23) "Being good" includes the above, but also means conforming to ideals and to conditions necessary for group functioning
18					
19					

The concept of stages also has some very important, general implications.

In the accompanying box, the two theories of Freud and of Piaget appear almost as opposites. The important stages in the Freudian scheme are crowded into the first few years of life. For Piaget, the important transformations take place about the time of adolescence.

Erikson's (1956) stages can be considered as an elaboration of those of Freud. The five stages shown in the box are followed by three others, not shown, that develop in late adolescence or early adulthood. With luck, the young adolescent may attain a secure sense of identity. If that happens, he can safely risk genuine intimacy both in important friendship and in a later marriage. Having solved these problems, he need not remain fixated on his own personal concerns and can now freely commit his energy to productive activity. With these matters settled, he can hope to attain a genuine integrity, seeing himself and the world in a sober, realistic light, but with an unshakable basic confidence.

The stages proposed by Havighurst (1962) are empirical rather than theoretical. They are proposed descriptions of what we actually find as we follow the development of children.

The most recent proposal is that of Kohlberg (1963a). Like Havighurst, Kohlberg is trying chiefly to describe the types of comments made by children of different ages as they discuss moral and ethical problems. Kohlberg's ideas, however, reflect those of Piaget to a great extent. In contrast to Freud, Kohlberg attaches chief significance to the transformations which occur in the midteens.

Our chart does not include those who explain character primarily as an aspect of learning. For such theorists, character formation should be a continuous process, although a process that is by no means smooth. Gradually, however, by fits and starts, and with the occasional regression, the child comes to develop a different way of behaving. There is no emphasis on qualitative stages that can be sharply differentiated.

Each Stage as a Necessary Forerunner of the Next

In the minds of their proponents, these stages are not to be regarded merely as convenient descriptions, telling us what to expect at different ages. One stage, on the contrary, actually grows out of the previous stage. To take an anatomical example, the stage theorists do not merely say that hair develops *after* the skin has attained a certain structure. Going much farther, they say that hair simply cannot develop until the skin has attained the specified structure. Similarly, in the realm of primitive sex behavior, Harlow (1962) found that not only does infantile sex play precede adult sexual activity, but that, without the childish grooming and playing, adult sex behavior will not develop at all. Erikson does not merely say that the child will usually learn autonomy and initiative before he acquires a pattern of industry. Going much farther, he claims that the attainment of industry, and the avoidance of inferiority, becomes possible only if the child has had reasonable success in working out the problems of the earlier stages. The other theorists similarly hold that one stage does not merely succeed another, but that each is a genuine transformation of an earlier stage.

Stages as Convenient Descriptions

Not everyone, of course, takes this extreme position with respect to stages. Some psychologists are content to point out that some behavior is typical of two-year-olds and other behavior typical of adolescents. They do not contend that each and every child must work his way through each stage before reaching the next. Most children do manage tricycles before graduating to bicycles, but—*must* they?

Even this less extreme notion of stages has much significance for the teacher. It is comforting and useful for us to know that the behavior we see before us is typical of a particular age, and that it will probably change and present us with a new pattern of worries and opportunities later on. To us, as to the parent, it is comforting and encouraging to know that "life is like that" and that our trouble is not a special visitation conjured up for our particular bedevilment.

The far-reaching claims of the more extreme theories of stages, however, have even more significance for the work of the teacher. Childish behavior is still inevitably transient and it is still to be relished, or endured, as something that is bound to pass. But in the extreme views, it is much more than that. These immature ways of doing things constitute the very essence from which the more adequate behavior is to be developed. These early flounderings are to be welcomed and exploited. Obviously, moreover, we must often wait while the timetable of changes follows its own inner sequence. If this theory is correct, we are doomed to failure if we try to rush things. And we ignore an opportunity that will never knock again if we do not take advantage of the stage now present.

SUMMARY

The facets of character that have been measured can be broken down into external conformity, external friendliness, inner friendliness, zest and commitment, reliance on inner controls, and understanding the implications of behavior. The instruments which reveal these factors include interviews, projective tests, inventories, ratings, and performance tests. These tend to measure freedom from character defect rather than possession of the more exciting features of character. Whatever traits they measure seem to remain fairly constant from one testing period to another.

Character has proved to be an intriguing mystery for many of the major psychological theorists. The Freudians visualize one or two basic urges, lodged in the id, and focusing on any outlet that will bring pleasurable release. The ego develops to keep the energy focused on realistic and safe outlets. During the fierce struggle involved in the Oedipus complex, the superego also develops. By conscious or unconscious controls, the superego tries to keep the id's energy focused on morally acceptable outlets. From the superego's efforts at unconscious controls come such processes as repression, displacement, and an unconscious identification with the parent of the same sex. Some attempts at displacement result in guilt and anxiety, and the distress from these forces leads the growing individual into more acceptable ways of behaving.

Other psychologists consider the learning of moral behavior to be similar to other forms of learning. Psychologists influenced by Clark Hull imagine a limited number of primitive drives (hunger, pain avoidance) and a larger number of acquired drive-states (need to be near parents). The reduction of any one of these drive-states results in the reinforcing of any act just committed. This power of reinforcing also spreads to neutral stimuli (secondary reinforcement). Much of moral learning comes from reduction of dependency and love needs and from the reduction of guilt or anxiety. This theory attempts to explain both the normal course of character development and the frequent bizarre or devious side effects.

A third group of psychologists lean heavily on reinforcement, but make less use of elaborate drive-states. They take for granted such processes as reinforcement and imitation and try to use these processes to explain both the successes and failures so frequently seen in character development. In doing this they stress the complexities involved in social reinforcement.

Other theorists, taking their lead from Piaget, stress the development of mental structures or concepts. They hold that the difference between the amoral, punishment-conscious child and the

moral adult lies in the latter's more accurate grasp of moral ideas, and in his understanding of his own moral make up. Before the child acquires the necessary understanding, he may achieve a blind conformity that makes things fairly comfortable for himself and for his elders. But he cannot clearly foresee the outcomes of his behavior nor can he see his true responsibility for these outcomes nor relate either of these to a clear concept of himself as a moral person.

The concept of stages, so prominent in the views of Piaget, also plays a part in the psychoanalytic theories. In both kinds of views, one stage is the necessary forerunner of the next. Other theorists admit that behavior shows typical sequences but question that the second stage depends on having passed through the first.

SUGGESTIONS FOR FURTHER READING

The Measurement of Character

Most of the general texts listed in Chapter 3 provide some discussion of measuring character. See especially Anastasi; Cronbach; Freeman; Remmers (1963); Remmers, Gage, and Rummel, 1960; and Thorndike and Hagen.

Harris, D. B., A scale for measuring attitudes of social responsibility in children, *Journal of Abnormal and Social Psychology*, 1957, **55**, 322–326.

Krathwohl, D. R., B. S. Bloom, and B. B. Masia, *Taxonomy of Educational Objectives*, Handbook II: *The Affective Domain*. New York: David McKay Company, Inc., 1964.

Remmers, H. H., *An Introduction to Opinion and Attitude Measurement*. New York: Harper & Row, Publishers, Inc., 1954. A section on attitude measurement is reprinted in Remmers, pp. 505–509.

Stern, G. G., Measuring noncognitive variables in research on teaching, in N. L. Gage, ed., *Handbook of Research on Teaching*. Skokie, Ill.: Rand McNally, 1963, pp. 398–447.

Yarrow, Marian R., The measurement of children's attitudes and values, in P. H. Mussen, ed., *Handbook of Research Methods in Child Development*. New York: John Wiley & Sons, Inc., 1960, pp. 645–687.

General Treatments of Character Development

Hartshorne, H., and M. A. May, A summary of the work of the Character Education Inquiry, *Religious Education*, 1930, **25**, 607–619; 754–762. Modified version in Kuhlen, pp. 432–441.

Jones, V., Character education, *Encyclopaedia of Educational Research*, 3d ed. New York: The Macmillan Company, 1960, pp. 184–191.

Peck, R. F., and R. J. Havighurst, *The Psychology of Character Development*. New York: John Wiley & Sons, Inc., 1960. Section on developmental levels reprinted in Morse, pp. 122–129.

Stevenson, H. W., ed., Child psychology, *Yearbook National Society for the Study of Education*, 1963, **62**, Part I. See especially the following chapters: Chapter 7, L. Kohlberg, "Moral Development and Identification"; Chapter 8, W. W. Hartup, "Dependence and Independence."

In 1957 the *British Journal of Educational Psychology* began a symposium on "The Development of Children's Moral Values." Of the various contributions, the following have considerable bearing on the problems and theories of character development:

Eysenck, H. J., The contribution of learning theory, *British Journal of Educational Psychology*, 1960, **30**, 11–21.

Hemming, J., Some aspects of moral development in a changing society, *British Journal of Educational Psychology*, 1957, **27**, 77–88.

Hilliard, F. H., The influence of religious education upon the development of children's moral ideas, *British Journal of Educational Psychology*, 1959, **29**, 50–59.

Morris, J. F., The development of adolescent value judgments, *British Journal of Educational Psychology*, 1958, **28**, 1–14.

The Psychoanalytic View

Bronfenbrenner, U., Freudian theories of identification and their derivatives, *Child Development*, 1960, **31**, 15–40. Reprinted in Stendler, pp. 102–121.

Bruner, J. S., Freud and the image of man, *American Psychologist*, 1956, **11**, 463–466. Reprinted in Rosenblith, pp. 5–8.

Erikson, E. H., *Childhood and Society*, 2d ed. New York: W. W. Norton & Company, Inc., 1963. One section, "Eight Ages of Man" reprinted in Stendler, pp. 242–255.

White, R. W., Competence and the psychosexual stages of development, in M. R. Jones, ed., *University Nebraska Symposium on Motivation*. Lincoln, Neb.: University Nebraska Press, 1960, **8**, 97–141. Portions reprinted in Rosenblith, pp. 213–221.

Social Learning

Bandura, A., and R. H. Walters, *Social Learning and Personality Development*. New York: Holt, Rinehart and Winston, Inc., 1963b.

Hill, W. F., Learning theory and the acquisition of values, *Psychological Review*, 1960, **67**, 317–331. Reprinted in Kuhlen, pp. 91–107.

Theories of Piaget

Bobroff, A., The stages of maturation in socialized thinking and in the ego development of two groups of children, *Child Development*, 1960, **31**, 321–338. Reprinted in Morse, pp. 315–323.

Durkin, Dolores, Children's concepts of justice: a further comparison with the Piaget data, *Journal of Educational Research*, 1959, **52**, 252–257. Reprinted in Seidman, pp. 559–567.

Medinnus, G. R., Objective responsibility in children: a comparison with Piaget data, *Journal of Genetic Psychology*, 1962, **101**, 127–133. Modified version in Kuhlen, pp. 426–431.

EXERCISES AND QUESTIONS FOR DISCUSSION

1. Think of someone that you know fairly well and rate him on each of the dimensions or factors that emerged from the Peck and Havighurst study.

Is your rating on one of these dimensions really independent of your rating on the others or, having rated him on one, do you find that you have, in effect, also rated him on some of the others? How well do these dimensions cover his character? Are there some important things about his character that are in no way brought out by the ratings?

2. List a few character tests that might well be used by the teacher; some that the teacher should be careful not to use.

3. What do you think of the Freudian theory (a) as the "truth"; (b) as a rigorous scientific explanation of observed facts; (c) as a working, imaginary model to make sense out of general behavior?

4. As you were growing up what changes took place in your ideas of "good" and "bad," "right" and "wrong"? See if these remembered changes fit in with any of the theories discussed. Can you trust your memory to portray these changes? What would the different theories predict about the trustworthiness of your memory with regard to these matters?

5. As inconspicuously as possible, listen in on a child trying to get (and keep) the attention of an adult who is reading. As far as possible, list each act performed by the child. Also list the adult response that followed each act. Which of these acts would seem likely to become more frequent? Which seem headed for extinction?

CHAPTER 10

▶ *The Inner Controls of Character and the Forces That Shape Them*

Whatever his theoretical orientation, any student of character would stress the importance of inner controls. If the child is to attain a reasonable degree of socialization, it is not enough that he should behave when under the eye of parent, teacher, or policeman. True morality must come from the operation of conscience or some other machinery which the child carries around with him (White and Lippitt, 1960, pp. 198–222) and which will function even when no one is looking (Peck and Havighurst, 1960).

THE CONTROLS IN THEIR THEORETICAL SETTING

Whatever the agreement on the necessity of some internal machinery or system of control, we are not surprised when we find different theorists emphasizing different kinds of controls. Psychoanalytic psychologists emphasize the feelings of *anxiety* and *guilt*, the structure of the *superego*, *conscience* and *ego-ideal*, and the process of *identification*. The more materialistic proponents of learning theory see the controls simply as internal connections by which the student is led to respond in one way rather than another. The Hullians invoke guilt or anxiety and identification only to help account for the formation of such connections. Other learning theorists make little reference to guilt or anxiety, but do rely heavily on internal tendencies to imitate. The followers of Piaget, although admitting the existence of guilt feelings, place greater stress on concepts of *self-blame* and a more balanced *self-criticism*. This latter term implies an intellectual appreciation of the situation, an appreciation that may be lacking in primitive feelings of guilt.

Guilt and Anxiety as Controls

The powerful feelings associated with guilt and anxiety have appealed to laymen and to psychologists alike as effective agencies for the control of conduct. As we have seen, these inner states receive different interpretations from the different theorists.

Psychoanalytic Views. To the Freudian, anxiety is one of the powerful forces with which the ego must constantly deal (Hall and Lindzey, 1957). Anxiety comes to the ego in several forms, and each form calls for some outlet. *Reality anxiety* is the simple fear of a real menace, such as the fear of the advancing aggressor or of the height from which we may fall. This fear may focus on a simple outlet such as flight or withdrawal. *Neurotic anxiety* is the fear of other drives or urges. Sensing some urge that has led to punishment in the past, we feel that same punishment working upon us again. The energy of this anxiety may be focused upon the inhibition of the frightening urge. Guilt is *moral anxiety*, arising from the fear of the conscience. The energy from this guilt is most suitably released when we obey the conscience and refuse to carry out the act that would give it offense.

Under the circumstances just set forth, the operation of moral anxiety or guilt would be quite straightforward. In actual practice, however, there are often complications. One complication arises when the guilt feelings become too intense. When faced with such excessive anxiety, the ego typically erects one of the familiar defense mechanisms (see Chapter 13). It then proceeds to deal with the distorted feelings. When this happens the energy behind the real guilt feelings may never be directed to its normal outlet.

A further complication arises from the fact that the basic force underlying guilt is not really directed to reform. This underlying drive comes from the agressive urges within the id, now redirected toward the self. To satisfy these primitive urges, it is not necessary that we reform. It is only necessary that we feel pain or anxiety. As soon as this pain or anxiety comes into existence, it satisfies the aggressive urge. As pain or anxiety, however, it becomes a problem with which the ego must deal. The exercise of moral restraint is the natural way for the ego to deal with this anxiety, unless, of course, the anxiety becomes so intense as to call for distortion.

The Place of Anxiety in Learning Theory. In the Freudian view, guilt and anxiety work by forcing the ego to take some action. In this there is little emphasis on the resulting reductions in anxiety. To the extent that the anxiety is reduced, as a matter of fact, there would be less need for the ego to take moral action (Kohlberg, 1963b).

Hullian theorists, in contrast to the Freudians, regard guilt or moral anxiety primarily as a drive-state that can be reduced. It is from the reduction of this drive-state, as from the reduction of any drive-state, that we get the all-important reinforcement. Any act that reduces our sense of guilt, and its attendant anxiety, will be reinforced. In owning up to a misdeed, for instance, the child may reduce his guilt distress. The act of owning up would thus be reinforced. Other moral behavior such as making restitution, apologizing, or turning away from wrongdoing can similarly reduce the anxiety of guilt and can become more and more strongly entrenched as habitual ways of doing things.

The followers of Skinner have little to say about guilt as a phenomenon.

They point out, however, that some of the *external indicators of guilt* actually serve as means of obtaining direct reinforcement. With confession or self-blame, for instance, the person gains release from the third degree or from other forms of inquisitions. This release means tremendous reinforcement. Under less stressful circumstances, voluntary or spontaneous confession may lead to praise or certainly to a mitigation of typical punishment. This pattern of reinforcement would suggest that the outward indicators of guilt, certainly, and perhaps the guilt itself, could be learned in the same way that we learn to avoid the hot stove.

The Cognitive Approach. The cognitive theorists (Kohlberg, 1963a) do not deny the guilt that is seen in the primi-tive wincing of the child who has done wrong. This is just as real as the pain of a burn or the distress of loneliness. Such primitive distress, moreover, may help in the later development of morality. Nor do the cognitive theorists deny the significance of the kind of guilt that leads to confession. Although it may be largely a technique to regain parental regard, it, too, may play a part in the attainment of true morality. But in admitting these things, the cognitive theorists still attach chief importance to the concepts and ideas that grow up along with these emotional aspects of guilt and that later become interwoven with them.

Many of the cognitive theorists consider that the guilt felt by the adolescent is by no means the same thing as that felt by the young child, and, unlike other

---

► *Confession Not Always a Direct Outgrowth of Wrongdoing*

The children taking part in this study were 69 girls and 69 boys in grade six. Groups of boys and groups of girls were assembled and given booklets containing the first part of four stories. An investigator read a story aloud as the children followed. The children were asked to complete the story. Other stories were then treated in the same way. The stories dealt with aggressive themes.

A few days later each child individually worked at a miniature shooting gallery. He was encouraged to try for a high score and then left alone. The situation permitted cheating and it was only by cheating that a high score could be obtained. Immediately after this experience, each child completed four stories similar to those completed initially.

In one or more of the completed stories most children (131 of 138) introduced some element of confession. In 77 percent, the hero confessed voluntarily before being questioned. The other confessions (admissions) followed questioning. Girls included more confession themes than boys.

While in the shooting gallery, 52 of the boys (75 percent) and 44 of the girls (64 percent) cheated.

The noncheaters used more confession themes both before and after temptation than did the cheaters. This was especially marked in the case of the girls.

SOURCE: Freda G. Rebelsky, W. Allinsmith, and R. E. Grinder, Resistance to temptation and sex differences in children's use of fantasy confession, *Child Development*, 1963, **34**, 955–962.

theorists, they think it unwise to explain adult morality in terms of the kinds of feelings observed in early childhood.

Self-blame and Self-criticism

Self-blame is a somewhat intellectualized form of guilt. It goes beyond mere pain, fear, or anxiety. These feelings could occur after an accident even though the child himself is in no way at fault. Even when, in objective fact, he is at fault, he could feel this blind anxiety without actually realizing his fault or without admitting it to himself or to others. Self-blame implies that the feeling of distress is accompanied by a clear admission of wrongdoing, certainly to the self, perhaps also to others, in the form of *confession*.

To the followers of Piaget, the young child is almost limited to such primitive inner controls as self-blame and the attendant fear of punishment. During this egocentric stage the child can visualize only his own concerns. Morality begins and ends with whether or not *he* has obeyed the rules or, at the other extreme, whether or not he has rendered himself liable to punishment.

Intellectual Aspects of Self-criticism. According to Piaget (1932) and his associates, *self-criticism* is a much more significant control than self-blame, but this calls for an intellectual grasp of matters that is seldom available to the preadolescent. It is only when he has emerged from this egocentric stage and when he can see other people as important in their own right that the adolescent can see the distress of others in reasonably objective fashion. While we are still in the egocentric stage we see our victim's distress as linked to our intentions. If we can show that we were not really at fault, his distress takes on a different complexion and strikes us as being less important.

To attain true self-criticism, the older student must see the distress of others as an objective reality, no matter who is to blame. He must also see this distress as something that any person of good will would seek to remedy, again, no matter who is to blame. Just as he must see the other's predicament objectively, so must he see his own part in objective fashion. If he is responsible, he must see this unflinchingly. He must also see how this behavior violates his concept of himself. To say this, of course, is to say that he must have a clear concept of himself as a moral person or as a person to whom this sort of behavior is reprehensible.

The young person capable of true self-criticism will typically feel the need to make amends or rectify his wrongdoing whenever that is still possible. Through his more adequate intellectual grasp of things, moreover, he becomes susceptible to additional pain. Some of this additional pain comes from his clearer intellectual appreciation of the victim's objective predicament. He would feel this pain no matter who had caused the victim's hurt. Additional pain comes from his disappointment as he realizes that he himself has fallen short of the behavior demanded by his concept of a moral being.

Self-criticism and General Moral Concepts. The kind of guilt just described can come into play only after the child can grasp some fairly complex ideas. These ideas or concepts, moreover, are not necessarily tied to guilt, but have much broader application. The adolescent experiencing this form of guilt is also capable of more general moral ideas. When he has reached this stage, he can also feel moral indignation over wrongs done to others, quite apart from his own life. He can also form disinterested moral judgments regarding the behavior of characters in literature or in hypothetical case studies.

To the followers of Piaget, this intellectualized form of guilt, experienced by the adolescent, is a much more effective inner control than the mechanisms seen in the young child. Primitive self-blame, for instance, does not contain the urge to rectify the misdeed or to make restitution, nor does it contain any feature from which this concept could plausibly be derived.

Identification as an Inner Control

In discussing the basic theories of psychoanalysis, we have already considered some important features of identification. In this theory (Bronfenbrenner, 1960) the child's identification with the same-sex parent plays a crucial role. Without it, the superego would never develop, and it is only through identification that the superego achieves access to the energy system of the id.

Not all theories, of course, attach so much theoretical significance to the process of identification. The followers of Hull see it as developing from powerful dependency needs. Skinnerian psychologists regard identification as something that we create by our patterns of reinforcement. When we see a child adopting our values, for instance, we feel happy about it and express our approval. When we see him adopting a more shoddy set of values, we fail to reinforce him. We thus lead him to the adoption of values, interests, and concerns that coincide with ours.

Whatever the genesis of identification, many theorists see in it a powerful inner control that influences the child's social behavior. Identification is what keeps him from doing what he thinks his father would not do. Faulty identifica-tion could lead to aimlessness and weakness. Identification with the parent of the opposite sex could lead to rejection of his own sex role and to serious maladjustment.

Types of Identification. Along with the identification that a child feels for one parent or the other, some investigations (Bandura and Walters, 1959) have stressed general identification with the home. The child profoundly influenced by this control may not be able to indicate how his mother will react, or what his father will think, but he does have a clear idea of the values and attitudes that are important to the family as a group. This kind of identification is discussed in Chapter 11 in connection with delinquency.

Identification and Imitation. Identification refers primarily to an attitude or inner state. Insofar as it influences the child's behavior it acts as a genuine inner control that the child carries around with him. Imitation, on the other hand, merely refers to the fact that the child's behavior resembles that of some model. We know, for instance, about some identifiable features, or relatively unique features, in the behavior of some adult. Later on we see that those same identifiable acts are performed by another person, often a child. This objective fact of imitation does not necessarily imply any specific inner controls.

In the effort to explain the objective fact of imitation, some theorists do make use of inner controls. The Freudians consider that the imitation results largely from an earlier identification. One person imitates another because he identifies with that person. According to this theory, the identification which the child carries around with him controls many kinds of behavior, including imitative behavior.

► *Do Children Have a General Tendency To Imitate Adults of the Same Sex?*

It has been held that children, boys especially, are more likely to imitate an adult of the same sex. But how general is this tendency? A boy may imitate the same-sex adult in one situation, but will he do so consistently?

Hartup observed 44 girls and 50 boys between the ages of 3 and 6. The children moved dolls around in a play situation, as the investigator told a story. The mamma doll, or the papa doll, the little friend, and the doll representing the child himself, are in the yard. They go into the house for a drink. The mother (father) doll goes one way, the little friend another way. Which way does *this* doll (the child himself) go?

In general there was more imitation of same-sex parents than of opposite-sex parents.

If a boy did show himself more likely to imitate his father in one situation, he was somewhat more likely (r's from .30 to .45) to imitate him in other situations. For girls this was not so true (r's from .22 to .38). The boys who did imitate the mother, however, were not consistent from situation to situation.

SOURCE: W. W. Hartup, Patterns of imitative behavior in young children, *Child Development*, 1964, **35**, 183–191.

Hullians think that imitation is due to an internal tendency to imitate. This tendency, or way of behaving, has been built up because it has been reinforced in one way or another. This internal tendency is a type of inner control, but it differs markedly from the kind of control the Freudians attribute to identification. The tendency to imitate does not act as a positive force, pushing the child in one direction rather than another. On the contrary, it merely makes sure that he will respond in a particular way to behavior that he sees.

The psychologists influenced by Skinner (Bandura and Walters, 1963b) merely stress the objective fact of imitation and do not link this fact to any specific inner needs or attitudes. They make a great deal of the fact that children do imitate. They point out the conditions under which imitation is likely to occur.

But they do not push the matter much farther.

When considered as an objective phenomenon, and not linked to any specific inner state, imitation should be viewed not as an inner control but as an external force that shapes the actual behavior. By manipulating the situations to which the child is exposed, we can make him act in this way rather than that. Having made him act in one way rather than another, we can arrange for reinforcement and thus make him more likely to act that way in the future.

In the sections that follow, imitation will often be offered as an explanation which seems to deny the importance of inner controls. Having observed, for instance, that the considerate parents are blessed with gentle children, we shall ask: Does this mean that consideration brings about more effective identification or stronger guilt or a more clear-cut self-criticism? Or could it mean that these children are merely, perhaps automatically, imitating the qualities they see in their parents? Here imitation is offered in opposition to theories that stress inner controls.

INNER CONTROLS, PARENTS, AND MORALITY

It is always assumed, of course, that inner controls serve chiefly as intermediate links between forces and character. They are the product of some external forces that act on the child, and they, in turn, play a part in determining his character. We turn now to the various interrelations between the forces, the controls, and the character which may result. In this we must deal, at one time or another, with the effect of forces on controls, with the relation between controls and morality, and also with the more direct relation between forces and morality.

The Study of Parental Behavior

To study the forces which affect inner controls or morality, is, of course, to turn the spotlight on the doings of parents (Becker and others, 1959; Hoffman, 1963). It is toward this area of parent-child relations that many theorists have pointed their remarks. To the great dismay of parents, the rival theorists have often offered conflicting advice (Ryerson, 1961) and, at times, each has seemed to threaten horrible consequences unless his particular doctrine were adopted.

Parental Warmth. In the warm home we find good-natured affection for children, expressed freely and demonstratively. There is much praise and encouragement, moderate use of reason, but little reliance on punishment. This home is to be contrasted with the harsh situations in which children are regarded as a nuisance and in which control or management is synonymous with punishment.

Children from the warmer homes show much more evidence of the controls that have been discussed. They are more willing to confess misdeeds and they experience genuine sadness over their behavior, placing the blame directly on themselves. The product of the harsher home is less likely to own up to misdeeds. When he is caught red-handed, moreover, he seems to feel that he is not really culpable or that he has anything to be ashamed of. He thinks anyone would do what he did, but he just happened to get caught, largely through the fault of someone else. All in all, in contrast to the expectations of the "power" theory of identification, punishment does not seem to promote a strong or adult type of conscience. The children from the nonpunitive homes show much more adequate development in this respect.

It is comforting to know that children from these pleasant homes turn out well. We must not be too quick, however, to decide just what is causing what (Payne and Mussen, 1956). Some theorists would attribute the results to the warmth itself, holding that this permits the identification necessary for morality. Other theorists would minimize the influence of such an inner control as identification and would explain the facts in terms of imitation. They claim that the less moral children merely carry out the harshness and irresponsibility they see so dramatically portrayed in the home. The other children, in their attitude toward people, imitate the affectionate behavior that their parents display. Theorists of the cognitive persuasion would

Stanford University Photographic Dept.

ROBERT R. SEARS

call attention to the fact that indifferent parents employing harsh, inconsistent, and unreasoning discipline are themselves lacking in some basic understanding. The children growing up in this deprived environment also fail to acquire the concepts of moral notions necessary for reasonable behavior.

Parental Anxiety. Homes vary not only in the warmth and affection but also in anxiety. At one extreme we may find parents who are happy-go-lucky and casual. At the other extreme we find parents who are tense, anxious, and desperately concerned about whether things are good or bad and who worry about what other people will think. These two dimensions, by the way, could be quite independent of each other. The happy-go-lucky parents, giving no thought to the morrow, could be quite harsh and punitive when a child gets in the way of the activities of

the moment. Or they could be warm and indulgent. Conversely, some tense, anxious parents could also be cold and punitive. Others, equally anxious, could feel genuine warmth and could earnestly and fearfully express acceptance at every turn.

Such parental anxiety about morals, especially about sex morality, is linked with well-developed guilt feelings in the children. Having done wrong, such children are more likely to feel genuine moral anxiety. This capacity for guilt is related not, as the Freudians would expect, to the actual parental restriction of sex activity, but to sheer parental concern or anxiety about sex, whether or not this anxiety expresses itself in prohibition or restrictions (Kohlberg, 1963b).

Control through Love Withdrawal. In some homes the mother may exploit the child's dependent needs, rewarding the child by allowing him to be close to her or withdrawing love upon his bad behavior. Children treated in this way are especially likely to confess to wrongdoing even at an early age. As they grow older, moreover, they are better able to resist temptation when given an opportunity to cheat, steal, or disobey instructions. Not surprisingly, however, this technique of love withdrawal has such an effect only when the mother is somewhat affectionate in the first place—only when there is some actual love to be withdrawn.

It is difficult to know just what part is played by the inner controls in this relation. Guilt is present in these children who resist temptation, but it is difficult to see such guilt as the cause of self-restraint. If guilt springs from actual wrongdoing, we should see less of it when the temptation has been successfully resisted. Actually, judging from their comments in projective play, it is the children who resist temptation who seem most preoccupied with guilt and confession. Those who yield to temptation talk less about guilt. Perhaps the temptation stirs up some general anxiety about wrongdoing and this in turn elicits guilt. The fantasied confession may serve as a means of reducing the anxiety and of giving the child a stronger claim to the parental love that he is always so close to forfeiting. Such fantasies are likely to appear in children who have a high need for approval. They are also more typical of girls than of boys.

Self-criticism and the Parental Environment. Self-criticism involves a number of related concepts. These concepts, it will be remembered, deal with the notion of moral rules being necessary for effective group action, the idea of reciprocity or of something approaching the golden rule, the idea that effective morality calls for making amends whenever possible.

These ideas, so neatly linked with moral behavior, clearly develop with age. Few of the concepts just listed are ever found in preschool children. Over 75 per cent of twelve-year-olds, however, will stress one or more of these notions when talking about moral problems. This regular change is shown in Table 10.1.

The regular development of moral concepts with age, interestingly enough, seems to cut across child-rearing practices. True, the attainment of such concepts is related to the child's intelligence and to his general social class or to the milieu in which he lives. This development, however, is not linked to any specific things that parents do. Children growing up under a variety of disciplinary practices seem to develop rather similar ideas about the nature of morality. This somewhat surprising constancy also appears occasionally in the development of superficial values and in the nature of things liked or disliked. In one community, for instance, grade-seven pupils of different IQ levels, and even from different social class groupings, showed marked agreement in the way they ranked the immorality of such things as bullying, stealing, boasting, smoking, and losing one's temper (Goertzen, 1959).

TABLE 10.1. Change in Concepts of Morality with Age

Different Concepts of Morality	PERCENT OF ALL STATEMENTS SHOWING EACH CONCEPT OF MORALITY			
	Age 7	Age 10	Age 13	Age 16
What is meant by morality or being good?				
1. Obeying, and thus avoiding punishment	70	31	11	10
2. Doing things that help you avoid worry	23	28	13	8
3. Helping other people and securing their approval	7	22	25	23
4. Respecting authority	0	15	31	33
5. Fitting in with rules necessary for group living	0	3	15	20
6. Obeying a rational conscience	0	1	5	6

SOURCE: L. Kohlberg, The development of children's orientations toward a moral order: I. Sequence in the development of moral thought, *Vita Humana*, 1963a, 6, 11–33.

Sex Differences in Morality and Inner Controls

The inner controls stressed by the various theorists become especially intricate when they deal with the different roles played by the father and the mother, and to the different effect these roles may have on boys and on girls (McKee and Sherriffs, 1959).

As any parent knows, boys are different from girls in the matter of behavior and conformity. Boys are the chief trouble makers in the school. Until recently, moreover, if not even now, agressive juvenile delinquency has been largely a masculine enterprise. But the differences are not all one-sided. It is true that girls do conform more readily to social expectations. Boys, on the other hand, show more concern for moral rules and for objective ethical principles. Boys are more likely to stress these general principles in talking about moral issues. They are also more likely to be guided by the values and principles they have adopted. The girl's greater conformity, in contrast, stems not so much from the values she has espoused as from her greater orientation to the approval of others and from her greater sensitivity to the plight of those who may suffer from her behavior (Douvan, 1960). In judging the behavior of others, girls are more likely to condemn behavior because it is personally irritating. Boys are more likely to base their indignation on general rules. Boys are also more willing than girls to be controlled by the rules they impose on others (Kohlberg, 1963b).

Theoretical Expectations. Both the Freudians and the social-learning theorists would expect these differences. The Freudians expect a more stringent and objective superego to develop in boys. The superego, we remember, develops from the resolution of the Oedipus complex. In coming to terms with this complex, the boy is spurred on by the actual threat of castration. The girl, on the other hand, is driven chiefly by a resentment for the mutilation that she has already endured. The boy's more urgent danger demands a more effective superego as a protection. From the girl's less compelling fear we might expect a superego that is less tyrannical, less absolute, and more personal and relative.

The theorists who stress social learning point to our conspicuous folklore dealing with the vagaries of feminine logic, especially in moral matters. Not only is it more forgivable for a girl to decide moral issues in terms of her own feelings, but such perversities are often depicted as being cute, or delightfully feminine, if not actually attractive.

Sex differences do not stop with moral objectivity. In giving up their dependence and in becoming responsible adults, girls and boys face different risks. When the girl fails to attain responsibility, the trouble is most likely to be too much affection and control on the part of the parents. With the boy, the lack of a responsible attitude is most likely to come from too little authority and too little support on the part of the parents (Bronfenbrenner, 1961b).

Sex Role of Adults and Socialization of Children. Not only do boys differ from girls in moral matters, but men differ from women in their influence upon child morality. A number of the things that the mother does have been found to be related to the moral behavior of the child. The same is true for the father's activities. But the things that count in the mother's behavior are not the same as the things that count in the father's behavior. When there is no father in the home, boys tend to be less aggressive. Girls are unaffected. With respect to delinquency, surprising as it may seem, it is the father's kindliness that matters. Variations in nurturance from mother to mother are less important (Bandura and Walters, 1959).

At first glance, this emphasis on the nurturance and affection provided by the father seems quite paradoxical. In many theories, the boy's identification with the father is supposed to come from the latter's power and prestige, and only secondarily from love of the father, or from the pleasure of being in his company. But the child, in forming his image of the male role, does not rely exclusively on the experiences from his own home (Kohlberg, 1963b). Whatever the situation in their own homes, both boys and girls regard males as somewhat more formidable than females. For younger children, transgression against a male is a much more serious matter than transgression against a female. In the world in general, these larger, deeper-voiced creatures, more freely indulging in mysterious comings and goings, and more clearly linked with community activities, are not to be taken lightly. And this general impression is not upset even when by some accident the child's own parents may have reversed these roles (Hartley, 1960). In the same way, the fatherless child may unhesitatingly depict the typical family as having both father and mother—his own anomalous situation being considered beside the point.

It is possible that any father, no matter how henpecked, automatically acquires this general mantle of male prestige. Being thus adequately equipped, deservedly or otherwise, he need now only concentrate on the other ingredient of identification, namely nurturance. This, apparently, he must earn. There is no pervasive image of the loving, nurturant male to which he can lay easy claim. These possibilities might account for the fact that it is the affection shown by the father, and not his dominance, that differentiates the socialized child from his deliquent school mate (Bandura and Walters, 1959). To account for the fact that variations in maternal affection are less significant, we might advance a similar explanation. Perhaps, here again, any female, no matter how harsh and nagging she herself may be, can cash in on the stereotype of the tender, self-sacrificing mother.

INNER CONTROLS, CHARACTER, AND THE SCHOOLS

The school, of course, is only one of several forces that affect the character of the student (V. Jones, 1960). Prominent among the other forces we must acknowledge the home, with its early training (Freud, Erikson), the movies, television programs, and other entertainment to which the child is exposed (Bandura and Walters, 1963b; Heinrich, 1961), the casual experience on the street and in the community (Livson and Nichols, 1957), and, of course, the intimate association with playmates, at home, in the street, and at school (Piaget, 1932).

The School's Access to the Inner Mechanisms

Compared to the other agencies that play a part, just how much access do teachers have to the controls that shape character?

Rival Views from General Theory. If Freud or Erikson are right, much of the general shaping of character must have occurred long before the child comes to school. Something, of course, is left to the teacher. Some identifications must be developed. Someone should still point the way to more adequate adolescent adjustments. But the child has already worked out his basic style of dealing with his urges, his relations to others, and his relation to himself.

Offhand, it would seem that the cognitive theorists would attribute more influence to the school. If the crux of morality lies in the intellectual concepts that the student is able to grasp, surely the school should be quite influential. According to Piaget and Kohlberg, moreover, the ideas that are important to moral development do not really begin to develop until early adolescence. If this is true, the teacher should have the whole elementary school period in which to develop moral character.

But even here the picture is somewhat confused. Arguing from theoretical considerations, Piaget (1932) would warn us not to be too hopeful. He speculates that the basic moral concepts develop not from overt instruction but from broad-ranging interaction with age mates. He doubts if adults can do much to accelerate the notions that are thus formed. The little bit of evidence available, by the way, does not always support these speculations. If Piaget is right, we might expect that the greater the amount of social interaction, the greater the development of moral concepts. This, however, turns out not to be the case (Kohlberg, 1963b). Perhaps the pessimism of Piaget should be regarded with some degree of skepticism.

Social Reinforcement Available to the School. With respect to the simple mechanisms and controls stressed by the proponents of social learning, the school may be under a relative handicap when it turns to teaching moral tasks. Consider, for instance, the problems faced in managing the learning process while teaching the prudent and proper regulation of sexual behavior. Contrast these problems with those we face in teaching an academic task, such as the expansion of the expression $(a + b)^2$. In algebra the sequence of experiences is largely under our control. We can easily program a series of tasks so as to maximize the likelihood of success at each step. Not so with sexual behavior. Primitive animal make-up cares not whether we reply $a^2 + b^2$ or $a^2 + 2ab + b^2$, but it does take a fiercely partisan position about the alternatives in sexual behavior. The consequences of reinforcement which differentiate sexual restraint from sexual activity have strong physiological components and these completely elude the teacher's control. The consequences which differentiate an algebraic error from an acceptable response, on the other hand, are almost entirely social and symbolic, and are almost completely under the teacher's control. Most of the algebraic behavior will be under the teacher's eye and he can apply as rigid a schedule of reinforcement as he chooses. This is not true for sexual behavior. In applying his schedule of reinforcement to algebraic responses, the teacher encounters little competition from other people or other agencies. If other agencies do contest his decision about the adequacy of a response, the teacher has abundant prestige to bolster his position in these matters. In sexual behavior the teacher has no such monopoly of social reinforcement. Other people may readily comment on what the student does, or fails to do, in sexual matters. If such comments are at variance with those of the teacher, the latter can seldom pass as an unquestioned authority in matters of sex or romance. All in all, in each of the crucial factors in learning, the teacher is in a much more favorable position when he addresses himself to algebra than when he undertakes to bring about reasonable sexual restraint in the developing teenager.

Dependency and the Need for Affection

To say that we should be reasonable in our aspirations is not to say that we have no influence at all. We are bound to have some effect. Perhaps by taking thought we could do much more. At any rate, in an area as critical as this, we are bound to try.

Evidence and considerations of humanity both suggest that the teacher, in working for effective character, should strive mightily to meet the student's need for attention, affection, and regard. The evidence comes partly from a few classroom experiments (Sears and Hilgard, 1964) and partly from the general data in the field of parent-child relations. Some of the argument for generous acceptance and affection would also come from the drive-reduction theory of learning. When the powerful need for affection or attention remains unmet, several things can happen. In the first place, the frustration of the unfulfilled need can give rise to aggression. In giving way to this aggressive urge—possibly by picking on some younger child—the student may well force himself on the teacher's attention. Insofar as he succeeds in getting the teacher's attention, his need to be noticed will be partially met. This need reduction constitutes reinforcement. If at that moment the student had been picking on a younger child, this is the act that would be reinforced. Notice that each step in this unfortunate train of events would have been avoided if the student's need for attention or acceptance had been met in the first place.

The theorists who stress direct reinforcement would also warn us about the dangers in a harsh and punitive atmosphere. The dangerous side effects, ironically enough, come from the fact that, at unpredictable times, the harshness is bound to be alleviated and the persisting threat of punishment is bound to be reduced. The teacher may smile in spite of himself. This alleviation of the grim atmosphere provides one of the most powerful kinds of reinforcement. Such inadvertent reinforcement will encourage all acts being carried out at that moment, however desirable or undesirable. Inadvertent reinforcement of this type would be less likely to occur if the general tone were more pleasant to begin with.

The Teacher as a Model for Imitation or Identification

The teacher is a potential model. Through one mechanism or another his character and behavior may be reflected in the activities of his students. To some extent, this may come from a genuine identification. The student may carry around some image of the teacher, and this image may function as an inner control. The student's behavior, on the other hand, may come from automatic, unthinking imitation which is in no way dependent on a clear image of the teacher. Here we shall be concerned with the teacher's role as a model whether his influence as a model comes from identification as an inner control or from automatic functioning of imitation as an external force.

Conditions Favoring Imitation. People are likely to imitate behavior that they see. This certainly is true for children (Bandura and Walters, 1963b) and also for adults (Berkowitz, 1964). Chil-

► *Children's Imitation of Behavior That Is Rewarded*

This study is based on 40 boys and 40 girls from 3 to 5 years of age. Each child was assigned to one of the four groups. Three of the groups watched what seemed to be a television show of two boys playing together.

In the scene presented to one group (aggressor-rewarded) one boy became very aggressive. He interrupted the play of the other, took the toys, and made off, happily, with the other boy's toys and picnic treats.

A second group (aggressor-punished) saw the same kind of aggression, but in this case the victim turned on the aggressor and trounced him. The aggressor was forced to sit cowering in a corner while the other boy resumed his play.

A third group saw two boys in vigorous, nonaggressive play.

A fourth group saw no "television" program.

After the "television" program, each child spent 20 minutes in a room containing the articles that had appeared in the television programs. An experimenter, also in the room, noted his activities. From these notes a record was made up showing the number of aggressive acts similar to those witnessed and the number of acts that were aggressive but different from those seen.

	Program Seen			
	Aggressor Rewarded	Aggressor Punished	Vigorous Play: No Aggressor	Control (No Program)
BOYS				
Number of aggressive acts performed that were similar to those seen	16.2	7.8	10.0	(5.6)
Number of aggressive acts performed that were different from those seen	75.6	45.6	81.7	(62.0)
Total number of aggressive acts	91.8	53.4	91.7	(67.6)
GIRLS				
Number of aggressive acts performed that were similar to those seen	14.5	8.9	4.4	(4.9)
Number of aggressive acts performed that were different from those seen	44.1	44.7	36.7	(51.2)
Total number of aggressive acts	58.6	53.6	41.1	(56.1)

SOURCE: A. Bandura, Dorothea Ross, and Sheila A. Ross, Vicarious and imitative learning, *Journal of Abnormal and Social Psychology*, 1963b, 67, 601–607.

dren are more likely to imitate behavior portrayed by human beings than by cartoon characters, but they will imitate both. Boys are more likely to imitate a male model. For girls, the sex of the model is less important.

A character in a play or television show has a better chance of being imitated if he is shown as being successful and if he is presented in a general atmosphere of approval. A character who fails or who is punished or who is made to seem foolish will not be imitated. Indeed, this treatment of a character will lead children to avoid the acts he has portrayed even though they would ordinarily behave in this fashion themselves.

Behavior That May be Imitated. Most teachers will be reluctant to strike an artificial pose for the purpose of presenting an effective model. Such priggish behavior might in itself constitute an unfortunate model. The teacher should realize, however, that whatever his present make-up, he is likely to function as a model for an undetermined number of his pupils (Adelson, 1962). With respect to the major departments of his behavior, he might occasionally stop to ask if he would be happy to see a number of his students acting as he does.

Without trying to, the typical teacher can present an image of reasonable and unashamed decency and morality in a world where this is often a scarce commodity. Going beyond this valuable, but unexciting morality which most of us can exemplify, the occasional teacher might present a model of outstanding moral courage, magnanimity, kindness, or duty. Students can hardly fail, for instance, to notice the teacher who speaks out on some issue in the face of certain censure or who makes some dramatic sacrifice of leisure or promotion in the interests of job or duty. Such models

will be noticed and may be influential even when students fail to understand the issue at stake (Havighurst, 1962).

The Problem of a Facade. It is comforting to think of the moral good that we might accomplish merely by living up to our own moral ideals and without having to give deliberate thought about the impact of our behavior. Conversely, there may be some danger in putting on an act that is markedly at odds with our feelings. Presenting such an unnatural facade has been roundly criticized (Jersild, 1955; Rogers, 1961) as being ineffective and somewhat immoral. This fear of an artificial facade, however, may be carried too far. A teacher, in the face of some emergency, for instance, might well try to portray a calmness that he does not feel, sincerely hoping that his level-headedness might be imitated. For the same reason he may often show more forebearance or patience than his spontaneous inclinations would dictate.

The Male Teacher as a Model. Many children have very little association with a reasonable male model. On the one hand we hear about the upper middle-class home where the father is merely a weekend visitor. At the other extreme, we know of the occasional lower-class matriarchal home where the only males in evidence are the current, but transient, boy friends of the female members of the household. For either group, the male teacher might provide a valuable additional image of masculine behavior (Ostrovsky, 1959).

It should be useful for both sexes, of course, to see men as a normal part of their daily lives. The presence of the male teacher, however, has been considered especially important for boys. The special needs of boys may have been somewhat neglected in the current school. In the typical class most of the approval

► *Aspects of Adjustment Stressed by Men and Women*

As part of another investigation, 17 women and 22 men, all teaching in the same high school, were asked to nominate the three best-adjusted students in the school and the three poorest. They were then asked to give the characteristics of each student that led him to be named well-adjusted or poorly-adjusted.

	Percent of Teachers Mentioning a Given Area When Describing:			
	Well-adjusted Students		Poorly-adjusted Students	
Area Invoked	Women	Men	Women	Men
General emotional and personal adjustment (mature, good judgment vs. show-off, unstable)	82.3	100	82.4	81.8
Character control (good manners, honest, modest vs. unreliable, talebearer, liar)	94.1	72.7	82.4	63.6
Social-interpersonal (good mixer, friendly, likes people vs. lone wolf, shy, stand-offish)	88.2	77.3	70.6	63.6
Cultural, academic attainment (ambitious, industrious, persistent vs. no goals, lazy)	88.2	72.7	47.1	63.6
Ability and interests (ideas, creative vs. dull, slow to learn)	23.5	18.2	41.2	18.2

SOURCE: H. Beilin and Emmy Werner, Sex differences among teachers in the use of criteria of adjustment, *Journal of Educational Psychology*, 1957, **48**, 426–436.

goes to girls (Meyer and Thompson, 1956). Boys, moreover, stand in need of a special kind of support (Bronfenbrenner, 1961b). And there is some evidence that male teachers are more likely to provide the needed emphasis on independence and maturity (Beilin and Werner, 1957). Female teachers are more likely to stress conformity and modesty. Finally, boys are more likely to imitate a male model, and the presence of a male model does not reduce the imitative tendencies in girls.

Models from Literature and Subject Matter. If we face some embarrassment in casting ourselves as models, we can, with good conscience and with tremendous relief, turn to the great and vivid models of history and literature. In contrast to the faltering and confusing images that we ourselves may present, most of the inadvertent gaucheries of these historical characters have either been deleted from the story or have been subordinated to a minor place in the total structure. We will hope, of course, that literature or history does not become a mere vehicle for moral preachments. But even when taught for its essential content, the material may well present some of its conspicuous characters as worthy models.

We will be fortunate when we can find characters that exemplify the traits we have in mind and that do so with a minimum of confusion and hesitation. We should be careful, however, not to push this matter too far. Characters should still be presented in the round. As pointed out earlier, stylized caricatures or cartoon characters do not serve as compelling models. If literary characters are to function as effective ideals, moreover, they may have to form some link with live people who have played a part in the student's life. Obviously we cannot predict just which facet of the literary character will present this all important link. It may be that some minor aspect of the hero resembles some characteristic of a father who is beloved but insufficiently available. The attraction may come, on the other hand, from the very contrast with some earlier idol who has cruelly shown himself to have feet of clay. Since the particular link is so unpredictable, we would be wise to see that each character is presented in some detail, in the hope that some one of his characteristics may act as a connection with an important person in the life of some child.

In literature, as in life, the effective model must be successful. For young children, the success should be obvious and overt. The eight-year-old may not be impressed by the hero who loses the world but gains inner tranquility. Virtue should prosper in some tangible manner. The character selected as a model should also be portrayed in a generally approving manner and should carry a reason-able amount of prestige. In all this, by the way, we should not hope for miracles. We must face the fact that students exposed to biographical materials do not always identify with the characters presented (Lodge, 1956).

In the bulk of our teaching few of us will be willing to distort the story in the hope of getting a more pointed moral. At times, however, particularly at the high school level, we could use a literary work as a jumping off place for explicit discussion of moral concerns (Havighurst, 1962). High school students are often interested in moral issues for their own sake and could well regard the occasional play or story chiefly as an illustration of a moral question.

Developing Useful Cognitions

The development of cognitions or moral notions is seen as important not only by those who lay chief stress on cognitions as the prime sources of moral control but also by Freudians and other psychoanalysts who stress unconscious emotional drives.

Rational vs. Unconscious Controls. According to the psychoanalytical view, one of the chief problems in arranging for a rational morality is to bring more and more issues into the conscious court of the ego and thus to permit such problems to be considered on their rational and practical merits. It is the ego and the ego alone that uses logic and rational thought in dealing with impulses and inhibitions. As the Freudians would hasten to point out, of course, any major improvement in this matter is beyond the teacher's power or province.

As the child faces new problems, however, or, more accurately, as he faces new aspects of old problems, we may be able to help him see things as matters for rational consideration and not as things that must be settled by the ill-considered "I want it" of the id, or by a fearful, unthinking "No!" on the part of the superego.

The Freudian psychologist is not so naïve as to suggest that once we have brought these issues before the ego all will be well. Morality, apart from sheer prudence, counts for nothing with the ego. The case for morality will be dependably furthered only if the ego-ideal can successfully intervene on behalf of behavior satisfactory to the superego.

Clearly we can do something to help the ego-ideal in making its case known before a rational but hard-boiled ego, dedicated to the interests of the id. We can make sure that there are many worthy outlets or laudable courses of action that could be presented to the ego. It is not enough that the pupil see moral worth in becoming a priest or clergyman. He ought to see nobility in many crafts and ought to be intrigued by the laudable moral possibilities in plumbing, delivering mail, and protecting forests. He must see moral worth not only in routine obedience but also in occasional resistance.

Intrinsic Usefulness of Moral Concepts

For the Freudian psychologist, the place of moral concepts, although important, takes second place to the emotional forces at work. For the cognitive theorist, on the other hand, these cognitive structures are the chief ingredients of moral character. As these develop, or fail to develop, the subsequent character of the child is formed.

Toward the end of the elementary school we find an increasing interest in theoretical issues as they appear in moral matters (Kohlberg, 1963a). With or without the teacher's stimulation, children will think and argue about what is *right* or *fair* or what one *ought* to do under certain circumstances. In these discussions with themselves or with others, children could well use concepts and ideas to help them label and structure their spontaneous notions and perhaps to help them bolster or refine their amateur theories. Although the actual words may never be used, many of the discussions will revolve around the concept of reciprocity in obligations, the idea of implied contracts, the idea of objectivity in the application of moral rules, and around the ultimate basis of moral demands. Insofar as a student is already familiar with these abstractions and their labels, perhaps from other contexts, he should more readily reach out to use them in thinking about moral issues. He should also find the more precise abstractions immensely rewarding in enabling him to sharpen his own groping insights.

Whatever our limitations in other areas of moral instruction, we should surely be able to help supply the intellectual tools for the efficient manipulation of ideas having to do with morality. As in the area of personal adjustment (Chapter 13), this may be the area in which the school can move most freely and for which it has unique responsibilities not to be delegated to other agencies.

Direct Experience in Moral Training

In the business of running a school or a class, there are endless occasions during which pupils are involved in moral issues, either in accepting rulings, in discussing them, or in actually formulating policies and decisions. The teacher can do much either to intensify or to minimize these experiences. At the very least, in dealing with whatever issues are under consideration, he can use casual guidance and reinforcement toward more enlightened and more responsible behavior. Going further, he may deliberately encourage student participation and responsibility in many aspects of the classroom work, hoping to provide real-life experiences that may generate more socialized behavior and a more informed moral judgment. Here, of course, the teacher must remember his own ultimate responsibility for everything that is done in these real-life activities. He should remember also that some of the outcomes of these immature activities may be hard to defend. Punishments decreed by these juvenile tribunals, for instance, are often

---

► Incidental vs. Dramatic Approaches in Producing a Favorable Attitude

Prior to undergoing a nine-day period of survival training, groups of aircrewmen were given different indoctrinations to a new survival ration, made of a pemmican-like mixture. For this experiment, the men were divided into six groups of from 40 to 70 men each, each group being given a different kind of indoctrination.

After the maneuvers were over, the men answered a questionnaire indicating how well they liked the rations, how many bars of it had been eaten, whether or not they would eat them in the future. A scale of *rejection* or *dislike* was worked out, and an index of each man's rejection rate was computed.

Approach Used in Orientation	*Rejection Rates Following Different Approaches*
A. Coercive: Told that failure to try the new ration would be held against a man	21.9
B. Group explanation: Told about the nature of the ration and the psychological factors involved in getting used to it	25.6
C. Control: Given no indoctrination; merely assigned ration as part of exercises	26.6
D. Factual information: Told about the bars (as in B) but not told of psychological factors	27.7
E. Minimal orientation: Told the bar would be used, but little or nothing added	29.2
F. Individual explanation: Same as in B, but explanation given to one man at a time	31.9
G. Example: No direct explanation. Instructor ate ration and made favorable comments	32.9

Compared to Control Group (C), the rejection rate of Group A was significantly less and that of Groups F and G significantly greater.

SOURCE: E. P. Torrance, and R. Mason, Instructor effort to influence: an experimental evaluation of six approaches, *Journal of Educational Psychology*, 1958, 49, 211–218.

almost unbelievably harsh. For the bright students, more capable of deriving dependable principles from their experiences, such real-life experiences seem to be valuable. For the less able, the value is questionable (V. Jones, 1960).

In the field of direct instruction, the teacher may at times deliberately arrange for situations that call for courage, restraint, or big-heartedness. He may be able to arrange for a graduated curriculum, steadily increasing the stress to be endured, the temptation to be overcome. Here he can employ the techniques of shaping-up, reinforcing early behavior that is merely in the right direction, and gradually becoming more and more demanding in the behavior that he will accept. In such attempts at direct training there is some evidence of better results when the special experience is made an unobtrusive and incidental aspect of the general program. In the military situation, results are less fortunate when the authorities make a big thing of the new stressful or tempting experience and when they accompany it by sales talks and conspicuous models (Torrance and Mason, 1958).

Overt Discussion of Character

In exposing children to real-life situations that involve moral problems, the teacher may spend little or no time in the actual direct discussion of moral matters. Overt lessons on moral issues, however, do imply such direct discussions. Here we have in mind talk about attitudes, character, values, tolerance, and the like.

Disagreement about the Direct Approach. There is a tremendous amount of disagreement about the problem of direct instruction in morality. At the one extreme, we find the position of Sir Herbert Read (1960), maintaining that true morality must always be spontaneous or almost automatic. In the truest kind of morality, Read would say, we must act so that the left hand knoweth not what the right hand doeth. At the other extreme, we have Piaget's (1932) emphasis on moral judgment. In the truly adult morality, Piaget visualizes the person making a deliberate choice between rival values and in so doing being influenced by his idea of himself as a moral person.

Most people, presumably, will see some value in both positions. For much of the day-by-day *behavior* that has important moral aspects, many people would prefer unthinking spontaneity. For one thing, life is more efficient when these smiles of greeting, these casual expressions of interested concern, these minor acts of aid or rescue, are given in automatic, spontaneous fashion. More important, however, any evidence of studied calculation in these matters might reduce their moral acceptability. Most of us would experience a change of attitude on learning that the person who had listened to our remarks with such charming interest was really practicing an assignment on "taking an interest in what other people say." An excessive concern over the question of whether or not I am being a good child in this or that matter would betoken the prig.

Conversely, there are crucial situations in which a purely automatic act would also seem to be the actual negation of true moral behavior. In some circumstances, unthinking behavior which we judged to be correct would not bring the same moral approval as a similar act resulting from a genuine moral argument within the person.

To some extent this dilemma may be partially resolved by choosing the early years for concentrated attention on the automatic performance of uncontroversial moral acts and waiting until later for the emphasis on responsible moral judgment. According to Piaget (1932) and Kohlberg (1963a), the young child still lacks the cognitive or moral structure that would enable him to deal with these matters demanding reflection. In the early stages, while he is forming his immature ideas of right and wrong, he is at the mercy of authority and the approval of adults anyhow. Since those early ideas, by accident or by design, are formed in a purely arbitrary way, and since any standards, good or bad, that he does accept are accepted in an automatic manner, we may as well arbitrarily shape his ideas and standards toward automatic, moral decency. By incidental approaches we may get the pupil to behave in a more adequate fashion without his knowing that he is doing so. Later on, however, as more adequate cognitive and moral structures become available to the child, we can ask him to wrestle with such questions as personal loyalty versus public good, or the limits of moral responsibility.

Aspects of the Direct Approach. A large number of specific approaches have been tried in the attempt to improve character. Some of these approaches have required students to deal directly with important moral and ethical issues. In one investigation at the college level, students replied to a letter written by a man who knew he had only six weeks to live but who felt little physical distress (Toch and Cantril, 1957). As another device for bringing the problem of values and obligations into sharp focus, teachers have used illustrations from actual court cases (Miller, 1957).

In these direct approaches we will expect more success if the general morale of the class is high, if personal adjustment of each student is at a reasonable level (V. Jones, 1960), and if the self-concept of each student is sturdy enough to stand the risk of modification (Francis, 1962). A student who sees himself as a reasonably worthy person may be fairly willing to "try on" new attitudes. His classmate who doubts his own essential worth may hesitate to take any risks with an ego that is already tottering.

SUMMARY

True character calls for the development of inner controls which will function when no one is looking. A sense of guilt, often overtly expressed as self-blame, is one such control. In Freudian theory this guilt develops along with the superego. When not too intense it works to keep the child from doing wrong. When overstrong it may be forced to take on unpredictable disguises. For the Hullian, guilt serves chiefly as a drive-state that can be reduced by proper conduct. With this reduction of guilt comes reinforcement of the preceding behavior. Other learning theorists hold that the avowal of guilt is built up by the rewards that often follow confession.

Cognitive theorists stress the difference between primitive, childish guilt and the more intellectual adolescent self-criticism. The latter calls for a clear awareness of many issues and the ability to see the moral problems in objective fashion. It also involves an urge to rectify the wrong.

Several theories attach much significance to identification, regarding it as a direct moral agent or as a force that leads the child to imitate others. Identification with the parent of the same sex is often stressed. But identification with the home in general may also be important. For many, the related phenomenon of imitation is a problem to be explained. The proponents of direct reinforcement, however, take imitation at its face value and use it as an important explanation of much social and moral behavior.

Inner controls are developed through the work of some forces, found chiefly in the home. Parental warmth is related to the development of strong inner controls. Punishment has no such relation. Perhaps children merely imitate the consideration shown by parents. Perhaps the warmth facilitates identification. Guilt feelings are linked to parental anxiety and to conditional love. They are often evoked more strongly from mere exposure to temptation than from actual wrongdoing. Self-criticism, as a control, develops with fair uniformity, in spite of the varying child-rearing practices. Although boys are much more obstreperous in much outward behavior, they often have more compelling inner controls. This is in line with Freudian theory and with social expectation. Girls may get too much affection and support, boys too little. Children often react to the stereotype of the male or the female and not to the behavior they observe in their own homes.

In developing inner controls, the school may be handicapped compared to some other agencies. It enters the picture after much has already happened and has control of only a small part of the relevant reinforcement. But the teacher can have some important effects. To achieve these he should provide an atmosphere of warmth and acceptance. He will also serve as an effective model, especially when his behavior is successful and approved. The male teacher can provide a useful model when the child's world is almost male-less. Male teachers do stress unique and different values. The teacher will make use of the models in history and literature.

The school should be able to develop the moral concepts considered so important by some theorists. Those concepts should be developed in a rich background providing many illustrations. In the classroom there are intrinsic moral issues that provide practice. Others could be provided. Case studies from law courts might be useful. Overt discussion of moral matters should be useful, especially for older students. In this, of course, there is some danger of priggishness. The more direct approaches are likely to be most effective for the well-adjusted student.

SUGGESTIONS FOR FURTHER READING

General

Bandura, A., and R. H. Walters, *Social Learning and Personality Development*. New York: Holt, Rinehart and Winston, Inc., 1963b.

Francis, E. F., Fundamentals of character education, *School Review*, 1962, **70**, 345–357.

Glidewell, J. C., ed., *Parental Attitudes and Child Behavior*. Springfield, Ill.: Thomas Publishing Company, 1961.

Hess, R. D., and G. Handel, *Family Worlds; A Psychological Approach to Family Life*. Chicago: University of Chicago Press, 1959.

Jones, H. E., The longitudinal method in the study of personality, in I. Iscoe, and H. W. Stevenson, eds. *Personality Development in Children*. Austin, Tex.: University of Texas Press, 1960, pp. 3–27.

Jones, V., Character education, *Encyclopaedia of Educational Research*, 3d ed. New York: The Macmillan Company, 1960, pp. 184–191.

McCandless, B. R., *Children and Adolescents; Behavior and Development*. New York: Holt, Rinehart and Winston, Inc., 1962.

Sears, R. R., The growth of conscience, in

I. Iscoe and H. W. Stevenson, eds., *Personality Development in Children.* Austin, Tex.: University of Texas Press, 1960, pp. 92–111.

————, Eleanor E. Maccoby, and H. Levin, *Patterns of Child Rearing.* New York: Harper & Row, Publishers, Inc., 1957.

Stevenson, H. W., ed., Child psychology, *Yearbook National Society for the Study of Education,* 1963, 62, Part I. See especially

J. A. Clausen and Judith R. Williams, "Sociological Correlates of Child Behavior," Chapter 2; L. Kohlberg, "Moral Development and Identification," Chapter 7; W. W. Hartup, "Dependence and Independence," Chapter 8; A. Bandura and R. H. Walters, "Aggression," Chapter 9; B. K. Ruebush, "Anxiety," Chapter 11.

Journal Articles Dealing with Special Problems

Becker, W. C., and others, Factors in parental behavior and personality related to problem behavior in children, *Journal of Consulting Psychology,* 1959, 23, 107–118. Reprinted in Stendler, pp. 288–300.

Berkowitz, L., The effects of observing violence, *Scientific American,* 1964 (Feb.), 210, No. 2, 35–41.

Bronfenbrenner, U., The changing American child—a speculative analysis, *Journal of Social Issues,* 1961a, 17, 6–16. Reprinted in Morse, pp. 83–89.

Harris, D. B., and others, Personality differences between responsible and less responsible children, *Journal of Genetic Psychology,* 1955, 87, 103–109. Reprinted in Kuhlen, pp. 411-417.

McKee, J. P., and A. C. Sherriffs, Men's and women's beliefs, ideals, and self-concepts, *American Journal of Sociology,* 1959, 64, 356–363. Reprinted in Seidman, pp. 282–293.

Medinnus, G. R., Research implications of several parent-child concepts, *Marriage and Family Living,* 1959, 21, 329–333.

Meyer, W. J., and G. G. Thompson, Sex differences in the distribution of teacher approval and disapproval among sixth-grade children, *Journal of Educational Psychology,* 1956, 47, 385–396. Reprinted in Noll, pp. 442–453, and in Rosenblith, pp. 275–280.

Mitton, Betty L., and D. B. Harris, The development of responsibility in children, *Elementary School Journal,* 1954, 54, 268–277. Reprinted in Remmers, pp. 7–16.

Payne, D. E., and P. H. Mussen, Parent-child relations and father identification among adolescent boys, *Journal of Abnormal and Social Psychology,* 1956, 52, 358–362. Reprinted in Seidman, pp. 394–407.

Sears, R. R., Relation of early socialization experiences to aggression in middle childhood, *Journal of Abnormal and Social Psychology,* 1961, 63, 466–492. Reprinted in Stendler, pp. 195–223.

For References to Additional Reports

Van Egmond, E., Socialization processes and education, *Review of Educational Research,* 1961, 31, 80–90.

EXERCISES AND QUESTIONS FOR DISCUSSION

1. Spend some time in observing children at play. Bring in brief descriptions of incidents that illustrate as many as possible of the following conditions:

A. Misdeed followed by no statement or evidence of self-blame.

(1) It is your impression that the child really had no guilt feelings

(2) It is your impression that the guilt feelings were so intense that they could not be admitted

B. Misdeed followed by distorted or modi-

fied expression of self-blame.
   (1) Spontaneous denial of blame
   (2) Blaming someone else
   (3) Alibi
   (4) Admitting deed by disclaiming intention (accident)
   (5) Boastful admission ("Do it again.")
C. Fairly natural admission of fault.
   (1) With no overt apology
   (2) With simple apology ("I'm sorry.")
   (3) Apology and spontaneous attempt to take care of trouble
   (4) More deliberate decision to rectify or make restitution
D. Discussion of rules showing
   (1) Belief that rules are inflexible
   (2) Willingness to consider changing rules to suit personal convenience
E. Comment on any differences in age, sex, or presumed social background that seem to go along with the trends that may appear.

2. Outline a talk to parents on "The School's Responsibility for Character Education."
   3. Comment on the rival theories as developed in this chapter.
A. Which theory is favored by the author of the text?
B. Do you find yourself favoring one general theory rather than another? If so, try to get at
   (1) Your reasons — previous conviction? general plausibility? evidence from investigations?
   (2) If not, try to describe your overall position.
   4. Briefly outline the kind of character you would like to see in a child. Describe the ideal home for developing this character. Justify each of your recommendations by reference to data or theoretical principles.

CHAPTER 11

▶ *Morals and Society: Defect in Behavior and in Attitude*

Defective character is a serious matter both to the person himself and to his immediate associates. At times the evils almost begin and end with the harm done to the person himself and to those in close touch with him. At times, however, defects in character take on a broad social significance, threatening the disruption of social institutions and suggesting the need for concerted social action. It is the problems faced by the teacher in these areas that we now consider.

DELINQUENCY

One hears a great deal these days about the appalling amount of delinquency in our young people. It is difficult to know whether or not the actual picture is as black as the more vocal reporters would have us believe. Our estimates are based largely on the cases brought before the authorities. But these official figures may represent as few as 2 percent of all actual delinquencies (Murphy and others, 1946). If better police methods raised this figure to 3 percent, the result would be an apparent increase of 50 percent in the delinquency rate, even though the actual delinquency rate changed not at all. After making allowance for these problems, however, investigators claim that juvenile delinquency really is on the increase and is becoming more vicious (Gibbens, 1961; Scudder and Beam, 1961; Teeters and Matza, 1959). Both journalistic accounts and sober investigation (Wilkens, 1963) suggest, moreover, that delinquency can no longer be considered merely a product of poverty and slums. It is moving across the tracks into the wealthier neighborhoods, and it may actually be increasing with the improvement in the standard of living (United Nations, 1960).

282

Classroom Cheating

Immorality and disregard for rules is brought home to the teacher when he faces the problem of classroom cheating. Wherever investigations have been carried on, a certain amount of cheating has been discovered. Older students have definite ideas of which sort of cheating is clearly to be condemned (using notes in an examination) and which practices are to be winked at (getting information about a quiz just taken by a different section) (Anderson, 1957). There is some fear, however, that students are becoming less and less concerned about the immorality of cheating and are influenced merely by expediency (Trabue, 1962).

Background and Dynamics

Since delinquency is an extreme form of moral deficit, we should expect to see the general principles of socialization clearly at work in this area. When we look at the home of the delinquent, whether he comes from the slums or the suburbs (Glueck and Glueck, 1962), we find the harsh or indifferent parents and also, at times, the ineffectual father, or, more frequently, the father with little warmth or affection.

In the study of delinquency we also find the same rival theories that have been advanced to account for general moral defect. Delinquency has been attributed to lack of identification or to unorthodox identification; to simple cognitive defect in parent and child alike; to displaced aggression; and to the direct learning arising from the models presented and the reinforcement supplied. Some of these general theories, of course, call for modification or elaboration when applied to delinquency.

Delinquency and Family Identification. In the prevention of delinquency, the kind of identification that counts most is not so much identification with the same-sex parent as identification with the home in general. It is this family identification that most clearly distinguishes between the delinquent and the nondelinquent (Bandura and Walters, 1959). The delinquent has little grasp of the values that are important to his own family. Certainly he has no vivid sense of commitment to these values. This failure to identify with the family is also typical of the child who fails to confess his misdeeds and also of the child who does not feel any self-blame when he is clearly at fault.

Surprisingly enough, family identification, so clearly linked to other aspects of morality, turns out to have no relation to the tendency to resist temptation under laboratory conditions (Kohlberg, 1963b). When deliberately exposed to temptation in a contrived test, the children who strongly identify are just as likely to cheat as those who have little feeling for family values.

We cannot be sure about the explanation for this discrepancy, or, indeed, about the basic link between family identification and the lack of delinquency. Certainly we must not assume that the identification is the thing that actually prevents delinquency. Perhaps some other factor (interesting and interested parents) is the cause of both. Perhaps the factor that reduces delinquency does whatever it does by keeping children away from situations where they would be tempted into delinquency. If identifying children were actually subjected to temptation, as in the laboratory situation, they may yield just as readily as other children. Perhaps family identification does exert a pull in real life, but has less

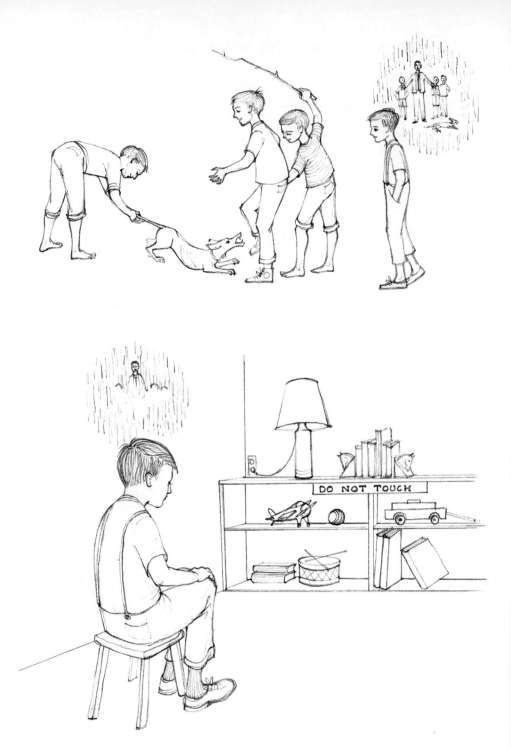

Fig. 11.1. Family values may seem more relevant in one situation than in another.

impact in the laboratory situation. A child on the verge of a delinquent act, for instance, might well visualize some other member of the family in a similar situation and might wonder how that person would act. When being observed for his ability to withstand temptation, however, the child is usually in a fairly contrived situation—disguised of course, but still artificial. He may never visualize other family members in this artificial situation and would hence have no clear model on which to base his conduct (Fig. 11.1).

Delinquency and Cognitive Defect. Theorists such as Rokeach, Piaget, and Kohlberg (Chapter 10) would stress the fact that the delinquent clearly lacks adequate cognitive controls. And much of the evidence (Bandura and Walters, 1959; Glueck and Glueck, 1950) suggests that this lack is his outstanding characteristic. In moral notions, delinquents resemble much younger children. Like younger children, they are susceptible chiefly to fear and to immediate punishment. The delinquent is remarkably deficient in self-criticism. If things go wrong, it is never his fault. He has a distorted picture of his own powers and no true appreciation of the probable consequences of various acts. He retains the tremendous egocentricism of the younger child. When given a choice between a small, immediate reward and a much larger one that might come later, he shows a preference for the small, immediate reward (Mischel, 1961). Deferred gratification is not for him.

Delinquency and Aggression. Very often the delinquency that brings the boy into court and thus gets him classified as a delinquent contains some element of aggression. For girls, of course, this is not so true. Girls are not so likely to turn up in court, and when they do,

the charge is more likely to be sexual delinquency.

In earlier Freudian theory, and in the earliest social-learning treatment (Dollard and others, 1939), aggression was regarded as a product of frustration. Aggression developed only when some basic urge was thwarted. Later, in his treatment of the death instinct, Freud revised his views to include aggression as a primitive urge. The revised view saw aggression as originally directed to the self, and aimed, indeed, at the destruction of the self. In an unloved, neglected infant, it is held, this death instinct might actually triumph. With the great majority of infants, however, this death urge is held in check by the positive energy of the id. As the child grows, this aggressive energy is directed to a succession of targets. First displaced toward parents, or to one of the parents (Oedipus complex), it is then fearfully redirected, partially to the self (guilt) and partially to others who may represent parents. The established social order, with its police and imposing property owners, may be an attractive substitute for parents, and it is often to these attractive targets that the delinquent's diverted hostility is energetically directed.

The social-learning theorists have retained their view that aggression is the product of frustration and in so doing have encountered a good deal of criticism. In general, this theory has seemed to claim too much. Very frequently, it is true, frustration does lead to an increase in the vigor of the responses. If your first nudge does not open the door, the next push is more energetic. And, obviously, an increase in vigor may change an otherwise gentle response—a pat on the head, into something that might readily seem aggressive.

It is also true that a child frustrated

in one activity will typically do something else. But it is hard to say just what that something else will be. He may attack someone. But he may also do something quite different. He may try an ingenious method of surmounting the frustration. He may cry or call for his mother. He may resort to some distracting solace such as thumb sucking or masturbation. Just which of these things he will do depends on which responses he has learned to make before the frustration occurs. If he has already been rewarded for vigorous marching to music, then he may turn to that in the face of severe frustration. If, earlier, he has had some success from fighting or from crying, he may fight or cry.

The theory also seems to be too extreme when it claims that frustration is the sole cause of aggression. One of the surest ways to instigate aggression is not to frustrate a person but rather to launch a direct attack on him (Buss, 1961).

Like the Freudians, the proponents of social-learning theory believe that much delinquency comes from displaced aggression. The delinquent has learned not to attack his parents or people who closely resemble them. As he moves toward people who show less resemblance to his parents, however, his hostility is more likely to break through and to be expressed in some overt act.

Delinquency as Direct Learning. High delinquency areas seldom have much to stimulate constructive activity or wholesome recreation. There is idleness, frustration, hopelessness, and much opportunity for furtive activity, to say nothing of countless examples, and overt instruction, in the criminal arts. According to some sociological theories, in fact, this general environment is the actual determining factor. For other theories, the deplorable conditions provide an outlet for the more important inner mechanisms.

To the proponents of direct reinforcement, it is not surprising that delinquency develops in settings such as these. We are certainly not surprised when children growing up in aggressive, primitive groups take on the hostile qualities they see portrayed. Similarly, we should not be surprised to see a child in our society take on the characteristics of his home or subculture. His parents, in administering frequent physical punishment, provide an early model of physical aggression. On the street he sees high-prestige figures engaging in violent aggression, and, too often, gaining admiration and material goods in the process. In some areas these models are seldom punished. Under these conditions children are exceedingly likely to imitate the delinquent acts they see.

Once entered upon, delinquent behavior is bound to bring a great deal of reinforcement. Detection and punishment is sporadic and often comes long after the event. Meanwhile there are the inevitable and powerful reinforcements from the thrill of successful risk taking and from being taken seriously by one's fellows. After all, much as we may lament the fact, many delinquent acts are fun. They bring a host of the *effectance results* (White, 1960) that meet powerful needs in most people. A boy gets interesting results when he throws snowballs at top hats, sends in a false alarm to the fire station, or actually sets fire to a building. Behavior that is so regularly reinforced and so sporadically punished may be extremely hard to extinguish.

The Prevention and Cure of Delinquency

A problem so extensive and so serious as delinquency is bound to attract a good deal of attention (Wilkins, 1961; Witmer, 1959). A small volume is re-

► *School Approaches in Combatting Juvenile Delinquency*

This investigation dealt with two elementary schools from a low income area in Washington, D. C. There were 1250 students and 43 teachers in the two schools.

The schools sent in 179 names of pupils who were behavior problems. The children were from all grades, kindergarten through grade six. The neighborhood was predominantly Negro. There were 34 white pupils (26 boys and 8 girls) and 145 Negro pupils (106 boys and 39 girls) in the group.

The Glueck Delinquency Scale was used to estimate the likelihood that each student would become a court case. Of the children considered unlikely to be delinquent, some 5 percent actually did come to have a court record within four years. Of those for whom delinquency was predicted, 30 percent came to have a court record.

The technical staff (psychologists, psychiatrists, social workers) studied the case of each child and made specific recommendations. Typically, these called for social work with child and family, or more intensive individual treatment such as psychotherapy or removal to a foster home. The technical staff worked out a treatment for each of the 179 children. To obtain a control group, however, the proposed treatment was deliberately withheld from 68 of these children (Untreated Group). For most of the children in the treated group the help consisted of interviews with a psychiatric social caseworker. Each of the treated children averaged about a dozen such interviews, and his parents about a dozen more.

Four years after the beginning of the project, the investigators were able to locate 165 children for whom they could get dependable records.

	Treated Group	Untreated Group	Combined
Total Number of Children	108	57	165
Number with Court or Police Record	42	14	56
Percent with Court or Police Record	40.7	24.6	

The difference would be significant at the 10-percent level, but not at the 5-percent level.

SOURCE: C. D. Tait and E. F. Hodges, *Delinquents, Their Families, and the Community* (Springfield, Ill.: Charles C Thomas Publishing Company, 1962).

quired merely to list the titles of the projects undertaken in any one year (Tait and Hodges, 1962).

General Community Programs. Often, when delinquency reaches a certain point, a community will mobilize almost all its resources. Recreation centers are established. Specialists are as-signed to police forces. Service clubs provide interested leaders. Frequently such an all-out program is followed by some feeling of improvement (Witmer, 1959). Lacking a control group, however, it is difficult to know just how much of the improvement can be attributed to the over-all program, and it is certainly impossible to know which particular facet should receive the credit.

In the famous Cambridge-Somerville attempt to curb delinquency (McCord and McCord, 1959), the emphasis was placed on intensive counseling. Potential delinquents were located and half of them were counseled systematically, whereas the rest of the boys were left to their own devices. Both groups were followed through the years and into adulthood. To the disappointment of everyone, there was no dependable differences in the delinquency rate of the two groups.

The School and Delinquency. Some recent studies from the United Kingdom (Dell, 1963) have held that a good school acts as a deterrent to delinquency. In his own study in Belfast, Dell found a correlation between poor schools and a high delinquency rate. Both of these factors, however, as might be expected, are related to the general quality of the neighborhood. When the influence of poverty is ruled out, the correlation drops from .56 to .29. If other common factors were also ruled out we might expect further reduction in the relation. The relation may come from the fact that the same factors responsible for good schools in the first place (interested parents, able children, favorable physical surroundings) might in themselves work for a reduction in delinquency.

In Dell's study, the schools, presumably, made no concerted attack on the problem of delinquency. A group of investigators, working in Washington, D.C., attempted to see what could be done by working through the schools (Tait and Hodges, 1962). Special workers in one school were assigned to work closely with potential delinquents. In another school there was no such effort. Here again, we find a grim failure. There was just as much, perhaps more, delin-quency on the part of the treated group as on the part of the untreated controls.

As we point out at the end of this chapter, there is some doubt that schools or school-like agencies provide the answer for the management of behavior that is about to break forth in delinquency. Cooperative arrangements with other groups may hold more promise.

PREJUDICE AND DISCRIMINATION

No one needs to be reminded about the problems of racial and minority discrimination. Such problems form a conspicuous part of our thinking, both with respect to education and to the whole realm of social relations. In contrast to the problem of delinquency, prejudice as an evil is not especially acute in the school-age population. It is true that students of all ages do come to adopt the discriminatory attitudes of their elders. But typically they are no worse than their elders in this respect, and often they are less rigid in their discriminatory beliefs. In contemplating more enlightened social measures, it is chiefly the bigotry of parents that we must fear. But prejudice and discrimination does exist in our students and is one of the problems that we face.

Aspects of Prejudice

Beliefs about other people can be true (almost everyone in England drives on the left side of the road) or false (almost all Jews have an exceptional flair for finance). These beliefs, true or false, may be regarded merely as amusing perversities (English traffic customs) or as mildly enviable traits (Italians are good singers; Hungarian women are beautiful) or as something to be condemned, feared, or scorned.

Exalting One's Own Group. For the most part, of course, we are rather unlikely to attribute enviable traits to other groups. We are much more likely to interpret any differences, real or imaginary, as being in our favor. In interpreting real or fancied differences in our own favor, we make good use of selective attention and selective recall. Jewish students, Negro students, and undifferentiated students, for instance, hearing accounts of the achievements of different "census groups" will note and remember the achievements of their own group (Gus-tafson, 1957). Much of this effect may come from the pre-existing structure (See Chapter 6) into which the ego-favoring material fits (Fitzgerald and Ausubel, 1963). When this effect does operate it appears to be more typical of minority groups than of the dominant group.

Along with selective perception and recall there is the group pride, or group respect, that leads any subgroup (Negro or white, Jewish or gentile), to consider its own members as basically superior to the members of other groups. Members of the dominant white group, by the way,

---

▶ *Attending to the Achievements of One's Own Group*

The students in this investigation were in grade ten in a large high school in Ohio. To get three comparable groups, a Negro student was first chosen. A search was then made for a Jewish student of the same sex, age, and intelligence and for a comparable white, non-Jewish student. The procedure was repeated until there were sixteen such trios, making three groups of sixteen students each.

All forty-eight students studied an account of contributions made to American culture. The contributions of Negroes, Jews, and of white gentiles were all stressed. Prior to the study of this material, the students were given a pretest dealing with the achievements of each of the three groups. The same test was given after the period of study, and again after a lapse of three weeks. The results show, first, how much the students gained after reading the material, and, second, what percentage of the material they retained over a period of three weeks.

AMOUNT THAT EACH GROUP LEARNED (AND REMEMBERED) ABOUT EACH TOPIC. (The first number under each topic gives the amount learned after one reading. The second number, in parentheses, gives the percent retained after a lapse of three weeks.)

	Topics		
Groups	Achievements of White, Gentiles	Achievements of Jews	Achievements of Negroes
White, Gentile Students	6.1 (57%)	7.9 (54%)	7.8 (46%)
Jewish Students	4.4 (21%)	6.1 (58%)	4.3 (51%)
Negro Students	3.5 (31%)	5.8 (59%)	9.7 (68%)

SOURCE: Lucille Gustafson, Relationship between ethnic group membership and the retention of selected facts pertaining to American history and culture, *Journal of Educational Sociology*, 1957, **31**, 49–56.

are often amazed to learn that a Negro student regards Negroes as superior to white people (Greenberg and others, 1957a). The bewildered white student is often inclined to consider this brash claim to be overcompensation, or mere whistling in the dark!

This moderate chauvinism may be the beginning of prejudice, but it is a long way from the sort of discrimination or intolerance that most people find disturbing. Many of us, in fact, would regard this prideful ethnocentrism as rather wholesome in moderate doses. We are not unduly distressed to learn that Navajo Indians or the members of some other distinctive group regard themselves as *the people*.

The Underdog Factor. Ethnocentric, disparaging views are most likely to be considered as serious prejudice when they are directed to some group that has already suffered because of those views. No outraged protest is likely to arise when most Scotsmen are accused of being parsimonious. The same charge made against Jews, however, might be viewed in a different light. Scotsmen have seldom been victimized. There are few demonstrations to protest when landlords discriminate against students (considered as one undifferentiated group) or against families with small children (again, all such families being treated as a group). Discrimination against Negroes, as Negroes, however, does arouse violent feelings of disapproval.

In trying to reduce the amount of prejudice in our students, however, we need worry very little about these fine shades in structure of prejudice. We will do well to concentrate on beliefs and attitudes that play a substantial part in day-by-day thoughts and that could lead to unacceptable distress to substantial numbers of people. We will be less concerned about a casual belief (Athabascan Indians don't go in for bathing) that, however questionable in fact, and however disparagingly directed to a whole minority group, still plays little part in the student's thoughts and certainly threatens no great sorrow to a group already badly treated.

In the United States, studies of prejudice have dealt preponderantly with negative feelings, or discriminatory practices, directed toward Jews or Negroes. To a lesser extent the studies also include such minority groups as Puerto Ricans, Mexicans, and people from Oriental countries.

The Correlates of Prejudice

Students in our schools readily acquire the ethnic beliefs and attitudes prevalent in their community. Anti-Negro feeling is especially marked in the less-favored economic groups, although, in some regions, students from wealthy homes (Young and others, 1960) also display marked prejudice. The more vicious kinds of beliefs are also more prevalent among the less educated groups, but many kinds of aversions and hesitations are equally prominent in the ranks of the better educated. Severe prejudice is more marked in rural than in urban areas (Lehmann, 1962). If anti-Negro feelings predominate in the community, the sexes share these attitudes equally (Young and others, 1960). When there is only moderate anti-Negro feeling, however, it is more likely to be found in males (Lehmann, 1962). In southern communities, women are likely to become less ethnocentric as they go through college. Men in the same communities, on the contrary, may become more ethnocentric with college. In general, the more prejudiced students come from overcontrolling homes. Their parents are more likely to feel inadequate, and these parents use their own parents as models to be followed. The prejudiced students feel sorry for themselves and consider that life has not given them an even break.

The factors that are typical of the students with marked anti-Negro feeling also hold for the students who have little interest in world problems in general. Here again we find less interest on the part of students from rural, southern backgrounds (Garrison, 1961).

Freudian Explanation of Prejudice

In the Freudian view, as we might expect, prejudice is a general symptom arising from early child-rearing practices. The tremendous aggression directed toward the parents has lead to punishment. As the superego develops, the child senses the immorality in the aggressive urges that are directed toward the parents. The superego takes steps to prevent the ego from ever being aware of the true nature of the urge. The powerful id-based urge still seeks some expression, however, and the aggression is (unconsciously) displaced to some safe victim who serves as a substitute for the parents. To make the disguise more perfect, this substitute should not resemble the parents too closely. It would be better if the persons to whom the hate is directed should differ from the parents in appearance, dialect, and in customs and should belong to a traditionally separate group. It is most important that the new hate object should not resemble the parents in the most outstanding attribute of parenthood, namely, power, authority, and dominance. Hence the frequency with which the displaced hate becomes focused on some minority group having a lowly or subjugated status. Insofar as the ego had a hand in selecting this substitute hate object, moreover, it would find it prudent to select a group that—in contrast to parents—is not in a position to strike back.

Intolerance of Ambiguity. The same child-rearing practices that forbid the child to express his hostility toward his parents also make him intolerant of ambiguity. Freudians make much of toilet training in this respect. Fussy, authoritarian parents may stress toilet training very early, before the child can clearly realize the importance of the difference between sitting on the toilet and sitting on mother's lap. From his point of view the child merely realizes that at one time a bowel movement will lead to praise; at other times to punishment. Not knowing what to expect, he anticipates punishment and comes to associate this punishment with uncertainty or ambiguity. Consequently he has a powerful need to see things in a clear-cut, good-or-bad, black-or-white relation. You are one of us, or you belong to a suspect group. There are no in-betweens.

According to the classical California study of prejudice (Adorno and others, 1950), the product of this training is the authoritarian personality. The authoritarian venerates authority and power, despises weakness, tolerance, or kindliness and wants to be sure just where he himself stands in the power structure. This classical investigation has been subjected to tremendous scrutiny, by the way, and there is some doubt that the famous F (fascist) scale measures all the things implied. To some extent it may merely indicate a tendency to agree with statements made on a questionnaire (McGee, 1962).

► *Childhood Intolerance: A Reflection of Parental Intolerance? or a Result of Parental Severity?*

This investigation was carried out in Columbus, Ohio, and is based on 161 children in grades six and seven. The children were given a *social distance* scale dealing with ten different ethnic groups. For each of the ethnic groups the child indicated how close a relationship he would welcome or approve. This gave a measure of the child's prejudice or ethnocentrism. The mothers of the children completed a modified form of an ethnocentrism scale from the Authoritarian Personality, and also answered a questionnaire dealing with their views on child-rearing practices. The latter scores were used to indicate whether the mother had an authoritarian or a permissive attitude in the upbringing of children.

When allowances were made for the mother's views in child rearing, the correlation between the mother's ethnocentrism and the child's ethnocentrism was .33. When allowances were made for the mother's ethnocentrism, the mother's authoritarian views on child rearing showed no correlation with the child's ethnocentrism ($r = -.01$).

SOURCE: D. L. Mosher and A. Scodel, Relationships between ethnocentrism in children and the ethnocentrism and authoritarian rearing practices of their mothers, *Child Development*, 1960, **31**, 369–376.

Prejudice as Something Learned

Not everyone, of course, subscribes to the Freudian view. Bandura and Walters, and others influenced by Skinner, point out that prejudice could develop from simple learning. Since children are prone to imitate, the child growing up in a prejudiced household would tend to imitate the behavior of his parents. To a great extent he would find agreement and reward whenever he spoke disparagingly of the groups disliked by his parents. Favorable comments about such groups would be met with argument or lack of reward. The attitudes thus imitated in the home circle are likely to be confirmed by neighbors and by his closest playmates. The generalized attitudes are sharpened, structured, and labeled by the never-failing pattern of insults and epithets so prominent in childhood play. In a momentary fit of anger, a child can hardly resist the chance to use such an epithet as "wop," "nigger" or "kike." If this vicious thrust hits home, it can acquire increased significance as a label around which the disparaging attitude can be structured.

In contrast to the Freudian view, this theory does not imply that prejudice is always permeated by aggression or hatred. Many people who hold extremely unflattering views of Negroes, for instance, may feel no marked ill will in the matter.

Data from Childhood Experience. As further support for their views, the advocates of the learning-theory approach point out that prejudice in children does not link up with the child-rearing practices of the parents (Mosher and Scodel, 1960) as the Freudian psychologists would predict. The prejudices of young children are more likely to reflect the overt prejudices frequently expressed by the parents. The overt prejudices seen in the adolescent, moreover, are those of his crowd or subculture (Livson and Nichols, 1957). Both kinds of data suggest the simple learning of the overt attitudes to which the child is exposed.

Prejudice and the Belief System

We have still to hear from those who consider prejudice to be partially, or largely, a cognitive defect. According to these theorists, the highly prejudiced person is less skillful in the use of abstractions. He has greater difficulty in solving problems, especially when there are several acceptable solutions to the same problem. He does not take kindly to the fact that there are continuous gradations between the bright and the dull, or between the honest and the dishonest.

Rokeach (1960) holds that prejudice is largely a matter of our belief system. To be able to distinguish the prejudiced from the less-prejudiced person, we should know three things about him. First, how *dogmatic* is he? Is he blind, for instance, to anything that would tend to upset his belief? Second, how *opinionated* is he? Does he accept or reject people because he sees them sharing or not sharing his beliefs? And third, is he for the most part an *acceptor* or *rejector* of other people? A person who is dogmatic, opinionated, and rejecting would show a good deal of overt prejudice toward the groups that, in his view, reject his opinions. Rokeach points out that some people (for example, English Communists)

▶ *Prejudice in Relation to Background*

Forty-three boys between the ages of 16 and 19 took a modified form of the tests in the Authoritarian Personality. On the basis of these scores the boys were classified into three clusters:

A. *Idealistic* (21 boys). Gentle, optimistic, trusting, unprejudiced
B. *Realistic* (14 boys). Favor rugged individualism and autonomy, conservative in politics
C. *Prejudiced* (5 boys). Despise weakness, dislike minority groups

	Characteristics of Parents and of the Home		
	Number of Years of Education for Parents	Percent of Fathers in Top Occupational Level	Index of Social Status of Home
Parents of Idealistic Boys	13.8	60%	52
Parents of Realistic Boys	14.8	54%	58
Parents of Prejudiced Boys	11.8	0	44

SOURCE: N. Livson and T. F. Nichols, Social attitude configurations in an adolescent group, *Journal of Genetic Psychology*, 1957, 91, 3–23.

who show little signs of the classical authoritarian personality, still show marked prejudice in the sense of rejecting those who disagree with them. Rokeach also maintains that an anti-Negro, white man would show more antipathy to a white man who challenged his views about Negroes than he would to a Negro who acquiesced with those views. Highly opinionated people reject the other fellow because of his beliefs and not because of his race.

Manipulating the Belief System

The belief system that the student brings to your class is a result of many factors. Much of it may come from automatic imitation or unconscious learning. Some of it, however, may be the result of deliberate manipulation by other people. The sustained discussions he has encountered may have been deliberately directed toward producing one belief rather than another or toward strengthening a belief system that has already begun to take shape.

The teacher should know something of the forces by which belief systems are modified. In the first place, the teacher should know the forces which have already been at work, and which are even now at work in the hands of other agencies. In the second place, if he is to influence the beliefs of his students, the teacher must know something of the problems faced and the techniques that may be used (Hovland, 1963; Sherif and Hovland, 1961). It is this second aspect that we emphasize in the following discussion. When we see how the principles can work for us, it should be easy to see how they could also be used by others. To illustrate the belief system, let us consider three hypothetical students having different views about Negro-white differences. A list, or suggested scale of views, appears in Table 11.1.

To the extreme racist, each of the possible views in Table 11.1 is either

TABLE 11.1. Hypothetical Scale of Beliefs Regarding Negro-White Differences

1. *Complete Equality*: Apart from such things as pigmentation and hair type, there are no systematic differences between Negroes and whites, except for those due to differences in experience or opportunity.

2. *Only Unimportant Differences*: Any average or group differences appearing after equal opportunity would have no social significance.

3. *Differences Dwarfed by Overlapping*: Any group or average difference that might appear would be inconsequential in the light of differences within groups.

4. *Differences Given Too Much Emphasis*: The possibility of significant group differences receives too much emphasis in much discussion.

5. *Differences on Existing Tests*: Under current conditions, more school failures are reported for Negroes.

6. *Some Refusal To Consider Differences*: Many responsible people have been too willing to deny any possibility of important genetic group differences.

7. *Some Important Genetic Differences*: Even when experience and opportunity have been equalized there will be some important average differences between the groups.

8. *Negro Inferiority*: As a group, Negroes are inferior with respect to many important qualities.

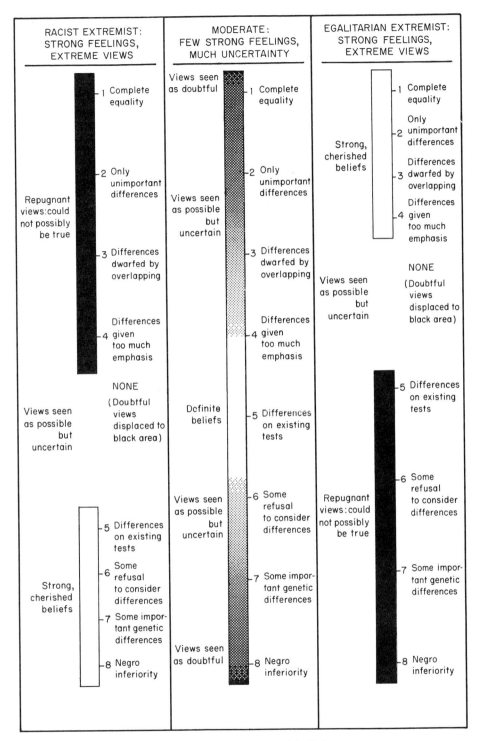

Fig. 11.2. Differences in the structure of belief systems.

completely accepted and cherished or completely rejected and detested. As indicated in Figure 11.2, his belief system is made up of black or white. Although we have set up a range of beliefs, he does not see them as spread out in a continuum. Certain beliefs, falling within a narrow range in our list, he accepts unquestioningly and with absolute certainty. There is a much wider range of beliefs in our list, however, that he violently rejects, and rejects with complete certainty. He does not see these beliefs as scattered over a range of uncertainty. At the moment there are no greys, no views that he regards as possible but unproved. Any such "grey" view offered to him will not be accepted as tentative or possible. If it bolsters the beliefs in the narrow white area of acceptance, it will be completely accepted and absorbed into that area. If it does not support the existing belief system, it will be displaced to the area of complete rejection.

To fit in with the views of Rokeach, we present to the right of Figure 11.2 the position of the egalitarian extremist. According to Rokeach the beliefs of such an extremist, like those of the rascist extremist, could be quite resistant to change and could be structured in a similar black and white manner. In contrast to Rokeach's position, however, the theory underlying the Authoritarian Personality would deny the possibility of an egalitarian extremist such as we portray here. According to this latter theory, ethnocentric racial bias and the rigid, narrow belief structure go hand in hand. The very forces making for a more liberal or egalitarian view, on the contrary, would at the same time inevitably produce a more flexible and varied belief system— one that would include a large grey area.

By including the egalitarian with a closed mind, we do not imply that Rokeach is right and that the authors of the Authoritarian Personality are wrong. We merely wish to show that, theoretically, the rigidity of the belief system could be independent of the nature of the belief.

The hypothetical moderate is presented as a contrast to both extremists. His belief system has little in the way of the pure white of complete acceptance. Nor is there much solid black of complete rejection. The dominant theme lies in the shades of grey representing degrees of probability. There is no necessary suggestion, by the way, that our moderate is good and the extremists are bad. Perhaps, in an issue such as this, placid, unemotional, suspended judgment is reprehensible.

Obdurate Anchor Points. If we should set out to deal with the racist extremist, we should consider the importance of the upper boundary of his accepted, cherished beliefs. This boundary acts as an *anchor point.* When the racist hears any new statement on this question, he evaluates the new statement in relation to the anchor point. If the new statement is seen as some distance from this anchor point, it will be vigorously displaced and moved farther up the scale to the zone of complete rejection. If, on the contrary, the new statement is seen as very close to the anchor point it will be accepted and incorporated into a slightly revised belief system. If we can present a view that is ever so slightly more liberal than one now held, we may not only succeed in getting this view accepted, but we may succeed in establishing a new anchor point. After that, a second view may be accepted if it is not too far removed from this more advanced anchor point.

This strategy for advancing the anchor point is effective but precarious. A statement that we consider to be quite close to the existing anchor point may strike our listener as being vastly different. We try him, for instance, on item 4 on our scale. We ask, "Although these worrisome differences may exist, do we need to emphasize them so much?" For all its seeming innocence, this statement might well be met with violent rejection. Over and over again, in dealing with highly charged issues, we find that a statement put forth as conciliatory is rejected with surprising vehemence. The old cliché, "Some of my best friends are Jews" is a case in point. When this was first seriously advanced it was undoubtedly offered as a friendly remark and as something that should establish the speaker as close to the democratic position. Typically, however, to one battling against anti-Semitism, it is seen not as conciliatory but as offensively antagonistic.

Moving the Anchor Point. As one technique for breaking the impasse, strategists make a point of presenting two views together, one clearly less moderate than the other. If we did not feel too hypocritical or Machiavellian in the matter, we might try something like this:

> Some people assume that by making a few improvements in the educational facilities for Negroes they could immediately boost the scores of all Negroes to the white level. You would think that if they had any pretense of having their feet on the ground, the most they would hope for right away would be a slight improvement for a few exceptional Negroes.

By pairing B (a slight boost for a few children) with A (complete equality for all children) we might convince our extremist that even if B is not very close to his accepted views, it is much closer than A is. So long as he recognizes such a *distinction,* he will not displace B *as*

far toward complete rejection as he will displace A. There is a chance then that B may escape complete rejection and come to be entertained in that, as yet, unpopulated grey area of "possible and uncertain." If so, this possible view may ultimately pull the white area of acceptance farther up the scale. Even if it merely remains in the newly established grey area, it may serve as a useful anchor point when subsequent statements are to be considered.

Worries about Craftiness. At several points in this discussion we stress rather involved and devious strategies. There is a suggestion of deception or trickiness. What should we think of this hint of duplicity? In thinking of the work of other agencies, we must clearly understand that such approaches are used, unconsciously at times, but with deliberate precision at other times. In deciding what we ourselves will do, we may face a different problem. We may be appalled at the prospect of using elaborate stratagems for the purpose of bringing people closer to social and moral decency. Surely in this area we should merely have to show the logic of the decent position! Having done this, we should have a right to expect people of good will to accept it. It is true that, when developing simple academic acceptability, you may be willing to adopt these patient, intricate, start-where-the-child-is maneuvers. You may rebel, however, if urged to use the same procedures when you are only asking the pupil for a modicum of humanity or asking him to get rid of degrading malice. Psychologically speaking, however, this process of inducing an enlightened or decent attitude is no different from the process whereby we help a child overcome his fear of diving boards or his aversion to spinach. Morally, of course, the two teaching tasks may strike you as being quite different. With respect to this moral dilemma, the psychologist, as psychologist, can offer little help.

Reducing Ambiguity. There are other things that will help us deal with this anchor effect. Our proposed statement or view is more likely to be allowed to remain in the grey "possible but uncertain" zone if we can get rid of any ambiguity. By use of concrete illustrations, for instance, we can try to make it clear just what we ask our extremist to accept and what we are not asking him to accept. In getting him to admit that *some* Negroes would profit *somewhat* from improved facilities, we could make it clear that we are not asking him to make this decision about all Negroes or about Negroes in general. We might try to restrict our discussions to the three most promising Negroes he knows.

With more intelligent extremists we might try to transform the black area of homogeneous disbelief into a grey area in which some beliefs are considered more outrageous than others. Once the greyness is partially established, we should be able to get him to sort out his disbeliefs more and more precisely. Some of these can be seen as more offensive than others. The others, by contrast, are seen as *somewhat* closer to the grey area of possible truth. Using these new secondary anchor points, we may be able to present modifications that are even closer to possible acceptance.

Persuading the Uncommitted. In our discussion so far we have assumed that we are dealing with a student who is already an extremist and who has views that are strongly entrenched and bolstered by powerful feelings. It is because of these important anchor points that our initial effects at persuasion may have little or no effect. But we are not always dealing with issues that already have these

sharply defined anchor points. Topics dealing with the world court, for instance, or with the differences between basic and applied science, may be rather new to the student. Regarding these he may have no cherished convictions that would serve as conspicuous anchor points.

Advantages for the First Speaker. In dealing with these unfamiliar issues for which the student has no strong commitment, it helps to be the first speaker. The first speaker is bound to set up some anchor points in the hitherto unstructured belief system. If he is reasonably adroit, moreover, these are likely to be the anchor points that will make the student more likely to favor the speaker's view. Conversely, these same anchor points, which he has just established, will make things more difficult for anyone coming later who argues for a contrary view.

The first speaker also has some opportunity to anticipate the other fellow's argument and to immunize students against it. By pointing out what the opponent is going to say, and by showing his "errors" in relation to the anchor points just established, the first speaker can make the students less likely to accept the second argument.

Here again there is a Machiavellian overtone. We are suggesting that we present the other fellow's argument solely for the purpose of knocking it down. What will happen if we play fair and give the opposing view, not in a snide attempt to undercut it but in a simple attempt to be honest? As moral individuals, of course, we may decide that we have no choice but to play fair in this way. Looking at the effectiveness of the device, however, as opposed to its moral claims, we see a complex picture. With people who, as a matter of principle, put a high premium on seeing both sides, the procedure might help. For most people, however, the presentation of the other fellow's side, with no attempt to demolish it, cannot be depended upon to be more effective (Jarrett and Sherriffs, 1953).

Pointing the Moral. Just as he cannot safely rely on impartiality to persuade, the avowed proponent of a given view should not rely on a subtle approach. He cannot safely let the facts speak for themselves, and he should not hesitate to draw the conclusion or to point the moral, however much he expects that the conclusion is blatantly obvious (Hovland and Mandell, 1952).

The teacher, in calling upon outsiders, will naturally seek someone who has prestige in the field. He will also make sure that the students are aware of the authority and competence of the speaker (Manis, 1961).

One way to persuade a student is to assign him the task of trying to persuade others. A student, in repeating or acting out an argument he has heard, will find himself affected by the argument he repeats. This, of course, has its dangers. As might be expected, some students may resent having to expound a view that is not their own. And those who resent it the most, change the least. But they all change to some extent (Janis and King, 1954).

The Work of the School in Reducing Prejudice

Schooling seems to do something toward reducing prejudice even when no special efforts are made in this direction. With increased schooling, at least, the cruder and cheaper ethnic stereotypes tend to fall off. Compared to relatively uneducated people, high school students are more likely to reject such ideas as,

"Jews are tricky" or, "There are differences between white and Negro blood" (Stember, 1961). College students have still less patience with such notions. We must hasten to add, however, that general education does not regularly reduce all unflattering ideas about minority groups. College people are even more likely than those with less education to link Jews with communism. The college graduate is also just as doubtful about the basic intellect of Negroes. Nor do the educated express any greater desire for close contact with members of minority groups, although they do, of course, come out for absence of legal discrimination. We can depend on education, it would seem, to reduce notions that are an affront to the general intellect, but we cannot be sure that general education will induce a more tolerant attitude or a warmer personal acceptance of minority groups.

The effect of education in reducing general prejudice probably varies tremendously from region to region and from one student group to another. In one Texas study, already mentioned (Young and others, 1960), male college seniors actually exceeded male freshmen in antipathy toward Negroes. For women, however, the reverse was true. This sex difference in susceptibility to education is quite consistent. In general, women are more likely than men to become less prejudiced as they receive more education (Stember, 1961). This is true even in regions—San Jose, California—where both sexes show a general decrease in prejudice with college (Plant, 1959).

The Effect of Specific Programs. Many schools have established special programs clearly directed to the reduction of prejudice and intolerance. These have met with varied success. An early summary by Mainer (1954) reported both successes and failures from a variety of studies. Many of these studies, unfortunately, were rather casually controlled and we cannot say for sure that even the successes came from the program itself.

Some of the special programs merely arrange for greater stress on the humanity, virtues, and achievements of the groups in question. These classes may be linked with regular lessons in history, geography, or literature (Hayes and Conklin, 1953). At times a simple, factual, neutral discussion has proved sufficient to improve the attitude of students (Miller and Biggs, 1958). In other studies, however, a simple, incidental discussion did little to bring about a real change in attitude. More dependable results were obtained when the lesson brought out vivid details in the lives of the group, thus presenting the members as ordinary people with universal needs and concerns (Williams, 1961). It may also be necessary, at times, to point the moral in fairly explicit fashion. Kagan (1952) found that a clear portrayal of the achievements and humanity of a given group (Jews in this instance) did little to change attitudes. To get a reduction in prejudice he had to introduce an overt discussion of prejudice.

Films. Ever since the classical investigation of Peterson and Thurstone (1933) it has been clear that highly charged motion pictures can bring about changes in attitude toward other nationalities. In these investigations, the motion pictures were powerful dramas, telling a convincing story for its own sake. There was no conspicuous preaching or pointing of the moral. Films overtly discussing the importance of better Negro-white relations (Kraus, 1962) have also proved effective. The effect was most pronounced when both a white and a Negro commentator took part.

THE BLANDNESS OF VALUES

Many articulate and responsible adults (Ginzberg, 1961) bemoan the softness, irresponsibility, and immaturity of today's adolescents. Our young people are held to be occupied exclusively with their own concerns. They seek a quiet security for themselves and their immediate circle. Even when they do react to the world's ills, they do so in an irresponsible manner. The anger of the angry young man is not the flaming anger of crusading protest, but the sullen, withdrawing pique of the child who cannot have his own way. Today's young folk are held to demand the continued indulgence of childhood. At their most trifling pain or inconvenience, the world must drop what it is doing and come rushing to the rescue with drugs and other palliatives. They demand the solace of early marriage while continuing their dependent status.

Many of these worries may merely reflect the age-old, jaundiced eye with which one generation views its successors. The expressed worries may be due partially to oversimplification. Many people, for instance, have worried about the adolescent's tremendous urge for conformity, and the prevalence of other-directed attitudes. Detailed studies, however, suggest (Riley and others, 1961) that the adolescent adopts this other-directed stance chiefly in his relations to the gang. In dealing either with broader civic problems or with important intimate relations, he may exhibit a good deal of autonomy.

Other worries may spring from sheer misconception. When Schuhle (1957), for instance, asked faculty members to estimate the values (reasons for going to college, activities considered important) held by individual students, he found

► *Teenage Attitudes*

From 1941 to 1958 a group at Purdue University carried on an opinion poll among teenagers in various sections of the country, drawing from city and rural youth of various social strata. The data represent a compilation over the years.

Questions (paraphrased)	Yes	No	Don't Know
Do Communist groups pose the greatest threat to U. S. Democracy?	76%	13%	11%
Are obedience and respect for authority the most important things for children to learn?	75	16	9
Is it best that the inevitable strong groups should dominate the inevitable weak?	20	61	19
Should police have the power to ban or censor movies and books?	60	27	13
Should the right of free assembly be denied to certain groups?	25	60	15
Does democracy depend basically on the existence of free business enterprise?	57	15	28
Is the average citizen justified in remaining aloof from dirty politics?	57	24	19
Should newspapers be allowed to print anything they choose apart from military secrets?	45	41	14
Should some people be prohibited from making speeches?	34	53	13

SOURCE: H. H. Remmers and D. H. Radler, Teenage attitudes, *Scientific American*, 1958 (June), **198**, 25–29.

that the faculty underestimated the seriousness of the purposes and of the values as expressed by the students themselves. Mallery (1962), in his interviews with high school students, found more serious concerns than he had been led to expect. The students accused the adult world of underrating student earnestness and of presenting the younger generation with an unchallenging diet of childish or trivial matters. Many teenagers were indignant at the emphasis on school grades and at the unnatural and frenzied concern about college entrance.

It is possible, however, that not all the worry comes from adult misunderstanding of student values. Over the years, the detailed investigations depict our young folk as benign but uninvolved (Franklin and Remmers, 1960; Jacob, 1957; Remmers and Radler, 1957; Remmers, 1963a). Clearly, they favor decency and fairness. They are for school integration and a fair deal, but these things are to be favored rather than fought for. There is no urge to strike a blow for civil liberties or for individual freedom in the face of governmental pressure. Many high school students actually approve wiretapping and search without warrant. They think it would be proper to deny freedom of the press to dissident or questionable groups. Our information on these topics, of course, is always out of date. By the time these words are read, the pendulum may have swung the other way, and worried adults may now be disturbed by the irresponsible and impetuous way in which young folks align themselves with social issues.

It is with the values and attitudes of adolescents that adults have been chiefly concerned. We are less worried or surprised when the expressed values of grade-school children cluster around glamorous possessions (cars and bikes), pets, gifts, and vacation plans (Amatora, 1960).

It is a serious mistake, of course, to lump all students together. Among college students, for instance, we are not surprised to find that the business majors are more conservative than arts students, or that there are wide ranges within each specialty (Morris and Will, 1959). There is some suggestion that the listlessness deplored in later adolescence is more typical of college students from private schools. Those from public schools may reflect the older values of individual responsibility, achievement, and service to society (Wilson, 1959).

The School's Influence on Attitudes

Anyone surveying the studies of the school's success in teaching character or values must come up with an impression of mixed results. Whereas in the teaching of algebra and English we can regularly expect some modest returns for our efforts, in the teaching of attitudes, unfortunately, we must be prepared to accept considerable risk (Freedman, 1960; V. Jones, 1954). Successes are reported, it is true, but, mingled with these optimistic accounts, there are a large number of failures. From the earliest summaries (Lichtenstein, 1934), through the more ambitious practical projects (Peters, 1948), to the most recent investigation

(Lehmann and Payne, 1963), we encounter perhaps more failures than successes. Jacob's review (1957, 1958) of some 350 investigations reported little change in college with respect to attitudes. If anything, the seniors, even more than freshmen, were addicted to a nice, safe conformity and showed even more fear of rocking the boat.

The Jacob report has been followed by a flood of other summaries and reports (Eddy, 1959). Some of the general trends have been confirmed (Freedman, 1960; McClintock and Turner, 1962). Some changes in attitude, however, are reported (Webster and others, 1962). There is a change toward independence of thought and to greater tolerance for expression of impulse. These latter changes, of course, are not quite the same thing as a change toward a more vigorous crusade for the moral and social values stressed by Jacob.

Specific Procedures in the Improvement of Attitudes. In many reports we get no more success from programs specifically directed to attitude change than from the general over-all exposure to education. The few favorable changes observed by Jacob (1957) at the college level were attributed not to courses specifically concerned with attitude, but to the general stress on attitudes and values throughout the whole college community. And since Jacob made his report, specific studies (Greenberg and others, 1957b) have supported his grim appraisal. Eglash (1957), after trying two different approaches to reduce opinionation in college students, found that neither had any observed effect. One experiment, directed to the general public, inaugurated a deliberate broad-scale effort to change the prevailing attitude toward mental disease (Cumming and Cumming, 1957). The approach had almost no success and produced a tremendous amount of community hostility.

But the results are not always grim and not always one-sided. College courses in abnormal psychology have been reported (Coslin and Kerr, 1962) to bring about an improvement in attitudes toward mental hygiene policies. Courses in child psychology (Walters, 1959) report changes in the attitude to child-rearing problems. Some favorable attitude change has been achieved by various films overtly preaching the importance of highway safety (Merril, 1962). In these films, by the way, the more gory and frightening treatments were less effective. Perhaps when fear becomes too intense, the student tends to tune the program out and in this way misses the message. The school's use of individual counseling to improve values and attitudes has met with only partial success (Callis, 1963; Patterson, 1963). The more careful the investigation, the less the success reported. Here, of course, we are dealing more with attempts to improve narrow attitudes toward school work and not with broad attitudes toward social values and moral questions.

Earlier experiments (See Chapter 12) laid great stress on the importance of group discussions for the changing of attitudes. It should be easier to persuade any one student to accept a given view if he can feel that his classmates and friends are also moving toward that view. A class discussion may show him the trends in the thinking of the others, and for this reason many people think that the discussion is more effective than a statement by a single speaker from outside the group. Although this claim has not gone unquestioned (Anderson, 1959), it seems probable that the views and values of classmates will have a tremendous influence (Coleman, 1960, 1961).

THE SCHOOLS AND OTHER AGENCIES IN THE DEVELOPMENT OF CHARACTER

At various points in the discussion of character (see also Chapter 10), we have stressed the variety of forces that work to form the student's character. At times we have noted the prevalent view that the school may not always be in a favorable position in comparison to other forces. Peck and Havighurst (1960), for instance, doubt that the school can hope for one tenth of the influence of the home. These same authors fear, moreover, that insofar as the school is effective, it would produce a morality built around a safe but irrational conformity to rules and to impositions in general. They doubt that the school would be as effective in fostering the more responsible and mature, but more risky, morality that comes from rational altruism. Other writers also feel some concern that the morality stressed by the schools might be of a compliant, passive type at the cost of the more positive and venturesome aspects of character.

A number of writers have held that the school can do most in the general area of character, and especially in the field of delinquency prevention, by working closely with other agencies. One of our greatest needs, it is held, is to restore in our young people a sense of intimate involvement in community, national, and international affairs (Lawhead, 1963). In many of these activities it would help if the student could regard himself as a responsible young adult and not as a legal infant, or as a dependent, in which the role of student must tend to cast him. Lack of such a sense of involvement is in itself a defect in moral development. Through such a lack of commitment, moreover, a student becomes an easier prey to delinquency or aimless gang action. His feeling of not belonging to anything significant invites him to seek excitement and expression in other areas.

For these and for other practical reasons, there is much advocacy of work experience and for genuine community participation on the part of students of high school age (Burchill, 1962; Havighurst and Stiles, 1961). The more drastic proposals, naturally enough, are directed to the problems of delinquent or predelinquent students. The general idea of involving agencies and people outside the schools, however, is applicable to the entire area of developing responsible citizens (Dubos, 1961; Mead, 1961).

When it is difficult to provide genuine community participation, there may be some advantage in such watered-down aspects of real life as camping or in institutions such as the old Civilian Conservation Corps organizations. Camping has been well regarded. The investigations going back over the years show some support for this favorable regard. "Integrated" camping, it is true, does not always lead to improved racial attitudes. Mussen (1950) found that the more aggressive boys actually increased in anti-Negro feeling as a result of an integrated camping experience. The more moderate boys, however, showed greater liking for Negroes after the camp. Responsibility, apparently, can be increased by a program in camping. That, at least, is the verdict of one unusually intensive scrutiny of the problem (Hyman and others, 1962) and of incidental reports (Bond, 1962).

Advantages Available to Other Agencies

If in teaching character we should be working closely with other agencies, we may find that those nonscholastic agencies have access to many forces and devices not always open to us.

Invoking a Sense of Commitment. Agencies outside the school might be more free to stress a sense of commitment that is not always open to the school. In the United States, particularly, the schools cannot readily link up with religious values. For this reason they may miss one powerful aid in bringing about a sense of commitment or of a purpose larger and more important than the individual himself. And to some writers this sense of a compelling commitment is an important aspect of morality. There are other types of commitment which for one reason or another are also less available to the school. Outside the school, the young adult can be completely committed to one political party or to the economic fortunes of one company. The school, however, is less able to invoke such types of commitment.

More Direct Selection of Personnel. Agencies outside the school might be in closer touch with the grass roots, enthusiasms, and values prevalent in the community. The selection of academic teachers must be made by professionals somewhat removed from the homes, and when this is done there is no guarantee of intimate connection between the teacher and the community. In the selection of people to staff the nonscholastic agencies, however, the prevailing values and commitments could find a ready outlet. The people taking part in these general programs could be chosen quite freely by laymen. Although the nonexpert would be at a loss in choosing a master of Latin or a teacher of physics, he is under little, if any, handicap in judging good sportsmanship, kindness, or magnaminity. Even in some areas of personal adjustment, the judgment of the layman may be as good as that of the expert. Undergraduates do as well as trained clinical psychologists in judging the mental hygiene significance of statements made by patients (Hunt and others, 1957). Grade teachers excel psychologists in predicting the things that children will approve or condemn (Goertzen, 1957). Specialized training in the interpretation of clinical symptoms has even led to reduced accuracy in this activity (Crow, 1957).

Greater Likelihood of Early Success. Some of the general principles of learning also point to possible advantages of the nonscholastic agency, especially in dealing with the delinquent or near-delinquent. Consider, for instance, the principle of maintaining a schedule of success (Chapter 5). The student tottering on the verge of delinquency will become more adequately socialized insofar as he can be led to make a succession of adequate reactions and insofar as he can be reinforced for each of those adequate reactions. To do this we wish to maximize his chances for early success. We should put him in some environment where, by good luck or good management, he will, some day, behave better than he is behaving today. At this point he should be led to experience *genuine* reinforcement. It is an open question if the predelinquent feels a marked glow from the approval of the typical teacher. On the contrary, in order to survive, he has often had to write off that kind of approval as unimportant.

When we think of conditions which favor success, we must realize that the school may not be our best hope for the delinquent. It is not the environment in which he is most likely to put his best foot forward. For the near delinquent, the school is the epitome of the difficult environments with which he must contend. Rejection of the school and all that it stands for is one of the most typical characteristics of the delinquent. For him, failure in scholastic tasks is the rule.

Less Dependence on Subtle Transfer. In attempting to get more adequate social behavior from the delinquent or predelinquent, we face the problem of transfer. Decent behavior within the school, of course, is important in its own right. But our most important problem is to get him to behave better in real life. If, in spite of the odds against us, we socialize him within the school, we must still depend on tremendous transfer if we hope for an improvement outside the school. It would seem better to have him learn this more reasonable behavior in a situation that more closely resembled real life and in one which permitted greater likelihood of early success.

The School as a Predictor of Delinquency

If the work of the school becomes merged with that of other agencies, especially in the critical problems of preventing delinquency, there is one area in which the teacher will prove especially useful. This is in the area of identifying pupils who run the risk of being delinquent. In study after study (V. Jones, 1960; Kvaraceus, 1961) teachers prove remarkably accurate in detecting predelinquent children. This is not surprising when we remember that the predelinquent's resentment of school is one of his most outstanding characteristics. He also does poorer school work than we would expect from his general mentality. Perhaps his attitude toward school is typical of his attitude toward the restrictions and obligations of civilization. At any rate, those who observe him in his reactions to school matters are quite successful in predicting how he will react to the legal and moral obligations imposed by society. To a considerable extent, the pupil who worries the teacher by his intransigency will also worry society.

SUMMARY

Defective morality assumes important social importance when it takes the form of delinquency, prejudice, or civic indifference. Some of the worrisome kinds of delinquency may well be on the increase and are becoming more prevalent in wealthier neighborhoods. Delinquents are likely to come from cold and rejecting parents who make much use of harsh and inconsistent punishment. Either imitation or lack of identification may be the root. In the Freudian view, delinquency is displaced aggression and is facilitated by inadequate or inappropriate identification. Hullian psychologists have held that the aggression behind delinquency comes from frustration of other impulses. As with the Freudians, delinquency is regarded as displaced aggression. Inadequate identification is also stressed. Poor identification with the home in general is often observed in delinquents. The proponents of direct reinforcement stress the unfortunate model provided in the homes and environments of delinquents and the pervasive reinforcement of delinquent acts. The cognitive theorists see delinquency largely as cognitive defect. They hold that the delinquent has the moral concepts of a much younger child.

Community efforts to reduce delinquency have often reported satisfactory progress, but in such experiments it is difficult to know what causes what. More careful studies typically report more discouraging results. Where there are good schools there is also less delinquency, but this may be an effect of the general community.

Prejudice in this country typically refers to derogatory attitudes toward Negroes and Jews, although also at times to similar attitudes toward other minority groups. Prejudice is especially severe in poorly educated, low-income, rural groups, although by no means confined to such groups. When prejudice is pronounced it is shared equally by men and women. When alleviation begins women improve first.

Freudian psychologists explain prejudice as displaced aggression caused by severe and rigid child-rearing. This displaces the primitive aggression toward a safe substitute and also renders the child intolerant of ambiguity and uncertainty. Other psychologists suggest that children directly learn the prejudice expressed by parents and the community. Cognitive psychologists consider prejudice to come from a belief system. In this view, the prejudiced person has a closed mind, dislikes those who hold opposing opinions, and rather dislikes people in general.

In attempting to modify prejudice, much can be done to change the belief system. Success often hinges on shifting the basic anchor points by which all new statements are judged and on presenting the new proposals in unambiguous form. In instilling attitudes originally, the first speaker has the advantage in being able to establish the all-important anchor points or reference points.

The products of schools and colleges reject the prejudiced ideas that offend the intellect, but they are not always better disposed toward minority groups. Specific attacks on prejudice have had varied success. Films and other approaches that present detailed living arrangements have often worked well. The successful programs have often presented rich detail (films) to bring out the humanity of the groups in question. Some programs have been quite explicit in attacking prejudice.

There is much concern about the uncommitted, bland attitude of youth.

This concern may have come from misconception. In any case, values may change abruptly in a few years. In attempting to change attitudes, school programs report both success and failure. With college there is more independence, and more tolerance for impulse expression, but not always an increase in serious social commitment. Specific college courses often change attitudes toward issues in child-rearing and mental hygiene.

In general, the school may be wise to link up with some other agency having more direct contact with the daily living of youth. Such agencies may be freer to invoke pressures (religion, political loyalty) and may promise more chance of initial success. This is especially true in such serious problems as delinquency.

SUGGESTIONS FOR FURTHER READING

Delinquency

Bandura, A., and R. H. Walters, Aggression, *Yearbook National Society for the Study of Education*, 1963a, **62**, Part I, 364–415.

——, and ——, *Adolescent Aggression*. New York: The Ronald Press Company, 1959.

Berkowitz, L., The effects of observing violence, *Scientific American*, 1964 (Feb.), **210**, No. 2, 35–41.

Glueck, S., and Eleanor Glueck, *Family Environment and Delinquency*. Boston: Houghton Mifflin Company, 1962.

Hathaway, S. R., *Adolescent Personality and Behavior: MMPI Patterns of Normal, Delinquent, Drop Out and Other Outcomes*, Minneapolis: University of Minnesota Press, 1963.

Lawhead, V. B., A curriculum for citizenship education, in A. Frazier, ed., *New Insights and the Curriculum, Yearbook Association for Supervision and Curriculum Development*, Washington, D. C.: National Education Association, 1963, pp. 263–282.

Nye, F. I., *Family Relationships and Delinquent Behavior*. New York: John Wiley & Sons, Inc., 1958.

Weeks, H. A., *Youthful Offenders at Highfields: An Evaluation of the Effects of the Short-Term Treatment of Delinquent Boys*. Ann Arbor, Mich.: University of Michigan Press, 1958.

Wilkins, L. T., Juvenile delinquency: a critical review of research and theory, *Educational Research*, 1963, **5**, 104–119.

Witmer, Helen L., ed., Prevention of juvenile delinquency, *Annals American Academy Political and Social Science*, 1959, **322**, 1–213.

Yablonsky, L., *The Violent Gang*. New York: The Macmillan Company, 1962.

Prejudice

Adorno, T. W., Else Frenkel-Brunswik, D. J. Levenson, and R. N. Sanford, *The Authoritarian Personality*. New York: Harper & Row, Publishers, Inc., 1950.

Clark, K. B., *Prejudice and Your Child*, 2d ed. Boston: The Beacon Press, 1963.

McCandless, B. R., *Children and Adolescents: Behavior and Development*. New York: Holt, Rinehart and Winston, Inc., 1962.

Stember, C. H., *Education and Attitude Change; The Effect of Schooling on Prejudice Against Minority Groups*. New York: Institute of Human Relations Press, 1961.

Values

Allen, E. A., Attitudes of children and adolescents in school, *Educational Research*, 1960, **3**, 65–80.

Coleman, J. S., The adolescent subculture

and academic achievement, *The American Journal of Sociology*, 1960, **65,** 337–347.

Freedman, M. B., *Impact of College, New Dimensions in Higher Education.* Washington, D. C.: U. S. Government Printing Office, 1960, No. 4.

Hovland, C. I., Yale studies of communication and persuasion, 1963. Printed in Charters, pp. 239–253. (A summary of earlier studies.)

Jacob, P. E., Does higher education influence student values? *NEA Journal,* 1958, **47,** 35–38. Reprinted in Seidman, pp. 670–679.

McConnell, T. R., Differences in student attitudes toward civil liberties, in R. L. Sutherland and others, eds., *Personality Factors on the College Campus.* Austin, Texas.: Hogg Foundation for Mental Health, University of Texas Press, 1962, pp. 29–42.

Mallery, D., *High School Students Speak Out.* New York: Harper & Row, Publishers, Inc., 1962.

Webster, H., Changes in attitudes during college, *Journal of Educational Psychology*, 1958, **49,** 109–117. Reprinted in Seidman, pp. 679–691.

EXERCISES AND QUESTIONS FOR DISCUSSION

1. In what way, if at all, do you think juvenile delinquency has changed in the last 60 years.

2. Think of a delinquent boy in the early teens. What kinds and what schedules of reinforcement might he be expected to obtain for various delinquent acts? From his refusal to indulge in delinquent acts?

3. From what you know about the psychology of learning and the psychology of character development, outline a promising approach for dealing with a group of teenagers (13–15) who seem headed for delinquency.

4. List some derogatory attitudes that would clearly come under the heading of prejudice. List some others that would not. What seems to be the crucial difference?

5. List your own attitudes that would be indicative of prejudice. Do these reflect the attitudes you remember in your home or general community in which you lived? Compare your present attitudes with those you remember in your parents or close friends. If you have given up any of the prejudices of your childhood, can you identify the factors responsible for the change?

6. Outline a strategy for reducing the bigotry of one of your pupils who is violently anti-Catholic.

7. Do you think the phrase "uncommitted generation" is applicable to your age group? What kinds of commitment do you seem to detect? What important types of commitment may be lacking?

CHAPTER 12

▸ The Class As a Social Group: Problems and Opportunities

A class is much more than a collection of individuals. It is also a social group (Jensen, 1960). To the members of the class, this group can be a very real thing. The group or class may have a character of its own, somewhat apart from the character of the individuals that make it up. Some of the assemblages in which you yourself take part, for instance, may be lively, vigorous, and noisy. Other groupings, even when they contain many of the same people, may be more subdued and thoughtful.

The group as such may have a marked influence on its members. Over and above the individual likes and dislikes, the group itself may induce loyalties or aversions in different students. In extreme cases the individual may so lose himself in the group that he has a clearer picture of the doings and achievement of the whole team or gang than of the things that he himself has done. Under other circumstances, the group, as a group, may be an object of hostility. In this latter situation, the student's dislike is not especially directed to Bill or Sam, but to some vague, corporate "they." "They" are the monsters who are scheming to undo him. It is on "them" that his imagined revenge descends.

Since we always deal with some actual group, we have many opportunities to help the students develop skill in working with groups. Experience in such group work is inevitable. By a little guidance or care, we can make sure that the experience is useful. As a by-product, we may be able to use a few powerful group forces to accomplish other purposes, such as the development of desirable attitudes or the attainment of social maturity.

309

Characteristics of the Classroom Group

In many ways the class resembles other familiar groups. Like the school board, or the neighborhood improvement association, it is a working group. The students do not merely drift together out of sociability or mutual attraction. They assemble on call for a particular purpose or series of purposes. The class differs from many other working groups, however, in the length of time its members spend together and in the variety and unpredictability of the tasks undertaken. Few other committees meet together for several hours each day. And most working groups, apart from the classroom groups, are task-oriented. They can clearly say, "This is (or is not) what we are here for." When the task is accomplished, the group can disband or adjourn. This is not true of the class. Here it is easier to predict the schedule and extent of meetings than the tasks to be taken on.

In this persistence of the group, irrespective of the tasks to be attempted, the class bears some resemblance to the family group. The members of the family are also unsure of the problems on which they will work from one day to the next, but they do know that the group will persist from day to day.

Although less task-oriented than the typical committee, the classroom group is much more of a business group than is the typical childhood gang or adolescent crowd. In these more spontaneous groups, the members drift together out of mutual attraction or common interests, if not by sheer accident. Here it is chiefly important to be together. The activities taken on are largely incidental. But the class has some of the features of these more spontaneous groups. On occasion the entire class, or most of it, may turn into such a group. And almost inevitably, the class will include several smaller groups of the spontaneous type.

SOCIOMETRIC RELATIONS

The *sociogram* can be used to bring out some important and interesting relations within the classroom group. This device employs a simple and direct approach. We merely ask the members of the group to give their preferences or choices. The choices are then diagramed to portray the various attractions, repulsions, and instances of disregard (Gardner and Thompson, 1956; Gronlund, 1959).

Collecting the Choices

To construct a sociogram you would ordinarily find out whom each pupil would choose to sit near, to work with, and to play with. Other activities, of course, could be substituted. In general, however, pupils should be asked to indicate preferred companions for familiar activities (playing, as opposed to an ocean voyage). Avoid activities that are extremely transitory (going to a particular football game). Also avoid activities that are affected by irrelevant practical matters. If you ask a pupil, "Whom would you like to have in your school bus?" he would have to consider the route the bus might take. If you are interested in general popularity or acceptance, be sure to choose some activity in which congeniality is important. Votes for class representative or for delegate to a convention should be used only when you are really interested in such problems.

In gathering sociometric data, try to find some practical purpose for requesting the preferences, and emphasize this purpose. Tell the students that there is to be a change in the seating arrangements; that the class will be divided into working committees; or that playtime teams will be formed. Make sure that they understand that their choices will be used in forming various subgroups, and afterwards, make sure that the choices are honored as far as possible.

For different age levels, ask for a different number of choices. At grade four or five you may get each pupil to list five choices in order of preference. Kindergarten children may find it difficult to go beyond one choice.

The Question of Rejections. It is always a touchy matter to ask pupils whom they would not like to be with. Many teachers prefer not to raise such

questions. It may happen, however, that you really wish to know if some children are consistently avoided or rejected. If so, you may be able to present this as an objective matter, pointing out that some substitutions may have to be made, and asking pupils to indicate those whom they would choose last.

Constructing the Sociogram

Table 12.1 shows how the sociometric choices can be assembled. From a brief study of the table we can pick up much important information. Cells along the diagonal have been x-ed out, since it is impossible for a pupil to choose himself. Notice that in this illustration, the boys gave most of their choices to

TABLE 12.1. The Sociometric Choices of Each Pupil

Pupils Making the Choices	BOYS CHOSEN					GIRLS CHOSEN				
	1 Bert	2 Dick	3 Sam	4 Bob	5 Pete	6 Dora	7 Ellen	8 Lana	9 Mary	10 Sue
1 Bert[a]	X		1	2	R		3			
2 Dick	R	X	1	2	3					
3 Sam			X	2	1	3				
4 Bob			1	X	2	3				
5 Pete	3		1	2	X			R		
6 Dora			3			X	1	2		
7 Ellen						1	X	2		3
8 Lana			3			2	1	X		
9 Mary						1	2		X	3
10 Sue		3	1			2				X
All Choices Received	1	1	7	4	3	6	4	2		2
Mutual Choices			3	2	2	3	2	2		
Rejections Received	1				1			1		

[a] The first line reads: Bert selected Sam as his first choice, Bob as his second choice, and Ellen as his third. He rejected Pete.

Mutual choices are in italics.

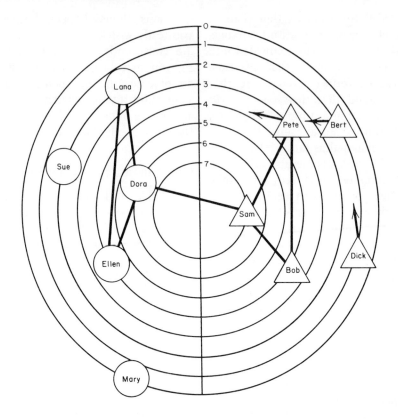

Fig. 12.1. A simple sociogram based on five boys and five girls.

other boys and the girls to other girls. The exceptions appear in the lower left and upper right quadrants. There are only seven such exceptions altogether. This sex cleavage often occurs even into the senior high school. It depends to some extent, of course, on what people are being chosen for.

The last three summary lines show how each pupil fared. In reaching these summary figures, no distinction has been made between first, second, or third choice. We could, of course, give more credit for a first choice, and less for a third, but this adds complications. By and large, moreover, the relative standing of each pupil would be unchanged by such weighting.

The summary shows that one boy, Sam, received seven choices, one girl, Dora, six choices. Mary was not chosen at all, and two boys, Bert and Dick, received only one choice each.

Mutual or reciprocated choices are italicized and these are also summarized. Such choices suggest actual or potential friendships and convey a different picture from one-way choices. Since the favorites, Sam and Dora, receive so many preferences, it is natural that their choices tend to be reciprocated. This does not always happen, however.

The sociogram gives a more vivid picture of these sociometric results. A sociogram for our ten pupils appears in Figure 12.1. This particular illustration is called a *target sociogram*. The pupils receiving the most choices—the stars—are placed near the center, those receiving fewer choices farther toward the edge. The straight lines connect mutual choices. The short arrows show that Dick rejects Bert, Bert rejects Pete, and Pete rejects Lana.

In our illustration we have used only ten pupils. In actual practice, of course, you will be concerned with much larger groups. With these larger groups the sociogram becomes much more complicated and the patterns more involved.

It is with these larger groups that we see more clearly the advantages of the graphic portrayal. Figure 12.2 shows a sociogram for twenty pupils. To save space, identifying numbers have been substituted for names. For this diagram the pupils were asked to give five choices. Notice that with more pupils and more choices, the number of mutual choices increases greatly. A sociogram for thirty or forty pupils would be quite complicated unless it happened to resolve itself into a number of relatively separate clusters.

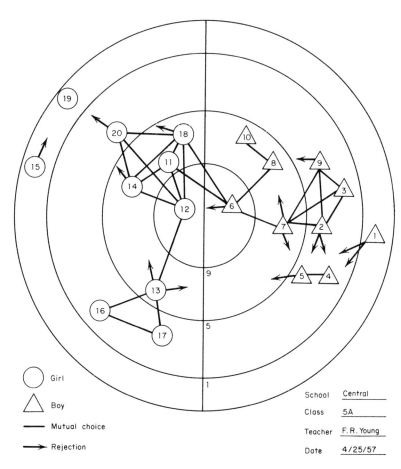

Fig. 12.2. A sociogram based on twenty pupils. Redrawn from N. E. Gronlund, *Sociometry in the Classroom* (New York: Harper & Row, Publishers, Inc., 1959), p. 73, Fig. 3.

Interpreting Sociometric Results

Offhand, you may well wonder how much importance you can attach to the choices shown in the sociogram. After all, they merely show what pupils write down on one particular day, and, what they write down for the teacher's eye. They do not necessarily show the way pupils actually group themselves. The choices, moreover, refer to some special kind of activity and not to one pupil's general liking for others or to his admiration for others or to the extent to which he defers to others.

Fortunately, in spite of the seemingly slender basis for sociometric results, they do have considerable meaning in actual practice. Although there is no strict necessity for it, they actually do reveal choices that are fairly prevalent throughout the classroom. The choices given by one half the class, or by one group, resemble those from the other half, or from another group (Marshall, 1958). The choices are also fairly consistent from week to week, especially for the extremes. This constancy is more typical for the upper grades than for younger pupils.

Along with their consistency, the results also seem to reflect actual behavior. If we go to the trouble to make a careful check on actual groupings and spontaneous choices of pupils, we will find, more often than not, that these reflect the results in the sociogram. And although pupils are not asked to select leaders, the pupils frequently chosen do have more potential for leadership and also have somewhat better social adjustment. Similarly, no pupil is asked to identify those classmates who have problems. Actually, however, the pupil receiving no votes will turn out, more often than not, to be the pupil who has difficulty in social adjustment.

Popularity

The distribution of popularity is something like that for income. As with income, we find a very few people in any group who are exceedingly popular. Trailing well behind these favored few, we find the vast bulk of the "also rans" who pick up one or two votes each. At the last, of course, are the few, 10 or 20 percent of pupils, who receive no votes whatever. These are called the isolates. As with income, most of us pile up much closer to the lower limit of popularity than to the upper limit.

At times, of course, the child who receives no votes may also be actively rejected. Number 19 in Figure 12.2, for instance, is in this category. She received no votes and is actively rejected by four of the girls. But isolation and rejection do not always go together. Many isolated pupils, numbers 1 and 15, for instance, are not rejected in any way. They are merely neglected. They just don't count. Conversely, rejection does not always mean lack of choices. A pupil chosen by many pupils could be rejected by many others. In Figure 12.2 you will notice that the most popular girl is rejected by the most popular boy. Number 8 is one of the most popular boys, as far as choices are concerned, but he is rejected by two other boys. Number 5 exceeds many pupils in number of choices received, but he is rejected by three other boys and by one girl.

Characteristics of Popular Students. Students frequently preferred are likely to be somewhat above average in intelligence. The bright child is much more likely to be chosen than the child of average intelligence (Dentler and Mackler, 1962). The extremely dull child certainly is seldom selected. Even in a special class for the mentally deficient, the duller children within this group will be

► *Popularity and Intelligence*

A total of 355 children in twelve classes (grades two to five) were asked to "write the names of five pupils in the class whom you feel are your best friends. Write your very best friend's name first." Later they were asked to "write the names of the five pupils whom you think will chose you as their best friends."

IQ Group	Number of Pupils	Average Number of Choices Received
Highest	18	6.3
Second Highest	95	4.9
Middle	147	4.2
Second Lowest	61	3.6
Lowest	11	2.8

The table shows the choices received by the different IQ groups.

The bright pupils selected 56 percent of their friends from among other bright pupils, and 44 percent from average or below-average pupils. The average or below average, conversely, made 55 percent of their choices from their own group. This slight trend, however, is not statistically significant.

For 167 pupils, the friends chosen lived closer to the "chooser" than those not chosen. For 49 pupils, the chosen friends lived farther away. The bright pupils who received only one choice were able to predict the chooser in 100 percent of the cases. Pupils of average intelligence were able to do this in only 67 percent of the cases. This trend also held for pupils receiving more than one choice, but was not so marked.

SOURCE: J. J. Gallagher, Social status of children related to intelligence, propinquity, and social perception, *Elementary School Journal*, 1958, **58**, 225–231.

neglected. As we might expect, intelligence is even more important in mutual choices. Friends choosing each other tend to be fairly close in intelligence.

In school achievement, as in intelligence, the low-scoring student, or the student headed for failure, is unlikely to be selected. Students with average achievement, however, are as likely to be popular as those with superior achievement. Indeed, in many cases, the average student may be somewhat more popular than the top-scoring student.

The popular student has better-than-average personal appearance and certainly tends to be free from marked physical handicap. He is also somewhat better adjusted emotionally. Popular children in the early grades, for instance, show less dependence on adults (McCandless and others, 1961). Older students who are frequently chosen usually have high aspirations for themselves and impress others as possessing a quiet self-confidence. The popular students are described by those choosing them as being genial, outgoing, honest, fair, loyal, and sincere.

As might be expected, the popular student is the one with social interests, interest in other people, and, among older students, interest in members of the opposite sex. Those who are seldom chosen often have strong interests in hobbies that can be pursued in solitude. Students are less likely to choose the girl who has pronounced interests in music, art, or literature or the boy who is especially fond of his workbench or laboratory.

The excessively talkative student faces the risk of being rejected. In the second grade, the most popular children are those making few, but mature, statements (Rosenthal, 1957). Older students are likely to apply such labels as noisy, conceited, "pesky," to those they reject (Feinberg, and others, 1958). These labels suggest the person who forces his opinions on others or who consistently intrudes himself into all conversations. Older students also describe the students they like as being quiet. Middle-class boys, in describing their friends, also note that they mind their own business.

But quietness, for all its importance, is not enough. True, the quiet, modest student is not likely to be rejected. But neither is he likely to be chosen. He may merely be ignored. The popular second-graders are not those who make no statements. They are those who make few, but mature statements. Among older students, those most frequently chosen are not only quiet but are described as being good conversationalists. Upper-income groups also stress social participation and capacity for leadership in those they select.

Home background plays a varying part. The parents of the popular student are likely to be outgoing, interested in sports, socially active themselves and glad to welcome friends of their children into the home. Children from broken homes, however, do not seem to lose out in popularity (Barr and Hoover, 1957). The role of social class is harder to determine. Mutual choices are likely to fall within social class or income groups. There may be some circumstances in which high SES children get more votes in general, but this tendency is by no means clear-cut. At all ages, children are more likely to associate with those who live fairly close or who are out-of-school acquaint-

---

► *Friendship Choice and Degree of Acquaintance*

This is the study of the friendship choices of 77 grade-nine students. Each of these students was given a list of all the grade-nine students (244) in the school and was asked to indicate which of these 244 he would like to have as one of his best friends. When he had made these choices he went over the list again and indicated how well he knew each of the 244 students. In doing this he was asked to ignore his likes or dislikes and to concentrate on degree of acquaintance.

On the average, each of the 77 "choosers" listed about 40 names as desired best friends. Most of these were selected from students known very well (65 percent) or fairly well (20 percent). A fair number, however, were chosen from people known only slightly (9 percent) or by sight only (6 percent).

Source: O. C. Scandrette, Social distance and degree of acquaintance, *Journal of Educational Research*, 1958, **51**, 367–372.

ances, and for young children, such proximity also affects sociometric choices. When merely indicating preferences, however, older students are not greatly affected by proximity. In selecting desired friends, as a matter of fact, high school students may chose people whom they know only by sight (Scandrette, 1958).

Mutual Choices of Friendships

Theoretically, popularity does not necessarily imply either friendships or mutual choices. A student could be chosen quite frequently and yet not be chosen by those he himself would select. A second student may receive few votes but each of these could represent a mutual choice. But, practically, as we might expect, the two things do tend to go together.

In the elementary grades, only a small fraction of all the choices are likely to be reciprocated. As children grow older, however, the proportion increases, and, in the secondary schools, a fair number of each student's choices go to those who also select him. This tendency, more prominent in girls than in boys, is probably an aspect of social maturity. As you get older, you are more likely to choose people whom you can get along with or who will respond to your advances.

A mutual choice, of course, does not necessarily mean a close friendship. At the lowest level, such a mutual choice might mercly suggest two people who know and admire each other, but who spend little time together. Going beyond that, such a choice might refer to the intimates who meet frequently and talk and joke freely. Beyond that again, there is the intense comradeship between people who spend much time together, who like each other, and who feel a great deal

of freedom and trust in the presence of each other. Typically, in any one situation, each person will have only one "buddy" of this order. But the college student may have one buddy on the campus and another in the home town.

It is probable that few mutual choices reach the stage of the most intense friendships. It is significant that, even in high school, relatively few mutual choices are of boy-girl type, whereas the most intense attractions are obviously of this type.

Boys, by the way, distinguish rather clearly between friends, on the one hand, and romantic attachments, on the other. When asked to describe an ideal *friend*, older boys, like younger boys, tend to describe another boy of about the same age. The older girl, however, unlike her younger sister, will picture her ideal friend as a boy somewhat older than herself. For older boys, it appears, there are friends and there is also a sweetheart. For older girls, on the other hand, there is a sweetheart and whatever else is necessary to fill in the details of life.

Close friends of the same sex tend to come from the same district and very often from similar socioeconomic groups. Friendships are most frequent within the same race and age groups. Mental age may be even more important than chronological age. Friends tend also to be comparable in physical vigor. As we might expect, interests are similar.

The qualities desired in friends turn out to be similar to those which make for popularity. Indeed, popularity itself is one of the traits often cherished in friends. Younger and older children look for different things in their friends (Horrocks, 1954). Children in the second grade stress physical appearance and home conditions. By the sixth grade, however, these factors become less im-

► *Aggression and Popularity*

The subjects in this investigation came from three schools, grades five and six in a white, upper-lower-class district in a New England city. Each pupil was asked to "list the three *boys* in your class that you would like to have for your best friends," and also to "list the three boys in your class that you wish were not in your class at all." Notice that only boys were to be chosen, but both boys and girls were asked to choose. A *popularity score* was obtained for each boy by subtracting the number of rejecting votes he received from the number of times he was nominated as a friend.

Each pupil then filled in a "guess who" booklet. He was told that in the booklet there were "some word pictures of boys in your class. Read each one and write down the names of the boys whom you think the picture fits." Pupils were told that they could write more than one name for any picture, and that they could use the same name for any number of pictures. They were also assured that the teacher would not see what they wrote. A boy's score for the different kinds of aggression consisted of the number of times his name was mentioned by the boys and girls in his class. Popularity and aggression scores were obtained for a total of seventy-four boys ranging in age from ten to thirteen.

Type of Aggression	Typical Description	Correlation with Popularity
Provoked Physical	"Here is a boy who will always fight back if you hit him first."	.31
Outburst	"This boy gets very, very mad at times."	−.21
Unprovoked Physical	"This boy starts a fight over nothing."	−.36
Verbal	"This boy often threatens other boys."	−.45
Indirect	"Here is a boy who breaks things that belong to others."	−.69

SOURCE: G. S. Lesser, The relationship between various forms of aggression and popularity among lower class children, *Journal of Educational Psychology*, 1959, **50**, 20–25.

portant and the chief stress is on cheerfulness, enthusiasm, friendliness, and popularity. At the high school level, friendliness and popularity are still important in choosing a friend of the same sex. High school students, planning on college, ask that their friends be good talkers, talented, and serious, whereas those not planning on college stress the good listener, the athlete, the lively, practical joker who is also neat and personable.

In choosing friends of the opposite sex, older students profess to be affected by a number of standards. Good manners stand high in the list for both sexes. Ability to converse and to dance are also listed frequently by both boys and girls. Boys want their girl friends to be considerate and, especially, to keep their tastes in entertainment within moderate financial limits. Girls are anxious that their escorts shall make a good impression with other people. Personality also comes high in both lists and, like all the rest of the traits mentioned, is more important than good looks or physique. Humor is mentioned favorably but far down the list. Reprehensible traits are also listed, and for both sexes these include untidiness (or at least unorthodox untidiness), conceit, and vulgarity. Boys also worry about the giggler and the girl who must always be entertained. Girls mention drinking and sponging as traits they abhor in their dates.

The Clique

Turn back to the sociogram in Figure 12.2 and look at the pattern of choices shown by boys 2, 3, 7, and 9. Here we find complete mutuality of choices. Each of the boys chooses, and is chosen by, each of the other three. Notice, too, that only one, number 7, has a mutual choice with anyone outside the group. Finally, observe how frequently the boys in this group reject boys outside the group. These characteristics suggest a self-sufficient, closely knit clique. The members of this clique feel very close to each other but have little to do with others, or may feel actual hostility to others.

Not all cliques have all these characteristics. At the secondary school level, for instance, we often find a typical adolescent crowd made up of a group of cliques. To a certain extent the cliques merge, the members of one clique having much to do with the members of another. The existence of the cliques becomes evident, however, when the larger group must be sorted into automobiles, restaurant booths, or theater seats. The larger crowd accepts the primary loyalty to the clique and shows little resentment unless things are carried too far.

Teachers often feel some worry about cliques that are too closely knit and too exclusive. This is especially true when the class consists of a few cliques having considerable prestige and a number of outsiders belonging to no small group. And in truth, it would seem better if the outsiders could feel a sense of belonging to some important group. Very often, however, the students left out, although somewhat envious, profess no resentment over the existence of a clique (Keislar, 1953).

Social Perception

How well do students detect the sort of thing that a sociogram brings out? Can the typical student predict who will be the most popular? Can he guess how many votes he himself will get? Does he know which particular students will vote for him and which, if any, will reject him? Obviously we will find great differences in such social perception. Older students have clearer ideas of these matters than younger students, partly perhaps, because mutual choices are more clearly established and more clearly recognized among older children. At almost all ages there is more success in estimating the popularity of others than in estimating one's own status, although toward the end of high school students may become surprisingly accurate in discerning their own popularity. Each student is more successful in detecting his general status than in knowing just who voted for him and who did not. Awareness of these matters, sometimes called *social empathy*, may play a part in successful leadership.

AUTHORITY AND THE PATTERN OF INFLUENCE

In any group that meets fairly frequently we are likely to find a definite power structure. This means that some people within the group will be very influential. Others will play a minor role. This power structure can be observed by several procedures (Flanders, 1960b). Often each member of the group could tell you which other members influence him and which other members he might expect to influence. With young children we often find fair agreement in these matters. If Jim says he can influence Bill, then Bill is likely to name Jim as one of the people who influences him (Gold, 1958).

In addition to this rather direct approach there are many other types of analyses, some of them exceedingly complex and technical (Glanzer and Glaser, 1959, 1961). Who does most of the talking? To whom do most people talk? Do most people remain silent until one particular person has spoken? After that, who follows suit? and in what order? (Fig. 12.3.)

Observations such as these might reveal a variety of patterns. Theoretically the influence could be distributed perfectly evenly. If there are twenty people, each could do precisely one twentieth of the talking. Most people in talking might address their remarks to the entire group, not singling out any one member in particular. Or if anyone is singled out, this would not always be the same person. Perhaps, for instance, remarks would always be addressed to the person who has just spoken. Such an even distribution, however, would be most unusual. Ordinarily we would find that some people do more than their share of talking, that most remarks, in turn, are addressed to a few people, perhaps to one person, and that there are some fairly frequent sequences, Bill making a statement and Jim and Sam fairly regularly following suit (Gibb, 1960). For young children, these power relations remain fairly constant from month to month (Gellert, 1961).

The unevenness in the distribution of influence could take several forms. We might find a very simple structure made up of one leader and a group of followers, no one of the latter having any more influence than any other. Or we might find several people each of whom exercises considerable influence over his own subgroup. In all this we may find that the pattern remains fairly constant from time to time and from one activity to another. Or we may find that the pattern changes with the topic under discussion or with the project being planned.

The Teacher's Place in the Authority Pattern

Even if he did nothing about it, the teacher's age, size, and legal status would point to him as a key figure in the power structure. Often he will find that most of the remarks are intended for his ear and that his reaction to things have a special significance. After all, the teacher should have more to contribute and should have a surer sense of the direction the class should be taking (Flanders, 1960a).

The teacher can never forget his very real legal and moral responsibilities to the adult community (Ladd, 1958). Unlike the secretary of the local improvement association, for example, the teacher cannot take the attitude that he is merely to help the group carry out its wishes. He is legally entrusted by some agency to accomplish a set of fairly def-

Fig. 12.3. To whom are most of the remarks addressed?

inite objectives. He is also given enough authority to permit him to carry out his assignment. He can delegate much of his authority if he so chooses. But he cannot actually relinquish either the authority or the responsibility.

GROUP-CENTERED TEACHING

Many people believe that the powerful group factors at work in any classroom should dominate the entire teaching process. These group forces are there. We cannot will them away. They constitute important educational tasks. To a great extent they can be utilized in the accomplishment of other educational tasks. Taking these things into account, some educators suggest that we organize our entire program around the group features of classroom life. They suggest that we delegate, not relinquish, a great deal of responsibility to the group and trust to group forces and our own occasional efforts to achieve the desired outcomes.

Actually, in most group-centered teaching, the delegation of responsibility is not as complete or drastic as we have implied. The teacher typically retains a good many responsibilities. He describes the general task facing the group. In most cases he supplies a fair amount of information, especially of a technical sort. He also makes sure that the group knows the external conditions under which it works—number of hours available, examinations to be taken, papers to be submitted. Over and above such mechanical matters, he often helps formulate an issue that he thinks is present but not clearly defined. At times he may try to keep the group oriented toward the problem at hand. At other times he may permit a new problem to replace the old. On still other occasions, suspect-

ing that the issue under discussion is gradually changing, he may get the group to consider whether it would be better to return to the old issue or to formulate the issue that appears to be taking over. Often he feels obligated to get the group to bring to the surface some troublesome but important question that they seem reluctant to face.

Seeing how much responsibility the teacher retains, we might wonder what is left to the group. First of all, within the limits which must be set, the group assumes considerable responsibility for setting the specific goals and the tasks on which they will work. After the goals have been set and the work is under way, the teacher may often make more than his share of comments and suggestions, but in some cases, the teacher might be indistinguishable from the students were it not for the fact that he is older and usually larger (Flanders, 1960a).

According to the proponents of the group-centered approach, it is not enough that the teacher encourage the group to take as much responsibility as possible in making the major decisions. He must also provide emotional support for the students (Gibb, 1960). He should accept each suggestion seriously, making liberal use of praise and encouragement. He may ask questions to be sure that the suggestion is completely understood or that it really contains what is in the student's mind. He does not use questions to bring out deficiencies or limitations in the suggestion. Scolding, sarcasm, or disparaging statements would be completely out of order. And naturally, the spirit of the group process would be nullified if the teacher had to call attention to his own status or authority or if he had to act defensively, or show that a certain suggestion is just what he had been trying to advocate all along.

Expected Advantages

To many people the group-centered approach has many inherent advantages. It automatically relieves the teacher of the fear that he is a tyrant or dictator and that he is merely inducing sullen assent to his wishes. Since the teacher accepts the goals of the group he has a clear feeling that he and the students are working jointly toward the same objectives.

Increased Group Cohesion. Experience with the group-centered approach should lead pupils to have a greater liking for group work, to feel more attraction toward their particular group, and to feel more tightly bound to their particular group. The evidence, although by no means unanimous (Tizard, 1953), gives general support for these hopes (Benne and Levit, 1953). Increased group cohesion is shown by the fact that pupils readily accept group decisions as their own and feel a personal responsibility to carry out the wishes of the group. When some job must be done, almost anyone handy is likely to do it. You can be sure that someone will do what is necessary, but ordinarily you cannot predict just who will do it (Gibb, 1960). In such a situation the group needs are paramount and there is little fear of being criticized for taking too much on one's self.

As one aspect of group cohesion, the early experiments in this area reported a marked reduction in scapegoating. With the group-centered approach pupils were less likely to pick on one unfortunate member of the group and to subject him to harassment and teasing (Lippitt and White, 1943).

Skill in Group Work. Throughout

► *Dependency and Popularity*

This study took place in a Hawaiian nursery school and involved a total of twenty-three boys and thirty-two girls between the ages of three and five. One of the most revealing measures of popularity was that of "free-play" choices. During free-play periods each child was observed for a period of time and his four most frequent playmates were listed. These lists were used to establish popularity. If Joe turned up as one of the most frequent playmates of Bill, of Sue, and of Ann, he would get a score of three. If Terry was on the most-frequent-playmate list of nine other children, he would receive a score of nine.

To get measures of dependency, each child was observed for fifteen periods of five minutes each. During this period all adult contacts were noted. Such contacts included asking for help in a physical problem, bids for attention, and bids for emotional support. To a considerable extent ($r = -.33$) the child making most bids for emotional support turned out to be the least popular. For girls, there was a similar relation ($r = -.38$) between *total* number of adult contacts and lack of popularity. For boys this relation was not so pronounced ($r = -.18$).

SOURCE: B. R. McCandless, Carolyn B. Bilous, and Hannah L. Bennett, Peer popularity and dependence on adults in preschool-age socialization, *Child Development*, 1961, 32, 511–518.

their lives, in school and out, your pupils will be immersed in group activities. They will take part in class work, in clubs, in committees, as members of working teams and playing teams, and in political and social activities of one kind or another. Some students will find that what they get out of life will hinge largely on their ability to work with groups. For all students, skill in this work will be a great asset. The group-centered approach automatically brings about much practice in such group activities, and it would be expected that some skill would develop.

Less Dependence on the Teacher. The pupil's dependence on the teacher can show up in two ways. As we have seen, it can show up in the classroom when all remarks are directed to the teacher and when only his comments are taken seriously. It can show up even more dramatically if the teacher leaves the room and the class work immediately disintegrates. The early experiments clearly showed much less dependence on the teacher with group-centered teaching (White and Lippitt, 1960). Pupils working under this approach went about their business in relaxed but purposeful fashion whether or not the teacher was in the room.

Mastery of Subject Matter

At one time it was almost taken for granted that pupils working toward goals of their own choosing would achieve more than those conforming to goals imposed from above. Unfortunately, however, this has not proved to be the case. From a large number of comparisons (Anderson, 1959; Stern, 1963) it appears that achievement is just about the same in group-centered and teacher-centered classes. If anything, there has been a slight advantage for the teacher-centered

Fig. 12.4. Different people require different degrees of psychological distance.

approach, but the difference, if any, is trifling. The two approaches are also on a par with respect to liking for the subject being taught.

Maintaining the Necessary Psychological Distance

Most people who are responsible for groups of subordinates find it necessary to maintain a certain amount of distance (Fiedler, 1958, 1962). Some people feel an intense need for a great deal of privacy or distance. Other people need much less and feel the need less urgently (Fig. 12.4). One man might go to some trouble to maintain exceptional distance

from his subordinates when he has one job, such as serving as captain of an ocean ship, but may get along comfortably with less distance when he is facing some other task.

Teachers, like other people, probably vary in this need for psychological distance. One teacher may work most effectively and most naturally when he can maintain a degree of privacy and when his important ideas and concerns can be kept to himself until he is ready to display them. Other teachers may feel natural and secure even when all their doubts and hesitations are exposed to the full light of student observation. The teacher who has a strong need for considerable distance may not relish some features of group-centered teaching. He might be more effective if in much of his instruction he frankly used a clear-cut teacher-centered approach.

No one should feel ashamed, by the way, over his need for some distance. Effective leadership usually calls for some distance. The question is just how much and how it can be attained. You should take stock of yourself as objectively as possible and try to decide how much you need. You should then work out a situation in which you can function effectively.

► *Psychological Distance and Leader Effectiveness*

This study made use of a new measure called *assumed similarity of opposites* (ASO). To get such a measure you ask a man, "Of all the people with whom you have ever worked, whom did you like the best?   B   Whom did you like the least?"   L   He then rates B on some forty characteristics (friendly-unfriendly; bold-timid; gloomy-cheerful). When he has finished his ratings for B, he rates L on the same list. To the rater B and L represent the extremes of liking versus disliking. Yet some raters will give almost the same ratings to B and to L. Such raters would have a high ASO score. Other raters will make widely differing ratings of the coworker they liked best and the one they liked least, thus obtaining a low ASO score. This latter man, who makes clear-cut distinctions between those he prefers and those he does not, is considered to have a strong tendency to remain impersonal and to maintain psychological distance.

With this measure available, the investigators studied a group of twelve high school basketball teams and another group of twenty-two student surveying parties made up of three or four men to a party. First, for each team or party, they tried to find the informal leader or the most influential member. The "leaders" then took the ASO test. Reversing the ASO score to get a measure of psychological distance, we find that in each case the "leader" with the greatest psychological distance tends to have the most successful group. For the basketball teams, the "distance" score of the "leader" correlated from .69 to .58 with games won. For the survey parties, "distance" correlated .51 with an instructor's rating of the party's success.

SOURCE: F. E. Fiedler, *Leader Attitudes and Group Effectiveness* (Urbana, Ill.: University of Illinois Press, 1958). Reprinted in D. Cartwright and A. Zander, *Group Dynamics: Research and Theory*, 2d ed. (New York: Harper & Row, Publishers, Inc., 1960), pp. 586–606.

Student Attitude toward the Group-Centered Approach

Students who have had much experience in group-centered teaching typically have considerable liking for working in groups. But this does not necessarily mean that they like the group-centered approach to which they have been exposed. This may have been the treatment that led to their relish for group work, but they may not like the treatment. If you embark on a program of group-centered teaching, therefore, you must not automatically expect to find all your students enthusiastic about this method. Actually some students, especially at first, will dislike the democratic features of group-centered teaching. Adults studying under the democratic procedure may actually resent the lack of positive leadership (Kelley and Thibaut, 1954; Sears and Hilgard, 1964). Some college students, probably those who will do the best work academically, will simply ignore the democratic features of the group approach and go blithely about the business of getting good grades (Johnson and Smith, 1953). From one elaborate experiment (Watson, 1953) we must conclude that it is extremely difficult to decide just who will get the most out of group work. In this study it was the student unusually concerned about fears and anxieties who seemed to profit from the group approach. Dislike for group-centered teaching, by the way, is by no means a symptom of an authoritarian personality. It is often the thoroughgoing liberal who places a low value on such group-centered work. Such students stress the frequent lack of intellectual stimulation.

The Case for Flexibility

There is every reason to recommend a great deal of flexibility in the use of group-centered teaching (Flanders, 1960a). What will work for one teacher may not work for another. Even the same teacher may find himself likely to use the democratic, group-centered approach with one group, but likely to use a more directive method with another group. In teaching a bright, well-behaved class, interested in the subject, you may find a group-centered approach the most natural procedure to adopt (Wandt and Ostreicher, 1953). In teaching a duller, more obstreperous group, with little interest in academic matters, you may find such an approach impractical. Even with the same type of class, the teacher's approach may shift from one subject to another. In directing a drill session, for instance, or in shepherding a group on a visit to a factory, the teacher may issue crisp, unambiguous orders. In planning a class election, on the other hand, he may appear to be merely one more member of the group and may seem willing to go along with any decision the class may reach.

Some teachers make no bones about the fact that they use different approaches under different conditions. Some may rigidly and successfully employ one approach throughout. Still others may profess to use the group-centered approach exclusively, but this claim may not be supported by people observing their instruction (Wandt and Ostreicher, 1953).

It would seem best to be open and aboveboard in this matter. Attempting to delude either yourself or your students could lead to trouble. Don't act as if you are following "our" goals when really you are imposing your own goals upon the students. When things are arbitrary, and often they may be, it might even be better to exaggerate the arbitrary features, perhaps relieving them with sardonic humor, than to act as if you were employing group-centered techniques when this is not the case.

Friendliness Possible in Many Approaches. We may be more reconciled to the possibility of flexibility if we remember that the group-centered approach is not the only method which permits warm, friendly human relations between teacher and student (Fig. 12.5). A teacher who has no intention of letting the group set the goals for his class can still be genial, warm, and human. Although he knows exactly what he wants the class to accomplish, and although he is determined that his own purposes shall prevail, he can try to do this by gentle persuasion, by jollying pupils along, and by kindly, but consistent, pressure. When he rejects a pupil's suggestion he can do it in a good-natured way. Many a teacher, inflexibly committed to certain intellectual goals, can maneuver his pupils toward those goals by a velvet touch that the pupils in no way resent and may even relish. Another teacher can be noisy, demanding, dominating, and even humorously abusive and yet by the vigor of his demands, and by his insistence that they meet his standards, he may convince the students that each and every pupil matters to him and has his genuine concern.

Fig. 12.5. Friendliness is possible with different approaches.

Many such assertive teachers, taken almost from the pages of *Life with Father*, succeed in creating an atmosphere of vast security and robust give and take. Many people, in retrospect, feel that life would have been somehow poorer if they had never been exposed to one of these noisy, demanding, but fair and interesting autocrats. By no stretch of the imagination, however, could such teachers be called democratic in the sense of permitting the pupils to set the goals.

GENERAL AIDS TO SATISFACTORY GROUP EXPERIENCE

For many children, guided group experience, if it comes at all, must come from the school. Successful experience of this kind may play an important part, not only in developing moderate skill in group work but in developing a reasonable attitude toward such work.

Group Pressures and the Urge To Conform

A group, working on an important issue, tends to be very intolerant of deviant or minority views. Much of the group's time is spent in trying to bring the dissenter into line. Clearly this is likely to occur in the jury situation when the hold-out is causing a great deal of inconvenience. But the group's demand for conformity will be seen even when there is no practical need for unanimity and when the minority could simply be outvoted. In many groups, the existence of divergent views seems to be distressing in some primitive fashion, quite apart from the practical implications of such divergent opinions.

Naturally, groups vary in this urge to bring the minority into line. Many groups may feel indulgent when they see an old and trusted member take a minority stand, but they would attack an untried newcomer if he showed the same departure from the majority position. Some groups are exceedingly demanding in the sense that they will not tolerate the slightest departure from the approved way of doing things. The cadet will be reprimanded, for instance, if his insignia is misplaced by a quarter of an inch. The "beatnik" will be ridiculed by his fellows if his conversation includes just a few phrases that would be intelligible to the "squares." Groups may also vary in the range of things on which a group passes judgment. In the military school, again, the organization passes judgment on many areas of a man's life—on his dress, his social graces, on his personality, and on his opinions. In other groups, a member may merely have to watch his step with respect to a few things. No one bothers about the rest of his life. Groups differ, moreover, in the intensity of the disapproval or approval. In some groups, a person's misstep may bring down official thunder. In other groups, he may encounter nothing more serious than a raised eyebrow. Finally, we will find differences in the extent to which the group presents a solid front to its members. In some circles the individual can expect unanimous approval or disapproval. In others he may merely sense a majority view offset by a number of dissenters (Jackson, 1960).

Insofar as he can exert any influence, what position should the teacher urge our groups to take in these matters? Should the group insist on an exact adherence to norms or should an approximation suffice? Should the norms cover the whole of the individual's life or should they cover only a few things for which the group has a legitimate concern? Should the group present a united front in these matters or should it admit some diversity in its opinions? Should the approval or condemnation be mild or severe?

Clearly these questions go beyond the province of psychology. The psychologist can note, however, that many writers from the 1950s on have lamented the tendency of large groups or organizations to control the whole life of the members, extending control or sanctions to style of clothes, the size of picture windows, the books read each month, and type of cheese preferred. These writers would urge us to persuade our groups to tolerate diversity and individuality in areas that do not greatly harm the group, or in which the group has no legitimate interest. Often the organization may properly demand that its members dress neatly, but it could permit its members to attain that neatness in suits of worsted as well as grey flannel.

On the other hand, the insecure or troubled person often feels more at ease when the group does take a hand in many areas of his life. He likes to feel that *everybody* cares a *great deal* about *everything* he does, even if that concern shows itself in occasional disapproval (Jackson, 1960). Perhaps under the ideal arrangement, young children, and the emotionally immature of all ages, should feel group demands for many areas of life. As maturity develops, however, groups should be encouraged to respect, and relish, individual behavior, and individuals should be encouraged to resist unwarranted group coercion.

There are some games and other artificial activities in which rigid adherence to a ritual is an essential part of the fun or satisfaction. There are also serious enterprises, such as diplomacy, in which a slight departure from protocol can have grave consequences. It is probably wise, therefore, that students have some group experience in which even the slightest infraction is noted and punished. In many situations, however, we could encourage groups to accept minor departures from norms and to be more moderate in their condemnations of the departures they do not accept.

Individual Urges To Conform. Most of us need very little pressure to bring us into line. As soon as we find ourselves in a minority position we feel uncomfortable and tend to re-examine our stand. Indeed, some people will change

their minds immediately if they find themselves at odds with the group. Others will retain their minority views, but find it necesary to persuade themselves that other people would really agree if they were free to express their honest opinions. Even in such seemingly objective things as judging the length of two lines, your judgment may be influenced by the opinion of others. You think that x is the longer line. But the vote seems to indicate that most people are voting for y. Will you change your vote? Most people will. This tendency to fit in with the majority varies, of course, from person to person. Those who resist are somewhat more intelligent, have stronger ego feelings, and are more individualistic in other ways. They are also more likely to be familiar with the material being judged (Crutchfield, 1955).

Small Groups or Large Groups?

In planning for a program of successful group experience you will want to take the size of the groups into account. There are important differences between smaller and larger groups (Thomas and Fink, 1963). A group of five, for instance, will reach a consensus more quickly than a group of twelve, especially if discussion time is limited. In a group of twelve, or even in a group of seven, there may be several people who do not contribute at all and whose ideas never come before the group. In groups of three, four, or five this is less likely. Here the shy person is less inhibited, and since his silence is more obvious in the small group, there is more pressure on him to take part. In the small group, moreover, there is less need for a clearly defined issue. Quite often a small group can be assigned a rather vague problem and still get somewhere. This is not so likely in the larger group. The small group lends itself to a different kind of atmosphere and a different kind of leadership. As the group gets larger and larger, we find more and more that one prolific contributor almost takes over. There is a "runner up," quite a distance behind, and then a very few who make some scattered contributions. The contributor in this case is likely to be a fairly positive fellow with a good deal of initiative and a liking for authority. The leadership that emerges in this larger group tends to be formal and authoritative. Added to all this is the fact that, at the high school level at least, most students report more satisfaction in their work and feel more confidence in the decisions reached when working with small groups. Finally, groups of twelve or larger tend to break up into small groups no matter how they are formed originally (Hare, 1952).

Oviously there are many advantages for the small group. The picture, however, is not completely one-sided. In the first place, there are fewer ideas or suggestions to be had from a small group. Although it will frighten many people into silence, the large group by sheer virtue of numbers will put out a larger number of suggestions. This trend holds for groups up to ninety or one hundred. The sense of ease and congeniality in the small group, moreover, is not always an unmixed blessing. Sometimes contention and opposition may prove useful, partly by bringing out genuine weakness in proposals and partly by stimulating some people to more adequate suggestions. In the small group we may not find the range of views and temperaments necessary for this salutary clash. In some cases, the larger group is less at the mercy of a really troublesome member. An obstreperous person who might wreck

a small group has more chance of being kept in line within a larger group. For one thing, sheer size may inhibit him as it does others. Even if it does not, however, there is more chance that the larger group may include someone who can deal with him (Thelen, 1949).

All in all, it would seem that the student of average, or less than average, dominance should have much experience in working with groups of three or four or five. He should also have occasional experience in somewhat larger groups, hoping that, when he really has something to say, he will gradually acquire the confidence to speak up in more formidable gatherings. Larger groups should be used freely when it is important to get as many different suggestions as possible, as, for instance, when a complex and costly project should be examined for flaws before it is finally set in motion.

Getting the Groups Started

At the beginning of the year, or when pupils are still getting to know each other, try to be sure that the people in any one group like each other. As far as possible, honor the sociometric choices they may have made. In forming any one group, start with an isolate and then add his first preference and, if possible, some pupil who has shown some spark of interest in him. Include one choice of each of these two pupils (Gronlund, 1959, Chapter 8). If you can avoid it, never have more than two isolates in a group. In later groupings, try to cut across cleavages that separate subgroups. In so doing, however, try to put two pupils from each clique or subgroup in your new group. For the most part, try not to include a pupil if some member of the group actively rejects him. If one pupil is rejected by most of the others, however, you cannot avoid this situation and may even have to use the rejected pupil as your starting point, treating him as you would an isolate.

To promote genuine group work you should get the pupils to talk to each other. Call on Joe to comment on Bill's suggestion. Get him to talk directly to Bill. But as far as possible you will be nondirective, providing praise or support when in order, encouraging pupils to talk about what is in their minds, but in no sense passing final judgment on contributions. Many people would urge that you get the pupils to talk occasionally about the actual group process, to comment on any changes they notice in the way the group tackles new problems, or in their own reactions to the way the group is working (Gronlund, 1959, Chapter 8).

Helping the Isolated or Rejected Pupil. Many steps have been proposed for increasing the popularity of the outsider. As we have suggested, one possibility is to place him in a small group that has the best chance of accepting him. Place him with those who show some inclination toward him. Success often breeds success, and popularity, popularity. Finding a measure of acceptance, he may throw off some of the defenses that made him unpopular.

Moderate acceptance or praise by the teacher may help (Flanders and Havumaki, 1960). Establishing the isolate as teacher's pet, of course, would not help him. But you can try to show him the same respect and friendly warmth as you show to all the other pupils. Admittedly, this advice is often easier to give than to follow. If you are honest with yourself you may find some rejected children very difficult to like. But you can try. It may help to realize that often the unattractive traits come not from malice or meanness but from insecurity and the rejection already experienced.

You might try to see if the rejected child has some skill or hobby that may place him in a more favorable light. Then try to arrange some project in which this skill or hobby would show up in a natural way. You might assign him some routine job in which he had a reasonable chance of success and in which he might show up as a more acceptable sort of person.

Beyond these safe and obvious steps, you can, if you feel enough confidence, try more radical and more risky treatment. Some teachers attempt to discuss the problem in some detail with the child himself or with his parents. Others have tried to talk to the other students either about the general problem of tolerance or even about this particular student. If you are skillful in these matters, you may decide to encourage a group discussion of popularity and its aspects. With luck and good management this may ventilate some of the unacknowledged fears and worries that lead pupils to reject others. Susie may come to realize that she dislikes Bill partly because something about him makes her think of parts of her own home life that she would prefer to forget. This is high-powered medicine, however, and you should feel no obligation to try it unless you have considerable confidence that you and your group can avoid the obvious dangers. You may find a mock drama somewhat less risky. Here the students, acting in make-believe manner, may freely take one role or another and may be encouraged to act out the difference between behavior that makes for popularity and that which leads to rejection. But even here there is some risk. You may be unearthing strong emotions that may prove tremendously disturbing to some of the students.

Children in an Australian orphanage, aged five to thirteen, were given a battery of personality tests and a test of sociometric status. From a total of fifty-two children, nine pairs were matched on age, sex, residence in the orphanage, general adjustment, and sociometric status. One member of each pair was then assigned to a play therapy group and the other member to a control group. The children in the control group were left on their own while the experimental children received play therapy. In the play therapy, the experimental children were encouraged to play freely with dolls and other objects representing their usual experiences. These were chosen to suggest many types of problems and to involve many aspects of personality.

The play therapy continued for twenty-seven weeks. For both groups, the tests and the sociograms were repeated after twelve weeks and after twenty-seven weeks.

	Number of Each Group Showing Improvement in Sociometric Status	
	After 12 weeks	After 27 weeks
Play Therapy Group	6	4
Control Group	0	0

SOURCE: F. N. Cox, Sociometric status and individual adjustment before and after play therapy, *Journal of Abnormal and Social Psychology*, 1953, **48**, 354–356.

One general word of caution: your laudable desire to increase the popularity, acceptance, and participation of your students could lead you to harass the quiet, withdrawn child who is really self-sufficient and who needs only a minimum of social activity. Like the professional hostess on shipboard, you should try to encourage the timid, lonely person who is just aching to take part but who lacks the nerve to take the plunge. But you should not torment the person longing for a few hours of quiet reading or loafing (White, 1961).

LEADERSHIP IN THE CLASSROOM

Whatever your decision about group-centered teaching—whether to use it exclusively, extensively, moderately, or not at all—you will face the problem of leadership in the classroom. As we have seen, some pattern of leadership is bound to emerge, either organized around you, or organized without respect to you. You will also have to exert some leadership either through one approach or through another. Finally, there is the real obligation to help the pupils develop greater skill as leaders.

The Emergent or De Facto Leader

As the power structure begins to develop within a group, one person will seem to acquire more than his share of influence. He may exert this influence by contributing ideas and information, by providing a friendly atmosphere, by making decisions, or verbalizing decisions toward which the group is moving, or by sheer labor (Bartlett, 1959). At times the group may elect such a person to some office, or some higher authority may appoint him to a position of official influence. But even if neither of these things occur, the person is clearly exercising leadership. Such a person is called an *emergent leader*.

The emergent leader is likely to have a general feeling of security. He is also likely to act spontaneously and confidently when the situation calls for action. In a minor emergency, for instance, while most of us stand around wondering what to do, the potential leader is likely to move confidently and unhesitatingly toward some proposed solution (Lippit and others, 1952). More often than not, his proposed solution is reasonably effective (Fig. 12.6). At least it does not turn out to be foolish, although its real effectiveness may never be known. To move spontaneously toward a reasonably acceptable solution, a person must not only have a measure of security or self-confidence but he must also have a certain amount of competence in the field. The experienced woodsman might "take command" readily and satisfactorily in a camping incident. His confidence may desert him, however, when he must deal with an unruly child in a public place. In this latter situation, moreover, the steps that first occur to him may lead to results that are clearly unacceptable. All in all, we would not be surprised if the person who is influential in one field (evaluating the intellectual worth of a given college course) may have less to say in a different field (planning the June-week dance).

The qualities necessary for influence vary from age to age. Among young children, the bossy, dominating youngster can have a marked influence on his companions. With adolescents, however, more subtlety is required. The influential high school student is more likely to persuade than to give outright commands.

These age changes in patterns of influence do not necessarily mean that the influential six-year-old cannot be an influential adolescent. For one thing, the important confidence and security may well persist from one age to another. Secondly, the bossy six-year-old may well turn into a persuasive adolescent.

The Official Leader

Many people are extremely influential and are still never named to office. The qualities necessary to be influential are not sufficient to insure official election or to encourage appointment by superiors. Consider the problem of getting elected. The influential person does not have to be talkative, genial, or enthusiastic. These qualities are important, however, when it comes to being elected. Indeed, to become elected, it is more important to be conspicuous and vigorous than to provide helpful direction. Friendliness and sociability also help but cannot be substituted for prominence and vigor. In view of the role of prominence, it is not surprising to find that sheer physical bulk may also help a little. Elected leaders are, on the average, a little taller and heavier than the nonleaders. For social leadership, general appearance plays a part. The leader is also somewhat ahead in intelligence and in scholastic or other achievement. He is more self-assured, more adventurous, and more capable of warm, human responses. He is persistent, industrious, tends to dominate, and has objectives that excel those of his fellows. He is likely to be aware of his own powers and limitations.

Fig. 12.6. The natural leader takes spontaneous action in an emergency.

Where such things are valued, he has often superior family background. In all this, the leader cannot depart too much from the norms of the group. He is only slightly more intelligent, slightly more dominant, slightly more adventurous. The one who is markedly out of line in any way is not likely to be elected.

Clearly there is an intricate relationship among friendships, social participation, and election to office. Friendships help with election and lead to participation. Conversely, many students specify high participation as something they require in their friends. Participation helps one become elected. Conversely, to participate in some councils or committee work one must be elected. It is not surprising then to find that the description of the elected leader is also a fair description of the student who is generally socially active—who goes to dances, attends meetings, and takes part in voluntary group activities. Like the leader, such a student has fairly high drives, is self-assured, and gives evidence of general social maturity. He is especially likely to have a favorable socioeconomic background.

Obviously there is no necessity that the appointed leader shall have demonstrated his ability to exert influence. The teacher, for instance, or the army officer have to be leaders, but they are seldom required to show that they could exert influence within the group they are asked to lead or that they could be formally elected by the group.

Some Problems for the Leader

In any position of leadership, there are unpleasant decisions to be made. Subordinates must be evaluated. Rewards must be passed out to some people and withheld from others. One person must be selected for a committee post and others must be disappointed. At times, some people must be promoted and others denied promotion or discharged. Most leaders, elected or appointed, are torn between the necessity of making unpleasant decisions and the conflicting need to be liked or to retain one's own self-respect. This is an age-old theme in high drama and in ordinary life. The good king, depressed by the need of imposing unwelcome or harsh decisions, willingly gives way to a less scrupulous successor and, through his very "goodness," opens the door to evil (West, 1957). The appointed college leader, contemplating decisions that are bound to displease some of his buddies, resigns his position of leadership.

If we examine existing leaders, by the way, we will find that these unpleasant duties give less trouble to emergent or elected leaders than to appointed leaders (Carter, 1951). The emergent leader regularly encountered these problems on his way up and he had to find some way of living with them in order to survive. The appointed leader, on the other hand, may have served no such apprenticeship and may find such problems thrust upon him with no effective advance warning.

The Tasks of the Group Leader

Whenever a group is working on some task, there is an opportunity and perhaps a need for leadership. As we have seen, moreover, some pattern of influence or leadership is almost bound to emerge. Some teachers will tend to do much of this leadership work themselves, and here the problem is merely one of doing the work effectively. Other teachers will tend to delegate these leadership activities to various students. Here there are two problems—that of insuring a measure of effective leadership right now and that of helping the current leader to develop some skill in this particular art (Jenkins, 1960). First, let us consider the problems involved in effective leadership, whether the leader is the teacher himself or one of the students.

Reaching a Satisfactory Decision. Often it is imperative that the group reach some decision. The committee must bring in a report, the jury must reach a verdict. It is hoped, of course, that the decision will turn out to be a good one. But that is often hard to decide and much of the immediate pressure will be toward reaching a decision that is reasonably satisfactory to the group.

In reaching this decision, the leader should go to some trouble to obtain as many views as possible. It is part of the democratic process that as many people as possible should be heard from. As a practical matter, moreover, the group can only consider the merits of those proposals that are expressed. A useful, unmentioned idea would be lost. The expression of one view, moreover, might lead a second member to think of something valuable that otherwise would never have occurred to him. Finally, there is a strategic value in encouraging the widespread expression of views. People are less likely to support a decision if they feel that they never had a chance to express their opinion in the matter. Those who had their full say in reaching the decision are more likely to support it, whether or not the decision is in accord with their views.

Using and Controlling the Pressures to Conformity. If he chooses, the leader can make use of both the group pressures and the individual urge to conform. Suppose, for instance, that you decide to try to change the attitude of your class. You

decide, in this case, to try to get the pupils to read something besides comic books. Theoretically, of course, you could try to persuade each pupil individually. But this would mean that you would be working against the pull of the group. As each pupil was about to change his views he would be held back by his ideas of what the group felt. In a genuine group discussion, on the other hand, the pressures are often reversed. Suppose that you are fortunate and the group as a whole does begin to lean slightly in your direction. If the group discusses the matter freely, the change should become apparent, and now the pressures to conform will lead each individual to go along with the changes taking place in the group. To make sure that the group changes would be apparent, the early investigators (Lewin, 1953, pp. 287–288) asked for an actual show of hands. This, of course, meant that each participant was asked to make a decision or commitment. Consequently, we cannot be sure that the persisting changes came from taking part in the discussion or from the fact of having made an overt decision.

Conformity may be made to serve many useful purposes. In searching for the best solution to a problem, however, conformity is often a downright evil. If everybody rushes to agree to the first suggestion, some important possibilities may never be considered. To take care of this problem, the group leader should go to some trouble to bring minority views to the surface (Maier and Solem, 1952). If someone should look hesitant or doubtful, he should be invited to speak up. Two things should follow. First, his view will be presented for consideration. Second, because of his stand, others might be more likely to do some dissenting.

► *Lecture vs. Discussion in Changing Attitudes*

This investigation was carried on during World War II and was concerned with the attempt to get housewives to make more use of the less popular beef products such as heart, kidneys, or sweetbreads. There were "six Red Cross groups of volunteers organized for home nursing." Three groups were given a forty-five minute lecture dealing with the nutritive qualities of the foods being discussed, the importance of the problem for the war effort, and specific procedures for making these meats more attractive. The lecturer gave out mimeographed recipes and told how much her family had enjoyed them.

In the other three groups the emphasis was on group discussion. The leader presented the general question and invited comments. He especially asked the women to comment on the problems that would be encountered in trying to use more meats of this kind. After the group had become involved in the discussion, the nutrition expert presented the same factual information about vitamins, economy, and methods for preparation. The groups were then asked to indicate by a show of hands how many were willing to try one of these meats within the next week.

Here, then, we have the effects of a lecture compared to the effects of group discussion, plus an overt group decision. Some 32 percent of the latter group actually did serve one of the meats, whereas only 3 percent of the lecture group did so.

SOURCE: K. Lewin, Studies in group decision, in D. Cartwright and A. Zander, eds., *Group Dynamics: Research and Theory* (New York: Harper & Row, Publishers, Inc., 1953), pp. 287–288.

Training for Leadership

One of the first tasks in training a pupil to become an effective leader is to help him to emerge as an influential person. To some extent this can be done by assigning him a position in which essential information passes through his hands. A student committee, for instance, is planning a yearbook or a display or some other project. One student is selected at random to act as a clearing house. He is not given any genuine responsibility, but is merely the one to go to for certain information. Very often this arbitrarily selected student will show more of a flair for leadership than his equally capable classmate who was not assigned this position. If the interest and capacity are potentially there, this seems a fairly simple way to bring it out (Leavitt, 1951).

At a more superficial level, of course, students can take turns in serving as appointed leaders. Here they will not necessarily develop intrinsic qualities of leadership, but they can gain experience in the effective direction of group activity.

When the student is actually in charge of a group, either through the wishes of the group or by assignment, how can he become more proficient in leading the group? It is reasonable to suppose that learning to be an effective leader is like learning any other skill. Remembering what was said earlier, we should stress the wisdom of keeping motivation or tension down to reasonable level, as very often the beginning leader is likely to be too tense. We should try to guarantee a measure of initial success. Perhaps we could arrange a graded series of tasks ranging from those which placed few demands on the leader to those which called for a considerable degree of competence. Successes should be brought out and made apparent. Perhaps we could point to some objective evidence of success—the extent and spirit of group participation, the results accomplished. Perhaps we would have to make do with our own unsupported statement that the job was well done.

All in all, some success can be expected in this process of training for leadership. As we have seen, trained leaders are better able to bring out and utilize minority opinion. On a broader scale, we find that trained leaders are often more successful in attaining a new or creative solution. Suppose, for instance, that a group of teachers is faced with a proposal. This project is attractive in most respects but it involves giving up the teachers' lounge. With untrained leadership there is likely to be outright rejection, or, less frequently, outright acceptance. With a trained leader, however, there is less likely to be outright rejection and more likely to be some compromise or "creative" plan that permits the general acceptance but avoids the complete loss of the lounge (Maier, 1953).

The training to be effective must not only bring about new kinds of skill. For most people it must also bring about a change in attitude. The leader, after all, will be asked to give up considerable measure of control and this may be a very frightening thing. To the untrained leader, the suggestions that will come from the group can be regarded as a criticism directed to him as a person, and the sensitive leader may feel a severe threat to his status or his ego.

DISCIPLINE AND THE GROUP PROCESS

The word "discipline" means many different things. One person, in using the word, may refer to self-discipline, or the process whereby a student comes to regulate his own behavior to fit in with larger purposes. A second person may use the term to refer to the problem of keeping children in line or keeping the schoolroom intact. In the first and larger sense, discipline is almost synonymous with the whole problem of character education (Chapters 9, 10, 11) and emotional development (Chapters 13, 14). The narrower problem of keeping order is the one considered here.

Keeping Order in the Classroom

This problem of keeping order, by the way, has too often been given a hush-hush treatment (Ladd, 1958). Many educators have written as if there were no problems of keeping order, or as if it were a problem only for completely worthless teachers, so that anyone who confessed to any difficulties would immediately put himself beyond the pale. Too often the topic has been pushed underground and has had a hearing only in the teachers' lounge room and behind the back of the educational leader.

This is too bad. Keeping order is a problem and also a worthy objective (Crawford and Harrington, 1961). Some degree of order is essential if you are to meet your responsibilities to the community and to the pupils. Many teachers will find some measure of orderliness necessary to their own peace of mind and efficiency. Actual investigations show, moreover, that this is a serious worry (Eaton and others, 1957). In one southwestern high school, four out of every five teachers made disciplinary reports covering 40 percent of the students. Women sent in twice as many as men, and the reports were especially numerous toward the end of the year. They dealt chiefly with lateness, truancy, classroom disturbance, and outright disobedience (Zeitlin, 1962). After poor salaries and lack of facilities, discipline is the concern most frequently aired by teachers when speaking frankly and anonymously (Ladd, 1958). Discipline is also the major worry of some 70 percent of beginning teachers.

Obviously you will hope that discipline in the larger sense, the development of social understanding, self-discipline, and consideration for others, will more and more take care of the problem of keeping order. That is a reasonable long-term goal. Meanwhile, however, you may have to take deliberate steps to maintain the degree of order needed right now.

Most experienced teachers frequently come up against this problem of keeping order. The successful teacher takes these matters in his stride, but few classes go by that do not call for some deliberate action on his part.

Discipline and the Task-oriented Attitude. Discipline presents one problem when the students are highly motivated and interested in the subject (Kounin and others, 1961) and quite another problem when motivation is low. When motivation is high, the student tends to judge the teacher's work impersonally, and the teacher's behavior is linked to the work to be learned. When motivation is high, moreover, students are not disturbed by a matter-of-fact admonition directed to one student. The students not admonished consider this a normal necessity for getting on with the work. In a poorly motivated class, however, such an admonition will start the other students thinking about fairness, meanness, and who will win out.

We must not imply that, merely by taking thought, the teacher can transform any class into a highly motivated group intent on the business of learning something. We shall profit from anything that we can accomplish in this matter, but we should not expect miracles. The teacher, of course, can do something toward establishing the idea that the pupils are in his class to learn. He can also keep his own efforts oriented to the task at hand. As far as the onlookers are concerned, a verbal reprimand is disturbing or distracting when the teacher stresses the fact that he does not like that behavior or that he won't stand for it. The reprimand is less disturbing to the other students and leaves a better taste if the teacher shows how the student's act interferes with the work at hand.

This task-oriented approach is perhaps one of the most important facets of good discipline. Keep the class moving toward the goal that is established. As far as possible prevent any interruptions to this progress. When someone does interrupt the progress, deal with it as an interruption and not as a challenge to you as a person. Don't let your personal feelings dominate. Ventilating them will prolong the interruption to the task and will distract the attention from the job and direct it to you and to your likes and tolerances.

When good disciplinarians are observed, it is easy to see this emphasis on progress toward the academic goal (Celler, 1948). These teachers keep their students busy with some worthwhile activities. There are few awkward lulls in which no one seems to know what to do. Such teachers also adapt their instruction to the circumstances that develop. If some pupils show unexpected confusion in trying to grasp a point, the teacher does not try to ignore the problem or try to gloss it over, but patiently tries to clear things up. These activities, of course, typically interfere with the prepared lesson plans, and the good disciplinarian has prepared for this possibility by having more than one way in which he can complete the lesson.

Good disciplinarians are somewhat more likely to use convenient physical equipment such as chalkboards, maps, projectors, and displays. More important, however, they use these things well. They go to some trouble to be sure that everyone can see and hear. In so doing, they not only get more pupils to see and hear but they also improve the rapport. Their concern helps the teacher and pupil establish a partnership in the task at hand.

These things that characterize the good disciplinarian are things that you would want to do whether or not discipline seemed to be a problem.

Avoiding Confusion or Appearance of Helplessness. Good disciplinarians seldom "teach" into irrelevant noise. If the shuffling or banging is inherent in getting settled, you should wait until the settling has taken place. If it has gone on too long, use some signal to bring it to a stop. But do not try to conduct actual instruction under these circumstances. Balky apparatus or film projectors can often contribute to the appearance of helplessness. If you are to use equipment that could get out of order, check it in advance. If it is very temperamental, have some alternative material ready. Go to some trouble to take care of routine tasks, such as passing papers and materials or the movement of pupils to and from the chalkboard. Don't let this become a

fetish to the neglect of intrinsic teaching, but keep it from being a frequent source of confusion.

A Confident and Natural Manner. You can't automatically become confident just by deciding that you will be, but there are some things you might remember that should help. First of all, you can expect that most behavior will be acceptable. Secondly, remember that not all offenses are direct attacks on you. Many of them are sheer thoughtlessness or exploitations of an inviting situation or even the expression of antagonism, not toward you but toward the school, toward adults, or toward the world in general. These offenses must be dealt with, but you can feel better about them if you don't take them personally.

Whatever you can or cannot do about increasing your own feeling of confidence, there are many things you can do to portray to good advantage the confidence that you do feel. Take praise, for instance. The ability to praise is often considered the mark of the secure and confident person. He can take note of the good work of others without feeling any threat to himself. Use praise whenever it is in order. This is good in itself and it also promotes an atmosphere of confidence and security.

Direct Psychological Contact. Confidence is often shown by the teacher's use of direct contact. Good disciplinarians (Celler, 1948), are anything but reticent in their relations with pupils. They encourage communication—almost insist upon it—and in general the communication they get is ready and free, rather than formal. Most of the time, the communication is friendly and objective, but sometimes there is a spirited interchange. Some teachers achieve directness by an assertive, almost aggressive tone.

By your manner or approach you should say to each student, "You are here and I am here and we have a job to do." Don't try to pretend that you are not there. Don't try to will the student into nothingness. And never forget about the task that confronts both of you.

To call attention to the fact that you are there, and very much so, *come out from behind the desk*. Move around the room freely, naturally, as if you enjoyed being there. Speak to the students, not at them, and certainly not at some spot on the opposite wall. As far as possible, speak directly to one student after another. Even if you do not get around to each one, you will accentuate the impression of directness when you are talking to some individual. When possible, call specific students by name.

Maintaining Necessary Psychological Distance. To urge you toward vigorous and direct contact with students is by no means to urge you to become excessively chummy or familiar. The two do not necessarily go together. A military officer could be forceful, vigorous, and direct in his official dealings with his men, and yet be completely unapproachable as a person. It is unlikely that this military relation would appeal to you as a teacher. But you may well need some measure of reserve or psychological distance if you are to operate freely and to remain reasonably comfortable. Certainly most experienced teachers would urge you not to become overly familiar, especially at first. You should try to decide how much psychological privacy or reserve you need and then deliberately try to maintain this. You yourself can be careful to stay within the limits you set. If you feel that a student is about to step over this line, you can hold him back politely, quietly, perhaps with a joke and a smile. But always do it directly and positively. Never try to protect yourself by retreating into nothingness.

Immediate Attention to Infractions. In keeping with this direct approach, the good disciplinarian tends to take immediate and unhesitating action whenever there is any serious, overt breach of the rules. Typically, he deals with this infraction by some very simple device, such as a gesture, a significant look, or one or two words of admonition. But, unlike his less effective colleague, he does not pretend that no infraction has occurred. Other students, watching the teacher ignore a definite incident, believe that the incident may well be repeated (Kounin and others, 1961). Such ignoring, however, may give a new teacher a reputation for kindliness.

There is always a problem, of course, in knowing just what to take seriously and what to treat lightly. In general, it would seem best to err on the side of noticing too much. If it is a borderline matter, make it clear that you see it, but treat it in exceedingly casual fashion. The twinkle in your eye can say, "I see you all right, but we are too busy with something else to stop and deal with you." This attitude suggests a sense of proportion in dealing with minor matters, yet preserves the all-important direct contact. It does not give the impression that you are pretending you are not there.

Sometimes, of course, a misdeed comes from genuine confusion or an honest mistake. In driving a car, for instance, you may have missed the sign that says this is a one-way street. Or the student may not really know that books should not be left on the window sills. These situations call not for punishment but for instruction.

► *Students' Views of Discipline*

A total of 141 girls and 135 boys from two Georgia high schools were asked to comment on recent behavior for which they had been reprimanded or on corrections they had recently received.

Misbehavior	Percentage of Mentions for Each Type of Behavior	
	Girls	Boys
Talking, Laughing	66	40
Inattention or Disturbing Class	4	15
Tardiness	5	3
Cutting Classes	3	6

In most cases (43 percent), students were merely reprimanded in class, but 16 percent were reprimanded in private. In some 3 percent of the cases the offender was sent to the principal. In all, 73 percent of girls and 79 percent of boys readily admitted the offenses, and 63 percent of the boys and 52 percent of the girls considered the punishment justifiable. Only a few (less than 10 percent) thought that discipline was too strict or too lax, but some 60 percent thought it was not sufficiently consistent.

SOURCE: K. C. Garrison, A study of student disciplinarian practices in 2 Georgia High Schools, *Journal of Educational Research*, 1959, **53**, 153–156.

In other situations, and these probably predominate in disciplinary matters, the culprit clearly knows he is in the wrong, and he knows why his behavior is wrong (Garrison, 1959). When you are caught exceeding the speed limit you really know that it is against the law, and you know it is dangerous. Jimmie really knows that when Billy walks down the aisle he should not trip him. Here instruction or explanation is superfluous.

Emphasis on Task Rather Than Infractions. Infractions are infractions because they interrupt our job. In treating them we do not wish to compound the evil by prolonging the interruption. Short, snappy, casual reprimands or admonitions have a great advantage in this respect. A tardy student can be admonished simply by looking him in the eye and pointing meaningfully to a clock or watch. Other delinquencies can be dealt with by a gesture, a wave of the hand, a snap of the finger, a grimace, or a brief "That's enough." Here there is almost no interruption to the basic activity in progress. The essential task and the minor misdemeanor retain their proper proportion.

The simple, casual device has a further advantage. It reduces the time that the student is forced to spend in an unflattering spotlight. Students readily become humiliated and resentful when subjected to a prolonged discussion of their misdoings, however sweet and reasonable the discussion may be. Adults similarly resent the lecture of the traffic policeman. A brief reprimand, even if it should be rough, is often less distressing.

Although the brief, casual reprimand can be vigorous, even rough, it should always carry some overtones of acceptance (Sears and Hilgard, 1964). Roughness and acceptance, in our culture, of course, are not at all contradictory. Exaggerated, semihumorous violence can convey much basic acceptance. The good-humored attack is a mark of friendship. Humor and a sense of proportion always help. A harsh, unrelieved punitive attitude is another matter. So is biting sarcasm. Threats and open hostility directed to one student tend to distract the whole class for some time. Behavior of this sort may also reduce the teacher's general academic prestige, especially if the teacher is not well established (Kounin and others, 1961).

The formal court-martial or student trial may give students useful practice in dealing with one of the unhappy aspects of social life. At one time or another, presumably, students must learn to deal with the breaker of rules. As a routine method of dealing with transgressions, however, this device has many disadvantages. As mentioned in Chapter 10, the decisions of some of these juvenile tribunals are almost unbelievably harsh. Reasonable decisions about misdeeds call for the utmost maturity and sagacity. Many societies select the wisest and most balanced of their elders to act as their judges. There is a danger that young people, given too much responsibility in these matters, may come to enjoy their censorious role.

Good Behavior as the Student's Obligation. Things should go much better if you expect good behavior as a matter of course. This should make for a natural and confident manner on your part. More important, moreover, this attitude represents a more wholesome moral relation. Reasonable behavior is something that the pupil owes to his classmates, to the school, and to the teacher.

Try to discourage any connection between the pupil's obligation to behave and his liking for you. You want the pupils to like you, of course. And this does have a favorable effect on behavior and on his judgments of your disciplinary acts (Kounin and others, 1961). But this liking is important in its own right. If you use your good standing as a device to get good behavior, you cheapen the relation and may give the erroneous impression that the pupil has the obligation to behave only when he likes the teacher.

Ultimate Sanctions. When you send a pupil to the principal, you run the risk of appearing to confess failure. And certainly this is a matter of last resort. Use it as such. But use it when really necessary. There are some infractions which really go beyond your jurisdiction, and the decisions about these should come from broader authority. In general, you should go as far as your skill and authority will permit you. But if these fail, and if a genuine disciplinary problem persists, don't just try to pretend it away. Good behavior on the pupil's part is more important than your feeling of success or failure. Your sense of failure, uncomfortable as it is, should not interfere with the need to take corrective action.

SUMMARY

The group has an individuality and an influence somewhat apart from the influence of the individuals making it up. The classroom is a working group but it has more continuity than most working groups and is less clearly directed to a single task.

Sociometric relations within a classroom may be easily determined and portrayed, if desired, in a sociogram. When reasonable precautions are taken, data obtained in this way are fairly reliable and reflect real-life social linkages. Children shown to be popular in these assessments are somewhat brighter than the average and have at least average academic success. They are above average in appearance and emotional adjustment. They are sociable and come from sociable parents. They may talk much or little, but when they do talk it is about matters of general interest. Friendship choices show the influence of intelligence, interests, and home background. An older student can tell fairly well who likes him and who does not. He can also tell something of the general popularity of his classmates.

Within a group there is some pattern of authority, indicating who influences whom. Young children agree fairly well on the relative influence of their classmates. Other lines of influence can be detected by observing communication patterns (to whom do people address their remarks?) These patterns, once established, may remain fairly constant for quite a period. Because of his age and legal position, the teacher is likely to be a key figure in the authority pattern, but he can delegate or rearrange this temporarily if he chooses. He cannot, of course, legally abdicate his powers.

To give children practice in group responsibility, and for other objectives, many teachers utilize group-centered teaching. In this arrangement, the group takes responsibility for many decisions, the teacher acting as consultant or as a member of the group. According to some views, the teacher is obligated to provide emotional support and is prohibited from sarcasm or personal derogation.

From this approach there is some suggestion of improved attitudes and greater group cohesion, perhaps more independence. Mastery of subject matter is no greater or no less than in other approaches. Students vary markedly in their reactions. There is much to suggest that the teacher should choose his own approach and in so doing consider his own need for psychological distance. Good teaching and friendly support are possible in many approaches.

The school may give valuable practice in dealing with group forces. On the one hand there is a strong group pressure to induce conformity, varying in intensity, in the areas covered, and in the degree of unanimity on the part of the group. Immature people seem to thrive when conformity pressure is quite marked. As students become older they may be better able to resist such pressures. The brighter and more sturdy are more likely to resist or rebel.

The pressures differ with the size of the group. The small group is more permissive and more efficient in structuring an ambiguous problem. The large group is more efficient in the relentless detection of defects. It is often wise to set a group up around an isolate, selecting those most likely to accept him. Other steps may be taken to increase the acceptance of the isolate and to increase the total amount of group interaction.

Leadership constitutes a twofold issue for the teacher. Leadership problems are present throughout daily work. The teacher also works to increase the pupil's skill in leadership. The person who automatically comes to exert leadership tends to be spontaneous, decisive. He contributes to the group by getting things decided and by advancing useful suggestions. The de facto leader may also be officially elected if he has the necessary friendliness and outgoing attitudes. The official leader has many unpleasant decisions to make and he may abdicate his responsibility because of this. The functioning leader faces the task of getting a representative decision, of collecting views to this end, and especially of encouraging the expression of minority views. If he has a clear idea of the decision he wants he can often use group pressures to promote that decision.

Training for leadership calls for a graded series of tasks to guarantee a reasonable series of successes, and a procedure for making the success apparent.

At one time or another discipline is a problem for every teacher. Those successful in managing this problem are noted for their determined orientation to the task on which the class is engaged. They keep the class busily and effectively at work on this problem, doing many things to point out the partnership in this task. They treat infractions as obstacles to the task and not as personal affronts to themselves. Such an approach leads pupils to see both the teacher and the misdemeanor in relation to the objectives. Good disciplinarians avoid lulls or the appearance of helplessness. They exude a confident and pleasant manner and seek direct psychological contact with as many individual students as possible, but they are not necessarily chummy with students.

Some infractions can be conspicuously ignored. Serious distractions call for immediate attention, preferably by some informal, casual device that offers the least possible interruption to the task at hand. Most of the time, the pupil is quite aware that his action is wrong. Lengthy explanations are typically unnecessary and are often intensely irritating. Elaborate formal inquiries should be considered for their training in judicial procedures. They have many disadvantages as disciplinary procedures.

The teacher should avoid giving the pupils the idea that he is prepared to bargain for their good behavior. Reasonable behavior is a moral obligation.

SUGGESTIONS FOR FURTHER READING

Measurement of Social Relations

Gronlund, N. E., *Sociometry in the Classroom*. New York: Harper & Row, Publishers, Inc., 1959.

Lindzey, G., and E. F. Borgatta, Sociometric methods, in G. Lindzey, ed. *Handbook of Social Psychology*. Reading, Mass.: Addison-Wesley Publishing Company Inc., 1954, pp. 405–448.

Remmers, H. H., Rating methods in research on teaching, in N. L. Gage, ed. *Handbook of Research on Teaching*. Skokie, Ill.: Rand McNally, 1963b, pp. 345–360.

Thompson, G. G., Children's groups, in P. H. Mussen, ed. *Handbook of Research Methods in Child Development*. New York: John Wiley & Sons, Inc., 1960, pp. 821–853.

Group Effects

Bartlett, C. J., Dimensions of leadership behavior in classroom discussion groups, *Journal of Educational Psychology*, 1959, **50**, 280–284. Reprinted in Morse, pp. 282–286.

Cartwright, D., and A. Zander, *Group Dynamics: Research and Theory*, 2d ed. New York: Harper & Row, Publishers, Inc., 1960.

Coleman, J. S., *The Adolescent Society; The Social Life of the Teenager and Its Impact on Education*. New York: The Free Press of Glencoe, 1961.

Grambs, Jean D., Understanding inter-group relations, Item 21 in *What Research Says to the Teacher*. Washington, D. C.: National Education Association, 1960.

Hare, A. P., E. F. Borgatta, and R. F. Bales, *Small Groups; Studies in Social Interaction*. New York: Alfred A. Knopf, Inc., 1955.

Henry, N. B., ed., The dynamics of instructional groups, *Yearbook National Society for the Study of Education*, 1960, **59**, Part II.

Klein, Josephine, *Working with Groups: The Social Psychology of Discussion and Decision*. London: Hutchinson & Co. (Publishers), Ltd., 1961.

Thibaut, J. W., and H. H. Kelley, *The Social Psychology of Groups*. New York: John Wiley & Sons, Inc., 1959.

Thomas, E. J., and C. F. Fink, Effects of group size, *Psychological Bulletin*, 1963, **60**, 371–384.

Group-Centered Approaches

Anderson, R. C., Learning in discussion: a resumé of the authoritarian-democratic studies, *Harvard Educational Review*, 1959, **29**, 201–215. Reprinted in Charters, pp. 153–162.

Flanders, N. A., Diagnosing and utilizing social structures in classroom learning, *Yearbook National Society for the Study of Education*, 1960a, **59**, Part II, 187–217.

Haring, N. G., and E. L. Phillips, *Educating Emotionally Disturbed Children*. New York: McGraw-Hill Book Company, Inc., 1962.

Sears, Pauline S., and E. R. Hilgard, The teacher's role in the motivation of the learner, *Yearbook National Society for the Study of Education*, 1964, **63**, Part I, 182–209.

Stern, G. G., Measuring noncognitive variables in research on teaching, in N. L. Gage, ed. *Handbook of Research on Teaching*. Skokie, Ill.: Rand McNally, 1963, 398–447.

White, R. K., and R. Lippit, *Autocracy and Democracy: An Experimental Inquiry*. New York: Harper & Row, Publishers, Inc., 1960.

Discipline

Ausubel, D. P., A new look at classroom discipline, *Phi Delta Kappan*, 1961b, **43**, 25–30.

Cutts, Norma E., and N. Moseley, *Teaching the Disorderly Pupil in Elementary and Secondary School*. New York: David McKay Company, Inc., 1957.

Kounin, J. S., P. V. Gump, and J. J. Ryan, III, Explorations in classroom management, *Journal of Teacher Education*, 1961, **12**, 235–246. Reprinted in Fullagar, pp. 533–549.

Laycock, S. R., *Mental Hygiene in the School; A Handbook for the Classroom Teacher*. Vancouver: Copp Clark, 1960.

McDonald, Blanche, and L. W. Nelson, *Successful Classroom Control*. Dubuque, Iowa: W. C. Brown Publishers, 1955.

Phillips, E. L., D. N. Wiener, and N. G. Haring, *Discipline, Achievement, and Mental Health, A Teacher's Guide to Wholesome Action*. Englewood Cliffs, N. J.: Prentice-Hall, Inc., 1960.

Sheviakov, G. V., and F. Redl, *Discipline for Today's Children and Youth*. Revised by Sybil K. Richardson. Washington, D. C.: National Education Association, 1956.

EXERCISES AND QUESTIONS FOR DISCUSSION

1. Comment on some of the advantages and difficulties in making a sociometric analysis of a class in grade one; in grade ten. Include the probable attitude of students toward such procedures and the problem of detecting pupils who are rejected.

2. What would you look for if you wanted to determine the cohesiveness of a group? if you wanted to determine the authority pattern within the group?

3. Compare the qualities that should lead to popularity with those helpful in *de facto* leadership and with those that lead to official election.

4. Outline a paper on "Conformity: Its Dimensions, Uses, and Dangers."

5. What sort of a group might prove best for each of the following tasks:

    (a) Looking for flaws in a plan that has been carefully worked out, but is up for a last-minute revision.

    (b) Providing a chance for a timid student to learn to express himself in public.

    (c) Keeping a noisy, aggressive student within bounds.

    (d) Writing a sketch for the school variety hour.

6. From those teachers whom you can remember, select the one best, and the one poorest, at keeping order. Try to pick them from the same general level. Analyze the differences and compare your analysis with that presented in the chapter.

CHAPTER 13

▶ *The Pupil's Adjustment:*
Observed and Projected

Along with its unique responsibilities for academic proficiency, the school shares with other agencies the obligation to promote personal adjustment. At the very least it must try to keep from actually injuring the personal adjustment of its pupils. Going farther, the school may assume much responsibility for positive gains in this area. No matter which of these objectives we espouse, nor in what degree, we need to know something of the nature of mental health, of the forces which affect it, and the means by which it can be fostered.

MENTAL HEALTH AND MENTAL ILLNESS

Most of us have a fairly clear idea of what is meant by general mental health. Certainly we have some definite notions about mental illness, and in analyzing our ideas of mental illness we

are bound to go some distance toward clarifying these general concepts of health. Let us look at some of these attempts (Scott, 1958).

Distortion of Reality

One conspicuous feature of mental ill health is a distorted view of important features of life. In extreme cases the victim may believe that he is John the Baptist or that he hears voices telling him what to do or that his neighbor is a spy working for the inhabitants of Mars. In less dramatic form, this distortion may show up in the person's refusal to face his own limitations or in his refusal to face some powerful hate, or fear, or off-beat desire. True enough, this latter type of distortion, the mere refusal to face our own nature, does not automatically mark us as mentally ill. Some of these distortions or defense

349

mechanisms may be extremely useful, for the time being, at least (Redlich, 1957). But such a willful and frantic blindness often lies behind anxieties, incapacities, hysterias, or psychosomatic ailments that do constitute symptoms of mental illness.

When the genuine psychotic distorts reality, he often does so in unmistakable fashion. We need waste little time in wondering whether our patient really is Abraham Lincoln or whether he does control the passage of the winds. The distortions of the nonpsychotic, however, may be more difficult to prove. How can we be sure that our client really is wracked by a hatred of his father which he refuses to admit? or that the high school girl is deceiving herself when she disclaims all wish to be popular with the other students? Are all such latter disclaimers self-deceptions? Or might there be some people who, even in their most basic selves, really feel no urge toward things like social acceptance?

In asserting that someone has acquired a distorted view of his own feelings or motives, we may merely be making inferences from a general pattern to the specific case. We believe that most people feel a need for moderate social acceptance, for instance, and we suspect that Susie is no different from anyone else. Alternatively our statement may be based on the unnaturalness of Susie's comments. Her denial may be too frequent or too vehement—she doth protest too much. We feel that anyone announcing a mere lack of interest would do so in more matter-of-fact fashion. At other times such a suspicion of distortion may be justified by later events. In a confidential setting, or even under great stress, the urge we have suspected may be admitted. After one successful social venture, Susie may change her attitude and seek such experiences in the future. True, the urge itself may have come with success, but we suspect that it was always there, being heretofore fearfully repressed.

Trouble in Handling Anxiety and Frustration

Fear, worry, tension, and concern are by no means synonymous with poor mental health. On the contrary, if a person were in a genuinely perilous situation and felt none of these things, he would be considered to be denying the existence of the peril and thus refusing to face the impressive reality of his fear. But there are different kinds of anxiety. The Freudians (Chapter 10), for instance, distinguish between moral anxiety (guilt), neurotic anxiety, and reality anxiety. Moral anxiety is treated in Chapter 10. Reality anxiety comes from the objective perils mentioned above. As such it implies no mental illness and it becomes significant for mental health only when it reaches excessive levels. As its name might imply, on the other hand, neurotic anxiety is almost always a problem in the field of mental hygiene. This is the anxiety that is likely to occur when there is no serious threat at all. The sufferer may be unable to name the object of his apprehension. He quails before some vague, unknown terror. In milder forms, our anxious person can tell what he fears, but his fear may be directed not to the real menace in the object but to some innocent aspect.

Typical Defense Mechanisms. When anxiety of any type becomes too intense, or when it cannot be dealt with in reasonable fashion, we are likely to adopt one or more of the familiar defense mechanisms. In Freudian psychology, these are the defenses which the ego erects to shield it from an anxiety with which it cannot deal. They serve to distort the menace and make it seem less of a threat to our safety or to our sense of self-respect (superego). These mechanisms appear so frequently in general discussions that a brief mention will serve here. *Repression* is treated in some detail in Chapter 9. Repression allays the immediate anxiety but invites the reappearance of the threatening urge in some unrelated disguise, perhaps passing itself off as the very opposite of the offensive urge (reaction formation). Unconscious *compensation* may also arise from a repressed idea. This may occur when the child refuses to admit a handicap and keeps directing his frenzied efforts to the very area in which he is deficient. Some forms of *identification*—that word of many meanings—can act as a defense mechanism when the child may try to ignore his own inadequacy by confusing his own self with that of some successful person or group. *Projection* can take either one of two forms. Distressed by some urge that strikes us as unworthy, we may seek solace by stressing the fact that other people are like that *too*. Going farther, however, we could get the idea that we are not at all hostile to our victim and that *all* the trouble comes from the victim's hostility to us. In *rationalization* we scrub up our motives and do the questionable things we want to do anyway, but for the most laudable of reasons. The id urge is thus permitted its release with no pain to the superego. Sometimes this takes the form of convenient ailments which excuse us from an unwelcome obligation or of pains that make our aggressive acts seem more pardonable. *Fantasy* is a very general device in which we seek the solace of imaginary success.

Unfortunate View of Self

Many of the defense mechanisms are frantic devices used to help us retain a favorable view of the self. Such subterfuges do not always work, however, and even when they do, the victim is left with a distorted view of the real self. To many clinicians this distorted or unhappy view of the self (Wylie, 1961) is the crux of mental ill health. At times the troubled person is unable to like the self that he seems to see. He feels ashamed, guilty, or regards himself as an inferior person, having no legitimate claim to the regard of other people. At other times, or perhaps even at the same time, he is driven to distort his view of the real self until it becomes a glamorized version of himself that no one else would ever recognize.

As opposed to this troubled approach, the more healthy person is willing to look at himself in fairly honest fashion. In examining this person that is himself, he undoubtedly sees much that distresses him. He sees himself making serious mistakes, entertaining hates and lusts that might make for general unhappiness, quailing before his obligations, and, in general, conducting himself in a fashion that is far from ideal. But he sees these qualities as minor defects in a person who, in general, can be liked, and a person who has a legitimate claim to be valued by other people.

Obviously, self-acceptance has an intimate relation to freedom from distortion. The person who likes the self he sees, in spite of the admitted quirks, has less need to distort the picture that is there. When the person cannot like the self that is tainted by such defects he may be driven to deny the defects or to gloss them over into some un-

Fig. 13.1. The importance of a reasonable and realistic view of the self.

realistic image. A reasonable amount of self-liking is one of the conditions which permits us to face our limitations openly and honestly, and thus to make realistic decisions regarding any matter in which any important frailties may play a part (Fig. 13.1).

Not that we should go overboard in this matter of admitting faults. To admit none whatever, of course, is, as we have seen, a suggestion of distortion or suppression. To dwell on one's faults endlessly and in seeming enjoyment, however, is also a mark of poor adjustment. It suggests that the person is fascinated by his inadequacies and is transforming his very unworthiness into a way of life.

Many people would insist that to avoid ill health we must not only like the self we find, but we must also see in that self some evidence of consistency, integrity, or style. A helter-skelter collection of traits or qualities would not do. The traits must fit into a pattern or unity that makes each of us an integrated individual.

Difficulties with Self-Control

Lack of self-control has long been identified with poor adjustment. Indeed, at one time, such self-control was regarded as the key test of emotional adjustment. A man with little control was at the low end of the scale. The man with much control was to be envied.

The contemporary view is by no means that simple. Overcontrol may be as crippling as no control at all. But we are still concerned with the problem of self-control (Fraiberg, 1959). Mental ill health may be associated with both the amount of control maintained and the type of the control that is used. Certainly, wholesome control does not lead to the elimination of basic drives. On the contrary, the wholesome personality is endowed with strong urges or drives. The happy, admirable person is well equipped with vigorous appetites and a full quota of needs. Some of these needs may act in relatively primitive form. Others may appear greatly modified. In either case, however, these drives still exist and for the most part constitute a considerable source of satisfaction. The happy and effective person has a rich emotional life. He has enthusiastic likes and loyalties. He may have equally vigorous aversions and dislikes. All in all, he is distinguished from his less fortunate colleague, not by a dearth of natural drives, but by an abundance of them.

The need for some control has also clearly been recognized. We have no use for the man who gives out with violent attacks or a flood of abuse at the slightest interference with his activity. We regard him as unsocial and immature. But we are also reluctant to approve the man who has controlled his aggressive tendencies to the point of complete suppression. Ordinarily we do not admire the man who lets people walk all over him, who never talks back, or who never protests unfair treatment.

In a proper balance between drive and control there should be evidence of a happy and spontaneous energy. The balanced individual goes joyfully and zestfully to his task. He does not move reluctantly before a nagging conscience, nor does he rush ahead in frenzy as if to escape some fearful panic. If the control is efficient and not too restricted, there is breadth and smoothness to his actions. He does not move ahead with awkward, pedantic caution, but proceeds at an even and unhurried rate. He takes minor obstacles in his stride. He gives major obstacles the attention they deserve and no more. The balanced person is strongly oriented to the present. He is not overpreoccupied with fighting yesterday's battles or in fearing tomorrow's hypothetical problems. The foreseeable problems he faces and takes steps to meet. The vague possibilities he tends to dismiss with very little attention.

Inadequate Relations with Other People

Social relations are related to mental health in at least two ways. First of all, to avoid ill health, we must have made some kind of adjustment to other people. We may avoid them. We may embrace them. But we should have worked out some approach that does not bring us too much distress. Secondly, our relations with other people often cast some light on other aspects of adjustment. They serve as an index by which other facets of mental health may be observed. Such relations may show whether or not we distort the world that confronts us, or may show how comfortable we feel about ourselves.

Balance between Belonging and Autonomy. To be comfortable with himself, and to be reasonably effective, a man must feel close relations with some other people, and yet be able to maintain a measure of independence or autonomy. To a certain extent, he should be able to lose himself in the family setting or in some group. But along with this he must have at least occasional views of himself as an individual and must see how he differs from those to whom he feels so close.

Indications of Belonging. A wholesome sort of belongingness is shown, first of all, in a feeling of identity in which we adopt as our own the goals and concerns of some person or groups of persons. In wholesome relations, moreover, this belongingness is seen to be reciprocated, and we feel that we are accepted by the other people. Few of us could go on being despised or rejected by those we value without being driven to distort the situation. Conversely, such lack of acceptance would suggest some basic inadequacy in our personal adjustment.

In wholesome personal relations we are able to accept help when it is necessary and to accept it graciously. It is only the individual whose self-esteem is tottering badly who feels injured or threatened by having to accept support or aid from others. In a similar way, we should be able to accept praise or commendation from others without too much embarrassment.

Typically, when our relations with others are in a happy state, we are not unduly plagued by a feeling of always being misunderstood. True enough, very few people may ever feel that they are completely understood. But under wholesome conditions a modicum of misunderstanding is accepted as the price of individuality, and is not resented or considered an intolerable situation. Certainly it does not become an obsession or a major source of unhappiness.

Excessive criticism of others, like the obsessive feeling of being misunderstood, may also be a sign of basic insecurity. The emphasis, of course, is on "excessive." Complete absence of critical feelings about others, far from being reassuring, would probably indicate that such feelings were being deliberately suppressed. Excessive concentration on the shortcoming of others, however, definitely suggests a basic uneasiness about one's self.

Indications of Autonomy. Most mental hygienists would worry about the man who is unable to work out satisfactory relations with other people. Recently, however, there has been a great deal of concern (see Chapter 11) about the man who goes too far in that direction. We would suspect some basic insecurity in the man who is completely other-directed (Riesman, 1950), who is never willing to swim against the stream, and who never asserts his own individuality in the face of group pressure. To attain a desirable degree of autonomy, each of us must be able to see how we differ from others, without feeling that this difference makes us outcasts from the group. We must also face genuine disagreements when they arise and face them with equanimity, without feeling the necessity of glossing over the differences, and without feeling unduly threatened by such disagreements. To retain our own individuality, we must often be prepared to resist the efforts of others to dominate us, if this domination appears to be going too far. Here there is an especial need for a fairly delicate balance. It would never do to be overly suspicious and to see any argument as an attempt to coerce us. Yet there must be some point at which we will resist coercion.

With all this we return to the paramount issue of not trying to hide from the facts. You are becoming convinced, for instance, that you have only moderate interest in other people, that basically you are a rather shy person in need of considerable privacy. If you suspect that this is really so, and not merely a screen for some more fundamental conflict, you should not try to talk yourself out of the urge. You may not always, or typically, give in to it. On the contrary, your sense of duty may force you to forgo your need for privacy. But even though you cannot indulge this urge, you should not pretend that it does not exist.

Lack of Effectiveness

Some people would refuse to consider a man well adjusted if he failed to exert himself to attain his goals, or even if his attainments fell far short of his potential (Jahoda, 1958; Scott, 1958).

This discrepancy might be regarded both as essential lack of adjustment in its own right and also as a symptom of some insecurity, some neurotic fear of success, or some perverted sense of satisfaction in failure.

The General Relation between Character and Mental Health

In discussing mental health, it is natural to concentrate on the evils to be avoided. Obviously, however, such a discussion must mention the positive goals of healthy mental life, and at times we must pay attention to the whole area of character treated in Chapters 9, 10, and 11.

Perhaps we should lay even greater stress on the positive goals and on desirable character when discussing mental health. It may be impossible to give an adequate description of mental health by merely listing the evils to be avoided. Perhaps this can be done only by stressing positive qualities to be attained. And to do justice to these positive qualities we must boldly relate the problem of mental health to that of character development (Smith, 1961).

There is much to be said for the emphasis on the positive approach (Jahoda, 1958). Mere absence of disease does little to stir the imagination. The important thing is what you do with your health when you have it. It

---

▶ *The Difference between the "Negative" (Minimal) and "Positive" (Enlarged) Aspects of Mental Health at Various Stages of Development*

	Kinds of Adjustment Apparent in Childhood		Adjustment Expected of the Adult
	Immediate Behavior of the Child	*Long-range Adjustment of the Child*	*Expected of the Adult*
Minimal Concept: (Mental health considered as the absence of illness)	Freedom from incapacitating symptoms	Good resistance to stress	Absence of mental disorder
Enlarged Concept: (Mental health considered as attaining positive values)	Enjoyable experience in day-to-day relation with self, family, others	Potential for effective, happy, zestful, creative childhood	Capacities for competent, happy, zestful, creative, responsible adulthood

SOURCE: M. B. Smith, Mental health reconsidered: a special case of the problem of values in psychology, *American Psychologist*, 1961, **16**, 299–306.

Fig. 13.2. Increased health brings more opportunity (and more necessity) for choice.

is possible, moreover, that this positive approach, or some aspects of it, is necessary for the more limited goal of merely avoiding illness. Illness is most likely to be avoided, perhaps, not by those who consciously seek to avoid it, but by those who throw themselves into some engrossing activity much bigger than themselves.

Against these very proper arguments we must place the problem of disagreement. Everyone agrees that illness is an evil. But not everyone agrees about what you should do when you are well (Fig. 13.2). One of the evils of illness lies in the fact that it limits our freedom of choice. In the views of some theorists, indeed, this freedom of choice, or the lack of it, is not only one feature of mental illness but the most critical feature which distinguishes mental health from mental illness (Bower, 1962). As soon as we correct this evil, however, and attain greater freedom of choice, we auto-matically invite a measure of disagreement. When we are well there are many different things we can do, and different people will have different ideas as to which of these things is most desirable. All in all, we will experience almost universal support when we attempt the very important task of trying to reduce the amount of serious mental ill health. We may encounter legitimate objections, however, when we begin to specify the positive attributes of mental health. Certainly we will have performed an outstanding service if we have brought our student to the point where he is free to choose from a variety of those positive objectives.

Much as we may wish to do so, however, we may not be able to separate our concepts of mental health from those of character (Edwards, 1957). We would hesitate, for instance, to rate a man as well adjusted if he were seriously deficient in character or if he failed to meet his ordinary obligations to society. But the converse does not necessarily hold (Block, 1962). A man could live an exemplary life and fulfill his social and personal obligations in a superior way and yet be plagued by an inner distress brought on by fears and feelings of guilt that had no basis in the world of reality. Some such men might be revered for their virtue or for their creative achievements, but they would not be considered well adjusted. Social desirability may be one necessary aspect of adjustment, but it is in no way a complete indication of such adjustment.

ASSESSING PERSONAL ADJUSTMENT

In studying any pupil, we must often make some estimate of his personal adjustment. Is he doing about as well as we would expect? Or does he show some sign that things are too much for him?

Informal Instruments

The precise measurement of personality is a complex technical matter. As it happens, however, there are also many less formidable devices, and many of these will prove quite convenient for classroom use.

General Observation. What are the signs that some pupil is finding the troublesome aspects of reality to be beyond his powers at the moment? (California State Department of Education, 1961). Although we would expect any child to make some use of the various defense mechanisms, we would be worried if he began to use such mechanisms to excess. Fantasy in moderation, for instance, would cause us little concern. If the child began to treat his fantasies too seriously, however, or to seek their

solace on too many occasions, we would suspect that his problems ranged beyond his skill. Similarly, an excessive use of rationalization, projection, or the other mechanisms would suggest that he is unable to achieve a genuine solution for the problem of his frustrations by objective methods.

Along with these signs that the child has already begun to hide from reality, there are a number of milder and more common ways of behaving, often seen when the child is on the point of beginning to distort the real world. Undue defiance may constitute a crude way of denying the existence of the threatening force. His vigorous assertion may give him a comforting illusion that he can escape the demands of society. Unusual surliness may act as a similar self-deception. Rejection by other children is also a sign (Bower, 1962). Not only does it show that the person in question is not accepted by those other children but it is also a sign of a more general lack of acceptance. Ironically enough, his very feeling of rejection may lead to behavior which will result in actual rejection. An undue urge for privacy may involve the same general mechanism. At any rate, it is true that children who are very prone to solitary activities are often those who have a marked feeling of general unacceptability. The child who feels rejected is also likely to make very obvious and persistent bids to gain adult attention. These bids may consist of showing off, tale bearing, acquiring injuries or ailments, or acting as the teacher's special assistant.

The Interview. Most of our conferences with individual students will not be used to get a precise picture of his mental health. They will be used, on the contrary, to help him with some project or to help him overcome some difficulties of an objective nature. They also remind the student that someone cares about him and his concerns. To some extent, however, these conferences will provide us with information about the student's personality and his more personal difficulties. For this general purpose, the conference or interview has some advantages. It permits us to follow unexpected leads and to explore features that seem of special interest.

With all its advantages, however, the interview is not a very dependable device for gaining precise information about the person's basic personality structure (Thorndike and Hagen, 1961a). It is notoriously subjective, and no two interviewers can be sure of coming up with similar reports on what is found. To some extent, this subjectivity may be reduced by the use of a *structured interview*. In this we use a prepared outline of the matters to be covered, but we can use our own convenience in deciding which questions to ask first. By using this structure we can be more sure that different interviewers will touch on the same area. The use of such a structure, of course, would not insure that each interviewer will give equal attention to the things the student says or that they will even make a similar report of what he has said.

Anecdotal Records. Often when we rate other people we must do so on the basis of general impression or of our recollection of past events. Under these circumstances we know before we begin our observations what we will be looking for. Rather than reporting from memory that this child is "much more dependent than average" we set out to observe the child in some fairly definite situation, say the nursery school playground. If we are interested in dependency, for instance, we might record the actual number of times he goes to the teacher for help, or note the different ways he asks for help. Our list might include items such as: "Stops playing with —— and looks expectantly at teacher." "Asks for help in matter-of-fact-fashion—in a whining way." "Sidled up to teacher and sought, or took, her hand." "Asked teacher to notice what he was doing." As pointed out in Chapter 3, we should distinguish between the *actual* behavior, on the one hand, and our interpretation on the other.

Typically, the observer watches for only a few forms of behavior during any one session. During that session there may be an attempt to record the number of times each kind of behavior occurred. In other procedures, the observer breaks the time up into short units, perhaps as short as thirty seconds. He then merely indicates whether the behavior in question (asking for help) occurred at all during that unit. He makes a similar check for successive short units.

Rating Scales and Checklists. General rating scales are discussed in some detail in Chapter 3. Naturally enough, such scales have been used quite extensively in the study of personality. The advantages and limitations discussed earlier apply to this area as well.

Standard Tests of Personality

A teacher has several reasons for knowing about published personality tests. For one thing, these are the instruments from which our systematic knowledge of personality has been derived. When the psychologist tells us something about various aspects of personality — adjustment, needs, and drives—he is usually talking about the things that have come through some kind of test, or the things that have been brought to light by them. When we know about these tests, we have a more dependable idea of what is being discussed. In the second place, the teacher may often have occasion to make practical use of the results of personality tests administered by others. These results should make more sense when one knows something about the instruments from which they were obtained. To a more limited extent, moreover, the teacher may administer some of these tests himself. Only a few personality tests, of course, can be used in this way by the teacher. Many of them have their own peculiarities and their own ways of being misunderstood. These tests should be given and interpreted only by a qualified psychologist or psychiatrist.

The Temperament or Adjustment Inventory. The *inventory* or *questionnaire* is the device most frequently used in the systematic studies of personal adjustment. A great many such inventories are available. Most of these are somewhat too technical for classroom use. Indeed, most publishers of such tests would hesitate to release them to anyone but a qualified psychologist or to someone working under a psychologist. The teacher may have occasion to look at the results of these tests, however, and should know something of their general make-up.

Most of these inventories or questionnaires provide either subtests or special keys so that we can study several different facets of personality or temperament. The particular facets measured vary from test to test. The authors of the *Guilford-Zimmerman Temperament Survey,* for instance, have tried to provide a subtest for each of the basic dimensions of personality. In their test they show how the student stands on ten of these

allegedly basic dimensions, namely: emotional stability; self-centeredness; friendliness (different from sociability or gregariousness); fondness for thinking; tolerance, or good opinion of people; masculinity-femininity. In the same way, the *IPAT High School Personality Questionnaire* is based on the sixteen factors of personality that have emerged from Cattell's (1956) studies.

The well-known *Minnesota Multiphasic Personality Inventory* also gives a number of separate scores. These, however, instead of being linked to traits that turned up from an analysis of test results, are based on pre-established psychiatric notions. Among these psychiatric concepts we find depressed mood; psychopathic deviate (indifference to convention, inconsiderate of others); fearfulness; suspiciousness; prevalence of hysterical symptoms (stomach upset); excessive worry about bodily functions; and schizophrenia (bizarre thoughts, divorced from reality). One of the scales of the *MMPI,* the K scale, is supposed to give a measure of defensiveness, the extent to which a person declines to reveal himself to others. Interestingly enough, good teachers seem to score high on this scale, and there has been some question as to whether it really means simple defensiveness or whether it represents something more like responsibility and ego-integration (Getzels and Jackson, 1963). In the MMPI, the person taking the test merely agrees, or disagrees, or expresses uncertainty regarding statements such as these: "I am usually tired when I get up in the morning. People often talk about me behind my back. I am frequently lost in thought."

In the *Edwards Personal Preference Schedule,* separate scales are organized around Murray's system of needs (see Chapter 4). The results tell us how

► *How Honestly Do People Reply to Inventory Questions?*

Married male graduate students answered the questions in three of the scales of the *Minnesota Multiphasic Personality Inventory* and in three scales from a different but comparable test (*Multi-dimensional Behavioral Inventory*). At the same time, but in a different room, the wife of each man went over the same scales and filled out each answer in the way that she thought would be true for her husband. At the time of taking the test, each man knew his wife was working with the test, but assumed, in most cases, that she was taking the test for herself.

The scales in question dealt with social introversion, social status, masculine-feminine temperament. A number of the items dealt with explicit behavior. "I frequently drive with one hand on the wheel. At a restaurant, I frequently wipe the silverware with a napkin. I often tell jokes in a conversation."

A "don't know" answer was permitted but the husbands answered "Yes" or "No" on from 87 to 96 percent of the items. For these items the wife's report agreed to the extent of 72 percent to 80 percent, depending on the scale.

SOURCE: S. R. Pinneau and A. Milton, The ecological veracity of the self-report, *Journal of Genetic Psychology*, 1958, **93**, 249–276.

much the person is affected by a need for order, for friendly relations with others, for achievement, and so forth.

Inventories such as these are answered by the person himself. Knowing this, we immediately begin to wonder how honestly he has answered. There is no question that many of these inventories can be faked. Students trying to do so can give either a favorable or unfavorable picture of themselves. To get around this, at least two steps may be taken. In the MMPI there is a built-in device for detecting the tendency to fake. The K scale, mentioned above, was originally developed as such an indication of faking. Edwards uses a different device to deal with deliberate faking. In his Personal Preference Schedule, he asks the student to choose between two descriptions which are intended to be equal in social desirability. This should take care of the student who is merely trying to create a good impression. But it would not necessarily take care of the person who is trying to make himself appear more nurturant than he really is, or who is trying to give himself a high score on achievement need, and who thinks he knows which answer will achieve this effect.

The fact that people are able to fake these tests does not necessarily mean that they will. In one investigation (Pinneau and Milton, 1958), for instance, the preferences, worries, whims, and idiosyncrasies reported by married men were largely confirmed by their wives and other adults who knew them.

Anxiety Inventories. One facet of the personality inventories has considerable information for the classroom teacher. This is the facet of anxiety in general, and test anxiety in particular. The *Taylor Manifest Anxiety Scale* was derived largely from the MMPI and has been used to indicate general tension and activation (see Chapter 4). This scale has been used quite extensively with college students and adults in general, and there is some evidence that it does reflect the level of activation or concern (Katzell and Katzell, 1962). A form for younger children, the *Children's Manifest Anxiety Scale* (Castaneda and others, 1956a), has been developed, but so far we cannot be sure just what this does reveal.

A special scale for test anxiety, the *Test Anxiety Scale for Children*, has been studied extensively by Sarason and others (1960). This test anxiety can be clearly distinguished from the kind of general anxiety that is measured by a *General Anxiety Scale for Children*, developed by the same authors.

Problem Checklists. As opposed to the more psychiatrically oriented inventories, there are a number of problem checklists which make no attempt to probe into the subtle mechanisms of maladjustment, but which merely attempt to reveal the problems that seem important to the student himself. The oldest of these is the *Mooney Problem Check List* (Psychological Corporation). This is designed for students in the teens and older. In this instrument, the student is merely presented with a list of possible worries (afraid of tests, being treated like an outsider, not good looking) and asked to check the items that bother him. A similar form, the *SRA Youth Inventory* (Science Research Associates) is also available for high school students, and one form, the *SRA Junior Inventory*, is intended for pupils in grades four to eight.

These simple devices are often useful in giving the student a better picture of himself. They also enable the teacher to see unusual or disturbing problems that may be acting on the pupil.

Some teachers use the results as a basis for a later interview. If an exceptional number of students indicate the same type of worry, moreover, there may be some point in checking to see if some peculiar influence is at work in the school or community.

Projective Tests. In contrast to many other forms of tests, the projective tests are intended to give the student the greatest possible opportunity to move in almost any direction he chooses. Instead of being asked to choose between one or two rigid alternatives, he is given almost complete freedom in responding. He is asked to describe an inkblot that is really meaningless and could be interpreted in any manner. He is asked to make up a story around a sketch that is deliberately ambiguous. He completes a simple sentence such as, "Most people _____." "When I am alone, I _____."

The best known of these projective devices is the *Rorschach Ink Blot Technique.* Everyone knows about these devices, but not everyone knows that the interpretation of the results is very complicated indeed. The investigator pays only moderate attention to what the student sees, although he is mildly concerned with the conventionality of the reports and the extent to which animals or human characters are seen. He is concerned instead with whether the response was based on a reaction to the whole blot or to one minor detail, whether the interpretation came from the form or shape, or from the color pattern, or from the texture; whether or not the interpretation implies movement of the elements. He also takes into account the number of different responses given.

Very elaborate methods of scoring and interpreting the Rorschach test (Klopfer and Davidson, 1962) have been worked out. From reaction to inkblots,

Rorschachers believe they can determine productiveness of the imagination, spontaneity, impulsiveness (or susceptibility to emotions), degree of control of emotions, and so forth. More important, perhaps, they believe that they can see these traits in relation to each other. They see, for instance, emotionality in relation to emotional control.

A method somewhat similar to the Rorschach is the *Thematic Apperception Technique* (Murray, 1938). In this method, the subject is shown a picture of an older man taking hold of the arm of a startled young woman. The subject is told that this is a test of fertility of the imagination. He is asked to give a story into which the picture would fit. The resulting story is supposed to give some insight into the hopes and fears and needs of the subject. A special group of such designs have been provided for adolescents (Symonds, 1948), and still other forms have been devised for young children. One of these, the *Children's Apperception Test*, makes considerable use of animals, on the assumption that children might more readily project their needs and fears into animals. So far the evidence suggests that the use of animals adds very little and that elementary school children give no different response to these than to the standard tests (Light, 1954).

The Blacky Pictures also rely on children's reactions to animals to bring out some aspects of development with special emphasis on psychosexual development as interpreted by the Freudians.

Along with these standardized published tests there has been much use of the child's expressive movements as revealed in painting, drawing, or writing to reveal characteristics of his personality (Harris, 1963). The *Machover Draw-a-person Test*, for instance, relies on this

procedure. So does the *H-T-P Test*, in which a student is asked to draw a house, a tree, and a person. These tests have been given to many children and the various features of the drawings have been studied and have been correlated with facts already known about the children.

Many people have been misled by the apparent simplicity of these tests. On the surface, it seems that one merely looks at the child's drawing and uses one's common sense. If there is a double padlock on the gate of the house he has drawn it is symbolic of fear. If there are large splotches of red under the trees he has painted, it shows a need for aggression, or certainly a preoccupation with violence. Actually these glib, spur-of-the-moment intuitions are most undependable. We must test many, many children and compare the various "signs" with other diagnoses before we can tell what it means when a child draws children that are bigger than the house or dogs that are bigger than either. Resist the temptation to jump to free and easy conclusions in these complicated and tricky matters.

Unlike the amateur who merely looks at a work of art and proceeds to hold forth on the personality of the one who created it, there have been several serious attempts to work out dependable rules for the interpretation of expressive movements. These more systematic efforts have been under critical study for some time but it is still too early to say how valuable they may prove to be (Henry, 1960; Miller, 1960).

Performance Tests. When using systematic observation you have little control over the detailed events that the child encounters. True, you can make sure that he will be in a playground or that he will be taking part in some project, but you do not control the precise experiences that he will face. In using performance tests, on the other hand, you arrange for some definite event and then see how the student will react to that specific situation (Murray, 1963). You arrange things, for instance, so that some stooge will contradict him, or that the teacher will be called from the room. At one time such tests were widely used in the study of character (see Chapter 9).

When the situations selected are meaningful, performance tests should have considerable validity. Here we do not have a statement of what the student says he does, or of what someone else thinks he might do. We have, on the contrary, an account of what he actually does in a certain situation. Such tests are often cumbersome to arrange, however, and many of them depend on successful deception. If the student knew he was being tested, he could readily make the proper response on this test occasion.

Approaches Using Several Instruments

Most psychologists, in attempting to get information about a student, would obviously make use of several different instruments. Lambert and Bower (1961), for instance, in working out a screening technique to detect the child who is emotionally disturbed, use a combination of (1) a rating or a checklist filled out by teachers (frequently gets into fights: Yes-No), (2) nominations by classmates (you are choosing people for a play. Someone has to play the part of a cruel boss. Who should it be? _____) and (3) a self inventory (thinking about yourself).

This elaborate procedure has been carefully developed. As this is being written it is too soon to say how well it works. If it does work out it should be most useful, partly because of its multiple approach, and partly because it attempts to reach all the way down to the kindergarten. And good self-inventories at the elementary school level are quite rare. Writing in 1961, for instance, Thorndike and Hagen (1961a, p. 589) suggest that none of the more technical personality inventories they had examined would be useful in the elementary school. Their report did not deal with the test anxiety scales or with the *Lambert-Bower Screening Device*.

The Classroom Use of Different Instruments

Most of the tests we have discussed will be useful to us chiefly by giving us an increased understanding of the nature of the personality studied by psychologists and by helping us to interpret the test results we may have occasion to study. Some few of them, however, we may use in the classroom either on our own or in cooperation with a specialist in these matters.

Obviously some consultations with individual pupils will take in the character of an interview. These should be useful and quite in order when used to bring out surface interests or troubles. The teacher would do well to avoid any suggestion of a probing interview searching for deep underlying causes. Not only are these likely to be fruitless when used by the amateur, but more serious, they may lead to greater resistance on the part of the student and to violent objection on the part of parents. The more psychiatrically oriented self-inventory is out-of-bounds for the classroom teacher. In some of the screening devices used for detecting children with emotional disturbances (Lambert and Bower, 1961), the teacher does play an important part in giving the tests and in supplying ratings. In this, however, the role is that of helper.

The general problem checklist type of inventory is perfectly suitable to classroom use and should prove profitable for many teachers.

Rating scales covering one area or another are bound to be used in the classroom. The suitability for classroom use would depend on the area of behavior being rated. Overt behavior, general approaches to other children, typical mood, and similar matters should be easily detected by the teacher and could readily be rated. Ratings that involve defense mechanisms or suppressed needs or unconscious wishes should be used with considerable caution, if at all.

The projective tests are to be avoided by the amateur. Indeed, even the typical experienced psychologist would hesitate to use these for serious purposes unless he had special training in the particular test being used. As indicated earlier, the home-made "projective tests," inviting glib, off-the-cuff interpretations, are especially to be avoided.

THE TEACHER VIEWS HIS TASK

Here, then, are the ailments that we would like our students to avoid. Here also, although less certainly, are the positive goals that we would like them to accomplish, and here are some of the instruments that can be used to detect ailments and to assess mental health. How serious is the problem that must be faced, and what is our role in it?

The Extent of Mental Ill Health

As is well known, mental ailments are very prevalent. Almost everyone has some trouble with unnecessary anxieties or employs some device for hiding from reality. In one densely settled section of Manhattan, for instance, about 50 percent of the adult population was judged to be in some psychiatric difficulty (Srole and others, 1962). Only 18 percent were considered really well. This is a crude average. Older people were much worse off, younger adults somewhat better. As is typically the case, the prevalence of such psychiatric trouble is much greater in the lower socioeconomic groups (Hollingshead and Redlich, 1958). Among younger adults in the New York study, the percentage of people considered "well" dropped from 24 percent for the upper social class, to 10 percent for the lowest. For about 8 percent of people, these troubles become so serious that the person is referred to a clinic. This figure is about the same as that observed during World War II, when about 6 percent of selective service registrants were so seriously disturbed that they were rejected for military service. Severe maladjustment among school children reaches about the same proportion. In the public schools about one child in twelve may be regarded as severely maladjusted (Kaplan, 1959, p. 57). At the college level the estimate is about the same—one student in ten (Farnsworth, 1961).

If these estimates are in any way dependable, the typical classroom may include two or three students who really need help. Some of these children may reveal their excessive tension by tics, unusual grimacing, nail biting, eneuresis, temper tantrums, or other easily observed behavior. Some of the more serious problems, however, are to be found in the quiet, well-behaved child who avoids trouble and who submits resignedly to the demands of the teacher or other children. Such children may readily escape notice, but may be more out of touch

► *The Extent of Mental Ill Health in the City*

The 1660 people studied in this investigation constituted a random sample of 110,000 people living in one district in central Manhattan. The district was about as crowded as the rest of Manhattan—about 380,000 people per square mile of residential land. The area included tenements (20 percent) and luxury apartments. Family incomes ranged from under $2500.00 per year for the lowest 10 percent to over $15,000.00 per year for the upper 10 percent. Those studied ranged from twenty to sixty years of age. Some two thirds had migrated to New York either from Europe or from other points of the United States. The sample was 99 percent white. Half were Catholic, one third Protestant, and one sixth Jewish.

During an interview in the home, a sixty-five page questionnaire was completed. The interview data were assessed independently by two psychiatrists and a mental health rating assigned by each.

SOME RESULTS OF MENTAL HEALTH RATINGS

	Percent Definitely Impaired
Total Group	20
Age: 20–30	15
30–50	23
50–60	31
Socioeconomic Status of Father	
Highest Groups	17–21
Three Lowest Groups	24–33

Those seriously impaired appeared comparable to patients in psychiatric clinics. About 2 percent were impaired to the extent of being incapacitated.

SOURCE: T. S. Langer and S. T. Michael, Life stress and mental health, Volume 2 of the *Midtown Manhattan Study.* (New York: Free Press of Glencoe, 1963). For a more detailed report, see L. Srole and others, Mental health in the metropolis (Volume 1 of the same series) (New York: McGraw-Hill Book Company, Inc., 1962).

with the real world than their more aggressive or more turbulent classmates.

Clearly mental health is a serious problem and something should be done about it. The teacher is one of the most identifiable influences in the life of the child and it is natural that all eyes should be turned toward him. The teacher himself must be aware of his conspicuous role. Indeed, in matching his own resources against the gravity of the problem, he must wonder if he is in anyway equal to the task that seems to confront him.

Limitations to the Teacher's Responsibility

In any balanced view of the problem, the responsibility of the teacher will be seen to be large. There are limits to that responsibility, however, and we should keep those limits in mind. We would be wise, moreover, if we encouraged the general public to remember those limits. After all we are still most uncertain about the success we might expect if the school and the teacher should make an all-out attack on the problem of teaching for mental health. The more ambitious experiments (Cowen and others, 1963) report mixed and modest results.

Even if the data did not give us pause, there are many theoretical considerations which should suggest limitations in our responsibility (Allinsmith and Goethals, 1962, Chap. 2). In the first place, we constitute only one of many forces that act on our students. As might be expected, we will see only a small fraction of the events that strongly stir the emotions or that set off intense frustrations. Such experiences are much more likely to occur in the home or in the playground (Fawl, 1959). The typical thwarting that we must impose seldom induces serious emotional stress. Severe disturbance, when it occurs, is more likely to be a characteristic of the student than of the situation under which it occurs. Some children may experience only a dozen upsets during an entire waking day. Others, encountering much the same experiences, may have ten times as many (Barker and Wright, 1954).

Above all, we should not permit ourselves to be overwhelmed or devastated by any single episode or short series of episodes. The temper tantrum or retreat to babyishness that we observe today does not mean mental disaster for the student. Turmoil and frustration is the order of the day. Most people surmount it. Even a prolonged lack of adjustment, although serious in its own right, must not be given too much significance. Such continued lack of adjustment is a serious school problem but it does not necessarily betoken poor out-of-school adjustment. Many children who show symptoms of maladjustment in the schoolroom will seem perfectly normal and well-adjusted in the home or in the out-of-school gang (Harris, 1960). Interestingly enough, a display of serious maladjustment in the school does not typically indicate subsequent maladjustment even in the school. Many of the seemingly disturbed children in grade three will seem perfectly normal in grade six (Harris, 1960). Most people, in school and out, have gone through periods in which their behavior would mark them as a bad risk. But for most people, and especially for most children, this is quite transitory. They pass through this episode and regain something approaching normal adjustment (MacFarlane and others, 1954). Notice that here we are speaking of disturbed behavior, or behavior that would have general psychiatric significance. The general temperament or style of personality, on the other hand, is much more likely to remain fairly constant from year to year. Such general characteristics as moodiness, cheerfulness, or irritability are more predictable from year to year.

In the special area of therapy, the teacher must see his role as strictly limited. As teachers we should never undertake to treat the children who are already seriously disturbed. Such students should be referred to a specialist. Treatment of such students is a difficult problem at the best and is no job for the amateur, no matter how well intentioned. These children are already hiding behind defenses. In our clumsy probings we may tear down these defenses and drive them behind even more impregnable barriers,

▶ On-again, Off-again Problems in Childhood

As part of the Berkeley Growth Study, an attempt was made to interview the group of children every year from the time the child in question was two years old until he was fourteen. The data reported in the table were based on 33 boys and 43 girls for whom at least eight annual interviews were obtained.

During the interview the mother mentioned, among other things, the problems that she observed in the behavior of the child. The question is: How consistent were these mentionings? Did the problems last over the twelve-year span? Or were they transitory?

| | Percent of Children for Whom Problem Was Mentioned | | |
Selected Problems Reported	On at Least One Visit	On Over Half the Visits	On Every Visit
For Boys			
Temper Tantrums	100	55	9
Being Oversensitive	85	42	0
Excessive Mood Swings	73	15	0
Finicky Eater	67	18	3
Physical Timidity	76	9	0
Excessive Emotional Dependence	70	6	0
Tics and Mannerisms	24	0	0
For Girls (Supplementary Data[a])			
Temper Tantrums	98	28	2
Finicky Eater	91	9	0
Physical Timidity	91	7	0

[a] For other problems the trends for boys and girls were similar.

The table shows that, with the exception of tics, all the problems listed became problems for at least two thirds of the children at one time or another. Some problems seemed fairly persistent, being more likely to be mentioned than not. The others, however, seemed quite transitory. After being mentioned in one interview they were most likely to be omitted in subsequent visits.

SOURCE: Jean W. MacFarlane, Lucile Allen, and Marjorie P. Honzik, *A Developmental Study of the Behavior Problems of Normal Children between Twenty-one Months and Fourteen Years* (Berkeley, Calif.: University of California Press, 1954).

thus complicating the task for the professional therapist.

The Teacher's Contributions

With so much excluded from our area of responsibility, what is left? Quite a bit. Even in the delicate matter of treatment, we need not forgo all analysis or all efforts to help. For the child having only moderate trouble in facing unpleasant events, the teacher can offer casual help and, while avoiding any deep, probing analysis, can do much in the way of helping him identify worrisome emotions. Suspecting a feeling of rage that is not quite admitted, the teacher may well say, "That must make you pretty mad," or, "You must find this hard to take, especially when you are tired (or hungry) (or worried about something else)." But the teacher would not extend such casual remarks to a search for the real, terrifying concern that is the basic underlying cause of a whole series of acts (Olson and Wattenberg, 1955).

Rather than attempt intensive therapy for those already in serious trouble, the teacher should concentrate on providing a general atmosphere which will encourage wholesome adjustment (Allinsmith and Goethals, 1962). His role is preventative and supportive rather than therapeutic.

In surveying our responsibilities we can be greatly heartened by the remarkable resilience of children. Fortunately, most pupils have tough little psyches. It is seldom that a single incident or single episode will produce any serious or lasting damage. When such damage does occur it comes from a persisting, unrelieved climate of stress, and from steady failure in the relations that are important to the child (Barker and Wright, 1954; Harris, 1960).

In offering recommendations for promoting mental hygiene, by the way, we are on somewhat more shaky ground than usual. In discussing other areas, such as academic development, we can frequently turn to experimental results which, for all their deficiencies, do provide a fair measure of assurance. In many areas of mental health, on the other hand, such experimental results are not always available. Much of what we have to say is based on the general opinion of psychiatrists, clinical psychologists, and others who have given much thought to the field (Olson and Wattenberg, 1955).

Interrelations with Other Aspects of Development

Mental health must always be developed along with other phases of educational growth, and each of these clearly affects, and is affected by, the problems of mental health. We have already shown how social adjustment overlaps with the idea of mental health. These two areas also interact. Adequate social relations make for more wholesome mental adjustment. Freedom from ordinary maladjustment, conversely, makes for more effective and more enjoyable relations with people. This is also clear in the special area of discipline. Reasonable discipline reduces some of the classroom frustrations and thus aids mental health. Many forms of general maladjustment, in turn, manifest themselves as problems in discipline.

The problem of developing academic skill is intricately related to the task of promoting mental health. The mastery of academic materials, for instance, can be a great boon to mental health. Increased academic mastery should add to the student's sense of his own worth and should increase his self-confidence and esteem. Such mastery should also enable him to solve many problems that, unsolved, would lead to dangerous frustration. Even when academic training does not lead to the solution of a problem, it can often be used to make the frustration easier to accept. Often, in teaching biology, history, or especially literature, we deal with truths which, in some cases, may be eminently reassuring, or which, in other instances, may point the way to a reasonable management of things that are difficult to face (Bower, 1962). With very little effort we could call attention to these features, and, without laboring the point, link them to the problems of everyday adjustment.

Academic tasks, on the other hand, typically induce their own share of frustration and a good deal of anxiety stems from academic failure or the fear of failure. Even under less drastic circumstances, much of what we do is bound to induce some frustration or distress. We cannot lead children into acceptable academic attainment without subjecting them to some stress and tension.

Insofar as there may be a clear-cut conflict between the claims of academic development and those of mental development, what should the classroom teacher do about it? Unfortunately, no one can be sure. It is possible, however, that in the long run the teacher should concentrate on the academic curriculum and do what he can in incidental fashion to promote mental health. Many other people, after all, share responsibility for over-all adjustment. The teacher, however, is almost alone in his responsibility for academic growth. If he falters here, no one stands ready to make up the deficit. In concentrating on this work, moreover, he can easily avoid undue risk to mental health. The frustrations need

not be excessive or continual, and, as we have seen, mild, occasional frustration is no great menace to mental well-being. Even if mental health were our sole concern, we might find it better not to pursue our goal too directly (Biber, 1961). Perhaps we can do most for mental health if, in the long run, we relegate it to the back of our minds and get on with academic tasks.

So much for the long run and for the general pervading attitude. Naturally, however, there will be interludes when the emphasis must be reversed. If serious lack of adjustment threatens, then we must forget about the demands of academic development and give every priority to the claims of mental health.

SUMMARY

At its lowest level, adjustment may mean the avoidance of many evils. We hope the pupil does not distort reality, that he can handle his anxieties without undue stress and without the necessity of making too much use of the defense mechanisms to distort the things that threaten him. To many theorists the most serious difficulty lies in the student's unfortunate view of himself as a person. This may come as a crippling feeling of unworthiness or as an unrealistic vision of a distorted and glamorized self. Self-control is a problem to be mastered but the control should be kept at reasonable level. Adjustment to others is a frequent cause of stress, and each student must strike his own balance between his need for autonomy and his need to belong.

Although we get most agreement when considering evils to be avoided, we must often include positive traits of character if we are to give a true picture of personal adjustment.

In the problem of assessing personal adjustment the teacher is often a bystander watching the professionals at work. Some understanding of the instruments the professional uses is necessary, however. The less formal instruments, such as casual interviews, anecdotal records, and rating scales will actually be used by the teacher. The more technical instruments take the form of inventories or questionnaires answered by the person himself and aimed at many facets of adjustment, including classroom anxiety. There are also the projective tests such as the *Rorschach Ink Blot Test* and the *Thematic Apperception Test* which are extremely difficult to give and to interpret. At times the more global performance tests are used, particularly for selection purposes. Most experts use a variety of instruments, including simple problem checklists.

The problems in the field of mental health are tremendous both for the teacher and for society in general. About one student out of ten may have worrisome problems of adjustment. The teacher must accept his fair share of responsibility, but he should not undertake the whole load. Direct studies promise only modest success. The turmoil most significant for adjustment, moreover, is not primarily a school affair. Adjustment is an up-and-down thing. A child not well adjusted in school may get along quite well elsewhere. A child in trouble now may do well later on. But the teacher can provide a supporting atmosphere and can ease up on the academic stress when general tension threatens the health of the student. The teacher can do much merely by increasing the academic proficiency of his charges. Such proficiency should help in over-all adjustment, and it is an area for which the teacher has unique responsibility.

SUGGESTIONS FOR FURTHER READING

Mental Health in the Schools

Allinsmith, W., and G. W. Goethals, *The Role of Schools in Mental Health*. New York: Basic Books, Inc., 1962.

Blaine, J. B., and others, *Emotional Problems of the Students*. New York: Appleton-Century-Crofts, 1961.

Joint Commission on Mental Illness and Health, *Action for Mental Health: Final Report*, 1961. New York: Basic Books, Inc., 1961.

Kanner, L., Early behavior problems as sign posts to later maladjustment, *American Journal of Psychiatry*, 1941, **97**, 1261–1271. Reprinted in Remmers, pp 318–325.

Kaplan, L., *Mental Health and Human Relations in Education*. New York: Harper & Row, Publishers, Inc., 1959.

Peck, R. F., Student mental health—the range of personality patterns in a college population, in R. L. Sutherland and others, eds., *Personality Factors on the College Campus*. Hogg Foundation for Mental Health. Austin, Texas: University of Texas Press, 1962, pp. 161–199.

Peck, R. F., and J. V. Mitchell, Jr., *Mental Health: What Research Says to the Teacher*. Washington, D. C.: National Education Association, 1962.

Ruebush, B. K., Anxiety, *Yearbook National Society for the Study of Education*, 1963, **62**, Part I, 460–516.

White, Mary A., and M. W. Harris, *The School Psychologist*. New York: Harper & Row, Publishers, Inc., 1961.

Additional References

Bower, E. M., Mental health in education, *Review of Educational Research*, 1962, **32**, 441–454.

Landsman, T., Factors influencing individual mental health, *Review of Educational Research*, 1962, **32**, 464–475.

McGuire, C., Cultural and social factors in mental health, *Review of Educational Research*, 1962, **32**, 455–463.

Morse, W. C., and C. O. Dyer, The emotionally and socially handicapped, *Review of Educational Research*, 1963, **33**, 109–125.

The Measurement of Personality

Bower, E. M., A process for identifying disturbed children, *Children*, 1957, **4**, 143–147. (This material also appears in the reference given below.)

California State Department of Education, *The Education of Emotionally Handicapped Children*. Sacramento, Calif.: The Department, 1961.

Cronbach, L. J., *Essentials of Psychological Testing*. New York: Harper & Row, Publishers, Inc., 1960.

Freeman, F. S., *Theory and Practice of Psychological Testing*, 3d ed. New York: Holt, Rinehart and Winston, Inc., 1962.

Messick, S., and J. Ross, eds., *Measurement in Personality and Cognition*. New York: John Wiley & Sons, Inc., 1962.

Mussen, P. H., ed., *Handbook of Research Methods in Child Development*. New York: John Wiley & Sons, Inc., 1960. The following chapters treat the problems of personality assessment: L. J. Yarrow, "Interviewing Children," Chapter 14; W. E. Henry, "Projective Techniques," Chapter 15; D. R. Miller, "Motivation and Affect," Chapter 17; U. Bronfenbrenner, and H. N. Ricciuti, "The Appraisal of Personality Characteristics in Children," Chapter 18.

Remmers, H. H., and N. L. Gage, The assessment and rating of pupil personality, in H. H. Remmers and others, eds., *Educational Measurement and Evaluation*. New York: Harper & Row, Publishers, Inc., 1955. Reprinted in Remmers, pp. 501–504.

Ross, A. O., *The Practice of Clinical Child Psychology*. New York: Grune & Stratton, Inc., 1959. Chapters 11 and 12 provide a discussion of projective tests.

Stern, G. G., Measuring noncognitive variables in research on teaching, in N. L. Gage, ed., *Handbook of Research on Teaching*. Skokie, Ill.: Rand McNally & Company, 1963, 398–447.

Thorndike, R. L., and Elizabeth P. Hagen, *Measurement and Evaluation in Psychology and Education*. New York: John Wiley & Sons, Inc., 1961a.

Sources of Additional References for Tests

Katzell, R. A., and Mildred E. Katzell, Development and application of structured tests of personality, *Review of Educational Research*, 1962, **32**, 51–63.

Ricciuti, H., Development and application of projective tests of personality, *Review of Educational Research*, 1962, **32**, 64–77.

EXERCISES AND QUESTIONS FOR DISCUSSION

1. Which of the various aspects of mental ill health do you consider the most worrisome for yourself? for people in general? Would some seem more serious for young children and some for older children?

2. Comment on the thesis that some of the defense mechanisms should be tolerated or even encouraged at times.

3. Think of some of the personality or interest tests you have taken. Do you remember feeling any urge to cheat or to fake a score? If so, would you have known how to do so? Would it be easier for some of the tests than for others?

4. As you see things now, which instruments do you hope to get most help from in measuring the adjustment of your pupils? Explain.

5. Discuss the school's opportunities and proper responsibilities in teaching for intellectual creativity, character, and personal adjustment.

CHAPTER 14

▶ *Teaching for Personal Adjustment*

The classroom activities are bound to have some effect on the mental health of the student. Whatever the teacher's objectives, he cannot avoid exerting some influence. Perhaps by making some deliberate effort he can help his students to deal more adequately with the stress and tension that they are bound to encounter.

In raising this question we run the risk of suggesting that tension or stress are great evils and things to be avoided at all costs. Clearly, such a suggestion would be most misleading. A certain amount of tension or stress may actually be necessary for basic physical well-being. Richter (1959) suggests that in our current civilization we are paying for our relative absence of stress by increases in arthritis and similar ailments. However that may be, many people realize their full powers only when under considerable tension. And, in actual fact, a certain amount of fear or anger can be pleasurable or exhilarating when allowed fairly free expression.

Effects of Excessive Stress

Stress is not always valuable or enjoyable or even manageable. All too often, excessive tension becomes a serious problem and threatens emotional well-being. Under such excessive tension the student may merely push ahead, blindly, stubbornly, using a single line of attack, often reconciling himself to failure and merely absorbing the resulting punishment. The desperate boy resorts to the unrelieved tension by uncontrolled fighting, losing out each time, and being punished each time, but refusing to break away from his stereotyped response or to attempt a new solution (Kubie, 1959). In less provocative situations, the harassed automobile driver endlessly presses the starter, knowing that he is foredoomed to failure, and almost admitting to himself, "This won't work, but it's what I'm going to do anyway."

This stereotyped and angry repetition of a failing response is, of course, occasionally reinforced. Sometimes the car

372

does start as a result of our foolish and desperate efforts. But it is one thing to adopt this procedure as a deliberate strategy and quite another thing to proceed in unthinking, self-punitive rage.

In addition to bringing about stereotyped repetition of a futile try, unrelieved tension may lead us to turn our backs on reality, to distort our perception of the forces behind the tension, or to become addicted to one or more of the troublesome defense mechanisms (Chapter 13).

KEEPING TENSION WITHIN BOUNDS

In teaching for mental health, the attempt to prevent excessive stress can never be the whole story. Ultimately the child should learn to deal with the many kinds of tension that will be inevitable in his life. It is only gradually, however, that he acquires skill in dealing with these tensions. Until he has acquired that skill, we should try to protect him from stress or frustration that is too severe for him to handle. This protecttion is demanded from sheer humanity. It would seem needlessly cruel to ask him to face problems that are beyond his power now, but which, either through maturation or learning, will be well within his capacity a few years hence. Apart from the immediate considerations of kindness or humanity, moreover, this moderate protection may also prevent some desperate plunge into self-deception from which there is no easy turning back. Finally, such partial tempering of the harshness of reality is an essential factor in the learning process itself. Competence in dealing with tension, like competence in most areas, comes from a series of successful performances, and from the reinforcements they bring. To achieve such a series of successes, we

must try, when it is within our power, to make sure that the early experiences with tension are not too difficult to cope with. Fortunately, in carrying out our humane urge to provide protection, we are also, for a time at least, helping to carry out our sterner resolve to develop skill.

Structuring the Experience of Tension

To be tolerable or enjoyable, the menace or tension should be clearly structured. It should be seen as being limited in the area that is threatened. It is not too difficult to deal with the threatened dunking in the lake if that is all that is at stake. Often danger may be faced without too much strain if it threatens only the person himself and not his family, or if it raises the possibility of an injury but offers no serious threat of loss of status or self-respect. Even when there is a threat to self-esteem we can often help the student to see that this serious threat has its limits. A student forced to withdraw from a full-time college program, for instance, may regard this as a limitless tragedy, completely shattering to his self-esteem. Without trying to minimize the very sad features of the situation, however, the teacher can point to the areas in which a major readjustment is required, and to those in which it is not. The change does call for a postponement of graduation, and this is a cruel blow. But it does not necessarily mean failure to graduate.

Tension is also more likely to be pleasurable or tolerable when it is perceived as being clearly temporary and having a fairly definite end point. The truth in the saying, "This, too, will pass," is too often overlooked in the midst of trouble, and the underlying truth, if not the saying, can bear repeating. Tension may be pleasurable when we know that the contest will end and that the trying expedition is scheduled for only a limited time. The stress or urgency is less tolerable when, far from having the appearance of a brief emergency, it threatens to continue on and on indefinitely.

Tension or arousal is often reported to be pleasurable or exhilarating when it is seen as a challenge that calls for all our new-found energy and our skill. The glow comes from a challenge that we have a chance to master, but which will demand all that we have. To transform the experience from a hideous menace to an acceptable challenge, we may merely need to remind the student of existing talents that he may have overlooked in the midst of his panic. A student quailing before the prospect of an oral report to the class could be reminded of his skill in photography and of the possibility of using slides. If the skill is actually lacking, we may be able to help the student acquire it. The smaller boy, in terror of the school bully, for instance, might consider lessons in boxing or junior jujitsu. The fearsome menace might then change its character and become an opportunity to demonstrate new skill and to acquire the admiration and gratitude of colleagues terrorized by the same menace. In helping the student to acquire more skill, however, we go beyond the technical problem of structuring the tension. The problem of thus modifying the student's skill is discussed in a later section.

Encouraging the Maximum Permissible Expression of Drives

A worrisome drive brings less tension and unpleasant stress when it is granted wholehearted expression. Fears which can be expressed in headlong, unashamed activity, such as a wild flight from a forest fire, may bring an exhilaration along with the very somber experience of danger. Contrived dangers, such as those found on roller coasters, often bring very intense fear, but the game calls for wholehearted expression of the panic, and the whole experience is somewhat thrilling. For some people, anger freely expressed in a quarrel or brawl is also pleasurable and may be deliberately sought.

Notice that many expressive actions do nothing to alleviate the actual situation. The shrieks do not stop the roller coaster. Tears do not bring back the dead. But even such nonadaptive behavior often has the power to make tension more endurable. People in the throes of terrific fear, as when civilians sit huddled in a bomb shelter, find some measure of relief in merely talking about their fears. The same thing is often true of hostility. Describing your anger may reduce your feeling of aggression. For young children, uninhibited crying provides a useful expression of emotion. Conversely, a child persuaded not to cry on the occasion of receiving one hurt may cry all the more frantically later on if he should receive a second hurt.

Clearly there are some drives that should not be expressed without some restriction. We cannot have people expressing all their hates and fears and lusts in completely uninhibited fashion. When natural, spontaneous expression is out of the question, however, we can often arrange for some partial or modified expression. Aggression, for instance, can be expressed in games. Sex needs can achieve a sublimated expression in parties, dancing, songs, or artistic productions.

Conscious Acceptance of Drives and Emotions. Frustration will be handled more comfortably and more efficiently if we are able to allow the frustrated idea to rise to consciousness. Frustration is harder to take and is more dangerous to experience when we repress the fearsome urge and try to pretend that we have no such wish or feeling. This admission to consciousness is one sort of outlet which should be available to all drives and emotions no matter how impractical, unflattering, or ugly.

In actual practice we can attain this partial expression by encouraging the child not to disown his wishes or emotions but to try to express these disturbing feelings in more and more acceptable fashion. Suppose, for instance, that a child has become annoyed at a playmate and among other manifestations of aggression he has shouted, "I hate you! I hate you! Some day I'll kill you!" What should we do? In our long-range objective for the child, we wish to modify this behavior. We do not wish him to go through life reacting to minor annoyances in this extreme way. But we should not try to talk him out of his feelings. We should not try to convince him that he did not hate his tormentor or the one who crossed him. Above all, we do not want him to think that he is wicked to have such feelings. And there is a distinct danger that, in discouraging his outward behavior, we may give him the idea that his feelings are also unworthy. Consequently, when trying to dissuade a child from the overt expression of an antisocial drive, we should take positive steps to indicate that there is nothing wrong with the wish itself. We should point out that it is natural for him to feel the way he does, and that almost anyone in a similar situation would feel very much the same way. We can then go on to suggest that things would be better if he expressed himself differently.

Absorbing Student Hostility. To what extent can the teacher permit his students to express their annoyance or anger, not only with the other students but also with the teacher himself? This is a crucial problem. It would be a most unusual teacher, and perhaps an ineffective one, who did not encounter some marked feelings of hostility on the part of his students. What should he do about it? We have suggested that the more the students are permitted to express this hostility, the easier it will be for them to deal with their feelings in an adequate manner. But might there be some practical difficulties? And, anyway, are we asking too much of the teacher?

In dealing with this problem you, as a teacher, can use many of the strategies that you would urge on your students. First of all, whenever there is evidence of such hostility, don't try to disguise the fact. On the other hand, don't take it too seriously. Remember that not all of expressed antagonism is directed to you as a person. Some of it, of course, may be. Most of us can expect to find that some people dislike us for what we really are. Much of the resentment you encounter, however, will come from the things that you must do in the performance of your duties. It would be directed to anyone carrying out the same functions. A very large portion of resentment against the teacher, moreover, is merely an expression of anger with adults in general and with parents in particular. Especially about the time of adolescence (Symonds, 1961) this hostility is the dominant emotion. Many adolescents, moreover, regard teachers, parents, and bosses as undifferentiated authority figures (Musgrove, 1964). You, in your sustained contact with pupils, are likely to catch the full brunt of their generalized annoyance at adults. If you can

► *The Conspicuous Place of Hostility (and Menace) in Adolescent Fantasy*

A number of adolescents (average age, fifteen) had taken the Symonds Adolescent Fantasy Test. Thirteen years later, twenty-eight of these took part in a follow-up, and again completed the Fantasy Test.

In this test, the subject sees an ambiguous sketch, as in the Thematic Apperception Test, and describes what he thinks might be going on. The different themes appearing in each account were then noted.

The table shows the number of people (as adolescents and as adults) who included each theme in at least one story. The most frequent themes are listed and are sorted into three general categories.

	Anger, Death, Violence		Altruism, Fond Relations, Romance		Achievement, Effort, Success	
	Adolescent	Adult	Adolescent	Adult	Adolescent	Adult
Hostility	26	15				
Punishment	25	23				
Being Attacked	21	10				
Eroticism			21	24		
Repentance	20	17				
Death (Not Criminal)	20	10				
Crime against Property	19	12				
Striving, Effort					19	19
Success					19	16
Planning					18	15
Jealousy			16	7		
Criminal Death	15	6				
Illness, Accident	15	9				
Separation			13	12		
Anger	12	13				
Disobedience, Rebellion	11	8				

SOURCE: P. M. Symonds, *From Adolescent to Adult* (New York: Columbia University Press, 1961).

absorb this undeserved, generalized hostility, you will be helping the students obtain some partial outlet for their disturbing emotions, thus making their anger easier for them to face (Ojemann, 1962).

In urging you to try to absorb this unmerited hostility in mature and adult fashion, we are by no means urging you to kowtow to it in abject surrender. Even though you preserve your equanimity, and even though you may see that this hostility has little to do with you, you may find it wise or necessary to pull the student up firmly, even sharply, if he oversteps the mark. As in dealing with the young child, you can accept his feelings, even the feelings which you in no way deserve, but may refuse to accept his manner of expressing them. Very often some correction may be absolutely necessary to preserve your own sense of self-respect, to assuage the sense of outrage felt by other students or other onlookers, and to help the student himself in his progress toward maturity.

Some of the overt hostility you encounter will be expressed in the form of gripes over some task you have assigned or some ruling you have made. If you are reasonably sure that the assignment or ruling must prevail anyhow, try to make this clear at the outset of the gripe session. Even when you are not committed in advance to the task you have assigned, you should still feel free to consider the objections on their merits, but to make your own decision as to what you will do about them. The fact that you have permitted the statement of objections does not mean that you must give in to them (Phillips and others, 1960).

In accepting and absorbing student hostility, you will again face the problem of your own security. If you are reasonably confident about your own worth as a person and about the importance of your mission, you will be in a much better position to take such hostility in your stride and to give your chief attention to your major work. If, however, your ego is already badly tottering, you may find a serious threat in even the most innocent grimace or expression of distaste. This general problem of the teacher's own security is treated in Chapter 16.

Meeting the More Basic Needs

As we might expect, it will be easier for a student to handle any one stressful episode if he is not asked to deal with other serious tensions at the same time. Conversely, if he is already frustrated in his attempts to satisfy some vital, basic need, he will have trouble in dealing

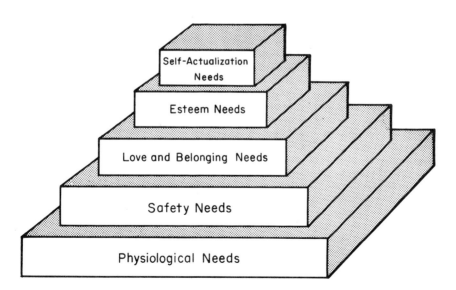

Fig. 14.1. Diagram of the hierarchy of needs. From H. J. Klausmeier, *Learning and Human Abilities: Educational Psychology* (New York: Harper & Row, 1961). Used with the permission of the publishers.

with the frustration of some less primitive desire. We are asking for trouble, for instance, if, when the child is already tired and hungry, we expect him to accept in graceful fashion the postponement of tomorrow's picnic.

Maslow (1948) has made much of the possibility that needs may fall into some sort of hierarchy, with the primitive needs at the base and with the more recent and deferrable needs superimposed (Fig. 14.1). In this hierarchy there are five levels of needs. Those having an A-1 priority are the physiological needs. Next on the list are the needs involved in avoiding danger or securing safety. Then there is the need to secure love from other people. One step beyond this is the need for esteem. For Maslow, esteem includes both the good opinion of other people and self-approval. Finally, there is the need for manipulation, or mastery or achievement or self-expression. By thus arranging needs in a hierarchy, Maslow seeks to emphasize the fact that a second-order need will be at a disadvantage in competing with a first-order need. A fairly strong urge toward artistic creation, for instance, might be ruled out by a weaker but more primitive need to avoid the contempt of others. Or, at the other end of the scale, when one is torn between the need for safety and the need for love, the former need may win out. We know, of course, that this does not always happen. The need for love may win out on occasion. This is so unexpected, so out of the ordinary, however, that it justifies a story or drama.

According to this view, a child should find it easier to manage the stress from unfulfilled creative urges if he is not already wrestling with the loss of esteem. He will find it easier to look honestly at his lack of popularity if he does not already feel a lack of parental love. He can better handle a fearsome experience (the approaching hypodermic needle) if he is not already tired and hungry.

A Warm, Accepting Manner

Of all the things that a teacher can do to make reality easier to face, perhaps the simplest is the trite business of liking the pupils and letting them know that they are important people in his life. The clear-cut conviction that one belongs, and is accepted, goes a long way toward transforming even the harshest reality into something that can be faced and dealt with, however sorrowfully. This important truth was clearly brought out in World War II by the reaction of children to bombing and to separation from parents (Jersild and Meigs, 1943). Surely these two problems represent reality in its most grim and formidable aspects. Fire, destruction of homes, death of parents, or a sudden move to a new environment and to life with strangers— these are pictures of reality which are exceedingly difficult to face. It is not surprising if children facing these ordeals should break down. Some children did. But some did not. And this is the important fact; the breakdown did not depend primarily on the severity of the shock or danger or on the extent of the separation. The children who adapted to these serious menaces were the children who had acquired a strong sense of belonging, especially of family belonging. The children who could not adjust themselves to those sudden terrors were those who lacked this strong sense of family security. They were the children who were secretly or openly worried about their status in the family. They were the children who were not sure that they were loved or wanted or that they really belonged. These factors of belonging and acceptance were much more important than the external stress to which the child was subjected.

It is not to be expected that the acceptance provided by the teacher will be so crucially important as that provided by the home. The teacher can do something, however, to add to the total feeling of acceptance or belonging and to provide a warm, human atmosphere.

Specifically this basic acceptance or liking may be shown by the frequent and ungrudging use of praise. This need not be expressed in the form of a fullsome speech or in a sugary manner. A frequent enthusiastic exclamation, interjected sincerely and under conditions that are reasonably appropriate, would seem more natural and more effective. We have suggested that the praise should be rea-sonably appropriate. This will probably vary with the students being taught. Young children can unembarrassedly accept praise for quite an ordinary performance. Older pupils may suspect the sincerity of praise that bubbles continuously. Here the most useful test would probably be that of sincerity. If you do feel an admiration for the student's performance, give free vent to your feeling. With young children, of course, we would urge you to develop a genuine appreciation for very ordinary achievement.

Praise, certainly solemn praise, is not the only means of providing an atmosphere of acceptance. Many teachers can be hearty, jovial, or even rough, and yet give the child a feeling of acceptance and belonging. Here the teacher's personality is crucial. Anything that puts a serious constraint on a natural manner of

---

▶ *The Teacher's Attitude toward Unpopular Children*

Each pupil in forty grade-six classes listed the five other pupils he would most prefer as work companions, play companions, or seating companions. The teacher in each of these classes indicated the three boys and the three girls she most preferred to have in her class and the three boys and three girls she least preferred to have in the class. The information was obtained toward the end of the school year. All forty teachers were women.

	Average Number of Choices Received by Pupils Preferred and Not Preferred by the Teacher	
	Boys	Girls
Pupils Most Preferred by Teacher	21	21
Pupils Least Preferred by Teacher	9	9

SOURCE: N. E. Gronlund, Relationship between the sociometric status of pupils and teachers' preferences for or against having them in class, *Sociometry*, 1953, 16, 142–150.

acting, would, to that very extent, reduce some of the indication of acceptance.

A warm, accepting attitude is especially important for pupils who have already come to think of the world as hostile, critical, and exacting. And there are many children who acquire this unfortunate attitude early in life and who come to school with all the apprehension, fearfulness, and even defiance which such an attitude engenders. For this child who has had to accept more criticism than he can absorb, or who has had to face standards which he does not know how to meet, the teacher should be especially generous in his acceptance. True enough, this may mean that he will have to relax his standards somewhat. In serious cases, however, it is better to relax standards than to risk the danger of forcing the child into a more drastic retreat from reality (Symonds, 1946).

The advice just given may be very difficult to carry out. Ironically enough, it is fairly easy to adopt this permissive, accepting attitude with bright, well-behaved children. Anyone seeing us teach in this situation would find us to be democratic, integrative, and helpful. Let us change to a more difficult situation, however, and we tend to change to a more dominative and demanding attitude (Wandt and Ostreicher, 1953). The children who are in most need of acceptance and liking are not those who are easy to like. If we follow our inclinations, we prefer the students who are already fairly popular (Gronlund, 1953). When we do surmount these difficulties we will often find our efforts rebuffed. Try to be friendly with children who have experienced extreme rejection over a long period and you will find that your advances are met with suspicion and distrust (Redl and Wineman, 1951).

All this implies a degree of security on the part of the teacher himself. The insecure person, for instance, is reluctant to praise. At the worst he feels, pathetic as it seems, that he is somehow putting himself at a disadvantage by freely expressing admiration for the act of another. Far from giving him pleasure, the other's success elicits fear, guilt, or envy. It is the secure, confident person who can take genuine satisfaction in the accomplishments of those around him without feeling that he is in some way belittling himself in the process.

Clearly there are many ways in which the teacher's lack of security will prevent him from feeling a reasonable degree of acceptance. The writer, in his early teaching experience, narrowly escaped serious trouble because of over-suspicion. On taking over a new job, he was told of the serious disciplinary problems he would face and was regaled with tales of the things the high school boys had done to his predecessor. As a result of this unfortunate indoctrination, he began the year on the defensive and regarded even mild irregularities as the beginning of outright rebellion. It was only by extremely good luck that he came to "drop his guard" and to accept the students for what they were, an exceptionally fine group of boys, although typically thoughtless and with an ordinary flair for obstreperousness.

The Importance of the General Atmosphere. In all this, the general pervading atmosphere is probably more important than any single isolated event. Most children can throw off the single traumatic experience with little trouble. It is the steady diet of frustration, failure, or harsh, unyielding reality that leads to trouble (Harris, 1960).

Remember that, despite your best efforts, most children will have their ups and downs in this matter of personal adjustment. One of the most important things, therefore, is to be sure that the child, on his upswing, will experience reinforcement for his new behavior (Dollard and Miller, 1950). At the time of his upswing he actually *is* better adjusted. Will that better adjustment pay off? Will the class be a place which will provide happiness for this new recruit to the world of superior adjustment? In short, is it the kind of place that a well-adjusted person would relish?

Since the upswing of each child may express itself in different ways, it is important that there should be some variety in the experiences to be had. In this way, each child will have a better chance to be successful in his own way.

Manifesting Adult Security

By possessing a generous measure of emotional security in his own make-up, the teacher will find it easier to provide liberal praise, to accept students in warm, human fashion, and to absorb some of the hostility that is almost bound to occur. In addition to providing these incidental aids, the teacher's own security also helps in very direct fashion to make reality easier for the child. For young children, especially, adult insecurity is a terrifying thing. For such children, the total stress felt in any situation is often determined, not so much by the objective menace as by the amount of adult anxiety expressed. Being unexpectedly forced to spend the night in the family car, for instance, can be a lark or a catastrophe depending on the attitude shown by the parents. Children's reaction to more serious predicaments, such as the father's loss of a job, may be governed almost entirely by the amount of parental anxiety. All in all, it would seem a

tremendous help if the pupil could live in a world that important adults find habitable or even enjoyable, a world filled with problems, of course, but problems susceptible to attack, a world in which teachers can feel reasonably secure.

The teacher's insecurity or apprehension may be infectious when he is terrified of some objective event, such as the visit of a supervisor, or the imminence of city-wide examinations. In more subtle situations, the teacher's doubts and minor worries may be magnified by the time they reach the student. In the counseling situation, for instance, the teacher may have mild reservations about the decision the student will ultimately make. This mild uncertainty on the part of the teacher may act as a severe threat to the student's entire ego. The secret here, of course, is to try to feel confident. Statistically, the decisions of most students, although far from ideal, are not disastrous.

We must not imply, of course, that the teacher, by sheer act of will, can automatically raise himself to new levels of security. The teacher's own security is a genuine problem and one that is most important in its own right (Chapter 16).

Ultimately the child should learn to deal with ambiguity and even with a measure of chaos, and this the well-adjusted child readily comes to do. For the child who is extremely uncertain, however, and who sees reality as a serious threat, a degree of order and structure is most reassuring. Such children welcome a fairly firm hand and like to know just what is expected in the way of discipline and control. There is some evidence that they learn more and make a better surface adjustment when the teacher clearly structures the tasks and makes it quite clear that the students are there to work (Haring and Phillips, 1962). This structure and control need not continue indefinitely. As adjustment develops, students can be asked to assume more responsibility and independence and more tolerance for the ambiguity and uncertainty that such freedom often brings.

DEVELOPING SKILL IN DEALING WITH STRESS AND TENSION

So far we have been trying to make sure that stress and worries of reality will not press too harshly on the student. But obviously this amelioration of reality is not the final answer. The great thing is to increase the pupil's ability to handle the stresses he is bound to encounter when there is no one at his side to temper the blast.

In the development of emotional adjustment, as in the development of character (Chapter 10), the school and the teacher face some serious, but not insurmountable, obstacles. With mental health and character we often lack the precise control that we can expect in teaching academic subjects. In teaching the management of stress, for instance, we cannot always arrange for a graded series of tasks. In spite of our best efforts, the emotional problems faced by the six-year-old may be more serious than any frustration he may encounter in all the rest of his life. In this area of adjustment we may also lack the precise control over reinforcement that we can usually expect in teaching algebra or Latin. As in the task of teaching character, moreover, direct motivation may be a problem when we turn to mental health. Although we can encourage children toward the deliberate aim to better themselves in English and French, we may

feel that an avid, deliberate search for naturalness or serenity would seem self-defeating or unduly calculating.

Practice in the Task Itself

In spite of the problems involved, it may be feasible at times to provide direct practice in the types of tension we wish the student to master. Whenever this is true we may adopt any of the formal means of ensuring a series of successful acts and of providing prompt reinforcement (Chapter 5).

A Program of Graded Tasks. As we have seen, the graded series of tasks is not always feasible. We cannot always hope to control many of the most significant experiences in the realm of tension. Some areas, however, permit such manipulation on our part. At times we can deliberately provide occasional stressful experiences that are within the capacity of the student and let him experience that positive joy of dealing successfully with the menace (Olson and Wattenberg, 1955). Successful exposure to an artificial, moderate stress can often make things easier for students when they encounter a genuine and serious threat (Torrance, 1958).

Whenever this approach is feasible there is much to recommend it. There is good reason to hope that in coping successfully with one stressful incident we acquire more competence to handle a similar or a more difficult situation (Klein, 1960). Perhaps each victory really does help us some other to win.

A Program of Reinforcement. In the minds of many theorists, reinforcement is the crucial factor in the development of any kind of skill (Bandura and Walters, 1963b; Staats and Staats, 1963), including the skill needed to handle stressful situations. According to this

► *Advance Preparation for an Unpleasant Experience*

A total of 416 aircrewmen took part in a seven-day survival experiment. As part of this experience they were supposed to use a new pemmican ration bar that is extremely nutritious but which is disliked by some men. Some 107 of these men had previously tried out the bar. After the exercise the men answered a questionnaire giving their reactions to the new ration bar.

Type of Experience with the New Bar	*Number of Men*	*Degree of Dislike*	*Average Number of Bars Eaten during the Experiment*
None	287	21.6	6.2
Had just tasted bar	22	21.0	7.2
Had tried it out and liked it	33	14.9	8.5
Had tried it out and disliked it	74	22.8	6.4
Total of those trying out the bar	107	20.0	7.6

SOURCE: E. P. Torrance, Sensitization versus adaptation in preparation for emergencies: prior experience with an emergency ration and its acceptability in a simulated survival situation, *Journal of Applied Psychology*, 1958, **42**, 63–67. (See the box by Torrance and Mason [Chapter 10] for a different aspect of this general investigation.)

view, one program of reinforcement can lead a person into more mature ways of behaving. A different program can force him to regress to more childish ways of reacting.

To use this all-important rule, we should try to make sure that the child is reinforced whenever he manages the stressful situation in a reasonably adequate way. First, we must get him to respond in some reasonable or acceptable fashion. Then we must reinforce him. But how do we get him to respond in reasonable or acceptable fashion in the first place? As we saw in Chapter 5, there are two chief means used to get the child to emit an acceptable response. You can guide him into it, or you can

temporarily lower your standards and employ the technique of shaping up.

Guidance. Sometimes, if the stressful situation is foreseen, it may be possible to supply the guidance before the student has a chance to make any response. In one experiment (Davitz, 1952), for instance, boys were guided toward constructive activities by being rewarded for this sort of work prior to the onset of stress. Another group, in contrast, was rewarded and praised for aggressive acts. Later both groups were subjected to stress and frustration. Each group reacted to the frustration by the behavior to which they had been guided. Often, of course, there is no opportunity to anticipate.

► *The Shaping of Behavior toward Maturity*

"Dee," a girl of 3½, insisted on crawling and remaining on the floor from her first day of attendance at nursery school. She paid little attention to the going or coming of her mother, but remained crouched on the floor, hiding her face whenever an adult approached. She moved around to get juice and food, but did so by crawling.

After two weeks, the two teachers initiated a shaping-up routine. Whenever Dee was on the floor and looked toward a teacher, the latter would be busy with something else. Whenever she made any approach to an upright posture, however, the teacher would immediately pay attention to her and talk cheerfully to her (but *not about* her posture). One of the two teachers made herself 100 percent available for this reinforcement.

In one week Dee spent most of the time on her feet. In two weeks she could not be distinguished from the other children. The teachers then reversed the procedure, ignoring Dee when she was standing or walking but talking to her cheerfully when she was crawling. With this treatment she spent 76 percent of the time on the floor on the first day, 82 percent of the second day. On the third day the procedure was switched again and reinforcement was given for the upright posture. On the next day she spent 62 percent of the time on her feet, and from then on she behaved normally for her age.

SOURCE: Florence E. Harris, Margaret K. Johnston, Susan C. Kelley, and M. M. Wolf, Effects of positive social reinforcement on regressed crawling of a nursery school child, *Journal of Educational Psychology*, 1964, **55**, 35–41.

Even when stress is already at work, however, exceedingly prompt action may still provide valuable guidance. Suppose, for instance, that a student has just been defeated in a tennis game and seems about to sulk or behave in some childish way. If you can help it, do not give him a chance to do this. Rush over to him, and while you are commenting on the good points in his play, unobtrusively push, guide, or maneuver him over to his opponent so that he is almost forced to shake hands. If a younger child has fallen in a puddle and is hovering between tears and laughter, lead him to laugh, if you can, by your manner. Laugh *with* him and not *at* him.

Shaping Up. In place of guidance, or along with it, we can often use the device of shaping up (Chapter 5) to increase the likelihood of reinforceable or acceptable behavior. In using this technique we reward early tries even when they are merely in the right direction. A student whose ability to manage his temper leaves much to be desired, may occasionally show something that can be praised, and this we should seize upon. A pupil who is not completely valiant on the diving board can be praised for the fact that ultimately he did make the jump. To a student, belatedly owning up to a misdeed, we can express our approval of the honesty and say little or nothing about the delay.

In trying to develop more mature methods of dealing with stress, you will find shaping up an extremely useful device. It has, however, at least two drawbacks. The first drawback lies in your own standards. You may find it exceedingly difficult to praise behavior that falls far short of your expectations. Indeed you may feel hypocritical or dishonest. In that case, try to decide how far you can go in this process. Could you commend a two-year old for owning up to his fear and yet making a valiant try to approach the menace? a three-year old? Would you commend a schizophrenic adult who made one feeble and pathetic effort to re-establish contact with the world? After considering particular illustrations, try to decide when shaping up becomes repugnant.

There is a second difficulty with shaping up. You do not always have a monopoly on the rewards or disparagements that may be administered. Other students, or bystanders, may have much to say and their reactions may carry much weight. Under these circumstances, shaping up is not under your complete control.

The reactions of other observers, by the way, present a continual problem in this matter of teaching for adjustment. At times the teacher may be able to influence these reactions. A student, for instance, has finally mustered up courage to make a public talk. It falls far short of a finished performance. But it is a resolute try in the face of severe tension. You yourself can applaud. Perhaps your applause may trigger off that of others. Perhaps, if that fails, an inconspicuous gesture may do the job.

No one else, of course, can tell you just how far you should be prepared to go in this matter of engineering a contrived success. In playing with the three-year old, you may readily let him break through the fence made by your arms, when his own unaided exertions would not produce that result. Later on you may have qualms on various grounds.

Such contriving may be wrong by some absolute moral standard. Even if it were not, you may shudder at what would happen if the student ever discovered the fraudulent basis of his cherished success.

Placing the Student on His Own. The devices just discussed are designed especially for the early stages in learning any task. By the use of these devices we may extract reinforceable behavior from the student even when he is a raw beginner. Gradually, but certainly, however, such devices must be withdrawn. Gradually we withdraw guidance, and less and less often do we feel we must point the way to the correct response before the student makes a move. Gradually, on the contrary, we require him to commit himself by some overt act, and then, and only then, do we let him find out whether he was right or wrong, clumsy or adroit.

Just as we gradually require the student to act on his own with no prompting on our part, so we also gradually tighten up the standards by which we greet his performance. Gradually we cease to make allowances for his lack of experience, and gradually we ask him to accept standards that are more adult and objective. Not only is this necessary if he is to acquire reasonable proficiency, but the frustration involved in trying to meet rigorous standards is part of the reality with which he should be asked to cope.

Effecting a Reasonable Transition. Clearly, in learning any one task, the pupil must leave the stage of guidance and protection and must come to be on his own and to accept more exacting standards. Obviously, however, the transition should not be too abrupt. If the transition should be too abrupt, it would probably reveal itself by a definite increase in the evidence of frustration. In young children, this frustration might express itself in unprovoked weeping or generalized anger. Faced with a specific task which is too frustrating at the moment, the child may loiter or postpone his start on the task. Other evidences of distaste may appear, or he may work around the task with a show of token movements or other useless reactions. Frustration may also reveal itself, however, in undue expenditure of energy. The child may attack an ordinary task almost aggressively. In severe frustration, even more serious behavior problems may develop. Ailments, exhibitionism, or destructive tendencies may appear.

When any of the many signs of frustration reach a point at which serious stress is suspected, ease up in the rate of transition. Provide more guidance and move back for the time being to a less exacting attitude. In doing this, it would be well if there were not too obvious a connection between, say, the temper tantrum and our "retreat." It would be well if we could change the intensity of the stress and do it in our stride without seeming to alter our approach. But this is a secondary matter. When behavior problems or other evidences of frustration appear, the important thing is to reduce the frustration. Just how gracefully we can arrange the reduction is another and a lesser problem.

Extinction. In most of our efforts, of course, we will be working in a positive direction. We will have a fair idea of a more adequate form of adjustment, and we will be working toward that goal. At other times, however, we may chiefly be concerned with eliminating some undesirable behavior. We want the child to stop whining or tale-bearing. We hope that he will replace these ways of behaving with something much better. At the moment, however, we chiefly want him to stop doing this.

Under such circumstances, the proponents of direct reinforcement would advocate simple extinction procedures. Try to be sure that the child gets no reinforcement following the behavior you wish to eliminate. Make sure that he gets no reinforcement from you, and do what you can to keep him from being reinforced by others. There are reports of using this procedure for the successful elimination of behavior ranging from temper tantrums (Williams, 1959) to mere nosy interference (Bandura and Walters, 1963b). When setting out to use extinction, by the way, we should prepare ourselves to encounter considerable expression of the frustration discussed above. Most people (and rats) undergoing extinction show signs of such general, undirected frustration.

Teaching by Transfer

It is often impossible and undesirable to expose children deliberately to much of the actual stress that we wish them to master. We cannot deliberately give them practice in adjusting to the death of a parent or to the pangs of unrequited love. To develop competence in dealing with these tasks for which we can provide no direct experience, we must rely on transfer of some kind. Even in using easier versions of the real task, we are relying to some extent on the powers of transfer. We invoke transfer much more clearly when we turn to literature, biography, or drama as a source of experience from which students may derive ability to deal with the stresses and frustrations of the real world. As in portraying character (Chapter 11), moreover, these literary sources often provide experience into which the pupil enters to a marked extent. He really is the hero, or the victim, and shares the urges and tensions in most vivid form. To a considerable extent these literary treatments structure the basic conflict much more clearly than can be done in real life. However subtly portrayed, the essential issues are typically not obscured by mere haphazard irrelevancies as in everyday life.

Although the student may experience the basic stress in compelling fashion, we cannot be sure that the literary selection will call for a realistic, overt response available to the child. Nor does the literary work provide appropriate reinforcement for any token responses that might occur. Consequently there is little chance to develop a realistic pattern of overt behavior in any dependable way. In developing the sheer willingness to admit the existence of distressing emotions and fearful menaces, written descriptions can do a great deal. Most people are quite eager to apply literary portrayals to their own concerns. Few of us can read a lucid analysis without thinking, "That's me," or, "I wouldn't feel that way."

If the transfer is to be at all effective, and even so we must not expect guarantees of effectiveness, we should try to find several examples of any particular point we wish to develop. To delineate reasonable adjustment to severe frustration, for instance, we might look for motion pictures of soldiers encountering blindness, as one illustration, and perhaps stories of boys having to sacrifice cherished pets, as another. We should not put all our faith in one example, or even a few examples, no matter how convincing. The student may react to the details of a specific example and not to the basic concept set forth.

In the academic realm, transfer is often facilitated when students are able to work out or acquire a convincing generalization or a working rule. Theoretically, this should hold in using transfer to develop skill in dealing with tension. After being exposed to the training situation, the students might well be asked to work out or consider rules which were the key to the successful adjustment, and which, when neglected, led to failure.

Instruction in the Principles of Mental Hygiene

So far, we have discussed the things that a teacher might do in the course of the ordinary school day. The devices described are those that might be sandwiched in with lessons and with informal playground activity. It is possible, however, that these incidental techniques, important as they are, should be supplemented by a frontal attack and that we should organize classes frankly aimed at more adequate adjustment (Morse and Dressel, 1960). Ojemann (1961) reports a group of experiments in which students were encouraged to approach social subjects from a "causal" approach—Why do people act the way they do? What are the deep, underlying motives of the nonvoter? Such students were better able to adopt a tolerant attitude, or a more objective attitude, toward the behavior of others, and were also considered more able to cope with the stresses in their own lives.

Bullis (1953) and his colleagues see great promise in the Human Relations Club that they have used for some years. In these classes there is much group discussion of interpersonal tensions, worries, and stresses. In such courses there is an opportunity to use films, books, and

► *Using a Formal Course To Improve Emotional Adjustment*

Four classes of grade-six pupils had been enrolled in a special course designed to increase the understanding of the causes of behavior, and to encourage pupils toward thinking of the reasons underlying behavior, rather than merely condemning or approving the behavior they observed. Some of the pupils had been in the special program for one year and the rest for two years. A control group of four classes had had the regular grade-six program. For all pupils in the special program the average IQ was 105.9. For those in the regular program the average was 105.4.

Each pupil took the Children's Manifest Anxiety Scale, a Security-Insecurity Rating Scale, and a test designed to bring out the *discrepancy* between the pupil's concept of the person he thought he ought to be and the kind of person he thought he actually was.

	Number of Pupils	Amount of Anxiety	Amount of Insecurity	Amount of Discrepancy between Ideal and Real Self
Regular Program	86	15.0	24.1	7.9
One Year of Special Program	53	15.5	24.0	8.0
Two Years of Special Program	45	11.9[a]	22.4[a]	7.2

[a] These two averages are significantly different from the averages of either of the other groups. No other differences are significant.

SOURCE: P. Bruce, Relationship of self-acceptance to other variables with sixth-grade children oriented in self-understanding, *Journal of Educational Psychology*, 1958, 49, 229–238.

booklets directed to students in various grades (see "Suggestions for Further Reading" at the end of chapter). Along with these approaches, we learn of the use of psychodrama or role playing, in which students are asked to take a part in some play dealing with adjustment difficulties (Weinreb, 1953). It would seem wise, however, to undertake these more ambitious projects only in cooperation with someone who is in a position to assume some responsibility for psychiatric treatment.

DEALING WITH ANGER AND AGGRESSION

The processes that produce aggression are discussed in Chapter 11. There it is pointed out that anger is likely to arise when we are subjected to an attack. We are also likely to get angry when prevented from satisfying other important needs. When unable to escape pain, we may even turn on an innocent bystander. We are likely to become angry at those who refuse to accept us, or who spurn our affection. Failure in our creative efforts may lead us to attack other people or even vent our anger on a balky wrench or on a knot that refuses to unsnarl.

Anger, in turn, may act as a threat or frustration to some of our needs. Some kinds of anger may threaten the loss of the esteem in which we are held and may be a severe blow to our cherished self-concept.

Reducing the Occasion for Anger

In helping students deal with the problem of anger, we can make good use of the general rules for handling stress or tension. There are also some additional considerations that have bearing on the special problem of anger (Horowitz, 1963).

To reduce the likelihood of serious anger in your students, try to avoid a fussy, worrisome or overmoralistic attitude. A prolonged, preachy, or semi-nagging discussion can infuriate a child (see section on "Discipline," Chapter 12). In "explaining" why he can't go out to play, or why he must put up with this frustration, it does little good to remind him of *all* the reasons for the frustration. By *dwelling* on these reasons for doing things our way, we seem to imply that he is an unreasonable person or a bad boy for wanting to do something else. Thus, to his original frustration there is added a very serious threat to his self-esteem.

This does not mean that we must never stress the reasons that underlie our demands. When parents use reason in moderation, children are more likely to avoid delinquency and other defects of character (Kohlberg, 1963b). Reasons that are genuine, consistent, and easily grasped should serve a useful purpose, especially when we have to make an unwelcome demand or to insist on an irksome prohibition. A brief and fairly cheerful announcement of the reasons, moreover, should not add to the intrinsic distress coming from the request or prohibition. It is the prolonged, repetitive, perhaps nagging, elaboration of these reasons that keeps the child in an unflattering spotlight and arouses his resentment. An extended, semicomplaining, moralistic harangue, in fact, can induce more annoyance than the resented demand itself (Goodenough, 1931).

Danger Signals. Many children show in advance that they are on the verge of an explosion. If we can recognize this, we can often reduce the stress before the anger actually develops, or before it is expressed. We may be able to find some legitimate, or almost legitimate, excuse to interject a word of praise, or other expression of acceptance. This should help and may be worth a try even if we must lower our standards somewhat.

In this matter, it is most helpful to anticipate or abort the outburst. Offering acceptance or praise after the temper tantrum is a questionable matter since, in permitting the anger to pay off, we may well reinforce this way of acting (Chapter 10). Even so, when things become too frenzied we may have no other choice. If we can successfully anticipate and divert the anger, however, we avoid this very awkward dilemma.

Acceptable Outlets for Aggression

Perhaps more than most forms of tension, the aggressive needs can profit from some degree of expression. Certainly the student should be encouraged to admit these needs to himself with no sense of guilt. To wish to hurt or to wreak revenge or to kill does not make him evil. Carrying out those wishes, of course, would be evil.

As soon as the child has freely faced his feelings and his aggressive wishes, and as soon as he is convinced that you do not condemn him for his hates and resentments, it is safe to go on to discuss the sensible thing to do about them. Get him to see the rival claims of revenge, on the one hand, and of the more tender needs, or the need for esteem of others, or esteem of self, or the need to avoid punishment, on the other. Do not leave the matter until the claims of affection, prudence, and social obligations have been clearly recognized.

Announcement of Anger

I was angry with my friend,
  I told my wrath, my wrath did end.
I was angry with my foe,
  I told it not, my wrath did grow.

Blake's pithy summary of this problem has been supported by sober investigation (Thibaut and Coules, 1952). Two students, strangers to each other, were asked to cooperate in the solution of a problem. They faced each other through a glass partition and all communication was in the form of notes passed back and forth. As it happened, one "student" was really a stooge for the experimenter. As the work went on he became more and more abusive, finally writing a vicious, personal attack. This was repeated with the same stooge with a number of different students. Some of these students were permitted to reply to the personal attack; others were not. Some days later, those who had been permitted no outlet were still bothered by the situation and felt acute resentment against the attacker. Those who had been permitted to reply had more often dismissed the whole thing.

It is true, of course, that we cannot always reply "in kind." Under the lash of an unfair reprimand from the boss, we cannot always afford to let our blind anger express itself in all its fury. Later on, however, if the boss is reasonably human, we can announce, in a matter-of-fact way, that the experience was very hard to accept. Often this may lead to a quiet discussion of the whole matter on the part of both parties concerned, and this may provide some release. Even the mere fact that we made the announcement may provide some release and may reduce the need for prolonged fantasies in which we seek an unrealistic and pathetically inadequate outlet for our pent-up rage.

Games or Contests. The device of unemotional announcement is one which older students may properly practice. For younger children, however, it may require a grasp of relations which are somewhat too complicated. This is especially true if there is no clear insight as to the exact nature of the aggressive need. In the face of such vague, poorly directed, aggressive needs, we may turn to games, contests, or general physical activity to provide a considerable measure of release. These activities should make the general frustration less pressing. Such devices, however, should not replace the more deliberate and rational expression of any aggressive needs which may be clearly understood.

DEALING WITH FEAR

In this discussion we refer to fear (Dasgupta, 1962) of some fairly specific menace, real or imaginary, and not to general free-floating anxiety. As with any form of tension or stress, the important thing is to try to make sure that the student sees the menace as a temporary situation that he can handle. This we can do by reducing the stress itself, by adding to relevant skill, or by showing the relevance of skill already possessed.

Fear is less likely to reach troublesome proportions when the child's basic security is in good order. Small children in the hospital, for instance, will handle their inevitable fears much better and recover from the anxiety much sooner, if they have had daily visits from parents and have received general psychological support (Prugh and others, 1953).

Forewarning and Explanation

When a child is about to undergo serious stress, such as an operation, mere forewarning or explanation cannot be expected to abolish fear or greatly to reduce it (Jessner and others, 1952). When dealing with milder stress, however, it often helps to have a moderate length of time to consider the oncoming menace (Jersild, 1954). Not only does this permit practical defenses, but it gives us a chance to erect psychological barricades. We can figure out ways of reacting to the danger and can at least brace ourselves against it. Certainly children who are warned to expect a loud noise, or who know that the boat will soon move, are often much less agitated than other children to whom the new stimulus is a complete surprise.

At times, an understanding of the mechanics of the menace may help. It may help to know what rattlesnakes can do and what they cannot do. By knowing what the menace can do and what it cannot do, we tend to localize its menacing qualities. Unexplained, it is a vast general "threat," perhaps threatening everything that we value. Explained, it is a limited menace, serious enough perhaps, but demanding our attention at only certain points.

In dealing with fear it is especially important to provide as much outlet as prudence, safety, and self-respect will permit. Certainly the student should admit his fear to himself. Perhaps he can also find acceptable ways of mentioning it to certain others. For some people, a humorous description of the agitation provides a partial solution.

Graduated Practice

In providing practice with fearsome experiences we can often arrange for a graduated series of tasks. The child can be asked to jump from diving platforms of slightly greater heights, to go on visits of gradually increasing duration, to speak before audiences that become more formidable by gradual degrees.

Although we can graduate the intensity of the menace, it is much better when the child himself controls the task that he must face, and when he is perfectly sure that the menace is completely under his control. When the student realizes that he can take as much or as little of the menace as he chooses, he can have no doubt that the threat can be kept at a level consistent with his skill. This would be true, for instance, if he knew he was free to withdraw at will to the shallow end of the swimming pool, if he could control the volume of the frightening sound, if he could, of his own will, move toward, or retreat from, the fearsome caged snake. If we are to maintain this arrangement, of course, we must not even express disappointment when he retreats. But we can be quite effusive about his more resolute tries.

SOCIAL REJECTION OR NEGLECT

Among the evils to be faced, we must consider the seeming negative danger of being neglected. The need for esteem or recognition has a rather low priority in the Maslow heirarchy. It is not likely to assert itself when one is striving fearfully to avoid pain, to escape danger, or to regain the love of one held dear. But as these latter needs become less active, the student finds it more and more important to be recognized as an individual having a personality and a value apart from his significance as a mere member of a group.

There are two quite different situations in which the teacher can help meet the need for recognition. Clearly the teacher can go out of his way to provide some acknowledgment of the quiet student who shuns the spotlight and never puts himself forward. Often such a student has such a powerful need for recognition that he cannot stand the risk of a rebuff. He protects himself against that risk by never making any bid for attention. A quiet, unobtrusive acknowledgment of his individuality may not only bring great joy at the moment, but also, in showing such acknowledgment can be had, may make him less afraid of admitting his need to himself and may give him confidence to make some moderate effort to satisfy it.

At the other end of the scale, the teacher can help the rambunctious child who expresses his need for recognition by a turbulent clamor. Here we do not face the problem of acknowledging his presence. That we cannot avoid. Our problem, on the contrary, is to see that this furious behavior is a demand for attention, and not, as it may appear to be, a hard-boiled display of wild disregard for the opinion of others. We should avoid trying to squelch him. But we should try, whenever possible, to give him much attention when he puts himself forward in acceptable fashion. We should make a less effusive response to his more tumultuous overtures.

LOSS OF SELF-ESTEEM: FAILURE AND THE FEAR OF FAILURE

Failure and the fear of failure hit at a wide range over the Maslow hierarchy. Clearly such failures deny the need for self-expression and mastery. Typically, although not necessarily, they direct a cruel blow to the need for self-esteem. At times they bring a loss, or an imagined loss, in the esteem of others. And, so fluid is the hierarchy, they may even seem to threaten the more primitive need for love.

Examinations. It is possible that examinations would be fearsome things even if there were no threat of failure. There may be external features which would incite tension under any circumstances. But whatever the basic reason, examinations clearly present a hazard to the typical pupil (Redl and Wattenberg, 1959). This fear of examinations, or test anxiety, can be distinguished from general anxiety (Sarason and others, 1960). The general distress induced by examinations is likely to be severe if the subject itself is frightening or if, when proctoring, rigid rules or time limits are conspicuous (Stephens, 1959). It is in this latter respect that the teacher can often help. An inescapable examination can be made less fearful if the teacher can act in a cheerful manner and encourage the students to exploit the humorous possibilities in the situation. There is also room for the structuring and delimiting of the menace and for showing that performance on this particular test is not the sole determiner of one's academic worth. As a minor means of reducing the stress of examinations some teachers have encouraged students to make notes on the examination questions. In these notes they express themselves freely and candidly about the ambiguity or unfairness of the item in question. There is

► *Attempting To Relieve Examination Stress*

Women college students in five classes took part in this experiment. At the beginning of the term all students (152) took the Manifest Anxiety Scale. At the time of the first test, each class was divided into an experimental (comment-invited) group, and a control (comment-prohibited). The test was of the multiple-choice type. Beside each question there were some blank spaces. For the comment-invited group, the instructions said, "Put an X through the best answer for each item. Feel free to make any comments about the items in the space provided." The others were told to mark the right item but not to make any marks in the space provided.

If there is any help from freedom to make comments, it should show up toward the end of the examination. When all classes were grouped together, the comment-invited group did show a superiority on the second half of the examination.

Students for one class were divided into those above the median in general anxiety (Manifest Anxiety Scale) and those below the median.

The table shows the number of *errors* made in each half of the examination.

	Average Number of Errors	
	First Half of the Examination	Second Half of the Examination
Students High in Initial Anxiety		
Comment-invited	9.6[a]	7.2[a]
Comment-prohibited	9.0	8.8
Students Low in Initial Anxiety		
Comment-invited	7.2	7.4
Comment-prohibited	8.4	6.8

[a] The difference between these two scores is significant. (The report does not say whether or not the difference in the last line is significant.)

SOURCE: A. D. Calvin, F. J. McGuigan, and M. W. Sullivan, A further investigation of the relationship between anxiety and classroom examination performance, *Journal of Educational Psychology*, 1957, **48**, 240–244. Reprinted in Seidman, pp. 421–425.

some evidence that this method of dealing with the irritation permits the student to direct his efforts more effectively to the basic task of answering the questions (Calvin and others, 1957; McKeachie and others, 1955).

Competition. An undue emphasis on competition may prove a source of stress for the student who regularly loses. It may also be stressful for the overly anxious student who frequently wins. The emphasis should be on keeping competition within reasonable bounds. It would be foolish and unnecessary to try to eliminate competition completely. Very often it provides zest and pleasant challenge (see discussion in Chapter 4). When team competes against team, there may be a pleasant increase in appreciation of teammates (Myers, 1962). We should try to make sure that as many children as possible can enjoy a reasonable amount of spirited competition. Competition of team against team, with its more moderate strain, may often be used to provide a graduated introduction to the more intensive individual competition. The emphasis on individual competition should be reduced when it seems too much for some of the pupils, or when undesirable social disruption threatens (Stendler and others, 1951).

The Experience of Failure

Failure, of course, is not always a complete evil and should not be regarded as such. Under favorable conditions men may indeed "rise on stepping stones of their dead selves to better things." And folk-wisdom has long insisted on profiting from mistakes. As we saw in the discussion of problem solving (Chapter 7), failure may often bring important information available in no other way. Without failure, for instance, we would never know our powers. Just as the engineer will never know the full strength of his beam until he has stressed it to the point of failure, so the jumper will never know how high he can jump until he makes an attempt that fails. The college student will never know how far he can go in mastering difficult subjects until he finally tries a course that proves too much for him.

It would be a great boon to our students and to our society if we could encourage people to regard failure in this way. Consider, for instance, the student who has made the second string team but not the first. Let us not talk him out of his inevitable regrets. But we could show him how his failure is a relative thing. Everyone is bound to fail if he tries things that are difficult enough.

He happened to fail here. This fact is much more significant in showing what he can do than what he cannot do.

More often than we do, we should go out of our way to encourage pupils to adopt a program of trying *until* they reach the point of failure. See how high we can build this tower *before* it topples. Let's challenge more and more capable teams *until* we seem to have met our match. At least once in your college career try a course that will call for everything you have and may call for more than you have. When failure is thus foreseen as the inevitable result of a progression of honest tries, it is much easier to take than when seen as something that sets us apart as a member of a shameful minority.

To encourage pupils to adopt this attitude toward life and challenge, we must be consistent and must provide generous rewards for resolute tries that fail. When a student has failed, moreover, we must help him to structure his failure and to see its limited impact. He must see the difference between failure in this particular task and failure as a person. Even when there is much ego-involvement, we can often help him to see that most of him has been unharmed even after this serious blow.

Like any other form of unresolved stress, failure can produce a stereotyped repetition of the very act that failed. In this, the pupil seems to get some perverted satisfaction of experiencing over and over again the failure and the punishment that accompanies it. At other times failure may lead to a chaotic variety of acts following each other in frantic haphazard fashion (Child and Waterhouse, 1952). Or it may be followed by a definite regression to more childish ways of acting.

In severe failure, the student becomes less sensible in setting his expectations for future success. Whereas his successful colleague will expect to do just a little better on the next trial, the failing student is more likely to set his aspirations ridiculously high or ridiculously low (Escalona, 1948; Frank, 1941).

Naturally, serious failure presents one of the strongest temptations to turn one's back on reality and to refuse to face the fact of failure. Either we actually perceive our performance as being more successful than it was (Nuttin, 1953) or we find some pathetic alibi to excuse our poor showing.

School Failure. The special problem of school failure has received a good deal of attention (Worth, 1960). Such a traumatic and conspicuous experience may well have many unfortunate effects. Many people have held that the blow is all the more deplorable in that the child who repeats a grade seldom does any better than his equally wobbly classmate who is promoted. This latter point is in dispute and it may be that the experience has different effects on different children (Worth, 1961).

Whether to fail a student or not is a most trying question and one in which the student's undoubted immediate distress must be balanced against the claims of his own total welfare, against academic standards, and against the rights of teachers in the succeeding grades. Adjudicating such claims goes far beyond the province of the psychologist. Once it appears that this student, for one reason or another, should remain in his grade, the teacher and the counselor face a genuine problem in mental hygiene. Although there should be no attempt to minimize the real problems encountered, there should be some effort to structure the distress and to show its limits. At its most probable worst, this decision will merely add a year to the twelve or so that he can expect to spend in school. Hard as it is, it is less serious than the other evil of endless frustration in a program for which he is not ready (assuming that the teacher considers that a second year will help avoid that problem).

If the teacher himself has been primarily responsible for the unpleasant medicine, he should be prepared to absorb considerable hostility both from the student and from those close to him. If his own security will permit, perhaps he can allow the unfortunate student some overt expression of resentment. Extensive counseling on the part of the teacher might not be effective under these conditions, however, and it might be better if someone else took on the major responsibility for helping the student face his ordeal.

Failing a whole grade, fortunately, is a tragedy that a student seldom confronts. There are many minor risks experienced every day, however, some of these being in tasks of the student's own devising. In a situation such as this the teacher not only can help make the failure more bearable once it has occurred but he may also be able to so regulate things as to keep the experience of failure within reasonable limits. If the tasks are those assigned by the teacher, he can often be sure that they occur in a reasonable gradation. If the student himself is determining his own projects, he, too, can be urged to be realistic in the succession of goals he sets himself. Although accepting the risk of failure without undue disturbance, the student can be encouraged to scale down the magnitude of each successive try. At times, of course, he must also be encouraged to scale down any final goal in which he is likely to invest much of his ego. In taking on tasks designed to see how far he is able to go—to provide information about his powers—there is no need to worry about unrealistic tasks. The unrealism will be apparent from the trial and the failure will convey this information. In adopting more absolute goals, goals in which his ego is already heavily committed, however, it is important that a degree of realism should prevail.

The Problem of Unfair Handicap. Failure and frustration may be hard enough to absorb under the best of conditions. They are likely to be especially distressing to a youngster who is battling toward a goal that seems legitimate, but who is held back by such things as physical handicap, lack of early cultural or educational opportunity, racial or cultural discrimination, or perhaps, simple poverty.

Naturally the teacher can offer a sympathetic understanding of the unhappy bafflement. Under favorable circumstances, moreover, he may help structure the frustration. The handicap is very real, and its presence is one of the unpleasant facts of life. It has a varied impact, however, and it may interfere only slightly with some of the student's important goals. It would be a great help if the student could see where he is hurt and where he is not. It is better to see the evil in this structured form, and not as a vague, horrible menace by which he is completely undone in every enterprise that matters. Although he cannot be expected to examine the frustration impersonally, we might try to keep him from seeing a sinister, malicious conspiracy if none really exists.

SUMMARY

In meeting his responsibilities for the mental health of his pupils, the teacher could not eliminate all stress, nor would he wish to. In the interests of humanity, however, and to expedite the acquisition of skill in handling stress, the teacher will wish to keep tension within very definite bounds. He can do this by structuring the tension so as to show its limits in extent and in time and by letting the student see the menace in relation to his skill. The teacher can also encourage any permissible expression of troublesome drives, as well as the conscious admission of those drives. In doing this he may reveal student hostilities not only to each other but to the teacher himself. For many teachers, especially the insecure teachers, this will be a difficult problem. Teachers should remember, however, that most of this is merely hostility to adults in general.

Frustration of any one need is easier to take if more basic needs have been fulfilled. Teachers can help provide the powerful need for acceptance and affection. This can be done in many ways, but it is likely to be difficult in the case of pupils who need it the most. The teacher's own security is a factor in this as in so many areas. One of the chief contributions of the teacher, as a matter-of-fact, is to supply the support of adult security.

The reduction of stress is only temporary and is chiefly a means toward giving the pupil more skill in handling stress. In this area, as in the teaching of character, the teacher may encounter difficulties, but should make a resolute try. In some areas the emotional tasks can be arranged so as to promote a sequence of successes with the attendant reinforcement. In other areas the teacher must rely on a flexible use of reinforcement to provide an adequate supply of that ingredient. Guidance and shaping up can be used to help. This means that at times the teacher must be prepared to reinforce a very ordinary performance.

Extinction procedure might be used to eliminate a specific superficial maladjustment.

In many areas, direct practice in handling stress is out of the question and we must rely on transfer. As in the teaching of character, literature and drama may be useful. We may also attempt to get some transfer from direct instruction in the principles of mental health.

Anger and hostility are important sources of stress, and they are things the student must learn to manage. The teacher will encounter less anger if he can avoid long, moralistic admonitions and try to reduce frustration upon the appearance of danger signals. An objective indication of acceptance might help. As in other emotions, the expression of anger in a permissible manner may help. When an overt statement is not possible or not in order, vigorous games may provide some outlet.

When some menace is imminent, fear may often be kept within bounds by making sure that more primitive stress (pain, fatigue) is at a minimum. Forewarning and explanation of the menace may help to structure and limit it and may help the pupil erect psychological defenses. Whenever possible, the extent of the menace (intensity of the noise, height of the jump) should be conspicuously under the pupil's control.

Lack of acceptance can be a trial. Fortunately we can take some direct action here. We should be alert to accept the shy child and also to accept the more subdued advances of the turbulent showoff.

Failure, and failure anxiety, constitute a serious threat. We should try to structure the experience of failure and let the pupil see that this is the inevitable outcome for anyone who really tests himself.

The anxiety connected with examinations has been reduced by encouraging students to express their feelings about the examination questions. When a student has experienced actual failure, he can sometimes be led to see that the experience, however tragic, does not blight his whole life. This is more difficult when the student links his failure with some unfair handicap (social class, poverty, physical defect, or prejudice on the part of others), but even here something can be done to show that the ordeal has definite limits.

SUGGESTIONS FOR FURTHER READING

Textbooks on Mental Hygiene in the Schools

Bernard, H. W., *Mental Hygiene for Classroom Teachers.* New York: McGraw-Hill Book Company, Inc., 1961.

Bonney, M. E., *Mental Hygiene in Education.* Boston: Allyn and Bacon, Inc., 1960.

Kaplan, L., *Mental Health and Human Relations in Education.* New York: Harper & Row, Publishers, Inc., 1959.

Laycock, S. R., *Mental Hygiene in the School; A Handbook for the Classroom Teacher.* Vancouver, B. C.: Copp Clark, 1960.

Redl, F., and W. W. Wattenberg, *Mental Hygiene in Teaching,* 2d ed. New York: Harcourt, Brace & World, Inc., 1959.

Brief Treatments of General Personal Adjustment

Lazarus, R. S., *Personality and Adjustment.* Englewood Cliffs, N. J.: Prentice-Hall, 1963.

Nixon, R. E., *The Art of Growing: A Guide to Psychological Maturity.* New York: Random House, Inc., 1962.

Stevenson, G. S., and H. Milt, *Master Your Tensions and Enjoy Living Again*. Englewood Cliffs, N. J.: Prentice-Hall, 1960.

For More Advanced Treatment

Allinsmith, W., and G. W. Goethals, *The Role of Schools in Mental Health*. New York: Basic Books, Inc., 1962.

Cameron, N. A., *Personality Development and Psychopathology*. Boston: Houghton Mifflin Company, 1963.

Brief Discussion of Special Topics

Horowitz, M., Hostility and its management in the classroom groups, in W. W. Charters, Jr., and N. L. Gage, eds. *Readings in the Social Psychology of Education*. Boston: Allyn Bacon, Inc., 1963, pp. 196–212.

Maslow, A. H., A theory of human motivation, *Psychological Review*, 1943, 50, 370–396. Reprinted in Baller, pp. 255–277; Remmers, pp. 300–317.

Ojemann, R. H., *Personality Adjustment of Individual Children: What Research Says to the Teacher*, No. 5. Washington, D. C.: National Education Association, 1962.

Peck, R. F., and J. V. Mitchell, Jr., *Mental Health: What Research Says to the Teacher*, No. 24. Washington, D. C.: National Education Association, 1962.

Pamphlets and Materials Suitable for High School Students

Leuba, C. J., *Personality: Interpersonal Relations and Self-understanding*. Columbus, Ohio: Charles E. Merrill Books, Inc., 1962.

Terhune, W. B., *Emotional Problems and What You Can Do about Them: First Aid to Wiser Living*. New York: William Morrow & Company, Inc., 1961.

Young, C., *Blondie*. New York: National Association for Mental Health, 1950.

A comic-book approach suitable for junior and senior high school pupils.

Science Research Associates, Chicago, Ill. publish the following series:

Alexander, F., What are you afraid of?

Henry, W. F., Exploring your personality.

Jenkins, Gladys G., How to live with parents.

Kirkendall, L. A., Understanding sex.

Menninger, W. C., Understanding yourself.

———, Making and keeping friends.

Remmers, H. H., What are your problems?

Schacter, Helen, Getting along with others.

Seashore, R. H., How to solve your problems.

Ullmann, Frances, Getting along with brothers and sisters.

Weitzman, E., Growing up socially.

Wrenn, C. G., How to increase your self-confidence.

Films and Tapes

Sound Films, 16 mm, black and white, available from the TV-Radio Department, Stephens College, Columbia, Missouri:

You do need friends (Program No. 4).

So you want to fight (Program No. 6).

A dreamer, aren't we all? (Program No. 12).

Tape: It's human to get frightened (9 min.) available from the Audio Visual Center, Kent State University, Kent, Ohio.

Sources for Additional Materials

World Federation for Mental Health, 162 East 78th Street, New York 21, New York, or 19 Manchester Street, London W1, England. Catalogs of films (World mental health films: international catalog, 2d edition, 1960), and also pamphlets and leaflets.

National Association for Mental Health, Inc., 1790 Broadway, New York 19, New York. List of Mental Health Publications and Audio-Visual Aids, and also inexpensive leaflets and pamphlets.

National Institute of Mental Health, Bethesda 14, Maryland. Pamphlets (The Teacher and Mental Health), and brief treatments of specific topics.

In many states the state department of education will maintain a library of films and tapes. A number of universities and public libraries also maintain a large rental collection. New items are being added frequently.

EXERCISES AND QUESTIONS FOR DISCUSSION

1. Recall a recent stressful experience, such as a humiliation or disappointment. Try to structure it to show those aspects which really were serious and those which were not. At the time, could anyone else have helped you see this structure?

2. How far do you think you could cheerfully go in letting children express their primitive or worrisome feelings? How far do you think you should go? How far do you think parents or other adults would want you to go?

3. There has been much talk at times of the dangers of a facade (see Chapter 10). In the light of this, what do you think about a teacher trying to manifest more security than he actually feels?

4. When faced with immature or maladjusted behavior on the part of a student, one group of psychologists would say, "Find out what is causing the behavior and treat the cause." A second group would say,

"Work out a program of reinforcing him" (giving him pleasant attention when he behaves better, and of not reinforcing him when he is worse). Comment on the two positions, giving something of the theoretical background of each. Do you think there is something to be said for both sides?

5. List some plays, movies, or TV shows that might be useful for a lesson in adjusting to or managing different kinds of stress. In each case ask whether the play might speak for itself or whether students would need help to grasp the point.

6. Recall some feelings of intense anger. What kind of expression might have been feasible in these instances? What risks do you see in each of the possible avenues of expression?

7. According to the text, what basic principle would you violate if you used physical force to keep a child from retreating from a frightening but harmless object?

PART FOUR

▶ *In the Larger Context*

CHAPTER 15

▶ *Supplementing the Classroom Approaches*

If our teaching is to have any effect at all it must have that effect on an individual student. In this sense we always teach individual students rather than classes or groups. In this sense, also, any teaching that is actually accomplished is necessarily individualized teaching.

This important and sobering fact has received great stress in discussions of teaching. It has also lead, as we shall see, to questionable and unrealistic inferences. But, however unrealistic some of the recommendations, the impressive fact is still with us and calls for serious consideration.

The Range of Differences

To realize the great impact of this problem we need only consider the extensive diversity among the individual children in any group. Even in one single characteristic such as height, or performance on one examination, we will find few, if any, children in any group who have precisely the same score. Now when we try to find two children who can be matched on a complete profile, or a complete pattern of abilities, we will find that we have taken on a difficult task. And if we try to take into account other things such as interests, needs, and worries, we could never hope to find a really homogeneous group.

A Problem and an Opportunity. This tremendous diversity inevitably presents a serious problem and we must wonder how we can deal with it. To some extent, we will try to eliminate diversity. We will try to make sure, for instance, that all our pupils will give the same answer to 8 + 6, will spell "pleasant" by the same succession of letters, and will keep to the same side of the street when driving a car.

But it would be a great mistake to

think of this inevitable variation and diversity merely as a problem with which we have to contend. This diversity, on the contrary, is a valuable and challenging thing. It gives us an opportunity to help develop a number of individuals, each with his own unique potential and each valuable in his own way. In this sense our problem is not to escape a distressing evil, but to take advantage of an opportunity and to help each of these diverse children to reach his capabilities.

Approaches to the Problem. To help the teacher both to deal with the difficulties and to exploit the opportunities presented by differences in children, we could, of course, arrange for completely individualized instruction. In this approach each child is taught on his own and, in the process of teaching him, there is no need to worry about children who are different. Group activities are introduced at times for their desirable effect on this individual, but never merely to simplify the process of instruction.

Throughout history much instruction has been carried on in this way, and highly individualized methods are not infrequent today (Anderson, 1962). By and large, however, such programs are the exception, and most teachers will be expected to teach a whole class at one time. Under these circumstances, the school administration typically takes a hand and employs one or more devices to help deal with the problem of individual differences. Such devices, of course, are never intended to eliminate individual differences—nobody would want that—but are designed to reduce such differences to a range that can be managed by the typical teacher.

ADMINISTRATIVE DEVICES

In many of the administrative arrangements for handling individual differences there are important psychological implications. From some thirty-five different arrangements that have been proposed (Shane, 1962), we select those that have most significance for the psychologist in his study of education.

The graded school is itself one of the oldest of such devices. Prior to this practice, as seen in the one-room rural school, pupils of all ages assembled in the same room and were taught by the same teacher. Even here, of course, there was bound to be some informal grouping based on age, or on level of performance, or, perhaps, on the reader or textbook being used. As any one school increased in population, these age groups or "reader" groups were frequently assigned to separate rooms and separate teachers.

Special Schools or Programs

At one extreme, special schools have been established to take care of the extreme ranges of differences. In other arrangements we see separate programs set up within a school. Separate schools are frequently established for the exceptionally dull child, and occasionally for the exceptionally bright child. There are also many separate schools for children with various physical handicaps, especially for those handicaps which call for special medical care or physical therapy during the day. Other schools are provided for children who are emotionally disturbed or in need of special psychiatric treatment.

For some types of defect or deficiency such separate programs seem clearly necessary. Often the deficiency so dominates the situation that ordinary instructional procedures cannot be used. There has been more argument, however, about special schools or programs for the exceptionally able (De Haan and Havighurst, 1961). Such schools may seem undemocratic, and may threaten

► *Student Attitude toward Special Programs for the Gifted*

Of some 200 honor graduates from a large high school (Evander) in New York City, 77 were interviewed and another 74 answered a questionnaire. Those who did not go to college were not included. Of these 151 students, there were 41 boys and 110 girls. (There were more girls, 3 to 2, enrolled in the school.) One girl out of every 22 enrolled made this honor group, whereas only one boy out of 39 did so.

Of these 151 honor students, 51 had IQ's less than 120, another 50 fell between 120 and 134, and the remaining 50 were over 135.

In this high school all promising students were involuntarily assigned to an honors program. As it turned out, each of the 151 students had had some experience in such a program.

	IQ Level		
	Below		*Above*
Attitude toward Being in the Honor Program	*120*	*120–134*	*135*
Enjoyed being in the program	88%	98%	85%
Would have made some effort to get in	66	78	66
Honor class resulted in too much work	4	4	2
Honor class should have been more demanding	20	29	21
Nonhonor classes easy to point of boredom	68	79	70
Some honor classes boring because too easy	22	40	45
Honors program led to occasional conceit or snobbishness	14	8	19
Felt some resentment from other students	36	38	36

SOURCE: M. M. Klein, What honors students think, *High Points*, 1958 (March), 40, 5–32.

a loss both to the students who are sent to the special school and to those who are left. The success of such programs is difficult to judge. Students going through them give a favorable report. Many of them, indeed, feel that the program could have been even more demanding (Klein, 1958).

Teaching in many of these programs calls for teachers with special interests, abilities, and training. Teaching the severely retarded child calls for exceptional dedication. Teachers lacking such dedication, but arbitrarily assigned to these classes, often feel persecuted and resentful.

Homogeneous Grouping

Some form of ability grouping or streaming is the most familiar device for reducing the range of differences within a class (Cochran and others, 1961; Shane, 1962). At one time, children were grouped simply by intelligence test scores. More recently, however, the grouping has come to be based on previous achievement and on general performance in the classroom. Experiments attempting to discover the advantage or disadvantage of grouping have produced a conflicting and confusing pattern of results (Ekstrom, 1961; Pattinson, 1963).

Certainly we cannot say, with any confidence, that children learn any more or any less when grouped according to ability. There is some suggestion that ability grouping may bring less wear and tear on the teacher. But such a system naturally means that someone must be chosen to teach the slow learning group, and many teachers resent this assignment.

Whatever the advantage of ability grouping, we should never expect it to solve all our problems (Goldberg and Passow, 1962). For one thing, the correlation between children's performances on any two tasks is never perfect. If children were closely grouped for today's lesson, we could not be sure that they would be so closely grouped for tomorrow's lesson in the same subject. They would be even less closely grouped in a different subject, or in a lesson studied much later.

Tyler (1962b) gives an interesting illustration of what happens even when pupils are narrowly grouped, and when as many as three separate criteria are used for the grouping. To be selected for the upper group, the seventh-grade pupils in his example had to be above 120 IQ, had to be able to read paragraphs at the grade-nine level, and had to show grade-nine ability in arithmetic reasoning. Yet in such closely related things as reading isolated words or in arithmetic computation the group showed wide dispersion, ranging from grade-six to grade-eleven performance in word meaning, and from grade-seven to grade-eleven performance in computation.

► *Difficulties in Getting Groups that are Really Homogeneous*

Pupils in grade five were grouped according to over-all reading scores in the Iowa Silent Reading Test. The total range before grouping was from a grade-two level to grade-nine level. After grouping there were from 18 to 29 students in each class.

The table shows the range found in the over-all performance of each group. It also shows the range on various subtests. Notice that the groups were so arranged that there is very little spread (about two grades for the most part) on over-all reading. On any particular subtest, however, the range for each group is quite large, and there is much overlapping between groups.

	Over-all Reading		Range of Scores in Certain Subtests			
Groups	Mean	Range	Rate	Compre-hension	Word Meaning	Sentence Meaning
A (Best)	6.7	5.7–9.0	2.1–12.7	3.8–11.1	4.5–8.5	4.4–10.3
B	5.2	4.6–5.6	1.8–12.7	2.5–11.1	2.9–7.9	2.9–8.4
C	4.0	3.6–4.6	1.8–12.7	2.0–6.5	1.9–6.1	1.9–7.5
D	3.3	2.0–3.6	1.8–7.4	2.0–6.0	1.9–3.8	1.9–9.5

SOURCE: I. H. Balow, Does homogeneous grouping give homogeneous groups? *Elementary School Journal*, 1963, 63, 28–32.

► *Does It Pay to Get an Earlier Start in Reading?*

Of some 5000 pupils entering grade one in a California school system, a total of 49 were already able to read. Their skill in reading ranged from grade-one level to midway between grades four and five.

Twenty-five of these pupils were available for study toward the end of grade three. To get a control group, a search was made of all the nonreaders at entrance who had taken the Stanford Binet test. From these a group was selected who approximated the early readers in intelligence.

A further study also revealed that the early readers were regularly farther ahead in the specific ability of reading than in general mental development.

	Early Readers	Control Group
Number of Cases	25	201
Median IQ	114.8	110.2
Range in IQ	91–161	70–191
Reading score toward end of grade 3	5.0	4.3

SOURCE: Dolores Durkin, An earlier start in reading? *Elementary School Journal,* 1963, 63, 147–151.

From these results it is clear that pupils closely grouped on one kind of ability will be found to vary considerably even in a closely related ability. When we turn to traits that are less closely related, we can expect a much wider range of differences in our "homogeneous" group. With respect to interest, for instance, or motivation or social adaptability, our homogeneous group would vary almost as much as any ungrouped classroom. The moral is clear. Grouping may reduce the range of differences in one or two characteristics, but it never completely eliminates differences even in those characteristics and may have almost no effect on other important characteristics.

Acceleration and Selective Promotion

By permitting able pupils to move forward at a more rapid rate, we will automatically do something to produce classes of more uniform academic ability. Theoretically, such a policy would make sure that all the pupils who were ready for grade four would be placed in grade four no matter what their age.

Selective promotion, when used, should have a somewhat similar effect. If this were practiced it should mean that the only pupils going on to grade four would be those ready for that grade. In actual practice, however, these theoretical gains do not appear (Cook and Clymer, 1962). Selective promotion means, of course, that some pupils will *not* be promoted. This matter of non-promotion raises other questions (see Chapter 14), and these other issues may be much more important than the mere problem of reducing the range of differences.

Acceleration of bright children can

be accomplished by permitting bright children to enter school early (Reynolds, 1962), by the simple use of double promotions whereby a pupil moves directly from (say) grade two to grade four, or by providing a special program whereby the able students accomplish more work in the same time (Rush and Clark, 1963). For the most part, these programs have worked fairly well (Klausmeier, 1963; Shannon, 1957). The accelerated children tend to excel their intellectual equals who were not accelerated, and they show few, if any, undesirable effects.

From the teacher's point of view, acceleration presents some problems. A child in grade four who has skipped grade three may need coaching in some of the important details he has missed. He may also need support while he is struggling with things that others understand and he does not. It is often surprising, however, to see how quickly bright children tend to correct these situations and catch up without any prolonged lag. Acceleration also poses other problems. At times, acceleration makes sense only if there is an intelligent follow-up. There is little point, for instance, in having a child study French conversation at an early age if he is not going to have the chance to continue this study for a reasonable period of time.

Team Teaching

In addition to its hope of reducing the many conflicting roles that the teacher must play, team teaching may provide one means of dealing with individual differences. Different members of the team, as seems wise and convenient, often attend to special interests, special ranges of ability, or special handicaps. Since this method can be extremely flexible it would seem, on the surface, to have many advantages over a more fixed schedule in which one teacher assumes charge of a single group for an entire year.

The Nongraded School

In a sense, the nongraded school is an about-face with respect to the problem of treating individual differences. As mentioned earlier, the use of grades represents one of the earliest administrative efforts to reduce the range of differences within a class. But in doing this, the arrangement may have seemed to have promised too much. Teachers may have assumed that all serious diversity had been eliminated and that, this being so, the class could be taught as a homogeneous unit. Clearly that has proved not to be the case. Meanwhile, moreover, the conspicuous class boundaries have made for much trouble and distress, especially when pupils fail to hurdle the artificial barriers between classes (Goodlad, 1962).

Certainly grade labels give a misleading picture of the true state of affairs. They imply that a given child is performing at (say) grade-six level in all respects. Few children would match this fictitious picture. Most children would be performing well below grade six in some subjects, well above in others. A teacher of a special subject such as art, or music, could never assume that all pupils in a given grade were even roughly comparable in his specialty. To get reasonably homogeneous groups in such special subjects, the teacher may have to reach into several different grades. Science clubs or dramatic groups also frequently cut across classes in recruiting their members.

To get away from the dangerous illusion created by fixed grades, many people would set up an "ungraded" school, arranging for a variety of groups in any one classroom. In these, diversity would be expected and highlighted and would clearly call for some deliberate treatment by the teacher.

THE TREATMENT OF DIFFERENCES WITHIN THE CLASSROOM

After the administrator has done his best, the teacher is bound to encounter a wide range of differences within the classroom. At times he may wish this range were less. At times he may exult in the opportunity for the development of diversity. But, either way, he must deal with the diversity that he finds.

Understanding Each and Every Child?

Teachers have often been urged to attempt a fairly complete understanding of each child. We are reminded that any learning that is done must be done by each child, and done within the total pattern of his interests, concerns, and abilities. From this, several writers have concluded that the teacher must have a clear picture of these forces as they operate in each child. The teacher should know each child's abilities, previous academic performance, hobbies, interests, worries, and vocational aims. He should also know much about the pupil's family and its place in the community, and certainly should know about the family attitude toward the pupil and his concerns (Nunnery and Gilliam, 1962; Prescott, 1957).

The Magnitude of the Assignment. The recommendation that the teacher undertake a complete understanding of each child seems hopelessly unrealistic. The complete understanding of even one individual is exceedingly hard to

come by. It takes a year or more and several thousand dollars for a psychoanalyst to attain a reasonable understanding of one person. Few parents would profess anything like a complete understanding of their own child.

When we think of the number of children with whom a teacher must deal, we must be skeptical of attaining even a moderate understanding of each child. In junior or senior high school, the typical teacher meets 156 students per day (NEA, 1963). The typical elementary school teacher meets about 30.

The Necessity of Understanding Each Child? Not everyone, of course, insists that the teacher must hope to have a complete understanding of each pupil. Highet (1950), after exhorting us to an intimate understanding of such special students as the genius, the weakling, or the off-beat excentric, explicitly warns us against feeling responsible for knowing every single pupil that well.

The evidence on the topic, although somewhat conflicting, does not suggest that a more intimate knowledge of pupils typically leads to superior teaching. One early study (Ojemann and Wilkinson, 1939) did report some gains from having teachers learn more about their pupils. A later study (Hoyt, 1955), however, found no gains in achievement, though occasional improvement in the pupil's attitude toward the teacher. Bush (1958), after reviewing the literature, suggested that the advantage, even when present, is by no means pronounced.

Along with the studies directly attacking this problem there is some indirect evidence which must suggest the wisdom of keeping an open mind on this question. As we might expect, studies show that the smaller the class, the more the teacher is likely to know about each child (McKenna, 1957). Yet, in study

► *Should the Teacher Have Complete Knowledge of Each Pupil?*

From a group of 135 grade-nine students, two groups of 33 each were selected. The selection procedures resulted in the same average age, IQ, and previous attainment for the two groups.

The students in the experimental group were given a number of personality and adjustment tests. Parents of these students were also interviewed. After making a summary of the information about each student, the investigator discussed this with the teacher, and on several other occasions consulted with the teachers regarding the students in the experimental group. (The 33 students in each group were scattered through several classes and a number of teachers were involved.)

The control group was given some of the tests, but the parents of these children were not interviewed. The results of the tests were not made available to the teachers, and there was no consultation between teacher and investigator about the control children.

	Experimental Group	Control Group	Difference Significant?
Average academic achievement at end of the year	3.2	3.0	Yes
Number of test items indicating disturbance—beginning of year	92.3	70.4	
—end of year	61.0	74.8	Yes
Teacher's rating for poor adjustment in class—beginning of year	3.3	3.1	
—end of year	2.3	2.9	Yes

SOURCE: R. H. Ojemann and F. R. Wilkinson, The effect on pupil growth of an increase in teachers' understanding of pupil behavior. *Journal of Experimental Education*, 1939, 8, 143–147.

after study, pupils in large classes learn as much as comparable children in small classes (Fleming, 1959; Herrick, 1960: Spitzer, 1954). Apparently the increased understanding does not automatically lead to greater attainment.

Possible Misconceptions about the Problem. At this point we seem to have something of a paradox. Clearly teaching, if it is to be effective, must have its influence on each separate individual. Yet deliberate efforts to take account of the individual and to adjust to his needs and interests do not always pay off. Sometimes they may. But often they do not, and even when they do, the gain is very slight.

Perhaps there has been a gap in our

In a different experiment at the grade-eight level, in two schools, each of six teachers taught three classes. For one of these classes (Maximum Information Condition), the teacher was given a folder for each student. This provided test results, personal data, and an interpretation of the information for each student. For this class, the teacher was also urged to secure additional information about each pupil. In a weekly conference with the investigator the teacher was encouraged to discuss individual pupils in this class and to go over the data available for each pupil. For a different class (tests only), the teacher was given the test results for each student, but no additional data. At the weekly conference regarding this class, the teacher was encouraged to get help with regard to test results, but was urged not to get additional data. For the third section (name only), the teacher was given no information about the students and was urged not to seek such information. In the weekly conference he was urged again to maintain this condition.

This same general procedure held for each of the six teachers. It was so arranged, however, that any given class would be taught by one teacher (say the teacher of mathematics) under maximum information, by another teacher under the test-only condition, and by a third teacher under name-only condition. Boys and girls of different IQ levels were so assigned that both sexes and all levels were equally represented in each class and in each condition. Each teacher, it will be remembered, taught under all conditions.

At the end of *one term* the teachers were tested to see how much they knew about the pupils. The teachers actually did know more about the pupils they were supposed to have studied.

When the total results were considered, there was no significant difference in the gains made under the different conditions. When the results were separated for subjects, the name-only condition seemed superior for English. There were no significant differences for mathematics or social studies.

Pupils taught under maximum-information condition had a better attitude toward the teacher. This effect was significant in one of two schools, and suggested in the other.

SOURCE: K. B. Hoyt, A study of the effects of teacher knowledge of characteristics on pupil achievement and attitudes toward class work, *Journal of Educational Psychology*, 1955, 46, 302–310. Reprinted in Noll, pp. 255–263.

thinking. Having said, "Each child learns as an individual," are we bound to conclude that each child must be treated as an individual in our teaching? Consider an analogy from nutrition. Obviously, each child must make use of his food on an individual basis. But this does not mean that each child's food must be provided on an individual basis. The person providing the food does not need to have a clear knowledge of each individual idiosyncrasy and caprice. The purveyor of food could offer a blanket cafeteria menu, disregarding the peculiarities of his individual clients. Under such an arrangement each consumer could adjust to that common menu in his own particular way. Different people

► *The Advantage of Smaller Classes?*

Students taking introductory psychology were enrolled either in one of two *large* classes (97 in one, and 127 in the other), or in one of six *small* classes (averaging 28 students). All classes used the same textbook, films, quizzes, and final examinations. Instructors met regularly to coordinate the work. All students were given a test at the beginning of the course and a regular final examination. Other students took a similar course in ten small sections (average 28) but this course was not coordinated with those in the remainder of the experiment.

Type of Instruction	Total Number of Students	Gain from Pretest to Post-test	Supplementary Final Examination
Large sections	224	3.3	58.0
Small sections	163	2.9	59.4
Small sections (Special Group)	290	3.1	

None of the differences is significant

Most students expressed the opinion that small classes are best.

SOURCE: J. P. De Cecco, Class size and co-ordinated instruction, *British Journal of Educational Psychology*, 1964, **34**, 65–74.

may eat different things, and even those who eat the same things might utilize what they eat in different ways.

Turning to the intellectual realm, it seems obvious that a single book or lecture or work of art, prepared without any thought of the differences among its possible patrons, often has different but useful effects on hundreds of different people. In spite of their differences, various people have each been able to get something out of the single mass of stimuli offered. But they probably get different things. From the same poem, one student may derive consolation or peace, and another an urge to go out and achieve.

Within the classroom, many of the things that the teacher may do, although carried out with no thought of the many differences among his students, may still have a valuable but different effect on most of those students. In some cases, indeed, such blanket treatment would be almost as effective in linking up with individual needs and peculiarities as a more elaborate treatment neatly tailored to the special needs of each student. To the extent that this second possibility holds, we would expect little or no gain if the teacher, by heroic exertion, had been able to know and remember each child's peculiarities and had been successful in arranging a separate approach to fit each child.

The Case for a New Strategy

We may have oversold the need for a complete understanding of each child. Starting with an important but limited notion, we may have built it up into a fetish. As a result of this fetish, intensive individual counseling is now likely to be recommended for any child who comes up for any attention whatever, even if he should be doing about as well as could be expected (Robinson, 1953).

Making a break from this individual-analysis-for-everyone approach, Passow and Goldberg (1962) suggest that differences between pupils may not be our chief worry. It may be more important, they contend, to deal with the differences in the subjects of instruction. Perhaps the typical teacher, even if he takes no special pains in the matter, will do a better job in handling the range of differences among his students than in doing justice to the differences he finds between one school subject and another.

It is possible that we should consider a complete about-face in this matter. Although never for a moment ignoring either the fact of individual differences, or the absolute need of treating such differences, we could consider a change in the strategy for dealing with this acknowledged problem.

Clearly there are at least two rival strategies to choose from. In one approach we commit ourselves to the ideal of completely individualized instruction and try to use this approach as far as possible, giving up only when we have to, with associated feelings of failure and guilt. We use group procedures only as an unwelcome substitute, for which we must apologize to ourselves and others. In the opposite approach, we realistically and unashamedly rely on group approaches, frankly stressed, as far as they will go, but supplement these with individual treatment when necessary and when feasible.

Efficient Use of the Teacher's Time. We should take care of the problem of individual differences, and we should, at the same time, be reasonably efficient in the use of the teacher's time. To do this

we suggest a priority list of procedures. Whenever they will work, use general procedures directed to the entire group. A general announcement of an assembly period, for instance, could be every bit as effective as a separate announcement to each child. When one single treatment will not work for all, try blanket projects in which each child can find a separate spot suited to his peculiarities. Or use standard individual practice materials in which each pupil follows his own course with little direct instruction from the teacher. Along with these steps, divide the class into convenient subgroups. Next in efficient use of the teacher's time would come special tutoring or sustained individual instruction. If reasonable individual instruction fails to bring results, consider referring the case to a specialist.

In all this there is one point that should never be misunderstood. On no account can consideration of cost be allowed to dominate the basic job of teaching. When it is necessary to give sustained individual attention, try to forget about the cost. Be like the doctor who treats each patient leisurely and painstakingly in spite of the line-up in his waiting room. There should be no sense of urgency, no hint of all the things you could be doing for the larger group, during the time you are spending with this one child.

Obviously it may be difficult to adopt these different attitudes. Some teachers may not be able to give chief thought to costs at one moment and to ignore such claims a few minutes later. Here, as in other matters, there may be some argument for team teaching. One teacher could be typically concerned with the matter of results-per-unit-of-effort. Another might find himself automatically attending to pronounced individual needs, with no thought of the cost involved.

Individual Reactions to Group Procedures. At times a single statement by the teacher may have a different effect on each pupil and yet, different as they are, each of these effects may be appropriate to the particular student. An announcement of a change in the class schedule, for instance, might well have different significance for different pupils. For some it may come as a welcome relief. For others, it may create problems. Typically, however, we would feel perfectly justified in making this announcement, once and for all, and letting each student deal with it on his own as far as he could. We would realize, of course, that a few students could not make an adequate adjustment on their own and would need individual help. But this we would supply as the need arose. Certainly we would not abandon the group approach and insist on an individual announcement to each student.

In many situations the individual student, each in his own way, reacts usefully to group procedures. In our discussions of the role of practice, it will be remembered, we stressed the highly individual reactions that occur when a student is merely listening to a lecture, or reading a book. Seldom, if ever, does each student react to a single statement in precisely the same way. Each one will respond in different ways and with different results. One student, hearing the beginning of a sentence, will correctly anticipate what is coming and will promptly be reinforced. A second student will make an erroneous guess about what is to follow. For him, the succeeding remark, already embedded in the talk or text, will act as a guide to show him what he ought to say. Here we have a fixed

procedure, applied uniformly to all students. Yet this blanket procedure brings about different reactions and differential treatment. The treatment that it brings to each student, furthermore, is appropriate to his special academic requirements.

In the process of using rhetorical questions, as in a drill on arithmetic, the teacher may also find that a fixed and blanket procedure will have different, and yet appropriate, effects on different students (see Chapter 5). The instructor poses a question and pauses briefly. During the pause, different students react differently. The informed students say the answer to themselves. Some other students react with a silent error. Still others find their minds a blank. At this point, the instructor gives the correct answer. He gives the same answer to each student in the class. Yet this single undifferentiated statement has a variety of results. To the student who has already thought of the correct answer, it provides the all-important reinforcement. This same statement guides the erring students away from their wrong answer and leads them into the correct response. Finally, for that third group of students who could think of nothing, this remark on the part of the teacher supplies a response to fill the empty space.

In many other group processes each student will automatically and unconsciously react to mass stimulation in a way that is moderately suitable for him. In a group exercise in problem solving, for instance, the timid newcomer to the material may be reluctant to commit himself, even silently, and is naturally led to take a spectator role. And, as it happens, such a role has proved useful in his stage of learning. The student who has some grasp of the material will make silent commitments to himself and may

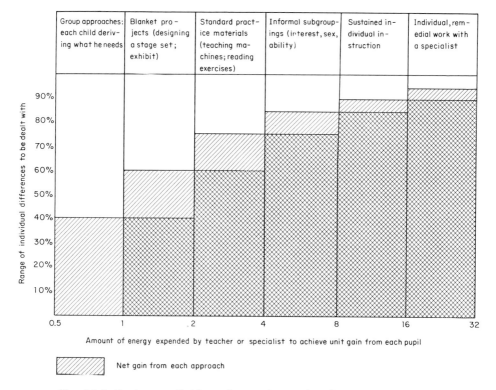

Fig. 15.1. Devices available to the teacher and to the specialist for taking care of individual differences. Devices are listed in order of per-pupil demand on the teacher's efforts. The least costly devices will take care of many of the individual differences.

vicariously share the reinforcement received by some more venturesome student who speaks out. The bolder student who announces his correct answer will be reinforced both for his correct solution and in his tendency to speak out when he thinks he has something to say (Fig. 15.1).

Experienced teachers have found simple ways to maximize these many individual reactions that occur in blanket group procedures. Ask your question first, for instance, before calling on a specific student. Each student is thus led to make a silent response. Having thus committed himself, each student will

share, in one way or another, the reinforcement pattern that is applied to the one who is asked to speak out.

To make sure that most individuals profit from these group exchanges, you should manipulate the tendency of some eager students to blurt out the answer as soon as it occurs to them. At one time you may suspect that most of the slower students are completely at a loss with respect to this question. In that case, permit the eager ones to explode. The answer thus emitted will provide guidance for the slower pupils who had no answer anyhow. Perhaps, on the other hand, you suspect, again on a very gen-

Fig. 15.2. Group projects permit different children to work in different ways.

eral basis, that the slower pupils are almost at the point of the answer. Then, wait for a moment before you yield to the forest of shaking hands, meanwhile gently shushing the more impatient ones into silence. In other circumstances, hesitations or pauses on your part may pointedly demand definite reactions from students. Sometimes by merely sweeping your eyes across the class you may remind some students that "You are in this too."

Use of Subgroups. Such general procedures cannot be expected to be effective for each and every student. At times, a sizable number will fail to respond in any useful manner. When you suspect that this might happen, it would seem wise to look for fairly large subgroups that, for a time at least, could be treated as a unit. In developing a certain project, for instance, you may have to use one approach to interest boys and quite a different approach to interest girls. But you might expect most (not all) of the boys to respond to a given kind of motivation. This may call for a sex grouping lasting perhaps only during the turn of a phrase, or perhaps, at the other extreme, demanding separate classrooms. At other times, an approach that works for those who have been in the class for some time might be lost on students recently transferred to the class.

Many other groupings will suggest themselves. For one purpose or another, we could establish groups, temporary or longer lasting, consisting of those who are at comparable stages of physical development, who have similar physical handicaps, who have or have not been to the museum, who are deficient in certain prerequisite experiences or interests or aptitudes. In general, it will often prove more efficient to arrange for groups that are moderately homogeneous, and to use blanket procedures for these

groups. Sometimes, of course, the trouble of arranging for such groups would more than offset any advantage that might be expected. It might be more efficient, for instance, to repeat an announcement individually to each latecomer than to go to the trouble of assembling all latecomers into one group.

In many cases the process of grouping can be very casual, at times consisting merely of a few parenthetical remarks addressed to one group. At other times the grouping process may call for elaborate testing or, perhaps, for the use of sociometry. At times the resulting group structure may dominate the whole situation. Under the latter circumstances, especially, team teaching might prove exceedingly valuable in giving each subgroup the special treatment that it requires.

Enrichment. Some subgroups can profit from additional work and many

teachers try to take care of this by arranging for differential assignments. This process of enrichment is not limited to large subgroups, of course, but could be geared to individual needs as well. Frequently, however, there will be several pupils, all of whom should profit from more work on the subject. These can be treated as a group.

As in other programs of subgrouping, these supplemental or differential assignments can often be accomplished in extremely casual fashion. "Anyone interested could . . ." "Those of you who have had chemistry should read . . ." "The people working on the 'gumshoe' project should . . ." At other times, such differentiation may involve separate reading lists or completely separate programs.

As we go farther and farther in the attempt to minister to individual needs, our concern for efficiency would suggest that, first of all, we try out more complex group approaches that are specifically designed to provide for a wide range of individual differences (Fig. 15.2). The older project method, at one time a complete way of life in American schools, is one such approach. The students in the class undertake some task that makes sense to them, such as planning a school fair or trying to learn the factors that affect housing restrictions. In the project selected are to be found separate tasks calling for a wide range of interests, aptitudes, and degrees of preparation. In a quite natural way, each student could fit into this general project, doing something that is consistent with his interests and abilities and that might be expected to help him develop in some useful way.

Prepared Individual Materials. Many prepared materials allow each child to proceed at his own rate and yet make only very general demands on the teacher's time. The newest of these are the teaching machines and programmed textbooks described in Chapter 5. In some tasks, these devices enable most children to save a good bit of time with no loss of comprehension. Along with these more recent provisions, there are many ancient arrangements whereby a student can use a set of standard practice tests in arithmetic, reading, or foreign languages. To judge from casual observation, even a child in grades three or four seems to get some enjoyment from going to the file, selecting the exercise that comes next on his schedule, taking the test, correcting his work, and recording the score.

Individualized Instruction. When intermediate devices fail to take care of varying students in our class, we have no choice but to turn to a brief or prolonged period of individual instruction. On the surface, as we have repeatedly stressed, this would seem the least efficient approach. While working with one child the teacher would have to neglect all the other students. But we must not make too much of this apparent neglect. Certainly we must not imply that the other pupils will be learning nothing unless the teacher is working with them. Much—often most—learning takes place when the student is working on his own. And in some subjects a very few minutes of individual instruction can profitably be followed by an extensive period of individual seat work, reading, or independent practice. It is difficult to say, of course, just how many minutes of independent practice should follow x minutes of instruction. Whenever this ratio is high, however, the teacher could devote a good deal of time to individual instruction with little or no loss of efficiency.

Under many circumstances, moreover, the teacher can do much individual work purely in passing. In the middle of some group activity, the teacher may frequently stop to help some student working at the chalkboard, or another student engaged in some construction work. From this interruption, the group that is momentarily deserted loses little and may even gain from the useful rest period provided.

In defending individualized instruction against the charge of complete inefficiency, we must also remember the effects of salutary eavesdropping or incidental learning. While a teacher is working with one student, others often listen. Such eavesdropping is especially tempting to the student who has a similar problem but who is reluctant to admit it. By listening to the teacher's discussion with Joe, it is possible for Jim, in circumstances devoid of threat, to wrestle silently with the same problem and, in this vicarious manner, to get some extremely valuable help.

Calling in the Specialist. At times the classroom teacher will have to do everything that is done in this process of individualizing instruction. After he has done what he can there may be no one else to whom he can turn. More and more, however, the services of a specialist are available for the child who does not adapt to the regular classroom approaches, or who does not respond to the individual attention the typical teacher is able to give. Such a specialist would seem exceedingly useful. Knowing that he was available for detailed individual help, the classroom teachers could be more confident in their orientation toward group approaches. From these group approaches they would expect normal reactions on the part of most students. They would be prepared, however, to deal with reasonable departure from normal behavior, and for the obdurate cases they would feel free to call in the person with special skill in diagnosing and treating the unusual case.

SUMMARY

Most educators are impressed by the fact that it is the individual pupil who learns. This conviction has led to many important innovations and to some excesses. In looking at the tremendous differences found within any one age group, we see both a problem and a challenge. At times we must reduce the diversity. At times we exploit it.

To help deal with individual differences, administrators have arranged for special schools, nongraded schools, special programs within schools, homogeneous grouping, team teaching, programs of selective promotion, and acceleration, including the early school admission of bright students. Judicious programs of acceleration have usually saved time for the bright student and have brought no discernible handicap. The dozens of studies on homogeneous grouping reveal no clear-cut advantage or disadvantage. It must be remembered, of course, that pupils closely grouped with reference to one subject are not necessarily grouped with reference to other subjects. Team teaching and the ungraded school are recent devices and have not been completely evaluated.

In dealing with the pupils he finds in any one classroom, the teacher has often been urged to attain a complete understanding of each child. This is considered an unrealistic assignment and one that is hard to justify on the basis of theory or empirical research. Different pupils can extract different but valuable features from one single lesson. As a realistic strategy, the teacher should rely primarily on group procedures that still permit different children to react at difference rates or in slightly different ways (see Chapter 5). Often a child will adopt an individual way of responding that is fairly useful for him. The able student will overtly commit himself; the less able may utilize the guidance in the overt comments of others. To supplement these blanket approaches, informal, transient subgroups might be useful: sex groups, interest groups, age groups, ability groups. The teacher can also make differential assignments, and provide general projects permitting varied activities. He can also make use of prepared materials for individual study (practice exercises, may have to resort to individual instruc- programmed devices). Finally the teacher tion, or summon the aid of a remedial specialist.

SUGGESTIONS FOR FURTHER READING

General Discussion

Fleming, C. M., Class size as a variable in the teaching situation, *Educational Research*, 1959, **1**, 35–48.

Fowler, W., Cognitive learning in infancy and early childhood, *Psychological Bulletin*, 1962, **59**, 116–152.

———, Teaching a two-year-old to read: an experiment in early childhood learning, *Genetic Psychology Monographs*, 1962, **66**, 181–283. This is an account of an ambitious project, containing an exceptionally complete bibliography (109 items). Some success is reported for the tremendous effort involved.

Kirk, S., and Bluma Weiner, *Behavioral Research on Exceptional Children*. Washington, D. C.: Council for Exceptional Children, National Education Association, 1963.

Reynolds, M. C., ed., *Early School Admission for Mentally Advanced Children*. Washington, D. C.: Council for Exceptional Children, National Education Association, 1962.

Tyler, F. T., ed., Individualizing instruction, *Yearbook National Society for the Study of Education*, 1962, **61**, Part I.

Sources for Additional Bibliography

Birch, J. W., and M. C. Reynolds, The gifted, *Review of Educational Research*, 1963, **33**, 83–98.

Cain, L. F., and S. Levine, The mentally retarded, *Review of Educational Research*, 1963, **33**, 62–82.

Evans, K. M., The teacher-pupil relationship, *Educational Research*, 1959, **2**, 3–8.

Leavitt, J. E., Teacher-pupil relationships, *Review of Educational Research*, 1959, **29**, 209–217.

EXERCISES AND QUESTIONS FOR DISCUSSION

1. Prepare an outline for a talk to parents on, "Accelerating the Bright Child: Advantages and Perils."

2. (a) Write down your own ideas on the value of any one of the administrative devices discussed. (b) Consult one of the summaries in "Suggestions for Further Reading" that reports the evidence on this topic. (c) Using the Education Index and other bibliographical sources, locate a recent investigation on this device. (d) Try to integrate or reconcile your own ideas, the ideas put forth in this chapter, and the evidence you can obtain.

3. Thinking chiefly of *the appeal to the teacher*, write a note on team teaching, homogeneous grouping, or the nongraded school.

4. Get together with some other student enrolled with you in a fairly large lecture class. Arrange for a series of inconspicuous signals. Four or five times during the lecture one of you should signal the other. At that time each of you should make a brief note of the thoughts running through your head. If possible, link these ideas with any statement made in the lecture. Show how these ideas were affected by subsequent points made in the lecture. Compare notes. Is there any resemblance in the two sets of responses? How do they differ? How do you regard the differences?

5. List four or five devices for maximizing valuable individual reactions to a single group presentation.

6. List some *specific* published materials for individual practice (for example, a certain series of graded reading exercises; a specific programmed textbook on algebra). Comment on the circumstances in which each could be used with profit.

CHAPTER 16

▶ *The Teacher and His Own Adjustment*

The first chapter of this book dealt with the experience of being a teacher and with the teacher's part in the general scheme of things. Inevitably in that discussion we had much to say about certain aspects of teaching that might turn out to be highly rewarding. We also raised some issues that threaten to be serious problems. Throughout the entire book, moreover, there are additional discussions of psychological tasks and problems that may bother the teacher.

So far we have considered these matters largely as objective facts. Now, however, we consider the teacher's adjustment to some of these facts, and his chance to take advantage of others. At this point we consider the teacher as a person in his own right. We do not ask, "How can we help you do a better job?" We ask instead, "How fares it with you? How can we help you to deal with your own frustrations and to lead a rich and rewarding life?" It would never do to forget that the teacher has an important life of his own and that his well-being is tremendously important in its own right.

A chapter such as this, of course, should never be regarded as treatment for people who are in serious trouble. It is not to be recommended to friends who have begun to lose contact with reality. Nor should you yourself depend on it if you suspect that you are losing your grip; or if your friends have advised you to see a doctor; or if in odd moments you feel that your suspicions of your colleagues are somewhat too intense, or extend to an excessive number of people; or if, again at odd moments, you wonder if your sudden tremendous burst of energy is quite normal. Under circumstances such as these, seek professional advice and do so without delay.

Extent of the Problem. It is difficult to know just how many teachers do experience serious trouble of a psychiatric nature. Semijournalistic accounts (Shipley, 1961) paint a shocking picture. In a more sober analysis of early surveys, Kaplan (1959) points out that teachers are less likely than the general public to be committed to some institution. Estimates over the past thirty years, however, suggest that as many as 10 percent of teachers might do well to consult a specialist and that another 15 percent are unusually nervous, although, as yet, in little danger of losing touch with the real world. Among the remaining three quarters of teachers there are many, of course, who have their share of problems, but these problems consist largely of the shynesses and sensitivities that plague many people but seldom threaten a major disruption.

SATISFACTIONS IN TEACHING: A BRIEF REVIEW

From the general description of teaching it is clear that different people will find different things that appeal to them. For some people it is the opportunity to indulge a taste for books and ideas and the experience of moderate autonomy. For others, especially, perhaps, for those devoting themselves to neglected groups, there is a sense of high adventure in helping the oncoming generation to develop its potentialities. Because of this feature, teaching has a powerful attraction to those who have a strong sense of social responsibility and who shrink from the exploitation of other people. Few people can doubt the social importance of some degree of education, and the teacher can feel sure that he is engaged in an important social enterprise. Whereas members of other occupations may have to resort to elaborate and ingenious arguments to show

the social value of their activities—improving the breed of horses, stabilizing the market, providing needed relaxation for the tired businessman—the teacher need go to no trouble to establish this point for his profession.

We must not, of course, give the impression that these values appeal to everyone. To many virtuous people, social usefulness has little immediate, primitive appeal. They are glad that other people are interested in such matters, but their own imagination is captivated by more surgent, glamorous activities in which any contribution to society is clearly a by-product, and in which an element of exploitation is part of the game.

Competition, although by no means absent, probably operates with less ferocity in teaching than in many professions. Typically there is less objective need to cut the other fellow down in order to enjoy moderate success. Certainly there is less of a clear tradition of competition in which the besting of a colleague is an essential part of the game, and the teacher, more than most people, can go about his work without worrying too much about what the other fellow is up to.

This lack of an open, clear-cut tradition of competition may, of course, be a two-edged sword. Often, it is true, it permits people so inclined to ignore problems of competition in many phases of their work. On the other hand, when an element of competition does appear, the lack of a clear-cut tradition may invite guilt-inspired, clandestine activities that are often less wholesome than the open, cutthroat activities of some other professions.

Again the familiar warning. This absence of violent competition would be the last thing that some people would want. For the vigorous, combatative "bonnie" fighters who have accomplished so much of this world's work, such seeming placidity would be boring in the extreme.

In satisfying the very human need for esteem, the teacher has a somewhat ambiguous position. As we point out later, he often feels lack of appreciation on the part of the general public. In many respects, however, the teacher has a fair opportunity to meet the need for the esteem of others. He is in a good position to secure the good opinion of his students. True, he usually cannot work directly toward this goal, but very often in the course of his daily work he may find incidental evidences of high regard from his students, or, less frequently, in the form of overt statements or formal testimonials.

In addition to the esteem of those directly in our charge, there is esteem (or lack of it) to be had from our colleagues and from our superiors. To the true craftsman, this is usually the esteem that counts most. The praise from our fellow-worker is a source of rich satisfaction. The criticism of our peers is something to be reckoned with. In this important matter, the teacher is probably on a par with people in most other professions. Gradually he is bound to achieve some sort of reputation (good or bad) in the eyes of his colleagues and superiors, and to some extent this will become evident to him.

This recital of the blessings of our craft would be incomplete without some mention of the more mundane advantages that we can expect. With respect to our working hours, we are in a somewhat ambiguous position. As we have seen, our work week is rather long. But to an unusual extent our schedule of hours is flexible and is under our own control. Although we must put in many hours, it is very often true that we can arrange those hours to suit ourselves. The long weekends and the summer vacations are not all free time, but they can be organized so as to give us fairly large blocks of free time if that is what we wish.

In the matter of physical health, the teacher is better off than most professions. In a typical year, 50 percent of teachers would have no absence due to illness, and less than 5 percent would have an illness of ten days or over. The average length of absence, including those who have no absence at all, is about a day and a half (NEA, 1957). There is, of course, much variation. Women have more absence than men, city teachers more than those in rural areas.

The financial plight of the teacher is well known. Clearly we are underpaid. There are some bright spots, however (NEA, 1963). Beginning salaries are not completely out of line with those in other professions. We do not face unpredictable layoffs, nor do we have much day-by-day uncertainty about our income. Pension systems of one kind or the other are now the rule (Stinnett and Haskew, 1962).

TEACHING AND ITS FRUSTRATIONS

Like any other worthwhile undertaking, teaching is not without its irritations and its headaches. This unlovely fact is to be expected and is taken for granted by all mature people. Any realistic view of a profession must include these obstacles and frustrations as well as the positive satisfactions to be gained.

It is clear that a disproportionately large number of teachers leave the profession each year, perhaps as many as 10 percent (Stinnett and Haskew, 1962). There is room for argument as to whether this is a good thing or a bad thing for the profession. It does suggest, however, that many people find some other activity more acceptable. Among those remaining in the profession, moreover, some 15 percent would not go into it again and some 12 percent are doubtful about the wisdom of their choice (Kaplan, 1959).

Teacher morale seems to be especially low for the ambitious, outgoing male who has a good opinion of himself and who is definitely trying to move from a very ordinary family background to better things (Suehr, 1962). Morale appears to be higher for women. Women have a greater sense of commitment to the profession, whereas more men regard teaching as a transitory matter or as a stepping-stone (Zimiles, 1962). On the average, the men who do leave the profession after a short period of service are somewhat more intelligent (Thorndike and Hagen, 1961b) and do tend to better themselves financially in their new job.

Dealing with Frustrations

Before considering specific vexations that trouble the teacher, let us review the more general ways of dealing with worries and stresses. Suppose, for instance, we are worried about the "low prestige" of the teaching profession. We feel that the public does not place us on a par with other professions, and this fact acts as a gnawing frustration to our very natural need for esteem. How can we deal with frustrations such as these?

Face the Fact of Frustration. First of all, if this real need is not adequately met, we must be willing to face the fact. We may be tempted to deny that we have any need for prestige. We may also be tempted to talk ourselves into be-

lieving that the prestige of the profession is much higher than it is. Both these steps should be avoided. We must face the fact of our need, if it is really there. We must also face the fact that the need is not being met, if that is the case. If objective evidence points to our lowly prestige (and, remember, this is an "if" statement), then we must accept the evidence. We should not try to gloss over it or try to search for pathetic exceptions which will blind us to the general picture.

Consider Remedial Action. Having faced the fact of our unsatisfied need for more public esteem, our next step is to decide if there is some reasonable means of remedying the situation. If we think that there is something that can be done about it and the effort is worthwhile, the logical thing to do is to take action. We should realize, by the way, that there is little objective evidence to guide us in this decision. It is highly unlikely, for instance, that we can command prestige merely by clamoring for it or by complaining that people do not "do right by us." There may be indirect methods of attaining this goal, however, and at present different teachers will reach different conclusions as to whether or not an increased measure of prestige is attainable.

Place the Frustration in Perspective. For some frustrations, remedial action may be impossible or impractical. Often, moreover, a good deal of frustration may remain after we have done all that we can to remedy the situation. What then? Then we must accept the facts and learn to live with them if we cannot change them. If we believe, for instance, that teaching is fated to receive less than its share of prestige, then we must try to accept the situation as one of the many unpleasant facts of life, such as disease,

▶ *Psychotherapy for Teachers?*

As the outgrowth of another project, the investigators located 200 teachers who had received at least two years of psychotherapy. Over 100 of these were interviewed and some 96 others filled in an inventory.

For most of the teachers, the decision to undergo therapy was quite a struggle. The final decision was motivated by intense personal problems or by a desire to live more zestfully. Many were helped in their decision by support from friends or relatives.

Benefits attributed to the therapy:

  Deeper insight into own anger (90 percent of group)

  First realization that own anger was a problem (66 percent)

  Deeper insight into nature of anxiety (90 percent)

  Less disturbance over the problem of handling anxiety (90 percent)

  Ability to engage in competition with better grace (many of the group)

  Less need of approval or adulation from others (many of group)

  Less distress when confronted with personal problems of students:

    Can offer help with assurance when that seems wise (90 percent) or can be comfortable in refusing to "treat" the problem when it seems to be one for the specialist (92 percent)

Considerable change in women's attitude toward their femininity. (Less change in men's attitude toward their masculinity.)

More candid in reporting sex problems

Concern about sex shifted from physical to emotional aspects

A control group, not experiencing therapy, reported similar types of improvement over the same period of time, but not to the same extent.

Supplementary Note: In this same article the editors of the *Phi Delta Kappan* report a survey of opinion from 68 teachers in one California high school. Some 90 percent of these teachers believed that unconscious factors play a big part in life. About 45 percent thought it would be a good idea if many teachers were psychoanalyzed, and over two thirds would themselves be willing to undertake psychoanalysis if they could spare the time and money.

SOURCE: A. T. Jersild, What teachers say about psychotherapy, *Phi Delta Kappan*, 1963, 44, 313–317.

pain, ingratitude, and death. It is there; we must live with it, and moreover, we must try to be happy in spite of it.

Seek Help. Many people (Laycock, 1960) recommend group discussions with those who share the frustrations. The usefulness of such discussions comes not only from the fact that misery likes company but also from the fact that various presentations cannot help but broaden the picture. From the descriptions other people offer, moreover, we may get a better picture of any trouble that seems to have a unique or suspicious impact on ourselves. Finally, there is some advantage in sheer ventilation. For people under stress, one of the simplest forms of relief is the act of talking about the stress in a permissive setting.

When any single frustration, or the

whole cluster of frustrations, looms up so frighteningly as to threaten our general well-being, there may be some gain from reading a shrewd and practical discussion of the problem of dealing with stress (Stevenson and Milt, 1959). Perhaps even a review of a chapter on mental health may help to regain perspective in this matter. But if the threat continues, or seems to grow, we should certainly seek professional help. Indeed, many teachers report benefits from psychotherapy even when they were not faced with some serious crisis (Jersild and others, 1962).

Perhaps because of the concern over the number of teachers leaving the profession, there has been much study of teachers' frustrations and worries (Havighurst and Neugarten, 1962; Rudd and Wiseman, 1962). The total list of dissatisfactions is extremely long (Blocker and Richardson, 1963). No doubt any other group of people would also produce an impressive array of troubles if frequently and solicitously urged to reveal their grievances.

The intelligent student will not be disturbed, of course, by the fact that more space is devoted to frustrations than to satisfactions. The prospective wayfarer needs only slight instruction to permit him to enjoy the satisfactions of his trip. With a minimum of briefing and sensitization, these rewards will be appreciated as soon as they are encountered. The obstacles to be faced, however, constitute a different story. Very often much instruction is necessary if these are to be dealt with adequately.

Uncertainty about Basic Functions. As we have seen, there are a great many different roles that teachers might be expected to fill. It is not surprising, therefore, to find that many teachers are confused about the basic work they are supposed to be carrying on (Allinsmith and Goethals, 1962). Sometimes the teachers really do not have any convictions. At other times they have a definite idea of what they should be doing, but see the general public, and especially the formal educational system, as having conflicting views. They think they should be eagerly pursuing one goal, but they suspect that others, especially their superiors, really want them to do something else.

In the minds of many of the teachers, a great deal of attention should be given to direct work with pupils, to satisfying relations with other teachers and with supervisors, and to a reasonable basis for professional advancement and recognition. They see their superiors, on the other hand, as giving a low priority to these matters. They feel that the administration attaches more importance to public relations, or relations with parents (the area of least importance to the teachers), than to the teacher's relations with pupils. Even when the administrators seem to pay attention to the "important" areas, the teachers see them still in opposition to the teacher's wishes. Teachers, for instance, would stress their own role of character models, and their responsibility for developing ability to think, love of learning, and the absorption of cultural values. They see the administrators, on the other hand, as largely concerned with preparing students for college and with the problem of keeping order in the classroom.

In this sense of conflict with the powers that be, the teachers may be largely mistaken. Those in charge of the system may not have the views attributed to them. Such a misapprehension, of course, does not in itself do away with the distress. If you really believe that your house is burning down, you are disturbed, no matter how ill-founded that belief. The possibility of misapprehension, however, does suggest a means of dealing with the frustration. If you should be disturbed by this sense of being at odds with important other people, the first thing to do is to find out exactly how much disagreement does exist. Very often there is much less than you may assume. Even when a systematic look does reveal substantial disagreement, you are in a much better position to deal with the problem, emotionally as well as practically, if you get a clear picture of the precise nature of such disagreement. Some aspects may call for overt remedial action or an attempt to convert people to your views. Other aspects may call for resigned acceptance or compromise. But these matters can be decided only when the extent of the actual disagreement is clearly seen.

Public Attitude toward the Profession. Many teachers are worried about the public view of the profession. In the minds of some people, as a matter of fact, we barely qualify as a profession (Havighurst and Neugarten, 1962; Wolpert, 1961). It is true that no one can say for sure just what makes a profession (Becker, 1962). But whatever the criteria may be, there is some feeling that teaching is lacking in some of them. It is held, for instance, that teaching includes too many diverse activities to be considered a single profession and that its members have too little to say as to who may enter the craft (Anderson, 1962; Lieberman, 1956).

Lack of Prestige. Whatever the fate of our aspirations to the status of a profession, many teachers feel some distress over the lowly prestige of teaching. Younger men leaving the profession give lack of prestige as one of the reasons (Thorndike and Hagen, 1961b). Compared to nurses, social workers, and psychologists, teachers are more given to worrying about matters of prestige (Charters, 1963, p. 748). Teachers also aspire to a higher status than do the other groups. To a greater extent than these other groups, they tend to underrate their true standing in the eyes of laymen.

Although the laymen may hold our profession in higher regard than teachers think they do, still the prestige accorded is by no means exalted. In nation after nation, teaching regularly falls below the prestige of a chartered accountant or army officer, and just above that of farm owner and operator. The teacher comes off somewhat better when people are asked to estimate his social status as a person, instead of the status of his work (Groff, 1962). Even here, however, he is below other professions (Warner and others, 1960).

Although our work is often accorded little prestige, especially, perhaps, in the eyes of the young (Allinsmith and Goethals, 1962), it is regularly considered to have great social importance. There is, of course, nothing paradoxical in this discrepancy. Of all the factors that contribute to occupational prestige in the minds of the young, social usefulness or moral worth come rather far down the list. An occupation is most likely to have prestige when it is regarded as being interesting and challenging, when it seems to demand rare abilities and originality, and when it is considered to have much influence in the world of affairs (Garbin and Gates, 1961). Clearly, teaching has no striking claim to these important correlates of prestige. When it comes to glamor, the decent Telemachus, conscientiously dedicated to common duties, cannot contend with the more surgent Ulysses in search of tasks not unbecoming men who strove with gods.

► *It's Nice To Have Telemachus*

How dull it is to pause, to make an end,
To rust unburnish'd, not to shine in use!
As tho' to breathe were life. Life piled on life
Were all too little, and of one to me
Little remains: But every hour is saved
From that eternal silence, something more,
A bringer of new things; and vile it were
For some three suns to store and hoard myself,
And this grey spirit yearning in desire
To follow knowledge, like a sinking star,
Beyond the utmost bound of human thought.
    This is my son, mine own Telemachus
To whom I leave the sceptre and the isle—
Well-loved of me, discerning to fulfil
This labour, by slow prudence to make mild
A rugged people, and thro' soft degrees
Subdue them to the useful and the good.
Most blameless is he, centred in the sphere
Of common duties, decent not to fail
In offices of tenderness, and pay
Meet adoration to my household gods,
When I am gone. He works his work, I mine.
   There lies the port: the vessel puffs her sail:
There gloom the dark broad seas. My mariners,
Souls that have toil'd and wrought, and thought with me—
That ever with a frolic welcome took
The thunder and the sunshine, and opposed
Free hearts, free foreheads—you and I are old;
Old age hath yet his honour and his toil;
Death closes all: but something ere the end,
Some work of noble note, may yet be done,
Not unbecoming men that strove with Gods.

SOURCE: "Ulysses" by Alfred, Lord Tennyson.

The Teacher Stereotype. Along with its lack of prestige, one frequently encounters an unflattering stereotype of the teacher (Charters, 1963; Furness, 1962). Mothers, in guessing at the need-structure of teachers, portray us as domineering, ultraconventional, and self-centered (Saltz, 1960). It may be that this stereotype is not as prevalent as it is thought to be (Belok and Dowling, 1961; O'Dowd and Beardslee, 1961). But if teachers believe it to be present, that belief could be disturbing.

In adjusting to this problem of the stereotype, again we might consider trying to get the facts. Is the stereotype true? If so, we might consider one strategy in dealing with the problem. If the stereotype is false, we might consider a different plan of attack. Unfortunately, it seems impossible to determine, at present, whether or not there is any truth in the stereotype. In spite of an impressive array of research (Getzels and Jackson, 1963) it is almost impossible to make any definite statements of *the* teacher's personality.

In dealing with both the lack of prestige and the prevalence of the stereotype, we should ask ourselves whether or not it is important that everyone should regard our profession as we do. In almost any other activity, the really dedicated practitioner must accept the fact that many other people regard some of his activities as boring, disgusting, if not actually insane. The novelist using his personal relations as grist for his story, the physiologist inducing diseases in experimental animals, the archeologist laboriously reassembling the sections of broken pottery, the mountain climber, and the astronaut—each of these must realize that many people will say, "Not for me." But must this realization of the indifference or aversion of others necessarily reduce our own dedication to our job or our enjoyment of it? The real devotee can accept the bewilderment or indulgent amusement of others merely as one of the inevitable differences in human tastes. Unless he is a little shaky about his own actual enjoyment of his craft, he should not need to feel that everyone thinks as highly of it as he does.

Social Treatment of the Teacher. Not only may teachers be disturbed by the public idea of what the teacher actually is like but they may also resent the general idea of what he should be like or of what is fit and proper for him as a teacher. Many teachers believe that

we are denied the full range of human feelings. They think it would seem inexcusable for us to feel anger or hostility toward the occasional monsters that get into our classrooms (Jersild, 1955). It would also be considered wrong to entertain, or certainly to express, any feeling of derogation or fleeting distaste for any of our charges. And much of the sardonic humor by which the medical intern is able to relieve his frustrations would seldom be permitted to us (Solomon, 1960).

If we are denied the earthy emotions of resentment and annoyance, we may be even more strenuously debarred from many of the frivolities and indulgences of ordinary social life. Certainly, at one time, our students would have us lead a staid and virtuous life. Even marriage during the school term would be improper in the minds of one third of our students. Another third are against smoking and over half would not have us drink. Regular church attendance is taken for granted (Cobb, 1952). Young people can be exceedingly stern, of course, in the conduct they demand from their elders, and many of us will understand this list of requirements but feel somewhat amused. Adult demands must be taken more seriously, however, and at one time these also imposed some restrictions on the teacher's social life (Kaplan, 1948). More recent evidence suggests that these may be lessening (Charters, 1963). Dating of students is still frowned on, but otherwise such associations are not curtailed. Smoking (in private) and dancing are less likely to be taboo. Church attendance is still expected for female teachers but not for males.

In these matters there is some suggestion that school board members and citizens in general make their decisions not on what they themselves think, but on what they think other people will think. Each person disowns such attitudes for himself but attributes them to the general public. If the truth of this matter could be brought out, it might make for more liberal policy.

Along with possible restrictions on social activities there is some evidence of social neglect (Havighurst and Neugarten, 1962). Many teachers feel that they play little part in the social life of the community and are considered to be people of no social importance (Metfessel and Shea, 1961; Remmlein and others, 1958). Whereas teachers would like more contact with adults, on an adult-adult basis, they are considered chiefly as teachers. They are introduced as, "Johnny's teacher, Mrs. Jones," and not as, "My friend, Mrs. Jones."

In many communities the teacher is expected to be useful, but not especially conspicuous (Grambs, 1957). He helps out rather than participates. This situation varies from community to community, of course, and a steady improvement may be in progress. In one recent study, sampling the state of Pennsylvania, there was evidence of considerable community participation and status on the part of

---

▶ The Teacher in Community Life

The teachers in this study consist of a sample drawn from twenty-two counties (sixty-six communities) in Pennsylvania. The sample was selected to reflect the general distribution of teachers (elementary, secondary, vocational, and so on). During an interview each teacher discussed the part he played in various organizations and was assigned a participation score. His participation score for *one* organization could range from 1 to 15. Total participation scores for one teacher ranged from less than 10 to more than 100.

Average Participation Scores of Various Groups

Top Business and Professional Men	65
Persons Identified as Civic Leaders	51
TEACHERS	50
"Natural" Leaders in Urban Groups	46
Semiprofessional, Managerial Workers	29
Clerical Workers	16
Elementary School Teachers	48
Vocational Teachers	55
Guidance Counselors	63
Teachers 20–25 Years of Age	38
Teachers over 30	51
Teachers Earning Less Than $4000	48
Teachers Earning over $6000	55

SOURCE: R. C. Buck, The extent of social participation among public school teachers, *Journal of Educational Sociology*, (April),[a] 1960, **33**, 311–319.

[a] In this volume there is a page 311 in both the March and April numbers.

teachers (Buck, 1960). The community participation score for teachers was almost as high as that for those classified as civic leaders.

In these matters, again, our sense of frustration depends on the situation as we perceive it and not upon the actual situation. Dependable data about the objective situation, however, should help us markedly in dealing with the frustration.

Obstacles to Basic Work. One very natural frustration on the part of many teachers is the feeling that they simply cannot get their work done. For this serious problem they see several reasons. Some teachers blame lack of interest on the part of students (McLaughlin and Shea, 1960; Solomon, 1960; Thorndike and Hagen, 1961b). Other teachers find the chief obstacle in the large classes, the amount of time and energy they must give to problems of discipline, the endless clerical tasks, and frequent interruptions to their classroom work. Still others feel that the chief difficulty lies in having to teach subjects for which they are really not prepared. A teacher who has majored in English, for instance, could find himself assigned to teach history or algebra.

Limited Knowledge of Results. Along with these factors which may reduce actual accomplishment, we face serious difficulties in becoming aware of what we have accomplished. As teachers, we are handicapped by the fact that the results of our activities are seldom immediate and definite (Peterson and others, 1948; Snow, 1963). Compare our work, for instance, to that of the machinist at the lathe. The results of his efforts are immediate and almost dramatic. As he manipulates the lathe, the wood or metal changes almost immediately. It changes, too, in a way that could not be mistaken. There is satisfaction from such immediate and definite results that must not be ignored.

The satisfaction available to the machinist is also to be had by most people who work with their hands. The carpenter, the dressmaker, and the typist can all see the results of their labor after only a moderate delay and in a fashion which needs little interpretation. Even when the results are not immediate, as in the case of the gardener, they are usually definite in character.

Some of the most important results of the teacher's work are neither immediate nor definite. Certainly those results do not make their presence felt automatically. We must search for them. We must give examinations or tests. We must send out follow-up questionnaires. Ordinarily, we must take some deliberate and perhaps elaborate step to see if we have achieved any results. Often, too, we wait for a considerable period of time. It is only at the end of the unit, of the term, or the year, or at the end of many years, that we know what we have accomplished.

This feeling of working in the dark deprives the teacher of many sources of satisfaction and, to that extent, leaves the creative needs partially unfulfilled. Fortunately this frustration is one that invites direct action. Much has already been said about the methods of testing and of obtaining dramatic records of academic growth. In so far as these devices can be adopted and automatically incorporated into regular practice, this need for self-expression will be partially met.

Irritating Working Conditions. The many extrinsic demands on the teacher's time can reduce his effectiveness and sense of accomplishment. They can also be irritating in their own right, even if they did not cut into the work that we consider important. Most lists of teachers' grievances include excessive clerical work, cafeteria duty, playground supervision, and responsibilities for many activities not clearly related to instruction. Many teachers believe that there are far too many staff meetings and that these are too long and too inconsequential.

A complete list of irritations, of course, would go rather far and would include frustrations brought on by poor equipment, inadequate janitor service, and difficulties in finding a parking place. Not surprisingly, several teachers feel that their life would be less stressful if they had a reasonable lounge room in which they could relax for a few moments, a few moments in which they could forget about students and their problems (Metfessel and Shea, 1961).

Dealing with Disturbing Working Conditions. Although many of these detailed chores are mildly irritating under any circumstances, they would be less serious if they were undertaken as a result of our own decision, or if they were forced upon us by objective practicalities. As the only adult in a one-room school, for instance, you would not welcome the problems that arose from playground disputes, minor injuries, arranging for supplies, and supplementing or supplying the janitorial services, but you would not feel unduly abused. In the one-room school, however, it is the practical circumstance that points the finger at you, whereas in the large school system, it is some administrator who does so. The decision, of course, may be quite objective. But for all you can see it could result from sheer administrative caprice. In picking you rather than someone else, moreover, he may seem to say that your time or your interests are not very important. This seeming slight can be more

irritating than the actual duties to be performed.

In dealing with these problems we may face a fairly narrow line between the demand for legitimate rights on the one hand, and a nagging never-satisfied attitude, on the other. A craftsman has the right to demand reasonable conditions for his work and reasonable tools with which to do it. On the other hand, the complaint about tools is the typical alibi of the poor workman. And, as in the fable, the true soldier can go on to conquer with the discarded sword of the chronic complainer.

The zealous worker, really committed to his task, will put up with necessary shortages and make do with his very inadequate tools. But don't permit yourself to be treated as an inconsequential person whose legitimate needs can be disregarded. You have every right to press your demands, and it is better to make a nuisance of yourself than to go around feeling persecuted or unjustly treated.

Problems of Professional Advancement. In any serious profession it is important that there be opportunities for professional growth and advancement. Many teachers feel dissatisfied with the arrangements open to them. Some of those queried have held that rewards should be based on duties and responsibilities and on demonstrated initiative, or even on the performance of students (Allinsmith and Goethals, 1962). They believe the present practice, on the contrary, puts far too much emphasis on degrees and on sheer length of service. In the minds of these teachers, administrators also seemed to neglect some important sources of reward. Increased autonomy, for instance, might be an effective reward for many teachers who had shown themselves capable. Some

► *The Woes of Teaching in England and in California*

The information for the California teachers was obtained from 27 schools in 5 counties. An investigator spoke to the teachers at a regular faculty meeting and asked them to fill out a questionnaire. A total of 793 teachers took part.

The information regarding the teachers in England is based on 590 reports. In this group 92 percent reported that, in spite of the listed annoyances, they found teaching to be a most satisfactory profession. This was especially true for teachers of quite young children and for teachers of adolescents. In general, as we move from younger to older pupils, we find less satisfaction for women, more for men.

Specific Dissatisfactions: (Rank of 1 means that this dissatisfaction was most serious for the group in question)	Teachers in California		Teachers in England	
	Secondary	Elementary	Men	Women
Low Salary	1	5	1	13
Inadequate Physical Equipment		4	3	2
Working Load: Large Classes	4	7	8	1
Heavy Teaching Load			4	3
Not Enough Time			9.5	5
Excessive Clerical Work	3	1		
Supervision of Cafeteria	8	2		
Too Many After-school Meetings	7	3		
Problems with Administrators				
Rigid School Organization			9.5	8
Poor Staff Relations	6	5	2	6
Frequent Class Interruptions		8		
Problems with Students				
Indifference to Learning	2	9	12	11
Discipline	5	6	16	18
Feeling of Professional Inadequacy			7	6
Lack of Training		10	5	4
Low Prestige of Teaching			6	15

SOURCE: California data from J. W. McLaughlin and J. T. Shea, California teachers' job dissatisfaction, *California Journal of Educational Research*, 1960, 11, 216–224. English data from W. G. A. Rudd and S. Wiseman, Sources of dissatisfaction among a group of teachers, *British Journal of Educational Psychology*, 1962, 32, 275–291.

form of public recognition would go a long way to boost morale. And, of course, the matter of salary should not be neglected, although actual salary (Mathis, 1959; Wynn and DeRemer, 1961) and salary policy, or the use of some sort of merit system, do not seem to play the major role in problems of morale.

Relations with Administrators. In many of the detailed annoyances already discussed, we can see a suggestion of almost chronic resentment against administrators or supervisors. Certainly many teachers are overtly critical of the administration in general (Allinsmith and Goethals, 1962). At one extreme they feel that teachers have too little to say in establishing policy, and at the other, they feel that the administration should come out with more clear-cut decisions. Although this seems like a conflicting demand, it is not necessarily completely paradoxical. Presumably the administration could permit teachers to help formulate a policy and could also make sure that the policy was translated into unmistakable rules whenever necessary.

In their dealings with parents, teachers often feel a lack of administrative support. The same complaint is often made with respect to discipline. Here the teachers suspect that principals and other superiors often let them down. They also feel that some supervisors would like to ignore disciplinary problems, and for this or for other reasons, refuse to develop any definite policy for dealing with disciplinary matters. The teacher is left to work out his own salvation, always facing the risk of subsequent disapproval.

The Clash between Ideals and Practice. As in the case of discipline, so in other matters, administrators and supervisors have been accused of being unrealistic, if not downright hypocritical, in urging ridiculous goals and standards on teachers. It is true, of course, that we do not always feel resentful in being reminded of ideals that are difficult to attain. Most people can profit from the Sabbath-day inspiration to higher things and then go back, without undue disturbance, to the less idealistic workaday world for the remainder of the week.

An extreme discrepancy between ideals and practice may readily cause resentment or frustrations under any circumstances. Even at the best, the hardworking teacher, fresh from some of the grim realities of the classroom, may feel annoyance at the easy picture painted by the supervisor who has no direct classroom responsibilities. The same teacher may also resent the glib advice of the textbook writer. The teacher will be especially resentful if he suspects his self-appointed advisor is not only unrealistic, but actually insincere.

This urge toward irresponsible, idealistic language has often appeared in the descriptions of the successful teacher. The acceptable teacher has been presented as a creature who would seem almost too good for this world. In recent years there have been suggestions that we tone down these idealistic descriptions and replace them with lists of traits that might conceivably be found in ordinary human beings (Jackson, 1962, Stephens, 1960a).

MAKING THE MOST OF TEACHING

The frustrations set forth at some length represent possible irritations that the teacher, or prospective teacher, must face. Each of these frustrations has seemed serious enough to lead some member of the profession to write it down or check it off from some list. These difficulties should be faced, and, as we have pointed out, studied to see if they are amenable to correction, or to see what kind of an adjustment is demanded.

Although obstacles must be faced they must not be allowed to dominate the picture. If the prospective traveler fearfully shuts his eyes to the difficulties he may encounter he is in serious trouble. If, however, he thinks of nothing but obstacles he may as well give up his trip. The chief emphasis must be on the positive satisfactions.

A Clear Picture of Personal Goals

To the extent that it is possible, each teacher or prospective teacher should look at his own needs and goals, as well as his own aversions and fears. Obviously, some of these may be hidden from him, but some may be partially visible if he only tries to see. These drives and goals should be analyzed to see just which facet is important and which is of less significance. Don't *disown* a need just because it seems unworthy or because someone else may be likely to sneer at it. If you do have a yen for security and safety rather than challenge, admit it to yourself. Be especially careful not to disown a drive just because it is often phrased in derogatory terms. In this conversation with yourself, try not to worry about how pretty the labels sound. Try to probe behind the labels and see how you stand with respect to the thing the label is supposed to represent. Don't worry about such linguistic niceties as the difference between the need "to dominate" and the need "to influence others." In your conversation with other people, of course, you may want to go to some trouble to be sure that your labels have a pleasant rather than an offensive sound. But not when you are just by yourself.

The fact that, in talking to yourself, you admit the existence of a powerful need, does not mean that you must decide to indulge this need. Take sex, for instance. After an honest look you may decide that sex needs are extremely strong in your case. You may also be convinced that in going in for teaching you are limiting your chance to gratify these needs. Yet you may well decide that the denial of this need is not a serious worry in the light of the other needs that may be met. It is one thing to decide that a need cannot be met, and quite another to try to convince yourself that it does not exist.

Suppose, now, that you have taken as close a look at yourself as circumstances will permit, and you can see a number of goals and aversions. You have decided that, in the light of this picture, teaching is an attractive enterprise. At this point, sort your goals out. You will find some that impel you into the profession. Verify these. Break them down into small units that can be attained in the foreseeable future. Keep these subgoals clearly in mind. Find some way of reminding yourself about them.

You will find other goals that you must adopt but for which you feel less enthusiasm. In some way or other try to come to terms with these.

Your goals, of course, should be in harmony with the important goals of those for whom you work. It would obviously be unethical to occupy a position of trust in which you were working directly counter to the main purposes of those who support you. But, fortunately, you can find a variety of goals among employing authorities, and you will encounter someone whose main purposes are in general harmony with your own.

To say that your goals must be in harmony with those of your employer does not mean that the goals must be identical. You may be strongly moved, for instance, to help children live their present lives as effectively as possible. Your superintendent or headmaster, on the other hand, may be concerned about producing future citizens. Yet there may be no conflict whatever between these two statements. In working toward your objective, you may also be working toward his.

Utilizing the Natural Forces in Teaching

There can be no doubt that learning is an exceedingly complex process. In many respects it may be fully as intricate as interplanetary navigation, computer programming, or neural surgery. And in these new complex processes we are impressed by the meticulous, conscious planning that must be given each detailed step in the process. Looking, now, at the process of learning under our direction, we may suspect that the management of this process is equally as demanding and precarious. Perhaps the management of learning calls for some well-thought-out decision to take care of each intricate step. Such a conclusion would be most misleading. We have only to look at a host of other processes that are complex enough in all conscience, but which, for all that, do not always call for deliberate, intelligent control. Swallowing, for instance, is complex and delicate enough. Fortunately, however, it calls for no conscious direction. Remembering the woes of the proverbial centipede, indeed, we may suspect that conscious direction would do more harm than good. In most species, the bearing and caring of the young is an exceedingly complex process, calling for definite procedures on the part of the mother. Ordinarily this is managed quite successfully, even when the maternal organism can have no clear idea of just what each act is supposed to accomplish. We should note that swallowing and parturition are vital for survival, and have been carried on with reasonable success for many generations. To guarantee this important success it is almost essential that there be dependable mechanisms that can be expected to work even in the absence of intelligent, deliberate decisions.

Spontaneous Forces in Teaching. Swallowing and the production of young are extreme examples of vital functions. Teaching cannot claim this immediate biological urgency. As a more relevant illustration, consider a child learning to talk. Talking, although not as vital as swallowing, has also been important in the survival of our species. And generation after generation, under widely varying circumstances, most children do *learn* the language of their parents. This fearsomely intricate process of learning has been successfully directed for thousands of years and in many different cultures. Typically it is managed by the mother, or similar adult. Now of all the mothers who have "taught" children to talk, there must be many who are unbelievably ignorant of the process they are managing. Surely the mother's success must come not from clear insight or from precise deliberate manipulation of the machinery of learning, but from some simple, primitive tendencies that we can be sure to find in mothers, or other adults, everywhere.

Some Prevalent Spontaneous Tendencies. Let us look at some of these blind, spontaneous tendencies by which even the ordinary mother leads her child to learn whatever language is spoken in the home. Even the most ordinary mother directs speech at her child. Without realizing what she is doing, she motivates and stimulates him. She talks to him for many reasons—for fun, to get him to stay out of the mud, or to come to dinner. But whatever her intention, these comments do act on the child as verbal stimuli. Similarly, when he comes out with "da da" or some other approximation to a recognizable word, she shows her spontaneous delight, and thus, without thinking, reinforces this behavior and makes him more likely to use the expression again. Similarly, without thinking, she supplies the phrase for which he is groping, thus supplying guidance. Very often she may also spend some time showing him how much better it is to express himself in this way rather than that.

Through these automatic, spontaneous tendencies the mother gets her child to learn the language of those around him. Could similar automatic, spontaneous tendencies be used by the teacher to get the child to learn to read? Is it so much more difficult to get a child to learn to read than to learn to speak? Probably not. The learning process is probably pretty much the same in the two tasks. If the child is to learn to read, someone should do for reading what the mother has done for talking. There should be, that is to say, someone who pays as much attention to reading as the mother pays to talking, someone who subjects the child to situations in which reading is appropriate, someone who is pleased when he reacts adequately to those situations, someone who comes to his aid when the correct response is beyond his immediate grasp.

Contribution of the Spontaneous Tendencies. It is held by some people (Smith and Hudgins, 1964; Stephens, 1960a) that such forces or tendencies automatically come into operation whenever an adult, enthusiastic about some field of knowledge, regularly consorts with growing children. If this view is correct, some instruction in the adult's special field will result even when this "teacher" makes no deliberate effort to instruct and when he is ignorant of what he is accomplishing. Complex as the teaching process is, the crude rudiments are taken care of by automatic tendencies found to some extent in all adults and conspicuously present in quite a few.

These primitive, automatic tendencies may hardly suffice, and any teacher will seek to refine and modify them and to make sure that they operate in more efficient fashion. But in this deliberate refinement you do not start from nothing. It should be comforting to realize that in managing this complex and awesome process, you do not always have to manipulate, in deliberate and conscious fashion, each minute aspect of the learning process operating within the child. On the contrary, put yourself in a situation in which teaching is in order, let yourself go, and, by virtue of the spontaneous urges to be found within you, *some* teaching will probably take place.

Indulging Primitive Tendencies and Needs. In deciding about yourself and teaching you must give much weight to thoughtful, rational considerations such as your idea of the purpose of education and the relative importance of this or that emphasis. Along with these important, rational factors, however, you should feel free to indulge the more primitive tendencies which, as we have just seen, play a tremendous part in teaching. Professor Burch (1957), for instance, has held that the chief *obligation* of the teacher is to give spontaneous expression to the educated man that he finds within himself. In other words, your job is chiefly to do what you, *as an educated person*, feel like doing. Notice that the idea of the educated person keeps cropping up. Not all your needs are to be spontaneously expressed, but only those that stem from you as an educated person.

But there are many such needs. Your need to pry into the intricacies of some subject, for instance, is one that you might properly express. Your need to bubble over about this subject is also a very natural need and one that you could quite properly indulge in many classroom situations. Surely there could be much satisfaction in a profession that asked one to develop an enthusiasm for a subject, largely of his own choosing, and also asked that he express his enthusiasm freely on many different occasions. There is more to teaching than that, probably, but this is one aspect, and one that should bring considerable reward.

Along with the concerns just mentioned, there are other warm, human nurturant needs evoked by the presence of children. The free indulgence of these can bring an immense earthy satisfaction with no sense of guilt. Some of these, it is true, although worthy and useful in moderation, may be dangerous and harmful in excess. A moderate need for nurturance, for example, might well work wonders in the classroom. Carried too far, however, it might stifle the growth of independence and might also regrettably frustrate the child's own need for self-expression. The need to dominate or to influence others, expressed in moderation, should help one carry out some of the teaching task. But this, again, when carried to extremes, could stultify initiative and induce a dangerous amount of frustration and resentment in the child (Peck and Mitchell, 1962).

Some psychologists (Jersild, 1955) would also recommend that the teacher give natural, unabashed expression to his anger and sorrow, thus introducing a natural, human tone into the environment and breaking the monotony of a steady diet of cheerfulness, sweetness, or artificial patience. It is true, perhaps that, when necessary, these needs can be indulged with no sense of shame, but, unlike the needs to nurture and to influence, they are not so vital in promoting the positive work of the classroom.

Using Guidance

Achievement in teaching, as in any activity, comes from a series of successful acts, each adequately reinforced. To keep those successes at a reasonable level, the beginning teacher should not hesitate to seek guidance at any reasonable opportunity. An experienced, intelligent, and understanding supervisor or older teacher can be of inestimable value. Many successful teachers attribute much of their professional happiness and effectiveness to the early guidance provided by an older hand. For the beginner, even an ordinary guide is often better than none. The ordinary guide has been over the path at least once and has survived thus far. That is something in the way of a recommendation.

Do what you can for yourself, of course, and steadily work toward the point where you can get along with less and less guidance. For a little while, however, when you are still learning the ropes, do not be ashamed even of playing the sedulous ape. When traversing especially difficult terrain, you may be forgiven if, like the inexperienced mountain climber, you deliberately place your feet in the precise tracks of your guide. On less treacherous paths, of course, you will be more free, and as you acquire competence, you will use your own judgment.

Relying on Independent Efforts

As in acquiring skill in any art, guidance is extremely useful at the outset when there would be a great likelihood of error were it not for guidance. With the growth of competence, however, errors fortunately become less likely. With this increase in skill, therefore, you can afford to let yourself go and risk the few errors that may lie in wait. With this minimum of competence you can rely more and more on sheer energy and application. After all, this energy and effort is bound to get you somewhere, even if somewhat inefficiently. Perfect technique, on the other hand, will be useless without enthusiastic application. For the teacher who has acquired a modicum of skill and confidence, therefore, the moral seems clear. Let yourself go!

Let yourself go as an educational reformer. There is room for reform. There is need for a host of enthusiastic voices calling attention to our lacks and urging their remedy.

Let yourself go as a student of education. Perhaps more than anything else, we need an insightful, lucid view of the essential nature of the educational process. Speculate, read, discuss. Announce your hypotheses. If you are cautious, you will announce them as hypotheses which need to be tested. But at any rate, publicize your hunch.

Let yourself go as a skeptic. We need more and more people who can pierce through wordy statements and see the assumptions that lie therein, and the hypotheses that must be tested before the statements can be accepted. If this is your strong suit, exercise it.

Above all, let yourself go as a teacher. In plunging on toward your objective, of course, you will make whatever use you can of the many techniques and minor devices that you may remember. Do this by all means. But these devices are your servants and not your master. They are merely minor refinements of the general process of teaching. Look at it this way. Most of the hundreds of "do's" and "don'ts" in this textbook, for instance, were developed from experiments performed since the year 1900. What did people do before they knew about these many restrictions? Was there any effective teaching prior to 1900? Assuredly so. The suggestions or restrictions set forth in this book are merely minor aids to a process that is much more fundamental than the minor suggestions.

SUMMARY

Teachers face the normal risks of maladjustment, although they probably fare somewhat better than people in many other lines of work. The profession carries more than its share of rewards. The lover of learning is actually paid for carrying on his affair. To those with strong social commitments, there is at the best an opportunity for high adventure, and at the least, the assurance of social worth. For those who shrink from the dog-eat-dog competition in other areas, there is the possibility of a more civilized life. Esteem is to be had from some sources, although not from all. Working conditions and salaries show some improvement over the past.

The frustrations of teaching are real and many people leave the profession each year. Frustrations can be dealt with when honestly faced. At times the irritating conditions can be corrected. At other times, they can be absorbed without disaster. Help is available when trouble threatens.

The worries that plague the teacher come in many forms. Very often the teacher is either uncertain about his basic function or feels that he is at odds with his superiors. He worries about his ambiguous social status, feeling that he is appreciated but patronized, and perhaps curtailed. He often sees little opportunity for professional advancement. He can never be sure just how much he is accomplishing, and he often works under difficult conditions.

Satisfaction in teaching should come with a clearer picture of goals and needs. There are also many earthy sources of satisfaction in the basic process of teaching. Much of what the teacher does, and should do, can be seen as the natural, spontaneous expression of the educated person he finds within himself. The typical teacher has a store of natural and academic urges that he can well afford to indulge and cultivate. The work accomplished in this way must, of course, be supplemented by deliberate undertakings.

In working out a satisfying relation to his job, the teacher should not hesitate to seek specific guidance at the outset. He should also be eager to throw off that guidance, and to let himself go as competence increases.

SUGGESTIONS FOR FURTHER READING

General

Gabriel, J., *An Analysis of the Emotional Problems of the Teacher in the Classroom.* Melbourne: F. W. Cheshire, Publishers, 1957.

Gage, N. L., ed., *Handbook of Research on Teaching.* Skokie, Ill.: Rand McNally, 1963. See especially the following chapters: Chapter 11, J. W. Getzels and P. W. Jackson, "The Teacher's Personality and Characteristics"; Chapter 14, W. W. Charters, Jr., "The Social Background of Teaching."

Havighurst, R. J., and Bernice L. Neugarten, *Society and Education,* 2d ed. Boston: Allyn and Bacon, Inc., 1962.

Jersild, A. T., *When Teachers Face Themselves.* New York: Bureau of Publications, Teachers College, Columbia University, 1955.

————, E. Allina Lazar, and Adele M. Brodkin, *The Meaning of Psychotherapy in the Teachers Life and Work.* New York: Bureau of Publications, Teachers College, Columbia University, 1962.

Peck, R. F., and J. V. Mitchell, Jr., *Mental Health: What Research Says to the Teacher,* No. 24. Washington, D. C.: National Education Association, 1962.

Stevenson, G. S., and H. Milt, *Master Your Tensions and Enjoy Living Again.* Englewood Cliffs, N. J.: Prentice-Hall, 1959. A brief excerpt is reprinted in Crow, pp. 579–585.

Witty, P. A., Mental health of the teacher, *Yearbook National Society for the Study of Education,* 1955, **54**, Part II, 307–333.

Problems and Frustrations of Teachers

Allinsmith, W., and G. W. Goethals, *The Role of Schools in Mental Health.* New York: Basic Books, Inc., 1962.

Groff, P. J., The social status of teachers, *Journal of Educational Sociology,* 1962, **36**, 20–25.

Kaplan, L., *Mental Health and Human Relations in Education.* New York: Harper & Row, Publishers, Inc., 1959.

Metfessel, N. S., and J. T. Shea, Fifty often overlooked areas of teacher frustration, *American School Board Journal* (June), 1961, **142**, 16–17.

Solomon, J. C., Neurosis of school teachers: a colloquy, *Mental Hygiene* (New York), 1960, **44**, 79–90.

Teaching as a Profession

Anderson, A. W., The teaching profession: an example of diversity in training and function, *Yearbook National Society for the Study of Education,* 1962, **61**, Part II, 140–167.

Lieberman, M., *Education as a Profession.* Englewood Cliffs, N. J.: Prentice-Hall, 1956.

Specific References

Wynn, D. R., and R. W. DeRemer, Staff

utilization, development and evaluation, *Review of Educational Research*, 1961, **31,** 393–405.

Zimiles, H., Mental health and school personnel, *Review of Educational Research*, 1962, **32,** 484–494.

EXERCISES AND QUESTIONS FOR DISCUSSION

1. Look over the needs suggested by Professor Murray (Chapter 4). List those that, as far as you can tell, seem important to you. Which of these might be met by the satisfactions of teaching? Which would be seriously impeded by the frustrations in teaching?

2. List the attitudes toward teaching and teachers that you encounter in casual conversations. Describe your reactions to the more important of these expressed attitudes. Are there some that boost your morale? Some that seem worrisome but which you can *genuinely* dismiss as unimportant? Some that you can deal with satisfactorily by charging up to a difference in tastes?

3. Write an outline for a talk on the problem of transiency in the teaching profession. Do you see any difficulties from the fact that many young folk enter for only a time? any advantages? any devices for avoiding the difficulties and exploiting the advantages?

4. Consider two teachers going into the profession, one for the fun of it, one from a high sense of duty. Describe the advantages and disadvantages, immediate and long-range, of the two attitudes.

APPENDIX

▶ *Some Elementary Statistics*

Here are the scores of two groups of students who have been asked to give the meanings of ten Spanish words. In Group A the first student got 7 words right, the second, 5. For the entire group the scores were as follows: 7, 5, 9, 7, 8, 6, 7, 6, 8, 7. The scores in Group B were 5, 8, 7, 9, 4, 8, 5, 9, 8, 10, 7, 3, 9, 7, 8, 4, 9, 3, 7, 8.

Which group made the better score?

With the scores arranged in this helter-skelter fashion, it is hard to make a comparison. There is no need to worry, by the way, over the fact that there are twenty students in Group B but only ten in Group A. It is quite in order to compare the standing of two groups even though there are more people in one group than in the other. There are many more men in New York than in Nevada, for instance, but we could still find out if the average Nevada man is taller or shorter than the average man in New York.

To get some order into the numbers, we might try ranking them.

Group A: 9, 8, 8, 7, 7, 7, 7, 6, 6, 5.
Group B: 10, 9, 9, 9, 9, 8, 8, 8, 8, 8, 8, 7, 7, 7, 7, 5, 5, 5, 4, 4, 3.

This makes things somewhat clearer but the numbers still seem rather disorderly. For one thing, it seems a little foolish to write one number over and over again. We might also feel some urge to match (say) the 8's in one group with the 8's in the other. We can take care of both of these problems by arranging a simple *frequency distribution.*

FREQUENCY DISTRIBUTIONS

First we make a list of the scores we have to deal with. In this list we make sure that there is a place, or score, for everyone. The highest score we have to arrange for is 10, the lowest 3. In this illustration it happens that our scores only go from 3 to 10, and there are no part scores. Here, then, we can find a place for every person merely by listing all possible scores from 10 through 3, as

TABLE A.1. Frequency Distributions for Successes in Identifying Spanish Words

List of Scores That Would Include All Students	Number of Students Getting Each of the Listed Scores	
	Group A	Group B
10		1
9	1	4
8	2	5
7	4	4
6	2	
5	1	3
4		2
3		1
Number of Students	$\overline{10}$	$\overline{20}$

in the left hand column of Table A.1. If, on the other hand, the scores ranged from 3 to 100 or so, this procedure would make for a very long list.

From our ranks we see that in Group A there was one score of 9, two scores of 8, and so forth. In the frequency distribution we show this by writing in the number of students who got each of these scores. This procedure saves us from writing down 7, 7, 7, 7. It also matches up the students in Group A who got a score of 7 with those in Group B who got the same score.

Here we have a frequency distribution for each group. These distributions give us all the information that was in the list of ranks. They present this information, moreover, in a more compact and systematic form. We avoid the wasteful repetition of scores. We can see at a glance how many of each group got a certain score. We are also forced to notice the fact that no one in Group B got a score of 6, and we are automatically impressed by the greater range of scores in Group B.

This example of frequency distributions is unduly simplified. As we have

noted, it deals with a very limited range of scores (10–3). It also ignores the possibility of part credit. There is no provision, for instance, for a student who got credit for 6.5 words. To take care of a much greater range of scores, and also to take care of partial scores, some modifications and elaborations would be necessary. But the principle would not be different.

By putting the scores in the form of frequency distributions we can get a clearer picture of the two groups. Group B, for instance, seems to fall into two clusters, the top cluster of fourteen students tending to exceed Group A, and a bottom cluster of six students tending to fall below Group A.

AVERAGES AND RANKS

Judgments that we can reach from general inspection are often very useful. For more detailed comparisons, however, we need a more precise measure. In comparing Group A with Group B *as a whole*, we would have to decide whether the good students in Group B more than offset the poor students. We need some kind of a measure which will take these things into account.

The Arithmetic Mean

When we wish to get a single number to describe the average score, or over-all score of each group, we often use the familiar *arithmetic mean*. This measure is so very familiar, indeed, that it is often called *the* average, in spite of the fact that it is only one of several ways that can be used to describe an average. To get the arithmetic mean we merely add the scores and divide by the number of cases. In doing this we could make use of the frequency distribution if we had already constructed one. For Group A we would add one 9, two 8's, four 7's, and so forth.

In our illustration you will find that both groups have an arithmetic mean of precisely 7. Using this more precise measure, then, we find that, on the average, there is no difference between the two groups. The superior scores in Group B are precisely offset or balanced by the very low scores in that group.

This concept of *balance* is extremely useful when we work a great deal with means. Suppose we had a weightless plank, 8 feet long, marked off to correspond to our scores (3–10). Suppose, further, that we had ten equal weights and placed these weights on the plank so as to match the frequency distribution of Group A. If, now, we placed this plank on a fulcrum it would balance precisely at the score of 7—remembering that the plank itself is supposed to be weightless. If we placed twenty weights for Group B in a similar way, the plank would also balance at the score of 7. It may help in several ways to remember that the mean is the point of balance (or point of zero moment). This fact may help you to visualize the mean. It is also useful in making short-cut calculations. By sheer inspection, for instance, we could tell that the mean for Group A is 7, since there is an obvious balance around this score. The mean for Group B is not so obvious, but by canceling high scores against low scores we can determine the point of balance fairly quickly and quite accurately. In more advanced treatments you will make much use of such procedures in calculating means.

The Median

The median is another measure that is used to indicate central tendency. The median is merely the point on the distribution which divides the group in such a way that half the students will be above the median and half below. In Group B, for instance, half the students have a score of 8 or above. Half have a score of 7 or less. The median would be 7.5, or the boundary score between 7 and 8. Notice that this median would remain the same no matter what happened to (say) the last six scores. If all six of these scores were 0, the median would still be 7.5. It would also remain at 7.5 if all six of these scores were changed to 5 or 6. On the other hand, if one single student were to drop from a score of 8 to a score of 7, the median would be greatly affected.

In these respects the median is quite different from the arithmetic mean. A change in any single score will have some effect—great or small—on the mean. With the median, on the other hand, changes in some scores (those toward the extremes) will have no effect whatever, whereas changes in other scores (those near the median) may have a marked effect. Sometimes this differential sensitivity of the median is considered an advantage. If you should be suspicious of

TABLE A.2. Percentile Ranks for Scores on Spanish Words, Based on Students in Group B

1	2	3	4	5	6
Score (Words Correct)	Number of Students Getting Each Score	Number of Students Falling below Each Score	Percent of Students Falling below Each Score	Number of Students Falling below Midpoint of Each Score	Percent of Students Falling below Midpoint of Each Score
10	1	19	95	19.5	97.5
9	4	15	75	17.0	85.0
8	5	10	50	12.5	62.5
7	4	6	30	8.0	40.0
6		6	30	6.0	30.0
5	3	3	15	4.5	22.5
4	2	1	5	2.0	10.0
3	1	0	0	0.5	2.5
	20				

the extreme scores in your distribution, for instance, you might not want to give them much weight. In that situation you might prefer the median. For most purposes, however, the mean, with its more uniform sensitivity and greater stability, is the preferred measure.

Percentile Ranks

A student in Group B who gets a score of 7.5 would just surpass 50 percent of the group. He would, of course, also fall just below 50 percent of the group, but it is not necessary to state the matter both ways. Since a score of 7.5 puts a person just above 50 percent of the group, we say that this score represents a *percentile rank* of 50. We also say that the person getting this score has a percentile rank of 50.

Just as we can translate a score of 7.5 into a percentile rank, so we can also translate any other score in the distribution into a percentile rank. The person who gets a score of 10 would exceed nineteen students (everyone except himself), or 95 percent of the group. He would have a percentile rank of 95.

Percentile ranks provide a very useful way of giving meaning to scores. You learn, for instance, that a student got 36 items right in a given test. You ask, "What does this mean? How good a score is this?" You are told that a person making this score would exceed 75 percent of the group taking the examination. This gives you some idea of the student's ability, especially if you know something of the group taking the examination.

Many of the *norms* provided in published tests are given in the form of percentile ranks. When you find out how many items the student got right on this test, you consult the table of norms provided (see Chapter 3) and learn that this score corresponds to a percentile rank of (say) 38. This means that the student getting this score would just exceed 38 percent of the group on which the norms are based.

The procedure for calculating percentile ranks is demonstrated in Table A.2, using the scores of the twenty students in Group B.

To get a rough general idea of percentile rank, look at columns 3 and 4. From column 3 we see that no one got a score *lower than* 3, one person got a score *lower than* 4, and so forth. In column 4 these numbers are turned into percentages. Looking at a score of 8, we see that the corresponding percentage in column 4 is 50, meaning that 50 percent of the group fell *below* this score. We could use such a rough percentile rank to give some meaning to scores. To show what it means to get nine words right, we could point out that the person getting this score just exceeds 75 percent of his group.

The percentile ranks that appear in published norms are based on the *general* idea used in our illustration. Such published percentile ranks, however, include a number of refinements to make the figures more precise. Obviously, such norms would be based on many more cases. Furthermore, it is assumed that, with a precise measure, we would not have (say) four people getting exactly a score of 7. A much more accurate measure would probably show a range of scores (6.8, 7.1, 7.2, etc.) clustering around 7. The published percentile ranks, therefore, show the percent of people below the midpoint represented by a given score. For these and other reasons, such published norms never quite reach 100, nor never fall as low as 0, although they may get very close to 100 (99.999) or very close to 0. Columns 4 and 5 show what these more precise percentile ranks would look like for our twenty students. If we had several thousand students instead of twenty, the differences between columns 3 and 5 would be less marked.

MEASURES OF DISPERSION

One of the most interesting things in the comparison of our two groups is the much greater dispersion, or spread, in Group B. Whereas the students in Group A form a tight cluster ranging over only a few points, those in Group B cover a wider range of scores.

Range

To compare the dispersion or spread in the two groups we could use the *range*. This is simply the difference between the highest and lowest score. The range for Group A is 4, for Group B, 7. The range, however, like the median, is greatly at the mercy of one or two scores. It is relatively insensitive, however, to changes in other scores. If the poorest student in Group A had happened to get a score of 3 instead of 5, the change in the score of this one student would increase the range from 4 to 6. On the other hand, the range would in no way be affected by extensive changes near the midpoint.

Standard Deviation

To avoid this difficulty, most statisticians use the *standard deviation* as a measure of dispersion. Unlike the range, this measure is influenced by every score. A change in one score would affect it a little, but only a little. The standard deviation indicates, on the average, how far each student's score departs from the mean. In Group A we note that four students are right at the mean. For them, the deviation from the mean is 0. Two students deviate by one score in the positive direction. One student is two steps above the mean. Similarly, two students are one step *below* the mean, and one student is two steps below.

So much for the individual deviations. The standard deviation is intended to give a general picture of these individual deviations. To obtain the standard deviation we simply collect all the individual deviations, including the 0 deviations, and average them. This average shows, in general, how the individual scores tend to depart from the mean.

In this process of averaging the individual deviations there is one complication that we must mention. In adding all the deviations together to get the average, we would find the plus deviations (those above the mean) and the minus deviations would always cancel each other out. (Remember that the mean *is* the point about which these deviations balance.) To prevent this from happening, all deviations are squared before being added. Since $(-x)$ $(-x)$ is x^2, all minus signs are thus eliminated. After averaging these squared deviations we take the square root of them.

In more extensive treatments of statistics you will want to know more about the ins and outs of this process of computing a standard deviation. For our purposes, however, you should regard it merely as a sort of average of the individual deviations. Each student's departure from the mean is noted and these individual departures are averaged to show in general whether the students tend to cluster closely around the mean, as in Group A, or whether, in general, they depart quite widely from the mean, as in Group B. The standard deviation for Group A happens to be 1.5 and that for Group B, 1.9.

Comparable Scores

The standard deviation has turned out to be an exceptionally useful measure. For one thing, it is an extremely convenient method of comparing scores in different traits. We know, for instance, that ten-year-old George is below average in both height and weight. More precisely, we know that he is only 4 feet 6 inches tall, whereas the average for his age is 4 feet 8½ inches. We also know that he weighs only 70 pounds as compared to an average of 85. He is thus 2½ inches below the average in height, and 15 pounds below the average in weight. But now we want to know if his deficiency in weight is excessive or whether this is just about what we might expect in view of his short stature. Is he farther behind in weight than he is in height? How does 2½ inches compare with 15 pounds?

We could, if we wished, use percentile ranks to answer this question. Suppose, in looking at the norms for ten-year-olds, we find that 4 feet 6 inches represents a percentile rank of 16, whereas 70 pounds represents a percentile rank of 12. From these it would appear that George surpasses 16 percent of ten-year-olds in height, but only 12 percent of ten-year-olds in weight. If we took this difference seriously we would decide that George is slightly farther behind in weight than in height.

As another rough-and-ready device, we might use the range. Discovering that the range in height for ten-year-olds is 15 inches, we could note that George falls below the group average by ⅙ of the range. Similarly, if the range in weight turned out to be 65 pounds, we would note that in weight he falls below the average by slightly more than ¼ of the total range.

But the range, as we have seen, is not a dependable measure of spread or dispersion. Change a single score and you could change the range quite markedly.

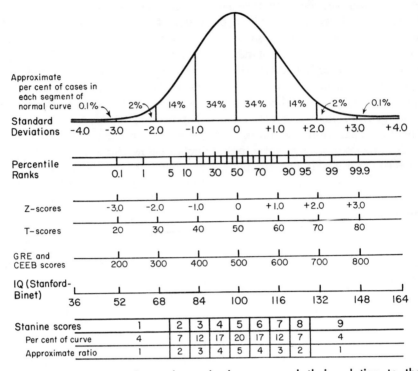

Fig. A.1. Frequently used standard scores and their relation to the normal curve of distribution.

It is much safer to use the standard deviation. And most comparable scores are based on the standard deviation or on something closely related to it. Suppose in our earlier illustration we find that the standard deviation for height is 2.4 and that for weight it is 15.6. Here we would note that George is just about 1 standard deviation below the average in both height and weight. Using this method of reckoning, we would conclude that he is no farther behind in one than in the other.

Z-scores or Sigma Scores. Speaking technically we would say that George had a z-score of −1.0 in both height and weight. A boy right at the mean would have a z-score of 0.0. A weight 2 standard deviations above the mean is equal to a z-score of 2.0. In the typical distribution, 98 percent of scores will be found between z-scores of −3.0 and +3.0. Notice that these z-scores come in the form of both positive and negative numbers. Notice, also, that the numbers themselves are small and that, to describe minor changes, we would often have to resort to fractions such as −1.8 or 2.63.

Standard Scores. To avoid the negative numbers and the awkward fractions that appear in z-scores, most publishers modify these scores in some way. Many of these are described as *standard scores.* Obviously, there would be no relative change in the scores if we added the same number, say 50 or 100 or 500 to each score. Obviously, also, no unfairness would result if we multiplied each score by any convenient number, say 10 or 15 or 100.

In Figure A.1 we see a number of the more frequently used standard scores. These are shown in relation to percentile ranks and also in relation to the normal curve and to the *stanine scores* described later.

One form of standard score is the *T-score*, in which each sigma score or z-score is multiplied by 10, and to which 50 is added to each of these increased scores. As a result, such scores have a mean of 50. About 98 percent of all T-scores will fall between 20 and 80. Obviously, these values of 50 and 10 are quite arbitrary. Scores for the Graduate Record Examination and the examination of the College Entrance Board, for instance, are treated differently. They are multiplied by 100 and have 500 added to them. This produces a mean of 500 and a range of from 200 to 800 for 98 percent of the scores.

Figure A.1 shows how these two forms of standard scores differ from the percentile ranks. Most of the percentile ranks (from less than 20 to more than 80) are crowded into a space of 1 standard deviation on each side of the mean. Clearly, percentile ranks near the extremes do not mean the same as those near the center. In percentile ranks the difference between 98 and 99 is quite large; the difference between 48 and 49 is minute. To go from 1 to 10 we have to cover the same distance as to go from 30 to 70.

Intelligence Quotients. As computed nowadays, the *intelligence quotient* is a type of standard score. With this score, however, the mean is set at 100 and the standard deviation at about 15 or 16. We say, "about" because this varies from one test to another. In the Stanford Binet it is 16, in the Wechsler tests it is 15. In

one similar military test, the General Classification Test, it is 20.

In using 100 as a mean, and 16 or thereabouts as the standard deviation, the IQ scales are trying to maintain some continuity with the older ideas of the intelligence quotient. When originally developed, the intelligence quotient was a true quotient and represented the ratio between the mental age and the chronological age. For the general population, these IQ's happened to have a mean of 100 and a standard deviation of 16. Over the years, many people came to feel at home with these particular numbers, just as we feel at home with numbers like 6 feet or 2 hours or 18 dollars. Rather than force people to adopt new units of measurement, these new deviation scores were calibrated to fit in with the old measures.

Stanine Scores. Stanine is one of the weird artificial labels we use so much these days. It comes from "standard nine." It was designed to get a standard score that would fit neatly into an IBM card. It was probably one of the first hints that everything of any importance just better had fit into an IBM card.

The boundaries between stanines are not computed from the standard deviation, but are set so as to include certain proportions of the normal curve. With a well-behaved normal curve, however, they end up as a type of standard score and can be read as such. Except for the extremes, each step corresponds to ½ of a standard deviation. A score of 5 represents a band around the mean. Notice, however, that stanines 1 and 9 take in a wide range of scores. A child with an IQ of 130, and one with an IQ of 160 or 170, would both be in the 9th stanine. Some statisticians think that this lumping of the extremes makes the scale too coarse. To get around this problem, scales of 10 and 11 steps are also used.

TABLE A.3. Heights and Weights of Children in One Grade-Six Class

	Height	Weight
A	4'10"	81
B	4'8"	86
C	4'8"	62
D	4'10"	91
E	4'7"	74
F	4'9"	94
G	4'11"	129
H	4'6"	72
J	4'10"	97
K	4'9"	88
L	5'0"	121
M	4'5"	63
N	4'5"	68
O	4'8"	75
P	4'8"	83
Q	4'4"	72
R	4'5"	70
S	4'7"	93
T	5'0"	90
U	4'10"	93
V	4'9"	91
W	4'10"	86
X	5'1"	93
Y	5'1"	99
Z	4'9"	104

MEASURES OF CORRELATION

Table A.3 lists the heights and weights of twenty-five children in grade six. Our problem is to see whether there is any relation between height and weight. We wish to see whether or not the two go together, and if so, to what extent.

Systematic Tables

The simplest way to get at this problem is to line the children up according to one of these variables (say height) and see if they also happen to line up with respect to the other variable. Notice that the heights go from 4 feet 4 inches to 5 feet 1 inch, or through a range of 9 inches. Quite arbitrarily, we break this range up into six class intervals as follows: 4 feet 4 inches–4 feet 5.99 inches; 4 feet 6 inches–4 feet 7.99 inches, and so forth, and use it as the basis for a frequency distribution. The first group will include all children 4 feet 4 inches and up to, *but not including* 4 feet 6 inches. Just to keep track of the original observations, we will, at this stage, identify each child along with his weight. Child A, for instance, is shown in the height group 4 feet 10 inches to 5 feet 0 inches, along with his weight of 81 pounds. After doing this for each child, we get the results shown in Table A.4. For convenience, the children are listed so that the heaviest children are at the top of each column.

TABLE A.4. Weight of Each Child Falling in Each Selected Height Range

4'4"	4'6"	4'8"	4'10"	5'0"	5'2"
		Z 104			
		F 94			
		V 91	G 129		
		K 88	J 97		
Q 72		B 86	U 93		L 121
R 70	S 93	P 83	D 91		Y 99
N 68	E 74	O 75	W 86		X 93
M 63	H 72	C 62	A 81		T 90
Mean Weight for each Column 68.2	79.7	84.2	96.3		100.7

Notice that in constructing Table A.4 we arranged things so that the groups would differ systematically in height. We deliberately set things up so that all the children to the right will be taller than those to the left. Differences such as these are called independent differences, or differences in the *independent variable* (height, in this case): The term *independent* refers to the fact that these differences do not "depend on," or arise from, the differences in weight. The differences in height would appear (because we arranged things this way) even if there were no difference in weight.

By arranging things this way we make sure that there will be differences in height. But do we at the same time automatically make sure that there will be differences in weight? By no means. In spite of all of our doings it might turn out that, on the average, the children in each of our height groups would have the same weight. Whether or not this will be

TABLE A.5. Correlation Chart of Height and Weight
(Identifying Letters Included)

Weight in Pounds

Weight	4'4"	4'6"	4'8"	4'10"	5'0"	5'2"	Total
130				G		L	2
120							
110			Z				1
100		S	F, V	J, D, U		T, X, Y	9
90			B, K, P	A, W			5
80							
70	Q, R	E, H	O				5
60	M, N		C				3
Total	4	3	8	6		4	25

Height in Feet and Inches

true *depends* on the relation between height and weight. Weight then is a *dependent variable*. Differences might turn up or they might not. It depends.

Simple Inspection

In our particular illustration, as seen in Table A.4, do we, in fact, find differences in weight as we move from left to right? From simple inspection it would appear that we do. We get the impression that, on the average, the groups to the right are heavier than those to the left. But most of us would not be happy with ordinary inspection. The answer would be clearer if we found the mean weight for each height group. These mean weights appear in the last row of Table A.4. Looking at these averages, we feel no doubt that when groups are arranged so that they are made to differ in height, then it turns out that they actually do differ in weight as well.

Before developing this matter further, let us tidy up Table A.4 a bit. This table gives us the necessary information, but it is awkward and calls for intensive

reading. It does not give much information in one quick glance. The picture would be clearer if we turn each column into a frequency distribution *for weight*, as in Table A.5. To show the relation with Table A.4, the identifying letters are retained in Table A.5. These are not really necessary, however, and an even neater arrangement is shown in Table A.6. Here the identifying letters are omitted, and in each cell we merely see the *number* of children who have that particular height and that particular weight.

Slope as an Index of Relation

Any one of the tables would show that weight differences are found when children are sorted according to height. To get a more vivid picture of this relation we could make a graph by plotting the average weights for each column. (These averages appear in Table A.4.) Such a graph is shown in Figure A.2. Here we see that the graph slopes upward (weight) as it moves from left to right (height).

TABLE A.6. Correlation Chart of Height and Weight (Identifying Letters Omitted)

Weight in Pounds	4'4"	4'6"	4'8"	4'10"	5'0"	5'2"	Total
130							
120				1	1		2
110							
100			1				1
90		1	2	3	3		9
80			3	2			5
70	2	2	1				5
60	2		1				3
Total	4	3	8	6	4		25

Height in Feet and Inches

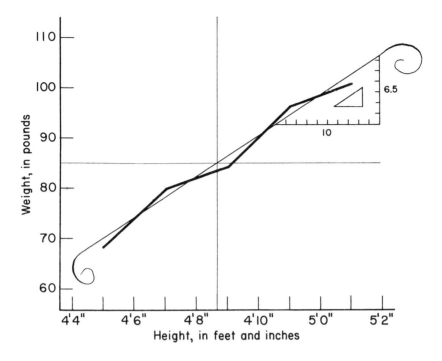

Fig. A.2. Correlation considered as an average slope.

By taking a few precautions, the slope of the graph in Figure A.2 can be used to show the *amount* or *extent* of the relation between height and weight. Since our graph wanders around a bit, we will find it better to get an average, or over-all slope. We could approximate this very well by stretching a black thread and moving it around until it came as close as possible to all the points on the graph, thus getting a straight line, shown as the lighter line in Figure A.2. By looking at the scale at the upper right, we can see that every time we *arrange for* an increase of 10 steps in height, it turns out that we *get* an increase of about 6.5 steps in weight. Our line, therefore, has a slope of 6.5 in 10, or .65. Provided that we have arranged for the necessary precautions, we can consider this slope of .65 as a *coefficient of correlation* of .65. A slope of this value means that the relation between height and weight is not perfect. If it were perfect, then every time we had a 10-step increase in height we would also have a 10-step increase in weight. This would give us a slope of 1.00, or a correlation of 1.00.

Let us look at a slope that shows less relation. Figure A.3 shows a comparable relation between height and mental age (for 12-year-old children). Here we see that an increase of 10 units in height is accompanied by a change of only 2 units in mental age. This is the same as a correlation of .20 and indicates a very low relation.

If the correlation between height and mental age had turned out to be zero, it would mean that no matter how much our groups differ in height, each group would have the same average men-

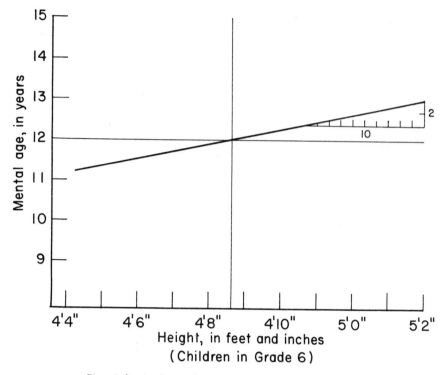

Fig. A.3. A slope showing a very low correlation.

tal age. Our graph, in that case, would move straight across the figure parallel to the base line, showing a slope of zero.

A slope, or correlation, can be negative as well as positive. At the elementary school level, for instance, we would probably find a negative relation between age, on the one hand, and amount of illness (days absent from school), on the other. If we sorted children according to age we would find that as we moved across from younger to older students there would be fewer and fewer days absence. This would produce a negative slope.

Try to think of a coefficient of correlation as a ratio which indicates the steepness of the graph. A correlation of .65 between height and weight does not mean that 65 percent of people will match up in height and weight, or that

we will have a 65 percent success in estimating weight from height. It merely means that a change of 1 unit in height will be accompanied by a change of .65 units in weight.

Precautions in Interpreting Correlations as Slopes. To use the slope of a graph as an index of the amount of correlation, we must, as we mentioned, take several precautions. First, we must use comparable scores for the two traits (height and weight in this case). We could not expect the slope to mean much if we used just any arbitrary scores or measures. Second, the steepest slope we can use to indicate correlation is a slope of 1.00. This may seem peculiar at first glance. Since a slope of 1.00 means a higher correlation than a slope of .50, then it might seem that a slope of 1.50

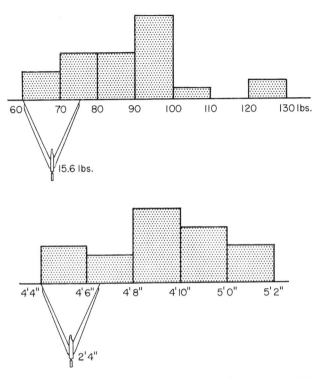

Fig. A.4. The two distances must be stepped off in comparable units.

should mean even more correlation. But it does not work out that way. The highest correlation we can get comes from a slope of 1.00 or a slope of −1.00, if it should happen to be a negative correlation.

If you wish to take these matters on faith, you can stop at this point, merely remembering that comparable units are always implied, and that the rule holds only up to a slope of 1.00. On the other hand, you may want to know the ins and outs of the matter, and if you do you should read the following brief explanation, and also, perhaps, a more advanced book on statistics.

Meeting the Problem of Comparable Scores. Such units as inches and pounds are quite arbitrary. We could not expect to get the same slope, for instance, if, instead of inches and pounds, we used millimeters and ounces. To get around this problem of arbitrary units, we make use of standard scores of the type discussed earlier (Fig. A.4). To show where a student stands in height, we show how far he is above or below the average for his group, and we do this in terms of standard deviations or z-scores. We say that in height this student is 1.8 standard deviations above the mean, or that he has a z-score of 1.8. In a similar way, we say that he has a z-score of, say, 2.3 in weight.

Under these arrangements each unit is expressed in terms of its own standard deviation. In our example, the standard deviation for height is 2.4 inches, and the standard deviation for weight is 15.6 pounds. In this group, to move through

2.4 inches of height is about the same thing as to move through 15.6 pounds of weight. For this reason, the scales are arranged so that 2.4 inches on the horizontal dimension covers the same space on the chart as 15.6 pounds on the vertical dimension.

The Maximum Possible Slope. Now we turn to our next question: Why does a slope of 1.00 mean a higher correlation than a slope of 1.50 or a slope of 5.0? Actually, if we were only interested in the changes in weight that go with changes in height, a slope of 5.0 really would be more impressive than a slope of 1.00. But, typically, we are not exclusively interested in the changes in weight that accompany changes in height. Often we are also interested in knowing what sort of changes in height we would get if we

moved from lighter to heavier children. With this question in mind, consider the slopes in Figure A.5. The slope of 5.00 shows that for each increase in height we get a tremendous increase in weight. But suppose we read the graph the other way. Starting from the origin, or point of intersection, we move up 10 units in weight. Now we move to the right along the height dimension until we come to the sloping line. Notice that for this increase of 10 units in weight we get an increase of only two units in height. In other words, moving past a slope of 1.00 to a greater slope, we have, it is true, suggested more pronounced changes in weight for each change in height, but in so doing we have reduced the change in height that goes along with each change in weight. Since the coefficient of corre-

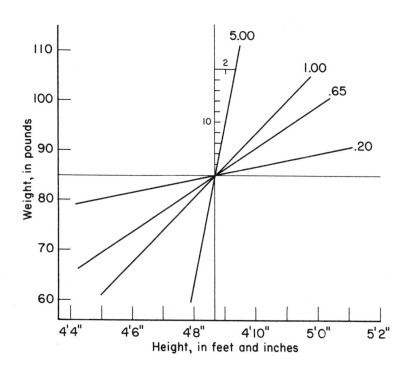

Fig. A.5. A slope of 1.00 represents the highest possible relation if both aspects of the relation are taken into account.

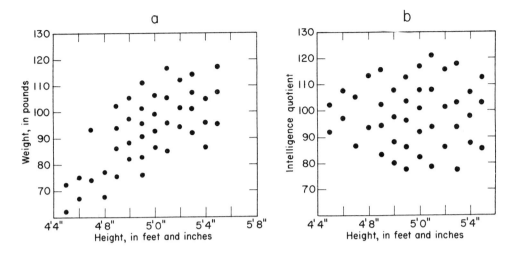

Fig. A.6. Correlation indicated by the lack of scatter.

lation must reflect both aspects of this relation between height and weight (it is, in fact, an average of these two relations), the very best relation it can show is indicated by a slope of 1.00.

Other Interpretations of the Coefficient of Correlation

Often, in describing quantities or amounts, you are not limited to a single approach. In describing the amount of water in the local reservoir, for instance, you could say how far the water is from the top or how far from the bottom. You could also state the volume in terms of gallons or acre-feet. Perhaps you might find "day's use" the most convenient measure. One of these is just as accurate as the other, and any one could be translated unambiguously into any other. Which will be the most useful depends on circumstances and on the previous experiences of the one receiving the information. You could also be influenced by the sheer preferences of the persons to whom you are speaking.

The coefficient of correlation is such a measure. It can be described in different ways. Although each tells the same story, different descriptions may appeal to different people.

Reduction in Scatter. Instead of thinking of a coefficient of correlation as a slope or as an average of two slopes, we could think of it as describing the reduction in the amount of scatter. A correlation chart, such as that shown in Table A.6, typically shows a good deal of scatter. In any one column, we have several entries scattered over quite a few rows. This is shown more simply in Figures A.6a, and A.6b. In both figures the scores or dots are scattered over a good deal of the chart. In Figure A.6a, however, the scores fall in a somewhat limited area. This area can be represented by a relatively thin ellipse. The axis of this ellipse slopes upward. In Figure A.6b, on the contrary, the scores cover much more territory. A line drawn around these scores would describe a fatter figure having no clearly marked axis. If there was a

TABLE A.7. Days of Illness in Relation to Age

	Number of Children with No Illness	Number of Children Ill One Day or More	Total Number of Children	Percent of Children Ill One Day or More
Children 13 Years or Older	1200	800	2000	40%
Children under 13 Years	900	2100	3000	70%
Total	2100	2900	5000	
Difference in Percent				−30

hint of such an axis, it would go straight across, parallel to the base line.

In this view, correlation would be indicated by the absence of scatter. Wide scatter would indicate a low correlation. With perfect correlation, there would be no vertical scattering whatever. Every single score would fall precisely on a straight line that rose regularly as we moved across the figure. In more precise treatments, this concept of scatter is linked up to the more fundamental idea of *error of estimate*. In this more technical sense, we can think of a high correlation as one that brings about a greater reduction in this error of estimate.

Difference in Percents. Taking a different look at this same coefficient of correlation, we can visualize a simple arrangement such as that shown in Table A.7. Here we are trying to see if there is any relation between age and days of absence due to illness. From the table we observe that young children seem to be likely to be ill at least once during the year. To get an idea of the extent of the relation we need merely get the percent of each age group that had absences due to illness. We note that 40 percent of older children had one or more illnesses, whereas 70 percent of younger children came in this category. The difference in

the percents is −30, the minus sign indicating that the older the child the fewer days of illness.

This difference of percent of −30 is quite comparable to a coefficient of correlation of −.30, except, of course, for the location of the decimal point. Like the coefficient of correlation, this difference in percents could range from 100 to −100. If the two groups were exactly comparable in illness, the difference in percents would be 0.

To see how the difference in percents compares to the regular coefficient of correlation, let us look at the data for the height and weight of 12-year-olds. This is shown in Table A.8 Here, instead of giving the precise height and weight for each child, we merely ask whether the child is above the median of the group in height (a tall child), or whether he is below the median in height. We also ask whether he is above the median in weight (a heavy child), or below the median in weight. Then we find out what percent of tall children are also heavy and what percent of short children are heavy. The *difference* in these percents is 66.7. This is quite comparable to the slope of .65 that we got when we treated the relation by using the actual height and weight of each child.

You may find it easier to think of correlations in this way than to think of them as slopes of lines. You learn, for instance, that there is a correlation of .55 between score on the Presto Aptitude Test and freshman grades in college. What does this mean? Think of the students divided into two groups, those above average on the Presto and those below average. Then ask how many from each of these groups "did well" as freshmen. Some of the low Presto group, of course, would do well as freshmen. But however many of this low group did well, there would be 55 percent *more* of the top group doing well according to the same criterion.

Precaution in the Use of Difference of Percents. Many students will merely wish to use the difference in percents as a rough general way of interpreting correlations. If you are in this group, you can leave the matter at this stage. It is possible, however, that you want to give this concept more thought. In that case, there are some cautions to keep in mind. In the first place, to make this concept strictly comparable to the coefficient of correlation, we should work it both ways. For our rough purposes we were content to find the difference in the percent of the two age groups having absences. To be more precise we should also find the percent of "no illness" children who were (say) older, (57.1 percent), and also the percent of "illness" children who were older (27.6 percent), and get the difference between these percents (29.5). This turns out to be quite comparable to the 30 percent we got in our first calculation. But it does not have to be. If there is any difference we should take the average (the geometric mean, in this case) of the two differences. When thus treated more completely, this method becomes a genuine *tetrachoric correlation* and is called the *phi coefficient of correlation.* In our discussion of this idea of correlation, you will remember, we were concerned merely with a useful and general way of thinking about coefficient of correlation. If you are going to do any more with this measure of correlation you will find methods of computation that are much more efficient than the steps we have gone through.

When taking this method seriously, we should also remember that this rough way of sorting the data—ignoring actual ages and actual days of illness—tends to

TABLE A.8. The Relation between Height and Weight for Twelve-year-old Children

	Number of Children below Median in Weight	Number of Children above Median in Weight	Total	Percent of Children above Median in Weight
Number of Children above Median in Height	2	10	12	83.3
Number of Children below Median in Height	10	2	12	16.6
Total	12	12	24	
Difference in Percent				66.7

underestimate the relation. Ordinarily we would get a higher correlation if we made use of the whole range of numbers.

SUMMARY

To deal with numbers in more efficient fashion, we can arrange them in frequency distributions and can calculate more precise measures such as means, medians, percentiles, and standard deviations. The frequency distribution gives a great deal of information in one eyeful, showing both the central trend of the data and the spread or dispersion. Either the mean or the median can be used when we need a single measure to describe the central tendency. The standard deviation is the favorite measure of dispersion.

Either a percentile rank or a standard score can be used to show where the individual stands within the distribution. Standard scores are frequently expressed as T-scores, or in other arbitrary forms such as IQ's, or the scores used in the Graduate Record Examination.

Provided we keep a few cautions in mind, a coefficient of correlation can be regarded as a slope. This shows how much change we can expect in one variable (weight) whenever we arrange for systematic changes in another variable (height). A coefficient of correlation is also something akin to a difference in percents. (What is the percent of tall children who are heavy as compared to the percent of short children who are heavy?) A high correlation can be interpreted in terms of the scatter in a correlation chart—the higher the correlation, the less the scatter.

SUGGESTIONS FOR FURTHER READING

Some treatment of statistics can be found in any of the textbooks listed under "Suggestions for Further Reading" in Chapter 3.

The following references deal more specifically with statistics:

Bartz, A., *Elementary Statistical Methods for Educational Measurement.* Minneapolis, Minn.: Burgess Publishing Company, 1958.

Bloomers, P., and E. F. Lindquist, *Elementary Statistical Methods in Psychology and Education.* Boston: Houghton Mifflin Company, 1960.

Cornell, F. G., *The Essentials of Educational Statistics.* New York: John Wiley & Sons, Inc., 1956.

Franzblau, A. N., *A Primer of Statistics for Non-statisticians.* New York: Harcourt, Brace & World, Inc., 1958.

Garrett, H. E., *Statistics in Psychology and Education,* 5th ed. New York: David McKay Company, Inc., 1958.

———, *Elementary Statistics,* 2d ed. New York: David McKay Company, Inc., 1962.

Guest, L., *Beginning Statistics.* New York: Thomas Y. Crowell Company, 1957.

Jordan, A. M., *Educational Psychology; Growth and Learning,* 4th ed. New York: Holt, Rinehart and Winston, Inc., 1956, Chapter 11.

Lindvall, C. M., Tests of statistical significance, *Phi Delta Kappan,* 1957, **38**, 314–316.

McIntosh, D. M., *Statistics for the Teacher.* New York: Pergamon Press, Inc., 1963.

McNemar, Q., *Psychological Statistics,* 3d ed. New York: John Wiley & Sons, Inc., 1962.

Nelson, M. J., E. C. Denny, and A. P. Coladarci, *Statistics for Teachers,* rev. ed. New York: Holt, Rinehart and Winston, Inc., 1956.

Noll, V. H., *Introduction to Educational Measurement.* Boston: Houghton Mifflin Company, 1957, Chapter 3.

Rummel, J. F., *An Introduction to Research Procedures in Education.* New York: Harper & Row, Publishers, Inc., 1958, Chapter 7.

Skinner, C. E., ed., *Essentials of Educational Psychology*. Englewood Cliffs, N. J.: Prentice-Hall, 1958, pp. 493–506.

Smith, G. M., *A Simplified Guide to Statistics for Psychology and Education*. New York: Holt, Rinehart and Winston, Inc., 1962.

Sorenson, H., *Fundamentals of Statistics*. New York: Vantage Press, 1961.

Townsend, E. A., and P. J. Burke, *Statistics for the Classroom Teacher, a Self-Teaching Unit*. New York: The Macmillan Company, 1963.

Tyler, Leona E., *Tests and Measurements*. Englewood Cliffs, N. J.: Prentice-Hall, 1963.

———, *Psychology of Human Differences*. New York: Appleton-Century-Crofts, 1956, Chapters 2 and 3.

Walker, Helen M., *Elementary Statistical Methods*. New York: Holt, Rinehart and Winston, Inc., 1943.

Special Aspects

A brief three-page article, How to read statistics, appears in Rosenblith (Readings), pp. 2–4.

To secure references to more advanced treatments consult:

Buckland, W. R., and R. A. Fox, *Bibliography of Basic Texts and Monographs on Statistical Methods*, 1945–1960, 2d ed. Edinburgh: Oliver & Boyd, Ltd., 1963.

EXERCISES AND QUESTIONS FOR DISCUSSION

1. A certain scientific team is made up of a director who earns $80 a day and four technical workers, earning $24, $20, $16, and $12 a day respectively. What is the mean salary? the median salary? To get a picture of the earning of the typical team member, should you use the median? or the mean?

A company is considering how many such teams it can afford. Which of the two measures should be used?

2. Arrange for a list of IQ's such as 160, 150, 140, 130, and so forth, down to 40. Using Figure A.1, estimate the percentile rank that corresponds to each IQ. Write a note explaining the things to keep in mind when translating IQ's to percentiles or vice versa.

3. There is a correlation of .60 between (x) the amount of money a state spends on education and (y) the average academic attainment of its students. Show how you might explain the meaning of this to a non-statistical friend.

REFERENCES

Adams, Georgia S., and T. L. Torgerson, *Measurement and Evaluation in Education, Psychology, and Guidance.* New York: Holt, Rinehart and Winston, 1964.

Adams, J. K., Laboratory studies of behavior without awareness, *Psychol. Bull.,* 1957, **54,** 383–405.

Adelson, J., The teacher as a model, in N. Sanford, ed., *The American College.* New York: Wiley, 1962, 396–417.

Adorno, T. W., Else Frenkel-Brunswik, D. J. Levenson, and R. N. Sanford, *The Authoritarian Personality.* New York: Harper & Row, 1950.

Ahmann, J. S., M. D. Glock, and Helen L. Wardeberg, *Evaluating Elementary School Pupils.* Boston: Allyn and Bacon, 1960.

Allen, E. A., Attitudes of children and adolescents in school, *Educ. Res.,* 1960, **3,** 65–80.

Allinsmith, W., and G. W. Goethals, *The Role of Schools in Mental Health.* New York: Basic Books, 1962.

Alper, Thelma G., Task-orientation and ego-orientation as factors in reminiscence, *J. exp. Psychol.,* 1948, **38,** 224–238.

———, Task-orientation vs ego-orientation in learning and retention, *Amer. J. Psychol.,* 1946, **59,** 236–248.

Amatora, Sister Mary, Expressed interests in later childhood, *J. genet. Psychol.,* 1960, **96,** 327–342.

American Association of Colleges for Teacher Education, *Roles and Relationships in Teacher Education,* 11th Biennial School for Executives. Washington, D. C.: The Association, 1963.

Anderson, A. W., The teaching profession: an example of diversity in training and function, *Yearb. nat. Soc. Stud. Educ.,* 1962, **61,** Part II, 140–167.

Anderson, H. H., ed., *Creativity and Its Cultivation.* New York: Harper & Row, 1959.

Anderson, R. C., Learning in discussions: resume of the authoritarian-democratic studies, *Harv. educ. Rev.,* 1959, **29,** 201–215.

Anderson, Scarvia B., Problem solving in multiple-goal situations, *J. exp. Psychol.,* 1957, **54,** 297–303.

Anderson, W. F., Attitudes of university students toward cheating, *J. educ. Res.,* 1957, **50,** 581–588.

Arnoult, M. D., Stimulus predifferentiation: some generalizations and hypotheses, *Psychol. Bull.,* 1957, **54,** 339–350.

Ausubel, D. P., *The Psychology of Meaningful Verbal Learning; An Introduction to School Learning.* New York: Grune & Stratton, 1963.

———, Learning by discovery: rationale and mystique, *Nat. Ass. second. Sch. Prin. Bull.,* 1961a (Dec.), **45** (No. 269), 18–58.

———, A new look at classroom discipline, *Phi Delta Kappan,* 1961b, **43,** 25–30.

———, The use of advance organizers in the learning and retention of meaningful verbal material, *J. educ. Psychol.,* 1960, **51,** 267–272.

———, *Theory and Problems of Child Development.* New York: Grune & Stratton, 1958.

———, S. H. Schpoont, and Lillian Cukier, The influence of intention on the retention of school materials, *J. educ. Psychol.,* 1957, **48,** 87–92.

Babitz, M., and N. Keys, An experiment in teaching pupils to apply scientific principles, *Sci. Educ.,* 1939, **23,** 367–370.

Baker, R. A., and S. W. Osgood, Discrimination transfer along a pitch continuum, *J. exp. Psychol.,* 1954, **48,** 241–246.

Baller, W. R., and D. C. Charles, *The Psychology of Human Growth and Development*. New York: Holt, Rinehart and Winston, 1961.

Balow, I. H., Does homogeneous grouping give homogeneous groups? *Elem. Sch. J.*, 1963, **63**, 28–32.

Bandura, A., Dorothea Ross, and Sheila A. Ross, A comparative test of the status envy, social power, and secondary reinforcement theories of identificatory learning, *J. abnorm. soc. Psychol.*, 1963a, **67**, 527–534.

———, ———, and ———, Vicarious and imitative learning, *J. abnorm. soc. Psychol.*, 1963b, **67**, 601–607.

Bandura, A., and R. H. Walters, Aggression, *Yearb. nat. Soc. Stud. Educ.*, 1963a, **62**, Part I, 364–415.

———, and ———, *Social Learning and Personality Development*. New York: Holt, Rinehart and Winston, 1963b.

———, and ———, *Adolescent Aggression*. New York: Ronald, 1959.

Barker, R. G., ed., *The Stream of Behavior: Explorations of Its Structure and Content*. New York: Appleton, 1963.

———, and H. F. Wright, *Midwest and Its Children; The Psychological Ecology of an American Town*. New York: Harper & Row, 1954.

Barr, J. A., and K. H. Hoover, Home conditions and influences associated with the development of high school leaders, *Educ. Admin. Superv.*, 1957, **43**, 271–279.

Barron, F., Creative vision and expression, in A. Frazier, ed., *New Insights and the Curriculum. Yearb. Ass. Superv. Curric. Develpm.* Washington, D. C.: NEA, 1963a, 285–305.

———, *Psychological Vitality and Creative Freedom*. Princeton, N. J.: Van Nostrand, 1963b.

———, The psychology of imagination, *Scient. American*, 1958 (Sept.), **199**, 150–166.

Bartlett, C. J., Dimensions of leadership behavior in classroom discussion groups, *J. educ. Psychol.*, 1959, **50**, 280–284.

Bartlett, Sir Frederick C., *Thinking: An Experimental and Social Study*. London: G. Allen, 1958; New York: Basic Books.

Bartz, A. E., *Elementary Statistical Methods for Educational Measurement*. Minneapolis: Burgess, 1958.

Bayley, Nancy, and E. S. Schaefer, Relationships between socioeconomic variables and the behavior of mothers toward young children, *J. genet. Psychol.*, 1960, **96**, 61–77.

Beach, F. A., The descent of instinct, *Psychol. Rev.*, 1955, **62**, 401–410.

Becker, H. S., The nature of a profession, *Yearb. nat. Soc. Stud. Educ.*, 1962, **61**, Part II, 27–46.

Becker, W. C., and others, Factors in parental behavior and personality related to problem behavior in children, *J. consult. Psychol.*, 1959, **23**, 107–118.

Beilin, H., and Emmy Werner, Sex differences among teachers in the use of the criteria of adjustment, *J. educ. Psychol.*, 1957, **48**, 426–436.

Belok, M., and F. R. Dowling, Teacher image and the teacher shortage, *Phi Delta Kappan*, 1961, **42**, 255–256.

Benne, K. D., and Grace Levit, The nature of groups and helping groups improve their operation, *Rev. educ. Res.*, 1953, **23**, 289–308.

Benschoter, Reba P., and D. C. Charles, Retention of classroom and television learning, *J. appl. Psychol.*, 1957, **41**, 253–256.

Berdie, R. F., and others (Symposium), Tests: tools of value, *Teachers Coll. Rec.*, 1962, **64**, 183–203.

Bereday, G. Z. F., and J. A. Lawreys, eds., *The Education and Training of Teachers: The Yearbook of Education*. New York: Harcourt, 1963.

Berkowitz, L., The effects of observing violence, *Scient. American*, 1964 (Feb.), **210**, No. 2, 35–41.

Berlyne, D. E., *Conflict, Arousal, and Curiosity*. New York: McGraw-Hill, 1960.

———, The influence of complexity and novelty in visual figures on orienting responses, *J. exp. Psychol.*, 1958, **55**, 289–296.

Bernard, H. W., *Mental Hygiene for Classroom Teachers*, 2d ed. New York: McGraw-Hill, 1961.

Biber, Barbara, The integration of mental health principles in a school setting as part of a program of primary prevention, in G. Caplan, ed., *Prevention of Mental Disorders in Children*. New York: Basic Books, 1961, pp. 323–352.

Bindra, D., *Motivation: A Systematic Reinterpretation*. New York: Ronald, 1959.

Binet, A., and Simon, T., Méthodes nouvelles pour le diagnostic du niveau intellectuel des anormaux, *L' Année psychologique*, 1905, **11**, 191–244. A translated, modified version, "The development of the Binet-Simon Scale," appears in Rosenblith, pp. 286–290.

Binter, A. R., Two ways of teaching per cent, *Elem. Sch. J.*, 1963, **63**, 261–265.

Birch, H. G., and H. S. Rabinowitz, The negative effect of previous experience on productive thinking, *J. exp. Psychol.*, 1951, **41**, 121–125.

Birch, J. W., and M. C. Reynolds, The gifted, *Rev. educ. Res.*, 1963, **33**, 83–98.

Birney, R. C., and R. C. Teevan, eds., *Reinforcement, An Enduring Problem in Psychology; Selected Readings*. Princeton, N. J.: Van Nostrand, 1961.

Black, H., *They Shall Not Pass*. New York: Morrow, 1963.

Blaine, G. B., Jr., C. C. McArthur, and others, *Emotional Problems of the Students*. New York: Appleton, 1961.

Block, J., Some differences between the concepts of social desirability and adjustment, *J. consult. Psychol.*, 1962, **26**, 527–530.

Blocker, C. E., and R. C. Richardson, Twenty-five years of morale research: a critical review, *J. educ. Sociol.*, 1963, **36**, 200–210.

Bloom, B. S., ed., *Taxonomy of Educational Objectives; The Classification of Educational Goals, by a Committee of College and University Examiners*. New York: McKay, 1956.

————, and Lois J. Broder, *Problem-solving Processes of College Students; An Exploratory Investigation*. Chicago: University of Chicago Press, 1950.

Bloomers, P., and E. F. Lindquist, *Elementary Statistical Methods in Psychology and Education*. Boston: Houghton Mifflin, 1960.

Bobroff, A., The stages of maturation in socialized thinking and in the ego development of two groups of children, *Child Develpm.*, 1960, **31**, 321–338.

Bond, Marjorie H., Teenage attitudes and attitude change as measured by the Q-technique, *J. educ. Sociol.*, 1962, **36**, 10–19.

Bonney, M. E., *Mental Hygiene in Education*. Boston: Allyn and Bacon, 1960.

Bourne, L. E., Jr., Effects of delay of information feedback and task complexity on the identification of concepts, *J. exp. Psychol.*, 1957, **54**, 201–207.

Bousfield, W. A., and B. H. Cohen, The occurrence of clustering in the recall of randomly arranged words of different frequencies-of-usage, *J. gen. Psychol.*, 1955, **52**, 83–95.

Bowen, R. O., *The New Professors*. New York: Holt, Rinehart and Winston, 1960.

Bower, E. M., Mental health in education, *Rev. educ. Res.*, 1962, **32**, 441–454.

————, A process for identifying disturbed children, *Children*, 1957, **4**, 143–147.

Brackbill, Yvonne, and M. S. Kappy, Delay of reinforcement and retention, *J. comp. physiol. Psychol.*, 1962, **55**, 14–18.

Breckenridge, Marian E., and Margaret N. Murphy, *Growth and Development of the Young Child*, 7th ed. Philadelphia: Saunders, 1963.

————, and E. L. Vincent, *Child Development; Physical and Psychologic Growth through Adolescence*, 4th ed. Philadelphia: Saunders, 1960.

Breed, F. S., Generalization in spelling, *Elem. Sch. J.*, 1937, **37**, 733–741.

Bronfenbrenner, U., The changing American child—a speculative analysis, *J. soc. Issues*, 1961a, **17**, 6–16.

————, Some familial antecedents of responsibility and leadership in adolescents, in L. Petrullo and B. M. Bass, eds., *Leadership and Interpersonal Behavior*. New York: Holt, Rinehart and Winston, 1961b. pp. 239–271.

————, Freudian theories of identification and their derivatives, *Child Develpm.*, 1960, **31**, 15–40.

————, and H. N. Ricciuti, The appraisal of personality characteristics in children, in P. H. Mussen, ed., *Handbook of Research Methods in Child Development*. New York: Wiley, 1960, pp. 770–817.

Brown, J. S., *The Motivation of Behavior*. New York: McGraw-Hill, 1961.

Brownell, W. A., and H. E. Moser, *Meaningful vs. Mechanical Learning; A Study in Grade III Subtraction*. Durham, N. C.: Duke University Press, 1949.

Brownfield, C. A., Deterioration and facilitation hypotheses in sensory-deprivation research, *Psychol. Bull.*, 1964, **61**, 304–313.

Bruce, P., Relationship of self-acceptance to other variables with sixth grade children oriented in self-understanding, *J. educ. Psychol.*, 1958, **49**, 229–238.

Bruner, J. S., Act of discovery, *Harv. educ. Rev.*, 1961, **31**, 21–32.

————, *The Process of Education*, Cambridge, Mass.: Harvard University Press, 1960.

————, Freud and the image of man, *Amer. Psychologist*, 1956, **11**, 463–466.

————, Jacqueline J. Goodnow, and G. A. Austin, *A Study of Thinking*. New York: Wiley, 1961.

Buck, R. C., The extent of social participation among public school teachers, *J. educ. Sociol.*, 1960, **33**, 311–319.

Buckland, W. R., and R. A. Fox, *Bibliography of Basic Texts and Monographs on Statistical Methods, 1945–1960*, 2d ed. Edinburgh: Oliver & Boyd, 1963.

Bugelski, B. R., *The Psychology of Learning*. New York: Holt, Rinehart and Winston, 1958.

————, and T. C. Cadwallader, A reappraisal of the transfer and retroaction surface, *J. exp. Psychol.*, 1956, **52**, 360–366.

Bullis, H. E., Are we losing our fight for improved mental health? *Progress. Educ.*, 1953, **30**, 110–114.

Burch, G. B., The problem of universals in the philosophy of education, *Educ. Theory*, 1957, **7**, 216–220.

Burchill, G. W., *Work-study Programs for Alienated Youth, A Casebook*. Chicago: Science Research Associates, 1962.

Burke, H. R., Raven's Progressive Matrices: a review and critical evaluation, *J. genet. Psychol.*, 1958, **93**, 199–228.

Buros, O. K., ed., *Tests in Print; a Comprehensive Bibliography of Tests for Use in Education, Psychology, and Industry*. Highland Park, N. J.: Gryphon Press, 1961.

Burt, Sir Cyril, Is intelligence distributed normally? *Brit. J. statist. Psychol.*, 1963, **16**, 175–190.

Burtt, H. E., A further study of early childhood memory, *J. genet. Psychol.*, 1937, **50**, 187–192.

Bush, R. N., The human relations factor: I. Principles of successful teacher-pupil relationship, *Phi Delta Kappan*, 1958, **39**, 271–273.

Buss, A. H., *The Psychology of Aggression*. New York: Wiley, 1961.

Buzzeli, J., and others, *Rewarding Creative Thinking: A Manual for Elementary Teachers*. Minneapolis: Minnesota State University College of Education, Bureau of Educational Research, 1959.

Byrns, Ruth, and V. A. C. Henmon, Entrance requirements and college success, *Sch. Soc.*, 1935, **41**, 101–104.

Cain, L. F., and S. Levine, The mentally retarded, *Rev. educ. Res.*, 1963, **33**, 62–82.

California State Department of Education, *The Education of Emotionally Handicapped Children*. Sacramento: The Dept., 1961.

Callis, R., Counseling, *Rev. educ. Res.*, 1963, **33**, 179–187.

Calvin, A. D., F. J. McGuigan, and M. W.

Sullivan, A further investigation of the relationship between anxiety and classroom examination performance, *J. educ. Psychol.*, 1957, 48, 240–244.

Cameron, N. A., *Personality Development and Psychopathology*. Boston: Houghton Mifflin, 1963.

Carroll, J. B., Language development, *Encyclopaedia of Educational Research*, 3d ed. New York: Macmillan, 1960, pp. 744–752.

Carter, L., and others, The behavior of leaders and other group members, *J. abnorm. soc. Psychol.*, 1951, 46, 589–595.

Cartwright, D., and A. Zander, *Group Dynamics; Research and Theory*, rev. ed. New York: Harper & Row, 1960.

Castaneda, A., B. R. McCandless, and D. S. Palmero, The children's form of the Manifest Anxiety Scale, *Child Develpm.*, 1956a, 27, 317–326.

———, D. S. Palmero, and B. R. McCandless, Complex learning and performance as a function of anxiety in children and task difficulty. *Child Develpm.*, 1956b, 27, 327–332.

Cattell, R. B., Validity and reliability: a proposed more basic set of concepts, *J. educ. Psychol.*, 1964, 55, 1–22.

———, Validation and intensification of the Sixteen Personality Factor Questionnaire, *J. clin. Psychol.*, 1956, 12, 205–214.

Celler, S. L., Practices associated with effective discipline, Unpublished EdD thesis, Johns Hopkins University, 1948.

Chansky, N. M., Learning: a function of schedule and type of feedback, *Psychol. Rep.*, 1960, 7, 362.

Chapanis, Natalia P., and A. Chapanis, Cognitive dissonance: five years later, *Psychol. Bull.*, 1964, 61, 1–22.

Charters, W. W. Jr., The social background of teaching, in N. L. Gage, ed., *Handbook of Research on Teaching*. Skokie, Ill.: Rand McNally, 1963, pp. 715–813.

Child, I. L., and I. K. Waterhouse, Frustration and the quality of performance: I. A critique of the Barker, Dembo, and Lewin experiment, *Psychol. Rev.*, 1952, 59, 351–362.

Chown, S. M., Rigidity: a flexible concept, *Psychol. Bull.*, 1959, 56, 195–223.

Churchill, Ruth, and Paula John, Conservation of teaching time through the use of lecture classes and student assistants, *J. educ. Psychol.*, 1958, 49, 324–327.

Clark, K. B., *Prejudice and Your Child*, 2d ed. Boston: Beacon Press, 1963.

Clausen, J. A., and Judith R. Williams, Sociological correlates of child behavior, *Yearb. nat. Soc. Stud. Educ.*, 1963, 62, Part I, 62–107.

Cobb, P. R., High school seniors attitudes toward teachers and the teaching profession, *Nat. Ass. second. Sch. Prin. Bull.*, 1952, (Jan.), 36, (No. 183), 140–144.

Cochran, J. R., and others, Grouping: promising approaches, *Educational Leadership*, 1961, 18, 410–434.

Cofer, C. N., ed., *Verbal Learning and Verbal Behavior; Proceedings*. New York: McGraw-Hill, 1961.

———, and Barbara S. Musgrave, eds., *Verbal Behavior and Learning: Problems and Processes; Proceedings*. New York: McGraw-Hill, 1963.

Coleman, J. S., *The Adolescent Society; The Social Life of the Teenager and Its Impact on Education*. New York: Free Press of Glencoe, 1961.

———, The adolescent subculture and academic achievement, *Amer. J. Sociol.*, 1960, 65, 337–347.

Coleman, W., and E. E. Cureton, Intelligence and achievement: the "jangle fallacy" again, *Educ. psychol. Measmt.*, 1954, 14, 347–351.

Coler, M. A., ed., *Essays on Creativity in the Sciences*. New York: New York University Press, 1963.

Cook, D. R., and W. D. Martinson, The relationship of certain course work in high school to achievement in college, *Personnel Guid. J.*, 1962, 40, 703–707.

Cook, W. W., and T. Clymer, Acceleration and retardation, *Yearb. nat. Soc. Stud. Educ.*, 1962, 61, Part I, 179–208.

Cornell, F. G., *The Essentials of Educational Statistics*. New York: Wiley, 1956.

Coslin, F., and W. D. Kerr, The effects of an abnormal psychology course on students' attitudes toward mental illness, *J. educ. Psychol.*, 1962, **53**, 214–218.

Cousins, N., Not so fast, *Sat. Rev.*, 1963 (July 6), p. 14.

Cowen, E. L., and others, A preventative mental health program in the school setting: description and evaluation, *J. Psychol.*, 1963, **56**, 307–356.

Cox, F. N., Sociometric status and individual adjustment before and after play therapy, *J. abnorm. soc. Psychol.*, 1953, **48**, 354–356.

Crawford, B. M., and E. R. Harrington, Development of a school policy on discipline, *Calif. J. educ. Res.*, 1961, **12**, 31–37.

Cremin, L. A., *The Transformation of the School; Progressivism in American Education, 1876–1957*. New York: Knopf, 1961.

Crofton, J. A., The effect on ability in woodwork of previous training in cardboard work, *Brit. J. educ. Psychol.*, 1957. **27**, 217–219.

Cron, G. W., and N. H. Pronko, Development of a sense of balance in school children, *J. educ. Res.*, 1957, **51**, 33–37.

Cronbach, L. J., *Educational Psychology*, 2d ed. New York: Harcourt, 1963.

———, *Essentials of Psychological Testing*, 2d ed. New York: Harper & Row, 1960.

———, R. Nageswari, and Goldine C. Gleser, Theory of generalizability: a liberalization of reliability theory. *Brit. J. statist. Psychol.*, 1963, **16**, 137–163.

Crow, W. J., The effect of training upon accuracy and variability in interpersonal perception, *J. abnorm. soc. Psychol.*, 1957, **55**, 355–359.

Crutchfield, R. S., Conformity and character, *Amer. Psychologist*, 1955, **10**, 191–198.

Cumming, Elaine, and J. Cumming, *Closed Ranks; An Experiment in Mental Health Education*. Cambridge, Mass.: Harvard University Press, 1957.

Cutts, Norma E., and N. Moseley, *Teaching the Disorderly Pupil, Elementary and Secondary School*. London: Longmans, 1957.

Dasgupta, S. K., An examination of the data on fear, *Agra U. J. Res.*, (Meerut, India), 1962, **10**, 35–43.

Davitz, J. R., The effects of previous training on postfrustration behavior, *J. abnorm. soc. Psychol.*, 1952, **47**, 309–315.

Day, R. H., Relative task difficulty and transfer of training in skilled performance, *Psychol. Bull.*, 1956, **53**, 160–168.

De Cecco, J. P., Class size and co-ordinated instruction, *Brit. J. educ. Psychol.*, 1964, **34**, 65–74.

Deese, J. E., *The Psychology of Learning*, 2d ed. New York: McGraw-Hill, 1958.

———, and G. W. Hardman, Jr., An analysis of errors in retroactive inhibition of rote verbal learning, *Amer. J. Psychol.*, 1954, **67**, 299–307.

DeHaan, R. F., and R. J. Havighurst, *Educating Gifted Children*, rev. and enlarged ed. Chicago: University of Chicago Press, 1961.

Dell, G. A., Social factors and school influence in juvenile delinquency, *Brit. J. educ. Psychol.*, 1963, **33**, 312–322.

Dentler, R. A., and B. Mackler, Mental ability and sociometric status among retarded children, *Psychol. Bull.*, 1962, **59**, 273–283.

Diederich, P. B., *Short-cut Statistics for Teacher-made Tests*. (Evaluation and Advisory Service Series, No. 5.) Princeton, N. J.: Educational Testing Service, 1960.

Dienes, Z. P., The growth of mathematical concepts in children through experience, *Educ. Res.*, 1959, **2**, 9–28.

Dollard, J., and N. E. Miller, *Personality and Psychotherapy, An Analysis in Terms of Learning, Thinking, and Culture*. New York: McGraw-Hill, 1950.

———, and others, *Frustration and Aggression*. New Haven, Conn.: Yale University Press, 1939.

Douvan, Elizabeth, Sex differences in adolescent character processes, *Merrill-Palmer Quart.*, 1960, **6**, 203–211.

Dressel, P. L., Critical thinking: the goal of education, *NEA J.*, 1955, **44**, 418–420.

Dubos, R. J., Adaptability for survival and growth, in E. Ginzberg, ed., *Values and Ideals of American Youth*. New York: Columbia University Press, 1961, pp. 3–13.

Duffy, Elizabeth, *Activation and Behavior*. New York: Wiley, 1962.

Dulles, R. J., The myth of underachievement, *J. educ. Sociol.*, 1961, **35**, 121–122.

Duncan, C. P., Recent research on human problem solving, *Psychol. Bull.*, 1959, **56**, 397–429.

———, Transfer in motor learning as a function of degree of first-task learning and inter-task similarity, *J. exp. Psychol.*, 1953, **45**, 1–11.

Duncker, K., On problem-solving, *Psychol. Monogr.*, 1945, **58**, No. 5.

Durkin, Dolores, An earlier start in reading? *Elem. Sch. J.*, 1963, **63**, 147–151.

———, Children's concepts of justice: a further comparison with the Piaget data, *J. educ. Res.*, 1959, **52**, 252–257.

Dyer, H. S., On the assessment of academic achievement, *Teachers Coll. Rec.*, 1960, **62**, 164–172.

Eason, R. G., and J. Branks, Effect of level of activation on the quality and efficiency of performance of verbal and motor tasks, *Percept. mot. Skills*, 1963, **16**, 525–543.

Eaton, M. T., G. Weathers, and B. N. Phillips, Some reactions of classroom teachers to problem behavior in school. *Educ. Adm. Superv.*, 1957, **43**, 129–139.

Eckstrand, G. W., and D. D. Wickens, Transfer of perceptual set, *J. exp. Psychol.*, 1954, **47**, 274–278.

Eddy, E. D., *The College Influence on Student Character*. Washington, D. C.: American Council on Education, 1959.

Educational Testing Service, *Developments*, 1961, **9**, No. 2.

———, *Making the Classroom Test: A Guide for Teachers* (Evaluation and

Advisory Service Series, No. 4). Princeton, N. J.: 1961.

———, *Selecting an Achievement Test: Principles and Procedures*, 2d ed. (Evaluation and Advisory Service Series, No. 3). Princeton, N. J.: 1961.

Edwards, A. L., *The Social Desirability Variable in Personality Assessment and Research*. New York: Holt, Rinehart and Winston, 1957.

Eglash, A., Changes in opinionation during a psychology course, *J. educ. Psychol.*, 1957, **48**, 164–165.

Eigen, L. D., High-school student reactions to programed instruction, *Phi Delta Kappan*, 1963, **44**, 282–285.

Ekstrom, Ruth B., Experimental studies of homogeneous grouping: a critical review, *Sch. Rev.*, 1961, **69**, 216–226.

Emmons, W. H., and C. W. Simon, The non-recall of material presented during sleep, *Amer. J. Psychol.*, 1956, **69**, 76–81.

Englander, M. E., A psychological analysis of vocational choice: teaching, *J. counsel. Psychol.*, 1960, **7**, 257–264.

Englehart, M. D., Operationally defined instructional objectives in relation to validity, *Yearb. nat. Council. Measmt. Educ.*, 1961, **18**, 15–21.

English, H. B., *Dynamics of Child Development*. New York: Holt, Rinehart and Winston, 1962.

Ennis, R. H., A concept of critical thinking, *Harv. educ. Rev.*, 1962, **32**, 81–111.

Entwisle, Doris R., Attensity: factors of specific set in school learning, *Harv. educ. Rev.*, 1961, **31**, 84–101.

———, Evaluations of study-skills courses: a review, *J. educ. Res.*, 1960, **53**, 243–251.

———, and W. H. Huggins, Interference in meaningful learning, *J. educ. Psychol.*, 1964, **55**, 75–78.

Erikson, E. H., *Childhood and Society*, 2d rev. and enlarged ed. New York: Norton, 1963a.

———, ed., *Youth: Change and Challenge*. New York: Basic Books, 1963b.

———, The problem of ego identity, *J.*

Amer. Psychoanal. Ass., 1956, **4**, 56–121.

Escalona, Sibylle K., An application of the level of aspiration experiment to the study of personality, *Teachers Coll. Contr. Educ.*, No. 937, 1948.

Estes, W. K., Learning, *Encyclopaedia of Educational Research*, 3d ed. New York: Macmillan, 1960, pp. 752–770.

——, The statistical approach to learning theory, in S. Koch, ed., *Psychology: A Study of a Science*. New York: McGraw-Hill, 1959, Vol. 2, pp. 380–491.

——, An experimental study of punishment, *Psychol. Monogr.*, 1944, **57**, No. 3.

Evans, K. M., The teacher-pupil relationship, *Educ. Res.*, 1959, **2**, 3–8.

Eysenck, H. J., The contribution of learning theory, *Brit. J. educ. Psychol.*, 1960, **30**, 11–21.

Farber, I. E., The things people say to themselves, *Amer. Psychologist*, 1963, **18**, 185–197.

——, The role of motivation in verbal learning and performance, *Psychol. Bull.*, 1955, **52**, 311–327.

Farnsworth, D. L., Mental health education: implications for teachers, *Teachers Coll. Rec.*, 1961, **62**, 263–273.

Fawl, C. L., Disturbances experienced by children in the natural habitats, Unpublished PhD dissertation, University of Kansas, 1959.

Feinberg, M. R., M. Smith, and R. Schmidt, An analysis of expressions used by adolescents at varying economic levels to describe accepted and rejected peers, *J. genet. Psychol.*, 1958, **93**, 133–148.

Feldhusen, J. F., Taps for teaching machines, *Phi Delta Kappan*, 1963, **44**, 265–267.

Ferguson, G. A., On transfer and the abilities of man, *Canad. J. Psychol.*, 1956, **10**, 121–131.

Festinger, L., *A Theory of Cognitive Dissonance*. New York: Harper & Row, 1957.

——, and V. Allen, *Conflict, Decision, and Dissonance*. Stanford, Calif.: Stanford University Press, 1964.

Fiedler, F. E., Leader attitudes, group climate, and group creativity, *J. abnorm. soc. Psychol.*, 1962, **65**, 308–318.

——, *Leader Attitudes and Group Effectiveness*. Urbana, Ill.: University of Illinois Press, 1958.

Findley, W. G., ed., The impact and improvement of school testing programs, *Yearb. nat. Soc. Stud. Educ.*, 1963, **62**, Part II.

——, Use and interpretation of achievement tests in relation to validity, *Yearb. nat. Council. Measmt. Educ.*, 1961, **18**, 23–34.

Fischer, J. H., *Report of the Advisory Committee on Pupil Records*. Albany, New York: University of the State of New York, State Education Department, 1961.

Fitzgerald, D., and D. P. Ausubel, Cognitive versus affective factors in the learning and retention of controversial material, *J. educ. Psychol.*, 1963, **54**, 73–84.

Flanders, N. A., Diagnosing and utilizing social structures in classroom learning, *Yearb. nat. Soc. Stud. Educ.*, 1960a, **59**, Part II, 187–217.

——, *Teacher influence, pupil attitudes, and achievement; final report* (U. S. Office of Educ. Coop. Res. Project, No. 397). Minneapolis: University of Minnesota, 1960b.

——, and Sulo Havumaki, The effect of teacher-pupil contacts involving praise on the sociometric choices of students, *J. educ. Psychol.*, 1960, **51**, 65–68.

Flavell, J. H., *The Developmental Psychology of Jean Piaget*. Princeton, N. J.: Van Nostrand, 1963.

Fleming, Charlotte M., Class size as a variable in the teaching situation, *Educ. Res.*, 1959, **1**, 35–48.

——, *Teaching: A Psychological Analysis*. New York: Wiley, 1958.

Forlano, G., School learning with various methods of practice and rewards, *Teachers Coll. Contr. Educ.*, No. 688, 1936.

——, and M. N. H. Hoffman, Guessing and telling methods in learning words of a foreign language, *J. educ. Psychol.*, 1937, **28**, 632–636.

Foster, Josephine C., As the child sees the teacher, *Childh. Educ.*, 1933, **9**, 283–288.

Fowler, W., Cognitive learning in infancy and early childhood, *Psychol. Bull.*, 1962a, **59**, 116–152.

———, Teaching a two-year-old to read: an experiment in early childhood learning, *Genet. Psychol. Monogr.*, 1962b, **66**, 181–283.

Fraiberg, Selma H., *The Magic Years: Understanding and Handling the Problems of Early Childhood*. New York: Scribner's, 1959.

Francis, E. F., Fundamentals of character education, *Sch. Rev.*, 1962, **70**, 345–357.

Frank, J. D., Recent studies of the level of aspiration, *Psychol. Bull.*, 1941, **38**, 218–226.

Franklin, R. D., and H. H. Remmers, Youth looks at civil liberties and the 1960 election, *Purdue Opin. Panel Poll Rep.*, 1960, No. 61.

Franzblau, A. N., *A Primer of Statistics for Non-statisticians*. New York: Harcourt, 1958.

Freedman, M. B., *Impact of College, New Dimensions in Higher Education.* Washington, D. C.: Govt. Printing Office, 1960, No. 4.

Freeman, F. S., *Theory and Practice of Psychological Testing*, 3d ed. New York: Holt, Rinehart and Winston, 1962.

French, W. M., and others, *Behavioral Goals of General Education in High School.* New York: Russell Sage, 1957.

Fry, E. B., *Teaching Machines and Programmed Instruction, An Introduction.* New York: McGraw-Hill, 1963.

Furness, Edna L., Portrait of the pedagogue in eighteenth century England, *Hist. Educ. Quart.*, 1962, **2**, 62–70.

Gabriel, J., *An Analysis of the Emotional Problems of the Teacher in the Classroom.* Melbourne: F. W. Cheshire, 1957.

Gage, N. L., ed., *Handbook of Research on Teaching.* Skokie, Ill.: Rand McNally, 1963.

Gagné, R. M., and R. C. Bolles, A review of factors in learning efficiency, in E. Galanter, ed., *Automatic Teaching: The State of the Art.* New York: Wiley, 1959, pp. 13–53.

———, Harriet Foster, and Miriam E. Crowley, The measurement of transfer of training, *Psychol. Bull.*, 1948, **45**, 97–130.

Gallagher, J. J., Social status of children related to intelligence, propinquity, and social perception, *Elem. Sch. J.*, 1958, **58**, 225–231.

Garbin, A. P., and F. L. Gates, Occupational prestige: an empirical study of its correlates, *Soc. Forces*, 1961, **40**, 131–136.

Gardner, E. F., and G. G. Thompson, *Social Relations and Morale in Small Groups.* New York: Appleton, 1956.

Gardner, M., *Mathematical Puzzles.* New York: Crowell, 1961.

Garrett, H. E., *Elementary Statistics*, 2d ed. New York: McKay, 1962.

———, *Statistics in Psychology and Education*, 5th ed. New York: McKay, 1958.

Garrison, K. C., Worldmindedness attitudes of college students in a southern university, *J. soc. Psychol.*, 1961, **54**, 147–153.

———, A study of student disciplinarian practices in 2 Georgia high schools, *J. educ. Res.*, 1959, **53**, 153–156.

Gellert, Elizabeth, Stability and fluctuation in the power relationships of young children, *J. abnorm. soc. Psychol.*, 1961, **62**, 8–15.

Gerberich, J. R., and others, *Measurement and Evaluation in the Modern School.* New York: McKay, 1962.

Gesell, A., and F. L. Ilg, *Child Development, An Introduction to the Study of Human Growth.* New York: Harper & Row, 1949.

Getzels, J. W., and P. W. Jackson, The teacher's personality and characteristics, in N. L. Gage, ed., *Handbook of Re-*

search on Teaching. Skokie, Ill.: Rand McNally, 1963, pp. 506–582.

———, and ———, Creativity and Intelligence, Explorations with Gifted Students. New York: Wiley, 1962.

Ghiselin, B., The Creative Process, A Symposium. Berkeley, Calif.: University of California Press, 1952.

Gibb, J. R., Sociopsychological processes of group instruction, Yearb. nat. Soc. Stud. Educ., 1960, 59, Part II, 115–135.

Gibbens, T. C. N., Trends in juvenile delinquency, Geneva: World Hlth. Organiz., WHO Public Health Papers, 1961, No. 5.

Gibson, Eleanor J., Perceptual development, Yearb. nat. Soc. Stud. Educ., 1963, 62, Part I, 144–195.

———, Improvement in perceptual judgments as a function of controlled practice or training, Psychol. Bull., 1953, 50, 401–431.

Ginzberg, E., ed., Values and Ideals of American Youth. New York: Columbia University Press, 1961.

Glanzer, M., and R. Glaser, Techniques for the study of group structure and behavior: II. Empirical studies of the effects of structure in small groups, Psychol. Bull., 1961, 58, 1–27.

———, and ———, Techniques for the study of group structure and behavior: I. Analysis of structure, Psychol. Bull., 1959, 56, 317–332.

Glidewell, J. C., ed., Parental Attitudes and Child Behavior. Springfield, Ill.: Charles C Thomas, 1961.

Glueck, S., and Eleanor Glueck, Family Environment and Delinquency. Boston: Houghton Mifflin, 1962.

———, and ———, Unravelling Juvenile Delinquency. New York: Commonwealth Fund, 1950.

Goertzen, S. M., Factors relating to opinions of seventh grade children regarding the acceptability of certain behaviors in the peer group, J. genet. Psychol., 1959, 94, 29–34.

———, A study of teachers' and psychologists' ability to predict seventh graders'

opinions of certain behaviors of their peer group, J. educ. Psychol., 1957, 48, 166–170.

Golann, S. E., Psychological study of creativity, Psychol. Bull., 1963, 60, 548–565.

Gold, M., Power in the classroom, Sociometry, 1958, 21, 50–60.

Goldberg, Miriam L., and A. H. Passow, The effects of ability grouping, Education, Boston, 1962, 82, 482–487.

Goodenough, Florence L., Anger in Young Children. Minneapolis: University of Minnesota Press, 1931.

———, and Leona E. Tyler, Developmental Psychology, 3d ed. New York: Appleton, 1959.

Goodlad, J. E., Individual differences and vertical organization of the school, Yearb. nat. Soc. Stud. Educ., 1962, 61, Part I, 209–238.

Goodnow, Jacqueline, J., and T. F. Pettigrew, Some sources of difficulty in solving simple problems, J. exp. Psychol., 1956, 51, 385–392.

Goslin, D. A., The Search for Ability: Standardized Testing in Social Perspective. New York: Russell Sage, 1963.

Grace, Gloria L., The relation of personality characteristics and response to verbal approval in a learning task, Genet. Psychol. Monogr., 1948, 37, 73–99.

Grambs, Jean D., Understanding intergroup relations, No. 21 in What Research Says to the Teacher. Washington, D.C.: NEA, 1960.

———, The roles of the teacher, in L. Stiles, ed., The Teacher's Role in American Society, Yearb. John Dewey Soc., 1957, 14, 73–93. New York: Harper & Row.

Grant, D. L., and N. Caplan, Studies in the reliability of the short-answer essay examination, J. educ. Res., 1957, 51, 109–116.

Green, J. A., Teacher-made Tests. New York: Harper & Row, 1963.

Greenberg, H., A. L. Chase, and T. M. Cannon, Jr., Attitudes of white and Negro high school students in a west

Texas town toward school integration, *J. appl. Psychol.*, 1957a, **41**, 27–31.

Greenberg, H., J. Pierson, and S. Sherman, The effects of single-session education techniques on prejudice attitudes, *J. educ. Sociol.*, 1957b, **31**, 82–86.

Groff, P. J., The social status of teachers, *J. educ. Sociol.*, 1962, **36**, 20–25.

Gronlund, N. E., *Sociometry in the Classroom*. New York: Harper & Row, 1959.

———, Relationship between the sociometric status of pupils' and teachers' preferences for or against having them in class, *Sociometry*, 1953, **16**, 142–150.

Grose, R. F., and R. C. Birney, eds., *Transfer of Learning, An Enduring Problem in Psychology*. Princeton, N. J.: Van Nostrand, 1963.

Gross, M. L., *The Brain Watchers*. New York: Random House, 1962.

Gruber, H. E., G. Terrell, and Michael Wertheimer, *Contemporary Approaches to Creative Thinking; A Symposium*. New York: Atherton, 1963.

Guba, E. G., P. W. Jackson, and C. E. Bidwell, Occupational choice and the teaching career, *Educ. Res. Bull.*, 1959, **38**, 1–12; 57.

Guest, L., *Beginning Statistics*. New York: Crowell, 1957.

Guilford, J. P., and R. Hoepfner, Current summary of structure-of-intellect factors and suggested tests, *Reports from the Psychological Laboratory*, Los Angeles: University of Southern California, 1963, No. 30.

Gustafson, Lucille, Relationship between ethnic group membership and the retention of selected facts pertaining to American history and culture, *J. educ. Sociol.*, 1957, **31**, 49–56.

Guthrie, E. R., *The Psychology of Learning*, rev. ed. New York: Harper & Row, 1952.

Hadfield, J. A., *Childhood and Adolescence*. Baltimore: Penguin, 1962.

Hall, C. S., and G. Lindzey, *Theories of Personality*. New York: Wiley, 1957.

Hall, J. F., *Psychology of Motivation*. Philadelphia: Lippincott, 1961.

———, Retroactive inhibition in meaningful material, *J. educ. Psychol.*, 1955, **46**, 47–52.

Hammer, E. F., *Creativity: An Exploratory Investigation of the Personalities of Gifted Adolescent Artists*. New York: Random House, 1961.

Hare, A. P., A study of interaction and consensus in different sized groups, *Amer. sociol. Rev.*, 1952, **17**, 261–267.

———, E. F. Borgatta, and R. F. Bales, eds., *Small Groups; Studies in Social Interaction*. New York: Knopf, 1955.

Haring, N. G., and E. L. Phillips, *Educating Emotionally Disturbed Children*. New York: McGraw-Hill, 1962.

Harlow, H. F., The heterosexual affectional system in monkeys, *Amer. Psychologist*, 1962, **17**, 1–9.

———, Mice, monkeys, men, and motives, *Psychol. Rev.*, 1953, **60**, 23–32.

———, and J. M. Warren, Formation and transfer of discrimination learning sets, *J. comp. physiol. Psychol.*, 1952, **45**, 482–489.

Harootunian, B., and M. W. Tate, The relationship of certain selected variables to problem solving ability, *J. educ. Psychol.*, 1960, **51**, 326–333.

Harris, C. W., ed., *Problems in Measuring Change*. Madison, Wis.: University of Wisconsin Press, 1963.

Harris, D. B., *Children's Drawings as Measures of Intellectual Maturity; A Revision and Extension of the Goodenough Draw-a-Man Test*. New York: Harcourt, 1963.

———, Child development, *Yearb. Amer. Ass. Coll. Teacher Educ.*, 1960, **13**, 28–44.

———, A scale for measuring attitudes of social responsibility in children, *J. abnorm. soc. Psychol.*, 1957a, **55**, 322–326.

———, ed., *The Concept of Development: An Issue in the Study of Human Behavior*. Minneapolis: University of Minnesota Press, 1957b.

————, and others, Personality differences between responsible and less responsible children, *J. genet. Psychol.*, 1955, 87, 103–109.

————, and others, The measurement of responsibility in children, *Child Develpm.*, 1954, 25, 21–28.

Harris, Florence R., and others, Effects of positive social reinforcement on regressed crawling of a nursery school child, *J. educ. Psychol.*, 1964, 55, 35–41.

Hartley, Ruth E., Children's concepts of male and female roles, *Merrill-Palmer Quart.*, 1960, 6, 83–91.

Hartshorne, H., and M. A. May, A summary of the work of the Character Education Inquiry, *Religious Educ.*, 1930, 25, 607–619; 754–762.

————, and ————, *Studies in the Nature of Character.* New York: Macmillan, 1928–1930.

Hartung, M. L., Teaching of mathematics in senior high school and junior college, *Rev. educ. Res.*, 1942, 12, 425–434.

Hartup, W. W., Patterns of imitative behavior in young children, *Child Develpm.*, 1964, 35, 183–191.

————, Dependence and independence, *Yearb. nat. Soc. Stud. Educ.*, 1963, 62, Part I, 333–363.

Haslerud, G. M., and Shirley Meyers, The transfer value of given and individually derived principles, *J. educ. Psychol.*, 1958, 49, 293–298.

Hathaway, S. R., *Adolescent Personality and Behavior; MMPI Patterns of Normal, Delinquent, Drop Out, and Other Outcomes.* Minneapolis: University of Minnesota Press, 1963.

Haubrick, V. F., The motives of prospective teachers, *J. Teacher Educ.*, 1960, 11, 381–386.

Havighurst, R. J., Developing moral character, *NEA J.*, 1962, 51, 28–30.

————, and Bernice L. Neugarten, *Society and Education*, 2d ed. Boston: Allyn and Bacon, 1962.

————, and L. J. Stiles, National policy for alienated youth, *Phi Delta Kappan*, 1961, 42, 283–291.

Hayes, Margaret L., and Mary E. Conklin, Inter-group attitudes and experimental change, *J. exp. Educ.*, 1953, 22, 19–36.

Heidbreder, Edna, An experimental study of thinking, *Arch. Psychol, N. Y.*, 1924, 11, No. 73.

Heinrich, K., *Filmerleben, Filmwirkung, Filmerziehung: Der Einfluss der Films auf die Aggressivität beim Jugendlichen. Experimentelle Untersuchungen und ihre lernpsychologischen Konsequenzen.* Berlin: Herman Schrroedel, 1961.

Hemming, J., Some aspects of moral development in a changing society, *Brit. J. educ. Psychol.*, 1957, 27, 77–88.

Henderson, K. B., The teaching of critical thinking, *Phi Delta Kappan*, 1958, 39, 280–282.

Hendrickson, G., and W. H. Schroeder, Transfer of training in learning to hit a submerged target, *J. educ. Psychol.*, 1941, 32, 205–213.

Hendrix, Gertrude, Learning by discovery, *Math. Teacher*, 1961, 54, 290–299.

————, A new clue to transfer of training, *Elem. Sch. J.*, 1947, 48, 197–208.

Henle, Mary, ed., *Documents of Gestalt Psychology.* Berkeley, Calif.: University of California Press, 1961.

Henry, N. B., ed., The dynamics of instructional groups, *Yearb. nat. Soc. Stud. Educ.*, 1960, 59, Part II.

Henry, W. E., Projective techniques, in P. H. Mussen, ed., *Handbook of Research Methods in Child Development.* New York: Wiley, 1960, pp. 603–644.

Herrick, V. E., Administrative structure and processes in curriculum development, *Rev. educ. Res.*, 1960, 30, 258–274.

Hess, E. H., Imprinting, *Science*, 1959, 130, 133–141.

Hess, R. D., and G. Handel, *Family Worlds: A Psychological Approach to Family Life.* Chicago: University of Chicago Press, 1959.

Highet, G., *The Art of Teaching.* New York: Knopf, 1950.

Hilgard, E. R., The place of Gestalt psychology and field theories in contemporary learning theory, *Yearb. nat. Soc. Stud. Educ.*, 1964a, **63**, Part I, 54–77.

Hilgard, E. R., ed., Theories of learning and instruction, *Yearb. nat. Soc. Stud. Educ.*, 1964b, **63**, Part I.

———, Motivation in learning theory, in S. Koch, ed., *Psychology: A Study of a Science*, Vol. V. New York: McGraw-Hill, 1963, pp. 253–283.

———, *Theories of Learning*, 2d ed. New York: Appleton, 1956.

———, and D. H. Russell, Motivation in school learning, *Yearb. nat. Soc. Stud. Educ.*, 1950, **49**, Part I, 36–68.

Hill, W. F., Contemporary developments within stimulus-response learning theory, *Yearb. nat. Soc. Stud. Educ.*, 1964, **63**, Part I, 27–53.

———, *Learning: A Survey of Psychological Interpretations*. San Francisco: Chandler, 1963.

———, Learning theory and the acquisition of values, *Psychol. Rev.*, 1960, **67**, 317–331.

Hilliard, F. H., The influence of religious education upon the development of children's moral ideas, *Brit. J. educ. Psychol.*, 1959, **29**, 50–59.

Hoehn, A. J., A study of social class differentiation in the classroom behavior of nineteen third grade teachers, *J. soc. Psychol.*, 1954, **39**, 269–292.

Hoffmann, B., *The Tyranny of Testing*. New York: Crowell, 1962.

Hoffmann, M. L., Childrearing practices and moral development: generalizations from empirical research, *Child Develpm.*, 1963, **34**, 295–318.

Holding, D. H., Transfer between difficult and easy tasks, *Brit. J. Psychol.*, 1962, **53**, 397–407.

Hollingshead, A. B., and F. C. Redlich, *Social Class and Mental Illness*, New York: Wiley, 1958.

Honkavaara, S., The "dynamic-affective" phase in the development of concepts, *J. Psychol.*, 1958, **45**, 11–23.

Hooker, D., *The Sequence in Human Fetal Activity*. Lawrence, Kansas: University of Kansas Press, 1952.

Horowitz, M., Hostility and its management in classroom groups, in W. W. Charters, Jr., and N. L. Gage, eds., *Readings in the Social Psychology of Education*. Boston: Allyn and Bacon, 1963, pp. 196–212.

Horrocks, J. E., The adolescent, in L. Carmichael, ed., *Manual of Child Psychology*. New York: Wiley, 1954, pp. 697–734.

Hovland, C. I., Yale studies of communication and persuasion, in W. W. Charters, Jr., and N. L. Gage, eds., *Readings in the Social Psychology of Education*. Boston: Allyn and Bacon, 1963, pp. 239–253.

———, and W. Mandell, An experimental comparison of conclusion-drawing by the communicator and by the audience, *J. abnorm. soc. Psychol.*, 1952, **47**, 581–588.

Hoyt, K. B., A study of the effects of teacher knowledge of pupil characteristics on pupil achievement and attitudes towards classwork, *J. educ. Psychol.*, 1955, **46**, 302–310.

Hughes, J. L., and W. J. McNamara, A comparative study of programmed and conventional instruction in industry, *J. appl. Psychol.*, 1961, **45**, 225–231.

Hughes, Marie M., and others, *Assessment of the Quality of Teaching in Elementary Schools, A Research Report*. Salt Lake City: University of Utah Press, 1959.

Humphrey, G., *Thinking; An Introduction to Its Experimental Psychology*. London: Methuen; New York: Wiley, 1951.

Hunt, J. McV., *Intelligence and Experience*. New York: Ronald, 1961.

Hunt, W. A., N. F. Jones, and E. B. Hunt, Reliability of clinical judgments as a function of clinical experience, *J. clin. Psychol.*, 1957, **13**, 377–378.

Hyman, H. H., C. R. Wright, and T. K. Hopkins, *Applications of Methods of Evaluation: Four Studies of the Encampment for Citizenship*. Berkeley, Calif.: University of California Press, 1962.

Iannaccone, L., Student teaching: a transitional stage in the making of a teacher, *Theory into Practice*, 1963, **2**, 73–80.

Isaacson, R. L., W. J. McKeachie, and J. E. Milholland, Correlation of teacher personality variables and student ratings, *J. educ. Psychol.*, 1963, **54**, 110–117.

Jackson, J. M., Structural characteristics of norms, *Yearb. nat. Soc. Stud. Educ.*, 1960, **59**, Part II, 136–163.

Jackson, P. W., The teacher and individual differences, *Yearb. nat. Soc. Stud. Educ.*, 1962, **61**, Part I, 75–90.

Jacob, P. E., Does higher education influence student values? *NEA J.*, 1958, **47**, 35–38.

———, *Changing Values in College; An Exploratory Study of the Impact of College Teaching*. New York: Harper & Row, 1957.

Jahoda, Marie, *Current Concepts of Positive Mental Health*. New York: Basic Books, 1958.

Janis, I. L., and B. T. King, The influence of role playing on opinion change, *J. abnorm. soc. Psychol.*, 1954, **49**, 211–218.

Jarrett, R. F., and A. C. Sherriffs, Propaganda, debate, and impartial presentation as determiners of attitude change, *J. abnorm. soc. Psychol.*, 1953, **48**, 33–41.

Jenkins, D. H., Characteristics and functions of leadership in instructional groups, *Yearb. nat. Soc. Stud. Educ.*, 1960, **59**, Part II, 164–184.

Jensen, G., The sociopsychological structure of the instructional group, *Yearb. nat. Soc. Stud. Educ.*, 1960, **59**, Part II, 83–114.

Jersild, A. T., What teachers say about psychotherapy, *Phi Delta Kappan*, 1963, **44**, 313–317.

———, *When Teachers Face Themselves*. New York: Teachers College, 1955.

———, Emotional development, in L. Carmichael, ed., *Manual of Child Psychology*, 2d ed. New York: Wiley, 1954, pp. 833–917.

———, Eve Allina Lazar, and Adele M.

Brodkin, *The Meaning of Psychotherapy in the Teacher's Life and Work*. New York: Teachers College, 1962.

———, and Margaret F. Meigs, Children and war, *Psychol. Bull.*, 1943, **40**, 541–573.

Jessner, L., G. E. Blom, and S. Waldfogel, Emotional implications of tonsillectomy and adenoidectomy on children, *Psychoanal. Stud. Child*, 1952, **7**, 126–169.

Johnson, D. McE., *The Psychology of Thought and Judgment*. New York: Harper & Row, 1955.

———, and H. C. Smith, Democratic leadership in the college classroom, *Psychol. Monogr.*, 1953, **67**, No. 11.

Joint Commission on Mental Illness and Health, *Action for Mental Health; Final Report, 1961*. New York: Basic Books, 1961.

Joint Committee on Testing, Some features to consider in choosing a published test, *Psychol. Bull., Supp.*, 1954, **51**, 1–38.

Jones, A., The relative effectiveness of positive and negative verbal reinforcers, *J. exp. Psychol.*, 1961, **62**, 368–371.

Jones, H. E., The longitudinal method in the study of personality, in I. Iscoe and H. W. Stevenson, eds., *Personality Development in Children*. Austin, Tex.: University of Texas Press, 1960, pp. 3–27.

Jones, Mary C., and P. H. Mussen, Self-conceptions, motivations, and interpersonal attitudes of early- and late-maturing girls, *Child Develpm.*, 1958, **29**, 491–501.

Jones, V., Character education, *Encyclopaedia of Educational Research*, 3d ed. New York: Macmillan, 1960, pp. 184–191.

———, Character development in children—an objective approach, in L. Carmichael, ed., *Manual of Child Psychology*, 2d ed. New York: Wiley, 1954, pp. 781–832.

Jordan, A. M., *Educational Psychology; Growth and Learning*, 4th ed. New

York: Holt, Rinehart and Winston, 1956.

Judd, C. H., The relation of special training to general intelligence, *Educ. Rev.*, 1908, **36**, 28–42.

Judson, A. J., and C. N. Cofer, Reasoning as an associative proccss: I. "Direction" in a simple verbal problem, *Psychol. Rep.*, 1956, **2**, 469–476.

——, ——, and S. Gelfand, Reasoning as an associative process: II. "Direction" in problem solving as a function of prior reinforcement of relevant responses, *Psychol. Rep.*, 1956, **2**, 501–507.

Kagan, H. E., *Changing the Attitude of Christian toward Jew: A Psychological Approach through Religion*. New York: Columbia University Press, 1952.

Kanner, L., Early behavior problems as signposts to later maladjustment, *Amer. J. Psychiat.*, 1941, **97**, 1261–1271.

Kaplan, L., *Mental Health and Human Relations in Education*. New York: Harper & Row, 1959.

——, New horizons in teacher-community relationships, *J. educ. Sociol.*, 1948, **21**, 417–427.

Katona, G., *Organizing and Memorizing*. New York: Columbia University Press, 1940.

Katzell, R. A., and Mildred E. Katzell, Development and application of structured tests of personality, *Rev. educ. Res.*, 1962, **32**, 51–63.

Kausler, D. H., A study of the relationship between ego-involvement and learning, *J. Psychol.*, 1951, **32**, 225–230.

Kawin, Ethel, *Parenthood in a Free Nation* (3 vols.). New York: Macmillan, 1963.

Keislar, E. R., The validity of the guess-who technique with large adolescent populations, *J. genet. Psychol.*, 1957, **91**, 131–135.

——, Girls' social groups rate each other, *Calif. J. educ. Res.*, 1953, **4**, 227–232.

——, and J. D. McNeil, Teaching scientific theory to first grade pupils by autoinstructional device, *Harv. educ. Rev.*, 1961, **31**, 73–83.

Kelley, H. H., and J. W. Thibaut, Experimental studies of group problem solving and process, in G. Lindzey, ed., *Handbook of Social Psychology*. Reading, Mass.: Addison-Wesley, 1954, pp. 735–785.

Kendler, H. H., and May F. D'Amato, A comparison of reversal shifts and nonreversal shifts in human concept formation behavior, *J. exp. Psychol.*, 1955, **49**, 165–174.

Kersh, B. Y., The motivating effect of learning by directed discovery, *J. educ. Psychol.*, 1962, **53**, 65–71.

Kirk, S., and Bluma Weiner, *Behavioral Research on Exceptional Children*. Washington, D.C.: Council for Exceptional Childrcn, NEA, 1963.

Kittell, J. E., An experimental study of the effect of external direction during learning on transfer and retention of principles, *J. educ. Psychol.*, 1957, **48**, 391–405.

Klausmeier, H. J., Effects of accelerating bright older elementary pupils: a follow up, *J. educ. Psychol.*, 1963, **54**, 165–171.

Klein, D. C., Some concepts concerning the mental health of the individual, *J. consult. Psychol.*, 1960, **24**, 288–293.

Klein, Josephine, *Working with Groups: The Social Psychology of Discussion and Decision*. London: Hutchinson, 1961.

Klein, M. M., What honor students think, *High Points*, 1958 (March), **40**, 5–32.

Klopfer, B., and H. H. Davidson, *The Rorschach Technique: An Introductory Manual*. New York: Harcourt, 1962.

Knight, F. B., and A. O. H. Setzafandt, Transfer within a narrow mental function, *Elem. Sch. J.*, 1924, **24**, 780–787.

Kohlberg, L., The development of children's orientations toward a moral order: I. Sequence in the development of moral thought, *Vita Humana*, 1963a, **6**, 11–33.

——, Moral development and identification, *Yearb. nat. Soc. Stud. Educ.*, 1963b, **62**, Part I, 277–332.

Köhler, W., *Gestalt Psychology, An Introduction to New Concepts in Modern Psychology*. New York: Liveright, 1947.

————, *The Mentality of Apes*. New York: Harcourt, 1926.

Koller, M. R., Heuristic devices for the teaching of sociology, *Sch. Soc.*, 1957, **85**, 312–313.

Komizar, B. P., "Need" and the needs—curriculum, in B. O. Smith and R. H. Ennis, eds., *Language and Concepts in Education*. New York: Random House, 1961, pp. 24–42.

Kounin, J. S., P. V. Gump, and J. J. Ryan, III, Explorations in classroom management, *J. Teacher Educ.*, 1961, **12**, 235–246.

Krasner, L., Studies of the conditioning of verbal behavior, *Psychol. Bull.*, 1958, **55**, 148–170.

Krathwohl, D. R., B. S. Bloom, and B. B. Masia, *Taxonomy of Educational Objectives*, Handbook II: *The Affective Domain*. New York: McKay, 1964.

Kraus, S., Modifying prejudice: attitude change as a function of the race of the communicator, *Audiovis. Commun. Rev.*, 1962, **10**, 14–22.

Krueger, W. C. F., The effect of overlearning on retention, *J. exp. Psychol.*, 1929, **12**, 71–78.

Kubie, L. S., Are we educating for maturity? *NEA J.*, 1959, **48**, 58–63.

Kvaraceus, W. C., Forecasting delinquency: a three-year experiment, *Except. Children*, 1961, **27**, 429–435.

Ladd, E. T., Perplexities of the problem of keeping order, *Harv. educ. Rev.*, 1958, **28**, 19–28.

Lambert, Nadine, and E. M. Bower, *Teachers' Manual: In-school Screening of Emotionally Handicapped Children*. Princeton, N. J.: Educational Testing Service, 1961.

Lambert, P., Team teaching for today's world, *Teachers Coll. Rec.*, 1963, **64**, 480–486.

Landsman, T., Factors influencing individual mental health, *Rev. educ. Res.*, 1962, **32**, 464–475.

Langemann, J. K., Let's abolish IQ tests, *PTA Magazine*, 1961 (Dec.), **56**, 7–10.

Langner, T. S., and S. T. Michael, *Life Stress and Mental Health, The Midtown Manhattan Study*, Vol. 2. New York: Free Press of Glencoe, 1963.

Laurendeau, Monique and A. Pinard, *Causal Thinking in the Child, A Genetic and Experimental Approach*. New York: International Universities, 1963.

Lawhead, V. B., A curriculum for citizenship education, in A. Frazier, ed., *New Insights and the Curriculum, Yearb. Ass. Superv. and Curric. Develpm.* Washington, D.C.: NEA, 1963, pp. 263–282.

Lawrence, D. H., The evaluation of training and transfer programs in terms of efficiency measures, *J. Psychol.*, 1954, **38**, 367–382.

————, and L. Festinger, *Deterrents and Reinforcement: The Psychology of Insufficient Reward*. Stanford, Calif.: Stanford University Press, 1962.

————, and W. R. Goodwin, Transfer in tracking behavior between two levels of speed, USAF Personnel Training Research Center, *Res. Bull.*, 1954, No. AFPTRCTR, 54–70.

Laycock, S. R., *Mental Hygiene in the School; A Handbook for the Classroom Teacher*. Vancouver, B. C.: Copp Clark, 1960.

Lazarus, R. S., *Personality and Adjustment*. Englewood Cliffs, N. J.: Prentice-Hall, 1963.

Leavitt, H. J., Some effects of certain communication patterns on group performance, *J. abnorm. soc. Psychol.*, 1951, **46**, 38–50.

Leavitt, J. E., Teacher-pupil relationships, *Rev. educ. Res.*, 1959, **29**, 209–217.

Leeds, Carroll H., Teacher behavior liked and disliked, *Education*, 1955, **75**, 29–37.

Leeper, R. W., Learning and the fields of perception, motivation, and personality, in S. Koch, ed., *Psychology: A Study of a Science*, Vol. 5. New York: McGraw-Hill, 1963, pp. 365–487.

Lehmann, I. J., Some socio-cultural differences in attitudes and values, *J. educ. Sociol.*, 1962, **36**, 1–9.

————, and Isabelle K. Payne, An exploration of attitude and value changes of college freshmen, *Personnel Guid. J.,* 1963, **41,** 403–408.

Lesser, G. S., The relationship between various forms of aggression and popularity among lower-class children, *J. educ. Psychol,* 1959, **50,** 20–25.

———, and F. B. Davis, *The Identification of Gifted Elementary School Children with Exceptional Scientific Talent.* Cooperative research project of Hunter College and the U. S. Office Educ. Proj. No. 392. New York: Hunter College Education Clinic, 1960.

Leuba, C. J., *Personality: Interpersonal Relations and Self-Understanding.* Columbus, Ohio: Merrill, 1962.

———, A preliminary experiment to quantify an incentive and its effects, *J. abnorm. soc. Psychol.,* 1930, **25,** 275–288.

Levin, G. R., and B. L. Baker, Item scrambling in a self-instructional program, *J. educ. Psychol.,* 1963, **54,** 138–143.

Levy, P. M., Ability and attainment: a new psychometric formulation of the concept of educational retardation, *Brit. J. statist. Psychol.,* 1962, **15,** 137–147.

Lewin, K., Studies in group decision, in D. Cartwright and A. Zander, eds., *Group Dynamics: Research and Theory.* New York: Harper & Row, 1953, pp. 287–288.

Lewis, D. J., Partial reinforcement: a selective review of the literature since 1950, *Psychol. Bull.,* 1960, **57,** 1–28.

Lichtenstein, A., Can attitudes be taught? *Johns Hopk. Univer. Stud. Educ.,* No. 21, 1934.

Lieberman, M., *Education as a Profession.* Englewood Cliffs, N. J.: Prentice-Hall, 1956.

Light, B. H., Comparative study of a series of TAT and CAT cards, *J. clin. Psychol.,* 1954, **10,** 179–181.

Lindley, R. H., Effects of controlled coding cues in short-term memory, *J. exp. Psychol.,* 1963, **66,** 580–587.

Lindvall, C. M., Tests of statistical significance, *Phi Delta Kappan,* 1957, **38,** 314–316.

Lindzey, G., and E. F. Borgatta, Sociometric measurement, in G. Lindzey, ed., *Handbook of Social Psychology.* Reading, Mass.: Addison-Wesley, 1954, pp. 405–444.

Lippitt, R., N. Polansky, and S. Rosen, The dynamics of power, *Hum. Relat.,* 1952, **5,** 37–64.

———, and R. K. White, The "social climate" of children's groups in, R. G. Barker and others, eds., *Child Behavior and Development.* New York: McGraw-Hill, 1943, pp. 485–508.

Livson, N., and T. F. Nichols, Social attitude configurations in an adolescent group, *J. genet. Psychol.,* 1957, **91,** 3–23.

Lloyd-Jones, Esther, and Mary V. Holman, Why people become teachers, in L. Stiles, ed., *The Teacher's Role in American Society, Yearb. John Dewey Soc.,* 1957, **14,** 235–246. New York: Harper & Row.

Lockhead, G. R., A re-evaluation of evidence on one-trial associative learning, *Amer. J. Psychol.,* 1961, **74,** 590–595.

Lodge, Helen C., The influence of the study of biography on the moral ideology of the adolescent at the eighth grade level, *J. educ. Res.,* 1956, **50,** 241–255.

Low, Camilla M., Determining the nature of the needs of youth, *Yearb. nat. Soc. Stud. Educ.,* 1953, **52,** Part I, 22–43.

Lumsdaine, A. A., Educational technology, programmed learning, and instructional science, *Yearb. nat. Soc. Stud. Educ.,* 1964, **63,** Part I, 371–401.

———, Instruments and media of instruction, in N. L. Gage, ed., *Handbook of Research on Teaching.* Skokie, Ill.: Rand McNally, 1963, pp. 583–682.

———, and R. Glaser, *Teaching Machines and Programmed Learning, A Source Book,* rev. ed. Dept. of Audio-Visual Instruction. Washington, D. C.: NEA, 1964.

Lyman, H. B., *Test Scores and What They Mean.* Englewood Cliffs, N. J.: Prentice-Hall, 1963.

Lysaught, J. P., and C. M. Williams, A

Guide to Programmed Instruction. New York: Wiley, 1963.

Macarthur, R. S., and W. B. Elley, The reduction of socioeconomic bias in intelligence testing, *Brit. J. educ. Psychol.*, 1963, **33**, 107–119.

McBain, W. N., Noise, the "arousal hypothesis," and monotonous work, *J. appl. Psychol.*, 1961, **45**, 309–317.

McCandless, B. R., *Children and Adolescents; Behavior and Development.* New York: Holt, Rinehart and Winston, 1962.

———, Carolyn B. Bilous, and Hannah L. Bennett, Peer popularity and dependence on adults in pre-school-age socialization, *Child Develpm.*, 1961, **32**, 511–518.

McClelland, D. C., and others, *The Achievement Motive.* New York: Appleton, 1953.

McClintock, C. G., and H. A. Turner, The impact of college upon political knowledge, participation, and values, *Hum. Relat.*, 1962, **15**, 165–176.

McConnell, T. R., Differences in student attitudes toward civil liberties, in R. L. Sutherland and others, eds., *Personality Factors on the College Campus.* Hogg Foundation for Mental Health. Austin, Tex.: University of Texas Press, 1962, pp. 29–42.

McCord, W., and Joan McCord, *Origins of Crime; A New Evaluation of the Cambridge-Somerville Youth Study.* New York: Columbia University Press, 1959.

McDonald, Blanche, and L. W. Nelson, *Successful Classroom Control.* Dubuque, Iowa: W. C. Brown, 1955.

McDougall, W. P., Differential retention of course outcomes in educational psychology, *J. educ. Psychol.*, 1958, **49**, 53–60.

MacFarlane, Jean W., Lucille Allen, and Marjorie P. Honzik, *A Developmental Study of the Behavior Problems of Normal Children between Twenty-one Months and Fourteen Years.* Berkeley, Calif.: University of California Press, 1954.

McGee, R. K., Response style as a personality variable: by what criterion? *Psychol. Bull.*, 1962, **59**, 284–295.

McGeoch, J. A., *The Psychology of Human Learning.* New York: Longmans, 1942.

———, and A. L. Irion. *The Psychology of Human Learning*, rev. ed., New York: McKay, 1952.

McGinley, Rev. L. J., Reality and responsibility, in E. Ginzberg, ed., *Values and Ideals of American Youth.* New York: Columbia University Press, 1961, pp. 307–315.

McGuire, C., Cultural and social factors in mental health, *Rev. educ. Res.*, 1962, **32**, 455–463.

———, and G. D. White, Social origins of teachers—in Texas, in L. Stiles, ed., *The Teacher's Role in American Society, Yearb. John Dewey Soc.*, 1957, **14**, 23–41. New York: Harper & Row.

McIntosh, D. M., *Statistics for the Teacher.* New York: Pergamon, 1963.

McKeachie, W. J., Research on teaching at the college and university level, in N. L. Gage, ed., *Handbook of Research on Teaching.* Skokie, Ill.: Rand McNally, 1963, pp. 1118–1172.

———, D. Pollie, and J. Speisman, Relieving anxiety in classroom examinations, *J. abnorm. soc. Psychol.*, 1955, **50**, 93–98.

———, and D. Solomon, Retention of general psychology, *J. educ. Psychol.*, 1957, **48**, 110–112.

McKee, J. P., and A. C. Sherriffs, Men's and women's beliefs, ideals, and self-concepts, *Amer. J. Sociol.*, 1959, **64**, 356–363.

McKenna, B. H., Greater learning in smaller classes, *NEA J.*, 1957, **46**, 437–438.

MacKinnon, D. W., The nature and nurture of creative talent, *Amer. Psychologist*, 1962, **17**, 484–495.

McLaughlin, J. W., and J. T. Shea, California teachers' job dissatisfactions, *Calif. J. educ. Res.*, 1960, **11**, 216–224.

McNemar, Olga W., An attempt to differentiate between individuals with high and low reasoning ability, *Amer. J. Psychol.*, 1955, **68**, 20–36.

McNemar, Q., *Psychological Statistics*, 3d ed. New York: Wiley, 1962.

Maddox, H., Advice on how-to-study versus the actual practices of university students, *Percept. mot. Skills*, 1963, **16**, 202.

Magoun, H. W., *The Waking Brain.* New York: Thomas Publishing, 1958.

Mahler, C., and H. Smallenburg, Effects of testing programs on the attitudes of students, teachers, parents, and the community, *Yearb. nat. Soc. Stud. Educ.*, 1963, **62**, Part II, 103–125.

Maier, N. R. F., An experimental test of the effect of training on discussion leadership, *Hum. Relat.*, 1953, **6**, 161–173.

———, Reasoning in humans, *J. compar. Psychol.*, 1930, **10**, 115–144.

———, and A. R. Solem, The contribution of a discussion leader to the quality of group thinking: the effective use of minority opinions, *Hum. Relat.*, 1952, **5**, 277–288.

Mainer, R. E., Attitude change in intergroup education programs, *Stud. higher Educ.*, *Purdue Univer.*, 1954, No. 83.

Maller, J. B., Coöperation and competition, *Teachers Coll. Contr. Educ.*, No. 384, 1929.

Mallery, D., *High School Students Speak Out; A Study of the Impact of High School Experience on Students.* New York: Harper & Row, 1962.

Malmo, R. B., Activation: a neuropsychological dimension, *Psychol. Rev.*, 1959, **66**, 367–386.

Maltzman, I., On the training of originality, *Psychol. Rev.*, 1960, **67**, 229–242.

———, and others, Experimental studies on the training for originality, *Psychol. Monogr.*, 1960, **74**, No. 6.

Manis, M., The interpretation of opinion statements as a function of recipient attitude and source prestige, *J. abnorm. soc. Psychol.*, 1961, **63**, 82–86.

Marshall, Helen R., Prediction of social acceptance in community youth groups, *Child Develpm.*, 1958, **29**, 173–184.

Martin, W. E., and Celia B. Stendler, *Child Behavior and Development*, rev. ed. New York: Harcourt, 1959.

Masling, J., and G. Stern, Changes in motives as a result of teaching, *Theory into Practice*, 1963, **2**, 95–104.

Maslow, A. H., "Higher" and "lower" needs, *J. Psychol.*, 1948, **25**, 433–436.

———, A theory of human motivation, *Psychol. Rev.*, 1943, **50**, 370–396.

Mason, G. P., Word discrimination and spelling, *J. educ. Res.*, 1957, **50**, 617–621.

Mason, W. S., R. J. Dressel, and R. K. Bain, Sex role and the career orientations of beginning teachers, *Harv. educ. Rev.*, 1959, **29**, 370–383.

Mathis, C., The relationship between salary policies and teacher morale, *J. educ. Psychol.*, 1959, **50**, 275–279.

Mead, Margaret, *The School in American Culture.* Cambridge, Mass.: Harvard University Press, 1962.

———, The young adult, in E. Ginzberg, ed., *Values and Ideals of American Youth.* New York: Columbia University Press, 1961, pp. 37–51.

———, Our educational emphasis in primitive perspective, *Amer. J. Sociol.*, 1943, **48**, 633–639.

Mearns, H., *Creative Power; The Education of Youth in the Creative Arts*, 2d rev. ed. New York: Dover, 1958.

Medinnus, G. R., Objective responsibility in children: a comparison with Piaget data, *J. genet. Psychol.*, 1962, **101**, 127–133.

———, Research implications of several parent-child concepts, *Marriage fam. Liv.*, 1959, **21**, 329–333.

Mednick, S. A., *Learning.* Englewood Cliffs, N. J.: Prentice-Hall, 1964.

———, The associative basis of the creative process, *Psychol. Rev.*, 1962, **69**, 220–232.

———, and J. L. Freedman, Stimulus generalization, *Psychol. Bull.*, 1960, **57**, 169–200.

Merril, I. R., Attitude films and attitude change, *Audiovis. Commun. Rev.*, 1962, **10**, 3–13.

Messick, W., and J. Ross, eds., *Measurement in Personality and Cognition.* New York: Wiley, 1962.

Metfessel, N. S., and J. T. Shea, Fifty often overlooked areas of teacher frustration, *Amer. Sch. Bd. J.*, 1961 (June), **142**, 16–17.

Meyer, W. J., and G. G. Thompson, Sex differences in the distribution of teacher approval and disapproval among sixth-grade children, *J. educ. Psychol.*, 1956, **47**, 385–396.

Miller, D. R., Motivation and affect, in P. H. Mussen, ed., *Handbook of Research Methods in Child Development.* New York: Wiley, 1960, pp. 688–769.

Miller, G. A., Information theory and memory, *Scient. American*, 1956a (Aug.), **195**, 42–46.

———, The magical number seven, plus or minus two: some limits on our capacity for processing information, *Psychol. Rev.*, 1956b, **63**, 81–97.

———, E. Galanter, and K. H. Pribram, *Plans and Structure of Behavior.* New York: Holt, Rinehart and Winston, 1960.

———, and Jennifer A. Selfridge, Verbal context and the recall of meaningful material, *Amer. J. Psychol.*, 1950, **63**, 176–185.

Miller, K. M., and J. B. Biggs, Attitude change through undirected group discussion, *J. educ. Psychol.*, 1958, **49**, 224–228.

Miller, L. N., Using law case materials to teach ethical behavior, *J. educ. Res.*, 1957, **51**, 39–42.

Miller, N. E., Theory and experiment relating psychoanalytic displacement to stimulus-response generalization, *J. abnorm. soc. Psychol.*, 1948, **43**, 155–178.

Milton, G. A., The effects of sex-role identification upon problem-solving skill, *J. abnorm. soc. Psychol.*, 1957, **55**, 208–212.

Mischel, W., Preference for delayed reinforcement and social responsibility, *J. abnorm. soc. Psychol.*, 1961, **62**, 1–7.

Mitton, Betty L., and D. B. Harris, The development of responsibility in children, *Elem. Sch. J.*, 1954, **54**, 268–277.

Moltz, H., Imprinting: empirical basis and theoretical significance, *Psychol. Bull.*, 1960, **57**, 291–314.

Moore, Shirley G., Displaced aggression in young children, *J. abnorm. soc. Psychol.*, 1964, **68**, 200–204.

Morgan, C. T., and J. E. Deese, *How To Study.* New York: McGraw-Hill, 1957.

Morris, B. R., and R. E. Will, The student attitude survey as a teaching aid, *Sch. Rev.*, 1959, **67**, 350–360.

Morris, J. F., Development of adolescent value-judgments, *Brit. J. educ. Psychol.*, 1958, **28**, 1–14.

Morse, H. T., and P. L. Dressel, *General Education for Personal Maturity; The Role of Courses in Personal Adjustment, Preparation for Marriage, and Vocational Planning.* Dubuque, Iowa: Brown, 1960.

Morse, W. C., and C. O. Dyer, The emotionally and socially handicapped, *Rev. educ. Res.*, 1963, **33**, 109–125.

Mosher, D. L., and A. Scodel, Relationships between ethnocentrism in children and the ethnocentrism and authoritarian rearing practices of their mothers, *Child Develpm.*, 1960, **31**, 369–376.

Munro, B. C., Meaning and learning, *Alberta J. educ. Res.*, 1959, **5**, 268–281.

Murphy, F. J., Mary M. Shirley, and Helen L. Witmer, The incidence of hidden delinquency, *Amer. J. Orthopsychiat.*, 1946, **16**, 686–696.

Murphy, G., Lois B. Murphy, and T. M. Newcomb, *Experimental Social Psychology*, 2d ed. New York: Harper & Row, 1937.

Murphy, Lois B., *The Widening World of Childhood.* New York: Basic Books, 1962.

Murray, H. A., Studies of stressful interpersonal disputations, *Amer. Psychologist*, 1963, **18**, 28–36.

———, *Explorations in Personality.* New York: Oxford, 1938.

Musgrove, F., Role-conflict in adolescence, *Brit. J. educ. Psychol.*, 1964, **34**, 34–42.

Mussen, P. H., *The Psychological Development of the Child*. Englewood Cliffs, N. J.: Prentice-Hall, 1963.

——, ed., *Handbook of Research Methods in Child Development*. New York: Wiley, 1960.

——, Some personality and social factors related to changes in children's attitudes toward Negroes, *J. abnorm. soc. Psychol.*, 1950, **45**, 423–441.

——, J. J. Conger, and J. Kagan, *Child Development and Personality*, 2d ed. New York: Harper & Row, 1963.

——, and Mary C. Jones, Self-conceptions, motivations, and interpersonal attitudes of late- and early-maturing boys, *Child Develpm.*, 1957, **28**, 243–256.

Myers, A., Team competition, success, and the adjustment of group members, *J. abnorm. soc. Psychol.*, 1962, **65**, 325–332.

NEA Research Division, The status of the American public school teacher, *Res. Bull.*, 1957, **35**, 1–63.

NEA, *Teaching Career Fact Book*. Washington, D.C.: The Association, 1963.

Nelson, M. J., E. C. Denny, and A. P. Coladarci, *Statistics for Teachers*, rev. ed. New York: Holt, Rinehart and Winston, 1956.

Newman, S. E., Student vs. instructor design of study method, *J. educ. Psychol.*, 1957, **48**, 328–333.

Nixon, R. E., *The Art of Growing: A Guide to Psychological Maturity*. New York: Random House, 1962.

Noll, V. H., *Introduction to Educational Measurement*. Boston: Houghton Mifflin, 1957.

Nunnally, J. C., *Educational Measurement and Evaluation*. New York: McGraw-Hill, 1963.

Nunnery, M. Y., and B. J. Gilliam, A study of secondary teacher knowledge of pupils as related to selected pupil characteristics, *Nat. Ass. second. Sch. Prin. Bull.*, 1962 (Oct.), **46**, (No. 276), 101–107.

Nuttin, J., *Tâche, Réussite et Échec; Théorie de la Conduite Humaine*, Publications Universitaires de Louvain, 1953.

Nye, F. I., *Family Relationships and Delinquent Behavior*. New York: Wiley, 1958.

Oakes, W. F., Use of teaching machines as a study aid in an introductory psychology course, *Psychol. Rep.*, 1960, **7**, 297–303.

O'Dowd, D. D., and D. C. Beardslee, Student image of the school teacher, *Phi Delta Kappan*, 1961, **42**, 250–254.

Ofchus, L. T., and W. J. Gnagey, Factors related to the shift of professional attitudes of students in teacher education, *J. educ. Psychol.*, 1963, **54**, 149–153.

Ojemann, R. H., Personality adjustment of individual children, No. 5 in *What Research Says to the Teacher*. Washington, D.C.: NEA, 1962.

——, Investigations on the effects of teaching an understanding and appreciation of behavior dynamics, in G. Caplan, ed., *Prevention of Mental Disorders in Children*. New York: Basic Books, 1961, pp. 378–397.

——, and F. R. Wilkinson, The effect on pupil growth of an increase in teacher's understanding of pupil behavior, *J. exp. Educ.*, 1939, **8**, 143–147.

Olander, H. T., Transfer of learning in simple addition and subtraction, *Elem. Sch. J.*, 1931, **31**, 358–369.

Olson, W. C., and W. W. Wattenberg, The role of the school in mental health, *Yearb. nat. Soc. Stud. Educ.*, 1955, **54**, Part II, 99–124.

Oppenheimer, J. R., Physics in the contemporary world, *Bull. Atomic Scientists*, 1948, **4**, 65–68; 85–86.

Osgood, C. E., G. J. Suci, and P. H. Tannenbaum, *The Measurement of Meaning*. Urbana, Ill.: University of Illinois Press, 1957.

OSS Assessment Staff, *Assessment of Men*. New York: Holt, Rinehart and Winston, 1948.

Ostrovsky, E. S., *Father to the Child, Case Studies of the Experiences of a Male*

Teacher with Young Children. New York: Putnam, 1959.

Overman, J. R., An experimental study of the effect of the method of instruction on transfer of training in arithmetic, *Elem. Sch. J.,* 1930, **31,** 183–190.

Page, E. B., Teacher comments and student performance: a seventy-four classroom experiment in school motivation, *J. educ. Psychol.,* 1958, **49,** 173–181.

Parnes, S. J., and A. Meadow, Evaluation of persistence of effects produced by a creative problem-solving course, *Psychol. Rep.,* 1960, **7,** 357–361.

———, and ———, Effects of "brainstorming" instructions on creative problem solving by trained and untrained subjects, *J. educ. Psychol.,* 1959, **50,** 171–176.

Parsley, K. M., Jr., and M. Powell, Achievement gains or losses during the academic year and over the summer vacation period: a study of trends in achievement by sex and grade level among students of average intelligence, *Genet. Psychol. Monogr.,* 1962, **66,** 285–342.

Passamanick, B., Determinants of intelligence, in S. M. Farber, and R. H. L. Wilson, eds., *Conflict and Creativity.* New York: McGraw-Hill, 1963.

Passow, A. H., and Miriam L. Goldberg, The talented Youth Project: a progress report 1962, *Except. Children,* 1962, **28,** 223–231.

Patrick, Catherine, Creative thought in poets, *Arch. Psychol.,* N.Y., 1935, **26,** No. 178.

Patterson, C. H., Program evaluation, *Rev. educ. Res.,* 1963, **33,** 214–224.

Pattinson, W., Streaming in the schools, *Educ. Res.,* 1963, **5,** 229–235.

Payne, D. E., and P. H. Mussen, Parent-child relations and father identification among adolescent boys, *J. abnorm. soc. Psychol.,* 1956, **52,** 358–362.

Peck, R. F., Student mental health—the range of personality patterns in a college population, in R. L. Sutherland and others, eds., *Personality Factors on the College Campus.* Hogg Foundation for Mental Health. Austin, Tex.: University of Texas Press, 1962, pp. 161–199.

———, and R. J. Havighurst, *The Psychology of Character Development.* New York: Wiley, 1960.

———, and J. V. Mitchell, Jr., Mental health, No. 24 in *What Research Says to the Teacher.* Washington, D.C.: NEA, 1962.

Peel, E. A., Learning and meaning, *Bull. Brit. Psychol. Soc.,* 1962, No. 48, 1–9.

———, *The Pupil's Thinking.* London: Oldbourne, 1961.

Penney, R. K., and A. A. Lupton, Children's discrimination learning as a function of reward and punishment, *J. comp. physiol. Psychol.,* 1961, **54,** 449–451.

Peters, C. C., *Teaching High School History and Social Studies for Citizenship Education: The Miami Experiment in Democratic Action-centered Education.* Coral Gables, Fla.: University of Miami Press, 1948.

Peterson, H. A., S. S. Marzolf, and Nancy Bayley, *Educational Psychology.* New York: Macmillan, 1948, p. 347.

Peterson, Ruth C., and L. L. Thurstone, *Motion Pictures and the Social Attitudes of Children.* New York: Macmillan, 1933.

Phillips, B. N., and M. Vere De Vault, Evaluation of research on cooperation and competition, *Psychol. Rep.,* 1957, **3,** 289–292.

Phillips, E. L., D. N. Wiener, and N. G. Haring, *Discipline, Achievement and Mental Health, A Teacher's Guide to Wholesome Action.* Englewood Cliffs, N. J.: Prentice-Hall, 1960.

Piaget, J., How children form mathematical concepts, *Scient. American,* 1953 (Nov.), **189,** 74–79.

———, *The Origins of Intelligence in Children.* New York: International Universities, 1952.

———, *The Moral Judgment of the Child.* New York: Free Press of Glencoe, 1948. Originally published in 1932.

Pidgeon, D. A., and A. Yates, Symposium: The use of essays in selection at 11+: IV. Experimental inquiries into the use of essay-type English papers, *Brit. J. educ. Psychol.*, 1957, **27**, 37–47.

Pinneau, S. R., and A. Milton The ecological veracity of the self-report, *J. genet. Psychol.*, 1958, **93**, 249–276.

Plant, W T., Changes in ethnocentrism associated with a four-year college education, *J. educ. Psychol.*, 1959, **49**, 162–165.

Poppleton, Pamela K., and K. Austwick, A comparison of programmed learning and note-taking at two age levels, *Brit. J. educ. Psychol.*, 1964, **34**, 43–50.

Porter, D., Some effects of year long taching machine instruction, in E. Galanter, ed., *Automatic Teaching: The State of the Art.* New York: Wiley, 1959, pp. 85–90.

Postman, L., The present status of interference theory, in C. N. Cofer, ed., *Verbal Learning and Verbal Behavior.* New York: McGraw-Hill, 1961, pp. 152–179.

———, and Lucy Rau, Retention as a function of the method of measurement, *Univer. Calif. Publ. Psychol.*, 1957, **8**, No. 3, 217–270.

Powell, J. P., Some remarks on "unteachable" and "unexaminable," *Educ. Res.*, 1963, **5**, 155–157.

Prentice, W. C. H., The systematic psychology of Wolfgang Köhler, in S. Koch, ed., *Psychology: A Study of a Science*, Vol. I. New York: McGraw-Hill, 1959, pp. 427–455.

———, Continuity in human learning, *J. exp. Psychol.*, 1949, **39**, 187–194.

Prescott, D. A., *The Child in the Educative Process.* New York: McGraw-Hill, 1957.

Pressey, S. L., Autoinstruction; perspectives, problems, and potentials, *Yearb. nat. Soc. Stud. Educ.*, 1964, **63**, Part I, 354–370.

———, and R. G. Kuhlen, *Psychological Development through the Life Span.* New York: Harper & Row, 1957.

Prugh, D. G., and others, A study of the emotional reactions of children and families to hospitalization and illness, *Amer. J. Orthopsychiat.*, 1953, **23**, 70–106.

Rasey, Marie J., *It Takes Time: An Autobiography of the Teaching Profession.* New York: Harper & Row, 1953.

Ray, W. S., Verbal compared with manipulative solution of an apparatus-problem, *Amer. J. Psychol.*, 1957, **70**, 289–290.

Read, Sir Herbert, Esthetics: enemy of violence? *Saturday Rev.*, 1960 (Dec. 4), **43**, No. 52, 9–11.

Rebelsky, Freda G., W. Allinsmith, and R. E. Grinder, Resistance to temptation and sex differences in children's use of fantasy confession, *Child Develpm.*, 1963, **34**, 955–962.

Redl, F., and W. W. Wattenberg, *Mental Hygiene in Teaching*, 2d ed. New York: Harcourt, 1959.

———, and D. Wineman, *Children Who Hate.* New York: Free Press of Glencoe, 1951.

Redlich, F. C., The concept of health in psychiatry, in A. H. Leighton, ed., *Explorations in Social Psychiatry.* New York: Basic Books, 1957, pp. 138–164.

Remmers, H. H., ed., *Anti-democratic Attitudes in American Schools.* Evanston, Ill.: Northwestern University Press, 1963a.

———, Rating methods in research on teaching, in N. L. Gage, ed., *Handbook of Research on Teaching.* Skokie, Ill.: Rand McNally, 1963b, pp. 329–378.

———, *An Introduction to Opinion and Attitude Measurement.* New York: Harper & Row, 1954.

———, and N. L. Gage, The assessment and rating of pupil personality, in H. H. Remmers, and others, eds., *Educational Measurement and Evaluation.* New York: Harper & Row, 1955.

———, ———, and J. F. Rummel, *A Practical Introduction to Measurement and Evaluation.* New York: Harper & Row, 1960.

———, and D. H. Radler, Teenage attitudes, *Scient. American*, 1958 (June), 198, 25–29.

———, and ———, *The American Teenager*. Indianapolis, Ind.: Bobbs-Merrill, 1957.

Remmlein, Madaline K., and others, Economic, legal and social status of teachers, *Rev. educ. Res.*, 1958, 28, 242–255.

Renner, K. E., Delay of reinforcement: a historical review, *Psychol. Bull.*, 1964, 61, 341–361.

Rethlingshafer, Dorothy, *Motivation as Related to Personality*. New York: McGraw-Hill, 1963.

Reynolds, M. C., ed., *Early School Admission for Mentally Advanced Children*. Washington, D.C.: Council for Exceptional Children, NEA, 1962.

Ricciuti, H., Development and application of projective tests of personality, *Rev. educ. Res.*, 1962, 32, 64–77.

Richey, R. W., and W. H. Fox, A study of some opinions of high school students with regard to teachers and teaching, *Bull. Sch. Educ. Ind. Univer.*, 1951, 27, No. 4.

Richter, C. P., Rats, man, and the welfare state, *Amer. Psychologist*, 1959, 14, 18–28.

Ricks, J. H., On telling parents about tests, *Psychol. Corporn. Test Serv. Bull.*, 1959, No. 54.

Riesman, D., R. Denney, and N. Glazer, *The Lonely Crowd; A Study of the Changing American Character*. New Haven, Conn.: Yale University Press, 1953.

Riley, D. A., and Laura W. Phillips, The effects of syllable familiarization on rote learning, association value, and reminiscence, *J. exp. Psychol.*, 1959, 57, 372–379.

Riley, Matilda W., J. W. Riley, Jr., and Mary E. Moore, Adolescent values and the Riesman typology: an empirical analysis, in S. M. Lipset and L. Lowenthal, eds., *Culture and Social Character*. New York: Free Press of Glencoe, 1961, 370–386.

Robinson, F. P., *Effective Reading*. New York: Harper & Row, 1962.

———, Guidance for all: in principle and practice, *Personnel Guid. J.*, 1953, 31, 500–504.

———, *Effective Study*. New York: Harper & Row, 1946.

Rock, I., Repetition and learning, *Scient. American*, 1958 (Aug.), 199, 68–72.

———, The role of repetition in associative learning, *Amer. J. Psychol.*, 1957, 70, 186–193.

Roe, K. V., H. W. Case, and A. Roe, Scrambled versus ordered sequence in autoinstructional programs, *J. educ. Psychol.*, 1962, 53, 101–104.

Rogers, C. R., *On Becoming a Person; A Therapist's View of Psychotherapy*. Boston: Houghton Mifflin, 1961.

Rokeach, M., R. Bonier, and others, *The Open and Closed Mind; Investigations into the Nature of Belief Systems and Personality Systems*. New York: Basic Books, 1960.

Rosenbloom, P. C., Teaching the strategy of problem-solving, in Rosalind L. Feierabend, and P. H. DuBois, eds., *Psychological Problems and Research Methods in Mathematics Training*. St. Louis: Washington University, 1959, pp. 30–36.

Rosenthal, F., Some relationships between sociometric position and language structure of young children, *J. educ. Psychol.*, 1957, 48, 483–497.

Ross, A. O., *The Practice of Clinical Child Psychology*. New York: Grune & Stratton, 1959.

Roth, R. H., Student reactions to programed learning, *Phi Delta Kappan*, 1963, 44, 278–281.

Rubenstein, H., and M. Aborn, Learning, prediction, and readability, *J. appl. Psychol.*, 1958, 42, 28–32.

Rudd, W. G. A., and S. Wiseman, Sources of dissatisfaction among a group of teachers, *Brit. J. educ. Psychol.*, 1962, 32, 275–291.

Ruebush, B. K., Anxiety, *Yearb. nat. Soc. Stud. Educ.*, 1963, 62, Part I, 460–516.

Rugg, H. O., *Imagination*. New York: Harper & Row, 1963.

Rummel, J. F., *An Introduction to Research Procedures in Education*. New York: Harper & Row, 1958.

Rush, R. R., and R. M. Clark, Four years in three: an evaluation, *Elem. Sch. J.*, 1963, **63**, 281–285.

Rust, Velma I., Factor analyses of three tests of critical thinking, *J. exp. Educ.*, 1960, **29**, 177–182.

Ryans, D. G., *Characteristics of Teachers, Their Description, Comparison and Appraisal*. Washington, D.C.: American Council on Education, 1960.

Ryerson, Alice J., Medical advice on child rearing, 1550–1900, *Harv. educ. Rev.*, 1961, **31**, 302–323.

Sachar, A. L., A climate of commitment, in E. Ginzberg, ed., *Values and Ideals of American Youth*. New York: Columbia University Press, 1961, pp. 317–323.

Saltz, Joanne W., Teacher stereotype: liability in recruiting? *Sch. Rev.*, 1960, **68**, 105–111.

Salzinger, K., Experimental manipulation of verbal behavior: a review, *J. gen. Psychol.*, 1959, **61**, 65–94.

———, Stephanie Portnoy, and R. S. Feldman, The effect of order of approximation to the statistical structure of English on the emission of verbal responses, *J. exp. Psychol.*, 1962, **64**, 52–57.

Sarason, S. B., and others, *Anxiety in Elementary School Children*. New York: Wiley, 1960.

Scandrette, O. C., Social distance and degree of acquaintance, *J. educ. Res.*, 1958, **51**, 367–372.

Schmidt, H. O., The effects of praise and blame as incentives to learning, *Psychol. Monogr.*, 1941, **53**, No. 3.

Schonell, Sir Frederick J., E. Roe, and E. G. Middletone, *Promise and Performance; A Study of Student Progress at University Level*. London: University of London Press, 1963.

Schuhle, W., Teachers' understanding of students' academic ideals, *J. higher Educ.*, 1957, **28**, 388–391; 408.

Scott, J. P., Critical periods in the development of social behavior in puppies, *Psychosom. Med.*, 1958, **20**, 42–54.

Scott, W. A., Research definitions of mental health and mental illness, *Psychol. Bull.*, 1958, **55**, 29–45.

Scudder, K. J., and K. S. Beam, *The Twenty Billion Dollar Challenge: A National Program for Delinquency Prevention*. New York: Putnam, 1961.

Sears, Pauline S., and E. R. Hilgard, The teacher's role in the motivation of the learner, *Yearb. nat. Soc. Stud. Educ.*, 1964, **63**, Part I, 182–209.

Sears, R. R., Relation of early socialization experiences to aggression in middle childhood, *J. abnorm. soc. Psychol.*, 1961, **63**, 466–492.

———, The growth of conscience, in I. Iscoe and H. W. Stevenson, eds., *Personality Development in Children*. Austin, Tex.: University of Texas Press, 1960, pp. 92–111.

———, Eleanor E. Maccoby, and H. Levin, *Patterns of Child Rearing*. New York: Harper & Row, 1957.

Seward, J. P., The structure of functional autonomy, *Amer. Psychologist*, 1963, **18**, 703–710.

Shane, H. G., The school and individual differences, *Yearb. nat. Soc. Stud. Educ.*, 1962, **61**, Part I, 44–61.

Shannon, D. C., What research says about acceleration, *Phi Delta Kappan*, 1957, **39**, 70–72.

Shaplin, J. T., and H. F. Olds, Jr., eds., *Team Teaching*. New York: Harper & Row, 1964.

Sherif, M., and C. I. Hovland, *Social Judgment: Assimilation and Contrast Effects in Communication and Attitude Change*. New Haven, Conn.: Yale University Press, 1961.

Sheviakov, G. V., and F. Redl, *Discipline for Today's Children and Youth*, rev. by Sybil K. Richardson. Washington, D.C.: NEA, 1956.

Shipley, J. T., *The Mentally Disturbed*

Teacher. Philadelphia: Chilton, 1961.

Silberman, H. F., Self-teaching devices and programmed materials, *Rev. educ. Res.*, 1962, **32**, 179–193.

Simmons, A. J., and A. E. Goss, Animistic responses as a function of sentence contexts and instructions, *J. genet. Psychol.*, 1957, **91**, 181–189.

Skelton, R. B., High-school foreign language study and freshman performance, *Sch. Soc.*, 1957, **85**, 203–205.

Skinner, B. F., Reinforcement today, *Amer. Psychologist*, 1958, **13**, 94–99.

———, Science of learning and the art of teaching, *Harv. educ. Rev.*, 1954, **24**, 86–97.

———, *Science and Human Behavior.* New York: Macmillan, 1953.

Skinner, C. E., P. L. Harriman, and others, eds., *Essentials of Educational Psychology.* Englewood Cliffs, N. J.: Prentice-Hall, 1958.

Smedslund, J., The acquisition of conservation of substance and weight in children: V. Practice in conflict situations without external reinforcement, *Scand. J. Psychol.*, 1961, **2**, 156–160.

Smith, A. J., E. M. Harrison, and R. Sobol, Productivity and recall in cooperative and competitive discussion groups, *J. Psychol.*, 1957, **43**, 193–204.

Smith, B. O., A concept of teaching, *Teachers Coll. Rec.*, 1960a, **61**, 229–241.

———, Critical thinking, *Yearb. Amer. Ass. Coll. Teacher Educ.*, 1960b, **13**, 84–96.

Smith, G. M., *A Simplified Guide to Statistics, for Psychology and Education.* New York: Holt, Rinehart and Winston, 1962.

Smith, H. P., A study of the problems of beginning teachers, *Educ. Admin. Superv.*, 1950, **36**, 257–264.

Smith, K. U., *Delayed Sensory Feedback and Behavior.* Philadelphia: Saunders, 1962.

Smith, L. M., and B. B. Hudgins, *Educational Psychology; An Application of Social and Behavioral Theory.* New York: Knopf, 1964.

Smith, M. B., "Mental health" reconsid-ered: a special case of the problem of values in psychology, *Amer. Psychologist*, 1961, **16**, 299–306.

Smith, W. I., and J. W. Moore, *Programmed Learning: Theory and Research, An Enduring Problem in Psychology.* Princeton, N. J.: Van Nostrand, 1962.

Smith, W. W., and others, Delayed visual feedback and behavior, *Science*, 1960, **132**, 1013–1014.

Smock, C. D., and Bess G. Holt, Children's reactions to novelty: an experimental study of "curiosity motivation," *Child Developm.*, 1962, **33**, 631–642.

Snow, R. H., Anxieties and discontents in teaching, *Phi Delta Kappan*, 1963, **44**, 318–321.

Solnit, A. J., *Modern Perspectives in Child Development; in Honor of Milton J. E. Senn.* New York: International Universities, 1963.

Solomon, D., and H. L. Miller, *Exploration in Teaching Styles.* Chicago: Center for the Study of Liberal Education for Adults, 1961.

Solomon, J. C., Neuroses of school teachers: a colloquy, *Ment. Hyg., N. Y.*, 1960, **44**, 79–90.

Sones, A. M., and J. B. Stroud, Review, with special reference to temporal position, *J. educ. Psychol.*, 1940, **31**, 665–676.

Sorenson, H., *Fundamentals of Statistics.* New York: Vantage, 1961.

Spaulding, R. L., Achievement, creativity and self-concept correlates of teacher-pupil transactions in elementary schools, in Celia B. Stendler, ed., *Readings in Child Behavior and Development.* New York: Harcourt, 1964, pp. 313–318.

Spence, K. W., *Behavior Theory and Conditioning.* New Haven, Conn.: Yale University Press, 1956.

Spitzer, H. F., Class size and pupil achievement in elementary schools, *Elem. Sch. J.*, 1954, **55**, 82–86.

Srole, L., and others, *Mental Health in the Metropolis: The Midtown Manhattan Study.* New York: McGraw-Hill-Blakiston, 1962.

Staats, A. W., Verbal and instrumental response-hierarchies and their relationship to problem-solving, *Amer. J. Psychol.*, 1957, **70**, 442–446.

——, and Carolyn K. Staats, *Complex Human Behavior: A Systematic Extension of Learning Principles*. New York: Holt, Rinehart and Winston, 1963.

Standlee, L. W., and W. J. Popham, Quizzes' contribution to learning, *J. educ. Psychol.*, 1960, **51**, 322–325.

Stein, M. I., and Shirley J. Heinze, *Creativity and the Individual: Summaries of Selected Literature in Psychology and Psychiatry*. New York: Free Press of Glencoe, 1960.

Stember, C. H., *Education and Attitude Change; The Effect of Schooling on Prejudice Against Minority Groups*. New York: Institute of Human Relations Press, 1961.

Stendler, Celia B., Dora Damrin, and Aleyne C. Haines, Studies in cooperation and competition: I. The effects of working for group and individual rewards on the social climate of childen's groups, *J. genet. Psychol.*, 1951, **79**, 173–197.

Stephens, J. M., Spontaneous schooling and success in teaching, *Sch. Rev.*, 1960a, **68**, 152–163.

——, Transfer of learning, *Encyclopaedia of Educational Research*, 3d ed. New York: Macmillan, 1960b, 1535–1543.

——, Educational psychology, *Annu. Rev. Psychol.*, 1959, **10**, 109–130.

——, *Educational Psychology; The Study of Educational Growth*, rev. ed. New York: Holt, Rinehart and Winston, 1956.

——, The influence of symbolic punishment and reward upon strong and upon weak associations, *J. gen. Psychol.*, 1941, **25**, 177–185.

——, The influence of different stimuli upon preceding bonds, *Teacher Coll. Contr. Educ.*, No. 493, 1931.

Stern, G. G., Measuring noncognitive variables in research on teaching, in N. L. Gage, ed., *Handbook of Research on Teaching*. Skokie, Ill.: Rand McNally, 1963, pp. 398–447.

Sterrett, M. D., and R. A. Davis, The permanence of school learning: a review of studies, *Educ. Adm. Superv.*, 1954, **40**, 449–460.

Stevenson, G. S., and H. Milt, *Master Your Tensions and Enjoy Living Again*. Englewood Cliffs, N. J.: Prentice-Hall, 1960.

Stevenson, H. W., ed., Child psychology, *Yearb. nat. Soc. Stud. Educ.*, 1963, **62**, Part I.

——, and E. F. Zigler, Discrimination learning and rigidity in normal and feebleminded individuals, *J. Pers.*, 1957, **25**, 699–711.

Stiles, L., ed., *The Teacher's Role in American Society*, *Yearb. John Dewey Society*, 1957, **14**, New York: Harper & Row.

Stinnett, T. M., and L. D. Haskew, *Teaching in American Schools; A Handbook for the Future Teacher*. New York: Harcourt, 1962.

Stone, L. J., and J. Church, *Childhood and Adolescence: A Psychology of the Growing Person*. New York: Random House, 1957.

Stovall, T. F., Classroom methods: lecture vs. discussion, *Phi Delta Kappan*, 1958, **39**, 255–258.

Stroud, J. B., Experiments on learning in school situations, *Psychol. Bull.*, 1940, **37**, 777–807.

Suehr, J. H., A study of morale in education utilizing incomplete sentences, *J. educ. Res.*, 1962, **56**, 75–81.

Symonds, P. M., with A. R. Jensen, *From Adolescent to Adult*. New York: Columbia University Press, 1961.

——, *The Symonds Picture-Story Test*. New York: Teachers College, 1948.

——, *The Dynamics of Human Adjustment*. New York: Appleton, 1946.

Taft, R., Selective recall and memory distortion of favorable and unfavorable material, *J. abnorm. soc. Psychol.*, 1954, **49**, 23–28.

Tait, C. D., Jr., and E. F. Hodges, Jr., *Delinquents, Their Families and the Community.* Springfield, Ill.: Charles C Thomas, 1962.

Tanner, J. M., *Education and Physical Growth; Implications of the Study of Children's Growth for Educational Theory and Practice.* London: University of London Press, 1961.

Taylor, C. W., and J. L. Holland, Development and application of tests of creativity, *Rev. educ. Res.,* 1962, **32,** 91–102.

Taylor, P. H., Children's evaluations of the characteristics of the good teacher, *Brit. J. educ. Psychol.,* 1962, **32,** 258–266.

Teeters, Negley K., and D. Matza, The extent of delinquency in the United States, *J. Negro Educ.,* 1959, **28,** 200–213.

Terhune, W. B., *Emotional Problems and What You Can Do about Them: First Aid to Wiser Living.* New York: Morrow, 1961.

Terrell, G., Manipulatory motivation in children, *J. comp. physiol. Psychol.,* 1959, **52,** 705–709.

Thelen, H. A., Group dynamics in instruction: principle of least group size, *Sch. Rev.,* 1949, **57,** 139–148.

Thibaut, J. W., and J. Coules, The role of communication in the reduction of interpersonal hostility, *J. abnorm. soc. Psychol.,* 1952, **47,** 770–777.

———, and H. H. Kelley, *The Social Psychology of Groups.* New York: Wiley, 1959.

Thomas, E. J., and C. F. Fink, Effects of group size, *Psychol. Bull.,* 1963, **60,** 371–384.

Thomas, R. M., *Judging Student Progress,* 2d ed. New York: McKay, 1960.

Thompson, G. G., Children's groups, in P. H. Mussen, ed., *Handbook of Research Methods in Child Development.* New York: Wiley, 1960, pp. 821–853.

———, and C. W. Hunnicutt, The effect of repeated praise or blame on the work achievement of "introverts" and "extroverts," *J. educ. Psychol.,* 1944, **35,** 257–266.

Thomson, S. D., The emerging role of the teacher aide, *Clearing House,* 1963, **37,** 326–330.

Thorndike, R. L., *The Concepts of Over- and Underachievement.* New York: Teachers College, 1963a.

———, The measurement of creativity, *Teacher Coll. Rec.,* 1963b, **64,** 422–424.

———, and Elizabeth P. Hagen, *Measurement and Evaluation in Psychology and Education,* 2d ed. New York: Wiley, 1961a.

———, and ———, Men teachers and ex-teachers: some attitudes and traits, *Teacher Coll. Rec.,* 1961b, **62,** 306–316.

Tiedeman, S. C., A study of pupil-teacher relationship, *J. educ. Res.,* 1942, **35,** 657–664.

Tizard, J., The effects of different types of supervision on the behavior of mental defectives in a shelterd workshop, *Amer. J. ment. Defic.,* 1953, **58,** 143–161.

Toch, H., and H. Cantril, A preliminary inquiry into the learning of values, *J. educ. Psychol.,* 1957, **48,** 145–156.

Tolman, E. C., *Collected Papers in Psychology.* Berkeley, Calif.: University of California Press, 1951.

Torbet, D. P., The attitude of a select group of Colorado secondary school teachers toward informal teacher-made tests as measured by a projective interview, *J. educ. Res.,* 1957, **50,** 691–700.

Torrance, E. P., *Guiding Creative Talent.* Englewood Cliffs, N. J.: Prentice-Hall, 1962.

———, The creatively gifted are cause for concern, *Gifted Child Quart.,* 1961a, **5,** 79–87.

———, Priming creative thinking in the primary grades, *Elem. Sch. J.,* 1961b, **62,** 34–41.

———, Sensitization versus adaptation in preparation for emergencies: prior experience with an emergency ration and its acceptability in a simulated survival situation, *J. appl. Psychol.*, 1958, **42**, 63–67.

———, and R. Mason, Instructor effort to influence: an experimental evaluation of six approaches, *J. educ. Psychol.*, 1958, **49**, 211–218.

Townsend, E. A., and P. J. Burke, *Statistics for the Classroom Teacher, a Self-teaching Unit.* New York: Macmillan, 1963.

Trabue, Ann, Classroom cheating—an isolated phenomenon? *Educ. Rec.*, 1962, **43**, 309–316.

Trow, W. C., The problem of transfer—then and now, *Phi Delta Kappan*, 1958, **40**, 68–71.

Tussing, L., *Study and Succeed.* New York: Wiley, 1962.

Tyler, F. T., Issues related to readiness to learn, *Yearb. nat. Soc. Stud. Educ.*, 1964, **63**, Part I, 210–239.

———, ed., Individualizing instruction, *Yearb. nat. Soc. Stud. Educ.*, 1962a, **61**, Part I.

———, Intraindividual variability, *Yearb. nat. Soc. Stud. Educ.*, 1962b, **61**, Part I, 164–174.

Tyler, Leona E., *Tests and Measurements.* Englewood Cliffs, N. J.: Prentice-Hall, 1963.

———, *The Psychology of Human Differences*, 2d ed. New York: Appleton, 1956.

Tyler, R. W., The impact of external testing programs, *Yearb. nat. Soc. Stud. Educ.*, 1963, **62**, Part II, 193–210.

Ullmann, C. A., Teachers, peers and tests as predictors of adjustment, *J. educ. Psychol.*, 1957, **48**, 257–267.

Ulmer, G., Teaching geometry to cultivate reflective thinking: an experimental study with 1239 high school pupils, *J. exp. Educ.*, 1939, **8**, 18–25.

Underwood, B. J., Forgetting, *Scient. American*, 1964a (March), **210**, No. 3, 91–99.

———, Laboratory studies of verbal learning, *Yearb. nat. Soc. Stud. Educ.*, 1964b, **63**, Part I, 133–152.

———, Ten years of massed practice on distributed practice, *Psychol. Rev.*, 1961, **68**, 229–247.

———, Verbal learning in the educative processes, *Harv. educ. Rev.*, 1959, **29**, 107–117.

———, Interference and forgetting, *Psychol. Rev.*, 1957, **64**, 49–60.

———, Speed of learning and amount retained: a consideration of methodology, *Psychol. Bull.*, 1954, **51**, 276–282.

———, and L. Postman, Extraexperimental sources of interference in forgetting, *Psychol. Rev.*, 1960, 67, 73–95.

———, and R. W. Schulz, *Meaningfulness and Verbal Learning.* Philadelphia: Lippincott, 1960.

United Nations, *Second Congress on Crime and the Treatment of Offenders*, Dept. Soc. Econom. Affairs, London, 1960.

Van Egmond, E., Socialization processes and education, *Rev. educ. Res.*, 1961, **31**, 80–90.

(Various), Abilities and attainment, I–IV, *Brit. J. statist. Psychol.*, 1963, **16**, 105–117.

Vernon, P. E., *Intelligence and Attainment Tests.* New York: Philosophical Library, 1961.

———, Education and the psychology of individual differences, *Harv. educ. Rev.*, 1958, **28**, 91–104.

Vinacke, W. E., *The Psychology of Thinking.* New York: McGraw-Hill, 1952.

Vincent, Elizabeth L., and Phyllis C. Martin, *Human Psychological Development.* New York: Ronald, 1961.

Von Wright, J. M., A note on the role of "guidance" in learning, *Brit. J. Psychol.*, 1957, **48**, 133–137.

Walker, Helen M., *Elementary Statistical Methods.* New York: Holt, Rinehart and Winston, 1955.

Wallach, M. A., Research on children's thinking, *Yearb. nat. Soc. Stud. Educ.*, 1963, **62**, Part I, 236–276.

Wallen, N. E., Development and application of tests of general mental ability, *Rev. educ. Res.*, 1962, **32**, 15–24.

———, and R. M. W. Travers, Analysis and investigation of teaching methods, in N. L. Gage, ed., *Handbook of Research on Teaching*, Skokie, Ill.: Rand McNally, 1963, pp. 448–505.

Walters, J., The effects of an introductory course in child development on the attitudes of college women toward child guidance, *J. exp. Educ.*, 1959, **27**, 311–321.

Walther, E. C., A study of participation in discussion as a factor in the learning of factual materials in social subjects, Unpublished dissertation, Johns Hopkins University, 1941.

Wandt, E., and L. M. Ostreicher, *Variability in Observed Classroom Behaviors of Junior High School Teachers and Classes*. N. Y. Office of Research and Evaluation, Division of Teachers Education, College of the City of New York, 1953, IV.

Wapner, S., and Thelma G. Alper, The effect of an audience on behavior in a choice situation, *J. abnorm. soc. Psychol.*, 1952, **47**, 222–229.

Warner, W. L., Marcia Meeker, and K. Eels, *Social Class in America*, new ed. New York: Harper & Row, 1960.

Watson, G. B., An evaluation of small group work in a large class, *J. educ. Psychol.*, 1953, **44**, 385–408.

———, The measurement of fair-mindedness, *Teachers Coll. Contr. Educ.*, No. 176, 1925.

Wattenberg, W., and others, Social origins and teaching role—Some typical patterns, in L. Stiles, ed., *The Teacher's Role in American Society, Yearb. John Dewey Soc.*, 1957, **14**, 42–60. New York: Harper & Row.

Webster, H., Changes in attitudes during college, *J. educ. Psychol.*, 1958, **49**, 109–117.

———, M. Freedman, and P. Heist, Personality changes in college students, in N. Sanford, ed., *The American College*. New York: Wiley, 1962, pp. 811–846.

Weeks, H. A., *Youthful Offenders at Highfields: An Evaluation of the Effects of the Short-term Treatment of Delinquent Boys*. Ann Arbor, Mich.: University of Michigan Press, 1963.

Weinreb, J., Report of an experience in the application of dynamic psychiatry in education, *Ment. Hyg., N. Y.*, 1953, **37**, 283–293.

Wertheimer, Max, Michael Wertheimer, ed., *Productive Thinking*, 2d ed. New York: Harper & Row, 1961.

West, J. V., and B. Fruchter, A longitudinal study of the relationship of high school foreign language and mathematics study to freshman grades, *J. educ. Res.*, 1960, **54**, 105–110.

West, Rebecca, *The Court and the Castle*. New Haven, Conn.: Yale University Press, 1957.

White, Mary A., and M. W. Harris, *The School Psychologist*. New York: Harper & Row, 1961.

White, R. K., and R. Lippitt, *Autocracy and Democracy: An Experimental Inquiry*. New York: Harper & Row, 1960.

White, R. W., Dangers of social adjustment, *Teachers Coll. Rec.*, 1961, **62**, 288–297.

———, Competence and the psychosexual stages of development, M. R. Jones, ed., *Nebraska Symposium on Motivation*, 1960, **8**, 97–141.

———, Motivation reconsidered: the concept of competence, *Psychol. Rev.*, 1959, **66**, 297–333.

Whitlock, G. H., L. C. Copeland, and A. M. Craig, Programming versus independent study in learning elementary statistics, *Psychol. Rep.*, 1963, **12**, 171–174.

Wickens, D. D., Stimulus identity as related to response specificity and response generalization, *J. exp. Psychol.*, 1948, **38**, 389–394.

Wilkins, L. T., Juvenile delinquency: a critical review of research and theory, *Educ. Res.*, 1963, **5**, 104–119.

———Crime, cause and treatment: recent research and theory, *Educ. Res.*, 1961, **4**, 18–32.

Wilkins, Minna C., The effect of changed material on ability to do formal syllogistic reasoning, *Arch. Psychol. N. Y.*, 1929, **16**, No. 102, 1–83.

Williams, C. D., The elimination of tantrum behavior by extinction procedures, *J. abnorm. soc. Psychol.*, 1959, **59**, 269.

Williams, H. M., Changes in pupils' attitudes towards West African Negroes, following the use of two different teaching methods, *Brit. J. educ. Psychol.*, 1961, **31**, 292–296.

Williams, J. D., Teaching problem-solving, *Educ. Res.*, 1960, **3**, 12–36.

Wilson, R. C., Creativity, *Yearb. nat. Soc. Stud. Educ.*, 1958, **57**, Part II, 108–126.

Wilson, W. C., Value differences between public and private school graduates, *J. educ. Psychol.*, 1959, **50**, 213–218.

Withall, J., and W. W. Lewis, Social interaction in the classroom, in N. L. Gage, ed., *Handbook of Research on Teaching*. Skokie, Ill.: Rand McNally, 1963, pp. 683–714.

Witmer, Helen L., ed., Prevention of juvenile delinquency, *Annals Amer. Acad. pol. soc. Science*, 1959, **322**, 1–213.

Witty, P. A., Mental health of the teacher, *Yearb. nat. Soc. Stud. Educ.*, 1955, **54**, Part II, 307–333.

Wohlwill, J. F., The teaching machine: psychology's new hobbyhorse, *Teachers Coll. Rec.*, 1962, **64**, 139–150.

Wolfle, D., Training, in S. S. Stevens, ed., *Handbook of Experimental Psychology*. New York: Wiley, 1951, pp. 1267–1286.

Wolpert, A. W., A survey and analysis of the status, problems, and potential of teaching as a profession, *Calif. J. educ. Res.*, 1961, **12**, 3–7.

Wood, B. D., and F. N. Freeman, *An Experimental Study of the Educational Influences of the Typewriter in the Elementary School Classroom*. New York: Macmillan, 1932.

Wood, Dorothy A., *Test Construction; Development and Interpretation of Achievement Tests*. Columbus, Ohio: Merrill, 1961.

Woodruff, A. D., *Basic Concepts of Teaching, with Brief Readings*. San Francisco: Chandler, 1962.

Woodworth, R. S., and H. Schlosberg, *Experimental Psychology*. New York: Holt, Rinehart and Winston, 1954.

Worth, W. H., When is grade repetition most profitable? *Alberta J. educ. Res.*, 1961, **7**, 217–222.

———, Promotion or non-promotion? *Educ. Admin. Superv.*, 1960, **46**, 16–26.

Wright, B., and Barbara Sherman, Who is the teacher? *Theory into Practice*, 1963, **2**, 67–72.

Wylie, Ruth C., *The Self-concept; A critical Survey of Pertinent Research Literature*. Lincoln, Neb.: University of Nebraska Press, 1961.

Wynn, D. R., and R. W. De Remer, Staff utilization development, and evaluation, *Rev. educ. Res.*, 1961, **31**, 393–405.

Yablonsky, L., *The Violent Gang*. New York: Macmillan, 1962.

Yarrow, L. J., Interviewing children, in P. H. Mussen, ed., *Handbook of Research Methods in Child Development*. New York: Wiley, 1960, pp. 561–602.

Yarrow, Marian R., The measurement of children's attitudes and values, in P. H. Mussen, ed., *Handbook of Research Methods in Child Development*. New York: Wiley, 1960, pp. 645–687.

Yates, A. J., Delayed auditory feedback, *Psychol. Bull.*, 1963, **60**, 213–251.

Young, P. T., *Motivation and Emotion; A Survey of the Determinants of Human and Animal Activity*. New York: Wiley, 1961.

Young, C., *Blondie*. New York: Nat. Ass. Mental Health, 1950.

Young, R. K., W. M. Benson, and W. H. Holtzman, Change in attitudes toward the Negro in a southern university, *J. abnorm. soc. Psychol.*, 1960, **60**, 131–133.

Zeitlin, H., High school discipline: four hundred forty-two teachers report on disciplinary problems in seven Phoenix high schools, *Calif. J. educ. Res.*, 1962, **13**, 116–125.

Zimiles, H., Mental health and school personnel, *Rev. educ. Res.*, 1962, **32**, 484–494.

▶ *Indexes*

NAME INDEX

This name index does *not* duplicate the alphabetical list of references, pages 462–492. It does provide reference pages (462–492) for associate authors, however, since there is no other alphabetical index for the latter. It also gives text mention for any author or other name.

SUBJECT INDEX